Linux Administration:
A Beginner's Guide,
Second Edition

STEVE SHAH

Osborne/McGraw-Hill

New York   Chicago   San Francisco
Lisbon   London   Madrid   Mexico City
Milan   New Delhi   San Juan
Seoul   Singapore   Sydney   Toronto

Osborne/**McGraw-Hill**
2600 Tenth Street
Berkeley, California 94710
U.S.A.

For information on translations or book distributors outside the U.S.A., or to arrange bulk purchase discounts for sales promotions, premiums, or fund-raisers, please contact Osborne/**McGraw-Hill** at the above address.

Linux Administration: A Beginner's Guide, Second Edition

4567890 CUS CUS 0198765432

Book p/n 0-07-213135-7 and CD p/n 0-07-213134-9
parts of
ISBN 0-07-213136-5

Publisher	**Proofreader**
Brandon A. Nordin	Pat Mannion
Vice President & Associate Publisher	**Indexer**
Scott Rogers	David Heiret
Acquisitions Editor	**Computer Designers**
Franny Kelly	Kelly Stanton-Scott
Project Editor	Roberta Steele
Janet Walden	**Illustrator**
Acquisitions Coordinator	Michael Mueller
Alexander Corona	**Cover Design**
Technical Editor	Amparo Del Rio
Art Chan	**Series Design**
Copy Editor	Peter F. Hancik
Emily K. Wolman	

This book was composed with Corel VENTURA™ Publisher.

ABOUT THE AUTHOR

Steve Shah started his technical life in 1986 as a programmer for the Apple II, hacking on BASIC and 6502 assembly (a frightening amount of which he still remembers). He added Systems Administrator to his title in 1992 when he was introduced to SCO UNIX. Today he gets to do both at ClickArray Networks (http://www.clickarray.com). In between work, sleep, and filddling around with some aspect of Linux that fascinates him, Steve enjoys spending time with his lovely wife, Heidi, and working on his DJ'ing skills.

Dedicated to Heidi, forever my better half.

AT A GLANCE

Part I　　**Installing Linux as a Server**

▼　1　Technical Summary of Linux Distributions and
Windows 2000 3
▼　2　Installing Linux in a Server Configuration . . 15
▼　3　GNOME and KDE 45
▼　4　Installing Software 69

Part II　　**Single-Host Administration**

▼　5　Managing Users 81
▼　6　The Command Line 111
▼　7　Booting and Shutting Down 149
▼　8　File Systems 167
▼　9　Core System Services 199
▼　10　Compiling the Linux Kernel 221
▼　11　Securing an Individual Server 241

Part III   Internet Services

▼ 12   DNS   257
▼ 13   FTP   305
▼ 14   Setting Up Your Web Server Using Apache .   335
▼ 15   SMTP   349
▼ 16   Post Office Protocol (POP)   383
▼ 17   The Secure Shell (SSH)   399

Part IV   Intranet Services

▼ 18   Network File System (NFS)   413
▼ 19   Network Information Service (NIS)   427
▼ 20   Samba   445
▼ 21   Printing   465
▼ 22   DHCP   481
▼ 23   Backups   495

Part V   Advanced Linux Networking

▼ 24   TCP/IP for System Administrators   511
▼ 25   Network Configuration   549
▼ 26   Advanced Linux Networking   559
▼ 27   The /proc File System   589

Part VI   Appendixes

▼ A   Programming Languages That Accompany
            Red Hat Linux   599
▼ B   Getting the Usual Done   605

▼   Index   611

▼   About the CD   645

CONTENTS

Acknowledgments xxi
Introduction xxiii

Part I

Installing Linux as a Server

▼ 1   Technical Summary of Linux Distributions and Windows 2000   3

Linux and Linux Distributions   4
Free Software and the GNU License   5
    What Is the GNU Public License?   5
    The Advantages of Free Software   6
The Major Differences Between Windows 2000 and Linux   7
    Single Users vs. Multiusers vs. Network Users   8
    Separation of the GUI and the Kernel   8
    The Network Neighborhood   9
    The Registry vs. Text Files   10
    Domains   11
    Active Directory   12
Other References   12
Summary   13

▼ 2   Installing Linux in a Server Configuration   15
      Before Installation   16
          Hardware   16
          Server Design   17
          Dual-Booting Issues   18
          Methods of Installation   19
          If It Just Won't Work Right   19
      Installing Red Hat Linux   20
          Creating a Boot Disk   21
          Starting the Installation   21
          Welcome to Red Hat Linux   25
          Finding Additional Help   43
      Summary   44

▼ 3   GNOME and KDE   45
      The History of X Windows   46
          The Downside   47
          Enter KDE and GNOME   48
          What This Means for Us   48
      About KDE   49
          Licensing Issues   49
          Starting X Windows and KDE   49
          KDE Basics   51
          The KDE Control Center   51
      About GNOME   59
          Starting X Windows and GNOME   59
          GNOME Basics   61
          The GNOME Configuration Tool   62
      Summary   67

▼ 4   Installing Software   69
      The Red Hat Package Manager   70
          Installing a New Package   71
          Querying a Package   72
          Uninstalling a Package   73
          gnorpm   73
      Compiling Software Yourself   74
          Getting and Unpacking the Package   74
          Looking for Documentation   75
          Configuring the Package   76
          Compiling Your Package   76

Installing the Package   77
Clean Up   78
Summary   78

Part II

Single-Host Administration

▼ 5   Managing Users   81
About Users   82
Home Directories   83
Passwords   83
Shells   84
Startup Scripts   85
Mail   85
User Databases   86
The /etc/passwd File   86
The /etc/shadow File   88
The /etc/group File   88
User Management Tools   89
Command-Line User Management   89
Using LinuxConf to Manipulate Users and Groups   95
SetUID and SetGID Programs   100
When a File Isn't Owned   101
Pluggable Authentication Modules (PAM)   101
How PAM Works   102
Downloading and Installing PAM   102
PAM's Files and Their Locations   104
Configuring PAM   105
Debugging PAM   109
Summary   110

▼ 6   The Command Line   111
An Introduction to BASH   112
Job Control   113
Environment Variables   114
Pipes   115
Redirection   116
Command-Line Shortcuts   116
Documentation Tools   118
The man Command   119
The texinfo System   120

File Listings, Ownerships, and Permissions 120
    Listing Files: ls 121
    File and Directory Types 121
    Change Ownership: chown 123
    Change group: chgrp 123
    Change Mode: chmod 124
File Management and Manipulation 126
    Copy Files: cp 126
    Move Files: mv 126
    Link Files: ln 127
    Find a File: find 127
    Convert and Copy a File: dd 128
    File Compression: gzip 129
    Make Special Files: mknod 130
    Create a Directory: mkdir 131
    Remove Directory: rmdir 131
    Show Present Working Directory: pwd 131
    Tape Archive: tar 132
    Concatenate Files: cat 133
    Display a File One Screen at a Time: more 134
    Disk Utilization: du 134
    Show the Directory Location of a File: which 134
    Locating a Command: whereis 135
    Disk Free: df 135
    Synchronize Disks: sync 135
Process Manipulation 136
    List Processes: ps 136
    Show an Interactive List of Processes: top 138
    Send a Signal to a Process: kill 139
Miscellaneous Tools 140
    Show System Name: uname 141
    Who Is Logged In: who 141
    Switch User: su 142
    Networking Tools 142
Editors 145
    vi 145
    emacs 146
    joe 146
    pico 146
Standards 147
Summary 147

▼ 7   Booting and Shutting Down   149
        LILO   150
        Configuring LILO   150
            Additional LILO Options   152
            Adding a New Kernel to Boot   154
        Running LILO   155
        The Steps of Booting   156
            rc Scripts   157
            Writing Your Own rc Script   159
            Enabling and Disabling Services   161
        Odds and Ends of Booting and Shutting Down   163
            fsck!   163
            "I Only See 'LI' When I Boot! What Happened?"   163
            Booting into Single-User ("Recovery") Mode   164
        Summary   165

▼ 8   File Systems   167
        The Makeup of File Systems   168
            i-Nodes   168
            Superblocks   169
            ext3 and ReiserFS   170
        Managing File Systems   171
            Mounting and Unmounting Local Disks   171
            Using fsck   176
        Adding and Partitioning a Disk   178
            Overview of Partitions   179
            Where Disks Exist   179
            Creating Partitions   180
            Making File Systems   186
        Network File Systems   187
            Mounting NFS Partitions   187
            Using the Automounter   188
        Quota Management   192
            Preparing a Disk for Quotas   193
            Configuring Quota Settings   195
            Managing Quotas   197
        Summary   198

▼ 9   Core System Services   199
        The init Service   200
            The /etc/inittab File   200
            The telinit Command   203

The inetd and xinetd Processes 203
The /etc/inetd.conf File 204
The /etc/xinetd.conf File 207
The syslogd Daemon 212
Invoking syslogd 212
The /etc/syslog.conf File 212
The cron Program 217
The crontab File 218
Summary 219

▼ 10   Compiling the Linux Kernel 221
What Exactly Is a Kernel? 223
Finding Kernel Source Code 224
Getting the Correct Version 224
Unpacking the Kernel Source Code 225
Building the Kernel 227
The make xconfig Process 227
Kernel Features and Modules 229
Compiling the Kernel 234
Installing the Kernel 235
It Didn't Work! 236
Patching the Kernel 237
Downloading and Unpacking Patches 237
Applying the Patch 238
Summary 239

▼ 11   Securing an Individual Server 241
TCP/IP and Network Security 243
The Importance of Port Numbers 243
Tracking Services 244
Using the netstat Command 245
Security Implications of netstat's Output 246
Shutting Down Services 247
Monitoring Your System 248
Making the Best Use of syslog 249
Monitoring Bandwidth with MRTG 250
COPS 250
TripWire 250
SATAN 251
Helpful Web Sites and Mailing Lists 251
CERT 251
BugTraq 252

Rootshell 252
Security Focus 252
Odds and Ends 252
Summary 253

Part III

Internet Services

▼ 12 DNS 257
Before DNS: The /etc/hosts File 259
The Guts of DNS 260
Domains and Hosts 260
Subdomains 262
in-addr.arpa Domain 263
Types of Servers 263
Installing a DNS Server 265
What to Download, Unpack, and Read 266
Configuring Clients 269
Client-Side DNS (a.k.a. the Resolver) 269
Getting Ready for DNS Servers: The named.conf File 271
The Specifics 272
Configuring Servers 284
Updating the named.conf File for a Primary Zone 285
Updating the named.conf for a Secondary Zone 286
Updating the named.conf File for a Caching Zone 287
DNS Records Types 288
Putting It All Together 292
A Complete Configuration 293
The DNS Toolbox 297
kill -HUP 298
host 298
dig 299
whois 299
Other References 302
Summary 302

▼ 13 FTP 305
The Mechanics of FTP 306
Client/Server Interactions 306
Getting the Latest wu-ftpd 307
Read the READMEs 308
Compiling and Installing wu-ftpd 308

Configuring wu-ftpd 310
    Controlling Access Through the /etc/ftpaccess File 311
    The Log File 322
    File Conversions on the Fly 323
    Configuring Host Access 326
Cookbook Access Solutions 326
    Anonymous Only 326
    Mixed Access 330
    Registered Users Only 331
Configuring a Virtual FTP Server 332
Summary 333

▼ 14   Setting Up Your Web Server Using Apache 335
The Mechanics of HTTP 336
    Headers 336
    Nonstandard Ports 337
    Process Ownership and Security 338
Installing the Apache HTTP Server 339
    Compiling Apache 340
    Starting Up and Shutting Down Apache 341
    Testing Your Installation 342
Configuring Apache 342
    Creating a Simple Root-Level Page 342
    Apache Configuration Files 344
    Common Configuration Changes 344
    Configuring Virtual Domains 345
Basic Troubleshooting with Apache 347
Summary 347

▼ 15   SMTP 349
The Mechanics of SMTP 350
    Rudimentary SMTP Details 350
    Security Implications 352
    SMTP vs. POP 354
    Recommended Texts 354
Finding and Installing Sendmail 355
    Downloading Sendmail 355
    Compiling Sendmail 356
Fast Configure for Red Hat 7 358
    Your Official Domain Name 358
    As Whom Do You Masquerade? 358
    Differing File Locations 359

The Right Way: Configuring Sendmail with MC Files 360
   Enough M4 for Sendmail 360
   The Sendmail Macros 363
   A Complete Sample Configuration 373
   Compiling Macros into a Configuration File 374
Installing Sendmail 374
Beyond the Primary Configuration File 375
   The Aliases File 375
   Spam Control: The "Access" Database 376
Real-Life Sendmail Issues 378
   mailq 378
   Is Sendmail Running? 379
   Where Does Sendmail Keep Its Queues and Spools? 380
   How to Remove Entries from the Queue 380
   Flushing the Queue 381
   Mail Logging 381
Summary 382

▼ 16 Post Office Protocol (POP) 383
The Mechanics of POP 385
   Reading Mail with Telnet 385
   Conflicts Between POP and Other Protocols 388
Qpopper 388
   Installing Qpopper 388
   Compiling Qpopper 389
   Setting Up Qpopper 391
Advanced Qpopper Configurations 393
   Server Mode 393
   Special Authentication 393
   Authenticated POP 394
   Publishing Bulletins 395
   Command-Line Options for Qpopper 396
Summary 397

▼ 17 The Secure Shell (SSH) 399
Public Key Cryptography 400
   Key Characteristics 402
   Cryptography References 403
SSH Versions and Distributions 404
   OpenSSH and OpenBSD 404
   Alternative Vendors for SSH Clients 405
   The Weakest Link 405

Downloading, Compiling, and Installing SSH   406
     Server Startup and Shutdown   408
Using SSH   409
     Applications Related to SSH   409
Summary   410

Part IV

Intranet Services

▼ 18   Network File System (NFS)   413
The Mechanics of NFS   414
     Mounting and Accessing a Partition   414
     Security Considerations for NFS   415
     Versions of NFS   415
Enabling NFS   416
     The Components of NFS   417
     Kernel Support for NFS   417
Configuring NFS Servers   417
     The /etc/exports Configuration File   418
     Telling the NFS Server Process About /etc/exports   419
     Common Problems   420
Configuring NFS Clients   420
     The mount Command   421
Common Uses for NFS Partitions   424
Troubleshooting NFS   425
     Stale File Handles   425
     Permission Denied   425
     Hard vs. Soft Mounts   425
Summary   426

▼ 19   Network Information Service (NIS)   427
Inside NIS   428
     The NIS Servers   429
     Domains   429
Configuring the Master NIS Server   430
     Establishing the Domain Name   430
     Starting NIS   431
     Editing the Makefile   431
     Using ypinit   434
Configuring an NIS Client   436
     Editing the /etc/yp.conf File   436
     Setting Up the Startup Script   437
     Editing the /etc/nsswitch.conf File   438
     Testing Your NIS Client Configuration   438

Configuring a Secondary NIS Server 439
    Setting the Domain Name 439
    Setting Up the NIS Master to Push to Slaves 439
    Running ypinit 440
NIS Tools 441
Using NIS in Configuration Files 441
Implementing NIS in a Real Network 442
    A Small Network 443
    A Segmented Network 443
    Networks Bigger than Buildings 444
Summary 444

▼ **20 Samba** **445**
The Mechanics of SMB 446
    Usernames and Passwords 446
    Encrypted Passwords 447
    The Differences Between smbd and nmbd 447
    Compiling and Installing Samba 448
    Red Hat 7 and RPM Installations 450
Samba Administration 451
    Starting and Stopping Samba 451
Using SWAT 452
    Setting Up SWAT 453
    The SWAT Menus 455
    Creating a Share 457
Using smbclient 457
    Browsing a Server 458
    Remote File Access 460
    Remote Printer Access 461
Using smbmount 462
Encrypted Password Support 462
    Allowing NULL Passwords 463
    Changing Passwords with smbpasswd 463
Troubleshooting Samba 463
Summary 464

▼ **21 Printing** **465**
The Basics of lpd 467
Installing LPRng 467
    Starting LPRng on Boot 469
    Fixing Man Pages for Red Hat 7 469
    Restarting LPD on a Live System 470
    Installing ifhp 470

Configuring /etc/printcap 471
    Sample /etc/printcap Files 473
    Implementing Your Changes 474
The /ETC/lpd.perms File 474
    The Format of /etc/lpd.perms 475
    Defaults 475
    Permission Keywords 476
    Example of /etc/lpd.perms 477
Clients of lpd 477
    lpr 477
    lpq 478
    lprm 478
Summary 479

▼ **22** DHCP 481

The Mechanics of DHCP 483
The DHCP Server 483
    Downloading, Compiling, and Installing a DHCP Server . . 483
    Configuring the DHCP Server 484
    A Sample dhcpd.conf File 490
    General Runtime Behavior 490
The DHCP Client Daemon 491
    Downloading, Compiling, and Installing a DHCP Client . . 491
    Configuring the DHCP Client 491
Summary 493

▼ **23** Backups 495

Evaluating Your Backup Needs 496
Managing the Backup Device and Files 498
    Using mknod to Create the Device Files 499
    Manipulating the Tape Device with mt 500
Command-Line Tools 501
    dump and restore 501
    tar 506
Summary 506

Part V

Advanced Linux Networking

▼ **24** TCP/IP for System Administrators 511

The Layers 512
    Packets 513
    TCP/IP Layers and the OSI Model 515

The Protocols 517
    Ethernet 517
    IP 517
    TCP 517
    UDP 518
    ICMP 519
Headers 519
    Ethernet 519
    IP 521
    TCP 525
    UDP 529
A Complete TCP Connection 530
    Opening a Connection 531
    Transferring Data 532
    Closing the Connection 533
How ARP Works 534
    The ARP Header: ARP Works with Other Protocols, Too! . . 535
Bringing IP Networks Together 536
    Hosts and Networks 536
    Netmasks 538
    Static Routing 541
    Dynamic Routing with RIP 543
Summary 548

▼ 25 Network Configuration 549
Modules and Network Interfaces 550
ifconfig 551
    Simple Usage 551
    Additional Parameters 553
Using Routers 554
    Simple Usage 555
    Displaying Routes 556
Summary 558

▼ 26 Advanced Linux Networking 559
IP Aliasing 561
Packet Filtering 562
    How Packet Filtering Works 563
    ipchains 566
    iptables 574
    Cookbook Solutions 577

IP Masquerading 583
   The Three-Line IP Masquerading Solution 586
   Masquerading Proxies 587
Summary 588

▼ **27** The /proc File System 589
What's Inside the /proc Directory? 590
   Tweaking Files Inside of /proc 591
Some Useful /proc Entries 591
   Enumerated /proc Entries 594
Common Reports and Settings Done with /proc 594
   SYN Flood Protection 594
   Issues on High-Volume Servers 595
   Debugging Hardware Conflicts 596
Summary 596

Part VI

Appendixes

▼ **A** Programming Languages That Accompany Red Hat Linux 599

▼ **B** Getting the Usual Done 605

▼   Index 611

▼   About the CD 645

ACKNOWLEDGMENTS

When I started the update to the second edition, I foolishly thought, "Hey, it's the second edition. Just bring it up to date and I'll be done." Yeah, right.

So, to the time commitments I already had at work, I added this project. And yet again I underestimated the effort required to get it done. You'd think I would've learned by now. Despite this, my wonderful wife Heidi has supported me all the way through it. This book is as much her creation as it is mine. *Thank you, Heidi. Where would I be without you?*

Before Heidi came to my rescue, my wonderful family made it possible for me to learn volumes about the world of technology around me. And for that, I thank my parents, Manjari and Jagdish Shah, as well as my sister Mona and her family, Paresh and Sangeet.

The people behind the scenes at Osborne/McGraw-Hill were also key to making this book happen. Franny Kelly, Alexander Corona, Janet Walden, and Emily Wolman were instrumental in turning my haphazard submissions into an organized work. Arthur Chan, my technical editor and friend, did an excellent job of making sure what went into print is technically sound. My thanks to all of you.

Last, but certainly not least, are my cohorts at ClickArray Networks who have made work not only a fun and exciting place, but a place where I can learn new and interesting things that have, in one way or another, found their way into this book.

INTRODUCTION

System administrators are a unique bunch. As a group, we are probably the most significant consumers of reference and training books, and we probably demand the most from them (at least, all of my peers do). And, of course, we get really annoyed with books that waste our time.

We're also a curious bunch. Most of my IT friends are gadget freaks (my wife included). We love to live on the edge of new technologies and find out what all the buzz is about before our users do. We like to do this for two very simple reasons—because it's fun, and because we need to understand the technology before the CEO reads about it in *BusinessWeek* and demands to know why we aren't running it.

And Linux, it seems, is one of those buzzes.

Diehards will argue that Linux has been a buzz since the mid-1990s (it's been available since 1991). I personally started using Linux in 1994 when some friends of mine suggested I make better use of my "huge" 340MB hard disk. I deployed Linux as a server operating system in 1995, when a coffee shop in my area decided to become a "cyber-cafe." In 1997, Linux became mature enough for me to deploy it as a primary server in a 100-user office environment, where server crashes meant being paged at any hour of the night. Linux held up well in all those roles, but even I will agree that it didn't hit the limelight until the big players of the industry decided it was noteworthy. (One of my favorite comic strips shows a penguin, the Linux mascot, strapped to a large jet engine labeled "IBM," with the caption, "How do you make a penguin fly?")

So, when IBM started porting DB2 to Linux, SGI adopted Linux as its primary desktop OS, and even Dell made Red Hat Linux a preinstallation option on servers...well, that's what started the *real* buzz.

WHO SHOULD READ THIS BOOK

The title of this book says it's a "beginners guide," and that's mostly true. What the title should really say is that it's a "beginners-to-Linux guide," because we do make a few assumptions about you, the reader.

First, we assume you are already familiar with the Windows environment. At the very least, you should be a strong user in Windows and know something about the networked Windows environment. Although you needn't be an NT or 2000 expert, some exposure to NT/2000 will help your understanding of the hairier concepts we discuss. We started with this assumption because we didn't want to waste time repeating what most folks from a Windows background already know, and instead focused on the new stuff that Linux brings to the table.

In addition to your Windows background, we assume that you're interested in having more information about the topics introduced here. After all, we're spending 30 or 40 pages on topics with entire books devoted to them! So several chapters include references to other texts. We urge you to take advantage of these references—no matter how advanced you think you're becoming, there is always more to learn.

WHAT'S IN THIS BOOK

Linux Administration: A Beginner's Guide is organized into five parts.

Part I: Installing Linux as a Server

The first part is targeted at folks with no experience in Linux and who want a hand installing it and getting rolling.

Chapter 1 focuses on the architectural differences between NT/2000 and Linux and will help you understand why some things in the Linux environment are the way they are. Chapter 2 puts a unique spin on an installation chapter: Instead of just regurgitating installation notes from the product, we help you specifically configure your Linux system as a server. Chapter 3 expands on the installation process by showing you how to set up the two most popular graphical environments for Linux, GNOME and KDE. We dedicated an entire chapter to this because we think it's important to have a pleasant working environment when you need to log into the server to take care of your administrative duties. Finally, Chapter 4 documents the process of installing software under Linux. We cover the two most popular methods (at least for system administrators): using RPMs and compiling the package yourself.

Part II: Single-Host Administration

The second part is geared toward the administration of features common to all Linux systems, not just servers. Some of these chapters, including 5 and 6, are really tutorials that help you use the system effectively. After all, what fun is a new operating system if you don't know how to use it? Chapter 7 starts getting into the nitty-gritty of startup and shutdown, as well as setting up Linux's boot manager, LILO. Chapter 8 takes a turn toward the disk and discusses the process of managing disks, creating partitions, and configuring quotas. Chapter 9 visits some of the lowest levels of the system that you'll work with as a system administrator: core system services. These include key processes such as `init`, the "Grandfather of All Processes." The somewhat tricky task of compiling a Linux kernel is documented in Chapter 10, which not only steps you through the process, but explains it as well. We close Part II with a chapter on basic system security.

Part III: Internet Services

In the third part, you'll study all the services needed to run an Internet site. This includes DNS, FTP, the Web, SMTP Mail, POP Mail, and Secure Shell (SSH)—Chapters 12 through 17, respectively. In each of these chapters we walk through downloading, compiling, and installing the service software, including the configuration process. Where appropriate, we even provide entire configuration files for common configurations.

Part IV: Intranet Services

The fourth part goes in the opposite direction of Part III. Rather than studying services for everyone on the Internet, we examine services offered only to people on your internal network. Starting with NFS in Chapter 18, we learn how to set up both the server and client sides. Then Chapter 19 explains the configuration of NIS clients and servers, including some cookbook solutions for a company-wide deployment. Chapter 20 is for those of you looking to replace NT/2000 in the server room with Samba. Printing solutions are discussed in Chapter 21, along with the LPD system. Chapter 22 describes DHCP, showing you how to configure both a server and a client component. Finally, we finish up by discussing the details of backups in Chapter 23. This includes some coverage of tools that come with Linux, as well as references to commercial packages.

Part V: Advanced Linux Networking

The fifth part moves into some of the more complex features of Linux networking. Chapter 24 begins with an in-depth look at TCP/IP from the point of view of a systems administrator. Chapter 25 helps you understand the command-line tools for configuring network cards and routing tables. Chapter 26 looks at the `ipchains` and `iptables` tools and their role in configuring IP masquerading and IP firewalls. Finally, Chapter 27 examines the **/proc** file system.

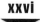

Part VI: Appendixes

Appendix A documents the programming languages that come with Red Hat Linux. Appendix B lists the many tools available for Linux that make it possible to use Linux as your primary desktop operating system.

Updates and Feedback

To get updates on errata issues regarding this book, visit http://www.planetoid.org/linux for more information. This is especially important if you find that some URLs I refer to have changed since I wrote a chapter.

I would also like to hear your feedback. Feel free to e-mail me at linuxadmin@planetoid.org. Unfortunately, due to the volume of e-mail I currently deal with (along with silly things like my day job), I may not have time to individually respond. If you have questions about Linux, I highly recommend you visit one of the many Linux-oriented Web sites that host piles of experts who are ready to help. A good place to start is the Linux home page at http://www.linux.org.

PART I

Installing Linux as a Server

CHAPTER 1

Technical Summary of Linux Distributions and Windows 2000

Unless you've been stranded on a deserted island somewhere or shunning the media and ignoring the trade press, you already have a pretty good idea of what Linux is and why you might be interested in it. So I won't bore you with the typical "History of Linux" introduction that you might find in other texts. Instead, we'll take a look at the technical differences between Linux and Windows 2000 (likely the platform for which you are considering Linux as a replacement). This chapter also explains the GNU (GNU's Not UNIX) license, which may help you understand why much of Linux is the way it is.

LINUX AND LINUX DISTRIBUTIONS

Usually people understand Linux to be an entire package of developer tools, editors, GUIs, networking tools, and so forth. More formally, such packages are called *distributions*. You've most likely heard of the Linux distributions named Red Hat, Caldera, and SuSE, which have received a great deal of press and have been purchased for thousands of installations. Noncommercial distributions of Linux such as Debian are less well known and haven't reached the same scale of popularity.

What's interesting about all Linux distributions is that almost all of the tools with which they ship were not written by the companies themselves. Rather, other people have released their programs with licenses, allowing their redistribution with source code. By and large, these tools are also available on other variants of UNIX, and some of them are becoming available under Windows as well. The makers of the distribution simply bundle them up into one convenient package that's easy to install. (Some distribution makers also develop value-added tools that make their distribution easier to administer or compatible with more hardware, but the software that they ship is generally written by others.)

So if we consider a distribution everything you need for Linux, what then *is* Linux exactly? Linux itself is the core of the operating system: the *kernel*. The kernel is the program acting as Chief of Operations. It is responsible for starting and stopping other programs (such as editors), handling requests for memory, accessing disks, and managing network connections. The complete list of kernel activities could easily be a chapter in itself, and in fact, several books documenting the kernel's internal functions have been written.

The kernel is known as a nontrivial program. It is also what puts the Linux into all those Linux distributions. All distributions use the exact same kernel, and thus the fundamental behavior of all Linux distributions is the same.

What separates one distribution from the next is the value-added tools that come with each one. For example, Red Hat includes a very useful tool called Xconfigurator that makes configuring the graphical interface a very straightforward task. Asking "Which distribution is better?" is much like asking "Which is better, Coke or Pepsi?" Almost all colas have the same basic ingredients—carbonated water, caffeine, and high fructose corn syrup—thereby giving the similar effect of quenching thirst and bringing on a small caffeine-and-sugar buzz. In the end, it's a question of personal preference.

FREE SOFTWARE AND THE GNU LICENSE

In the early 1980s, Richard Stallman began a movement within the software industry. He preached (and still does) that software should be free. Note that by free, he doesn't mean in terms of price, but rather free in the same sense as freedom. This meant shipping not just a product, but the entire source code as well.

Stallman's policy was obviously a wild departure from the early eighties mentality of selling prepackaged software, but his concept of free software was in line with the initial distributions of UNIX from Bell Labs. Early UNIX systems did contain full source code. Yet by the late 1970s, source code was typically removed from UNIX distributions and could be acquired only by paying large sums of money to AT&T. The Berkeley Software Distribution (BSD) maintained a free version but had to deal with many lawsuits from AT&T until it could be proven that nothing in the BSD was from AT&T.

The idea of giving away source code is a simple one: Users of the software should never be forced to deal with a developer who might or might not support that user's intentions for the software. The user should never have to wait for bug fixes to be published. More important, code developed under the scrutiny of other programmers is typically of higher quality than code written behind locked doors. The greatest benefit of free software, however, comes from the users themselves: Should they need a new feature, they can add it to the program and then contribute it back to the source, so that everyone else can benefit from it.

From this line of thinking has sprung a desire to release a complete UNIX-like system to the public, free of license restrictions. Of course, before you can build any operating system, you need to build tools. And this is how the GNU project was born.

 NOTE: GNU stands for GNU's Not UNIX—recursive acronyms are part of hacker humor. If you don't understand why it's funny, don't worry. You're still in the majority.

What Is the GNU Public License?

The most important thing to emerge from the GNU project has been the *GNU Public License (GPL).* This license explicitly states that the software being released is free, and no one can ever take away these freedoms. It is acceptable to take the software and resell it, even for a profit; however, in this resale, the seller must release full source code, including any changes. Because the resold package remains under the GPL, the package can be distributed for free and resold yet again by anyone else for a profit. Of primary importance is the liability clause: The programmers are not liable for any damages caused by their software.

It should be noted that the GPL is not the only license used by free software developers (although it is arguably the most popular). Other licenses, such as BSD and Apache, have similar liability clauses but differ in terms of their redistribution. For instance, the BSD license allows people to make changes to the code and ship those changes without having to disclose the added code. (The GPL would require that the added code be shipped.) For more information about other open-source licenses, check out http://www.opensource.org.

The Advantages of Free Software

If the GPL seems a bad idea from the standpoint of commercialism, consider the recent surge of successful freeware packages—they are indicative of a system that does indeed work. This success has evolved for two reasons: First, as mentioned earlier, errors in the code itself are far more likely to be caught and quickly fixed under the watchful eyes of peers. Second, under the GPL system, programmers can release code without the fear of being sued. Without that protection, no one would ever release his or her code.

This concept of course begs the question of why anyone would release his or her work for free. The answer is simple: Most projects don't start out as full-featured, polished pieces of work. They may begin life as a quick hack to solve a specific problem bothering the programmer. As a quick-and-dirty hack, the code has no sales value. But when this code is shared with others who have similar problems and needs, it becomes a useful tool. Other program users begin to enhance it with features they need, and these additions travel back to the original program. The project thus evolves as the result of a group effort and eventually reaches full refinement. This polished program contains contributions from possibly hundreds if not thousands of programmers who have added little pieces here and there. In fact, the original author's code is likely to be little in evidence.

Here's another reason for the success of generally licensed software: Any project manager who has worked on commercial software knows that the *real* cost of development software isn't in the development phase. It's really in the cost of selling, marketing, supporting, documenting, packaging, and shipping that software. A programmer carrying out a weekend lark to fix a problem with a tiny, kluged program lacks the interest, time, and backing money to turn that hack into a profitable product.

When Linus Torvalds released Linux in 1991, he released it under the GPL. As a result of its open charter, Linux has had a notable number of contributors and analyzers. This participation has made Linux very strong and rich in features. Torvalds himself estimates that since the v.2.2.0 kernel, his contributions represent only 5% of the total code base.

Since anyone can take the Linux kernel (and other supporting programs), repackage them, and resell them, some people have made money with Linux. As long as these individuals release the kernel's full source code along with their individual packages, and as long as the packages are protected under the GPL, everything is legal. Of course, this means that packages released under the GPL can be resold by other people under other names for a profit.

Why Commercial Software Doesn't Mean Liability

In the previous section, I mentioned something that tends to frighten a lot of IT managers: The GPL removes any and all liability from the programmer. You cannot sue someone who has released their code under the GPL because the code was unfit for your needs and caused you financial harm. So if no one is taking the heat for when things go wrong, why should the IT managers? Wouldn't it be better to purchase a commercial package so that you can point a finger at someone else?

No. And the reason is in the fine print. Take a look at that license you agreed to when opening up the software. Read it carefully, and you may be surprised to find that commercial software uses similar clauses to the GPL as far as liability issues are concerned. You can't sue a developer, the developer's company, or anyone else because the software you purchased failed to deliver and caused you financial harm.

For example, the Windows 2000 Professional End User License Agreement (EULA) has a paragraph that says Microsoft isn't liable for ". . .any special, incidental, indirect, or consequential damages whatsoever . . ." The third sentence in the EULA also states that "you agree to be bound by the terms of this EULA by installing, copying, or otherwise using the product."

Of course, this doesn't mean that you shouldn't buy commercial software. There are many packages that are worth their price (and yes, Microsoft even makes some of them). However, falling into the trap of "who's liable" isn't the right way to decide which software is best for your needs.

In the end, what makes a package from one person more valuable than a package from another person are the value-added features, support channels, and documentation. Even IBM can agree to this; it's how they made a bulk of their money between the 1930s and 1970s: The money isn't in the product, it's in the services that go with it.

THE MAJOR DIFFERENCES BETWEEN WINDOWS 2000 AND LINUX

As you might imagine, the differences between Microsoft Windows 2000 and the Linux operating systems cannot be completely discussed in the confines of this section. Throughout these chapters, topic by topic, we'll examine the specific contrasts between the two systems.

In some chapters, you'll find that we don't derive any comparisons because a major difference doesn't really exist.

But before we attack the details, let's take a moment to discuss the primary architectural differences between the two operating systems.

Single Users vs. Multiusers vs. Network Users

Windows 2000 was designed according to the "one computer, one desk, one user" vision of Microsoft's cofounder Bill Gates. For the sake of discussion, we'll call this philosophy *single-user*. In this arrangement, two people cannot work in parallel running (for example) Microsoft Word on the same machine at the same time. (On the other hand, one might question the wisdom of doing this with an overwhelmingly weighty program like Word!)

Linux borrows its philosophy from UNIX. When UNIX was originally developed at Bell Labs in the early 1970s, it existed on a PDP-7 computer that needed to be shared by an entire department. It required a design that allowed for *multiple users* to log in to the central machine at the same time. Various people could be editing documents, compiling programs, and doing other work at the exact same time. The operating system on the central machine took care of the "sharing" details, so that each user seemed to have an individual system. This multiuser tradition continued through today, on other UNIXs as well. And since Linux's birth in the early 1990s, it has supported the multiuser arrangement.

Today, the most common implementation of a multiuser setup is to support *servers*—systems dedicated to running large programs for use by many clients. Each member of a department can have a smaller workstation on the desktop, with enough power for day-to-day work. When they need to do something requiring significantly more CPU power or memory, they can run the operation on the server.

"But hey!" you may be arguing, "Windows 2000 can allow people to offload-compute heavy work to a single machine! Just look at SQL Server!" Well, that position is only half correct. Both Linux and Windows 2000 are indeed capable of providing services such as databases over the network. We can call users of this arrangement *network users,* since they are never actually logged into the server but rather send requests to the server. The server does the work and then sends the results back to the user via the network. The catch in this case is that an application must be specifically written to perform such server/client duties. Under Linux, a user can run any program allowed by the system administrator on the server without having to redesign that program. Most users find the ability to run arbitrary programs on other machines to be of significant benefit.

Separation of the GUI and the Kernel

Taking a cue from the Macintosh design concept, Windows 2000 developers integrated the graphical user interface (GUI) with the core operating system. One simply does not exist without the other. The benefit to this tight coupling of the operating system and user interface is consistency in the appearance of the system. Although Microsoft does not impose rules as strict as Apple's, with respect to the appearance of applications, most developers tend to stick with a basic look and feel among applications.

On the other hand, Linux (and UNIX in general) has kept the two elements—user interface and operating system—separate. The X Window System interface is run as a user-level application, which makes it more stable. If the GUI (which is very complex for both 2000 and Linux) fails, Linux's core does not go down with it. X Windows also differs from the 2000 GUI in that it isn't a complete user interface: It only defines how basic objects should be drawn and manipulated on the screen.

The most significant feature of X Windows is its ability to display windows across a network and onto another workstation's screen. This allows a user sitting on Host A to log in to Host B, run an application on Host B, and have all of the output routed back to Host A. It is possible for two people to be logged in to the same machine, running a Linux equivalent of Microsoft Word (such as ApplixWare, WordPerfect, or StarOffice) at the same time.

In addition to the X Windows core, a window manager is needed to create a useful environment. Linux distributions come with several window managers and include support for GNOME and KDE, both of which are available on other variants of UNIX as well. When set as default, both GNOME and KDE offer an environment that is friendly even to the casual Windows user.

So which is better—Windows 2000 or Linux—and why? That depends on what you are trying to do. The integrated environment provided by Windows 2000 is convenient and less complex than Linux, but it lacks the X Windows feature that allows applications to display their windows across the network on another workstation. Windows 2000's GUI is consistent but cannot be turned off, whereas X Windows doesn't have to be running (and consuming valuable memory) on a server.

The Network Neighborhood

The native mechanism for Windows folk to share disks on servers or with each other is through the Network Neighborhood. In a typical scenario, users *attach* to a share and have the system assign it a drive letter. As a result, the separation between client and server is clear. The only problem with this method of sharing data is more people-oriented than technology-oriented: People have to know which servers contain which data.

With Windows 2000, a new feature borrowed from UNIX has also appeared: *mounting*. By mounting a share, Windows makes the share look as if it were just another directory located on the user's local disk. This gives the illusion that a single unified directory structure exists, completely local to the machine. The downside to this mechanism under Windows 2000 is that it requires a reboot for each mount you want to do.

Linux, using the Network File System (NFS), has supported the concept of mounting since its inception. Unlike Windows 2000, mounting under Linux does not require a reboot. In fact, Chapter 8 discusses the Linux Automounter which dynamically mounts and unmounts partitions on an as-needed basis.

A common example of mounting partitions under Linux is with mounted home directories: The user's home directories reside on a server, and the client mounts the directories at boot time (automatically). So **/home** exists on the client, but **/home/username** exists on the server.

Under Linux NFS, the user never has to know server names or directory paths, and their ignorance is your bliss! No more questions about which server to connect to. Even better, users need not know when the need arises to change the server configuration. Under Linux, you can change the names of servers and adjust this information on client-side systems without making any announcements or having to reeducate users. Anyone who has ever had to reorient users to new server arrangements is aware of the repercussions that may occur.

Printing works much in the same way. Under Linux, printers receive names that are independent of the printer's actual host name. (This is especially important if the printer doesn't speak TCP/IP.) Clients point to a print server whose name cannot be changed without administrative authorization. Settings don't get changed without your knowing it. The print server can then redirect all print requests as needed. The Linux uniform interface will go a long way toward improving what may be a chaotic printer arrangement in your installation. It also means you don't have to install print drivers in several locations.

NOTE: If you intend to use Linux to serve Windows 2000/NT/98 clients via the Samba package, you'll still have to deal with notifying users about server shares and printer assignments. You can read more about Samba in Chapter 20.

The Registry vs. Text Files

I think of the Windows 2000 Registry as the ultimate configuration database—thousands upon thousands of entries, very few of which are completely documented, some located on servers and some located on clients.

"What? Did you say your Registry *got corrupted*?" <maniacal laughter> "Well, yes, we can try to restore it from last night's backups, but then Excel starts acting funny and the technician (who charges $50 just to answer the phone) said to re-install . . ."

If you're not getting my message, I'm saying that the Windows 2000 Registry system is, at best, very difficult to manage. Although it's a good idea in theory, I've never emerged without injury from a battle with the Registry.

Linux does not have a registry. This is both a blessing and a curse. The blessing is that configuration files are most often kept as a series of text files (think of the Windows .INI files before the days of the Registry). This setup means you're able to edit configuration files using the text editor of your choice rather than tools like **regedit**. In many cases, it also means you can liberally comment those configuration files so that six months from now you won't forget why you set something up in a particular way. With most tools that come with Linux, configuration files exist in the **/etc** directory or one of its subdirectories.

The curse of a no-registry arrangement is that there is no standard way of writing configuration files. Each application or server can have its own format. Many applications are now coming bundled with GUI-based configuration tools. So you can do a basic setup easily, and then manually edit the configuration file when you need to do more complex adjustments.

In reality, having text files to hold configuration information usually turns out to be an efficient method. Once set, they rarely need to be changed; even so, they are straight text files and thus easy to view when needed. Even more helpful is that it's easy to write scripts to read the same configuration files and modify their behavior accordingly. This is especially helpful when automating server maintenance operations, which is crucial in a large site with many servers.

> **NOTE:** A very interesting side effect of having configuration files exist as a series of text files is that configuration of these files can be automated. This is very useful in situations where a large number of workstations needs to be deployed or new workstations are added frequently. Even with tools like Norton Ghost, Windows installs simply cannot be automated or scripted.

Domains

For a group of Windows NT systems to work well together, they should exist in a domain. This requires a dedicated NT Server system configured as a Primary Domain Controller (PDC). Domains are the basis of the Windows NT security model.

The basis of Linux's network security model is NIS, Network Information Service. NIS is a simple database (based on text files!) which is shared with client workstations. Each primary NIS server (which by the way, does not require a complete dedicated system as a PDC usually does) establishes a domain. Any client workstation wanting to join this domain is allowed to do so, as long as it can set its domain name. To set the domain name, you must use the **root** user—Linux's equivalent to an Administrator user. Being part of the domain does not, however, immediately grant you rights that you would otherwise not have. The domain administrator must still add your login to the master NIS password list so that the rest of the systems in the network recognize your presence.

The key difference between NIS and NT domains is that the NIS server by itself does not perform authentication the way a PDC does. Instead, each host looks up the login and password information from the server and compares it to the user's entered information. It's up to the individual application to properly authenticate a user. Thankfully, the code necessary to authenticate a user is very trivial.

Another important difference is that NIS can be used as a general purpose database and thus hold any kind of information that needs to be shared with the rest of the network. (This usually includes mount tables for NFS and e-mail aliases.) The only limitation is that each NIS map can only have one key, and the database mechanism doesn't scale well beyond about 20,000 entries. Of course, a site with 20,000 users shouldn't keep them all in a single NIS domain, anyway!

A final note about NT domains and NIS: Neither is required for the base operating system to work. Nevertheless, they are key if you need to maintain a multiuser site with a reasonable level of security.

Active Directory

So how does NIS stack up to Active Directory? Good question. The answer is "it doesn't." Active Directory was designed to be much more than what NIS was designed for. This really places the two into different classes of applications.

Active Directory (AD) is designed to be a generic solution to the problem of large sites that need to have their different departments share administrative control—something that NT's Domain model did very poorly. (Setting up interdomain trusts under NT often required a great deal of patience and a willingness to fix "broken" trusts on a regular basis.) AD is also an opportunity for Microsoft to fix many of its broken naming schemes and move toward an Internet-centric scheme based on DNS. The result is quite beastly and requires a lot of time to master. Mark Minasi's book, *Mastering Windows 2000 Server, Second Edition*, (Sybex, 2000) dedicates well over 100 pages to the subject. However, in a smaller network, most folks will find that it looks and feels mostly like NT-style domains with some new whiz-bang features thrown in for good measure.

Don't get me wrong, though—AD is a strong step in the right direction for Windows 2000 and presents solid competition for the Linux camp to think about how directory services can be better integrated into their designs. But despite what Microsoft tells you, AD will not solve all the world's problems, let alone all of yours, in one easy step.

So does Linux have anything that compares to AD? Yes, actually, it does. Several implementations of LDAP (Lightweight Directory Access Protocol) now exist for Linux, and work is actively being done to allow NIS to tie into LDAP servers. (The radius authentication protocol is also becoming more common.) What makes LDAP interesting is that it is the same underlying technology that Active Directory uses in Win2k. This means that, in theory, it is possible to share LDAP databases between both your UNIX and Windows systems and possibly unify authentication between them. Well, in theory, anyway . . .

OTHER REFERENCES

If you are interested in getting under the hood of the technology revolution (and it's always helpful to know how things work), I recommend the following texts:

▼ *Computer: A History of the Information Machine,* by Martin Campbell-Kelly and William Aspray. (Harper Collins, 1997)

▲ *A Quarter Century of Unix,* by Peter Salus. (Addison-Wesley, 1994)

Neither of these texts discusses Linux specifically. *A Quarter Century of Unix* does tell the Linux history up to the point where the system was just becoming a serious player. Peter Salus writes an interesting discussion of why Linus Torvalds saw a need to create Linux in the first place.

To get the scoop on Linux itself, start with the Linux home page at http://www.linux.org.

SUMMARY

In this chapter, we covered three important topics: Linux distributions, the GNU license (GPL), and the major design differences between Windows 2000 and Linux. You should now have a sharp picture of what lies ahead.

Linux is a very powerful operating system, capable of many things. Perhaps its most important feature is its configurability—it's almost like Silly Putty! You can mold it into anything from basic to the most complex shapes. And breaking it is *not* easy to do. (The **planetoid.org** server was hosted on a Linux server that was up and running for over 450 days before the power supply died—and that was from someone tripping over the power cable! Suffice it to say, its stability is wonderful.) Be sure to keep this in mind as you read the remainder of this book and when you start working with Linux in any environment. Linux isn't just a productive, efficient operation system; it also gives you a chance to think creatively. Before letting yourself fall into the trap of believing that you have to get the feature you want from Uncle Bill [Gates], take a quick trip to the World Wide Web and find out if there isn't in fact a project already in existence that will solve your problem.

CHAPTER 2

Installing Linux in a Server Configuration

A key attribute in Linux's recent success is the remarkable improvement in installation tools. What once was a mildly frightening process many years back has now become almost trivial. Even better, there are many ways to install the software; CD-ROMs are no longer the only choice (although they are still the most common). Network installations are part of the default list of options as well, and they can be a wonderful help when installing a large number of hosts.

> **NOTE:**   The version of Red Hat Linux 7.0 that ships with this book is the "Publishers Edition." This means Red Hat had to make a special effort to get all of the package's source code in addition to their easy-to-install format onto a single CD. As a result, some of the less used packages had to be dropped. For the complete list, look at the README.publishers-edition file located in the root directory of the CD-ROM.

Most default configurations where Linux is installed are already capable of becoming servers. This is due to an unfortunate, slightly naive design decision: being designated a server means that the machine serves everything! From disk services to printers to mail to news to . . . it's all turned on from the start. As we all know, the reality is that most servers are dedicated to performing one or two tasks, and any other installed services simply take up memory and drag on performance.

In this chapter, we discuss the installation process as it pertains to servers. This requires us to do two things: differentiate between a server and client workstation and streamline a server's operation based on its dedicated functions.

We will go through this process for Red Hat Linux, which you will find on the CD-ROM that came with this book.

BEFORE INSTALLATION

Before getting into the actual installation phase, it is important that we take a moment and evaluate two things:

- ▼ The hardware the system is going to run on
- ▲ The server's ideal configuration to provide the services you need

Let's start by examining hardware issues.

Hardware

As with any operating system, before getting started with the installation process, you should determine what hardware configurations would work. Each commercial vendor publishes a hardware compatibility list (HCL) and makes it available on its Web site. (Red Hat's Web site is at http://www.redhat.com/support/hardware.) Be sure you obtain the latest version of the list so that you are confident in the hardware selected. In general, most popular Intel-based configurations work without difficulty.

A general suggestion that applies to all operating systems is to avoid cutting-edge hardware and software configurations. While they appear to be really impressive, they haven't had the maturing process some of the slightly older hardware has gone through. For servers, this usually isn't an issue since there is no need for a server to have the latest and greatest toys, such as fancy video cards. After all, our main goal is to provide a highly available server for our users, not to play Doom. (Although it should be noted that this author, during his less responsible days as a junior-level administrator, found that Linux is wonderfully stable even while running Doom and being a file server.)

Server Design

When a system becomes a server, its stability, availability, and performance become a significant issue. These three factors are usually improved through the purchase of more hardware, which is unfortunate. It's a shame to pay thousands of dollars extra to get a system capable of achieving in all three areas when you could have extracted the desired level of performance out of existing hardware with a little tuning. With Linux, this is not hard. Even better, the gains are outstanding!

The most significant design decision you must make when managing a server configuration is not technical but administrative. You must design a server to be *un*friendly to casual users. This means no cute multimedia tools, no sound card support, and no fancy Web browsers (when at all possible). In fact, it should be a rule that casual usage of a server is strictly prohibited—not only to site users but site administrators as well.

Another important aspect of designing a server is making sure that it has a good environment. As a system administrator, you must ensure the physical safety of your servers by keeping them in a separate room under lock and key (or the equivalent). The only access to the servers for nonadministrative personnel should be through the network. The server room itself should be well ventilated and kept cool. The wrong environment is an accident waiting to happen. Systems that overheat and nosy users who think they know how to fix problems can be as great a danger to sever stability as bad software (arguably even more so).

Once the system is in a safe place, installing battery backup is also crucial. Backup power serves two key purposes: to keep the system running during a power failure so that it may gracefully shut down, thereby avoiding file damage or loss; and to ensure that voltage spikes, drops, and other noises don't interfere with the health of your system.

Here are some specific things you can do to improve your server situation:

▼ Take advantage of the fact that the graphical user interface is uncoupled from the core operating system, and avoid starting X Windows (Linux's GUI) unless someone needs to sit on console and run an application. After all, like any other application, X Windows requires memory and CPU time to work, both of which are better off going to the server processes instead.

■ Determine what functions the server is to perform, and disable all other functions. Not only are unused functions a waste of memory and CPU, but they are just another issue you need to deal with on the security front.

▲ Unlike some other operating systems, Linux allows you to pick and choose the features you want in the kernel. (You'll learn about this process in Chapter 10.)

The default kernel will already be reasonably well tuned, so you won't have to worry about it; but if you do need to change a feature or upgrade the kernel, be picky about what you add and what you don't. Make sure you really need a feature before adding it.

> **NOTE:**   You may hear an old recommendation that you recompile your kernel to make the most effective use of your system resources. This is no longer true—the only reason to recompile your kernel is to upgrade or add support for a new device. Remember: Don't screw around (lightly) with what's stable and performs reasonably well.

Uptime

All of this chatter about taking care of servers and making sure silly things don't cause them to crash stems from a long-time UNIX philosophy: *Uptime is good. More uptime is better.*

The UNIX (Linux) **uptime** command tells the user how long the system has been running since its last boot, how many users are currently logged in, and how much load the system is experiencing. The last two are useful measures that are necessary for day-to-day system health and long-term planning. (For example, the server load has been staying high lately, so maybe it's time to buy a faster/bigger/better server . . . .)

But the all-important number is how long the server has been running since its last reboot. Long uptimes are a sign of proper care, maintenance, and, from a practical standpoint, system stability. You'll often find UNIX administrators boasting about their server's uptimes the way you hear car buffs boast about horsepower. This is also why you'll hear UNIX administrators cursing at system changes (regardless of operating system) that require a reboot to take effect. You may deny caring about it now, but in six months you'll probably scream at anyone who reboots the system unnecessarily. Don't bother trying to explain this phenomenon to a nonadmin, because they'll just look at you oddly. You'll just know in your heart that your uptime is better than theirs.

Dual-Booting Issues

If you are new to Linux, you may not be ready to commit to a complete system when you just want a test drive. All distributions of Linux can be installed on only certain partitions of your hard disk while leaving others alone. Typically, this means allowing Microsoft Windows to coexist with Linux.

Because we are focusing on server installations, we will not cover the details of building a dual-booting system; however, anyone with a little experience in creating partitions on a disk should be able to figure this out. If you are having difficulty, you may want to refer to the installation guide that comes with your distribution or another one of the many available beginner's guides to Linux.

Some quick hints: If a Windows 95 or Windows 98 partition currently consumes an entire hard disk as drive C:, you can use the **fips** tool to repartition the disk. Simply defragment and then run **fips.exe**. If you are using Windows NT/2000 with NTFS and have already allocated all the disk with data on each partition, you may have to move data around a bit by hand to free up a partition. Don't bother trying to shrink an NTFS partition, though; because of its complexity, it doesn't like being resized, and doing so will lead to corruption.

NOTE: From the perspective of flexibility, NTFS doesn't sound like a good thing, but in reality it is. If you have to run NT or 2000, use NTFS.

You may find using a commercial tool such as Partition Magic to be especially helpful, because it offers support for NTFS, FAT32, and regular FAT, as well as a large number of other file system types. Its user interface is also significantly nicer than `fips`.

Methods of Installation

With the improved connectivity and speed of both local area networks and Internet connections, it is becoming an increasingly popular option to perform installations over the network rather than using a local CD-ROM.

In general, you'll find that network installations become important once you've decided to deploy Linux over many machines and therefore require a fast installation procedure in which many systems can install at the same time.

Typically, server installations aren't well suited to automation, because each server usually has a unique task; thus each server will have a slightly different configuration. For example, a server dedicated to handling logging information sent to it over the network is going to have especially large partitions set up for the appropriate logging directories, compared to a file server that performs no logging of its own. (The obvious exception is for server farms where you have large numbers of replicated servers. But even those installations have their nuances that require attention to detail specific to the installation.)

Because of this, we will focus exclusively on the technique for installing a system from a CD-ROM. Of course, once you have gone through the process from a CD-ROM, you will find performing the network-based installations to be very straightforward.

If It Just Won't Work Right . . .

You've gone through the installation procedure . . . twice. This book said it should work. The installation manual said it should work. The Linux guru you spoke with last week said it should work.

But it's just not working.

In the immortal words of Douglas Adams, *don't panic*. No operating system installs smoothly 100% of the time. (Yes, not even the MacOS!) Hardware doesn't always work as advertised, combinations of hardware conflict with each other, that CD-ROM your friend burned for you has CRC errors on it (remember: it is legal for your buddy to burn you a copy of Linux!), or (hopefully not) the software has a bug.

With Linux, you have several paths you can follow for help. If you have purchased your copy from Caldera or Red Hat, you can always call tech support and reach a knowledgeable person who is dedicated to working through the problem with you. If you didn't purchase a box set, you can try contacting companies such as LinuxCare (www.linuxcare.com), which is a commercial company dedicated to providing help. Last, but certainly not least, is the option of going online for help. An incredible number of Web sites are available to help you get started. They contain not only useful tips and tricks but also documentation and discussion forums where you can post your questions. Obviously, you'll want to start with the site dedicated to your distribution: www.redhat.com for Red Hat Linux, and www.caldera.com for Caldera Linux. (Other distributions have their own sites. Check your distribution for its appropriate Web site information.)

Here are some recommended sites for installation help:

▼ **comp.os.linux.admin**   This is a newsgroup, not a Web site. You can read it through the Web at http://www.deja.com.

■ **http://www.ojichan.com/linux-admin/**   This site contains a book titled *Linux Administration Made Easy*. The book is geared toward cookbook administration tasks and contains some useful tips for installing Red Hat Linux. Unfortunately, the book lacks in more advanced areas of Linux administration—but then again, that's why you bought this book! ·

■ **http://www.linuxdoc.org/**   This site is a collection of wonderful information about all sorts of Linux-related topics, including installation guides. Just a warning, though: Not all documents are up to date. Be sure to check the date of any document's last update before following the directions. There is a mix of cookbook-style help guides as well as guides that give more complete explanations of what is going on.

▲ **http://www.thelinuxgurus.org/**   Here's a complete site for news, reviews, tips, and tricks. The site administrators have done an excellent job at bringing a lot of very useful information into one site.

INSTALLING RED HAT LINUX

In this section, we will document the steps necessary to install Red Hat Linux 7.0 on a stand-alone system. We will take a liberal approach to the process, installing all of the tools possibly relevant to server operations. Later chapters explain each subsystem's purpose and help you determine which ones you really need to keep.

You have two ways to start the boot process: you can use a boot floppy or the CD-ROM. This installation guide assumes you will boot off the CD-ROM to start the Red Hat installation procedure. If you have an older machine not capable of booting off the CD-ROM, you will need to use a boot disk and start the procedure from there.

NOTE: Using the boot disk alters the order of some of the installation steps, such as which language to use and whether to use a hard disk or CD-ROM for installation. Once past the initial differences, you will find that the graphical steps are the same.

> ### "But I Don't Want to Use the Graphical Installer!"
> Don't worry. Red Hat realized that there are still plenty of people who prefer text-based installation tools, and some who need to use them for systems that do not support graphics. If you fall into one of these categories, type **text** at the `boot:` prompt when starting Linux from either the CD-ROM or floppy.

If your system supports bootable CD-ROMs, this is obviously the faster approach. If your distribution did not come with a boot disk and you cannot boot from the CD-ROM, you will need to create the boot disk. We will assume you have a working installation of Windows to create the boot disk.

NOTE: Users of other UNIX operating systems can use the **dd** command to create the boot image onto a floppy disk. Follow the instructions that came with your distribution on using the **dd** command with your floppy device.

Creating a Boot Disk

Once Windows has started and the CD-ROM is in the appropriate drive, open an MS-DOS Prompt window (Start | Program Menu | MS-DOS Prompt), which will give you a command shell prompt. Change over to the CD-ROM drive letter and go into the **dosutils** directory. There you will find the **rawrite.exe** program. Simply run the executable; you will be prompted for the source file and destination floppy. The source file will be on the same drive and is called **/images/boot.img**.

You can find more detail on this process at http://www.redhat.com/support/manuals/RHL-7-Manual/install-guide/s1-steps-install-cdrom.html.

Starting the Installation

To begin the installation process, boot off the CD-ROM. This will present you with a splash screen introducing you to Red Hat 7.0. At the bottom of the screen will be a prompt that reads

```
boot:
```

If you do not press any key, the prompt will automatically time out and begin the installation process. You can press ENTER to start the process immediately.

If you have had some experience with Red Hat installations in the past and do not want the system to automatically probe your hardware, you can type in **expert** at the `boot:` prompt. For most installations, though, you will want to stick with the default.

If you don't have a mouse, or if the installer cannot find yours, you will be presented with a screen that asks whether you want to use the text mode installation or if you want to help the installer figure out what kind of mouse you have. Use the TAB key to select which choice you want, and press ENTER to continue. If you proceed with the text mode, you will find that the basic steps to the installation are similar to those of the graphical interface, and you should be able to follow along with this installation guide. If you need additional help, you can visit Red Hat's help page on the text-mode installation at http://www.redhat.com/support/manuals/RHL-7-Manual/install-guide/ch-textmode.html.

NOTE: As the initial part of the operating system loads and autodetects hardware, do not be surprised if it does not detect your SCSI subsystem. SCSI support is activated later on in the process.

Choosing a Language

The first menu will ask which language you want to use to continue the installation process (see Figure 2-1).

The interface works much like any other Windows-style interface. Simply point to your selection and click. When you are ready, click the Next button in the lower-right portion of the screen.

On the left side of the screen is context-sensitive help. If you don't want to see it, you can click the Hide Help button at the lower-left part of the screen.

Figure 2-1.   Selecting a language during installation

The Back button in the lower right of the screen is grayed out at this point, because there have been no prior options to select.

Selecting a Keyboard Type

This next menu allows you to select what kind of keyboard you have. The options are broken into three dialog boxes: The first lists the types of keyboards supported; the second lists available layouts the keyboard can have; and the third box allows you to enable *dead keys*, which enable you to type special characters with multiple keystrokes (e.g., Ñ and Ô). The bottom dialog box is meant for you to type in, thereby allowing you to test whether your keyboard works. You do not have to type anything there if you don't want to.

For most of us, the keyboard type will be one of the Generic options, the layout will be U.S. English, and the variant will be set to None (see Figure 2-2).

▼ **TIP:** If you ever want to change your keyboard layout or type, you can run the program **/usr/sbin/kbdconfig**.

When you are done, click Next to continue, or click Back to go back to the language selection menu.

Figure 2-2. Selecting a keyboard type

Selecting a Mouse

You now can select the type of mouse you want to use with the X Windows environment. More than likely, the autoprobe will have been able to identify what kind of mouse you have.

If you need to help Linux, simply pick your mouse type from the top menu box (see Figure 2-3). If you see the name brand of the mouse with a plus sign (+) to the left of it, clicking the plus sign will open a new level of choices for that particular brand.

If you have a serial mouse, you will also need to select the serial port it is using, which you can do in the lower box of the screen.

If you have a two-button mouse, click Emulate 3 Buttons at the bottom of the screen, because some features of the X Windows environment work with a three-button mouse only. The emulation allows you to click both buttons of a two-button mouse to simulate the third (middle) button.

TIP: If you change the type of mouse you have later, you can run **/usr/sbin/mouseconfig** to reconfigure your mouse.

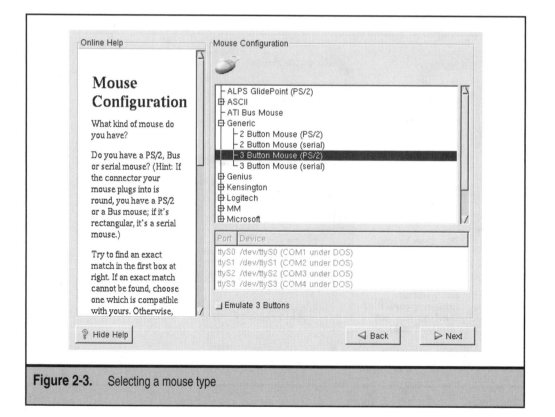

Figure 2-3. Selecting a mouse type

Welcome to Red Hat Linux

With the language and input devices selected, you are now ready to begin the actual installation phase of Red Hat Linux. This starts with a splash screen whose corresponding help bar tells you how to register Red Hat Linux if you purchased the boxed version.

Once you have read the information about registering, you can simply click Next to continue.

Upgrading or Installing?

Now you will see a screen that lets you pick how you want to install Red Hat Linux. If you are on an upgrade path, this selection is easy—simply click Upgrade and then click Next. You'll see some screens informing you of what is being currently upgraded.

For this chapter, we're assuming that you're doing a clean installation. This will wipe all the existing contents of the disk before freshly installing Red Hat 7.0.

Note that under the Install button is an option to install Linux in a Server configuration (see Figure 2-4). This method has all of the packages selected for you, as well as a

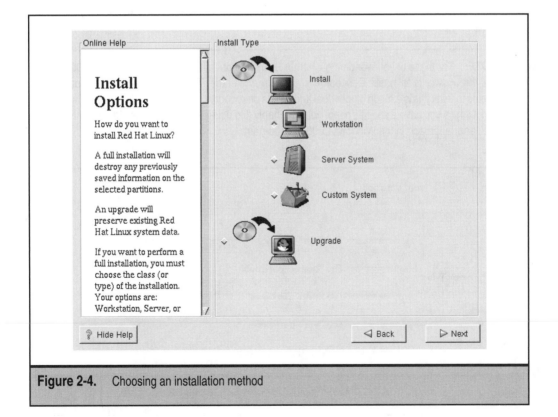

Figure 2-4.   Choosing an installation method

disk-partitioning scheme. For this chapter, you want to choose Custom so that you can fine-tune what you install and how you configure it.

Creating Partitions for Linux

Since you selected the custom installation, you will need to create partitions for Linux to install on. If you are used to the Windows installation process, you will find that this process is a little different from how you partition Windows into separate drives.

In short, each partition is *mounted* at boot time. The mount process makes the contents of that partition available as if it were just another directory on the system. For example, the root directory (/) will be on the first (*root*) partition. A subdirectory called **/usr** will exist on the root directory, but it will have nothing in it. A separate partition can then be mounted such that going into the **/usr** directory will allow you to see the contents of the newly mounted partition (see Figure 2-5).

Since all of the partitions, when mounted, appear as a unified directory tree rather than as separate drives, the installation software does not differentiate one partition from another. All it cares about is into which directory each file goes. As a result, the installation process automatically distributes its files across all the mounted partitions, as long as the mounted partitions represent different parts of the directory tree where files are usually placed. Under Linux, the most significant grouping of files is in the **/usr** directory where all of the actual programs reside. (In Windows terms, this is similar to **C:\Program Files**.)

NOTE: For those of you wondering whether Linux mounting is the same as Windows 2000 mounting, the answer is "almost." Conceptually, they are the same. The difference is that Windows 2000 seems to think this is a much bigger deal and insists on rebooting after mounting or unmounting a partition. Unless you have a specific need, you'll probably find doing things the same old way as NT 4 to be the saner approach in the Windows 2000 environment.

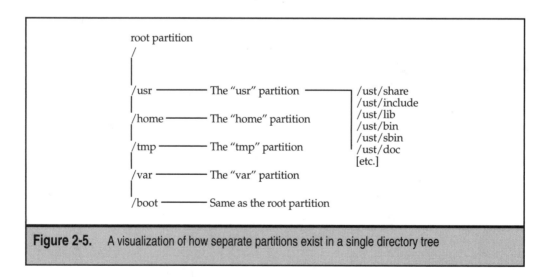

root partition
/

/usr ———————— The "usr" partition ———————— /ust/share
                                                /ust/include
/home ————————— The "home" partition   /ust/lib
                                                /ust/bin
/tmp ————————— The "tmp" partition   /ust/sbin
                                                /ust/doc
                                                [etc.]
/var ——————————— The "var" partition

/boot ——————————— Same as the root partition

Figure 2-5.   A visualization of how separate partitions exist in a single directory tree

Because you are configuring a server, you need to be aware of the additional large grouping of files that will exist over the life of the server. They are:

▼ **/usr**, where all of the program files will reside (similar to **C:\Program Files**).

■ **/home**, where everyone's home directory will be (assuming this server will house them). This is useful for keeping users from consuming an entire disk and leaving other critical components without space (such as log files).

■ **/var**, the final destination for log files. Because log files can be affected by outside users (for instance, individuals visiting a Web site), it is important to partition them off so that no one can perform a Denial of Service (DoS) attack by generating so many log entries that the entire disk fills up.

■ **/tmp**, where temporary files are placed. Because this directory is designed so that it is writable by any user (similar to the **C:\Temp** directory under Windows), you need to make sure arbitrary users don't abuse it and fill up the entire disk; you ensure this by keeping it on a separate partition.

▲ **Swap**. This isn't a user accessible file system, but it is where the virtual memory file is stored. Although Linux (and other UNIXs, as well) can use a normal disk file to hold virtual memory the way Windows does, you'll find that having it on its own partition improves performance.

Now you see why it is a good idea to create multiple partitions on a disk rather than a single large partition, which you may be used to doing under Microsoft Windows. As you become more familiar with the hows and whys of partitioning disks under Linux, you may choose to go back to a single large partition. At that point, of course, you will have enough knowledge of both systems to understand why one may work better for you than the other.

Now that you have some background on partitioning under Linux, let's go back to the installation process itself.

The installation screen gives you three options: automatically partition the disk, manually partition the disk with Disk Druid, or manually partition the disk with fdisk. You don't want the first, because you want tight control over how the disk gets allocated in a server environment. And while the method of using fdisk is extremely powerful, it can also be a bit daunting at first. (Don't worry: we do eventually go over it in Chapter 8.) So this leaves you with Disk Druid. Simply select Disk Druid and click Next. This will take you to Figure 2-6.

The Disk Druid partitioning tool was developed by Red Hat as an easy way to create partitions and associate them to the directories as which they will be mounted. When starting Disk Druid, you will see all of the existing partitions on your disk. Each partition entry will show the following information:

▼ **Mount point**   The location where the partition is mounted. Initially, this should not contain any entries.

Figure 2-6. The Disk Druid partitioning tool

■ **Device** Linux associates each partition with a separate *device*. For the purpose of installation, you need to know only that under IDE disks, each device begins with /dev/hd*XY*, where *X* is either:

a for IDE Master on the first chain

b for IDE Slave on the first chain

c for IDE Master on the second chain

d for IDE Slave on the second chain

and *Y* is the partition number of the disk. For example, /dev/hda1 is the first partition on the primary chain, primary disk. SCSI follows the same basic idea, except instead of starting with /dev/hd, each partition starts with /dev/sd and follows the format /dev/sd*XY*, where *X* is a letter representing a unique physical drive (**a** is for SCSI id 1, **b** is for SCSI id 2, and so on). The *Y* represents the partition number. Thus /dev/sdb4 is the fourth partition on the SCSI disk with id 2. The system is a little more complex than Windows, but each partition's location is explicit—no more guessing, "What physical device does E: correspond to?"

■ **Requested**   The minimum size that was requested when the partition was defined.

■ **Actual**   The actual amount of space allocated for that partition.

▲ **Type**   The partition's type. Linux's default type is Linux native, but Disk Druid also understands many others, including FAT, FAT32, and NTFS.

The second half of the screen shows the drive summaries. Each line represents a single drive and its characteristics. Among the information presented is:

▼ The drive name (without the preceding /dev/)

■ The disk geometry in *Cylinders/Heads/Sectors* format

■ Total size of the disk

■ Amount of disk that has been allocated (partitioned)

▲ Amount of available disk that can still be partitioned

In the middle of the screen are the menu choices for what you can do with Disk Druid. These buttons are:

▼ **Add**   Create a new partition.

■ **Edit**   Change the parameters on the highlighted partition.

■ **Delete**   Delete the highlighted partition.

■ **Reset**   Restore all of the changes you've made to the partition table but have not committed to.

■ **Make RAID Device**   This button will only appear if you have multiple disks that are identical in size and configuration. This installation guide does not cover RAID installations.

■ **Next**   Commit changes to disk.

▲ **Back**   Abort all changes made using Disk Druid and exit the program.

NOTE: The changes made within Disk Druid are not committed to disk until you click the Next button.

Adding a Partition   To create a new partition, click the Add button. This will bring up a dialog box where each of the elements in the dialog box should resemble those in Figure 2-7:

▼ **Mount point**   The directory where you want this partition to be automatically mounted at boot time.

■ **Size (Megs)**   The size of the partition in megabytes.

■ **Growable?**   By using the space bar to check this box, you are telling Disk Druid that you want to be able to grow this partition later. If you have an

Figure 2-7. The Add Partition dialog box

especially large disk, and you don't know how much to allocate to what, you may find it handy to size each partition as you need it now and select the growable option. Thus, as the system gets used and you see which partitions need more space than others, you can easily grow the necessary partitions without repartitioning your disk.

- ■ **Type** The type of partition that will reside on that disk. By default, you will want to select Linux Native except for the swap partition, which should be Linux Swap.
- ▲ **Allowable Drives** Specifies onto which drives the partition should be created.

Once you are done entering all of the information, click OK to continue.

At a minimum, you need to have two partitions: one for holding all of the files and the other for swap space. Swap space is usually sized to be double the available RAM if there are fewer than 128MB of RAM, or the exact same amount of RAM if there are more than 128MB.

Realistically, you will want to separate partitions for **/usr**, **/var**, **/home**, and **/tmp** in addition to a root partition. Obviously, you can adjust this equation based on the purpose of the server.

Other Partition Manipulation Tasks   Once you have gone through the steps of adding a partition, and you are comfortable with the variables involved (mount points, sizes, types, devices, and so on), the actual process of editing and deleting partitions is quite simple. Editing an entry means changing the exact same entries that you established when you added the partition, and deleting an entry requires only that you confirm you really want to perform the deletion.

NOTE: One last detail that we have intentionally omitted is the process of adding network drive mounts (NFS). This requires a more complete explanation and is covered in Chapter 8.

Formatting Partitions

The screen for formatting partitions will present you with a list of all the newly created partitions (see Figure 2-8). Because you are wiping the disk of previous installations, you want to select all of the partitions to be formatted. (More accurately, Red Hat will be creating a *file system* on it.)

TIP: If you are using an older drive, and you aren't sure about its reliability, click the Check For Bad Blocks While Formatting option, which is below all of the partitions. This will cause the formatting process to take significantly longer, but at least you will know for sure whether the disk is reliable.

Installing LILO

LILO is the *boot manager* for Linux. If you aren't already familiar with what it does, a boot manager handles the process of actually starting the load process of an operating system.

Figure 2-8. Formatting partitions

If you're familiar with Windows NT, you have already dealt with the NT Loader (NTLDR), which presents the menu at boot time, allowing you to select whether you want Windows NT or Windows NT (vga only). LILO effectively does the same thing, just without flashy menus.

The Red Hat tool's screen for setting up LILO has three sections (see Figure 2-9). The top of the screen allows you to select whether you want to make a boot disk. For obvious reasons, it is a good idea to have one.

The middle block of the screen allows you to select whether you want to have LILO set up on the master boot record (MBR) or the first partition on which Linux resides. The MBR is the very first thing the system will read when booting a system. It is essentially the point where the built-in hardware tests finish and pass off control to the software. If you choose to have LILO installed here, LILO will load with a `boot:` prompt when you turn on or reboot your system, and it will allow you to select which operating system to load. In a server configuration, there should be only one choice!

If you are already using another boot loader and prefer it, then you will want to place LILO on the first sector of the root partition. This will allow your preferred boot loader to run first and then pass control off to LILO, should you decide to start Linux.

The middle block also has an option to Use Linear Mode. This applies only to some SCSI drives or drives that are accessed in LBA mode.

Figure 2-9.   Setting up LILO

The last option in the middle block is a box that allows you to enter kernel parameters to be used at boot time. Most people can ignore this box. If the documentation for a particular feature or device requires you to pass a parameter here, add it; otherwise, leave it blank.

Finally, the bottom part of the screen allows you to select which operating systems LILO will allow you to select at boot time. On a system that is configured to support both Windows and Linux, you will see your choices here. Since your system is set up only for Linux, you will see one choice.

> **NOTE:**   The exception is for SMP-based systems that will have two choices. The first choice, linux, is set up to support multiple processors. In the event this doesn't work out for you, linux-up will also be available; it will utilize only one processor, but at least it will get you up and going.

Setting Up Networking

Now Red Hat is ready to configure your network interface cards (see Figure 2-10).

Each interface card you have will be listed as a tabbed menu on the top of your screen. Ethernet devices are listed as eth0, eth1, eth2, and so on. For each interface, you can either configure it using DHCP or set the IP address by hand. If you choose to configure by

Figure 2-10.   Configuring networking

hand, be sure to have the IP, netmask, network, and broadcast addresses ready. Finally, click Activate On Boot if you want the interface to be enabled at boot time.

On the bottom half of the screen, you'll see the configuration choices for giving the machine a host name, gateway, and related DNS information.

> **NOTE:** Even if you are not part of a network, you can fill in the host name. If you don't fill in a host name, your computer will be known as localhost.

Once you have all of this filled in, simply click Next to continue.

Time Zone Configuration

The time zone configuration screen (see Figure 2-11) allows you to select in which time zone the machine is located. If your system's hardware clock keeps time in UTC, be sure to click the System Clock Uses UTC button so that Linux can determine the difference between the two and display the correct local time.

Figure 2-11.   Configuring your time zone

Creating Accounts

The Red Hat Installation tool creates one account for you called root. This user account is similar in nature to the Administrator account under Windows NT/2000: The user who is allowed access to this account has full control of the system.

Thus, it is crucial that you protect this account with a good password. Be sure not to pick dictionary words or names as passwords, as they are easy to guess and crack.

Part of protecting root means not allowing users to log in as the root user over the network. This keeps crackers from being able to guess your root password by using automated login scripts. In order to allow legitimate users to become the root user, you need to log in as yourself, and then use the **su** (switch user) command. Thus, setting the root password isn't enough if you intend to perform remote administration; you will need to set up a real user, as well.

In general, it is considered a good idea to set up a normal user to do day-to-day work anyway. This gives you the protection of not being able to accidentally break configuration files or other important components while you're just surfing the Net or performing nonadministrative tasks. The exception to this rule is, of course, certain server configurations where there should never be any users besides the root user (for example, firewalls).

In Figure 2-12, you see the screen that lets you set the root password as well as create new users.

Begin by picking a root password and entering it into the Root Password box at the top of the screen. Enter it again in the Confirm box right below; this protects you from locking yourself out of the system in case you make a typo. The text Root Password Accepted will appear below the password boxes once you have entered a password twice the same way.

> **NOTE:** You do not need to add the root user.

The remainder of the screen is meant for creating a new user. To do so, simply enter their username in the Account Name box, their real name in the Full Name box, and their password in the Password and Password (confirm) boxes. Click Add to insert this new user into the list below these boxes. Click Next to continue.

> **NOTE:** If you make any mistakes while adding new users, you can delete and edit them, as well.

Authentication Configuration

Linux keeps its list of users in the **/etc/passwd** file. Each system has its own copy of this file, and a user listed in one **/etc/passwd** file cannot log into another system unless they

Figure 2-12. Setting up a root password and configuring a new user

have an entry in the other **/etc/passwd** file. To allow users to log in to any system in a network of computers, Linux uses the Network Information System (NIS) to handle remote password file issues.

In addition to listing users, the **/etc/passwd** file contains all of the passwords for each user in an encrypted format. For a very long time, this was acceptable since the process of attacking such files to crack passwords was so computationally expensive, it was almost futile to even try. Within the last few years, affordable PCs have gained the necessary computational power to present a threat to this type of security, and therefore a push to use *shadow passwords* has come. With shadow passwords, the actual encrypted password entry is not kept in the **/etc/passwd** file but rather in a **/etc/shadow** file. The **/etc/passwd** file remains readable by any user in the system, but **/etc/shadow** is readable by the root user only. Obviously, this is a good step up in security.

Another method to arise has been a technique utilizing the MD5 hashing function. (Don't worry about the details of MD5—all you need to concern yourself with is the fact that it is better than the stock method.) Unless you have a specific reason not to do this, be sure to check the Enable MD5 Passwords and Enable Shadow Passwords checkboxes (see Figure 2-13).

If your site has an existing NIS infrastructure, enter the relevant NIS domain and server name in this window. If you don't know or if you want to deal with this later, you can safely ignore this step.

Another option is to use a Lightweight Directory Access Protocol (LDAP) server for storing passwords. This is ideal for an environment where you have many thousands of users accessing many servers and NIS doesn't cut it performance wise. If you aren't sure about LDAP or whether you have an LDAP server, you can skip this step.

Finally, if you are in a Kerberos environment, you will need to enable the Kerberos authentication method. If you go this route, contact your Kerberos administrator for the appropriate realm names, KDC, and admin server. If you aren't sure about what Kerberos is, then you probably don't need it.

Figure 2-13. Configuring authorization

Once you have selected all checkboxes and filled out the relevant entries, click Next to continue to the next screen.

Selecting Package Groups

This is where you can select what packages get installed onto the system. Red Hat categorizes these packages into several high-level descriptions, which allows you to make a quick selection of what type of packages you want installed and safely ignore the details. You can also select to install all of the packages that come with Red Hat, but be warned: A full install can be upwards of 1.5GB of software!

Looking at the choices (Figure 2-14), you see the menu of top-level groups that Red Hat gives you. You can simply pick the groups that interest you; you can scroll to the bottom and pick Everything to have all of the packages installed; or you can click a button at the bottom of the screen labeled Select Individual Packages. Once you have made your decisions, simply click Next.

If you choose Select Individual Packages, you'll see a screen like that shown in Figure 2-15. On the left side of the screen, you'll see the logical groupings of packages, and on the right side of the screen you'll see the packages that exist in that group. When you click a package, the bottom of the screen will show the name of the package and a brief

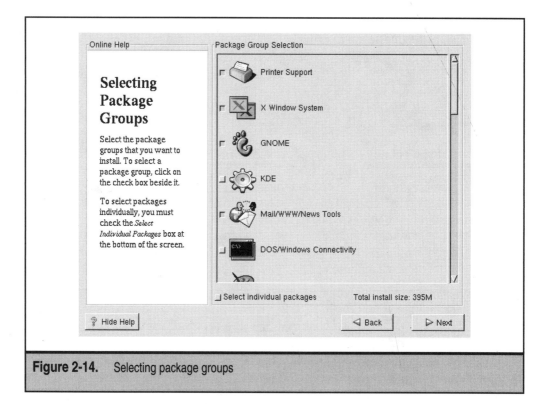

Figure 2-14.   Selecting package groups

Figure 2-15. Selecting individual packages

description of it. Right above the description is a button to click if you want that package installed.

If you opted to select individual packages, Red Hat will go through and verify that all of the prerequisites necessary for these packages are met. If any are not met, you will be shown these packages in a screen that looks like Figure 2-16.

If there are any packages that need to be installed to allow all of your selected packages to work, simply make sure that the button labeled Install Packages To Satisfy Dependencies is selected.

Click Next when you're done picking packages.

Configuring X Windows

X Windows is the basis for Linux's graphical user interface. It is what communicates with the actual video hardware. Programs such as KDE and GNOME (which you are more likely to have heard about; if not, read the next chapter) use X Windows as a standard mechanism for communicating with the hardware.

What makes X Windows interesting is that it is not coupled with the base operating system. In fact, the version of X that Linux uses, Xfree86, is also available for many other UNIX-based systems, such as those from Sun. This means it is possible to run a server

Figure 2-16. Resolving prerequisite packages

without ever starting the graphical environment, and as I mentioned earlier in this chapter, it is often a good idea to do so. By having the GUI turned off, you save memory and system resources that can instead be used for the actual server processes.

Of course, this doesn't change the fact that many nice administrative tools are available under X Windows only, so getting it set up is still a good idea.

Red Hat will begin by trying to sense the type of network card and monitor you have. If you have a brand name monitor and card, you'll likely have the easiest time. If Linux cannot determine the type of video card and monitor, you will be prompted for the necessary information.

> **TIP:** Have the frequency information about your monitor information. Trying to send your monitor too high of a frequency can cause physical damage. This author managed to toast his first color monitor this way, back when monitors were far less robust and before X Windows configuration tools existed.

Once Red Hat has the necessary information, you'll see a screen similar to Figure 2-17.

There are five choices under the description of the hardware configuration: Test This Configuration, Customize X Configuration, Use Graphical Login, Skip X Configuration, and a drop-down tab defaulted to GNOME for selecting the default desktop.

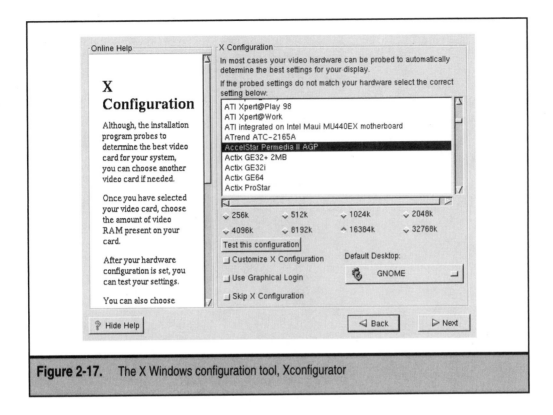

Figure 2-17.   The X Windows configuration tool, Xconfigurator

The first choice is a button that, when pressed, will immediately test your X Windows configuration. It will let you verify that the settings work. The second is a toggle switch that, when turned on, lets you select X Windows resolution and colors. By default, Xconfigurator tries to use the highest resolution with the maximum number of colors available. For some people, this resolution setting is too high and makes fonts hard to read.

The choice of using a graphical login is just that: You can have X Windows automatically start up on boot so that the first login everyone sees is graphical instead of text based. This choice is often nice for the novice user who has a Linux system at his or her desk.

The next option is if you don't have a need for X Windows, or if you want to configure it later, you can click the button to not configure X Windows.

Finally, if you do want X Windows, you can select your default desktop to be either GNOME or KDE. This, of course, depends on whether you opted to only install one of them earlier in the installation process.

When you're done selecting, click Next to continue. This will bring you to the screen shown in Figure 2-18. Here you can select the resolution you want to work with. Be sure to test the resolution before continuing. Click Next to continue.

Figure 2-18.   Choosing your resolution

And It's Off!

Red Hat will now go through the process of installing all of the packages you have selected as part of the installation process. Depending on the speed of your hard disk,
CD-ROM, and machine, this could take from just a few minutes to 20 minutes. A status
indicator (see Figure 2-19) will let you know how far the process has gotten and how
much longer the system expects to take.

Boot Disk Creation

Once the installation process is complete, Red Hat gives you the option of creating a boot
disk. Unless you are familiar with recovering a Linux system already (in which case I
highly doubt you're reading this book), you should take a moment and create one.

Following the directions as shown in Figure 2-20, simply insert a blank disk into your
drive and click Next. If you don't want to create a boot disk, click the button labeled Skip
Boot Disk Creation, and then click Next.

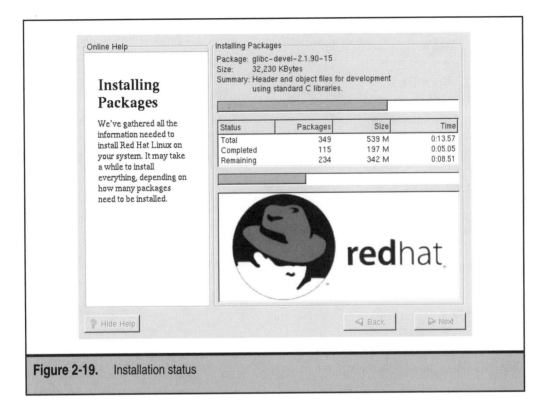

Figure 2-19.   Installation status

And You're Done!

That's it! The installation process is over. You'll be prompted to press a key to reboot the system. As the system reboots, be sure to remove any CD-ROMs or floppy disks you have in your system that are capable of booting before your hard disk is.

Finding Additional Help

If you are still having problems with the installation, be sure to visit Red Hat's Web site (http://www.redhat.com) and take a look at the manuals available for Red Hat 7.0 (http://www.redhat.com/support/manuals/). There you will find the official installation guide for all possible variations in the installation process. You will also find the latest errata, security updates, and notes regarding the Red Hat 7.0 distribution.

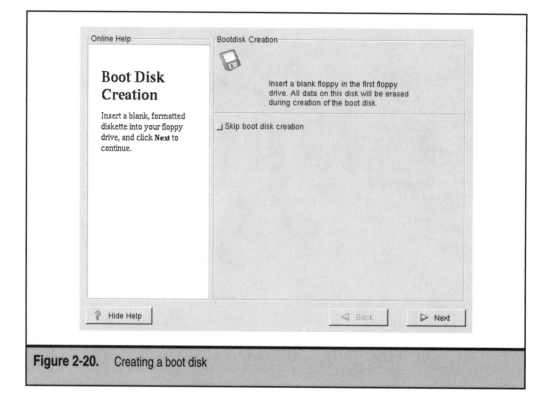

Figure 2-20.   Creating a boot disk

SUMMARY

In this chapter, we discussed the process of building up a server, choosing the right hardware, establishing the right environment, and finally, installing Red Hat 7.0. All of the commentary before we got to the actual process of installing Red Hat Linux applies to any server you build, regardless of operating system.

The steps for installing Red Hat itself are also quite straightforward. Anyone who witnessed the procedure from prior versions should have noted how much easier the process has become and how many fewer configuration choices need to be made to get going. What makes Linux wonderful is that even though those options are no longer part of the installation process, you can still change them and tweak them to your heart's content once you've completed the install and have started the system for real.

Don't forget to search those places I mentioned earlier in the chapter if you need help, and once you become a Linux whiz, don't forget to help others.

CHAPTER 3

GNOME and KDE

GNOME and KDE are getting a lot of press these days, because they offer a truly easy-to-use interface to UNIX-based operating systems, most notably Linux. In this chapter, we will go over various tips and tricks to make GNOME and KDE work better for you. Since most distributions come with one (or both) preinstalled, you won't have to deal with an installation or configuration process before you can jump in and start using them.

Before we get into the fun stuff, though, we need to step back and understand a little more about the X Window System and how it relates to GNOME and KDE. This will give you a better idea of the big picture of Linux and one of its fundamental architectural differences with Windows NT.

NOTE: This chapter assumes you are logged in as root. However, all of the changes we talk about here can apply to any user.

THE HISTORY OF X WINDOWS

The designers of UNIX-based operating systems, like Linux, take a very different view of the world when it comes to user environments than do those behind Microsoft Windows or even Macintosh OS. UNIX folk believe the interface they present the user should be 100% independent of the core operating system. As a result, Linux's kernel is completely decoupled from its user interface. This allows us to select the interface that works best for us, rather than be stuck with the dictated vision of someone else or potentially random "market research."

More important, however, is the stability that comes from having such a large program independent of the core operating system. If the GUI crashes under Windows or MacOS, you have to reboot. Under Linux, you can kill the GUI and restart it without affecting any other services being offered by the system (such as network file services).

In the mid-1980s, an OS-independent foundation for graphical user environments was created and called X Windows. "X" (as it is commonly abbreviated) simply defines the method by which applications can communicate with the graphical hardware. Also established was a well-defined set of functions programmers could call on to perform basic window manipulation.

The simple definition of how windows are drawn and mouse clicks are handled did not include any model of how the windows should look. (In fact, X Windows in its natural state has no real appearance. It doesn't even draw lines around windows!) Control of appearance was passed off to an external program called a *window manager*. The window manager took care of drawing borders, using color, and making the environment pleasant to the eye; the window manager was required only to use standard calls to the X Windows subsystem to draw on the screen. The window manager *did not* dictate how the application itself utilized the windows. This meant application programmers had the flexibility to develop a user interface most intuitive for the application.

Because the window manager was external to the X Windows subsystem, and the X Windows application programmers interface (API) was open, any programmer who wanted to develop a new window manager could, and many did. In the context of today, we might associate this form of openness with MP3 players, like WinAMP, that allow developers to build "skins" for the base player.

The icing on the cake was the relationship between applications and X Windows. Typical applications were written to communicate directly with X Windows, thereby working with any window manager the user opted to use. Figure 3-1 shows this relationship.

The Downside

As technically interesting and versatile as X Windows is, it is a pain in the backside to program for. A Windows programmer might equate programming for X Windows to programming for the original MS Windows prior to the visual tools and MFC libraries. For example, writing a simple program to bring up a window, display the text "Hello World," and then offer a button to allow the user to quit could easily be several hundred lines long under both X and MS Windows!

And here the UNIX folks took a lesson from the Macintosh OS and MS Windows families (who, it should be noted, borrowed their ideas from Xerox's work back in the late 1970s): Failure to offer a reasonably consistent user interface for both the user and the programmer that is easy to use and easy to develop for means a loss of user base.

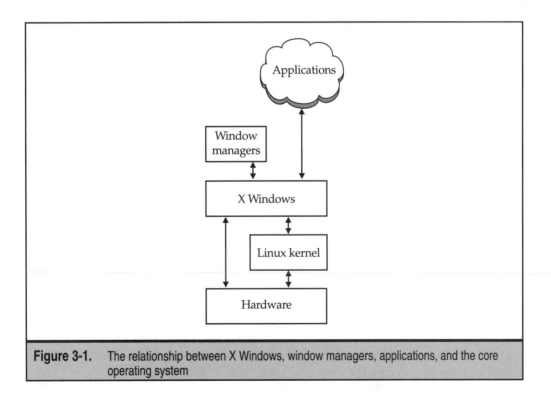

Figure 3-1.   The relationship between X Windows, window managers, applications, and the core operating system

Commercial UNIX vendors tried to fix this problem with the Common Desktop Environment so their users would get a consistent look and feel, and an improved library for X Windows called Motif was developed, as well. For Linux, both of these developments presented a problem, because they went against the ideal of being open source. To make matters even more unpleasant, they weren't much better than what was available before.

Enter KDE and GNOME

With unfriendly programming environments and unfriendly user interfaces, X Windows had the potential to one day turn into a legacy interface. This would be extremely unfortunate, because it offers a design that was (and still is) leaps and bounds better than other commercial offerings. The protocol is open, which means anyone who wants to write an X client or X server is welcome to. And, of course, one of the best features of X Windows is that it allows applications to be run on one host but be displayed on another host.

In the latter 1990s, two groups came out of the woodwork with solutions to the problems with X Windows: GNOME and KDE. *KDE* offers a new window manager and necessary libraries to make writing applications for it much easier. *GNOME* offers a general framework for other window managers and applications to work with it. Each has its own ideas for how things should work, but because they both work on top of X Windows, they aren't entirely incompatible.

NOTE: Despite what you might hear in newsgroups and on Web sites, the two groups are not "at war" with each other. Rather, they welcome the open competition. Each group can feed off of each other's ideas, and in turn, both groups can offer two excellent choices for us, the users.

What This Means for Us

The keywords in the previous section were "not entirely incompatible." In order for KDE and GNOME to offer features such as drag and drop, they must offer a uniform way for applications to communicate with each other and a set of developer libraries to do so. Unfortunately, because the two methods are different, they aren't compatible.

What this means for applications can be a little confusing. Depending on the functionality the application calls on from its libraries, it may still work in the other environment as long as the libraries exist. A good example is the **ksysv** program. It was written with KDE in mind, but because the functionality it relies on is 100% available in the library, a system that is running GNOME but has KDE libraries available (such as Red Hat) will allow the application to run without a problem. On the other hand, if an application relied on the KDE window manager itself, the application would not work under GNOME.

As users, this means that picking one environment over the other has the possibility of locking us out of getting to use certain applications. As of this writing, this hasn't been too much of an issue. In fact, there is work going on between both groups on improving the level of compatibility between them. That leaves us with having to make a choice. If you aren't sure about what you like better, try both. See which you like better rather than depending on the opinion of some Web page or (even worse) this author! What I use is irrelevant. What you like is what matters. And that's what having two competing systems is all about.

ABOUT KDE

KDE is a desktop environment (the K Desktop Environment). It is slightly different from typical window managers that we have mentioned: Instead of just describing how the interface should look, KDE also provides a set of libraries that, if used, allow an application to take advantage of some of the special features the window manager has to offer. This includes things like drag-and-drop support, standardized printing support, and so on.

The flip side to this technique of window management is that once an application is designed to run with KDE, it requires KDE in order to work. This is a big change from earlier window managers where applications are independent of the window manager.

From a programmer's point of view, KDE offers a library that is much easier to work with than working directly with the X interface. KDE also offers a standardized object-oriented framework that allows one set of tools to build on another, something that was not available with X Windows alone.

For this section, we will assume that KDE has already been installed on your system. This is true for Caldera, since it only offers KDE, and, if you opted for using it during the install process, for Red Hat, too.

NOTE: For more details and information on KDE, visit their Web site at http://www.kde.org.

Licensing Issues

Until recently, there were some problems with the license restrictions imposed by the developers of the Qt library, which is what KDE is based on. This prohibited commercial usage of KDE without paying fees for it. The GNOME project started because of this restriction.

Recently, Qt's license was revised. The revised license, known as the QPL, is now more open and does allow for commercial usage; however, it is different from the GPL and Berkeley-style licenses used by the majority of the packages that ship with Linux distributions. Like any documentation, it is worth taking a read if you think you may have issues with it.

You can find out more about this license by visiting KDE's Web site.

Starting X Windows and KDE

When setting up X Windows, you may have had a choice of starting up the system straight into X. If so, all you need to do is log in and you're there—you're using KDE and X Windows. If that option was not selected, you will have a text-based login prompt. To get into the X Windows environment, simply log in and run **startx**, like so:

```
[root@ford /root]# startx
```

In a few moments, you will be in KDE. Your screen will probably look something like Figure 3-2.

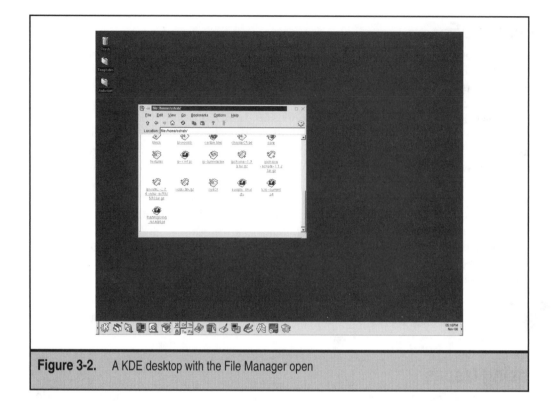

Figure 3-2.   A KDE desktop with the File Manager open

If your screen doesn't look like that, but rather it displays the GNOME banner window on startup, then you need to edit the file that decides which window manager you start. To do this, exit out of GNOME by clicking the bear claw in the lower-left corner of the screen and selecting logout. This will bring you back into text mode. Edit the **.xinitrc** file using your favorite editor. If you don't have a favorite, try **pico**, like so:

```
[root@ford /root]# pico .xinitrc
```

NOTE: If you aren't familiar with **pico**, don't worry. All of the available commands are always shown at the bottom of the screen. Any command that starts with the caret symbol (^) means you use the CTRL key along with other keys specified. For example, ^X means CTRL-X.

Most likely, the file will be empty. If that is the case, simple add the following content:

```
#!/bin/sh
startkde
```

If the file is not empty, go to the very last line. It will probably begin with the string **exec**, which tells the system to execute a program. Change that line so that it reads **startkde** instead.

KDE Basics

KDE shares many qualities with other graphical desktops, such as Windows or MacOS. It has a desktop on which files and folders can exist. One key point to note is that because Linux places all of the hard disks on the system into a unified directory tree, you won't find a special icon allowing you to browse a particular disk like you can under My Computer.

At the bottom of the screen, you will find KDE's *kpanel*. The leftmost "K" button is the equivalent of the Windows Start Button. By clicking it, you will be presented with a menu showing you a number of applications that can be started by simply clicking the appropriate menu entry.

What makes the kpanel different from the Windows Start menu is that it is also a shortcut bar to commonly used applications. You can configure the bar to have any shortcuts you like by clicking the K button and selecting Panel. Under this menu is a number of configuration options.

If you want to hide the panel altogether, you can do so by clicking the arrows on the far right or the left side of the panel. This will make the panel hide in that direction. Click the arrow again to bring the panel back.

The KDE Control Center

The KDE Control Center is a lot like the Control Panel for Windows, except it is specifically geared toward desktop configuration items (see Figure 3-3).

The Control Center offers an impressive array of tools for configuring KDE to your heart's delight. This includes support for a variety of themes, colors, backgrounds, screen savers, certain applications, and certain types of hardware. The best way to see all it has to offer is to go through it and play—this is one of the rare opportunities you have as a system administrator to play with the interface without breaking your system.

In this section, we will step through several common tasks, giving you an idea of what can be done and the typical method for figuring out how to do it. As mentioned earlier, the interface is very Windows-like, so getting around in it should be relatively easy.

Using Multiple Desktops

One of the most powerful tools you have at your disposal is the virtual desktop. The only dangerous thing about it is your aggravation when you work on systems that don't have this feature.

The essence of virtual desktops is that they allow you to effectively have multiple screens at the same time. All you need to do is select which screen you want to use by clicking the virtual desktop selector at the bottom of the screen.

Most KDE installations default to four virtual screens. If you want to adjust that, do the following:

1. Open the Control Center.
2. Select Applications.

3. Select Panel.

4. Select Desktops from the tab-style window on the right side of the Control Center (see Figure 3-4).

5. Move the Visible slider to the right to increase the number of desktops. (Of course, you can also move it left to reduce the number of desktops.)

6. Click the Apply button at the bottom of the window to make the changes take effect.

If each desktop has a specific purpose, you can also change the label of the desktop by highlighting it and changing the desktop name field on the same panel. In Figure 3-4, you can see that desktop 1 has been renamed Misc., and desktop 2 has been renamed StarOffice, while the other desktops have remained untouched.

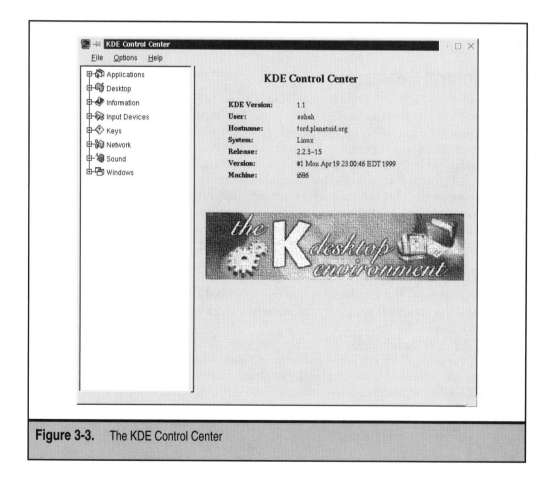

Figure 3-3.   The KDE Control Center

Figure 3-4. Setting up additional desktops

TIP: If you prefer keyboard shortcuts, you can set up a shortcut that allows you to move from one desktop to another in the Control Center under the Keys | Global Keys menu. Simply click the action you want (switch desktop) and then select the key combination you want to use to move around. Like a lot of folks who used the fvwm window manager for a long time, I personally prefer using CTRL-arrow key to jump from one desktop to another.

Starting Other Applications

There are multiple ways to start a new application. As a system administrator, you are likely to have a command window up (better known as an "xterm"), so you may find it convenient to simply run the application from there. In fact, most of this book assumes you are running applications from that prompt. Simply open a terminal window box by either clicking the icon of a terminal on the desktop panel or clicking the K menu, selecting

Utilities, and then clicking Terminal. This starts up kterm, which is functionally equivalent to an xterm. Once open, you can enter the name of the command you wish to run there and press ENTER.

NOTE: Many commands discussed in this book must be run from a terminal window.

Under KDE, you can also bring up the equivalent of the Run option under the Windows Start menu by pressing ALT-F2. This brings up a small window in the center of your screen where you can type in the command you want to run (see Figure 3-5). The window automatically goes away once you press ENTER to execute the command or ESC to abort.

The last way is to search through the directory listing using the file browser and double-clicking the application name you want. This method is, of course, the most tedious, but it can be useful if you can't remember the name of the application. Common directories to check are **/usr/bin**, **/usr/sbin**, **/bin**, **/sbin**, and **/usr/X11R6/bin**.

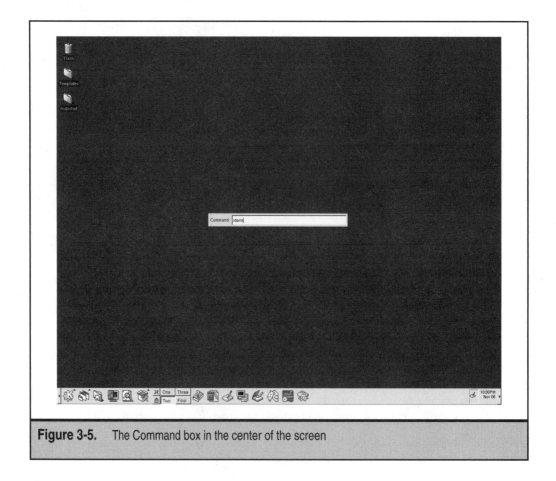

Figure 3-5. The Command box in the center of the screen

Changing the Color Scheme

If you're fussy about your desktop environment, you'll probably want to change the appearance of your desktop color scheme. With KDE's Control Center, this is quite easy. Begin by bringing the Control Center up and then clicking the Desktop option in the left window. This will bring up a window that looks like Figure 3-6.

Changing Your Background   Click the Background menu option under Desktop. This will bring up a configuration panel like the one in Figure 3-7.

To change your background, simply select either a color or wallpaper from the respective menu. If you choose a wallpaper, you can test what the wallpaper will look like before committing to it by clicking Apply at the bottom of the screen. If you like what you see, you can keep the change by clicking OK. If you don't, simply set it back to the original and click Apply again.

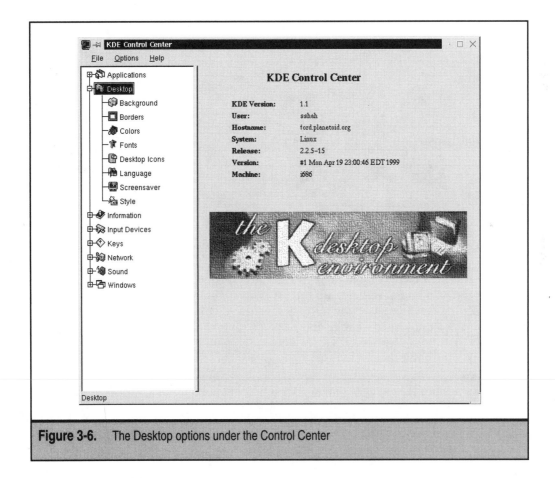

Figure 3-6.   The Desktop options under the Control Center

Figure 3-7. Changing your background configuration panel

Changing Colors To change the colors, click the Colors menu option under Desktop. This will bring up a configuration panel like the one in Figure 3-8.

Simply click the color combination you like best. If you want to create a new combination, click the Add button underneath the list and give your new settings a name. Highlight this setting and then select the color you want to give each widget in the right side of the panel. For example, to change the color of normal text, open the Widget Color drop-down box. Select Normal Text. The bar underneath the drop-down box will show the current color. Click the bar to bring up a color wheel so you can select the new color you like best.

As always, click Apply once you are done.

Figure 3-8.   Changing colors under KDE

Changing the Screen Saver   To change the screen saver, click the Screensaver option under Desktop. This will bring up a configuration panel like the one in Figure 3-9.

In the menu box, select the screen saver you like. A demo of it will appear in the picture of the monitor in the same panel. You can try out a full-screen version of the screen saver by clicking Test. If that screen saver has configuration options, the Setup button will also be available so you can configure it.

From this menu, you can also choose to lock your screen in addition to starting the screen saver. This is very handy if you need to leave your workstation in a non-private location, like an office.

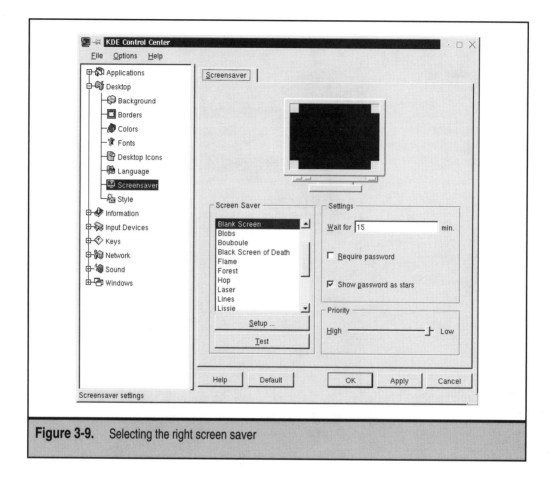

Figure 3-9.   Selecting the right screen saver

But the most fun feature is the corner activation. Looking at the picture of the monitor carefully, we see that the four corners of the screen have little gray boxes. Clicking the boxes reveals a menu that lets us pick Ignore, Save Screen, or Lock Screen. The default value is Ignore. However, by selecting either Save Screen or Lock Screen, you can then move the cursor to that corner and immediately cause that action to happen. For example, I have the lower-right corner of my screen set to Save Screen. When I want to immediately activate my screensaver, I simply move my mouse into that corner and *shazaam!*—my screensaver is active. The lower-left corner is set to Lock Screen. So if I know I'm going away from my desk for a long time, I can immediately lock my screen by moving my mouse into the lower-left corner.

The default behavior for the screen saver is to activate after the number of minutes specified in the screen saver configuration window. Setting any of the corners to activate the screen saver does not invalidate the default behavior.

ABOUT GNOME

Like KDE, GNOME (GNU Network Object Model Environment) offers a complete desktop environment and application framework to make development as well as usage easier. What makes GNOME different is how it achieves these goals. Unlike KDE, GNOME is not a window manager. GNOME provides development libraries and session management—foundation features that we as users don't see. On top of this foundation is a window manager that takes care of the general appearance of the desktop. The default window manager is Sawfish, but there are several choices available.

NOTE: According to the official Web site, the correct pronunciation of GNOME is guh-NOME. This is because the *G* in GNOME stands for GNU, and the correct pronunciation of GNU is "guh-new." In the same paragraph, the GNOME team states that no one will be offended if you pronounce it "NOME."

From a developer's point of view, GNOME is very interesting. It defines its interfaces with the rest of the world through the CORBA technology. Thus, any development system that can communicate using CORBA can be used to develop GNOME-compliant applications. (For more information, see their developer's Web pages at http://www.gnome.org.)

For users, this holds the potential for many applications to be developed to take advantage of the features in GNOME. Of course, like KDE, GNOME also works with existing X Windows applications quite nicely.

NOTE: If you do not have GNOME installed, you can download the application and installation directions from the GNOME Web site at http://www.gnome.org. Precompiled packages for various distributions are also available at their Web site.

Another difference you'll find between GNOME and KDE is that GNOME offers multiple distributions. The base distribution (the one that comes with Red Hat) is quite nice and is what we examine in this section; however, other companies have begun spinning their own versions that have their own benefits. One of the more popular alternatives is Helix (http://www.helixcode.com) which offers a smoother window manager and upgrade tool. (One of the founding members of the Helix team worked on the initial Macintosh user interface. However, Helix *is not* is a clone of the Mac's user interface.)

Starting X Windows and GNOME

If you are using Red Hat Linux and have opted for its defaults, you already have GNOME installed as your default GUI. Depending on how X Windows is configured, you may already have a graphical login prompt. In that case, logging in will automatically place you in the X Windows environment. If you have a text-based login, simply run **startx** in order to bring X up, like so:

```
[root@ford /root]# startx
```

This should bring up a screen that looks something like Figure 3-10.

If the default GUI that starts is not GNOME, you can change your personal settings to use GNOME by editing the **.xinitrc** file in your home directory. Begin by trying to exit out of the window manager. If you are in KDE (represented by a big "K" in the lower-left corner), click the K to bring up a menu. In that menu should be an option to log out. If you're really stuck, you can also press CTRL-ALT-BACKSPACE to kill the underlying X Windows manager. This will bring you back into text mode. Edit the **.xinitrc** file using your favorite editor. If you don't have a favorite, try **pico**, like so:

```
[root@ford /root]# pico .xinitrc
```

NOTE: If you aren't familiar with **pico**, don't worry. All of the available commands are always shown at the bottom of the screen. Any command that starts with the caret symbol (^) means you use the CTRL key along with other keys specified. For example, ^X means CTRL-X.

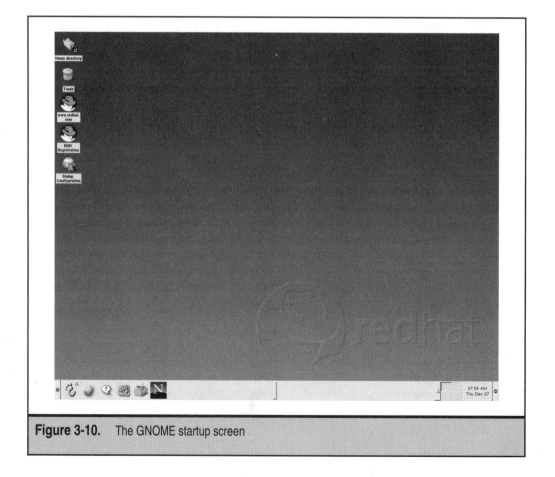

Figure 3-10. The GNOME startup screen

Most likely, the file will be empty. If that is the case, simple add the following content:

```
#!/bin/sh
gnome-session
```

If the file is not empty, go to the very last line. It will probably begin with the string **exec**, which tells the system to execute a program. Change that line so that it reads **gnome-session** instead.

GNOME Basics

If you are familiar with GUI interfaces, the GNOME desktop should make you feel right at home. There are two significant differences: the first is that there is no My Computer icon on the desktop. This is because Linux does not have the concept of separate drive letters for each partition. Rather, all of the partitions are made available in a single directory tree, thereby eliminating the need to select a drive.

The second big difference is the panel at the bottom of the screen. This panel is like the MS Windows panel on steroids; it shows what applications are currently running, as well as the date and time, and the bear claw button at the left side of the panel is similar to the Start button. The big difference is that this panel is completely configurable: You can move things around in it, dock dynamic applications, set up shortcuts to other applications, and move around your virtual desktops. If you don't want it in the way for a particular task, simply click the right or left arrow buttons at each end of the panel and it will slide out of the way until you click the arrow button again.

By default, the buttons available on the panel (see Figure 3-11) are, from left to right, the GNOME Start Menu, Screen Locking Tool, help system, a terminal emulation program (sometimes referred to as an "xterm"), the GNOME Configuration Tool, and Netscape Communicator.

If you want to change the panel's appearance, click the bear claw in the lower-left corner of your screen and select the Panel menu. It will bring up a series of submenus that allow you to configure various aspects of the panel, including being able to dock running programs into it (applets) and set up new shortcuts (launchers).

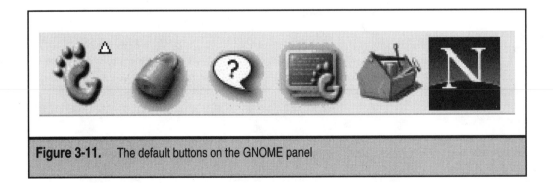

Figure 3-11.   The default buttons on the GNOME panel

The GNOME Configuration Tool

The GNOME Configuration Tool allows you to control the appearance and behavior of GNOME, similar to the way that the Windows Control Panel works. To start the GNOME Configuration Tool, click the panel button that looks like a toolbox.

TIP: If you aren't sure what a particular button does, simply leave the mouse pointer on the button for a few seconds. A small description will pop up right next to the pointer. The description will automatically disappear once you move the mouse off the button.

If you don't see the toolbox button on your panel, you can try clicking the bear claw on the bottom-left corner of your screen. This will bring up a menu containing the Settings option. Selecting Settings will bring up a submenu in which one of the options is the GNOME Configuration Tool. Highlight that menu option to start the tool.

Once started, the GNOME Configuration Tool will look something like Figure 3-12.

Control Center

File   Help

- Desktop
  - Background
  - Panel
  - Screensaver
  - Theme Selector
  - Window Manager
- Document Handlers
  - Default Editor
  - Mime Types
  - URL Handlers
- Multimedia
  - Sound
- Peripherals
  - CD Properties
  - Keyboard
  - Mouse
- Sawfish window manager
  - Appearance
  - Focus behavior
  - Matched Windows
  - Meta

G N O M E

Control Center

Operating System: Linux   version: #2 Sun Oct 15 15:56:34 PDT 2000
Distribution Version: Red Hat Linux release 7.0 (Guinness)
Processor Type: i686
User Name: sshah
Host Name: arthur

Figure 3-12.   The GNOME Configuration Tool

In this section, we will step through several common tasks. They should give you an idea of what can be done and the typical method for figuring out how to do it. As we mentioned earlier, the interface is very Windows-like, so getting around in it should be relatively easy.

Changing the Background

To change your background settings, click the Desktop menu and then the Background menu. This will bring up a panel that looks like Figure 3-13.

The Background panel is broken up into two groups, Color and Wallpaper. The Color group allows you to set the background color. If you like, you can select two colors and do a gradient between them, either horizontally or vertically. To select the color itself, click the box immediately underneath the string Color 1 or Color 2; this will bring up a color wheel from which you can choose any color you like.

To change the wallpaper, click the Browse button in the Wallpaper group to see a list of available wallpapers. Once you have found the one you like, simply select it and click Apply to make the change take effect.

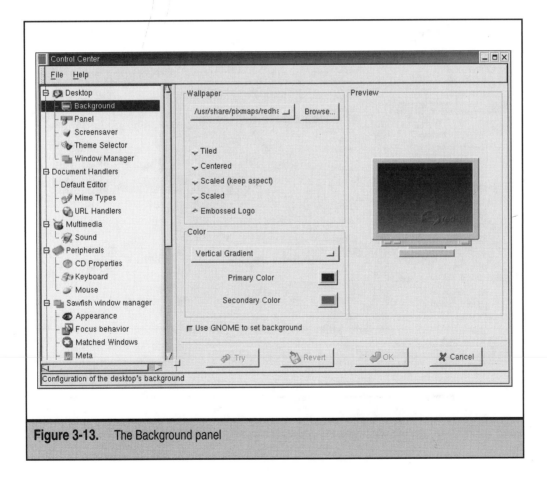

Figure 3-13.   The Background panel

Setting the Screen Saver

To set the screen saver under GNOME, click the Desktop menu and then the Screensaver menu. This will bring up a panel that looks like Figure 3-14.

Once there, choosing a screen saver is very easy. Simply select the module you like best from the list shown. A sample of what the screen saver will look like will appear in the Screen Saver Demo, located in the same window. If there are any configuration parameters available for the screen saver, a button will become undimmed immediately beneath the listing of possible screen savers.

The global screen saver settings are on the lower half of the screen saver panel. There, you can select how long the system should wait before starting the screen saver and how long it should wait before it uses advanced power management features to try to turn off the monitor.

Figure 3-14. The Screen Saver panel

Themes

Themes are the way GNOME allows you to configure the appearance of your window manager. These changes go beyond simply changing colors; they can change the appearance of the desktop, windows, borders, and fonts for all applications. (Users of MacOS 8 or WinAMP should be at home with this technology.) If you aren't sure how significant a change you can make, visit the themes Web site at http://www.themes.org.

To get to the Themes menu in the GNOME Control Center, simply click the Desktop menu and then click the Themes Selector menu. This will bring up a panel that looks like Figure 3-15.

By default, GNOME comes with only the default theme. If you are interested in changing the theme, you can visit http://www.themes.org and download new ones.

Once you have a theme selected, you can click the Preview button to see what the theme will look like on your screen before committing to it.

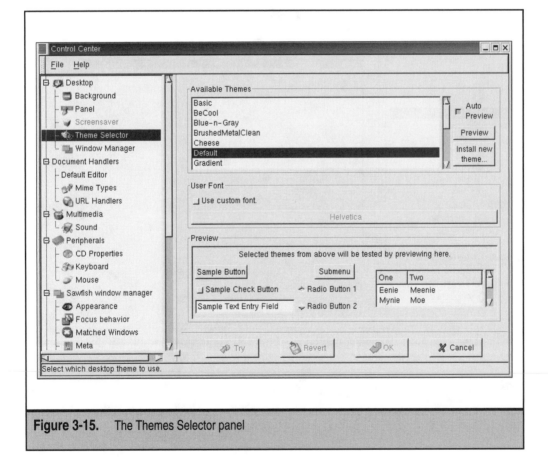

Figure 3-15.   The Themes Selector panel

Window Manager

As we mentioned earlier in this section, GNOME does not specify the window manager that must be used with it. All window managers perform the same basic tasks, but the little differences in interface, style, and appearance are what set them apart. The default that ships with Red Hat that works with GNOME is Enlightenment.

To change your window manager from the Control Center, click the Desktop menu and then the Window Manager menu. This will bring you to a panel that looks like Figure 3-16.

If you want to get a better idea of what the screen will look like with a different window manager, you can click the Try button at the bottom of the window. If you decide that the look is not quite what you are interested in, you can go back to your original settings by clicking Revert.

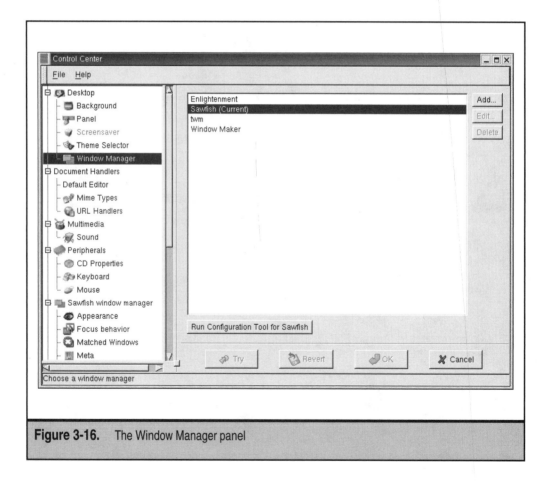

Figure 3-16. The Window Manager panel

SUMMARY

In this chapter, you learned about the X Windows environment, specifically KDE and GNOME. Some key points are

▼   The X Windows environment is *not* part of the core operating system.

■   Window managers run on top of X Windows, and we can pick whatever window manager works best for us.

■   The KDE environment is a combination of both a window manager and application framework for developing GUI applications.

■   KDE's control panel is called the Control Center and can be found by clicking the K icon in the lower-left corner of the window.

■   KDE's Web site is http://www.kde.org.

■   GNOME defines an application framework for other window managers and libraries. Therefore, you can use multiple window managers, such as Enlightenment and Window Maker.

▲   GNOME's Web site is http://www.gnome.org.

GNOME and KDE represent significant advancements in the quality of graphical user interfaces for Linux and UNIX as a whole. Hopefully, the comfort of working in these two environments is enough to convince even more folks to turn their dual-boot configurations into single-boot Linux configurations.

CHAPTER 4

Installing Software

Given that a great deal of systems administration centers around installing the software necessary to provide a service, it is important that we discuss the mechanisms for installing new packages as well as compiling those packages that ship as source code.

In general, most applications have very similar installation patterns. Keeping an eye out for the typical sources of information, as well as a healthy dose of common sense, will make most installation processes go smoothly. Thus, the intent of this chapter is to not only show cookbook formulas for installing certain types of packages, but also to include troubleshooting strategies.

> **NOTE:** All of the packages that are discussed in this book have already been tested to see if they work under Linux and if they compile and install nicely. You shouldn't have problems with the installation process, but versions change, and different hardware configurations can cause software to break. It's always better to know and understand than simply hope it works.

In this chapter, we will discuss the two most common methods of installation: using the Red Hat Package Manager (RPM) and compiling the source code yourself. All of the commands entered in this chapter are entered as the root user. The easiest way to do this is to log in as root. (Chapter 6 will show you how to change your user ID to someone else's ID using the **su** command.) In general, if you have logged in as someone other than root, begin by opening a terminal window. At the prompt, type **su - root** there.

THE RED HAT PACKAGE MANAGER

The Red Hat Package Manager's primary function is to allow the installation and removal of files (typically precompiled software). It is wonderfully easy to use, and several graphical interfaces have been built around it to make it even easier. Red Hat, Caldera, and other distributions have started using this tool to distribute their software. In fact, almost all of the software mentioned in this book is available in RPM form. The reason we go through the process of compiling software ourselves in other chapters is so that we can compile time options that are not available in an RPM.

Basically, an RPM file is a collection of all the files necessary for a particular program to run. It also includes descriptions of the program, version information, and the necessary scripts to perform the installation itself.

> **NOTE:** In this context, we are assuming that the RPM files contain pre-compiled binaries. Several groups, such as Red Hat, also make source code available as an RPM but it is uncommon to download and compile source code in this fashion.

The RPM tool performs general management of all of the RPM packages that are installed on a given host. This includes tracking which packages are installed, their version numbers, and their file locations. All of this information is kept in a simple database file on the host.

In general, software that comes in the form of an RPM is less work to install and maintain than software that needs to be compiled. The trade-off is that by using an RPM, you accept the default parameters supplied in the RPM. In most cases, these defaults are acceptable. However, if you need to be more intimately aware of what is going on with a service, you may find that compiling the source yourself will prove more educational about what package components exist and how they work together.

But assuming that all you want to do is install a simple package, RPM is perfect. There are several great resources for RPM packages, including the following:

▼ http://www.rpmfind.net

■ ftp://ftp.redhat.com/pub/contrib

▲ http://www.linuxapps.com

Of course, if you are interested in more details about RPM itself, you can visit the RPM Web site at http://www.rpm.org. RPM comes with Red Hat Linux (and derivatives) as well as Caldera Linux. If you aren't sure if RPM comes with your distribution, check with your vendor.

NOTE: Although the name of the package says "Red Hat," the software can be used with other distributions as well. In fact, RPM has even been ported to other operating systems, such as Solaris and IRIX! The source code to RPM is open-source software, so anyone can take the initiative to make the system work for them.

Installing a New Package

The easiest way to install a new package is to use the **-i** option with RPM. For example, if we downloaded a package called **bc-1.05a-4.i386.rpm** and wanted to install it, we would type

```
[root@ford /root]# rpm -i bc-1.05a-4.i386.rpm
```

If the installation went fine, we would not see any errors or messages. This is the most common method of installing RPMs. On the other hand, if the package already exists, we would see this message:

```
error: package bc-1.05a-4 is already installed
```

Some packages rely on other packages. A game, for example, may depend on SVGA libraries having already been installed. In those instances, you will get a message indicating which packages need to be installed first. Simply install those packages and then come back to the original package.

If you need to upgrade a package that already exists, use the **-U** option, like so:

```
[root@ford /root]# rpm -U bc-1.05a-4.i386.rpm
```

Some additional command-line options to RPM are listed in Table 4-1.

Command-Line Option	Description
--force	This is the sledgehammer of installation. Typically, you use it when you're knowingly installing an odd or unusual configuration, and RPM's safeguards are trying to keep you from doing so. The --**force** option tells RPM to forgo any sanity checks and just do it, even if it thinks you're trying to fit a square peg into a round hole. Be careful with this option.
-h	Prints hash marks to indicate progress during an installation. Use with the -**v** option for a pretty display.
--percent	Prints the percentage completed to indicate progress. It is handy if you're running RPM from another program, like a Perl script, and you want to know the status of the install.
-nodeps	If RPM is complaining about missing dependency files, but you want the installation to happen anyway, passing this option at the command line will cause RPM to not perform any dependency checks.
--test	This option does not perform a real installation; it just checks to see whether an installation would succeed. If it anticipates problems, it displays what they'll be.
-v	Tells RPM to be verbose about its actions.

Table 4-1.   RPM Command-Line Options

For example, to force the installation of a package regardless of dependencies or other errors, we would type:

```
[root@ford /root]# rpm -i --force -nodeps packagename.rpm
```

where **packagename.rpm** is the name of the package being installed.

Querying a Package

Sometimes it is handy to know which packages are currently installed and what they do. You can do that with the RPM query options.

To list all installed packages, simply type

```
[root@ford /root]# rpm -qa
```

Be ready for a long list of packages! If you are looking for a particular package name, you can use the **grep** command to specify the name (or part of the name) of the package, like so:

```
[root@ford /root]# rpm -qa | grep -i 'name'
```

> **NOTE:** The **-i** parameter in **grep** tells it to make its search case-insensitive.

If you just want to view all of the packages one screen at a time, you can use the **more** command, like so:

```
[root@ford /root]# rpm -qa | more
```

To find out which package a particular file belongs to, type

```
[root@ford /root]# rpm -qf filename
```

where **filename** is the name of the file that you want to check on.

To find out the purpose of a package that is already installed, you must first know the name of the package (taken from the listing in **rpm -qa**) and then specify it, like so:

```
[root@ford /root]# rpm -qi packagename
```

where **packagename** is the name of the package that you want information about.

To find out what files are contained in a package, type

```
[root@ford /root]# rpm -qlp packagename
```

where **packagename** is the name of the package that you want information about.

Uninstalling a Package

Uninstalling packages with RPM is just as easy as installing them. In most cases, all you will need to type is

```
[root@ford /root]# rpm -e packagename
```

where **packagename** is the name of the package as listed in **rpm -qa**.

gnorpm

For those of us who like a good GUI tool to help simplify our lives, there is **gnorpm**. Although it was meant to run under the GNOME environment, it works quite nicely under

KDE as well. It performs all of the functions that the command-line version does without forcing you to remember command-line parameters. Of course, this comes at the price of not being scriptable, but that's why we have the command-line version, too.

COMPILING SOFTWARE YOURSELF

One of the key benefits of open-source software is that you have the source code in your hands. If the developer chooses to stop working on it, you can continue. If you find a problem, you can fix it. In other words, you are in control of the situation and not at the mercy of a commercial developer you can't control. But having the source code means you need to be able to compile it, too. Otherwise all you have is a bunch of text files that can't do much.

Although almost every piece of software in this book is available as an RPM, we step through the process of compiling it ourselves so that we can pick and choose compile time options, which is something that we can't do with RPMs. Thus, it's a good idea to become comfortable with compiling packages yourself.

In this section, we will step through the process of compiling the Secure Shell (SSH) package, a tool that allows secure connections to remote hosts. (SSH is covered in Chapter 17.) SSH is a typical package; you'll find that most other packages that you need to compile follow the same general pattern.

Getting and Unpacking the Package

Software that comes in source form is generally made available as a *tarball*—that is, it is archived into a single large file and then compressed. The tools used to do this are **tar** and **gzip**: **tar** handles the process of combining many files into a single large file, and **gzip** is responsible for the compression.

NOTE: Do not confuse **gzip** with WinZip. They are two different programs that use two different (but comparable) methods of compression. It should be noted, though, that WinZip does know how to handle tarballs.

Typically, a single directory is selected in which to build and store tarballs. This allows the system administrator to keep the tarball of each package in a safe place in the event he or she needs to pull something out of it later. It also lets all the administrators know which packages are installed on the system in addition to the base system. A good directory for this is **/usr/local/src**, since software local to a site is generally installed in **/usr/local**.

When unpacked, most tarballs create a new directory for all of its files. The SSH tarball (**ssh-2.0.13.tar.gz**), for example, creates the subdirectory **ssh-2.0.13**. Most packages follow this standard. If you find a package that does not follow it, it is a good idea to create a subdirectory with a reasonable name and place all the unpacked source files there. This allows multiple builds to occur at the same time without the risk of the two builds conflicting.

Begin by downloading the SSH tarball. You can fetch it from the official SSH site at http://www.ssh.fi.

To unpack the SSH tarball, first move the file into the **/usr/local/src** directory, like so:

```
[root@ford /root]# mv ssh-2.0.13.tar.gz /usr/local/src
```

NOTE: This assumes that the SSH tarball is called **ssh-2.0.13.tar.gz**, and it was downloaded into the **/root** directory.

Once there, use the **cd** command to change directories to **/usr/local/src**, like so:

```
[root@ford /root]# cd /usr/local/src
```

Then unpack the tarball with the following command:

```
[root@ford src]# tar -xvzf ssh-2.0.13.tar.gz
```

The **z** parameter in the **tar** command invokes **gzip** to decompress the file before the untar process occurs. The **v** parameter tells **tar** to show the name of the file it is untarring as it goes through the process. This way you'll know the name of the directory where all the sources are being unpacked. We should now have a directory called **/usr/local/src/ssh-2.0.13**. We can test this by using the **cd** command to move into it:

```
[root@ford src]# cd /usr/local/src/ssh-2.0.13
```

Looking for Documentation

Once you are inside the directory with all of the source code, begin looking for documentation. *Always read the documentation that comes with the source code!* If there are any special compile directions, notes, or warnings, they will most likely be mentioned here. You will save yourself a great deal of agony by reading the relevant files first.

So then, what are the relevant files? Typically there are two files in a distribution: README and INSTALL, both of which are located in the root of the source code directory. The README file generally includes a description of the package, references to additional documentation (including the installation documentation), and references to the author of the package. The INSTALL file typically has directions for compiling and installing the package.

These are not, of course, absolutes. Every package has its quirks. The best way to find out is to simply list the directory contents and look for obvious signs of additional documentation. In the case of SSH, there is a file named SSH2.QUICKSTART. Guessing from the filename, it probably has cookbook directions for getting SSH2 configured, compiled, and installed. Some packages use different capitalization: readme, README, ReadMe, and so on; some introduce variations on a theme: README.1ST or README.NOW, and so on.

Another common place for additional information is a subdirectory that is appropriately called "doc" or "documentation." In the case of SSH, the only directories that exist are **apps**, **include**, and **lib**.

To view a text file, use the **more** command:

```
[root@ford ssh-2.0.13]# more README
```

To view the text file in an editor, use the **pico** command:

```
[root@ford ssh-2.0.13]# pico README
```

> **TIP:**   To get a quick list of all the directories in a source tree, enter the command:
> ```
> [root@ford ssh-2.0.13]# ls -l | grep drwx
> ```

Configuring the Package

Most packages ship with an autoconfiguration script; it is safe to assume they do unless their documentation says otherwise. These scripts are typically named "configure," and they take parameters. There are a handful of stock parameters that are available across all configure scripts, but the interesting stuff occurs on a program-by-program basis. Each package will have a handful of features that can be enabled or disabled or that have special values set at compile time, and they must be set up via **configure**.

To see what configure options come with a package, simply run

```
[root@ford ssh-2.0.13]# ./configure --help
```

Yes, those are two dashes (– –) before the word "help."

In the case of SSH, we'll see a long list of features that can be enabled and disabled. (See Chapter 17 for an explanation of what the options mean with respect to SSH.)

One commonly available option is **--prefix**. This option allows you to set the base directory where the package gets installed. By default, most packages use **/usr/local**. Each component in the package will install into the appropriate directory in **/usr/local**. For example, the server component of SSH is called sshd, which gets installed into **/usr/local/sbin**.

With all of the options you want set up, a final run of **configure** will create a special type of file called a *makefile*. Makefiles are the foundation of the compilation phase.

Compiling Your Package

Compiling your package is the easy part. All you need to do is run **make**, like so:

```
[root@ford ssh-2.0.13]# make
```

The **make** tool reads all of the makefiles that were created by the configure script. These files tell **make** which files to compile and the order in which to compile them—which is crucial since there could be hundreds of source files.

Depending on the speed of your system, the available memory, and how busy it is doing other things, the compilation process could take a while to complete, so don't be surprised.

As **make** is working, it will display each command it is running and all of the parameters associated with it. This output is usually the invocation of the compiler and all of the parameters passed to the compiler—it's pretty tedious stuff that even the programmers were inclined to automate!

If the compile goes through smoothly, you won't see any error messages. Most compiler error messages are very clear and distinct, so don't worry about possibly missing an error. If you do see an error, don't panic. Most error messages don't reflect a problem with the program itself, but usually with the system in some way or another. Typically, these messages are the result of inappropriate file permissions (see the **chmod** command in Chapter 6), or files that cannot be found. In the latter case, make sure your path has at the very least the **/bin**, **/sbin**, **/usr/bin**, **/usr/sbin**, **/usr/local/bin**, **/usr/local/sbin**, and **/usr/X11R6/bin** directories in it. You can see your path by issuing the following command:

```
[root@ford ssh-2.0.13]# echo $PATH
```

See Chapter 6 for information on environment variables so that you can set your path correctly.

In general, slow down and read the error message. Even if the format is a little odd, it may explain what is wrong in plain English, thereby allowing you to quickly fix it. If the error is still confusing, look at the documentation that came with the package to see if there is a mailing list or e-mail address you can contact for help. Most developers are more than happy to provide help, but you need to remember to be nice and to the point. (In other words, don't start an e-mail with a one paragraph rant about why their software is terrible!)

Installing the Package

Similar to the compile stage, the installation stage typically goes smoothly. In most cases, once the compile is done, all you need to run is

```
[root@ford ssh-2.0.13]# make install
```

This will start the installation script (which is usually embedded in the makefile). Because **make** displays each command as it is executing it, you will see a lot of text fly by. Don't worry about it—it's perfectly normal. Unless you see an error message, the package is installed.

If you do see an error message, it is most likely because of permissions problems. Look at the last file it was trying to install before failure, and then go check on all the permissions required to place a file there. You may need to use the **chmod**, **chown**, and **chgrp** commands for this step; see Chapter 6 for additional details.

Clean Up

Once the package is installed, you can do some cleanup to get rid of all the temporary files created during the installation. Since you have the original source code tarball, it is okay to simply get rid of the entire directory from which you compiled the source code. In the case of SSH, you would get rid of **/usr/local/src/ssh-2.0.13**. Begin by going one directory level above the directory you want to remove. In this case, that would be **/usr/local/src**.

```
[root@ford ssh-2.0.13]# cd /usr/local/src
```

Now use the **rm** command to remove the actual directory, like so:

```
[root@ford src]# rm -rf ssh-2.0.13
```

CAUTION: The **rm** command, especially with the **-rf** parameter, is very dangerous. It recursively removes an entire directory without stopping to verify *any* of the files. Run as the root user, this has the potential to really cause problems on your system. Be very careful and make sure you are erasing what you mean to erase. There is no "undelete" command.

SUMMARY

In this chapter, you learned how to install software under Linux using the RPM method and by compiling software yourself. Hopefully, this information should alleviate any fears you have of dealing with an open-source system!

The key points to remember are

▼   The typical install command with RPM is **rpm -i** *packagename.rpm*.

■   The typical upgrade command with RPM is **rpm -U** *packagename.rpm*.

■   The typical package remove command with RPM is **rpm -e** *packagename*.

■   Most source code is shipped as *tarballs*, which can be unpacked with the **tar** command.

■   Once untarred, reading the documentation that comes with the package is very important.

■   Configure the package with the **./configure** command.

■   Compile the software by running the **make** command.

▲   Install compiled software by running the **make install** command.

PART II

Single-Host Administration

CHAPTER 5

Managing Users

Under Linux, every file and program must be owned by a *user*. Each user has a unique identifier called a *user ID* (UID). Each user must also belong to at least one *group*, a collection of users established by the system administrator. Users may belong to multiple groups. Like users, groups also have unique identifiers called *group IDs* (GIDs).

The accessibility of a file or program is based on its UIDs and GIDs. A running program inherits the rights and permissions of the user who invokes it. (Set-UID and Set-GID, discussed in "SetUID and SetGID Programs" later in this chapter, create an exception to this rule.) Each user's rights can be defined in one of two ways: a *normal user* or the *root user*. Normal users can access only what they own or have been given permission to run; permission is granted because the user either belongs to the file's group or because the file is accessible to all users. The root user is allowed to access all files and programs in the system, whether or not root owns them. The root user is often called a *superuser*.

If you are accustomed to Windows, you can draw parallels between that system's user management and Linux's user management. Linux UIDs are comparable to Windows SIDs (system IDs), for example. In contrast to Windows NT, you may find the Linux security model maddeningly simplistic: Either you're root or you're not. Normal users cannot have root privileges in the same way normal users can be granted Administrator access under NT. You'll also notice the distinct absence of Access Control Lists (ACLs) in Linux. Which system is better? Depends on what you want and whom you ask.

In this chapter, we will examine the technique of managing users for a single host. Managing users over a network will be discussed in Chapter 19. Let's begin by exploring the actual database files that contain information about users. From there we'll examine the system tools available to manage the files automatically.

ABOUT USERS

In Linux, everything has an owner attached to it. Given this, it is impossible for a Linux system to exist without users! At the very least, it needs one root user; however, most Linux distributions ship with several special users set up. These users work well as self-documentation tools since each user owns all of the files related to his or her username—for example, the user www is set up to own all files related to World Wide Web service. These users are configured in such a way that grants access only to a select few, so you do not have to worry about their abuse.

TIP: When possible, run applications without root privileges. (The Apache server, for example, knows how to give up root privileges before it starts accepting connections.) The benefit of doing this is that if an application is found to have a security problem, it cannot be exploited to gain system privileges.

A few things need to be set up for a user's account to work correctly. In this section, we discuss those items and why they need to be there. The actual process of setting up accounts is discussed in "User Management Tools," later in the chapter.

Home Directories

Every user who actually logs in to the system needs a place for configuration files that are unique to the user. This place, called a *home directory*, allows each user to work in a customized environment without having to change the environment customized by another user—even if both users are logged in to the system at the same time. In this directory, users are allowed to keep not only their configuration files but their regular work files as well.

For the sake of consistency, most sites place home directories at **/home** and name each user's directory by his or her login names. Thus, if your login name were sshah, your home directory would be **/home/sshah**. The exception to this is for system accounts, such as a root user's account. Here, home directories are usually set to be either **/** or something specific to the need for that account (e.g., the www account may want its home directory set to **/usr/local/apache** if the Apache Web server is installed). The home directory for root is traditionally **/** with most variants of UNIX. Many Linux installations use **/root**.

The decision to place home directories under **/home** is strictly arbitrary—but it does make organizational sense. The system really doesn't care where we place home directories so long as the location for each user is specified in the password file (discussed in "The /etc/passwd File," later in this chapter). You may see some sites use **/u** or break up the **/home** directory by department, thereby creating **/home/engineering**, **/home/accounting**, **/home/admin**, etc., and then have users located under each department. (For example, Dr. Bosze from engineering would be **/home/engineering/bosze**.)

Passwords

Every account should either have a password or be tagged as impossible to log in to. This is crucial to your system's security—weak passwords are often the cause of compromised system security.

The original philosophy behind passwords is actually quite interesting, especially since we still rely on a significant part of it today. The idea is simple: Instead of relying on protected files to keep passwords a secret, the system would encrypt the password using an AT&T-developed (and National Security Agency–approved) algorithm called Data Encryption Standard (DES) and leave the encrypted value publicly viewable. What originally made this secure was that the encryption algorithm was computationally difficult to break. The best most folks could do is was a brute force dictionary attack where automated systems would iterate through a large dictionary and rely on the nature of users to pick English words for their passwords. Many people tried to break DES itself, but since it was an open algorithm that anyone could study, it was made much more bulletproof before it was actually deployed.

When users entered their passwords at a login prompt, the password they entered would be encrypted. The encrypted value would then be compared against the user's password entry. If the two encrypted values matched, the user was allowed to enter the system. The actual algorithm for performing the encryption was computationally cheap enough that a single encryption wouldn't take too long. However, the tens of thousands of encryptions that would be needed for a dictionary attack would take prohibitively long. Along with the encrypted passwords, the password file could then also keep information about the user's home directory, UID, shell, real name, and so on without having to worry about system security being compromised if any application run by any user would be allowed to read it.

But then a problem occurred: Moore's Law on processor speed doubling every 18 months held true, and home computers were becoming fast enough that programs were able to perform a brute force dictionary attack within days rather than weeks or months. Dictionaries got bigger and the software got smarter. The nature of passwords needed to be reevaluated.

Shadow passwords were one solution. In the shadow password scheme, the encrypted password entries were removed from the password file and placed in a separate file called **shadow**. The regular password file would continue to be readable by all users on the system, and the actual encrypted password entries would be readable only by the root user. (The login prompt is run with root permissions.) Why not just make the regular password file readable by root only? Well, it isn't that simple. By having the password file open for so many years, the rest of the system software that grew up around it relied on the fact that the password file was always readable by all users. Changing this would simply cause software to fail.

Another solution has been to improve the algorithm used to perform the encryption of passwords. Some distributions of Linux have followed the path of the FreeBSD operating system and used the MD5 scheme. This has increased the complexity of being able to crack passwords, which, when used in conjunction with shadow passwords, works quite well. (Of course, this is assuming you make your users choose good passwords!)

> **TIP:** Choosing good passwords is always a chore. Your users will inevitably ask, "What then, O Almighty System Administrator, makes a good password?" Here's your answer: a non-language word (not English, not Spanish, not German, not human-language word), preferably with mixed case, numbers, and punctuation—in other words, a string that looks like line noise. Well, this is all nice and wonderful, but if a password is too hard to remember, most people will quickly defeat its purpose by writing it down and keeping it in an easily viewed place. So better make it memorable! I prefer the technique of choosing a phrase and then picking the first letter of every word in the phrase. Thus, the phrase "coffee is VERY GOOD for you and me" becomes ciVG4yam. The phrase is memorable even if the resulting password isn't.

Shells

When users log in to the system, they expect an environment that can help them be productive. This first program that users encounter is called a *shell*. If you're used to the Windows side of the world, you might equate this to command.com, Program Manager, or Explorer (not to be confused with Internet Explorer, which is a Web browser).

Under UNIX, most shells are text based. The shell we discuss in further detail in Chapter 6 is the default shell for the root user, the Bourne Again Shell, or BASH for short.

Linux comes with several shells from which to choose—you can see most of them listed in the **/etc/shells** file. Deciding which shell is right for you is kind of like choosing a favorite beer—what's right for you isn't right for everyone, but, still, everyone tends to get defensive about his or her choice!

What makes UNIX so interesting is that you do not have to stick with the list of shells provided in **/etc/shells.** In the strictest of definitions, the password entry for each user doesn't list what shell to run so much as it lists what program to run first for the user. Of course, most users prefer that the first program run be a shell, such as BASH.

Startup Scripts

Under DOS, we are used to having the **autoexec.bat** and **config.sys** files run automatically when we start up the system. Since DOS is a single-user system, the two programs not only perform system functions such as loading device drivers, but they also set up our working environment.

UNIX, on the other hand, is a multiuser environment. Each user is allowed to have his or her own configuration files; thus the system appears to be customized for each particular user, even if other people are logged in at the same time. The configuration file comes in the form of *shell script*—a series of commands executed by the shell that starts when a user logs in. In the case of BASH, it's the file **.bashrc**. (Yes, there is a period in front of the filename—filenames preceded by periods, also called *dot files*, are hidden from normal directory listings unless the user uses a special option to list them.) You can think of shell scripts in the same light as batch files, except shell scripts can be much more capable. The **.bashrc** script in particular is similar in nature to that of **autoexec.bat**.

When you create a user's account, you should provide a default set of dot files to get the user started. If you use the tools that come with Linux, you don't need to worry about creating these files—the tools automatically do this for you. However, there is nothing stopping you from customizing these files to make them site specific. For example, if you have a special application that requires an environment variable to be set, you can add that to the dot files that are copied to new user's home directories.

Mail

Creating a new user means not only creating the user's home directory and setting up the environment. It also means making it possible for the user to send and receive e-mail. Setting up a mailbox under Linux is quite easy, and if you use the tools that come with Linux to create the account, you don't even have to do this yourself!

Mailboxes are kept in the **/var/spool/mail** directory. Each user has a mailbox that is based on his or her login name. Thus, if a user's login is jyom, his mailbox will be **/var/spool/mail/jyom**. All mailboxes should be owned by their respective owners with the permissions set such that others cannot read its contents. (See the `chown`, `chmod`, and `chgrp` commands in Chapter 6 for details on how to do this.)

An empty mailbox is a zero-length file. To create a zero-length file anywhere in the system, you simply use the **touch** command like so:

```
[root@ford /root]# touch myfile
```

This will create a new file called **myfile** in the current directory.

USER DATABASES

If you're already used to Windows 2000 user management, you're familiar with the Active Directory tool that takes care of the nitty-gritty details of the user database. This tool is convenient, but it makes developing your own administrative tools trickier, since the only other way to read or manipulate user information is through a series of LDAP calls.

In contrast, Linux takes the path of traditional UNIX and keeps all user information in straight text files. This is beneficial for the simple reason that it allows you to make changes to user information without the need of any other tool but a text editor such as **pico**. In many instances, larger sites take advantage of these text files by developing their own user administration tools so that they can not only create new accounts but also automatically make additions to the corporate phone book, Web pages, and so on.

However, users and groups working with UNIX style for the first time may prefer to stick with the basic user management tools that come with the Linux distribution. We'll discuss those tools in "User Management Tools" later in this chapter. For now, let's examine how Linux's text files are structured.

The /etc/passwd File

The **/etc/passwd** file stores the user's login, encrypted password entry, UID, default GID, name (sometimes called GECOS), home directory, and login shell. The file keeps one user per line, and each entry for the user is delimited by a colon. For example:

```
sshah:boQavhhaCKaXg:100:102:Steve Shah:/home/sshah:/bin/tcsh
```

> **NOTE:** Although modern distributions of Linux allow for logins to be longer than eight characters, it is generally considered a bad idea to do so. This is because some tools don't work quite right with longer logins, and some versions of UNIX get quite finicky with them.

Earlier in this chapter, we discussed the details of the password entry. In the code listing above, you can actually see what a DES-encrypted password looks like (the information following the first column). Many sites disable accounts by altering the encrypted password entry so that when the disabled account's user enters her password, it won't match the value in the password file. The guaranteed method of altering passwords for this reason is to insert an asterisk (*) into the entry. The above entry, for example, could be altered to boQavhhaCKaXg*.

> *TIP:* When disabling accounts in this manner, you may find it helpful not only to add an asterisk char-
> acter, but also to add a string to indicate why the account was disabled in the first place. For example, if
> you catch a user downloading pirated software, you could disable his account by changing the en-
> crypted entry to `boQavhhaCKaXg*caught pirating`.

The UID must be unique for every user, with the exception of the UID zero. Any user who has a UID of zero has root (Administrative) access and thus has full run of the system. Usually, the only user who has this specific UID has the login root. It is considered bad practice to allow any other users or usernames to have a UID of zero. This is notably different from the Windows NT and 2000 models, in which any number of users can have Administrative privileges.

> *NOTE:* Some distributions of Linux reserve the UID -1 (or 65535) for the user nobody.

The user's name can be any free-form text entry. Although it is possible for nonprintable characters to exist in this string, it is considered bad practice to use them. Also, the user's name may not span multiple lines.

> *NOTE:* Although the entire line for a user's password entry may not span multiple lines, it may be lon-
> ger than 80 characters.

The user's home directory appears as discussed earlier in this chapter. Ditto for the last entry, the user's shell. A complete password file for a system, then, might look like this:

```
root:AgQ/IJgASeW1M:0:0:root:/root:/bin/bash
bin:*:1:1:bin:/bin:
daemon:*:2:2:daemon:/sbin:
adm:*:3:4:adm:/var/adm:
lp:*:4:7:lp:/var/spool/lpd:
sync:*:5:0:sync:/sbin:/bin/sync
shutdown:*:6:0:shutdown:/sbin:/sbin/shutdown
halt:*:7:0:halt:/sbin:/sbin/halt
mail:*:8:12:mail:/var/spool/mail:
news:*:9:13:news:/var/spool/news:
uucp:*:10:14:uucp:/var/spool/uucp:
operator:*:11:0:operator:/root:
games:*:12:100:games:/usr/games:
gopher:*:13:30:gopher:/usr/lib/gopher-data:
ftp:*:14:50:FTP User:/home/ftp:
pop:*:15:15:APOP Admin:/tmp:/bin/tcsh
```

```
nobody:*:99:99:Nobody:/:
sshah:Kss9Ere9b1Ejs:500:500:Steve Shah:/home/sshah:/bin/tcsh
hdc:bfCAblvZBIbFM:501:501:H. D. Core:/home/hdc:/bin/bash
jyom:*:502:502:Mr. Yom:/home/jyom:/bin/bash
```

The /etc/shadow File

The speed of home computers began making dictionary attacks against password lists easier for hackers to accomplish. This led to the separation of the encrypted passwords from the **/etc/passwd** file. The **/etc/passwd** file would remain readable by all users, but the passwords kept in the **/etc/shadow** file would be readable only by those programs with root privileges, such as the login program.

In addition to the encrypted password field, the **/etc/shadow** file contains information about password expiration and whether the account is disabled. The format of each line in the **/etc/shadow** file contains the following:

▼ Login name

■ Encrypted password

■ Days since Jan. 1, 1970, that the password has been changed

■ Days before the password may be changed

■ Days after which the password must be changed

■ Days before the password is about to expire that the user is warned

■ Days after the password is expired that the account is disabled

■ Days since Jan. 1, 1970, that the account has been disabled

▲ Reserved field

Each user has a one-line entry with a colon delimiter. Here's an example:

```
sshah:boQavhhaCKaXg:10750:0:99999:7:-1:-1:134529868
```

Entries with a -1 imply infinity. In the case where a -1 appears in the field indicating the number of days before a password expires, you are effectively tagging a user as never having to change his or her password.

The /etc/group File

As you know, each user belongs to at least one group, that being their default group. Users may then be assigned to additional groups if needed. The **/etc/passwd** file contains each user's default GID. This GID is mapped to the group's name and other members of the group in the **/etc/group** file. The format of each line in the **/etc/group** file is

▼ Group name

- Encrypted password for the group
- GID number
▲ Comma-separated list of member users

Again, each field is separated by a colon. An entry looks similar to this:

```
project:baHrElKPNjrPE:102:sshah,hdc
```

Also like the **/etc/passwd** file, the group file must be world-readable so that applications can test for associations between users and groups. Group names should not exceed eight characters, and the GID should be unique for each group. Finally, the comma-separated list of users is used only for users for whom particular groups are not their default group.

If you want to include a group that does not have a password, you can set the entry like this:

```
project:baHrElKPNjrPE:102:sshah,hdc
```

If you want a group to exist, but you don't want to allow anyone to change his working group to this group (good for applications that need their own group but no valid reason exists for a user to be working inside that group), use an asterisk in the password field. For example:

```
project:*:102:
```

USER MANAGEMENT TOOLS

The wonderful part about having password database files that have a well-defined format in straight text is that it is easy for anyone to be able to write his or her own management tools. Indeed, many site administrators have already done this in order to integrate their tools along with the rest of their organization's infrastructure. They can start a new user from the same form that lets them update the corporate phone and e-mail directory, LDAP servers, Web pages, and so on. Of course, not everyone wants to roll their own tools, which is why Linux comes with several prewritten tools that do the job for you.

In this section, we discuss user management tools that work from both the command-line interface and the graphical user interface (GUI). Of course, learning how to use both is the preferred route, for you never know under what circumstances you may one day find yourself adding users.

Command-Line User Management

You can choose from among six command-line tools to perform the same actions performed by the GUI tool: **useradd**, **userdel**, **usermod**, **groupadd**, **groupdel**, and

groupmod. The obvious advantage to using the GUI tool is ease of use. However, the disadvantage is that actions that can be performed with it cannot be automated. This is where the command-line tools become very handy.

> **NOTE:** Linux distributions other than Red Hat may have slightly different parameters than the tools used here. To see how your particular installation is different, read the man page for the particular program in question.

useradd

As the name implies, **useradd** allows you to add a single user to the system. Unlike the GUI tool, there are no interactive prompts. Instead, all parameters must be specified on the command line. Here's how you use this tool:

```
useradd [-c comment] [-d homedir] [-e expire date] [-f inactive time]
[-g initial group][-G group[,...]] [-m [-k skeleton dir]] [-M]
[-s shell] [-u uid [-o]] [-n] [-r] login
```

Don't be intimidated by this long list of options! We'll examine them one at a time and discuss their relevance.

Before you dive into these options, take note that anything in the square brackets is optional. Thus, to add a new user with the login sshah, we could issue a command as simple as this:

```
[root@ford /root]# useradd sshah
```

Default values are used for any unspecified values. (To see the default values, simply run **useradd -D**; we will discuss how to change the defaults shortly.) Table 5-1 shows the command options and their descriptions.

For example, to create a new user whose name is H.D. Core, who is a member of the admin and support groups (default group admin), and who prefers using the Turbo C Shell and wants the login name hdc, we would use this line:

```
[root@ford /root]# useradd -c "H. D. Core" -g admin -G support -s /bin/tcsh hdc
```

userdel

userdel does the exact opposite of **useradd**—it removes existing users. This straightforward command has only one optional parameter and one required parameter:

```
userdel [-r] username
```

By running the command with only the user's login specified on the command line, for example, **userdel** sshah, all of the entries in the **/etc/passwd** and **/etc/shadow** files, and references in the **/etc/group** file, are automatically removed. By using the optional parameter (e.g., **userdel -r** sshah) all of the files owned by the user in his home directory are removed as well.

Option	Description
`-c comment`	Allows you to set the user's name in the GECOS field. As with any command-line parameter, if the value includes a space, you will need to put quotes around the text. For example, to set the user's name to Steve Shah, you would have to specify `-c` `"Steve Shah"`
`-d homedir`	By default, the user's home directory is **/home/***login* (e.g., if my login is sshah, my home directory would be **/home/sshah**). When creating a new user, the user's home directory gets created along with the user account. So if you want to change the default to another place, you can specify the new location with this parameter—for example, `-d` `/home/sysadmin/sshah`.
`-e expire-date`	It is possible for an account to expire after a certain date. By default, accounts never expire. To specify a date, be sure to place it in *MM/DD/YY* format (specify 00 for the year 2000 for this system)—for example, use `-e` `04/01/00` to expire on April 1, 2000.
`-f inactive-time`	This option specifies the number of days after a password expires that the account is still usable. A value of 0 (zero) indicates that the account is disabled immediately. A value of –1 will never allow the account to be disabled, even if the password has expired (e.g., `-f` 3 will allow an account to exist for three days after a password has expired). The default value is –1.
`-g initial-group`	Using this option, you can specify the default group the user has in the password file. You can use a number or name of the group; however, if you use a name of a group, the group must exist in the **/etc/group** file—for example, `-g` `project`.
`-G group[,...]`	This option allows you to specify additional groups to which the new user will belong. If you use the `-G` option, you must specify at least one additional group. You can, however, specify additional groups by separating the list with a comma. For example, to add a user to the project and admin groups, you should specify `-G` `project,admin`.

Table 5-1. Command Options and Their Descriptions

Option	Description
`-m [-k skel-dir]`	By default, the system automatically creates the user's home directory. This option is the explicit command to create the user's home directory. Part of creating the directory is copying default configuration files into it. These files come from the **/etc/skel** directory by default. You can change this by using the secondary option **-k skel dir**. (You must specify **-m** in order to use **-k**.) For example, to specify the **/etc/adminskel** directory, you would use **-m -k** /etc/adminskel.
`-M`	If you used the **-m** option, you cannot use **-M**, and vice versa. This option tells the command NOT to create the user's home directory.
`-n`	Red Hat Linux creates a new group with the same name as the new user's login as part of the process of adding a user. You can disable this behavior by using this option.
`-s shell`	A user's login shell is the first program that runs when a user logs in to a system. This is usually a command-line environment, unless you are logging in from the X Windows login screen. By default, this is the Bourne Shell (**/bin/bash**), though some folks like other shells such as the Turbo C Shell (**/bin/tcsh**). This option lets you choose whichever shell you would like to run for the new user upon login. (A list of shells is available in **/etc/shells**.)
`-u uid`	By default, the program will automatically find the next available UID and use it. If for some reason you need to force a new user's UID to be a particular value, you can use this option. Remember that UIDs must be unique for all users.
`Login`	Finally, the only parameter that *isn't* optional! You must specify the new user's login name.

Table 5-1.   Command Options and Their Descriptions *(continued)*

usermod

usermod allows you to modify an existing user in the system. It works in much the same way as **useradd**. The exact command-line usage is as follows:

```
usermod [-c comment] [-d homedir] [-m] [-e expire date]
[-f inactive time] [-g initial group]
[-G group[,...]] [-l login] [-s shell]
[-u uid] login
```

Every option you specify when using this command results in that particular parameter being changed about the user. All but one of the parameters listed here are identical to the parameters documented for the **useradd** program. That one option is **-l**.

The **-l** option allows you to change the user's login name. This and the **-u** option are the only options that require special care. Before changing the user's login or UID, you must make sure the user is not logged in to the system or running any processes. Changing this information if the user is logged in or running processes will cause unpredictable results.

Here's an example of using **usermod** to change user hdc such that her comment field reads H.D. Core instead of H.D.C:

```
[root@ford /root]# usermod -c "H.D. Core" hdc
```

groupadd

The group commands are similar to the user commands; however, instead of working on individual users, they work on groups listed in the **/etc/group** file. Note that changing group information does not cause user information to be automatically changed. For example, if you remove a group whose GID is 100 and a user's default group is specified as 100, the user's default group would not be updated to reflect the fact that the group no longer exists.

The **groupadd** command adds groups to the **/etc/group** file. The command-line options for this program are as follows:

```
groupadd [-g gid] [-r] [-f] group
```

Table 5-2 shows command options and their descriptions.

Suppose, for example, that you want to add a new group called research with the GID 800. To do so, you would type the following command:

```
[root@ford /root]# groupadd -g 800 research
```

groupdel

Even more straightforward than **userdel**, the **groupdel** command removes existing groups specified in the **/etc/group** file. The only usage information needed for this command is

```
groupdel group
```

Option	Description
-g *gid*	Specifies the GID for the new group as *gid*. By default, this value is automatically chosen by finding the first available value.
-r	By default, Red Hat searches for the first GID that is higher than 499. The -r options tell **groupadd** that the group being added is a system group and should have the first available GID under 499.
-f	When adding a new group, Red Hat Linux will exit without an error if the specified group to add already exists. By using this option, the program will not change the group setting before exiting. This is useful in scripting cases where you want the script to continue if the group already exists.
group	This option is required. It specifies the name of the group you want to add to be *group*.

Table 5-2.   More Command Options and Their Descriptions

where *group* is the name of the group to remove. For example, if you wanted to remove the research group, you would issue this command:

```
[root@ford /root]# groupdel research
```

groupmod

The **groupmod** command allows you to modify the parameters of an existing group. The options for this command are

```
groupmod -g gid -n group-name group
```

where the -g option allows you to change the GID of the group, and the -n option allows you to specify a new name of a group. Additionally, of course, you need to specify the name of the existing group as the last parameter.

For example, if the superman research group wanted to change its name to batman, you would issue the command:

```
[root@ford /root]# groupmod -n batman superman
```

Using LinuxConf to Manipulate Users and Groups

The LinuxConf package is a remarkably powerful configuration tool that you will find yourself using for many different tasks. One of its features is its ability to create, delete, and modify user and group information.

To start LinuxConf, be sure you are logged in as the root user and have started the X Windows environment. If you are using GNOME with Enlightenment (Red Hat's default), you will see LinuxConf as a menu choice at the bottom-left corner menu. If it doesn't appear there (or if you aren't using the default window manager), you can start LinuxConf by entering the command **linuxconf** from a terminal window.

Once you have started LinuxConf, you can scroll to the section on user management, which should look like Figure 5-1.

From this window, you can perform the three basic functions: add, modify, and delete users and groups.

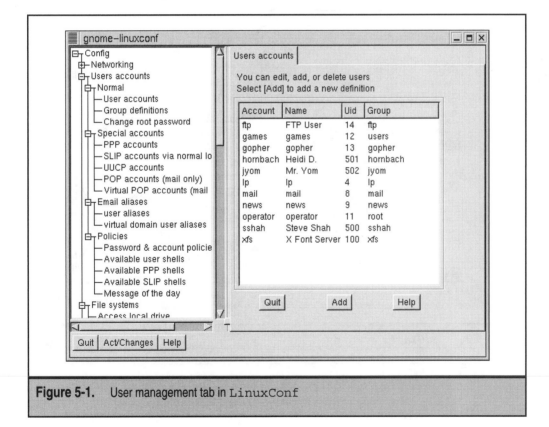

Figure 5-1. User management tab in LinuxConf

Adding a User

To add a user, begin by clicking the Add button at the bottom of the `LinuxConf` opening window. This will change the window as shown in Figure 5-2.

Every field except those in which the word "(opt)" (for optional) appears must be filled out. This includes the new account's login name and the user's real name. All other fields have default values associated with them. These parameters correlate to the entries in the **useradd** program.

Along with the basic user parameters, `LinuxConf` allows you to set some parameters regarding the user's permission to access some applications and e-mail settings if the user needs her e-mail forwarded to another address. These options are available via the window's tabs. Figure 5-3 shows the Privileges tab.

After you have established the parameters to your liking, click the Accept button at the bottom of the window. The next window asks you to set the user's initial password.

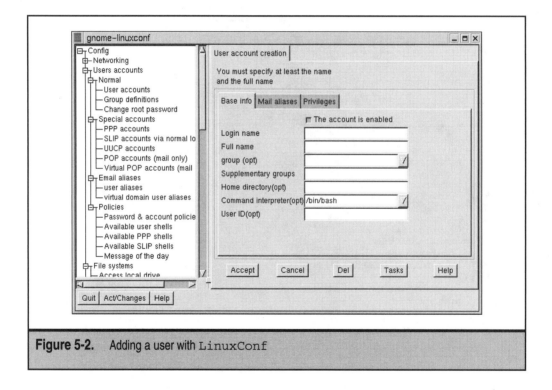

Figure 5-2.   Adding a user with `LinuxConf`

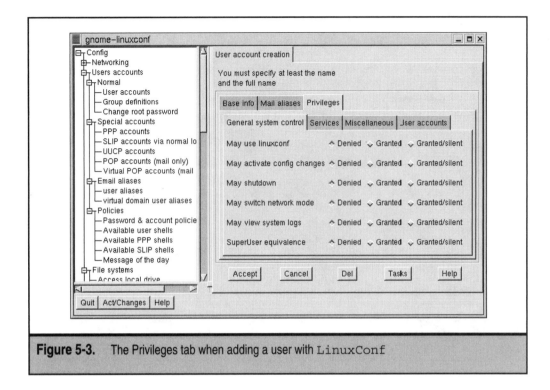

Figure 5-3. The Privileges tab when adding a user with `LinuxConf`

Once the password is set up, you are returned to the list of existing users, complete with your new addition.

Modifying a User

Modifying a user's settings is quite simple. In `LinuxConf`'s opening window, select the user whose settings you wish to modify. You'll see a window similar to that shown in Figure 5-4, which looks similar to the add user settings, except it's filled out. All the fields in the window are modifiable. After all of the modifications are made, click Accept.

NOTE: Remember that before you change a user's login or UID, make sure the user is not logged in or running any processes.

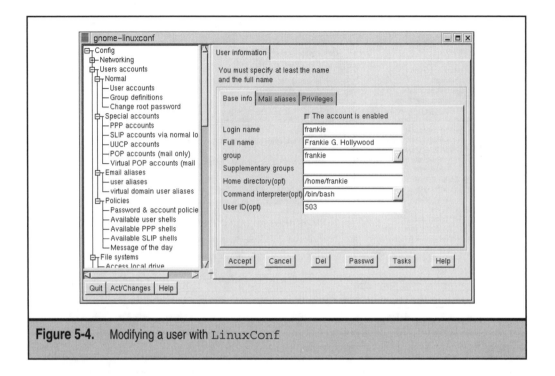

Figure 5-4. Modifying a user with `LinuxConf`

Deleting a User

To delete a user, click the username from the user list as shown in Figure 5-1. Once you see the user's information, you should notice a button labeled Del at the bottom of the window. Clicking this button begins the account removal process (see Figure 5-5).

Once you have decided what to do with the user's home directory, click Accept to bring you back to the user list. If you choose to archive the user's home directory, a **gzip**ped **tar** file containing the data can be found in the **/home/oldaccounts** directory.

Adding a Group

To add a new group, click Group Definitions on the left side of the `LinuxConf` opening window. This will bring up the list of current groups on the right of the window (see Figure 5-6).

If you click the Add button, you'll see a window in which you can fill in the name of a new group to be created. Although the window displays multiple fields, the only required field is the name of the group you want to create. All others have working defaults

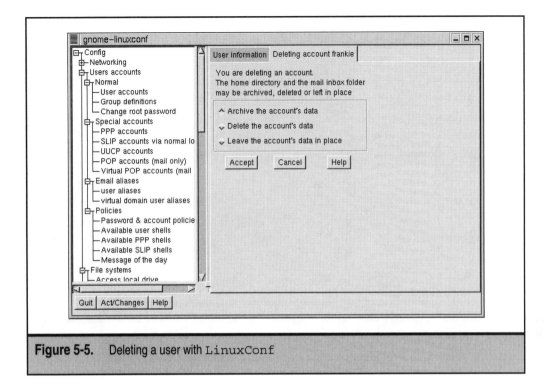

Figure 5-5.   Deleting a user with `LinuxConf`

that the system will supply for you. After you're finished, click Accept, and you will be brought back to the list of groups, which should include the new group you added.

Modifying a Group

Similar to modifying a user, to modify a group you simply select the name of the group you wish to edit from the group list to open a window similar to the add group window. This time, the fields will be filled out with the group's existing values. Simply change the fields you want and click Accept for the changes to take effect.

Deleting a Group

To delete a group, select the group from the list of groups shown in Figure 5-6. You'll see the details of the group, below which will include a button labeled Del. Click Del to open a screen requiring you confirm your decision. Click Yes, and you'll see the list of groups, minus the group you just deleted.

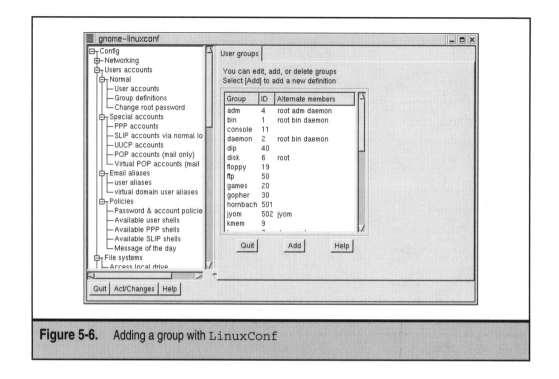

Figure 5-6.   Adding a group with `LinuxConf`

SETUID AND SETGID PROGRAMS

Normally, when a program is run by a user, it inherits all of the rights (or lack thereof) that the user has. If the user can't read the **/var/log/messages** file, neither can the program. Note that this permission can be different than the permissions of the user who owns the program file (usually called *the binary*). For example, the `ls` program (which is used to generate directory listings) is owned by the root user. Its permissions are set such that all users of the system can run the program. Thus, if the user sshah runs `ls`, that instance of `ls` is bound by the permissions granted to the user sshah, not root.

However, there is an exception. Programs can be tagged with what's called a *SetUID bit*, which allows a program to be run with permissions from the program's owner, not the user who is running it. Using `ls` as an example again, setting the SetUID bit on it and having the file owned by root means that if the user sshah runs `ls`, that instance of `ls` will run with root permissions, not with sshah's permissions. The *SetGID bit* works the same way, except instead of applying the file's owner, it is applied to the file's group setting.

To enable the SetUID bit or the SetGID bit, you need to use the **chmod** command, which is covered in detail in Chapter 6. To make a program SetUID, prefix whatever permission value you are about to assign it with a 4. To make a program SetGID, prefix whatever permission you are about to assign it with a 2. For example, to make the **/bin/ls** a SetUID program (which is a bad idea, by the way), you would use this command:

```
[root@ford /root]# chmod 4755 /bin/ls
```

WHEN A FILE ISN'T OWNED

The title of this section is a bit misleading. A file is always owned, no matter what. A more accurate title would be: "When a File's Owner's UID Doesn't Map To an Entry in the **/etc/ passwd** File"—but my editor wouldn't go for that.

When a user is created, it gets a new and unique UID. Any files created by that user are owned by that user. To keep things easy, Linux doesn't use the user's name, but the UID, to set file ownership. The system then uses the **/etc/passwd** file to perform a mapping between the user's UID and login so that it can make directory listings more human readable.

So what happens when a user is removed from the **/etc/passwd** file but files still exist that were owned by him? Nothing special, really. The most visible effect will be when you perform a directory listing on the file in question. Instead of showing you the owner of the file, it'll show a number. This number represents the UID that owns this file. If a new user is created with the same UID as the old user, the same UID will show up as the owner, making it appear as if the new user owns the file. Because of this behavior, it is important that you make sure you delete all of the files owned by a user when removing that user's account.

PLUGGABLE AUTHENTICATION MODULES (PAM)

One of the problems with the UNIX method of authentication is that it is always the same thing no matter what—passwords. While this worked great for a very long time, people have needed to become more sophisticated for a variety of reasons. This led to a number of very ugly hacks to abstract the authentication mechanism. Taking a cue from Solaris, Linux folks created their own implementation of *Pluggable Authentication Modules* (PAM).

The idea behind PAM is that instead of applications reading the password file, they would simply ask PAM to perform the authentication. PAM could then use whatever authentication mechanism the system administrator wanted. For many sites, the mechanism of choice is still a simple password file. And why not? It does what we want. Most users understand the need for it, and it's a well-tested method to get the job done. However, some sites have needed to expand on this.

A popular example of exceptions to the rule is still password-based, but instead of using standard UNIX passwords, another method of storing passwords was needed. For some sites, this is based on a database, thereby allowing for a larger number of users. For others, it is adapting to an existing system (like an NT server acting as a PDC).

In this section, we discuss how PAM is set up under Red Hat Linux. While the placement of files may not be exactly the same in your distribution, the underlying configuration files and concepts still apply.

How PAM Works

PAM is to other programs as a DLL is to a Windows application—it is just a library. When programs need to perform authentication on someone, they call a function that exists in the PAM library.

When invoked, PAM checks the configuration file for that application. If there isn't a configuration file, it uses a default configuration file. This configuration file tells the library what types of checks need to be done in order to authenticate the user. Based on this, the appropriate module is called on. (Red Hat folks can see these modules in the **/lib/security** directory.)

This module can check any number of things. It can simply check the **/etc/passwd** file or the **/etc/shadow** file, or it can perform a more complex check like calling on a LDAP server.

> **NOTE:** The PAM Web site (http://www.kernel.org/pub/linux/libs/pam/) offers a complete list of available modules.

Once the module has made the determination, an "authenticated/not authenticated" message is passed back to the calling application.

If this feels like a lot of steps for what should be a simple check, you're almost correct. While it feels like a lot of steps, each module here is very small and does its work very quickly. From a user's point of view, there should be no noticeable performance difference between an application that uses PAM and one that does not. From a system administrators and developers point of view, the flexibility this scheme offers is incredible and a very welcome addition.

Downloading and Installing PAM

Many distributions, most notably Red Hat, Caldera, and SuSE Linux, come with PAM pre-installed. You can check if PAM is already installed by looking for PAM's modules somewhere in your directory tree. These modules start with **pam_** and therefore should be easy to find.

Unless you find a good reason to reinstall or upgrade PAM, don't. Yet if you do need to download and install PAM yourself (or you want to upgrade your version of PAM), visit http://www.kernel.org/pub/linux/libs/pam/ to download the latest version. In this example, we will download and compile Linux-PAM-0.72.

Begin by going to http://www.kernel.org/pub/linux/libs/pam/pre/library/ and fetching the **Linux-PAM-0.72.tar.gz** file. (For this discussion, we will assume you have downloaded it to the **/usr/local/src** directory.)

Once there, unpack the archive with the **tar** command like so:

```
[root@ford src]# tar -xvzf Linux-PAM-0.72.tar.gz
```

This will create a Linux-PAM-0.72 directory. Use the **cd** command to get into this directory. There, you will find a file called README. This file contains complete directions on how to install this package should you need more information than what is provided here. A quick way to read this file is by using the **more** command, like so:

```
[root@ford Linux-PAM-0.72]# more README
```

Now take a look at the directory contents again. This time, notice that there is a **default.defs** file that contains default configuration information necessary for compiling and installing the package. Since we're using a Red Hat system, we want this to be the default of pointing to the **defs/redhat.defs** file.

Now we're ready to actually compile the software. Since this distribution of PAM is Linux-specific, we don't need to run **configure**; just run **make** like so:

```
[root@ford Linux-PAM-0.72]# make
```

However, the first time running **make** will return a warning that looks like this:

```
*WARNING*: If you are running a system that is dependent
on PAM to work. DO NOT make sterile NOR make remove.
These options will delete the PAM files on your system
And make it unusable!

If you are in any doubt, just do 'make all' (or just
'make'). It is likely that this is the SAFEST thing to do...
```

This message means exactly what it says—do not run **make remove**—this will remove your existing PAM installation and render your system unusable if you currently need PAM. However, since we aren't going to do that, we continue with just a simple **make** again:

```
[root@ford Linux-PAM-0.72]# make
```

You will see a lot of things fly by your screen—this is okay. It is simply the compiler going through and compiling each file that makes up the package. You will get used to this as you compile more software downloaded from the Internet.

With PAM compiled, we are ready to do an install. Simply run

```
[root@ford Linux-PAM-0.72]# make install
```

and you are off.

PAM's Files and Their Locations

On a Red Hat–style installation, PAM puts her configuration files in certain places. These file locations and their definitions are listed in Table 5-3.

Looking at the list of file locations in Table 5-3, one has to ask why PAM needs so many different configuration files. "One configuration file per application? That seems crazy!" Well, maybe not. The reason why PAM allows this is that not all applications are created equal. For instance, a POP mail server that uses the Qpopper mail server may want to allow for all of a site's users to fetch mail, but the login program may only want to allow certain users to be able to log in to the console. To accommodate for this, PAM needs a configuration file for POP mail that is different from the configuration for the login program.

File Location	Definition
`/sbin/pam_filter`	Filters that have the opportunity to examine all of the input and output from a user and a running application. This is a very discrete way of setting up logs and traps, but it is rarely used.
`/sbin`	Supplementary tools that may be called on from library functions.
`/lib`	The actual PAM library that manages the authentication process. Depending on the application's configuration, it calls on the appropriate module in the **/lib/security** directory.
`/lib/security`	Dynamically loaded authentication modules called by the actual PAM library.
`/usr/include/security`	Special header files for developers.
`/etc/security`	Configuration files for the modules located in **/lib/security**.
`/etc/pam.d`	Configuration files for each application that uses PAM. If an application that uses PAM does not have a specific configuration file, the default is automatically used.

Table 5-3. Locations of PAM Configuration and Library Files

Configuring PAM

The configuration files that we will be discussing here are the ones located in the **/etc/pam.d** directory. If you want to change the configuration files that apply to specific modules in the **/etc/security** directory, you should consult the documentation that came with the module. (Remember, PAM is just a framework. Specific modules can be written by anyone.)

The nature of a PAM configuration file is very interesting because of its "stackable" nature. That is, every line of a configuration file is evaluated during the authentication process (with the exceptions shown next). Each line specifies a module that performs some authentication task and returns either a success or failure flag. A summary of the results is returned to the application program calling PAM.

NOTE: By "failure," we do not mean the program did not work. Rather, we mean that when some process was done to verify whether a user could do something, the return value was "NO." PAM uses the terms "success" and "failure" to represent this information that is passed back to the calling application.

Each file consists of lines in the following format:

```
module_type    control_flag    module_path    arguments
```

where **module_type** represents one of four types of modules: **auth**, **account**, **session**, or **password**. Comments must begin with the hash (#) character. Table 5-4 lists these module types and their functions.

The **control_flag** allows us to specify how we want to deal with the success or failure of a particular authentication module. The control flags are described in Table 5-5.

Module Type	Function
Auth	Instructs the application program to prompt the user for a password and then grants both user and group privileges.
Account	Performs no authentication, but determines access based on other factors such as time of day or location of the user. For example, the root login can be given only console access this way.
Session	Specifies what, if any, actions need to be performed before or after a user is logged in (e.g. logging the connection).
Password	Specifies the module that allows users to change their password. (if appropriate).

Table 5-4. Module Types and Their Functions

Control Flag	Description
Required	If this flag is specified, the module MUST succeed in authenticating the individual. If it fails, the returned summary value must be failure.
Requisite	This flag is similar to **required**, however if **requisite** fails authentication, modules listed after it in the configuration file are not called, and a failure is immediately returned to the application. This allows us to require certain conditions to hold true before even accepting a login attempt (e.g., the user is on the local area network and cannot come from over the Internet).
Sufficient	If a **sufficient** module returns a success and there are no more **required** or **sufficient** control flags in the configuration file, PAM returns a success to the calling application.
Optional	This flag allows PAM to continue checking other modules even if this one has failed. You will want to use this when the user is allowed to log in even if a particular module has failed.

Table 5-5.　Control Flags and Their Descriptions

The *module_path* specifies the actual directory path of the module that performs the authentication task. For a full list of modules, visit PAM's Web site (http://www.kernel.org/pub/linux/libs/pam).

The final entry in a PAM configuration line is *arguments*. These are the parameters passed to the authentication module. Although the parameters are specific to each module, there are some generic options that can be applied to all modules. These arguments are described in Table 5-6.

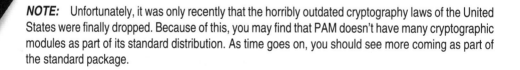

NOTE: Unfortunately, it was only recently that the horribly outdated cryptography laws of the United States were finally dropped. Because of this, you may find that PAM doesn't have many cryptographic modules as part of its standard distribution. As time goes on, you should see more coming as part of the standard package.

Argument	Description
Debug	Sends debugging information to the system logs.
no_warn	Does not give warning messages to the calling application.
use_first_pass	Does not prompt the user for a password a second time. Instead, the password they entered the first time determine their eligibility to enter the system. (This is for configurations where two different modules require a password to continue.)
try_first_pass	This option is similar to **use_first_pass**, where the user is not prompted for a password the second time. However, if the existing password causes the module to return a failure, the user is then asked to enter a second password, and the module is tried again.
use_mapped_pass	Passes the password from a previous module into the current one, much like **use_first_pass**. However, the password is then used to generate an encryption or decryption key.

Table 5-6.   PAM Arguments and Their Descriptions

An Example PAM Configuration File

Let's examine a sample PAM configuration file, **/etc/pam.d/login**:

```
#%PAM-1.0
auth       required    /lib/security/pam_securetty.so
auth       required    /lib/security/pam_pwdb.so shadow nullok
auth       required    /lib/security/pam_nologin.so
account    required    /lib/security/pam_pwdb.so
password   required    /lib/security/pam_cracklib.so
password   required    /lib/security/pam_pwdb.so shadow nullok use_authtok
session    required    /lib/security/pam_pwdb.so
```

We can see that the first line begins with a hash symbol and is therefore a comment. Thus we can ignore it. Let's go on to line 2:

```
auth        required    /lib/security/pam_securetty.so
```

Since the **module_type** is **auth**, PAM will want a password. The **control_flag** is set to **required**, so this module must return a success, or the login will fail. The module itself, **pam_securetty.so**, verifies that logins on the root account can only happen on the terminals mentioned in the **/etc/securetty** file. There are no arguments on this line.

```
auth        required    /lib/security/pam_pwdb.so shadow nullok
```

Similar to the first **auth** line, line 3 wants a password for authentication, and if the password fails, the authentication process will return a failure flag to the calling application. The **pam_pwdb.so** module checks the **/etc/passwd** file and with the **shadow** parameter, it checks the **/etc/shadow** file as well. The **nullok** parameter tells it that having no password is okay. (Normally empty passwords mean that the account is locked.)

```
auth        required    /lib/security/pam_nologin.so
```

In line 4, the **pam_nologin.so** module checks for the **/etc/nologin** file. If it is present, only root is allowed to log in; others are turned away with an error message. If the file does not exist, it always returns a success.

```
account     required    /lib/security/pam_pwdb.so
```

In line 5, since the **module_type** is **account**, the **pam_pwdb.so** module acts differently. It silently checks that the user is even allowed to log in (e.g., "has their password expired?"). If all the parameters check out okay, it will return a success.

```
password    required    /lib/security/pam_cracklib.so
```

The **module_type** of **password** in line 6 means that this module will only be applied during password changes. The **pam_cracklib.so** module performs a variety of checks to see whether a password is "too easy" to crack by potential intruders.

```
password    required    /lib/security/pam_pwdb.so shadow nullok use_authtok
```

Line 7 offers another example of the versatility of the **pam_pwdb.so** module. With the **module_type** set to **password**, it will perform the actual updating of the **/etc/passwd** file. The **shadow** parameters tell it to check for the existence of the **/etc/shadow** file and update that file if it does exist. The **nullok** parameter allows users to change their passwords from empty entries to real passwords. The last option, **use_authtok**, forces **pam_pwdb.so** to use the password retrieved from a previous **module_type** entry of **password**.

```
session     required    /lib/security/pam_pwdb.so
```

The final usage of the **pam_pwdb.so** module is for **module_type session**. This time, it sends login successes and failures to the system logs.

The "Other" File

As we mentioned earlier, if PAM cannot find a configuration file that is specific to an application, it will use a generic configuration file instead. This generic configuration file is called **/etc/pam.d/other**. By default, the "other" configuration file is set to a paranoid setting so that all authentication attempts are logged and then promptly denied. It is recommended you keep it that way.

"DOH! I Can't Log In!"

Don't worry—screwing up a setting in a PAM configuration file happens to everyone. Consider it part of learning the ropes. First thing to do: Don't panic. Like most configuration errors under Linux, you can fix things by booting into single-user mode (see Chapter 7) and fixing the errant file.

If you've screwed up your login configuration file and need to bring it back to a sane state, here is a safe setting you can put in:

```
auth        required      /lib/security/pam_unix_auth.so
account     required      /lib/security/pam_unix_acct.so
password    required      /lib/security/pam_unix_passwd.so
session     required      /lib/security/pam_unix_session.so
```

This setting will give Linux the default behavior of simply looking into the **/etc/passwd** file for a password. This should be good enough to get you back in, where you can make the changes you meant to make!

Debugging PAM

Like many other Linux services, PAM makes excellent use of the system log files. (You can read more about them in Chapter 9.) If things are not working the way you want them to work, begin by looking at the end of the log files and see if PAM is spelling out what happened. More than likely, it is. You should then be able to use this information to change your settings and fix your problem.

> **TIP:** If you are running in X Windows, you can monitor the log file in real time by using the **tail** command in a window like so:
> ```
> [root@ford /root]# tail -f /var/log/messages
> ```
> where **/var/log/messages** is the name of the log file that you want to monitor. If you aren't sure which file to check, start with **/var/log/messages**. Then check the **/var/log** directory and see what other files are there. You can use the **tail** command with any of them.
> In another window, try doing what you are testing out. If there are any messages generated by PAM, you will see them in your **tail** window immediately.

SUMMARY

This chapter documents the nature of users under Linux. Much of what you read here also applies to other variants of UNIX, which makes administering users in heterogeneous environments much easier with different UNIX's than NT/UNIX.

Following are the most significant issues covered in this chapter:

▼   Each user gets a unique UID.

■   Each group gets a unique GID.

■   The **/etc/passwd** file maps UIDs to usernames.

■   Linux handles encrypted passwords in multiple ways.

■   Linux includes tools that help you administer users.

■   Should you decide to write your own tools to manage the user databases, you'll now understand the format for doing so.

▲   PAM, the Pluggable Authentication Modules, is Linux's generic way of handling multiple authentication mechanisms.

These changes are pretty significant for an administrator coming from the Windows 98/NT/2000 environment and can be a little tricky at first. Not to worry, though—the UNIX security model is quite straightforward, so you should quickly get comfortable with how it all works.

If the idea of getting to build your own tools to administer users appeals to you, definitely look into books on the Perl scripting language. It is remarkably well suited for manipulating tabular data (such as the **/etc/passwd** file). With Perl's networking facilities and NT/2000 support, Linux even lets you build a cross-platform **adduser** tool that can create and set up both UNIX and NT accounts. With so many books on Perl out there, each with a slightly different angle and assuming a slightly different level of programming background, it's tough to make a single book recommendation. Take some time and page through a few books at your local bookstore.

CHAPTER 6

The Command Line

Over time, it's been UNIX's command-line options that have given the system its power and flexibility. Casual observers of UNIX gurus are often astounded at the results of a few carefully entered commands. Unfortunately, this power makes UNIX less intuitive to the average user. For this reason, graphical user interfaces (GUIs) have become the de facto standard for many UNIX tools.

More experienced users, however, find that it is difficult for a GUI to present all of the available options. Typically, doing so would make the interface just as complicated as the command-line equivalent. The GUI design is often oversimplified, and experienced users ultimately return to the comprehensive capabilities of the command line.

> **TIP:**   Before you start debating which interface is better, remember that both types of interface serve a purpose. Each has its weaknesses and benefits. In the end, the person who chooses to master both methods will come out ahead.

Before we begin our study of the command-line interface under Linux, understand that this chapter is far from an exhaustive resource. Rather than trying to cover all the tools without any depth, we have chosen to describe thoroughly a handful of tools we believe to be most critical for day-to-day work.

> **NOTE:**   For this chapter, we assume that you are logged in as root user and have started the X Windows environment. If you are using the GNOME environment (which is the default behavior of the latest versions of Red Hat Linux) you can start an "X terminal." Click the GNOME footprint in the lower-left corner of your screen, select Utilities, and then select Color Xterm. All of the commands you enter in this chapter should be typed into the window that appears after Color Xterm is selected.

AN INTRODUCTION TO BASH

In Chapter 5, we learned that one of the parameters for a user's password entry is their *login shell*, which is the first program that runs when a user logs in to a workstation. The shell is comparable to the Windows Program Manager, except that the shell program used, of course, is arbitrary.

A *shell* is simply a program that provides an interface to the system. The Bourne Again Shell (BASH) in particular is a command-line–only interface containing a handful of built-in commands, the ability to launch other programs, and the ability to control programs that have been launched from it (job control). Think of it as a command.com or a cmd on steroids.

A variety of shells exist, most with similar features but different means of implementing them. Again for the purpose of comparison, you can think of the various shells as Web browsers; among several different browsers, the basic functionality is the same—displaying content from the Web. In any situation like this, everyone proclaims that their shell is better than the others, but it all really comes down to personal preference.

In this section, we'll examine some of BASH's built-in commands. A complete reference on BASH could easily be a book in itself, so we'll stick with the commands that most affect the daily operations of a systems administrator. However, I do recommend that you eventually study BASH's operations. There's no shortage of excellent books on the topic.

Job Control

When working in the BASH environment, you can start multiple programs from the same prompt. Each program is a *job*. Whenever a job is started, it takes over the *terminal*. (This is a throwback to the days when actual dumb terminals such as VT-100s and Wyse-50s were used to interface with the machine.) On today's machines, the terminal is either the straight-text interface you see when you boot the machine or the window created by the X Window System on which BASH runs. (The terminal interfaces in X Window System are called a pseudo tty, or pty for short.) If a job has control of the terminal, it can issue control codes so that text-only interfaces (the Pine mail reader, for instance) can be made more attractive. Once the program is done, it gives full control back to BASH, and a prompt is redisplayed for the user.

Not all programs require this kind of terminal control, however. Some, including programs that interface with the user through the X Window System, can be instructed to give up terminal control and allow BASH to present a user prompt, even though the invoked program is still running. In the following example, Netscape Navigator receives such an instruction, represented by the ampersand suffix:

```
[root@ford /root]# netscape &
```

Immediately after you press ENTER, BASH will present a prompt. This is called *backgrounding* the task. Folks who remember Windows NT prior to version 4 will remember having to do something similar with the Start command.

If a program is already running and has control of the terminal, you can make the program give up control by pressing CTRL-Z in the terminal window. This will stop the running job altogether and return control to BASH so that you can enter new commands.

At any given time, you can find out how many jobs BASH is tracking by typing this command:

```
[root@ford /root]# jobs
```

The running programs that are listed will be in one of two states: running or stopped. If a job is stopped, you can start it running in the background, thereby allowing you to keep control of the terminal. Or a stopped job can run in the foreground, which gives control of the terminal back to that program.

To run a job in the background, type

```
[root@ford]# bg number
```

where **number** is the job number you want to background. To run a job in the foreground, type

```
[root@ford]# fg number
```

where **number** is the job number you want in the foreground.

NOTE: You cannot background a task that requires interaction through the terminal window.

Environment Variables

Every instance of a shell that is running has its own "environment"—settings that give it a particular look, feel, and, in some cases, behavior. These settings are typically controlled by *environment variables*. Some environment variables have special meanings to the shell, but there is nothing stopping you from defining your own and using them for your own needs. It is with the use of environment variables that most shell scripts are able to do interesting things and remember results from user inputs as well as program's outputs. If you are already familiar with the concept of environment variables in Windows NT/2000, you'll find that many of the things that you know about them will apply to Linux as well; the only difference is how they are set, viewed, and removed.

Printing Environment Variables

To list all of your environment variables, use the **printenv** command. For example:

```
[root@ford /root]# printenv
```

To show a specific environment variable, specify the variable as a parameter to **printenv**. For example, here is the command to see the environment variable OSTYPE:

```
[root@ford /root]# printenv OSTYPE
```

Setting Environment Variables

To set an environment variable, use the following format:

```
[root@ford /root]# variable=value
```

where **variable** is the variable name, and **value** is the value you want to assign the variable. For example, here is the command to set the environment variable FOO with the value BAR:

```
[root@ford /root]# FOO=BAR
```

Once the value is set, use the **export** command to finalize it. The format of the **export** command is as follows:

```
[root@ford /root]# export variable
```

where **variable** is the name of the variable. In the example of setting FOO, we would enter this command:

```
[root@ford /root]# export FOO
```

TIP: You can combine the steps for setting an environment variable with the export command, like so:
```
[root@ford /root]# export FOO=BAR
```

If the value of the environment variable you want to set has spaces in it, surround the variable with quotation marks. Using the above example, to set FOO to "Welcome to the BAR of FOO.", we would enter

```
[root@ford /root]# export FOO="Welcome to the BAR of FOO."
```

Unsetting Environment Variables

To remove an environment variable, use the **unset** command:

```
[root@ford /root]# unset variable
```

where **variable** is the name of the variable you want to remove. For example, here is the command to remove the environment variable FOO:

```
[root@ford]# unset FOO
```

NOTE: This section assumed that you are using BASH. There are many other shells to choose from; the most popular alternatives are C-Shell (csh) and its brother Turbo C-Shell (tcsh), which use different mechanisms for getting and setting environment variables. For more information, read the manual page (see "The Man Command" section later in this chapter) for the shell you prefer. We document BASH here since it is the default shell of all new Linux accounts.

Pipes

Pipes are a mechanism by which the output of one program can be sent as the input to another program. Individual programs can be chained together to become extremely powerful tools.

Let's use the **grep** program to provide a simple example of pipes usage. The **grep** utility, given a stream of input, will try to match the line with the parameter supplied to it and display only matching lines. For example, if we were looking for all environment variables containing the string "OSTYPE", we could enter this command:

```
[root@ford /root]# printenv | grep "OSTYPE"
```

The vertical bar (|) character represents the pipe between **printenv** and **grep**.

The command shell under Windows also utilizes the pipe function. The primary difference is that all commands in a Linux pipe are executed concurrently, whereas Windows runs each program in order, using temporary files to hold intermediate results.

Redirection

Through *redirection,* we can take the output of a program and have it automatically sent to a file. The shell rather than the program itself handles this process, thereby providing a standard mechanism for performing the task. (Using redirection is much easier than having to remember how to do this for every single program!)

Redirection comes in three classes: output to a file, append to a file, and send a file as input.

To collect the output of a program into a file, end the command line with the greater than symbol (>) and the name of the file to which you want the output redirected. If you are redirecting to an existing file and you want to append additional data to it, use two > symbols back-to-back (>>) followed by the filename. For example, here is the command to collect the output of a directory listing into a file called **/tmp/directory_listing**:

```
[root@ford /root]# ls > /tmp/directory_listing
```

Continuing this example with the directory listing, we could append the string "Directory Listing" to the end of the **/tmp/directory_listing** file by typing this command:

```
[root@ford /root]# echo "Directory Listing" >> /tmp/directory_listing
```

The third class of redirection, using a file as input, is done by using the less than sign (<) followed by the name of the file. For example, here is the command to feed the **/etc/passwd** file into the **grep** program:

```
[root@ford /root]# grep 'root' < /etc/passwd
```

Command-Line Shortcuts

One of the difficulties in moving to a command-line interface, especially from command-line tools such as command.com, is working with a shell that has a good number of shortcuts. These refinements may surprise you if you're not careful. This section explains the most common of the BASH shortcuts and their behaviors.

Filename Expansion

Under UNIX-based shells such as BASH, wildcards on the command line are expanded *before* being passed as a parameter to the application. This is in sharp contrast to the default mode of operation for DOS-based tools, which often have to perform their own wildcard expansion. The UNIX method also means that you must be careful where you use the wildcard characters.

The wildcard characters themselves in BASH are identical to those in command.com: the asterisk (*) matches against all filenames, and the question mark (?) matches against single characters. If you need to use these characters as part of another parameter for whatever reason, you can *escape* them by preceding them with a backslash (\ ) character. This causes the shell to interpret the asterisk and question mark as regular characters instead of wildcards.

NOTE: Most UNIX documentation refers to wildcards as *regular expressions*. The distinction is important since regular expressions are substantially more powerful than just wildcards alone. All of the shells that come with Linux support regular expressions. You can read more about them in either the shell's manual page or in the book *Mastering Regular Expressions* by Jeffrey E. F. Friedl (O'Reilly and Associates, 1997).

Environment Variables as Parameters

Under BASH, you can use environment variables as parameters on the command line. (Although command.com does this as well, it's not a common practice and thus is an often forgotten convention.) For example, issuing the parameter **$FOO** will cause the value of the FOO environment variable to be passed rather than the string "$FOO".

Multiple Commands

Under BASH, multiple commands can be executed on the same line by separating the commands with semicolons (;). For example, to execute this sequence of commands on a single line

```
[root@ford /root]# ls -l
[root@ford /root]# cat /etc/passwd
```

you could instead type the following:

```
[root@ford /root]# ls -l ;cat /etc/passwd
```

Backticks

How's this for wild: You can take the output of one program and make it the parameter of another program. Sound bizarre? Well, time to get used to it—this is one of the most useful and innovative features available in all UNIX shells.

Backticks (`) allow you to embed commands as parameters to other commands. You'll see this technique used often in this book to take a number sitting in a file and pass that number as a parameter to the **kill** command. A typical instance of this occurs when the DNS server, **named**, needs to be killed. When **named** starts, it writes its process identification number into the file **/var/run/named.pid**. Thus, the generic way of killing the **named** process is to look at the number in **/var/run/named.pid** using the **cat** command, and then issue the **kill** command with that value. For example:

```
[root@ford /root]# cat /var/run/named.pid
253
[root@ford /root]# kill 253
```

One problem with killing the **named** process in this way is that it cannot be automated—we are counting on the fact that a human will read the value in **/var/run/named.pid** in order to **kill** the number. Another issue isn't so much a problem as it is a nuisance: It takes two steps to stop the DNS server.

Using backticks, however, we can combine the steps into one *and* do it in a way that can be automated. The backticks version would look like this:

```
[root@ford /root]# kill `cat /var/run/named.pid`
```

When BASH sees this command, it will first run **cat /var/run/named.pid** and store the result. It will then run **kill** and pass the stored result to it. From our point of view, this happens in one graceful step.

NOTE: So far in this chapter, we have looked at features that are internal to BASH. The remainder of the chapter explores several common commands accessible outside of BASH.

DOCUMENTATION TOOLS

Linux comes with two superbly useful tools for making documentation accessible: **man** and **info**. Currently, a great deal of overlap exists between these two documentation systems because many applications are moving their documentation to the **info** format. This format is considered superior to **man** because it allows the documentation to be hyperlinked together in a Web-like way, but without actually having to be written in HTML format.

The **man** format, on the other hand, has been around for decades. For thousands of utilities, their man (short for *manual*) pages are their only documentation. Furthermore, many applications continue to utilize **man** format because many other UNIX-like operating systems (such as Sun Solaris) use **man** format.

Both the **man** and **info** documentation systems will be around for a long while to come. I highly recommend getting comfortable with them both.

TIP: Many Linux distributions also include a great deal of documentation in the **/usr/doc** or **/usr/share/doc** directory.

The man Command

We mentioned quite early in this book that man pages are documents found online that cover the use of tools and their corresponding configuration files. The format of the **man** command is as follows:

```
[root@ford /root]# man program_name
```

where **program_name** identifies the program you're interested in. For example:

```
[root@ford /root]# man ls
```

While reading about UNIX and UNIX-related information sources (newsgroups and so forth), you may encounter references to commands followed by numbers in parentheses—for example, **ls(1)**. The number represents the *section* of the manual pages (see Table 6-1). Each section covers various subject areas, to accommodate the fact that some tools (such as **printf**) are commands in the C programming language as well as command-line commands.

To refer to a specific **man** section, simply specify the section number as the first parameter and then the command as the second parameter. For example, to get the C programmers' information on **printf**, you'd enter this:

```
[root@ford /root]# man 3 printf
```

Manual Section	Subject
1	User tools
2	System calls
3	C library calls
4	Device driver information
5	Configuration files
6	Games
7	Packages
8	System tools

Table 6-1.   **man** Page Sections

To get the command-line information, you'd enter this:

```
[root@ford /root]# man 1 printf
```

By default, the lowest section number gets printed first.

Unfortunately, this organization is sometimes difficult to use. You may find it helpful to use the graphical interface for this library of documentation, developed as part of the GNOME project; it's called **gnome-help-browser**. Look for a large icon for this interface on the toolbar at the bottom of your screen or in the menu selection at the lower-left corner of your screen. If you don't have this icon, you can always start it from a terminal window yourself with this command:

```
[root@ford /root]#  gnome-help-browser
```

TIP: A handy option to the **man** command is **-k** preceding the command parameter. With this option, **man** will search the summary information of all the man pages and list pages matching your specified command, along with their section number. For example: [root@ford /root]# **man -k printf**

The texinfo System

Another common form of documentation is *texinfo*. Established as the GNU standard, texinfo is a documentation system similar to the hyperlinked World Wide Web format. Because documents can be hyperlinked together, texinfo is often easier to read, use, and search.

To read the texinfo documents on a specific tool or application, invoke **info** with the parameter specifying the tool's name. For example, to read about **emacs**, type:

```
[root@ford /root]# info emacs
```

In general, you will want to verify that a man page exists before using **info** (there is still a great deal more information available in **man** format than in texinfo). On the other hand, some man pages will explicitly state that the texinfo pages are more authoritative and should be read instead.

FILE LISTINGS, OWNERSHIPS, AND PERMISSIONS

Managing files under Linux is different than managing files under Windows NT/2000, and radically different from managing files under Windows 95/98. In this section, we discuss basic file management tools for Linux. We'll start with specifics on some useful general-purpose commands, and then step back and look at some background information.

Listing Files: ls

The `ls` command is used to list all the files in a directory. Of more than 26 available options, the ones listed here are the most commonly used. The options can be used in any combination. See the texinfo page for a complete list.

Option for `ls`	Description
-l	Long listing. In addition to the filename, shows the file size, date/time, permissions, ownership, and group information.
-a	All files. Shows all files in the directory, including hidden files. Names of hidden files begin with a period.
-1	Single column listing.
-R	Recursively lists all files and subdirectories.

To list all files in a directory with a long listing, type this command:

```
[root@ford /root]# ls -la
```

To list a directory's non-hidden files that start with *A*, type this:

```
[root@ford /root]# ls A*
```

File and Directory Types

Under Linux (and UNIX in general), almost everything is abstracted to a file. Originally this was done to simplify the programmer's job. Instead of having to communicate directly with device drivers, special files (which look like ordinary files to the application) are used as a bridge. Several types of files accommodate all these file uses.

Normal Files

Normal files are just that—normal. They contain data or executables, and the operating system makes no assumptions about their contents.

Directories

Directory files are a special instance of normal files. Directory files list the location of other files, some of which may be other directories. (This is similar to folders in Windows.) In general, the contents of directory files won't be of importance to your daily operations, unless you need to open and read the file yourself rather than using existing applications to navigate directories. (This would be similar to trying to read the DOS File Allocation Table directly rather than using command.com to navigate directories, or using the findfirst/findnext system calls.)

Hard Links

Each file in the Linux file system gets its own *i-node*. An i-node keeps track of a file's attributes and its location on the disk. If you need to be able to refer to a single file using two separate filenames, you can create a *hard link*. The hard link will have the same i-node as the original file and will therefore look and behave just like the original. With every hard link that is created, a *reference count* is incremented. When a hard link is removed, the reference count is decremented. Until the reference count reaches zero, the file will remain on disk.

> **NOTE:** A hard link cannot exist between two files on separate partitions. This is because the hard link refers to the original file by i-node, and a file's i-node may differ among file systems.

Symbolic Links

Unlike hard links, which point to a file by its i-node, a *symbolic link* points to another file by its name. This allows symbolic links (often abbreviated *symlinks*) to point to files located on other partitions, even other network drives.

Block Devices

Since all device drivers are accessed through the file system, files of type *block device* are used to interface with devices such as disks. A block device file has three identifying traits:

▼ It has a major number.

■ It has a minor number.

▲ When viewed using the **ls -l** command, it shows **b** as the first character of the permissions.

For example:

```
[root@ford /root]# ls -l /dev/hda
brw-rw----   1 root       disk        3,   0 May  5  1998 /dev/hda
```

Note the **b** at the beginning of the file's permissions; the **3** is the major number, and the **0** is the minor number.

A block device file's major number identifies the represented device driver. When this file is accessed, the minor number is passed to the device driver as a parameter telling it which device it is accessing. For example, if there are two serial ports, they will share the same device driver and thus the same major number, but each serial port will have a unique minor number.

Character Devices

Similar to block devices, character devices are special files that allow you to access devices through the file system. The obvious difference between block and character devices is that block devices communicate with the actual devices in large blocks, whereas character devices work one character at a time. (A hard disk is a block device; a modem is a character device.) Character device permissions start with a **c**, and the file has a major and a minor number. For example:

```
[root@ford /root]# ls -l /dev/ttyS0
crw-------   1 root      tty        4,  64 May  5  1998 /dev/ttyS0
```

Named Pipes

Named pipes are a special type of file that allows for interprocess communication. Using the **mknod** command (discussed later in this chapter), you can create a named pipe file that one process can open for reading and another process can open for writing, thus allowing the two to communicate with one another. This works especially well when a program refuses to take input from a command-line pipe, but another program needs to feed the other one data and you don't have the disk space for a temporary file.

For a named pipe file, the first character of its file permissions is a **p**. For example:

```
[root@ford /root]# ls -l mypipe
prw-r--r--   1 root      root          0 Jun 16 10:47 mypipe
```

Change Ownership: chown

The **chown** command allows you to change the ownership of a file to someone else. Only the root user can do this. (Normal users may not give away file ownership or steal ownership from another user.) The format of the command is as follows:

```
[root@ford /root]# chown [-R] username filename
```

where **username** is the login of the user to whom you want to assign ownership, and **filename** is the name of the file in question. The **filename** may be a directory as well.

The **-R** option applies when the specified **filename** is a directory name. This option tells the command to recursively descend through the directory tree and apply the new ownership not only to the directory itself, but to all of the files and directories within it.

Change group: chgrp

The **chgrp** command-line utility lets you change the group settings of a file. It works much like **chown**. Here is the format:

```
[root@ford /root]# chgrp [-R] groupname filename
```

where **groupname** is the name of the group to which you want to assign **filename** ownership. The **filename** may be a directory as well.

The **-R** option applies when the specified **filename** is a directory name. As with **chown**, the **-R** option tells the command to recursively descend through the directory tree and apply the new ownership not only to the directory itself, but also to all of the files and directories within it.

Change Mode: chmod

Permissions are divided into four parts. The first part is represented by the first character of the permission. Normal files have no special value and are represented with a hyphen (-) character. If the file has a special attribute, it is represented by a letter. The two special attributes we are most interested in here are directories (**d**) and symbolic links (**1**).

The second, third, and fourth parts of a permission are represented in three-character chunks. The first part indicates the file owner's permission. The second part indicates the group permission. The last part indicates the world permission. In the context of UNIX, "world" means all users in the system, regardless of their group settings.

Following are the letters used to represent permissions and their corresponding values. When you combine attributes, you add their values. The **chmod** command is used to set permission values.

Letter	Permission	Value
R	Read	4
W	Write	2
X	Execute	1

Although **chmod** does have more readable formats for permissions, it's important that you understand the numbering scheme because it is used in programming. In addition, not everyone uses the letter-naming scheme. It is often assumed that if you understand file permissions, you understand the numeric meanings as well.

Following are the most common combinations of the three permissions. Other combinations, such as **-wx**, do exist, but they are rarely used.

Letter	Permission	Value
- - -	No permissions	0
r - -	Read only	4
rw -	Read and write	6
rwx	Read, write, and execute	7
r - x	Read and execute	5
- - x	Execute only	1

For each file, three of these three-letter chunks are grouped together. The first chunk represents the permissions for the owner of the file, the second chunk represents the permissions for file's group, and the last chunk represents the permissions for all users on the system. Table 6-2 describes some common file permission setups.

Permission	Numeric Equivalent	Description
`-rw-------`	600	Owner has read and write permissions. Set for most files.
`-rw-r--r--`	644	Owner has read and write permissions; group and world have read only permission. Be sure you want to let other people read this file.
`-rw-rw-rw-`	666	Everyone has read and write permissions. Not recommended; this combination allows the file to be accessed and changed by anyone, anywhere on the system.
`-rwx------`	700	Owner has read, write, and execute permissions. Best combination for programs the owner wishes to run (files that result from compiling a C or C++ program).
`-rwxr-xr-x`	755	Owner has read, write, and execute permissions. Everyone else has read and execute permissions.
`-rwxrwxrwx`	777	Everyone has read, write, and execute privileges. Like the 666 setting, this combination should be avoided.
`-rwx--x--x`	711	Owner has read, write, and execute permissions; everyone else has execute only permissions. Useful for programs that you want to let others run but not copy.
`drwx------`	700	This is a directory created with the **mkdir** command. Only the owner can read and write into this directory. Note that all directories must have the executable bit set.
`drwxr-xr-x`	755	This directory can be changed only by the owner, but everyone else can view its contents.
`drwx--x--x`	711	A handy combination for keeping a directory world-readable but restricted from access by the **ls** command. File can be read only by someone who knows the filename.

Table 6-2. File Permission Combinations

FILE MANAGEMENT AND MANIPULATION

This section covers the basic command-line tools for managing files and directories. Most of this will be familiar to anyone who has used a command-line interface. Same old functions, but new commands to execute.

Copy Files: cp

The **cp** command is used to copy files and has a substantial number of options. See its man page for additional details. By default, this command works silently, only displaying status information if an error condition occurs. Following are the most common of options for **cp**.

Option for cp	Description
-f	Force copy; do not ask for verification.
-i	Interactive copy; before each file is copied, verify with user.

To copy **index.html** to **index-orig.html**, use the following command:

```
[root@ford /root]# cp index.html index-orig.html
```

To interactively copy all files ending in **.html** to the **/tmp** directory, type this command:

```
[root@ford /root]# cp -i *.html /tmp
```

Move Files: mv

The **mv** command is used to move files from one location to another. Files can be moved across partitions as well. That requires a copy operation to occur, so that move command may take longer. Following are the most common options for **mv**:

Option for mv	Description
-f	Force move
-i	Interactive move

To move a file from **/usr/src/myprog/bin/*** to **/usr/bin**, use this command:

```
[root@ford /root]# mv /usr/src/myprog/bin/* /usr/bin
```

There is no explicit rename tool, so we can use **mv**. To rename **/tmp/blah** to **/tmp/bleck**, type this command:

```
[root@ford /root]# mv /tmp/bleck /tmp/blah
```

Link Files: ln

The **ln** command lets you establish hard links and soft links. (See "File and Directory Types" earlier in this chapter.) The general format of **ln** is as follows:

```
[root@ford /root]# ln original_file new_file
```

Although **ln** has many options, you'll never need to use most of them. The most common option, **-s**, creates a symbolic link instead of a hard link.

To create a symbolic link so that **/usr/bin/myadduser** points to **/usr/local/bin/myadduser**, issue this command:

```
[root@ford /root]# ln -s /usr/local/bin/myadduser /usr/bin/myadduser
```

Find a File: find

The **find** command lets you search for files based on various criteria. Like the tools we have already discussed, **find** has a large number of options that you can read about on its man page. Here is the general format of **find**:

```
[root@ford /root]# find start_dir [options]
```

where **start_dir** is the directory from which the search should start. Table 6-3 shows the most common options used with **find**.

To find all files in **/tmp** that have not been accessed in at least seven days, use the following command:

```
[root@ford /root]# find /tmp -atime 7 -print
```

Type this command to find all files in **/usr/src** whose names are core and to remove them:

```
[root@ford /root]# find /usr/src -name core -exec rm
```

To find all files in **/home** which end in **.jpg** and are over in 100K in size, issue this command:

```
[root@ford /root]# find /home -name "*.jpg" -size 100k
```

The –exec Parameter

One of the most useful parameters to **find** is **-exec**. It allows **find** to execute a command on any file it finds. The name of the file is passed to the command using the string "{}", and the end of the command is entered as \;. For example, to look for the string 'tcp' in all of the files in **/usr/include/netinet** using **grep**, use this command:

```
[root@ford /root]# find /usr/include/netinet -name "*.h" -exec grep 'tcp' {} \; -print
```

Option for `find`	Description
`-mount`	Do not search file systems other than the one from which search starts.
`-atime n`	File was accessed at least n*24 hours ago.
`-ctime n`	File was changed at least n*24 hours ago.
`-inum n`	File has i-node n.
`-amin n`	File was accessed n minutes ago.
`-cmin n`	File was changed n minutes ago.
`-empty`	File is empty.
`-mmin n`	File was modified n minutes ago.
`-mtime n`	File was modified n*24 hours ago.
`-nouser`	File's UID does not correspond to a real user in **/etc/passwd**.
`-nogroup`	File's GID does not correspond to a real group in **/etc/group**.
`-perm mode`	File's permissions are exactly set to **mode**.
`-size n [bck]`	File is at least n *b*locks/*c*haracters/*k*ilobytes. One block equals 512 bytes.
`-print`	Print the filenames found.
`-exec cmd`	On every file found, execute **cmd**. Important: Be sure to always follow every **cmd** with the \; characters, or BASH will become confused.
`-name name`	File's name should be **name**. You can use regular expressions here.

Table 6-3.   Common Options Used with `find`

Convert and Copy a File: dd

The **dd** command reads the contents of a file and sends it to another file. What makes it different from **cp** is that **dd** can perform on-the-fly conversions on the file and accept data from a tape or floppy drive or other device. When **dd** accesses a device, it does not assume anything about the file system and instead pulls the data in a raw format. Thus, **dd** can be used to generate images of disks even if the disk is of foreign format.

Table 6-4 shows the most common parameters for **dd**.

Option for dd	Description
`if=infile`	Specifies the input file as *infile*.
`of=outfile`	Specifies the output file as *outfile*.
`count=blocks`	Specifies *blocks* as the number of blocks on which **dd** should operate before quitting.
`ibs=size`	Sets the block size of the input device to be *size*.
`obs=size`	Sets the block size of the output device to be *size*.
`Seek=blocks`	Skips *blocks* number of blocks on the output.
`Skip=blocks`	Skips *blocks* number of blocks on the input.
`Swab`	Converts big-endian input to little endian or vice-versa.

Table 6-4. Common Parameters for **dd**

To generate an image of a floppy disk (especially useful for foreign file formats), use the following command:

```
[root@ford /root]# dd if=/dev/fd0 of=/tmp/floppy_image
```

File Compression: gzip

NOTE: `gzip` does not share file formats with either PKZip or WinZip; however, WinZip can decompress `gzip` files.

In the original distributions of UNIX, the tool to compress files was appropriately called **compress**. Unfortunately, the algorithm was patented by someone hoping to make a great deal of money. Instead of paying out, most sites sought and found another compression tool with a patent-free algorithm: **gzip**. Even better, **gzip** consistently achieves better compression ratios than **compress** does. Another bonus: Recent changes have allowed **gzip** to uncompress files that were compressed using the **compress** command.

TIP: The filename extension usually identifies a file compressed with `gzip`. These files typically end in .GZ (files compressed with **compress** end in .Z).

Optional parameters used most often with `gzip` are as follows; see the man page for a complete list.

Option for `gzip`	Description
`-c`	Write compressed file to the **stdout** (thereby allowing the output to be piped to another program)
`-d`	Decompress
`-r`	Recursively find all files that should be compressed
`-9`	Best compression
`-1`	Fastest compression

Note that **gzip** compresses the file in place, meaning that after the compression process, the original file is removed, and the only thing left is the compressed file.

To compress a file and then decompress it, use this command:

```
[root@ford /root]# gzip myfile
[root@ford /root]# gzip -d myfile.gz
```

Issue this command to compress all files ending in **.html** using the best compression possible:

```
[root@ford /root]# gzip -9 *.html
```

Make Special Files: mknod

As discussed earlier, Linux accesses all of its devices through files. A file that the system understands as an interface to a device must be of type block or character and have major and minor numbers. To create this kind of file with the necessary values, you use the **mknod** command. The **mknod** command can also be used to create named pipes.

Here's the command format:

```
[root@ford /root]# mknod name type [major] [minor]
```

where **name** is the name of the file; **type** is either **b** for block device, **c** for character device, or **p** for named pipe. If you choose to create a block or character device (when installing a device driver that requires it), you need to specify the **major** and **minor** numbers. The documentation accompanying that driver should tell you what values to use for the major and minor numbers.

To create a named pipe called **/tmp/mypipe**, use this command:

```
[root@ford /root]# mknod /tmp/mypipe p
```

Create a Directory: mkdir

The **mkdir** in Linux is identical to the same command in other UNIXs, as well as in MS-DOS. The only option available is **-p**, which will create parent directories if none exist. For example, if you need to create **/tmp/bigdir/subdir/mydir** and the only directory that exists is **/tmp,** using **-p** will cause **bigdir** and **subdir** to be automatically created along with **mydir.**

To create a directory called **mydir,** use this command:

```
[root@ford /root]# mkdir mydir
```

NOTE: The **mkdir** command cannot be abbreviated to **md** as it can be under DOS.

Remove Directory: rmdir

The **rmdir** command offers no surprises for those familiar with the DOS version of the command; it simply removes an existing directory. The only command-line parameter available for this is **-p**, which removes parent directories as well. For example, in a directory named **/tmp/bigdir/subdit/mydir,** if you want to get rid of all the directories from **bigdir** to **mydir,** you'd issue this command alone:

```
[root@ford /tmp]# rmdir -p bigdir/subdir/mydir
```

To remove a directory called **mydir,** you'd type this:

```
[root@ford /root]# rmdir mydir
```

NOTE: The **rmdir** command cannot be abbreviated to **rd** as it can under DOS.

Show Present Working Directory: pwd

It is inevitable that you will sit down in front of an already logged in workstation and not know where you are in the directory tree. To get this information, you need the **pwd** command. It has no parameters, and its only task is to print the current working directory. The DOS equivalent is typing **cd** alone on the command line; however, the BASH **cd** command takes you back to your home directory.

To get the current working directory, use this command:

```
[root@ford src]# pwd /usr/local/src
```

Tape Archive: tar

If you are familiar with the PKZip program, you are accustomed to the fact that the compression tool reduces file size but also consolidates files into compressed archives. Under Linux, this process is separated into two tools: **gzip** and **tar**.

The **tar** program combines multiple files into a single large file. It is separate from the compression tool, so it allows you to select which compression tool to use or whether you even want compression. Additionally, **tar** is able to read and write to devices in much the same way **dd** can, thus making **tar** a good tool for backing up to tape devices.

NOTE: Although the name of the **tar** program includes the word "tape," it isn't necessary to read or write to a tape drive when creating archives. In fact, you'll rarely use **tar** with a tape drive in day-to-day situations (backups aside). The reason it was named **tar** in the first place was that when it was originally created, limited disk space meant that tape was the most logical place to put archives. Typically, the **-f** option in **tar** would be used to specify the tape device file, rather than a traditional Unix file. You should be aware, however, that you can still **tar** straight to a device.

Here's the structure of the **tar** command, its most common options, and several examples of its use:

```
[root@ford /root]# tar [commands and options] filename
```

Option for tar	Description
-c	Create a new archive.
-t	View the contents of an archive.
-x	Extract the contents of an archive.
-f	Specify the name of the file (or device) in which the archive is located.
-v	Be verbose during operations.
-z	Assume the file is already (or will be) compressed with **gzip**.

To create an archive called **apache.tar** containing all the files from **/usr/src/apache**, use this command:

```
[root@ford src]# tar -cf apache.tar /usr/src/apache
```

To create an archive called **apache.tar** containing all the files from **/usr/src/apache**, and to show what is happening as it happens, enter the following:

```
[root@ford src]# tar -cvf apache.tar /usr/src/apache
```

To create a **gzip**ped compressed archive called **apache.tar.gz** containing all of the files from **/usr/src/apache**, and to show what is happening as it happens, issue this command:

```
[root@ford src]# tar -cvzf apache.tar.gz /usr/src/apache
```

To extract the contents of a **gzip**ped **tar** archive called **apache.tar.gz**, and to show what is happening as it happens, use this command:

```
[root@ford /root]# tar -xvzf apache.tar.gz
```

If you like, you can also specify a physical device to **tar** to and from. This is handy when you need to transfer a set of files from one system to another and for some reason you cannot create a file system on the device. (Or sometimes it's just more entertaining to do it this way.) To create an archive on the first floppy device, you would enter this:

```
[root@ford /root]# tar -cvzf /dev/fd0 /usr/src/apache
```

To pull that archive off of a disk, you would type

```
[root@ford src]# tar -xvzf /dev/fd0
```

Concatenate Files: cat

The **cat** program fills an extremely simple role: to display files. More creative things can be done with it, but nearly all of its usage will be in the form of simply displaying the contents of text files—much like the **type** command under DOS. Because multiple filenames can be specified on the command line, it's possible to concatenate files into a single, large continuous file. This is different from **tar** in that the resulting file has no control information to show the boundaries of different files.

To display the **/etc/passwd** file, use this command:

```
[root@ford /root]# cat /etc/passwd
```

To display the **/etc/passwd** file and the **/etc/group** file, issue this command:

```
[root@ford /root]# cat /etc/passwd /etc/group
```

Type this command to concatenate **/etc/passwd** with **/etc/group** into the file **/tmp/complete**:

```
[root@ford /root]# cat /etc/passwd /etc/group > /tmp/complete
```

To concatenate the **/etc/passwd** file to an existing file called **/tmp/orb**, use this:

```
[root@ford /root]# cat /etc/passwd >> /tmp/orb
```

Display a File One Screen at a Time: more

The **more** command works in much the same way the DOS version of the program does. It takes an input file and displays it one screen at a time. The input file can either come from its **stdin** or from a command-line parameter.

Additional command-line parameters, though rarely used, can be found in the man page.

To view the **/etc/passwd** file one screen at a time, use this command:

```
[root@ford /root]# more /etc/passwd
```

To view the directory listing generated by the **ls** command one screen at a time, enter this:

```
[root@ford /root]# ls | more
```

Disk Utilization: du

You will often need to determine where and by whom disk space is being consumed, especially when you're running low on it! The **du** command allows you to determine the disk utilization on a directory-by-directory basis. Here are some of the options available:

Option for du	Description
-c	Produce a grand total at the end of the run.
-h	Print sizes in human readable format.
-k	Print sizes in kilobytes rather than block sizes. (Note: Under Linux, one block is equal to 1K, but this is not true for all UNIXs.)
-s	Summarize. Print only one output for each argument.

To display the amount of space each directory in **/home** is taking up in human readable format, use this command:

```
[root@ford /root]# du -sh /home/*
```

Show the Directory Location of a File: which

The **which** command searches your entire path to find the name of the file specified on the command line. If the file is found, the command output includes the actual path of the file. This command is used to locate fully qualified paths.

Use the following command to find out which directory the **ls** command is in:

```
[root@ford /root]# which ls
```

You may find this similar to the **find** command. The difference here is that since **which** only searches the path, it is much faster. Of course, it is also much more limiting than **find**, but if all you're looking for is a program, you'll find it to be a better choice of commands.

Locating a Command: whereis

The **whereis** tool searches your path and displays the name of the program and its absolute directory, the source file (if available), and the man page for the command (again, if available).

To find the location of the program, source, and manual page for the command **grep**, use this:

```
[root@ford /root]# whereis grep
```

Disk Free: df

The **df** program displays the amount of free space, partition by partition. The drives/partitions must be mounted in order to get this information. NFS information can be gathered this way, as well. Some parameters for **df** are listed here; additional (rarely used) options are listed in the **df** manual page.

Option for df	Description
-h	Generate free space amount in human readable numbers rather than free blocks.
-l	List only the local mounted file systems. Do not display any information about network mounted file systems.

To show the free space for all locally mounted drivers, use this command:

```
[root@ford /root]# df -l
```

To show the free space in a human readable format, for the file system in which our current working directory is located, enter

```
[root@ford /root]# df -h .
```

To show the free space in a human readable format for the file system on which **/tmp** is located, type this command:

```
[root@ford /root]# df -h /tmp
```

Synchronize Disks: sync

Like most other modern operating systems, Linux maintains a disk cache to improve efficiency. The drawback, of course, is that not everything you want written to disk will have been written to disk at any given moment.

To schedule the disk cache to be written out to disk, you use the **sync** command. If **sync** detects that writing the cache out to disk has already been scheduled, the kernel is instructed to immediately flush the cache. This command takes no command-line parameters.

Type this command to ensure the disk cache has been flushed:

```
[root@ford /root]# sync ;  sync
```

PROCESS MANIPULATION

Under Linux (and UNIX in general), each running program comprises at least one process. From the operating system's standpoint, each process is independent of the others. Unless it specifically asks to share resources with other processes, a process is confined to the memory and CPU allocation assigned to it. Processes that overstep their memory allocation (which could potentially corrupt another running program and make the system unstable) are immediately killed. This method of handling processes has been a major contributor to the stability of UNIX systems: User applications cannot corrupt other user programs or the operating system.

This section describes the tools used to list and manipulate processes. They are very important elements of a system administrator's daily work.

List Processes: ps

The **ps** command lists all the processes in a system, their state, size, name, owner, CPU time, wall clock time, and much more. There are many command-line parameters available, and the ones most often used are described in Table 6-5.

The most common set of parameters used with the **ps** command is **-auxww**. These parameters show all the processes (regardless of whether they have a controlling terminal), each process's owners, and all the processes' command-line parameters. Let's examine the output of an invocation of **ps -auxww**.

```
USER       PID %CPU %MEM   VSZ   RSS TTY       STAT START    TIME COMMAND
root         1  0.0  0.3  1096   476 ?         S    Jun10    0:04 init
root         2  0.0  0.0     0     0 ?         SW   Jun10    0:00 [kflushd]
root         3  0.0  0.0     0     0 ?         SW   Jun10    0:00 [kpiod]
root         4  0.0  0.0     0     0 ?         SW   Jun10    0:00 [kswapd]
root         5  0.0  0.0     0     0 ?         SW<  NJun10    0:00 [mdrecoveryd]
root       102  0.0  0.2  1068   380 ?         S    Jun10    0:00 /usr/sbin/apmd -p 10 -w 5
bin        253  0.0  0.2  1088   288 ?         S    Jun10    0:00 portmap
root       300  0.0  0.4  1272   548 ?         S    Jun10    0:00 syslogd -m 0
root       311  0.0  0.5  1376   668 ?         S    Jun10    0:00 klogd
daemon     325  0.0  0.2  1112   284 ?         S    Jun10    0:00 /usr/sbin/atd
root       339  0.0  0.4  1284   532 ?         S    Jun10    0:00 crond
root       357  0.0  0.3  1232   508 ?         S    Jun10    0:00 inetd
root       371  0.0  1.1  2528  1424 ?         S    Jun10    0:00 named
root       385  0.0  0.4  1284   516 ?         S    Jun10    0:00 lpd
```

```
root        399  0.0  0.8  2384 1116 ?          S    Jun10   0:00 httpd
xfs         429  0.0  0.7  1988  908 ?          S    Jun10   0:00 xfs
root        467  0.0  0.2  1060  384 tty2       S    Jun10   0:00 /sbin/mingetty tty2
root        468  0.0  0.2  1060  384 tty3       S    Jun10   0:00 /sbin/mingetty tty3
root        469  0.0  0.2  1060  384 tty4       S    Jun10   0:00 /sbin/mingetty tty4
root        470  0.0  0.2  1060  384 tty5       S    Jun10   0:00 /sbin/mingetty tty5
root        471  0.0  0.2  1060  384 tty6       S    Jun10   0:00 /sbin/mingetty tty6
root        473  0.0  0.0  1052  116 ?          S    Jun10   0:01 update (bdflush)
root        853  0.0  0.7  1708  940 pts/1      S    Jun10   0:00 BASH
root       1199  0.0  0.7  1940 1012 pts/2      S    Jun10   0:00 su
root       1203  0.0  0.7  1700  920 pts/2      S    Jun10   0:00 BASH
root       1726  0.0  1.3  2824 1760 ?          S    Jun10   0:00 xterm
root       1728  0.0  0.7  1716  940 pts/8      S    Jun10   0:00 BASH
root       1953  0.0  1.3  2832 1780 ?          S    Jun11   0:05 xterm
root       1955  0.0  0.7  1724  972 pts/10     S    Jun11   0:00 BASH
nobody     6436  0.0  0.7  2572  988 ?          S    Jun13   0:00 httpd
nobody     6437  0.0  0.7  2560  972 ?          S    Jun13   0:00 httpd
nobody     6438  0.0  0.7  2560  976 ?          S    Jun13   0:00 httpd
nobody     6439  0.0  0.7  2560  976 ?          S    Jun13   0:00 httpd
nobody     6440  0.0  0.7  2560  976 ?          S    Jun13   0:00 httpd
nobody     6441  0.0  0.7  2560  976 ?          S    Jun13   0:00 httpd
root      16673  0.0  0.6  1936  840 pts/10     S    Jun14   0:00 su -sshah
sshah     16675  0.0  0.8  1960 1112 pts/10     S    Jun14   0:00 -tcsh
root      18243  0.0  0.9  2144 1216 tty1       S    Jun14   0:00 login -- sshah
sshah     18244  0.0  0.8  1940 1080 tty1       S    Jun14   0:00 -tcsh
```

Option for `ps`	Description
`-a`	Show all processes with a controlling terminal, not just the current user's processes.
`-r`	Show only running processes (see the description of process states later in this section).
`-x`	Show processes that do not have a controlling terminal.
`-u`	Show the process owners.
`-f`	Display parent/child relationships among processes.
`-l`	Produce a list in long format.
`-w`	Show a process's command-line parameters (up to half a line).
`-ww`	Show all of a process's command-line parameters, despite length.

Table 6-5.   Command-Line Parameters for `ps`

The very first line of the output provides column headers for the listing, as follows:

▼ **USER**   Who owns what process.

■ **PID**   Process identification number.

■ **%CPU**   Percentage of the CPU taken up by a process. Note: For a system with multiple processors, this column will add up to more than 100%.

■ **%MEM**   Percentage of memory taken up by a process.

■ **VSZ**   The amount of virtual memory a process is taking.

■ **RSS**   The amount of actual (resident) memory a process is taking.

■ **TTY**   The controlling terminal for a process. A question mark in this column means the process is no longer connected to a controlling terminal.

▲ **STAT**   The state of the process:

S   Process is sleeping. All processes that are ready to run (that is, being multitasked, and the CPU is currently focused elsewhere) will be asleep.

R   Process is actually on the CPU.

D   Uninterruptible sleep (usually I/O related).

T   Process is being traced by a debugger or has been stopped.

Z   Process has gone zombie. This means either (1) the parent process has not acknowledged the death of its child using the `wait` system call; or (2) the parent was improperly `kill`ed, and until the parent is completely `kill`ed, the `init` process (see Chapter 9) cannot reap the child itself. A zombied process usually indicates poorly written software.

In addition, the STAT entry for each process can take one of the following modifiers: W = No resident pages in memory (it has been completely swapped out); < = High-priority process; N = Low-priority task; L = Pages in memory are locked there (usually signifying the need for real-time functionality).

▼ **START**   Date the process was started.

■ **TIME**   Amount of time the process has spent on the CPU.

▲ **COMMAND**   Name of the process and its command-line parameters.

Show an Interactive List of Processes: top

The `top` command is an interactive version of `ps`. Instead of giving a static view of what is going on, `top` refreshes the screen with a list of processes every 2 to 3 seconds (user adjustable). From this list, you can reprioritize processes or `kill` them. Figure 6-1 shows a `top` screen.

```
The Orb                                                            _ □ ×
  11:53pm  up 3 days,  1:00,  4 users,  load average: 0.00, 0.00, 0.00
  64 processes: 61 sleeping, 3 running, 0 zombie, 0 stopped
  CPU states: 13.0% user,  2.7% system,  0.0% nice, 84.1% idle
  Mem:  257880K av,  254704K used,   3176K free,  89580K shrd, 103980K buff
  Swap: 128516K av,      0K used, 128516K free                 50084K cached

  PID USER      PRI  NI  SIZE  RSS SHARE STAT  LIB %CPU %MEM   TIME COMMAND
  519 root       17   0 30556  29M  1640 S       0 12.2 11.8  10:09 X
19285 root        3   0  1012 1012   824 R       0  1.3  0.3   0:00 top
  535 root        2   0  2268 2268  1608 S       0  0.9  0.8   0:20 enlightenmen
  608 root        1   0  3332 3332  2624 S       0  0.7  1.2   0:16 gnomepager_a
 6630 root        0   0  2784 2784  1384 R       0  0.3  1.0   0:05 xterm
  552 root        0   0  1408 1408  1156 S       0  0.1  0.5   0:12 xscreensaver
    1 root        0   0   476  476   408 S       0  0.0  0.1   0:04 init
    2 root        0   0     0    0     0 SW      0  0.0  0.0   0:00 kflushd
    3 root        0   0     0    0     0 SW      0  0.0  0.0   0:00 kpiod
    4 root        0   0     0    0     0 SW      0  0.0  0.0   0:04 kswapd
    5 root      -20 -20     0    0     0 SW<     0  0.0  0.0   0:00 mdrecoveryd
  105 root        0   0   460  460   400 S       0  0.0  0.1   0:00 apmd
  256 bin         0   0   364  364   300 S       0  0.0  0.1   0:00 portmap
  303 root        0   0   592  592   492 S       0  0.0  0.2   0:00 syslogd
  314 root        0   0   752  752   388 S       0  0.0  0.2   0:00 klogd
  328 daemon      0   0   472  472   400 S       0  0.0  0.1   0:00 atd
  342 root        0   0   592  592   504 S       0  0.0  0.2   0:00 crond
```

Figure 6-1.   The `top` program in action

The `top` program's main disadvantage is that it's a CPU hog. On a congested system, this program tends to complicate system management issues. Users start running `top` to see what's going on, only to find several other people running the program as well, slowing down the system even more.

By default, `top` is shipped so that everyone can use it. You may find it prudent, depending on your environment, to restrict `top` to root only. To do this, change the program's permissions with the following command:

```
[root@ford /root]# chmod 0700 /usr/bin/top
```

Send a Signal to a Process: kill

This program's name is misleading: it doesn't really kill processes. What it *does* do is send *signals* to running processes. The operating system, by default, supplies each process a standard set of *signal handlers* to deal with incoming signals. From a system administrator's standpoint, the most important handler is for signals number 9 and 15, kill process and terminate process, respectively. When `kill` is invoked, it requires at least one parameter: the process identification number (PID) as derived from the `ps` command. When passed only the PID, `kill` sends signal 15. Some programs intercept this signal and perform a number of actions so that they can shut down cleanly. Others just stop running in their tracks. Either way, `kill` isn't a guaranteed method for making a process stop.

Signals

The optional parameter available for **kill** is **-n**, where the *n* represents a signal number. As system administrators, we are most interested in the signals 9 (kill) and 1 (hang up).

The kill signal, 9, is the impolite way of stopping a process. Rather than asking a process to stop, the operating system simply kills the process. The only time this will fail is when the process is in the middle of a system call (such as a request to open a file), in which case the process will die once it returns from the system call.

The hang up signal, 1, is a bit of a throwback to the VT100 terminal days of UNIX. When a user's terminal connection dropped in the middle of a session, all of that terminal's running processes would receive a hang up signal (often called a SIGHUP or HUP). This gave the processes an opportunity to perform a clean shutdown or, in the case of background processes, to ignore the signal. These days, a HUP is used to tell certain server applications to go and reread their configuration files (you'll see this in action in several of the later chapters). Most applications simply ignore the signal.

Security Issues

The power to terminate a process is obviously a very powerful one, making security precautions important. Users may only kill processes they have permission to kill. If non-root users attempt to send signals to processes other than their own, error messages are returned. The root user is the exception to this limitation; root may send signals to all processes in the system. Of course, this means root needs to exercise great care when using the **kill** command.

Examples of kill

Use this command to terminate process number 2059:

```
[root@ford /root]# kill 2059
```

For an almost guaranteed kill of process number 593, issue this command:

```
[root@ford /root]# kill -9 593
```

Type the following to send the HUP signal to the **init** program (which is always PID 1):

```
[root@ford /root]# kill -1 1
```

MISCELLANEOUS TOOLS

The following tools don't fall into any specific category we've covered in this chapter. They all make important contributions to daily system administration chores.

Show System Name: uname

The **uname** program produces some system details that may be helpful in several situations. Maybe you've managed to remotely log in to a dozen different computers and have lost track of where you are! This tool is also helpful for script writers, because it allows them to change the path of a script based on the system information.

Here are the command-line parameters for **uname**:

Option for uname	Description
-m	Print the machine hardware type (such as i686 for Pentium Pro and better architectures).
-n	Print the machine's host name.
-r	Print the operating system's release name.
-s	Print the operating system's name.
-v	Print the operating system's version.
-a	Print all of the above.

To get the operating system's name and release, enter the following command:

```
[root@ford /root]# uname -s -r
```

NOTE: The **-s** option may seem wasted (after all, we know this is Linux), but this parameter proves quite useful on almost all UNIX-like operating systems, as well. At an SGI workstation, **uname -s** will return IRIX, or SunOS at a Sun workstation. Folks who work in heterogeneous environments often write scripts that will behave differently based on the OS, and **uname** with **-s** is a consistent way to determine that information.

Who Is Logged In: who

On systems that allow users to log in to other users' machines or special servers, you will want to know who is logged in. You can generate such a report by using the **who** command:

```
[root@ford /root]# who
```

The **who** report looks like this:

```
sshah     tty1      Jun 14 18:22
root      pts/9     Jun 14 18:29 (:0)
root      pts/11    Jun 14 21:12 (:0)
root      pts/12    Jun 14 23:38 (:0)
```

A Variation on who: w

The **w** command displays the same information that **who** does and a whole lot more. The details of the report include who is logged in, what their terminal is, where they are logged in from, how long they've been logged in, how long they've been idle, and their CPU utilization. The top of the report also gives you the same output as the **uptime** command.

Switch User: su

Once you have logged in to the system as one user, you need not log out and back in again in order to assume another identity (root user, for instance). Instead, use the **su** command to switch. This command has only two command-line parameters, both of which are optional.

Running **su** without any parameters will automatically try to make you the root user. You'll be prompted for the root password and, if you enter it correctly, will drop down to a root shell. If you are already the root user and want to switch to another ID, you don't need to enter the new password when you use this command.

For example, if you're logged in as yourself and want to switch to the root user, type this command:

```
[sshah@ford ~]$ su
```

If you're logged in as root and want to switch to, say, user sshah, enter this command:

```
[root@ford /root]# su sshah
```

The optional hyphen (-) parameter tells **su** to switch identities and run the login scripts for that user. For example, if you're logged in as root and want to switch over to user sshah with all of his login and shell configurations, type this command:

```
[root@ford /root]# su - sshah
```

Networking Tools

If you are starting your experience with Linux in an already networked environment, you may find some of these tools handy for getting around. However, if you need to configure your network first, you should read Chapters 24 and onward first.

telnet

As we've mentioned in earlier chapters, Linux understands the concept of multiple users logged into the same workstation at the same time. So in order to allow for someone to log in to another host from remote, the **telnet** command was created.

The format of the command is as follows:

```
[sshah@ford ~]$ telnet oid
```

where **oid** is the name of another computer running either Linux or a variant of UNIX. Once you run the command, you will get a login prompt from that machine. Logging in to that machine enables you to run programs on the other host just as if you were running them on your own. If you aren't sure where you are logged in, use the **uname** command (discussed earlier) to find out where you are.

Remote Shell: rsh

As we've seen with **telnet**, you must enter a username and password in order to log in to another host. For many people who found the need to log in to other hosts often, this became a nuisance. They wanted the other host to automatically trust them so that when issued a remote login request, the system would allow them access without asking for a login and password. The double-win with a feature like that is the ability to automate tasks that require one host to invoke a program on another host.

To accommodate this, the **rsh** command was created. In its simplest form, specify the name of the host you wish to log in to the way you would for **telnet**. For example:

```
[sshah@ford ~]$ rsh oid
```

If you set up your configuration files so that **oid** knows to trust you, the system will automatically give you a shell prompt. If the configuration file does not automatically trust you, you will need to enter your password again.

To set up the configuration file, edit the **.rhosts** file (yes, there is a period in front of the filename) in your home directory. When there, create a line that looks like this:

```
host_to_trust       your_username
```

If I want to be able to **rsh** from **ford** to **oid** without being prompted for a password, I would create the following file in a **.rhosts** file in my home directory on **oid**:

```
ford sshah
```

And I'd be ready to go!

Remote X Windows Displays

In Chapter 1, I said that X Windows offers the ability to display content on other hosts' screens. This makes it possible to log in to a server that has a special program on it and have the display redirected to the screen in front of you.

Allowing this to happen is a two-step process. The first step is telling your machine that it should allow connections from another host for X Windows displays. This is done with the **xhost** command:

```
[sshah@ford ~]$ xhost +trillian
```

where **trillian** is the name of the host we want to allow X Windows displays to come from in addition to our own host.

Now that you have allowed trillian to display to your host, log in to trillian using either **rsh** or **telnet**, and set your DISPLAY environment variable like so:

```
[sshah@trillian ~]$ DISPLAY="ford:0"; export DISPLAY
```

This will redirect all X Windows displays to the host **ford**. If you have two hosts to try this with, an easy test to see if it worked is to start Netscape on the remote host and watch it display its content on your host. Neat trick, isn't it?

Once you are done with whatever work is required to allow other hosts to display to your screen, you need to explicitly disallow future connections like so:

```
[sshah@ford ~]$ xhost -trillian
```

If you want to disallow everyone, you can use the following shortcut:

```
[sshah@ford ~]$ xhost -
```

CAUTION: Some people will tell you that a shortcut to disallowing everyone is to just issue the command (note the plus sign here, as opposed to the minus sign in the command above):

```
[sshah@ford ~]$ xhost +
```

Don't do it! This is a dangerous command because it allows anyone to connect to your machine and display things on it. Typically, this leads to all kinds of practical jokes, but the potential for something more serious to happen is there. Be sure to specify from which hosts you allow X connections, and remember to undo it when you are done.

Mail Preferences: mail, pine, and mutt

Like everyone else, Linux folk need to read their e-mail. And as you can imagine, you have plenty of choices with which you can do so. We discuss some GUI-based POP mail readers in Appendix B; here, we give mention to command-line tools.

The one tool that you will always be able to find is called—you guessed it—**mail**. Simply run **mail** from the command line like so:

```
[sshah@ford ~]$ mail
```

and you'll see what mail you have available to read. Because this tool does not require any screen formatting, it is well suited for those instances where you are troubleshooting a host so broken it has no terminal control.

To exit the **mail** program, type **q** and press ENTER. If you want more information about **mail**, check out its man page. As you'll see, for a tool that looks very simple, it actually offers quite a bit of capability.

Another popular tool is **pine**, which actually takes control of your terminal window and makes the display look much nicer. Being a fully menu-driven program where all of your options are always listed on a menu in front of you, **pine** tends to be a very popular choice for people new to Unix.

From a practical point of view, **pine** is ideal for communicating with people who use all sorts of other mail tools since it understands all of the popular standards in use today (such as MIME attachments). **pine** also offers a very powerful filing system with which you can archive your mail easily and find it again at a later date.

My personal favorite mail tool is **mutt**. To quote **mutt**'s author, "All mail clients suck. This one just sucks less." **mutt** is another tool that looks simple on the outside but offers a wealth of capability. Unlike **pine**, **mutt** is much less menu-oriented. For folks who are used to the UNIX environment, this is a very welcome feature because it allows for very efficient use. Doubly useful is that **mutt** offers excellent memory management and can therefore handle extremely large mailboxes. More than once, I've used **mutt** to clean up someone's mailbox that Outlook choked on.

ftp

Linux offers a very handy command-line version of the FTP client. Anyone used to the Windows version of the FTP client that runs under command.com will feel right at home with this since the Windows version adopted the standard commands in use by the UNIX community since the late 70s.

To start the FTP client, simply run **ftp** at the command line like so:

```
[sshah@ford ~]$ ftp remotehostname
```

where **remotehostname** is the name of the host that you would like to FTP to/from.

EDITORS

Editors are by the far the bulkiest of common tools, but they are also the most useful. Without them, making any kind of change to a text file would be a tremendous undertaking. Regardless of your Linux distribution, you will have gotten a few editors. You should take a few moments to get comfortable with them before you're busy fighting another problem.

NOTE: Not all distributions come with all of the editors listed here.

vi

The **vi** editor has been around UNIX-based systems since the 1970s, and its interface shows it. It is arguably one of the last editors to actually use a separate command mode and data entry mode; as a result, most newcomers find it unpleasant to use. But before you give **vi** the cold shoulder, take a moment to get comfortable with it. In difficult situations, you may not have a pretty graphical editor at your disposal, and **vi** is ubiquitous across all UNIX systems.

The version of **vi** that ships with Linux distributions is VIM (VI iMproved). It has a lot of what made **vi** popular in the first place and many features that make it useful in today's typical environments (including a graphical interface if X Windows is running).

To start **vi**, simply type

```
[root@ford /root]# vi
```

The easiest way to learn more about **vi** is to start it and enter **:help**. If you ever find yourself stuck in **vi**, press the ESC key several times and then type **:qu!** to force an exit without saving. If you want to save the file, type **:wq**.

emacs

It has been argued that **emacs** is an operating system all by itself. It's big, feature-rich, expandable, programmable, and all-around amazing. If you're coming from a GUI background, you'll probably find **emacs** a pleasant environment to work with at first. On its cover, it works like Notepad in terms of its interface. Yet underneath is a complete interface to the GNU development environment, a mail reader, a news reader, a Web browser, and even a psychiatrist (well, not exactly).

To start **emacs**, simply type

```
[root@ford /root]# emacs
```

Once **emacs** has started, you can visit the psychiatrist by pressing ESC-X and then typing **doctor**. To get help using **emacs**, press CRTL-H.

joe

Of the editors listed here, **joe** most closely resembles a simple text editor. It works much like Notepad and offers on-screen help. Anyone who remembers the original WordStar command set will be pleasantly surprised to see that all those brain cells hanging on to CTRL-K commands can be put back to use with **joe**.

To start **joe**, simply type

```
[root@ford /root]# joe
```

pico

pico is another editor inspired by simplicity. Typically used in conjunction with the **pine** mail reading system, **pico** can also be used as a stand-alone editor. Like **joe**, it can work in a manner similar to Notepad, but **pico** uses its own set of key combinations. Thankfully, all available key combinations are always shown at the bottom of the screen.

To start **pico**, simply type

```
[root@ford /root]# pico
```

STANDARDS

One argument you hear regularly against the usage of Linux is that there are too many different distributions, and that by having multiple distributions, there is fragmentation. This fragmentation will eventually lead to different versions of incompatible Linux's.

This is, without a doubt, complete nonsense that plays on "FUD" (Fear, Uncertainty, and Doubt). These types of arguments usually stem from a misunderstanding of the kernel and distributions. However, the Linux community has realized that it has grown past the stage of informal understandings about how things *should* be done. As a result, two types of standards are actively being worked on.

The first standard is the File Hierarchy Standard (FHS). This is an attempt by many of the Linux distributions to standardize on a directory layout so that developers have an easy time making sure their applications work across multiple distributions without difficulty. As of this writing, Red Hat is almost completely compliant, and it is likely that most other distributions are as well.

The other standard is the Linux Standard Base Specification (LSB). Like the FHS, the LSB is a standards group that specifies what a Linux distribution should have in terms of libraries and tools.

A developer who only assumes that a Linux machine complies with the LSB and FHS is guaranteed to have an application that will work with all Linux installations. All of the major distributors have joined these standards groups, including companies like Red Hat, Caldera, SuSE, VA Linux, and Turbo Linux. This should ensure that all desktop distributions will have a certain amount of common ground that a developer can rely on.

From a system administrator's point of view, these standards are interesting but not crucial to administering a Linux network. However, it never hurts to learn more about both. For more information on the FHS, go to their Web site at http://www.pathname.com/fhs. To find out more about the LSB, check out http://www.linuxbase.org.

SUMMARY

In this chapter, we discussed Linux's command-line interface through BASH, many command-line tools, and a few editors. As you continue through this book, you'll find many references to the information in this chapter, so be sure that you get comfortable with working at the command line. You may find it a bit annoying at first, especially if you are used to a GUI for performing many of the basic tasks mentioned here—but stick with it. You may even find yourself eventually working faster at the command line than with the GUI!

Obviously, this chapter can't cover all the command-line tools available to you as part of your default Linux installation. I highly recommend taking some time to look into some of the reference books available, which give complete documentation on this subject. *Linux: The Complete Reference,* Fourth Edition, by Richard Petersen (Osborne/McGraw-Hill, 2001) is an excellent choice for a solid, thorough guide that covers everything available on your Linux system. For a helpful but less comprehensive approach to the considerable detail of Linux systems, try *Linux in a Nutshell,* Third Edition, edited by Ellen Siever (O'Reilly and Associates, 2000). In addition, there are a wealth of texts on shell programming at various levels and from various points of view. Get whatever suits you; shell programming is a skill well worth learning even if you don't do system administration.

CHAPTER 7

Booting and Shutting Down

A s operating systems have become more complex, the process of starting up and shutting down has become more comprehensive. Anyone who has undergone the transition from a straight DOS-based system to a Windows 2000–based system has experienced this transition firsthand: Not only is the core operating system brought up and shut down, but also an impressive list of services must be started and stopped. Like Windows 2000, Linux comprises an impressive list of services that are turned on as part of the boot procedure.

In this chapter, we step through the processes of starting up and shutting down the Linux environment. We discuss the scripts that automate this process as well as the parts of the process for which modification is acceptable.

> *CAUTION:* Apply a liberal dose of common sense in following this chapter with a real system. As you experiment with modifying startup and shutdown scripts, bear in mind that it is possible to bring your system to a nonfunctional state that cannot be recovered by rebooting. Don't try new processes on production systems; make backups of all the files you wish to change; and most important, have a boot disk ready in case you make an irreversible change.

LILO

LILO, short for Linux Loader, is a boot manager. It allows you to boot multiple operating systems, provided each system exists on its own partition. (Under PC-based systems, the *entire* boot partition must also exist beneath the 1024-cylinder boundary.) In addition to booting multiple operating systems, with LILO you can choose various kernel configurations or versions to boot. This is especially handy when you're trying kernel upgrades before adopting them.

The big picture with LILO is straightforward: A configuration file (**/etc/lilo.conf**) specifies which partitions are bootable and, if a partition is Linux, which kernel to load. When the **/sbin/lilo** program runs, it takes this partition information and rewrites the boot sector with the necessary code to present the options as specified in the configuration file. At boot time, a prompt (usually `lilo:`) is displayed, and you have the option of specifying the operating system. (Usually, a default can be selected after a timeout period.) LILO loads the necessary code from the selected partition and passes full control over to it.

> *NOTE:* If you are familiar with the NT boot process, you can think of LILO as comparable to the OS loader (NTLDR). Similarly, the LILO configuration file, **/etc/lilo.conf**, is comparable to BOOT.INI.

CONFIGURING LILO

The LILO configuration file is **/etc/lilo.conf**. In most cases, you won't need to modify the file in any significant way. When you do need to change this file, the options are quite plain and simple to follow. Let's begin by reviewing a simple configuration. The file shown here is probably quite similar to what is already in your default **lilo.conf** file:

```
boot=/dev/hda
prompt
timeout=50
image=/boot/vmlinuz-2.2.5-15
        label=linux
        root=/dev/hda2
        read-only
other = /dev/hda1
        label = dos
        table = /dev/hda
```

The first line, **boot=/dev/hda**, tells LILO where to write the boot sector. Usually, this is the first sector of the boot drive: **/dev/hda** for IDE-based disks, and **/dev/sda** for SCSI-based disks. This sector is better known as the *Master Boot Record (MBR)*. The purpose of the MBR is to inform PC designers of what to load first in order to start the operating system. Once loaded, the program stored in the MBR is expected to take over the boot process.

When you want another program (such as the NT OS loader) to handle the MBR, you can specify that the boot sector be written to another partition. Then control can be passed to this partition from the code specified in the MBR.

Returning to our configuration file, we see the next command is **prompt**. This instruction tells LILO to give the **lilo:** prompt at boot time. At this prompt, the user can either type in the name of the boot image that is to start, or press TAB to list the available options. By default, LILO will wait indefinitely for user input unless a timeout command is specified.

The **timeout=50** command tells LILO to wait for 50 deciseconds (5 seconds) before selecting the default boot image and starting the boot process.

The next line begins a small block. With the line

```
image=/boot/vmlinuz-2.2.5-15
```

we are indicating a specific boot image. This being the first block, it will be the default boot image. The image to boot is the file **/boot/vmlinuz-2.2.5-15**, which is a Linux kernel. Inside the block is the line **label=linux**, which is the name that is displayed if the user asks for a list of available boot options at the **lilo:** prompt.

Also inside the block is the line

```
root=/dev/hda2
```

which tells LILO the partition on which the **/boot/vmlinuz-2.2.5-15** file is located.

If you aren't sure which partition holds your kernel, go to the kernel's directory and enter

```
df .
```

This will produce a response similar to the following:

```
[root@ford /boot]# df .
Filesystem            1k-blocks       Used Available Use% Mounted on
/dev/hda2               108870       56119     47129  54% /
```

The first column, where the entry begins with a **/dev**, is the device where your kernel is located. In this example, the kernel (which is located in the **/boot** directory) exists on the **/dev/hda2** partition. (See Chapter 8 for more information about partitions.)

The last option in the block is **read-only**, which tells LILO to mount the root file system with read-only permissions when starting the kernel. This is necessary so that the root file system can check itself for corruption during the boot process. Once this is done, the root file system is automatically remounted with read/write access.

This ends the first block. A block is separated from the next block by a line beginning with either **image=** or **other=**. In our example, the next block starts with **other=/dev/hda1**. For this example, the **/dev/hda1** partition, as it turns out, is set up with a complete DOS installation. (This could just as well be Windows 95, Windows NT, or Windows 2000.) As in the preceding block, we see the **label=** line; however, that's where the similarities end. The next line is **table=/dev/hda**, which specifies where table information can be found for the operating system on the partition we are trying to boot (**/dev/hda1**).

> **NOTE:** Although DOS and Windows are the most common "other" operating systems in a dual-boot configuration, they are not the only options you have. LILO can be used to boot any other operating system that understands partitions.

Additional LILO Options

In addition to the options discussed above, a number of other options can be placed in the **lilo.conf** file. This section describes the most common options. With these, you should be able to configure most (if not all) of your systems without a problem. For those rare situations requiring additional configuration, you can read the man page on **lilo.conf**; it gives a brief rundown of all the available options.

Global Options in lilo.conf

The following global options are applicable to the entire configuration file, not just one particular block.

default=*name*   Specifies the default operating system that should boot. If this is not specified, the first block is the default.

`message=message-file`	You can specify that a message (whose text is in **message-file**) be displayed before presenting a `lilo:` prompt. This message cannot be longer than 64K, and if it is changed, the map file must be rebuilt. (See the upcoming section "Running LILO.")
`prompt`	Forces LILO to display a `lilo:` prompt and wait for user response. Automated reboots cannot be done if this option is specified and the `timeout` option is not.
`timeout=deciseconds`	Specifies the number of deciseconds (tenths of a second) to wait at a prompt before selecting the `default` boot option and continuing with the boot process.

Per-Block Options

The options listed in this section apply only to specific blocks that designate bootable operating systems.

`Image=image name`	Specifies which Linux kernel to boot.
`Other=image name`	Specifies other arbitrary operating systems to boot.
`Table=device name`	For a particular block, specifies which device stores the partition table.
`Label=name`	The name of the block that should be displayed if the user requests a list at the `lilo:` prompt. This label should be unique across all blocks.
`password=password`	Indicates that an image should be booted only if the `password` is correctly specified by the user.
`restricted`	User must enter a password if any command-line parameters are passed to the kernel. (This is especially important if you need to password-protect the single-user mode environment.)

NOTE: If you opt to use either the **password** or **restricted** option, you should set the permissions on your **/etc/lilo.conf** file so that only root can read it. With the default permission setup, the file can only be changed by root, but anyone can read it. The command to set the read permission to root only is

`[root@ford /root]# chmod 600 /etc/lilo.conf`

Kernel Options

Options can be passed to the kernel from LILO. Such options may include the request to boot into single-user mode (the most common usage of this feature). If you need to pass kernel options only once in a while (such as requesting to go into single-user mode), you can pass these parameters at the `lilo:` prompt. For example, at `lilo:` you might enter `linux s` to start the kernel image with the `linux` label and pass the parameter `s` to it. This boots Linux into single-user mode. Obviously, these options apply to Linux kernels only.

`append=string`	Append *string* to any command-line parameter the user specifies.
`literal=string`	Similar to **append**, except *string* replaces the passed parameters of a user's command line rather than being appended.
`read-only`	Specifies that the root file system should be mounted read-only. After the kernel loads and runs a check on it using the **fsck** tool, the root file system is remounted read/write.

Adding a New Kernel to Boot

In Chapter 10, we discuss the process of compiling new kernels to boot with. Part of that process requires adding an entry into the **/etc/lilo.conf** file so that LILO knows about the new kernel. More important, this entry allows you to keep the existing, working configuration in case the new kernel doesn't work as you'd like it to. You can always reboot and select an older kernel that does work.

For the sake of discussion, let's assume you've compiled the 2.3.12 because you're feeling dangerous and want to try the new Toxygene Network Protocol by Dr. Alex Paterson. You have compiled the new kernel, **vmlinuz-2.3.12**, and it is placed in the **/boot** directory. Your first step is to append the relevant information to the **/etc/lilo.conf** file. This block would look something like this:

```
image=/boot/vmlinuz-2.3.12
    label=linux-2.3.12
    root=/dev/hda2
    read-only
```

If we append this to the end of the **/etc/lilo.conf** file, however, **vmlinuz-2.3.12** won't become the default kernel file that gets booted. In order for this to happen, we must do one of two things: Either we make this block the first block, or we use the **default** command. For our example, we'll use the **default** command. Because this command cannot be part of a block, we insert it at the beginning of the file, as shown here:

```
default=vmlinux-2.3.12
```

And that's it! Here's the final **/etc/lilo.conf** file:

```
default=vmlinux-2.3.12
boot=/dev/hda
prompt
timeout=50
image=/boot/vmlinuz-2.2.5-15
        label=linux
        root=/dev/hda2
        read-only
other = /dev/hda1
        label = dos
        table = /dev/hda
image=/boot/vmlinuz-2.3.12
        label=linux-2.3.12
        root=/dev/hda2
        read-only
```

Now that the **/etc/lilo.conf** file is edited and saved, all you need to do is run LILO.

RUNNING LILO

Now that you are familiar with your **/etc/lilo.conf** file, it's time to actually run the LILO boot manager program and let it do its important work. Usually this is a relatively uneventful process.

In most cases, you will simply need to run LILO without any parameters. The result will look something like this:

```
[root@ford /boot]# lilo
Added linux *
Added dos
```

LILO has taken the information from **/etc/lilo.conf** and written it into the appropriate boot sector.

Viewing the man page on LILO reveals many command-line options. Most of them, however, have **lilo.conf** equivalents, so we won't examine them here. Table 7-1 lists the most important options for the **lilo** command.

LILO Command Option	Description
`-t`	Tests the configuration without actually loading it. The `-t` option alone doesn't tell you much, but when used with the `-v` option (defined below), you can see exactly what LILO would do.
`-C config-file`	By default, LILO looks for the **/etc/lilo.conf** configuration file. You can specify an alternate file with this command-line option.
`-r root-directory`	Tells LILO to **chroot** to the specified directory before doing anything. The **chroot** command will change the root directory to the directory specified in *root-directory*. Typically, this option is used when booting from a floppy to repair a broken system, so that LILO knows which directories to search for files. (For example, if you boot from a floppy and mount the root file system to the **/mnt** directory, you will probably want to run LILO as `lilo -r /mnt`.)
`-v`	Makes LILO verbose about what it's doing.

Table 7-1. Command-Line Options to LILO

THE STEPS OF BOOTING

In this section, I'll assume you are already familiar with the boot process of other operating systems and thus already know the boot cycle of your hardware. We'll begin with the Linux boot loader (usually LILO for PCs).

Kernel Loading   Once LILO has started and you have selected Linux as the operating system to boot, the very first thing to get loaded is the kernel. Keep in mind that no operating system exists in memory at this point, and PCs (by their unfortunate design) have no easy way to access all of their memory. Thus, the kernel must load completely into the first megabyte of available RAM. In order to accomplish this, the kernel is compressed. The head of the file contains the code necessary to bring the CPU into protected mode (thereby removing the memory restriction) and decompress the remainder of the kernel.

Kernel Execution   With the kernel in memory, it can begin executing. It knows only whatever functionality is built into it, which means any parts of the kernel compiled as modules are useless at this point. At the very minimum, the kernel must have enough code to set up its virtual memory subsystem and root file system (usually, the ext2 file system). Once the kernel has started, a hardware probe determines what device drivers should be initialized. From here, the kernel can *mount* the root file system. (You could draw a parallel of this process to that of Windows' being able to recognize and access its C: drive.) The kernel mounts the root file system and starts a program called **init**.

NOTE: Obviously, we've omitted discussion of the many details of Linux kernel startup; these details are really only of interest to kernel developers. However, if you are curious you can visit the Kernel Hackers Guide at http://www.redhat.com:8080.

The init PROCESS   The **init** process (which we'll examine more closely in Chapter 9) is the first non-kernel process that is started, and therefore it always gets the process ID number of 1. **init** reads its configuration file, **/etc/inittab**, and determines the *runlevel* where it should start. Essentially, a runlevel dictates the system's behavior. Each level (designated by an integer between 0 and 6) serves a specific purpose. A runlevel of **initdefault** is selected if it exists; otherwise you are prompted to supply a runlevel value.

The runlevel values are as follows:

0	Halt the system
1	Enter single-user mode (no networking is enabled)
2	Multiuser mode, but without NFS
3	Full multiuser mode (normal operation)
4	Unused
5	Same as runlevel 3, except using an X Windows login rather than a text-based login
6	Reboot the system

When it is told to enter a runlevel, **init** executes a script as dictated by the **/etc/inittab** file. The default runlevel depends on whether you indicated the system should start with a text-based or X Windows login during the installation phase.

rc Scripts

In the preceding section, we mentioned that the **/etc/inittab** file specifies which scripts to run when runlevels change. These scripts are responsible for either starting or stopping the services that are particular to the runlevel.

Because of the number of services that need to be managed, **rc** scripts are used. The main one, **/etc/rc.d/rc**, is responsible for calling the appropriate scripts in the correct order for each runlevel. As you can imagine, such a script could easily become extremely uncontrollable! To keep this from happening, a slightly more elaborate system is used.

For each runlevel, a subdirectory exists in the **/etc/rc.d** directory. These runlevel sub-directories follow the naming scheme of **rcX.d**, where *X* is the runlevel. For example, all the scripts for runlevel 3 are in **/etc/rc.d/rc3.d**.

In the runlevel directories, symbolic links are made to scripts in the **/etc/rc.d/init.d** directory. Instead of using the name of the script as it exists in the **/etc/rc.d/init.d** directory, however, the symbolic links are prefixed with an **S** if the script is to start a service, or with a **K** if the script is to stop (or kill) a service. (See Chapter 6 for information on symbolic links.) Note that these two letters are case sensitive. You must use capitals or the startup scripts will not recognize them.

In many cases, the order in which these scripts are run makes a difference. (You can't use DNS to resolve hostnames if you haven't yet configured a network interface!) To enforce order, a two-digit number is suffixed to the **S** or **K**. Lower numbers execute before higher numbers; for example, **/etc/rc.d/rc3.d/S50inet** runs before **/etc/rc.d/rc3.d/S55named** (**S50inet** configures the network settings, and **S55named** starts the DNS server).

The scripts pointed to in the **/etc/rc.d/init.d** directory are the workhorses; they perform the actual process of starting and stopping services. When **/etc/rc.d/rc** runs through a specific runlevel's directory, it invokes each script in numerical order. It first runs the scripts that begin with a **K**, and then the scripts that begin with an **S**. For scripts starting with **K**, a parameter of **stop** is passed. Likewise, for scripts starting with **S**, the parameter **start** is passed.

Let's peer into the **/etc/rc.d/rc2.d** directory and see what's there:

```
[root@ford rc2.d]# ls -l
total 0
lrwxrwxrwx   1 root     root           15 Aug 11  1998 K15httpd ->> ../init.d/httpd
lrwxrwxrwx   1 root     root           15 Jul 29  1998 K15sound ->> ../init.d/sound
lrwxrwxrwx   1 root     root           16 Jun 10 09:36 K20rstatd ->> ../init.d/rstatd
lrwxrwxrwx   1 root     root           17 Jul 29  1998 K20rusersd ->> ../init.d/rusersd
lrwxrwxrwx   1 root     root           15 Jul 29  1998 K20rwhod ->> ../init.d/rwhod
lrwxrwxrwx   1 root     root           16 Sep 27  1998 K30ypbind ->> ../init.d/ypbind
lrwxrwxrwx   1 root     root           19 Sep 27  1998 K34yppasswdd ->> ../init.d/yppasswdd
lrwxrwxrwx   1 root     root           13 Jul 29  1998 K35smb ->> ../init.d/smb
lrwxrwxrwx   1 root     root           16 Sep 27  1998 K35ypserv ->> ../init.d/ypserv
lrwxrwxrwx   1 root     root           15 Feb 22 22:20 K45named ->> ../init.d/named
lrwxrwxrwx   1 root     root           14 Jul 29  1998 K50inet ->> ../init.d/inet
lrwxrwxrwx   1 root     root           16 Jul 29  1998 K55routed ->> ../init.d/routed
lrwxrwxrwx   1 root     root           13 Jul 29  1998 K60atd ->> ../init.d/atd
lrwxrwxrwx   1 root     root           15 Jun 10 09:32 K85netfs ->> ../init.d/netfs
lrwxrwxrwx   1 root     root           17 Jun 10 09:35 K89portmap ->> ../init.d/portmap
lrwxrwxrwx   1 root     root           14 Jun 10 09:29 S05apmd ->> ../init.d/apmd
lrwxrwxrwx   1 root     root           17 Jul 29  1998 S10network ->> ../init.d/network
lrwxrwxrwx   1 root     root           16 Jul 29  1998 S20random ->> ../init.d/random
lrwxrwxrwx   1 root     root           16 Jul 29  1998 S30syslog ->> ../init.d/syslog
lrwxrwxrwx   1 root     root           15 Jul 29  1998 S40crond ->> ../init.d/crond
lrwxrwxrwx   1 root     root           16 Jun 10 09:33 S45pcmcia ->> ../init.d/pcmcia
lrwxrwxrwx   1 root     root           13 Jul 29  1998 S60lpd ->> ../init.d/lpd
lrwxrwxrwx   1 root     root           18 Jul 29  1998 S80sendmail ->> ../init.d/sendmail
lrwxrwxrwx   1 root     root           13 Jun 10 09:39 S90xfs ->> ../init.d/xfs
lrwxrwxrwx   1 root     root           19 Jun 10 09:34 S99linuxconf ->> ../init.d/linuxconf
lrwxrwxrwx   1 root     root           11 Jul 29  1998 S99local ->> ../rc.local
```

Thus, when **K35smb** is invoked, it really starts

```
/etc/rc.d/init.d/smb stop
```

instead. If **S90xfs** is invoked,

```
/etc/rc.d/init.d/xfs start
```

is what really gets run.

Writing Your Own rc Script

In the course of keeping a Linux system running, you will, at some point, need to modify the startup or shutdown scripts. There are two roads you can take to doing this:

▼   If your change is to be affected at boot time only, and the change is small, you may want to simply edit the **/etc/rc.d/rc.local** script. This script gets run at the very end of the boot process.

▲   On the other hand, if your addition is more elaborate and/or requires that the shutdown process explicitly stop, you should add a script to the **/etc/rc.d/init.d** directory. This script should take the parameters **start** and **stop** and act accordingly.

Of course, the first option, editing the **/etc/rc.d/rc.local** script, is the easier of the two. To make additions to this script, simply open it in your editor of choice and append the commands you want run at the end. This is good for simple one- or two-line changes.

If you do need a separate script, however, you will need to take the second option. The process of writing an **rc** script is not as difficult as it may seem. Let's step through it using an example, to see how it works. (You can use our example as a skeleton script, by the way, changing it to add anything you need.)

Assume you want to start a special program that pops up a message every 60 minutes and reminds you that you need to take a break from the keyboard (a good idea if you don't want to get carpal tunnel syndrome!). The script to start this program will include the following:

▼   A description of the script's purpose (so we don't forget it a year later!)

■   Verification that the program really exists before trying to start it

▲   Acceptance of the **start** and **stop** parameters and performance of the required actions

Given these parameters, here's the script we will write. (Notice that lines starting with a number sign (#) are only comments and not part of the script's actions, except for the first line.)

```
#!/bin/sh
#
```

```
# Carpal          Start/Stop the Carpal Notice Daemon
#
# description: Carpald is a program which wakes up every 60 minutes and
#              tells us that we need to take a break from the keyboard
#              or we'll lose all functionality of our wrists and never
#              be able to type again as long as we live.
# processname: carpald

# Source function library.
. /etc/rc.d/init.d/functions

[ -f /usr/local/sbin/carpald ] || exit 0

# See how we were called.
case "$1" in
  start)
        echo -n "Starting carpald: "
        daemon carpald

        echo
        touch /var/lock/subsys/carpald
        ;;
  stop)
        echo -n "Stopping carpald services: "
        killproc carpald

        echo
        rm -f /var/lock/subsys/carpald
        ;;
  status)
        status carpald
        ;;
  restart|reload)
        $0 stop
        $0 start
        ;;
  *)
        echo "Usage: carpald start|stop|status|restart|reload"
        exit 1
esac

exit 0
```

Once you have a new script written, simply add the necessary symbolic links (symlinks, as described in Chapter 6) from the appropriate runlevel directory to have the script either start or stop. In our sample script, we want it to start only in either runlevel 3 or runlevel 5. This is because we are assuming these are the only two runlevels during which we will do normal day-to-day work. Lastly, we want the daemon to be shut down when we go to runlevel 6 (reboot). Here are the commands we enter to create the required symlinks:

```
[root@ford /root]# cd /etc/rc.d/rc3.d
[root@ford rc3.d]# ln -s ../init.d/carpal S99carpal
[root@ford rc3.d]# cd ../rc5.d
[root@ford rc5.d]# ln -s ../init.d/carpal S99carpal
[root@ford rc5.d]# cd ../rc6.d
[root@ford rc6.d]# ln -s ../init.d/carpal K00carpal
```

Notice that for runlevels 3 and 5, we used the number 99 after the **S** prefix; this ensures that the script will be one of the last things to get started as part of the boot process. For runlevel 6, we wanted the opposite—**carpald** should shut down before the rest of the components. (The sequence for starting components generally goes from most critical to least critical, whereas shutting components down goes from least critical to most critical.)

Seems rather elaborate, doesn't it? Well, the good news is that because we've set up this **rc** script, we won't ever need to do it again. More important, the script will automatically run during startup and shutdown and be able to manage itself. The overhead up front is well worth the long-term benefits.

Enabling and Disabling Services

At times, you may find that you simply don't need a particular service to be started at boot time. This is especially true if you are considering Linux as a replacement for a Windows NT File and Print server.

As described in the preceding sections, you can cause a service not to be started by simply renaming the symbolic link in a particular runlevel directory; rename it to start with a **K** instead of an **S**. Once you are comfortable with working the command line and the symbolic links, you'll find this to be the quickest way of enabling and disabling services.

While getting your feet wet in this process, however, you may find the graphical interface, **ksysv**, easier to deal with. Although it was designed for use with the KDE environment, it will work with the default installed GNOME environment under Red Hat Linux 6.0. To start it, simply open an xterm window and type in the **ksysv** command. A window will pop up displaying all of your options, including a help section if you need it (see Figure 7-1).

Although the GUI tool is a nice way to do this task, you may find yourself in a situation where there is no graphical interface (e.g., you have logged in to a co-located server and cannot redirect X Windows through the firewall). In that case, you will need to move the symlinks by hand in the **/etc/rc.d** directory.

Figure 7-1. The opening window for `ksysv`

Disabling a Service

To disable a service, you must first find out two things: the name of the service and the runlevel at which it starts. More than likely, you'll already know the name of it, and also more than likely, the service is started in both runlevels 3 and 5. If you aren't sure about the runlevel, use the `find` command (see Chapter 6) to find it. For example,

```
[root@ford rc.d]# find . -name "*nfs*" -print
```

will find all files containing the string "nfs". You'll likely get three hits (locations containing the sought file), the first being in the **init.d** directory. Recall that this is the main script that does the work, though it is not directly called. We do not want to remove this script in the event that we want to enable it again in the future. Going back to the results of the `find` command, we'll see that we got two hits in the **rc3.d** and **rc5.d** directories.

To remove the service, simply `cd` into those directories and rename the symlink so that instead of starting with an **S**, they start with a **K**. By renaming the symlink, you'll be able to come back later and easily enable it without having to try and figure out the correct order that entry should be in (e.g., should it be **S35nfs** or **S45nfs**?).

Enabling a Service

Enabling a service works just like disabling a service. You find the scripts that actually run at the appropriate runlevels, except instead of changing them from an **S** to a **K**, you'll change them *to* a **S** from a **K**.

If the symlink you are looking for does not exist but the appropriate script in the **init.d** directory does exist, you can simply add a new symlink in the **rc3.d** and **rc5.d** directories. Be sure to use the correct format for the filename (see previous sections for details).

ODDS AND ENDS OF BOOTING AND SHUTTING DOWN

Starting up and shutting down a Linux server is always troubling. This is because typical Linux servers run for very long periods of time without needing a reboot and thus, when they do need a reboot, something bad has usually happened.

Thankfully, Linux does an excellent job of self-recovery. It is rare to have to deal with a system that will not boot correctly, but that is not to say that it'll never happen—and that's what this section is all about.

fsck!

The File System ChecK (**fsck**) tool is automatically run on every boot. Its purpose is similar to that of Windows' Scandisk: to check and repair any damage on the file system before continuing the boot process. Because of its critical nature, **fsck** is traditionally placed very early in the boot sequence.

If you were able to do a clean shutdown, **fsck** will run without incident. However, if for some reason you had to perform a hard shutdown (such as having to press the reset button), **fsck** will need to run through all of the local disks listed in the **/etc/fstab** file and check them. (And it isn't uncommon for the system administrator to be cursing through the process!)

If **fsck** does need to run, don't panic. It is unlikely you'll have any problems. However, if something does arise, **fsck** will prompt you with information about the problem and ask whether or not you want to repair them. See Chapter 8 for more details on the repair process. In general, you'll find that answering "yes, go ahead and repair it" is the right thing to do.

In the eight years I have administered UNIX systems, the only disks that **fsck** could not repair were those that were physically damaged or improperly terminated on a SCSI chain.

"I Only See 'LI' When I Boot! What Happened?"

This is one of the more aggravating situations because it seems like you did everything right—what the heck happened? Thankfully, LILO makes an effort to tell us where the problem is based on the number of characters it prints of the "LILO" string.

The most common of these errors is when LILO only prints the first two characters of the string ("LI") and then stops. When this happens, it is usually the case that the entire boot partition does not exist in the first 1024 cylinders. Unfortunately, that means having to repartition your disk and reinstalling Linux.

As you are installing Linux again, be sure that the first partition you select to boot from exists completely below the 1024-cylinder mark. This is due to a limitation in LILO that has been corrected in newer versions but has not been widely made available in new Linux distributions such as Red Hat.

NOTE: Why isn't LILO more verbose? The thing to remember about boot loaders is that they have very little space to work with. They must fit completely within the first tiny bit of disk, and this means giving up on cute things like graphical interfaces and wordy explanations of what's going on.

Booting into Single-User ("Recovery") Mode

Under Windows, the concept of "Recovery Mode" was borrowed from a long time UNIX feature of booting into single-user mode. What this means for you under Linux is that if something gets broken in the startup scripts that affects the booting process of a host, it is possible for you to boot into this mode, make the fix, and then allow the system to boot into complete multi-user mode (normal behavior).

To boot into single-user mode, you must be at the `lilo:` prompt that is presented to you at boot time. When there, press the TAB key so that your choices of kernels are presented to you. The first kernel listed is your default kernel that is booted. Enter the name of the kernel followed by a space and an **s**. For example:

```
lilo: linux s
```

When you press ENTER after this, the Linux kernel will boot as normal except when it gets to the point where it starts the `init` program it will only go through runlevel 1 and then stop. (See previous sections in this chapter for a description of all the runlevels.) Depending on the system configuration, you will either be prompted for the root password or simply given a shell prompt. If prompted for a password, enter the root password and press ENTER, and you will get the shell prompt.

NOTE: Red Hat 7 users who have the graphical boot manager will need to press CTRL-X in order to switch back to text mode where there will be a `boot:` prompt. From there, you can enter the name of the kernel followed by an **s** to get into single-user mode.

At this time, you'll find that almost all the services that are normally started are not running. This includes network configuration. So if you need to change the IP address, gateway, netmask, or any network-related configuration file, you can. This is also a good time to run **fsck** manually on any partitions that could not be automatically checked and recovered. (The **fsck** program will tell you which partitions are misbehaving, if any.) A common problem that is easy to fix at this point is getting the DNS client-side configuration fixed right. (A typical symptom of bad client DNS configuration is that the system seems to hang for minutes on starting up services like Sendmail and NFS.) Simply edit the **/etc/resolv.conf** file and enter the correct IP address of your DNS server, and you're off.

> **NOTE:**   In single-user mode of many Linux distributions, only the root partition will be automatically mounted for you (Red Hat 7 will try to mount all of the partitions for you). If you need to access any other partitions, you will need to mount them yourself using the **mount** command. You can see all of the partitions that you can mount in the **/etc/fstab** file.

Once you have made any changes you need to make, simply press CTRL-D. This will exit single-user mode and continue with the booting process. Multiuser mode (runlevel 3 or 5, depending on whether you have X Windows set to automatically come up) should run.

If you need to reboot instead of continuing the boot process, remember that you need to unmount all of your disks by hand using the **unmount** command. Once you get to the point where the root partition is the only one left, simply remount it with read-only access like so:

```
[root@ford /root]# mount -o ro /
```

Then to reboot, simply run the **reboot** command.

SUMMARY

LILO is Linux's extremely flexible boot loader capable of starting not only Linux, but other operating systems as well, most notably the many variants of Windows. This chapter's comparisons of LILO to the Windows NT boot process may help you understand the LILO process. Part of what makes LILO so useful is its simplicity and its capacity to be automated.

In this chapter, we covered the following key issues:

▼   Working with the **/etc/lilo.conf** configuration file

■   Running LILO so that it can install itself onto the boot sector (MBR)

■   The general startup process under Linux, including **rc** scripts

■   The process of creating your own **rc** script

▲   Recovering from a hard shutdown

One final reminder: Like any crucial system component, LILO should be learned on a non-production system before taking your hand to it in a working environment. A mistake made while working with any tool that affects the boot process, regardless of operating system, may be difficult to correct. Unless, of course, you like risk taking. (If you do, I have this cactus farm in Brazil . . .)

CHAPTER 8

File Systems

L inux is built upon the foundation of *file systems*. They are the mechanisms by which the disk gets organized, providing all of the abstraction layers above sectors and cylinders. In this chapter, we'll discuss the composition and management of these abstraction layers supported by the default Linux file system, ext2.

In this chapter, we will cover the many aspects of managing disks. This includes creating partitions, establishing file systems, automating the process by which they are mounted at boot time, and dealing with them after a system crash. In addition to the basics, we examine some of the more complex features of Linux, such as mounting network file systems, managing quotas, and the Automounter.

NOTE: Before beginning your study of this chapter, you should already be familiar with files, directories, permissions, and owners in the Linux environment. If you haven't yet read Chapter 6, it's best to read that chapter before continuing.

THE MAKEUP OF FILE SYSTEMS

Let's begin by going over the structure of file systems under Linux. It will help to clarify your understanding of the concept and let you see more easily how to take advantage of the architecture.

i-Nodes

The most fundamental building block of many UNIX file systems (including Linux's ext2) is the *i-node*. An i-node is a control structure that points to either other i-nodes or to data blocks.

The control information in the i-node includes the file's owner, permissions, size, time of last access, creation time, group ID, etc. (For the truly curious, the entire kernel data structure is available in **/usr/src/linux/include/linux/ext2_fs.h**—assuming, of course, that you have the source tree installed in the **/usr/src** directory.) The one thing an i-node *does not* keep is the file's name.

As mentioned in Chapter 6, directories themselves are special instances of files. This means each directory gets an i-node, and the i-node points to data blocks containing information (filenames and i-nodes) about the files in the directory. Figure 8-1 illustrates the organization of i-nodes and data blocks in the ext2 file system.

As you can see in Figure 8-1, the i-nodes are used to provide *indirection* so that more data blocks can be pointed to—which is why each i-node does not contain the filename. (Only one i-node works as a representative for the entire file; thus it would be a waste of space if every i-node contained filename information.) For example, my 6GB disk contains 1,079,304 i-nodes. If every i-node consumed 256 bytes to store the filename, a total of about 33MB would be wasted in storing filenames, even if they weren't being used!

Each indirect block can point in turn to other indirect blocks if necessary. With up to three layers of indirection, it is possible to store files as large as 2GB on an ext2 file system.

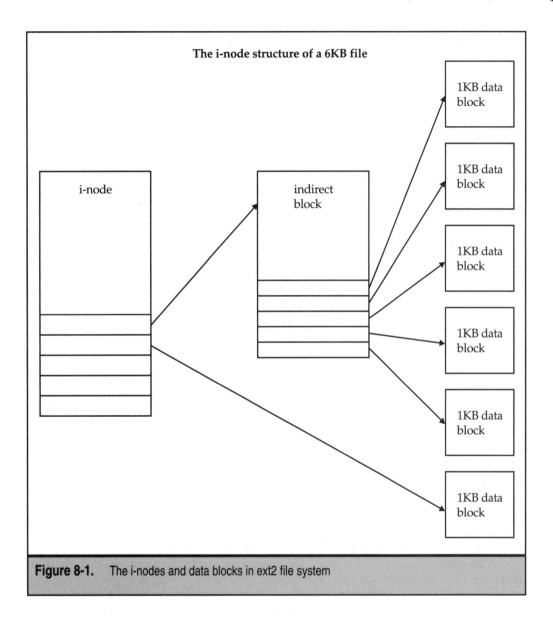

Figure 8-1.   The i-nodes and data blocks in ext2 file system

Superblocks

The very first piece of information read from a disk is its *superblock*. This small data structure reveals several key pieces of information, including the disk's geometry, the amount of available space, and, most important, the location of the first i-node. Without a superblock, a file system is useless.

Something as important as the superblock is not left to chance. Multiple copies of this data structure are scattered all over the disk to provide backup in case the first one is damaged. Under Linux's ext2 file system, a superblock is placed after every *group* of blocks, which contains i-nodes and data. One group consists of 8192 blocks; thus the first redundant superblock is at 8193, the second at 16385, and so on.

ext3 and ReiserFS

As of this writing, the ext2 file system is somewhere around seven years old. This means two things for us as system administrators: First and foremost, ext2 is rock solid. It is a well tested subsystem of Linux and has had the time to be very well optimized. Second, other file systems that were considered experimental when ext2 was created have matured and become available to Linux.

The two file systems that are the current candidates to replace ext2 in the next few years are ext3 and ReiserFS. Both offer significant improvements in performance and stability, but the most important component of both of them is that they have moved to a new way of getting the data to the disk. This new method is called *journaling*. Traditional file systems (such as ext2) must search through the directory structure, find the right place on disk to lay out the data, and then lay out the data. (Linux can also cache the whole process, including the directory updates, thereby making the process appear faster to the user.)

The problem with this method of doing things is that in the event of an unexpected crash, the **fsck** program has to go in and follow up on all of the files that are on the disk in order to make sure that they don't contain any dangling references (for example, i-nodes that point to other, invalid i-nodes or datablocks). As disks expand in size and shrink in price, the availability of these large capacity disks means more of us will have to deal with the aftermath of having to **fsck** a large disk. And as anyone who has had to do that before can tell you, it isn't fun. The process can take a long time to complete, and that means downtime for your users.

With journaling file systems, the new way of getting data out to disk, instead of finding the right place, the file system simply writes the data out in any order it can, as fast as it can. Each time, it logs the location of these datablocks. You can think of it like using the same spiral notebook for multiple classes without pre-partitioning the notebook. It would be wiser to simply take notes for each class in chronological order instead of grouping all of one class together. A journaled file system is like such a notebook, with the beginning of the notebook containing an index telling you which pages contain all the notes for a single class. Once the data is written, the file system can go move things around to make them optimal for reading without risking the integrity of the file.

What this means to you as a system administrator is that the amount of time it takes for the disk to write out data is much less, while at the same time the safety of getting the data written out to disk quickly means that in the event of a system crash, you won't need to run **fsck**. Think of how much faster you could recover a system if you didn't have to run **fsck** on a 70G disk! (Haven't had to run **fsck** on a big disk before? Think about how long it takes to run Scandisk under Windows on large disks.)

Unfortunately, as of the 2.4 kernel series, these two new file systems aren't ready for primetime quite yet. But don't be surprised if you see them in the 2.6 series (or 3.0?).

In the meantime, if you want to learn more about the ext2 file system, I highly recommend taking a look at *Linux Kernel Internals*, edited by Michael Beck (Addison-Wesley, 1998). Although the book is a bit dated in many aspects of the kernel (it was written for the 2.0 series), the parts about the ext2 file system still hold true.

MANAGING FILE SYSTEMS

The process of managing file systems is trivial—that is, the management becomes trivial *after* you have memorized all aspects of your networked servers, disks, backups, and size requirements with the condition that they will never again have to change. In other words, managing file systems isn't trivial at all.

There aren't many technical issues involved in file systems. Once the systems have been created, deployed, and added to the backup cycle, they do tend to take care of themselves for the most part. What makes them tricky to manage are the administrative issues—such as users who refuse to do housekeeping on their disks, and cumbersome management policies dictating who can share what disk and under what condition, depending of course on the account under which the disk was purchased, and . . .. (It sounds frighteningly like a *Dilbert* cartoon strip, but there is a good deal of truth behind that statement.)

Unfortunately, there's no cookbook solution available for dealing with office politics, so in this section we'll stick to the technical issues involved in managing file systems—that is, the process of mounting and unmounting partitions, dealing with the **/etc/fstab** file, and performing file-system recovery with the **fsck** tool.

Mounting and Unmounting Local Disks

Linux's strong points include its flexibility and the way it lends itself to seamless management of file locations. Partitions are mounted so that they appear as just another subdirectory. Even a substantial number of file systems look, to the user, like one large directory tree. This characteristic is especially helpful to the administrator, who can relocate partitions to various servers but can have the partitions still mounted to the same location in the directory tree; users of the file system need not know about the move at all.

The file-system management process begins with the root directory (see Figure 8-2). The partition containing the kernel and core directory structure is mounted at boot time. This single partition needs to have all the required utilities and configuration files to bring the system up to single-user mode. Many of the directories on this partition are empty.

As the boot scripts run, additional partitions are mounted, adding to the structure of the file system. The mount process overlays a single subdirectory with the directory tree of the partition it is trying to mount. For example, let's say that **/dev/hda1** is the root partition. It has the directory **/usr,** which contains no files. The partition **/dev/hda3** contains all the files that we want in **/usr,** so we mount **/dev/hda3** to the directory **/usr**. Users can now

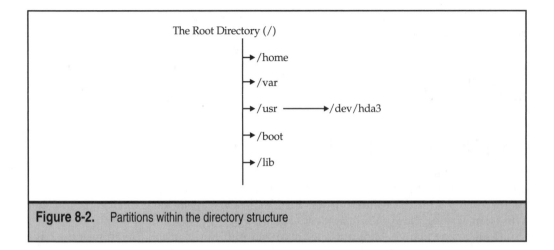

Figure 8-2.   Partitions within the directory structure

simply change directories to **/usr** to see all the files from that partition. The user doesn't need to know that **/usr** is actually a separate partition.

Keep in mind that when a new directory is mounted, the **mount** process hides all the contents of the previously mounted directory. So in our **/usr** example, if the root partition did have files in **/usr** before mounting **/dev/hda3,** those **/usr** files would no longer be visible. (They're not erased, of course—once **/dev/hda3** is unmounted, the **/usr** files would become visible once again.)

Using the mount Command

Like many command-line tools, the **mount** command has a plethora of options, most of which you won't be using in daily work. You can get full details on these options from the **mount** man page. In this section, we'll explore the most common uses of the command.

The structure of the **mount** command is as follows:

```
mount [options] device directory
```

where **[options]** may be any of those shown in Table 8-1.

Option for mount	Description
-a	Mounts all the file systems listed in **/etc/fstab** (this file is examined later in this section).

Table 8-1.   Options Available for the **mount** Command

Option for mount	Description
`-t fstype`	Specifies the type of file system being mounted. Linux can mount file systems other than the ext2 standard, most notably FAT, VFAT, and FAT32. The **mount** command can usually sense this information on its own.
`-o options`	Specifies **options** applying to this **mount** process. These are usually options specific to the file system type (options for mounting network file systems may not apply to mounting local file systems).

Table 8-1.   Options Available for the **mount** Command *(continued)*

The **options** available for use with the **mount -o** parameter are shown in Table 8-2.

Option for the mount -o Parameter (for Local Partitions)	Description
`ro`	Mounts the partition as read-only.
`rw`	Mounts the partition as read-write (default).
`exec`	Permits the execution of binaries (default).
`noatime`	Disables update of the access time on i-nodes. For partitions where the access time doesn't matter (such as news spools), this improves performance.
`noauto`	Disables automatic mount of this partition when the **–a** option is specified (applies only to the **/etc/fstab** file).
`nosuid`	Disallows application of **setuid** program bits to the mounted partition.
`sb=n`	Tells **mount** to use block **n** as the superblock on an ext2 file system.

Table 8-2.   Options Available for Use with the **mount   -o** Parameter

The following **mount** command mounts the **/dev/hda3** partition to the **/usr** directory with read-only privileges:

```
[root@ford /root]# mount -o ro /dev/hda3 /usr
```

Unmounting File Systems

To unmount a file system, use the **umount** command. Here's the command format:

```
umount [-f] directory
```

where **directory** is the directory to be unmounted. For example:

```
[root@ford /root]# umount /usr
```

unmounts the partition mounted on the **/usr** directory.

When the File System Is in Use There's a catch to **umount**: If the file system is in use (that is, when someone has a file open on that partition), you won't be able to unmount that file system. To get around this, you have three choices:

▼ You can use the **lsof** program (available at **ftp://vic.cc.purdue.edu/pub/tools/unix/lsof**) or **fuser** to determine which processes are keeping the files open, and then kill them off or ask the process owners to stop what they're doing. (Read about the **kill** parameter in **fuser** on the **fuser** man page.) If you choose to kill the processes, be sure you understand the repercussions of doing so (read: don't get fired for doing this).

■ You can use the **-f** option with **umount** to force the unmount process. Any processes with open files on the partition will be left hanging, and data may be lost.

▲ The safest and most proper alternative is to bring the system down to single-user mode and then unmount the file system. In reality, of course, you don't always get this luxury.

The /etc/fstab File

As mentioned earlier, **/etc/fstab** is a configuration file that **mount** can use. This file contains a list of all partitions known to the system. During the boot process, this list is read and the items in it are automatically mounted.

Here's the format of entries in the **/etc/fstab** file:

```
/dev/device /dir/to/mount       fstype    parameters    fs_freq      fs_passno
```

Table 8-3 defines each element in an **/etc/fstab** entry.

/etc/fstab File Entry	Definition
/dev/device	Indicates the partition to be mounted (e.g., **/dev/hda3**).
/dir/to/mount	Designates the directory on which to mount the partition (e.g., **/usr**).
fstype	Specifies the type of file system (e.g., ext2).
parameters	Indicates the parameters to be supplied in the **-o** option of the **mount** command.
fs_freq	Tells the **dump** command how often the file system needs to be backed up.
fs_passno	Tells the **fsck** program at boot time to determine the order in which the file systems should be checked. (Note that all file systems are checked before they are mounted.)

Table 8-3.   Each Element in an **/etc/fstab** Entry

Following is a sample **/etc/fstab** file:

```
/dev/hda2           /                     ext2    defaults        1 1
/dev/hda8           /home                 ext2    defaults        1 2
/dev/hda7           /tmp                  ext2    defaults        1 2
/dev/hda5           /usr                  ext2    defaults        1 2
/dev/hda6           /var                  ext2    defaults        1 2
/dev/hda1           /usr/local            ext2    defaults        1 2
/dev/hda3           swap                  swap    defaults        0 0
/dev/fd0            /mnt/floppy           ext2    noauto          0 0
/dev/cdrom          /mnt/cdrom            iso9660 noauto,ro       0 0
/dev/hdc            /mnt/cdrom2           iso9660 noauto,ro       0 0
none                /proc                 proc    defaults        0 0
none                /dev/pts              devpts  mode=0622       0 0
```

Let's take a look at a few details of **/etc/fstab** that haven't been mentioned yet, most notably the entry of **swap** for **/dev/hda3**, and the **none** for **/proc** and **/dev/pts**. In general, you'll never have to touch these file systems once the system is installed, so don't worry about them.

▼   The **/dev/hda3** partition is where virtual memory resides. Unlike Microsoft Windows and similar systems, in Linux the virtual memory can be kept on a separate partition from the root partition. This is done to improve performance, since the swap partition can obey rules different than a normal file system. Since the partition doesn't need to be backed up or checked with **fsck** at boot time, the last two parameters on it are zeroed out. (Note that a swap partition can be kept in a normal disk file, as well. See the man page on **mkswap** for additional information.)

■ The **none** entry in conjunction with **/proc** is for the **/proc** file system (see Chapter 27 for details). This is a special file system that provides an interface to kernel parameters through what looks like any other file system. Although it appears to exist on disk, it really doesn't—all the files represent something that is in the kernel. Most notable is **/dev/kcore**, which is the system memory abstracted as a file. People new to the **/proc** file system often mistake this for a large unnecessary file and accidentally remove it, which will cause the system to malfunction in many glorious ways. Unless you are sure you know what you are doing, it's a safe bet to leave all the files in **/proc** alone.

▲ The last entry in a **/etc/fstab** file, **/dev/pts**, is for a new mechanism to improve implementation for network terminal support (**ptys**). This entry is necessary if you intend to allow remote login to your host via **rsh**, **telnet**, **rlogin**, or **ssh**.

If you use the LinuxConf configuration tool, you don't have to edit this **/etc/fstab** file directly. However, like anything else in system management you should know how this file is organized in case you need to edit it by hand.

TIP: When mounting partitions with the **/etc/fstab** configured, you can run the **mount** command with only one parameter: the directory you wish to mount to. The **mount** command checks **/etc/fstab** for that directory; if found, **mount** will use all parameters that have already been established there. For example, here's the command to mount a CD-ROM given the **/etc/fstab** shown earlier:

```
[root@ford /root]# mount /mnt/cdrom
```

Using fsck

The **fsck** tool, short for **F**ile **S**ystem **C**hec**K**, is used to diagnose and repair file systems that may have become damaged in the course of daily operations. Such repairs are usually necessary after a system crash in which the system did not get a chance to fully flush all of its internal buffers to disk. (Although this tool's name bears a striking resemblance to one of the expressions often uttered after a system crash, that this tool is part of the recovery process is *strictly* coincidence.)

Usually, the system runs the **fsck** tool automatically during the boot process (much in the same way Windows runs Scandisk) if it detects a partition that was not cleanly unmounted. Linux makes an impressive effort to automatically repair any problems it runs across and in most instances does take care of itself. The robust nature of the ext2 file system helps in such situations. Nevertheless, it may happen that you get this message:

```
*** An error occurred during the file system check.
*** Dropping you to a shell; the system will reboot
*** when you leave the shell.
```

At this point, you need to run **fsck** by hand and answer its prompts yourself.

If you do find that a file system is not behaving as it should (log messages are excellent hints to this situation), you may want to run **fsck** yourself on a running system. The only downside is that the file system in question must be unmounted in order for this to work. If you choose to take this path, be sure to remount the file system when you are done.

NOTE: **fsck** isn't the proper title for the ext2 repair tool; it's actually just a wrapper. The **fsck** wrapper tries to determine what kind of file system needs to be repaired and then runs the appropriate repair tool, passing any parameters that were passed to **fsck**. In ext2, the real tool is called **e2fsck**. When a system crash occurs, you may need to call **e2fsck** directly rather than relying on other applications to call it for you automatically.

Parameters Available for e2fsck

The parameters available for **e2fsck** are shown in Table 8-4.

Parameter for `e2fsck`	Description
`-b superblock`	Specifies the superblock number from which **e2fsck** should read partition information. In most instances, **e2fsck** is able to find it at block 1, but if that block becomes corrupted, you'll need to specify an alternative number. Superblocks occur at every 8192 blocks, so the next superblock is at 8193, then 16385, and so on.
`-c`	Runs the badblocks program on the disk before running **e2fsck**. This searches the entire disk block-by-block and verifies the block's integrity. This is a very thorough way of checking a disk, but it is *extremely* time consuming.
`-f`	Forces a check to run even if it thinks the file system is already clean.
`-y`	Tells **e2fsck** to automatically assume that all prompts from **e2fsck** are to be answered Yes.

Table 8-4.   Parameters Available for `e2fsck`

For example, to run **e2fsck** on the **/dev/hda3** file system, you would run:

```
[root@ford /root]# e2fsck /dev/hda3
```

To force a check and automatically answer Yes to any prompts that come up, you would enter this command:

```
[root@ford]# e2fsck -f -y /dev/hda3
```

What If I Get Errors?

First, relax. The **fsck** check rarely finds problems that it cannot correct by itself. When it does ask for human intervention, telling **fsck** to execute its default suggestion is often enough. Very rarely does a single pass of **e2fsck** not clear up all problems.

On the rare occasions when a second run is needed, it *should not* turn up any more errors. If it does, you are most likely facing a hardware failure. Remember to start with the obvious: Check for reliable power and well-connected cables. Anyone running SCSI systems should verify that they're using the correct type of terminator, that cables aren't too long, that SCSI IDs aren't conflicting, and that cable quality is adequate. (SCSI is especially fussy about the quality of the cables.)

The lost+found Directory

Another rare situation is when **e2fsck** finds segments of files that it cannot rejoin with the original file. In those cases, it will place the fragment in the partition's **lost+found** directory. This directory is located where the partition is mounted, so if **/dev/hda3** is mounted on **/usr**, then **/usr/lost+found** correlates to **/dev/hda3**.

Anything can go into a **lost+found** directory—file fragments, directories, and even special files. When normal files wind up there, a file owner should be attached, and you can contact the owner and see if they need the data (typically, they won't). If you encounter a directory in **lost+found**, you'll most likely want to try and restore it from the most recent backups rather than trying to reconstruct it from **lost+found**.

At the very least, **lost+found** tells you if anything became dislocated. Again, such errors are extraordinarily rare.

ADDING AND PARTITIONING A DISK

The process of adding a disk under Linux on the Intel (x86) platform is relatively easy. Assuming you are adding a disk that is of similar type to your existing disks (e.g., adding an IDE disk to a system that already has IDE drives or adding a SCSI disk to a system that already has SCSI drives), the system should automatically detect the new disk at boot time, and all that is left is partitioning it and creating a file system on it.

If you are adding a new type of disk (like a SCSI disk on a system that only has IDE drives), you may need to compile in support for your SCSI card to the kernel. (Note that most Linux distributions come with support for many popular SCSI cards as part of the standard installation. If you didn't recompile the kernel from the original installation, it is unlikely that you will need to recompile the kernel to add support.) To compile in support for a new type of disk, see Chapter 10. Be sure to step through all of the relevant menus and mark the appropriate driver to be compiled either into the base kernel or as a module (assuming it can be compiled as a module).

Once the disk is in place, simply boot the system and you're ready to go. If you aren't sure about whether the system can see the new disk, run the **dmesg** command and see whether the driver loaded and was able to find your disk. For example:

```
[root@ford /root]# dmesg | more
```

Overview of Partitions

For the sake of clarity, and in case you need to know what a partition is and how it works, let's do a brief review of this subject. Every disk must be *partitioned*. *Partitions* divide up the disk, and each segment acts as a complete disk by itself. Once a partition is filled, it cannot (without special software) automatically overflow onto another partition. Usually, the process of partitioning a disk accomplishes one of two goals: Either the user needs two different operating systems installed and each operating system requires its own partition, or it may be prudent that the usage of space on one partition not interfere with space dedicated to other tasks on other partitions.

An example of the latter occurs in user home directories. When users of the system are not the administrators of the system, the administrator must ensure that users don't consume the entire disk for their personal files. This takes up room needed for logging purposes and temporary files, causing the system to misbehave. To prevent this, a special partition is created for user files so that they don't overflow into protected system space.

NOTE: It is acceptable to partition a disk so that only one large partition is taking up the entire disk. But beware: If this is the boot partition, the entire partition must fit within the 1024 cylinder boundary, or you will not be able to boot. See the LILO chapter (Chapter 7) for more information.

Where Disks Exist

Under Linux, each disk is given its own device name. IDE disks start with the name **/dev/hdX**, where X can range from *a* through *z*, with each letter representing a physical device. For example, in an IDE-only system with one hard disk and one CD-ROM, both on the same IDE chain, the hard disk would be **/dev/hda**, and the CD-ROM would be **/dev/hdb**. Disk devices are automatically created during system installation.

When partitions are created, new devices are used. They take the form of **/dev/hdXY**, where X is the device letter (as described just above), and Y is the partition number. Thus, the first partition on the **/dev/hda** disk is **/dev/hda1**, the second partition would be **/dev/hda2**, and so on.

SCSI disks follow the same basic scheme as IDE, except instead of starting with **/dev/hd**, they start with **/dev/sd**. Therefore, the first partition on the first SCSI disk would be **/dev/sda1**, the second partition on the third SCSI disk would be **/dev/sdc2**, and so on.

Creating Partitions

CAUTION: The process of creating partitions is irrevocably destructive to the data already on the disk. Before creating, changing, or removing partitions on any disk, you must be *very* sure of what's on the disk being modified, and you need to have a backup if that data is still needed.

During the installation process, you probably used a "pretty" tool to create partitions. Unfortunately, Linux platforms don't ship with a standard utility for creating and managing partitions. A basic mechanism that does exist on all Linux distributions is **fdisk**. Though it's small and somewhat awkward, it's a reliable partitioning tool. Furthermore, in the event you need to troubleshoot a system that has gone really wrong, you should be familiar with basics such as **fdisk**. The only real downside to **fdisk** is its lack of a user interface.

NOTE: An easier-to-use wrapper called **cfdisk** exists as well. However, this tool may not be available in an emergency situation, so it's best to learn how to use **fdisk** despite its awkwardness.

For this sample run, let's assume that we want to partition the **/dev/hdb** device, a 340MB IDE hard disk. (Yes, they do still exist.) We begin by running **fdisk** with the **/dev/hdb** parameter:

```
[root@ford /root]# fdisk /dev/hdb
```

which outputs a simple prompt:

```
Command (m for help):
```

Let's use **m** to see what our options are. This menu is reasonably self-explanatory:

```
Command (m for help): m
Command action
   a   toggle a bootable flag
   b   edit bsd disklabel
   c   toggle the dos compatibility flag
   d   delete a partition
   l   list known partition types
   m   print this menu
```

```
n    add a new partition
o    create a new empty DOS partition table
p    print the partition table
q    quit without saving changes
s    create a new empty Sun disklabel
t    change a partition's system id
u    change display/entry units
v    verify the partition table
w    write table to disk and exit
x    extra functionality (experts only)
Command (m for help):
```

We begin by looking at the existing partition, using the **p** command (print the partition table):

```
Command (m for help): p
Disk /dev/hdb: 16 heads, 63 sectors, 665 cylinders
Units = cylinders of 1008 * 512 bytes
    Device Boot      Start       End     Blocks   Id  System
/dev/hdb1    *           1       664    334624+    6  FAT16
Command (m for help):
```

We have a little legacy system here, don't you think? Time to upgrade this disk—we start by removing the existing partition using the **d** command (delete a partition):

```
Command (m for help): d
Partition number (1-4): 1
Command (m for help):
```

And we use the **p** (print the partition table) command to verify the results:

```
Command (m for help): p
Disk /dev/hdb: 16 heads, 63 sectors, 665 cylinders
Units = cylinders of 1008 * 512 bytes
    Device Boot      Start       End     Blocks   Id  System
Command (m for help):
```

No partition there. Time to start creating partitions. For the sake of discussion, we'll pretend this disk is large enough to accommodate a full workstation configuration. To set this up, we need to create the partitions shown in Table 8-5.

So now that we know which partitions to create, let's do it! We start with the root partition. Given that we have only 340MB to work with, we'll keep root small—only 25MB.

Partition	Description
/	The root partition is for those core system files necessary to bring a system to single-user mode. Once established, the partition's contents shouldn't vary at all and definitely shouldn't need to grow. The intent is to isolate this file system from other file systems, to prevent interference with core operations.
/usr	This partition is used for system software such as user tools, compilers, X Windows, and so forth. Because we may one day need to find a bigger home for our system software, we put this in a separate partition.
/var	The **/var** partition is used to hold files that change a lot—this usually includes spool directories (mail, print, etc.) and log files. What makes this partition worrisome is that external events can make its contents grow beyond allocated space. Log files from a Web server, for instance, can grow quickly and beyond your control. To keep these files from spilling over into the rest of your system, it's wise to keep this partition separate. (A type of attack via the network can be mounted by artificially generating so much activity on your server that the disk fills up with system logs and the system behaves unreliably.)
/tmp	Similar to **/var**, files in **/tmp** can unexpectedly consume substantial space. This can occur when users leave files unattended or application programs create large temporary files. Either way, maintaining this partition is a good safety mechanism.
/home	If you need to store home directories on your disk, especially for users whose disk consumption needs to be restricted, you'll definitely want to have this separate partition.
swap	The swap partition is necessary to hold virtual memory. Although it isn't required, swap is often a good idea in case you do exhaust all your physical RAM. In general, you'll want this partition to be the same size as your RAM.

Table 8-5.   Disk Partitions

```
Command (m for help): n
Command action
   e   extended
   p   primary partition (1-4)
p
```

```
Partition number (1-4): 1
First cylinder (1-665, default 1): 1
Last cylinder or +size or +sizeM or +sizeK (1-665, default 665): +25M
Command (m for help):
```

Notice the first prompt is for whether we want a primary or extended partition. This is because of a goofy mess created long ago (pre-Linux) when hard disks were so small that no one thought more than four partitions would ever be needed. When disks got bigger and backward-compatibility was an issue, we needed a trick to accommodate more partitions. The last partition would be an "extended" partition, unseen by the user but able to contain additional partitions.

The next question: Which partition number? (You can see the limit of four primary partitions as part of the question.) We start with one, picking the default starting cylinder, and then specify that we want 25MB allocated to it.

To create the second partition for swap, we type the following:

```
Command (m for help): n
Command action
   e   extended
   p   primary partition (1-4)
p
Partition number (1-4): 2
First cylinder (52-665, default 52): 52
Last cylinder or +size or +sizeM or +sizeK (52-665, default 665): +16M
Command (m for help):
```

This time, the prompts are identical to those used for the previous partition, with slightly different numbers. However, by default, **fdisk** is creating ext2 partitions. We need this partition to be of type **swap**. To do this, we use the **t** (change partition type) command:

```
Command (m for help): t
Partition number (1-4): 2
Hex code (type L to list codes): L
 0  Empty            16  Hidden FAT16    61  SpeedStor       a6  OpenBSD
 1  FAT12            17  Hidden HPFS/NTF 63  GNU HURD or Sys a7  NeXTSTEP
 2  XENIX root       18  AST Windows swa 64  Novell Netware  b7  BSDI fs
 3  XENIX usr        24  NEC DOS         65  Novell Netware  b8  BSDI swap
 4  FAT16 <32 <N     3c  PartitionMagic  70  DiskSecure Mult c1  DRDOS/secFAT-
 5  Extended         40  Venix 80286     75  PC/IX           c4  DRDOS/secFAT-
 6  FAT16            41  PPC PReP Boot    80  Old Minix       c6  DRDOS/secFAT-
 7  HPFS/NTFS        42  SFS             81  Minix / old Lin c7  Syrinx
 8  AIX              4d  QNX4.x          82  Linux swap      db  CP/M / CTOS .
 9  AIX bootable     4e  QNX4.x 2nd part 83  Linux           e1  DOS access
 a  OS/2 Boot Manag  4f  QNX4.x 3rd part 84  OS/2 hidden C:  e3  DOS R/O
 b  Win95 FAT32      50  OnTrack DM      85  Linux extended  e4  SpeedStor
 c  Win95 FAT32 (LB  51  OnTrack DM6 Aux 86  NTFS volume set eb  BeOS fs
 e  Win95 FAT16 (LB  52  CP/M            87  NTFS volume set f1  SpeedStor
```

```
 f  Win95 Ext'd (LB 53  OnTrack DM6 Aux 93  Amoeba           f4  SpeedStor
10  OPUS            54  OnTrackDM6      94  Amoeba BBT       f2 DOS secondary
11  Hidden FAT12    55  EZ-Drive        a0  IBM Thinkpad hi  fe  LANstep
12  Compaq diagnost 56  Golden Bow      a5  BSD/386          ff  BBT
14  Hidden FAT16    5c  Priam Edisk
Hex code (type L to list codes): 82
Changed system type of partition 2 to 82 (Linux swap)
Command (m for help):
```

The first question is, of course, what partition number do we want to change to? Since we want the second partition to be the swap, we entered **2**. The next prompt is a bit more cryptic: the hexadecimal code for the correct partition. My wife has to remind me what day it is sometimes, so you can imagine that I don't remember all these hexadecimal codes. The **L** command lists all available partition types. We spot 82 for Linux Swap, so we enter that, and we're done.

NOTE: It used to be that Linux's swap partition was limited to 128M. This is no longer the case. You can create a swap partition as large as 2GB.

Now for creating **/usr**. We'll make it 100MB in size:

```
Command (m for help): n
Command action
   e   extended
   p   primary partition (1-4)
p
Partition number (1-4): 3
First cylinder (85-665, default 85): 85
Last cylinder or +size or +sizeM or +sizeK (85-665, default 665): +100M
Command (m for help):
```

So at this point, we have three partitions: **root**, **swap**, and **/usr**. We can see them by entering the **p** command:

```
Command (m for help): p
Disk /dev/hdb: 16 heads, 63 sectors, 665 cylinders
Units = cylinders of 1008 * 512 bytes
   Device Boot    Start      End     Blocks   Id  System
/dev/hdb1            1       51      25672+   83  Linux
/dev/hdb2           52       84      16632    82  Linux swap
/dev/hdb3           85      288     102816    83  Linux
Command (m for help):
```

Now we need to create the extended partition to accommodate **/tmp**, **/var**, and **/home**. We do so using the **n** command, just as for any other new partition:

```
Command (m for help): n
Command action
   e   extended
   p   primary partition (1-4)
e
Partition number (1-4): 4
First cylinder (289-665, default 289): 289
Last cylinder or +size or +sizeM or +sizeK (289-665, default 665): 665
Command (m for help):
```

Instead of designating a megabyte value for the size of this partition, we enter the last cylinder number, thus taking up the remainder of the disk. Let's see what this looks like:

```
Command (m for help): p
Disk /dev/hdb: 16 heads, 63 sectors, 665 cylinders
Units = cylinders of 1008 * 512 bytes
   Device Boot    Start      End    Blocks   Id  System
/dev/hdb1            1        51    25672+   83  Linux
/dev/hdb2           52        84    16632    82  Linux swap
/dev/hdb3           85       288   102816    83  Linux
/dev/hdb4          289       665   190008     5  Extended
Command (m for help):
```

Now we're ready to create the last three partitions:

```
Command (m for help): n
First cylinder (289-665, default 289): 289
Last cylinder or +size or +sizeM or +sizeK (289-665, default 665): +100M
Command (m for help): n
First cylinder (493-665, default 493): 493
Last cylinder or +size or +sizeM or +sizeK (493-665, default 665): +45M
Command (m for help): n
First cylinder (585-665, default 585): 585
Last cylinder or +size or +sizeM or +sizeK (585-665, default 665): 665
Command (m for help):
```

Note that for the very last partition, we again specified the last cylinder instead of a megabyte value, so that we are sure that we have allocated the entire disk. One last **p** command shows us what our partitions now look like:

```
Command (m for help): p
Disk /dev/hdb: 16 heads, 63 sectors, 665 cylinders
Units = cylinders of 1008 * 512 bytes
   Device Boot    Start      End    Blocks   Id  System
/dev/hdb1            1        51    25672+   83  Linux
/dev/hdb2           52        84    16632    82  Linux swap
/dev/hdb3           85       288   102816    83  Linux
/dev/hdb4          289       665   190008     5  Extended
/dev/hdb5          289       492   102784+   83  Linux
```

```
/dev/hdb6          493      584    46336+  83  Linux
/dev/hdb7          585      665    40792+  83  Linux
Command (m for help):
```

Perfect. We commit the changes to disk and quit the **fdisk** utility by using the **w** (write table to disk and exit) command:

```
Command (m for help): w
The partition table has been altered!
Calling ioctl() to re-read partition table.
Syncing disks.
WARNING: If you have created or modified any DOS 6.x
partitions, please see the fdisk manual page for additional
information.
[root@ford /root]#
```

If we needed to write an **/etc/fstab** file ourselves for this configuration, it would look something like this:

```
/dev/hdb1      /          ext2     defaults    1 1
/dev/hdb2      swap       swap     defaults    0 0
/dev/hdb3      /usr       ext2     defaults    1 2
/dev/hdb5      /home      ext2     defaults    1 2
/dev/hdb6      /var       ext2     defaults    1 2
/dev/hdb7      /tmp       ext2     defaults    1 2
none           /proc      proc     defaults    0 0
none           /dev/pts   devpts   mode=0622   0 0
```

Making File Systems

With the partitions created, we need to put file systems on them. (If you're accustomed to Microsoft Windows, this is akin to formatting the disk once you've partitioned it.)

Under Linux, we use two tools for this process: **mke2fs** to create ext2 file systems, and **mkswap** to create swap file systems. There are many command-line parameters available for the **mke2fs** tool, many of which are needed only if you have an unusual situation. And if you have such an unusual need, I'm confident you don't need this text for guidance on creating file systems!

The only command-line parameter you'll usually have to set is the partition onto which the file system should go. To create a file system on the **/dev/hdb3** partition, we would issue the command

```
[root@ford /root]# mke2fs /dev/hdb3
```

and the result would look something like this:

```
[root@ford /root]# mke2fs /dev/hdb3
mke2fs 1.14, 9-Jan-1999 for EXT2 FS 0.5b, 95/08/09
Linux ext2 file system format
```

```
File system label=
25792 inodes, 102816 blocks
5140 blocks (5.00%) reserved for the super user
First data block=1
Block size=1024 (log=0)
Fragment size=1024 (log=0)
13 block groups
8192 blocks per group, 8192 fragments per group
1984 inodes per group
Superblock backups stored on blocks:
        8193, 16385, 24577, 32769, 40961, 49153, 57345, 65537, 73729, 81921,
        90113, 98305
Writing inode tables: done
Writing superblocks and file system accounting information: done
[root@ford /root]#
```

Setting up swap space with the **mkswap** command is equally straightforward. The only parameter needed is the partition onto which the swap space will be created. To create swap space on **/dev/hdb2**, we would use

```
[root@ford /root]# mkswap /dev/hdb2
```

and the result would look something like this:

```
[root@ford /root]# mkswap /dev/hdb2
Setting up swapspace version 0, size = 17027072 bytes
[root@ford /root]#
```

NETWORK FILE SYSTEMS

Network file systems make it possible for you to dedicate systems to serving disks while letting clients handle the compute-intensive tasks of users. Centralized disks mean easier backup solutions and ready physical security. Under Linux (and UNIX as a whole), disk centralization is accomplished through the Network File System (NFS). In this section, we'll discuss client-side issues of NFS, leaving the server-side issues until later in this book (Chapter 18).

Mounting NFS Partitions

Mounting NFS partitions works much the same way as mounting local partitions. The only difference is in how the partition is addressed. On local disks, partitions are addressed by their device name, such as **/dev/hda1**. In NFS mounts, partitions are referenced by their hostnames and export directories. Thus, if the server named technics is allowing your host to mount the directory **/export/SL1200/MK2** and you want to mount this to **/projects/topsecret1**, you would use this command:

```
[root@ford /root]# mount technics:/export/SL1200/MK2 /projects/topsecret1
```

As you can see, it's not necessary for your local directory to have the same name as the server's directory.

With NFS come some additional options you can use in conjunction with the **mount** command's **-o** option, as shown in Table 8-6.

Here's an example of an NFS mount in the **/etc/fstab** file:

```
denon:/export/DN2000F  /proj/DN2k nfs bg,intr,hard,wsize=8192,rsize=8192 0 0
```

Using the Automounter

As your site grows, you'll find that maintaining mount tables becomes increasingly complicated. You may find it appropriate to standardize on a particular set of NFS mounts for all systems to save yourself some work, but this has the side effect of wasting system resources for both the client and server.

Option for the MOUNT -o Parameter (for NFS Partitions)	Description
soft	"Soft mounts" the partition. If the server fails, the client will time out after a designated interval and cause the requested operation to fail.
hard	"Hard mounts" the partition. The client will wait as long as it takes for the server to come back after a failure. If the server comes up, no data will be lost.
timeo=n	Sets the timeout value to be **n** seconds.
wsize=n	Sets the write buffer size to **n** bytes. Default is 1024; recommended value is 8192.
rsize=n	Sets the read buffer size to **n** bytes. Default is 1024; recommended value is 8192.
bg	Backgrounds the mount. If the mount does not initially work, lets the mount process go into the background and keep trying. If you are placing any NFS mount points in an **/etc/fstab** file, you should definitely include this option.

Table 8-6.   Options You Can Use in Conjunction with the **mount** Command's **-o** Option

To combat this problem, you can use the *Automounter* subsystem. As its name implies, it automatically mounts partitions as they are needed. When used in conjunction with NIS (see Chapter 19), you can produce a centralized set of maps that apply to your entire site, deploying the Automounter to mount only those partitions needed by users at the time they are needed.

A good example of this is home directories. Say that for a variety of technical reasons, my company currently needs to allow everyone in engineering to put their home directories on their local systems rather than having them all reside on a central server (like a Network Appliance, http://www.netapps.com box). However, we want to allow anyone to be able to log in to anyone else's system and have their home directory available to them. If we were to use **/etc/fstab** for this, every new person in engineering would require a lot of people to get their **/etc/fstab**'s updated, which is bound to be an error-prone task. Even worse, having to mount several dozen home directories every time would be a waste of resources, especially if other engineers are not logging in to other people's machines all the time.

By using the Automounter in conjunction with NIS, I can maintain a very simple **/etc/fstab** on each host and run the Automounter daemon. When someone logs in to the system, the login program will try to access her home directory. Automounter will intercept this request, go look up where that user's home directory is located, mount it, and then let the login process continue. The process happens so quickly the user doesn't realize that her home directory was just dynamically mounted for her. Once the user logs off, Automounter will notice that there hasn't been any activity on that partition for a while and automatically unmount it. Neat, huh?

And of course, conveniently, all popular distributions of Linux are currently shipping with the Automounter subsystem already set up, ready to accept your configuration files.

The Slightly Bigger Picture

Let's begin by taking a closer look at the steps taken by the Automounter so that we better understand how it works.

When Automounter starts, it looks for a file called **/etc/auto.master**. This file tells it what *maps* it will need to read for what directory. For example, the **auto.master** file might contain an entry that looks like this:

```
/home           auto.home
```

This tells Automounter that for any directory accessed in the **/home** directory, it should consult the **/etc/auto.home** file to find out what partition it should mount.

The **auto.home** file is called a *mapfile*. Mapfiles in this context are simply text files that map user's names to the location of their home directories. The first column of the file contains the *key*, which is simply the user's login. This value is what is used to search the mapfile.

```
sshah           orb:/export/home/sshah
```

Options in Centralized Storage

Just because you can do something doesn't always make it sensible to do it. In my example of home directories, there is a technical need to allow the engineering staff to keep their home directories local to their system. The side effect of this is that backups tend to be more troublesome, and should the user's system go down, their data becomes unavailable until either a restore occurs or the system is brought back online. Because of this, it is often a better idea to stick to centralized storage with systems like Network Appliance's, EMC, or Auspex's disk servers. Unlike traditional NFS servers (such as a Linux-based or Sun server), these systems are dedicated servers that offer many additional features, including high availability. And since people cannot log in to them, they are much less likely to crash. The downside to centralized storage systems is that they tend to be very expensive. But once you get one, you'll never give it up.

Also note that there is a lot of competition growing in the field of dedicated disk servers, many of which are substantially cheaper than NetApps and Auspex's solutions. This is often because they don't offer the same feature set and performance—look at your choices carefully. This isn't to say that NetApps and Auspex are the only games in town, but as of this writing, they are still solid choices. To use an old cliché, "No one ever got fired for buying NetApps."

In this example, sshah is the key.

Combining the two files together (**auto.master** and **auto.home**), the Automounter will do the following when someone tries to access the directory **/home/sshah**:

1. Check if **/home/sshah** is already mounted.
2. If not, create the directory **/home/sshah**.
3. Mount **orb:/export/home/sshah** to **/home/sshah**.

Don't worry if it takes you a few minutes to wrap your head around this concept—it isn't terribly intuitive. But once you get it and see why this feature is useful, you'll wonder how you ever managed a network without it.

Starting the Automounter

Because the Automounter relies on NFS, before using it you'll need to be sure you can do normal NFS mounts. Once you have this working, just make a simple change to your startup scripts to deploy the Automounter: Make sure the **autofs** script (found in **/etc/rc.d/init.d** under Red Hat Linux) is started when the system enters runlevel 3. You can do this with a graphical runlevel editor such as **tksysv** or **ksysv**, or you can add the symlink to the **init** script into the **rc3.d** directory yourself. Just remember to make the symlink number sufficiently high to start after all the networking systems start. (Under Red Hat Linux, you could create a symlink from **/etc/rc.d/rc3.d/S72autofs** to **/etc/rc.d/init.d/autofs**.)

If you need to start the Automounter by hand, run this command:

```
[root@ford /root]# /etc/rc.d/init.d/autofs start
```

Use this same command to stop the Automounter daemon, by changing the **start** option to **stop**.

Configuring /etc/auto.master

The Automounter's primary configuration file is **/etc/auto.master**. The format of this file is as follows:

```
#
# Sample /etc/auto.master file
# (lines which begin with a '#' are comments)
#
/mount/point            map-file           global-options
/home            auto.home
/usr/local       auto.local
/misc            auto.misc
```

The first column tells you the mount point; the second column lists the files containing details about the mapping for that mount point; and the last column contains any NFS options you want to apply to all mounts.

The map files look a little different from the **auto.master** file. For example, here's the **auto.misc** file:

```
#
# auto.misc
#
# This is an automounter map and it has the following format
# key [ -mount-options-separated-by-comma ] location
# Details may be found in the autofs(5) manpage
kernel          -ro,soft,intr           ftp.kernel.org:/pub/linux
cd              -fstype=iso9660,ro      :/dev/cdrom
# the following entries are samples to pique your imagination
#floppy         -fstype=auto            :/dev/fd0
#floppy         -fstype=ext2            :/dev/fd0
#e2floppy       -fstype=ext2            :/dev/fd0
#jaz            -fstype=ext2            :/dev/sdc1
```

Here, the first column is the key, the second column holds the **mount** options, and the last column is the location from which to mount. If the location entry begins with a colon, it's a signal to the system that the mount is local. Thus, **/misc/cd** would mount **/dev/cdrom** with the following **mount** options:

```
-fstype=iso9660,ro
```

> **NOTE:**   Unlike NFS, which requires that the directory already exist in order for you to mount it, the Automounter does not. In the case of the **/misc** mount point, all that needs to exist is the **/misc** directory. All subdirectories would be created by the Automounter daemon as needed.

If you change any of the map files while the Automounter is running, you'll need to restart the Automounter so that it can reread the configuration files. This is done by using **autofs** as follows:

```
[root@ford /root]# /etc/rc.d/init.d/autofs reload
```

Alternatives to the Linux Automounter

The Linux Automounter didn't always look like this. In fact, the first Automounter for Linux was actually done through a system called AMD, which is short for (you guessed it) Auto-Mounter Daemon. What made AMD so popular was that it was the first truly cross-platform Automounter tool. Regardless of UNIX, you were bound to find an AMD port for it.

However, there was trouble in paradise. There were little problems (such as performance) with AMD, and the fact that Sun had standardized on a different format made it fall out of favor in the Linux community. As a result, the Linux-specific implementation of Automounter looked a lot like Sun's, especially in map-file compatibility.

However, if you find yourself working with other UNIXs that still use Automounter (such as FreeBSD), fear not. Several tools exist to allow you to quickly (and painlessly) convert one file format to the next. Read the man page for AMD for more information. Note that most installations of Linux do not install AMD by default.

QUOTA MANAGEMENT

In any multiuser environment, you're bound to run across users who—either refusing to play fair or because they're oblivious to common courtesy—practice the fine art of disk hogging, taking up more than a reasonable amount of disk space.

This problem can be managed in several ways. The first and most obvious solution is to beg and plead. This rarely works. The second approach is peer pressure: You regularly and publicly post the amounts of disk space being hogged by these users. If people are at all sensitive to what others think of them, this may work. The final and most successful technique is to institute *disk quotas,* allowing each user to consume a certain amount of disk space and no more. Enforcement is done by the operating system.

Disk quotas are usually the best option for system administrators, because the quotas are automated and don't require that you confront the offending users. However, technical and/or political barriers may be standing in the way of using them. (For instance, the CEO may not like being told she can use only 5MB of the server disk space.) Quotas are, of course, optional—your system will be quite happy to hum along without them. Whether they will work in your environment is up to you and your management.

Preparing a Disk for Quotas

Preparing to use disk quotas works in two steps. Step 1 is a one-time setup to configure your system to use disk quotas. This setup ensures that the necessary software to enforce quotas will be in place and ready for every startup. Step 2 is to make the necessary settings in the **/etc/fstab** file, and add the necessary files in each partition for which you want quota control. Step 2 must be repeated for every partition you want under quota control.

Setting Up the Boot Process

You'll be happy to know that most Linux distributions (including Red Hat) have quota support enabled as part of the standard installation. As a result, you shouldn't have to change anything. If you do need to change the startup scripts, first be sure that you've read the chapter on LILO and **rc** scripts (Chapter 7). We will assume here that you're already familiar with those two topics.

To start the quota manager, add the following lines to the end of your startup scripts (**rc.local** is a reasonable candidate):

```
# Check quota and then turn quota on.
  if [ -x /usr/sbin/quotacheck ]
        then
                echo "Checking quotas. This may take some time."
                /usr/sbin/quotacheck -avug
                echo " Done."
        fi
        if [ -x /usr/sbin/quotaon ]
        then
                echo "Turning on quota."
                /usr/sbin/quotaon -avug
        fi
```

Then reboot your system to test that your startup changes are working and that the system can bring itself back up correctly without any human assistance.

Configuring Individual Partitions

Disk quotas work on either a per-user or per-group basis, with each partition allowing for their own quotas. For example, it's possible for each user to have a quota associated with their home directories on one partition and another quota on another partition for a group project they're part of.

For each partition on which you want a quota, you'll need to set up three things: the **usrquota** option, the **grpquota** option, and the quota database.

The usrquota Option   Edit the **/etc/fstab** file so that, for each partition needing quotas, the **mount** options contain the **usrquota** option. For example, if **/dev/hda5** is mounted to the **/home** directory and you want that directory to have user quotas, the **/etc/fstab** entry would be something like this:

```
/dev/hda5    /home    ext2    defaults,usrquota 1    1
```

The grpquota Option   Partitions needing group quota support should have the **grpquota** option in the **/etc/fstab** file, just like the **usrquota** option as described above. (Note that it's acceptable to have both options enabled.) For example, if **/dev/hda5** is mounted to the **/home** directory and you want that directory to have group quotas, the **/etc/fstab** entry would be similar to this:

```
/dev/hda5    /home    ext2    defaults,grpquota 1    1
```

The Quota Database   Create the database files to store the user and group quota information. These files are empty, they are positioned at the root of each partition to have quotas, they should be readable only by the root user, and they must be named **quota.user** and **quota.group**.

To create these files with the appropriate permissions, use the **su** command to become the root user, go to the root of the partition, and use the **touch** command to create the files necessary to hold the quota database. For example, to set quota controls over **/dev/hda5**, which gets mounted to **/home**, use the **cd** command to go into the **/home** directory and type the following:

```
[root@ford /root]# cd /home
[root@ford /home]# touch quota.user
[root@ford /home]# touch quota.group
[root@ford /home]# chmod 600 quota.user
[root@ford /home]# chmod 600 quota.group
```

Now you're ready to configure individual quota settings.

NOTE: The first time you turn on quotas, while the initial database files are still empty, the **quotaon** command will report that the **quota.user** and **quota.group** files have invalid arguments. This is acceptable; the message will continue to occur until you add at least one user to each database via the **edquota** command.

Configuring Quota Settings

Creating, modifying, and removing quotas on either a per-user or per-group basis is done via the **edquota** command. In this section, we'll look at the usage of this command and run through some examples as well. First, some terminology:

▼ **Soft Limit**   This requested limit is placed on a user or group. If the user's account exceeds the soft limit, a grace period can be imposed as to how long the account can exist over the soft limit. During this time phase, users can be warned that their accounts are over the limit.

■ **Hard Limit**   This limit is imposed by the operating system and cannot be overrun. Any attempts to write data beyond the hard limit are denied.

▲ **Grace Period (Time Limit)**   When a user's account exceeds the soft limit, a clock starts tracking. After the grace period expires, the user cannot access the account. The length of this grace period should depend on the environment. A common value is one week. To keep the account from being disabled, the user needs to remove or compress files until his or her disk consumption falls below the soft limit.

Command-Line Options of edquota

The **edquota** command has only three options when used to manage per-user quotas:

-u *login*	Sets the quota information for the named user.
-t	Sets the grace period of a partition. Use it in conjunction with -u or -g to set all the grace periods for users or groups, respectively. Note: If users/groups exist on the same partition, they cannot have different grace periods.
-g *group*	Sets the quota information for the named group.
-p *login*	Allows you to clone one user's (user *login*) information to another user. Must be set in conjunction with the -u option.

When you invoke the **edquota** command, it brings up the configuration information for the particular user, group, or grace period you want to add or edit. By default, the **vi** editor is used to display human-readable information. If you prefer another editor, such as **emacs** or **pico**, you can simply change the EDITOR environment variable before running **edquota**. For example, if you're using BASH (the root user's default shell), you would enter this command:

```
[root@ford]# EDITOR=pico;export EDITOR
```

Once the **edquota** information is on screen, you can edit it, save the document, and quit. The **edquota** process takes that information and places it into the database. Note that **edquota** uses the **/etc/passwd** file to determine the location of a user's home directory.

Examples of edquota

To place a quota on user heidi (a well-known disk hog on my network), I would use the following command:

```
[root@ford]# edquota -u heidi
```

This will bring up the editor with a file that looks like the following:

```
Quotas for user heidi:
   /dev/hda2: blocks in use: 0, limits (soft = 0, hard = 0)
              inodes in use: 0, limits (soft = 0, hard = 0)
```

Zeros in all the limits means there is no quota on heidi's account at the moment. Notice that there is a limit value for i-nodes as well as blocks. Remember that one block is equal to 1K under Linux, and i-nodes are the control information needed to store files. You will usually only need a few i-nodes per file, and more as the file grows larger.

So, to set heidi's soft block limit to 5000, the hard block limit to 6000, the soft i-node limit to 2500, and the hard i-node limit to 3000, I would edit the file to look like this:

```
Quotas for user heidi:
   /dev/hda2: blocks in use: 0, limits (soft = 5000, hard = 6000)
              inodes in use: 0, limits (soft = 2500, hard = 3000)
```

CAUTION: The **edquota** command generates a unique name for the temporary file used to edit this information. Keep this file—do not write over the **quota.user** or **quota.group** file with this information! The **edquota** utility will take care of integrating quota information into those two files for you.

To change the quota for heidi, rerun **edquota -u heidi** and change the limits. In this instance, I found that putting disk quotas on your spouse is a bad idea, so I went back and changed the quota values to zero.

Another example of using **edquota** is to clone one user's settings to apply to another user. For example, if we want to clone the user jyom so that user ebosze gets the same quota values, we would enter this command:

```
[root@ford]# edquota -p jyom ebosze
```

Here's one more example: To apply quota settings to a large number of users at once, you can use a little one-line script to do it. Let's assume that all of the affected users have their UIDs at greater than (or equal to) 500, and that at least one user has had their quota set up manually. For our example, we'll call this user artc. The magic line is

```
[root@ford]# edquota -p artc `awk -F: '$3 >> 499 print $1' /etc/passwd`
```

Managing Quotas

Once you have your quotas enabled and working, there are three tools available to help you manage things: `quotacheck`, `repquota`, and `quota`.

The quotacheck Command

The `quotacheck` command verifies the integrity of the quota database. In the script presented earlier for turning on the quota subsystem, we used this technique to do the verification before using `quotaon` to turn on the quotas.

The options you can pass to `quotacheck` are as follows:

`-v`	Turns on verbose mode. This presents useful and interesting information as the quota databases are checked.
`-u uid`	Checks the allocation of the user whose UID is *uid*.
`-g gid`	Checks the allocation of all users whose GID is *gid*.
`-a`	Checks all file systems that have quotas (as determined by the **/etc/fstab** file).
`-r`	Used in conjunction with `-a.` Checks all partitions with quotas, except the root partition.

The repquota Command

The `repquota` command generates a summary report of quota usage on the system. This command takes the following options:

`-a`	Reports on all file systems.
`-v`	Reports on all quotas, even if there is no usage.
`-g`	Reports on quotas for groups only.
`-u`	Reports on quotas for users only.

The quota Command

Finally, the `quota` command is for users. It allows them to view the quota limitations placed on them. It takes the following options:

`-g`	Prints quotas on groups of which the user is a member.

`-u`	Prints quota information about the specific user (default).
`-v`	Prints quota information as it pertains to the user for all file systems that support quotas.
`-q`	Prints a message to the user if he is over quota.

For example, if user sshah were to run **quota -v**, he would see the following:

```
[sshah@ford ~]% quota -v
Disk quotas for user sshah (uid 500):
     File system blocks    quota   limit    grace   files  quota  limit  grace
     /dev/hda8        0        0       0                0      0      0
     /dev/hdb1        0     5000    5100                0   1000   1100
```

SUMMARY

In this chapter, we covered the process of administering your file systems, from creating them to applying quotas to them. With this information, you're armed with what you need in order to manage a commercial-level Linux server in a variety of environments.

Like any operating system, Linux undergoes changes from time to time. Although the designers and maintainers of the file systems go to great lengths to keep the interface the same, you'll find some alterations cropping up from time to time. Sometimes they'll be interface simplifications. Others will be dramatic improvements in the file system itself. Keep your eyes open for these changes. Linux provides a superb file system that is robust, responsive, and in general a pleasure to use. Take the tools we have discussed in this chapter and find out for yourself.

CHAPTER 9

Core System Services

Regardless of distribution, network configuration, and overall system design, every Linux system has five core services: **init**, **inetd**, **xinetd**, **syslog**, and **cron**. The functions performed by these services may be simple, but they are also fundamental. Without their presence, a great deal of Linux's power would be missed.

In this chapter, we'll discuss each one of the core services, its corresponding configuration file, and the suggested method of deployment (if appropriate). You'll find that the sections covering these simple services are not terribly long, but don't neglect this material. We highly recommend taking some time to get familiar with their implications (perhaps during those lovely commutes through traffic every morning). Many creative solutions have been realized through the use of these services. Hopefully, this chapter will inspire a few more.

THE INIT SERVICE

The **init** process is the patron of all processes. *Always* the first process that gets started in any UNIX-based system (such as Linux), **init**'s process ID is always 1. Should **init** ever fail, the rest of the system will most definitely follow suit.

The **init** process serves two roles: The first is being the ultimate parent process. Because **init** never dies, the system can always be sure of its presence and, if necessary, make reference to it. The need to refer to **init** usually happens when a process dies before all of its spawned children processes have completed. This causes the children to inherit **init** as their parent process. A quick execution of the **ps -af** command will show a number of processes that will have a parent process ID (PPID) of 1.

The second job for **init** is to handle the various runlevels by executing the appropriate programs when a particular runlevel is reached. This behavior is defined by the **/etc/inittab** file.

The /etc/inittab File

The **/etc/inittab** file contains all the information **init** needs for starting runlevels. The format of each line in this file is as follows:

```
id:runlevels:action:process
```

NOTE: Lines beginning with the number symbol (#) are comments. Take a peek at your own **/etc/inittab**, and you'll find that it's already liberally commented. If you ever do need to make a change to **/etc/inittab** (and it's unlikely that you'll ever need to), you'll do yourself a favor by including liberal comments to explain what you've done.

Table 9-1 explains the significance of each of the four items in the **/etc/inittab** file's line format.

Table 9-2 defines the options available for the *action* field in the **/etc/inittab** file.

/etc/inittab Item	Description
id	A unique sequence of 1–4 characters that identifies this entry in the **/etc/inittab** file.
runlevels	The runlevels at which the process should be invoked. Some events are special enough that they can be trapped at all runlevels (for instance the CTRL-ALT-DEL key combination to reboot). To indicate that an event is applicable to all runlevels, leave **runlevels** blank. If you want something to occur at multiple runlevels, simply list all of them in this field. For example, the **runlevels** entry **123** specifies something that runs at runlevels 1, 2, and 3.
action	Describes what action should be taken. Options for this field are explained in Table 9-2.
process	Names the process (program) to execute when the runlevel is entered.

Table 9-1.   Description of Each Item in the **/etc/inittab** File's Line Format

Values for *action* Field in /etc/inittab File	Description
respawn	The process will be restarted whenever it terminates.
wait	The process will be started once when the runlevel is entered, and **init** will wait for its completion.
once	The process will be started once when the runlevel is entered; however, **init** won't wait for termination of the process before possibly executing additional programs to be run at that particular runlevel.
boot	The process will be executed at system boot. The **runlevels** field is ignored in this case.
bootwait	The process will be executed at system boot, and **init** will wait for completion of the boot before advancing to the next process to be run.

Table 9-2.   Options Available for the *action* Field in the **/etc/inittab** File

Values for *action* Field in /etc/inittab File	Description
ondemand	The process will be executed when a specific runlevel request occurs. (These runlevels are **a**, **b**, and **c**.) No change in runlevel occurs.
initdefault	Specifies the default runlevel for **init** on startup. If no default is specified, the user is prompted for a runlevel on console.
sysinit	The process will be executed during system boot, before any of the **boot** or **bootwait** entries.
powerwait	If **init** receives a signal from another process that there are problems with the power, this process will be run. Before continuing, **init** will wait for this process to finish.
powerfail	Same as **powerwait**, except that **init** will not wait for the process to finish.
powerokwait	If **init** receives the same type of signal as **powerwait**, when a file called **/etc/powerstatus** exists with the string "OK" in it, this process will be executed, and **init** will wait for its completion.
ctrlaltdel	The process is executed when **init** receives a signal indicating that the user has pressed CTRL-ALT-DEL. Keep in mind that most X Windows servers capture this key-combination, and thus **init** will not receive this signal if X Windows is active.

Table 9-2.　　Options Available for the *action* Field in the **/etc/inittab** File *(continued)*

Now let's look at a sample line from an **/etc/inittab** file:

```
# If power was restored before the shutdown kicked in, cancel it.
pr:12345:powerokwait:/sbin/shutdown -c "Power Restored; Shutdown Cancelled"
```

In this case:

▼ **pr** is the unique identifier

■ **1, 2, 3, 4,** and **5** are the runlevels from which this process can be activated

■ **powerokwait** is the condition under which the process is run

▲ The **/sbin/shutdown** ... command is the process

The telinit Command

It's time to fess up: The mysterious force that tells **init** when to change runlevels is actually the **telinit** command. This command takes two command-line parameters: One is being the desired runlevel that **init** needs to know about, and the other is **-t** *sec*, where *sec* is the number of seconds to wait before telling **init**.

NOTE: Whether **init** actually changes runlevels is its decision. Obviously, it usually does, or this command wouldn't be terribly useful.

It is extremely rare that you'll ever have to run the **telinit** command yourself. Usually, this is all handled for you by the startup and shutdown scripts.

NOTE: Under most UNIX implementations (including Linux), the **telinit** command is really just a symbolic link to the **init** program. Because of this, some folks prefer running **init** with the runlevel they want rather than using **telinit**. Personally, I find that using **telinit** to change runlevels self-documents much more nicely.

THE INETD AND XINETD PROCESSES

The **inetd** and **xinetd** programs are daemon processes. You probably know that daemons are special programs that, after starting, voluntarily release control of the terminal from which they started. The only mechanism by which daemons can interface with the rest of the system is through interprocess communication (IPC) channels, by sending entries to the system-wide log file, or by appending to a disk file.

The role of **inetd** is as a "superserver" for other network server-related processes, such as **telnet** and **ftp**. It's a simple philosophy: Not all server processes (including those that accept new **telnet** and **ftp** connections) are called upon so often that they require a program to be running in memory all the time. So instead of constantly maintaining potentially dozens of services loaded in memory waiting to be used, they are all listed in **inetd**'s configuration file, **/etc/inetd.conf**. On their behalf, **inetd** listens for incoming connections. Thus only a single process needs to be in memory.

A secondary benefit of **inetd** falls to those processes needing network connectivity but whose programmers do not want to have to write it into the system. The **inetd** program will handle the network code and pass incoming network streams into the process as its standard-in (**stdin**). Any of the process's output (**stdout**) is sent back to the host that has connected to the process.

NOTE: Unless you are programming, you don't have to be concerned with **inetd**'s **stdin/stdout** feature. On the other hand, for someone who wants to write a simple script and make it available through the network, it's worth exploring this very powerful tool.

As a general rule of thumb, low-volume services (such as Telnet) are usually best run through the **inetd**, whereas higher-volume services (such as Web servers) are better run as a stand-alone process that is always in memory ready to handle requests.

As of Red Hat 7.0, the Red Hat distribution started using a newer version of **inetd** called **xinetd**. The **xinetd** program accomplishes the same task as the regular **inetd** program, yet it includes a new configuration file format and some additional features.

Unfortunately, **xinetd** uses a format that is very different than the classic **inetd** configuration file format. (Most if not all other variants of UNIX, including Solaris and FreeBSD, use the classic **inetd** format.) This means that if you have an application that relies on **inetd**, you may need to provide some hand adjustments to make it work. Of course, you should definitely contact the developers of the application and let them know of the change so that they can release a newer version that works with the new **xinetd** configuration format, as well.

In this section, we will begin with covering the classic **inetd** format. You will find this format to still be in use with other Linux distributions and versions of Red Hat older than 7.0. We will then cover the **xinetd** format in a separate section so that the differences between the two are clear.

The /etc/inetd.conf File

The **/etc/inetd.conf** file is the configuration file for **inetd**. Its structure is very simple: Each line represents a service. Any line beginning with the number symbol (#) is a comment. The format of a service description line follows.

```
srvce_name sock_type protocol wait/nowait user srvr_prog srvr_prog_args
```

Table 9-3 explains each element of the service descriptions in **/etc/inetd.conf**.

Column Name	Description
srvce_name	The name of the service being offered. This has a correlation to the **/etc/services** file, which maps the name of the service to the port on which it is offered. If you need to add something new to **/etc/inetd.conf**, you'll also need to add a corresponding entry to **/etc/services**. (Don't worry, the format of the **/etc/services** file is inconsequential.)

Table 9-3.　Elements of the Service Descriptions in **/etc/inetd.conf**

Column Name	Description
sock_type	Socket type can be either **stream** or **dgram**. The **stream** value refers to connection-oriented (TCP) data streams (for example, **telnet** and **ftp**). The **dgram** value refers to datagram (UDP) streams (for example, the **tftp** service is a datagram-based protocol). Other protocols outside the scope of TCP/IP do exist; however, you'll rarely encounter them.
protocol	This will be a value as defined in the **/etc/protocols** file—typically **tcp**, **udp**, or **rpc/tcp** for RPC-based TCP services, and **rpc/udp** for RPC-based UDP services.
wait/nowait	May be either **wait** or **nowait**. For any stream (TCP)-based connections, you should use **nowait**. For other connections, the value depends on the type of datagram connection supported by the process. The **wait** value means the client will connect to the server and wait for a response before dropping the connection. (This is often called a "single-threaded" server, because it can only handle one request at a time.) The **nowait** value means the client will disconnect once it has sent its information.
user	The process will run as the service defined in this entry. *Be very careful with this entry*—an incorrect choice may constitute a security hazard. In general, try to select services that can be run as a nonroot user. If you must run a service that has to start as root, be sure the program is well designed, and read all of its documentation to ensure that you have it configured correctly.
srvr_prog	This is the full path of the program that is to be executed when connected to.
srvr_prog_args	The name of the program, plus the arguments that go with that program. For example, let's say the full path to **srvr-prog** (defined in the previous entry) is **/usr/bin/in.fingerd** and you want to pass the **-l** option to it. In this case, **srvr_prog** would read **/usr/bin/in.fingerd**, and **srvr_prog_args** would read **in.fingerd -l**.

Table 9-3. Elements of the Service Descriptions in **/etc/inetd.conf**

Now here is an example entry from the **/etc/inted.conf** file:

```
#
# These are standard services.
#
ftp     stream  tcp     nowait  root    /usr/sbin/tcpd  in.ftpd -l -a
telnet  stream  tcp     nowait  root    /usr/sbin/tcpd  in.telnetd
```

In this example, you see two service entries: **ftp** and **telnet**. Both are stream-TCP services that are immediately run as the root user when invoked. Notice that instead of the service being called directly, it is called via the **/usr/sbin/tcpd** program, better known as TCP Wrappers. The TCP Wrappers program accepts the connection on behalf of the program, logs the request, and checks both the **/etc/hosts.allow** and **/etc/hosts.deny** files to determine whether the client host is allowed to connect to these services. If everything checks out, control of the connection is passed to the appropriate daemon.

> **NOTE:** TCP Wrappers is an external program and not part of the base **inetd** package.

Security and inetd.conf

You'll find that in most installations of Linux, many services are turned on by default. If your system will be available to the Internet at large (this includes being connected via dial-up PPP), the first thing you'll want to do is turn everything off! *Never* assume that just because your system is unadvertised to the public, other people won't find it. On the contrary—tools to scan large networks for systems potentially vulnerable to security attacks are easily found and utilized.

The first step to turning off services is to comment out every unnecessary service in the **/etc/inetd.conf** file. For example, is it necessary that you offer a gopher server? Will you ever use it? Will your users ever use it? If not, then comment it out.

> **NOTE:** In general, you'll find that it's easier to comment out everything (effectively turning off the network services) and then selectively turning on services again after you've had a chance to think about the implications of doing so.

Once you've made the desired changes to **/etc/inetd.conf**, you'll need to alert the daemon that the configuration file has changed. This is done by sending the HUP signal to the daemon. Begin by finding the process ID for **inetd.conf** with the following command:

```
[root@ford /root]# ps auxw | grep inetd | grep -v grep
```

This will have output resembling the following:

```
root       359  0.0  0.1  1232   168 ?        S    Jun21   0:00 inetd
```

The second column tells us the process number (here, 359). To send the HUP signal, we use the **kill** command. (Naming this program **kill** is misleading, unfortunately. In reality, it only sends signals to processes. By default, it sends the signal requesting that a program terminate.)

Here's how to send a HUP signal with the **kill** command:

```
[root@ford /root]# kill -1 359
```

where you'd replace **359** with the process number you derived from your system.

> *TIP:* Another way to send a HUP signal to **inetd** without needing to find its process ID first is via the **killall** command, like so: [root@ford /root]# **killall -1 inetd**

The /etc/xinetd.conf File

The **/etc/xinetd.conf** file consists of a series of blocks that take the following format:

```
blockname
{
    variable = value
}
```

where **blockname** is the name of the block that is being defined, **variable** is the name of a variable being defined within the context of the block, and **value** is the value assigned to the **variable**. Every block can have multiple variables defined within.

One special block exists which is called "default." Whatever variables are defined within this block are applied to all other blocks that are defined in the file.

An exception to the block format is the **includedir** directive, which tells **xinetd** to go read all the files in a directory and consider them to be part of the **/etc/xinetd.conf** file.

Like the **/etc/inetd.conf** file, any line that begins with a number sign (#) is the start of a comment. The stock **/etc/inetd.conf** file that ships with Red Hat 7.0 looks like this:

```
#
# Simple configuration file for xinetd
#
# Some defaults, and include /etc/xinetd.d/

defaults
{
        instances               = 60
        log_type                = SYSLOG authpriv
        log_on_success          = HOST PID
        log_on_failure          = HOST RECORD
}
```

```
includedir /etc/xinetd.d
```

Don't worry if all of the variables and values aren't familiar to you yet; we will go over those in a moment. Let's first make sure you understand the format of the file.

In this example, the first four lines of the file are comments explaining what the file is and what it does. After the comments, you see the first block: **defaults**. The first variable that is defined in this block is **instances**, which is set to the value of 60. Four variables in total are defined in this block, the last one being **log_on_failure**. Since this block is titled **defaults**, the variables that are set within it will apply to all future blocks that are defined. Finally, the last line of the file specifies that the **/etc/xinetd.d** directory must be examined for other files that contain more configuration information. This will cause **xinetd** to read all of the files in that directory and parse them as if they were part of the **/etc/xinetd.conf** file.

Variables and Their Meanings

The variable names that are supported by **xinetd** are as follows:

Variable	Description
Id	This attribute is used to uniquely identify a service. This is useful because services exist that can use different protocols and need to be described with different entries in the configuration file. By default, the service ID is the same as the service name.
Type	Any combination of the following values may be used: **RPC** if this is an RPC service, **INTERNAL** if this service is provided by **xinetd**, or **UNLISTED** if this is a service not listed in the **/etc/services** file.
Disable	This is either the value **yes** or **no**. A **yes** value means that although the service is defined, it is not available for use.
socket_type	Valid values for this variable are **stream** to indicate that this service is a stream-based service, **dgram** to indicate that this service is a datagram, or **raw** to indicate that this service uses raw IP datagrams. The **stream** value refers to connection-oriented (TCP) data streams (for example, telnet and ftp). The **dgram** value refers to datagram (UDP) streams (for example, the tftp service is a datagram-based protocol). Other protocols outside the scope of TCP/IP do exist; however, you'll rarely encounter them.

Variable	Description
`Protocol`	Determines the type of protocol (either **tcp** or **udp**) for the connection type.
`Wait`	If this is set to **yes**, only one connection will be processed at a time. If this is set to **no**, multiple connections will be allowed by running the appropriate service daemon multiple times.
`User`	Specifies the username under which this service will run. The username must exist in the **/etc/passwd** file.
`Group`	Specifies the group name under which this service will run. The group must exist in the **/etc/group** file.
`Instances`	Specifies the maximum number of concurrent connections this service is allowed to handle. The default is no limit if the **wait** variable is set to **nowait**.
`Server`	The name of the program to run when this service is connected.
`server_args`	The arguments passed to the server. In contrast to **inetd**, the name of the server should not be included in **server_args**.
`only_from`	Specifies the networks from which a valid connection may arrive. (This is the built-in TCP Wrappers functionality.) You can specify this in one of three ways: a numeric address, a host name, or a network address with netmask. The numeric address can take the form of a complete IP address to indicate a specific host (e.g., 192.168.1.1). However, if any of the ending octets are zeros, the address will be treated like a network where all of the octets that are zero are wildcards (e.g., 192.168.1.0 means any host that starts with the numbers 192.168.1). Alternately, you can specify the number of bits in the netmask after a slash (e.g., 192.168.1.0/24 means a network address of 192.168.1.0 with a netmask of 255.255.255.0). For more information on IP addresses, network addresses, and netmasks, read Chapter 24.
`no_access`	The opposite of **only_from** in that instead of specifying the addresses from which a connection is valid, this variable specifies the addresses from which a connection is invalid. It can take the same type of parameters as **only_from**.

Variable	Description
`log_type`	Determines where logging information for that service will go. There are two valid values: **SYSLOG** and **FILE**. If **SYSLOG** is specified, you must also specify to which syslog facility to log, as well (see "The syslogd Daemon," later in this chapter, for more information on facilities). For example, you can specify: `log_type = SYSLOG local0` Optionally, you can include the log level, as well. For example: `log_type = SYSLOG local0 info` If **FILE** is specified, you must specify to which filename to log. Optionally, you can also specify the soft limit on the file size. The soft limit on a file size is where an extra log message indicating that the file has gotten too large will be generated. If the soft limit is specified, a hard limit can also be specified. At the hard limit, no additional logging will be done. If the hard limit is not explicitly defined, it is set to be 1% higher than the soft limit. An example of the **FILE** option is as follows: `log_type = FILE /var/log/mylog`
`log_on_success`	Specifies which information is logged on a connection success. The options include **PID** to log the process ID of the service that processed the request, **HOST** to specify the remote host connecting to the service, **USERID** to log the remote username (if available), **EXIT** to log the exit status or termination signal of the process, or **DURATION** to log the length of the connection.
`Port`	Specifies the network port under which the service will run. If the service is listed in **/etc/services**, this port number must equal the value specified there.
`Interface`	Allows a service to bind to a specific interface and only be available there. The value is the IP address of the interface that you wish this service to be bound to. An example of this is binding less secure services (such as Telnet) to an internal and physically secure interface on a firewall and not allowing it the external, more vulnerable interface outside the firewall. (See Chapter 26 for more details on firewalls.)

Variable	Description
cps	The first argument specifies the maximum number of connections per second this service is allowed to handle. If the rate exceeds this value, the service is temporarily disabled for the second argument number of seconds. For example: cps = 10 30 This will disable a service for 30 seconds if the connection rate ever exceeds 10 connections per second.

You do not need to specify all of the variables in defining a service. The only required ones are

▼ `socket_type`

■ `user`

■ `server`

▲ `wait`

An Example of a Simple Service Entry

Using the finger service as an example, let's take a look at one of the simplest entries possible with **xinetd**:

```
# default: on
# description: The finger server answers finger requests. Finger is \
#        a protocol that allows remote users to see information such \
#        as login name and last login time for local users.
service finger
{
        socket_type     = stream
        wait            = no
        user            = nobody
        server          = /usr/sbin/in.fingerd
}
```

In Red Hat 7.0, you can find this file in **/etc/xinetd.d/finger**.

THE SYSLOGD DAEMON

With so much going on at any one time, especially with services that are disconnected from a terminal window, it's necessary to provide a standard mechanism by which special events and messages can be logged. Linux uses the **syslogd** daemon to provide this service.

The **syslogd** daemon provides a standardized means of performing logging. Many other UNIXs employ a compatible daemon, thus providing a means for cross-platform logging over the network. This is especially valuable in a large heterogeneous environment where it's necessary to centralize the collection of log entries to gain an accurate picture of what's going on. You could equate this system of logging facilities to the Windows NT System Logger.

The log files that **syslogd** stores to are straight text files, usually stored in the **/var/log** directory. Each log entry consists of a single line containing the date, time, hostname, process name, process PID, and the message from that process. A system-wide function in the standard C library provides an easy mechanism for generating log messages. If you don't feel like writing code but want to generate entries in the logs, you have the option of using the **logger** command.

As you can imagine, a tool with **syslogd**'s importance is something that gets started as part of the boot scripts. Every Linux distribution you would use in a server environment will already do this for you.

Invoking syslogd

If you do find a need to either start **syslogd** manually or modify the script that starts it up at boot, you'll need to be aware of **syslogd**'s command-line parameters, shown in Table 9-4.

The /etc/syslog.conf File

The **/etc/syslog.conf** file contains the configuration information that **syslogd** needs to run. This file's format is a little unusual, but the default configuration file you have will probably suffice unless you begin needing to seek out specific information in specific files or sent to remote logging machines.

Log Message Classifications

Before you can understand the **/etc/syslog.conf** file format itself, you have to understand how log messages get classified. Each message has a *facility* and a *priority*. The facility tells us from which subsystem the message originated, and the priority tells us how important the message is. These two values are separated by a period.

Both values have string equivalents, making them easier to remember. The string equivalents for facility and priority are listed in Tables 9-5 and 9-6, respectively.

Parameter	Description
-d	Debug mode. Normally, at startup, **syslogd** detaches itself from the current terminal and starts running in the background. With the **-d** option, **syslogd** retains control of the terminal and prints debugging information as messages are logged. It's extremely unlikely that you'll need this option.
-f *config*	Specifies a configuration file as an alternative to the default **/etc/syslog.conf**.
-h	By default, **syslogd** does not forward messages sent to it that were really destined for another host. *Caution:* If you use this parameter, you run the risk of being used as part of a denial of service attack.
-l hostlist	This option lets you list the hosts for which you are willing to perform logging. Each host name should be its simple name, not its fully qualified domain name (FQDN). You can list multiple hosts, as long as they are separated by a colon; for example, -l toybox:ford:oid.
-m interval	By default, **syslogd** generates a log entry every 20 minutes as a "just so you know, I'm running" message. This is for systems that may not be busy. (If you're watching the system log and don't see a single message in over 20 minutes, you'll know for a fact that something has gone wrong.) By specifying a numeric value for interval, you can indicate the number of minutes **syslogd** should wait before generating another message.
-r	By default, as a security precaution, the **syslogd** daemon refuses messages sent to it from the network. This command-line parameter enables this feature.
-s domainlist	If you are receiving **syslogd** entries that show the entire FQDN, you can have **syslogd** strip off the domain name and leave just the host name. Simply list the domain names to remove in a colon-separated list as the parameter to the -s option. For example, -s x-files.com:conspiracy.com:wealthy.com

Table 9-4.   **syslogd** Command-Line Parameters

Facility String Equivalent	Description
`auth`	Authentication messages.
`authpriv`	Essentially the same as **auth**.
`cron`	Messages generated by the **cron** subsystem (see "The cron Program," later in this chapter).
`daemon`	Generic classification for service daemons.
`kern`	Kernel messages.
`lpr`	Printer subsystem messages.
`mail`	Mail subsystem messages (including per mail logs).
`mark`	Obsolete, but you may find some books that discuss it; **syslogd** simply ignores it.
`news`	Messages through the NNTP subsystem.
`security`	Same thing as **auth**; should not be used.
`syslog`	Internal messages from **syslog** itself.
`user`	Generic messages from user programs.
`uucp`	Messages from the UUCP (UNIX to UNIX CoPy) subsystem.
`local0 - local9`	Generic facility levels whose importance can be decided based on your needs.

Table 9-5. String Equivalents for the Facility Value in **/etc/syslog.conf**

NOTE: The priority levels are in the order of severity according to **syslogd**. Thus **debug** is not considered severe at all, and **emerg** is the most crucial. For example, the combination facility-and-priority string **mail.crit** indicates there is a critical error in the mail subsystem (for example, it has run out of disk space). **syslogd** considers this message more important than **mail.info**, which may simply note the arrival of another message.

syslogd also understands wildcards. Thus, you can define a whole class of messages; for instance, **mail.*** refers to all messages related to the mail subsystem.

Priority String Equivalent	Description
debug	Debugging statements.
info	Miscellaneous information.
notice	Important statements, but not necessarily bad news.
warning	Potentially dangerous situation.
warn	Same as **warning**; should not be used.
err	An error condition.
error	Same as **err**; should not be used.
crit	Critical situation.
alert	A message indicating an important occurrence.
emerg	An emergency situation.

Table 9-6.   String Equivalents for Priority Levels in **/etc/syslog.conf**

Format of /etc/syslog.conf

Here is the format of each line in the configuration file:

```
facility/priority combinations separated by commas     file/process/host to log to
```

For example:

```
kern.info, kern.emerg /ver/log/kerned
```

The location to which **syslogd** can send log messages is also quite flexible. It can save messages to files and send messages to FIFOs, to a list of users, or (in the case of centralized logging for a large site) to a master log host. To differentiate these location elements, the following rules are applied to the location entry:

▼   If the location begins with a slash (/), the message is going to a file.

■   If the location begins with a pipe (|), the message is going to a FIFO.

▲   If the location begins with an @, the message is going to a host.

Table 9-7 shows examples of location entries according to these rules.

Location Style	Description
`/var/log/logfile`	A file. Note: If you prefix the filename with a dash, `syslogd` will not synchronize the file system after the write. This means you run the risk of losing some data if there is a crash before the system gets a chance to flush its buffers. On the other hand, if an application is being overly verbose about its logging, you'll gain performance using this option. Remember: If you want messages sent to the console, you need to specify **/dev/console**.
`|/tmp/mypipe`	A pipe. This type of file is created with the **mknod** command (see Chapter 6). With `syslogd` feeding one side of the pipe, you can have another program running that reads the other side of the pipe. This is an effective way to have programs parsing log output, looking for critical situations, so that you can be paged if necessary.
`@loghost`	A host name. This example will send the message to **loghost**. The `syslogd` daemon on **loghost** will then record the message.

Table 9-7.   Examples of Location Entries

If you enter no special character before the location entry, **syslogd** assumes that the location is a comma-separated list of users who will have the message written to their screen.

If you use an asterisk (*), **syslogd** will send the message to all of the users who are logged in.

As usual, any line that begins with a number symbol (#) is a comment.

Now let's look at some examples of configuration file entries:

```
# Log all the mail messages in one place.
mail.* /var/log/maillog
```

This example shows that all priorities in the mail facility should have their messages placed in the **/var/log/maillog** file.

Consider the next example:

```
# Everybody gets emergency messages, plus log them on another
# machine.
*.emerg                                    @loghost,sshah,hdc,root
```

In this example, you see that any facility with a log level of **emerg** is sent to another system running **syslogd** called **loghost**. Also, if the user hdc, sshah, or root is logged in, the message being logged is written to the user's console.

You can also specify multiple selectors on a single line for a single event. For example:

```
*.info;mail.none;authpriv.none                  /var/log/messages
```

Sample /etc/syslog.conf File

Following is a complete **syslog.conf** file:

```
# Log all kernel messages to the console.
# Logging much else clutters up the screen.
#kern.*                                          /dev/console

# Log anything (except mail) of level info or higher.
# Don't log private authentication messages!
*.info;mail.none;authpriv.none                   /var/log/messages

# The authpriv file has restricted access.
authpriv.*                                       /var/log/secure

# Log all the mail messages in one place.
mail.*                                           /var/log/maillog
# Everybody gets emergency messages, plus log them on another
# machine.
*.emerg                                          *

# Save mail and news errors of level err and higher in a
# special file.
uucp,news.crit                                   /var/log/spooler

# Save boot messages also to boot.log
local7.*                                         /var/log/boot.log
```

THE CRON PROGRAM

The **cron** program allows any user in the system to schedule a program to run on any date, at any time, or on a particular day of week, down to the minute. Using **cron** is an extremely efficient way to automate your system, generate reports on a regular basis, and perform other periodic chores. (Not-so-honest uses of **cron** include having it invoke a system to have you paged when you want to get out of a meeting!)

Like the other services we've discussed in this chapter, **cron** is started by the boot scripts and is most likely already configured for you. A quick check of the process listing should show it quietly running in the background:

```
[root@ford /root]# ps auxw | grep cron | grep -v grep
root        341  0.0  0.0  1284  112 ?         S    Jun21   0:00 crond
[root@ford /root]#
```

The **cron** service works by waking up once a minute and checking each user's **crontab** file. This file contains the user's list of events that they want executed at a particular date and time. Any events that match the current date and time are executed.

The **crond** command itself requires no command-line parameters or special signals to indicate a change in status.

The crontab File

The tool that allows you to edit entries to be executed by **crond** is **crontab**. Essentially, all it does is verify your permission to modify your **cron** settings and then invoke a text editor so you can make your changes. Once you're done, **crontab** places the file in the right location and brings you back to a prompt.

Whether or not you have appropriate permission is determined by **crontab** by checking the **/etc/cron.allow** and **/etc/cron.deny** files. If either of these files exists, you must be explicitly listed there for your actions to be effected. For example, if the **/etc/cron.allow** file exists, your username must be listed in that file in order for you to be able to edit your **cron** entries. On the other hand, if the only file that exists is **/etc/cron.deny**, unless your username is listed there, you are implicitly allowed to edit your **cron** settings.

The file listing your **cronjobs** (often referred to as the **crontab** file) is formatted as follows. All values must be listed as integers.

```
Minute Hour Day Month DayOfWeek Command
```

If you want to have multiple entries for a particular column (for instance, you want a program to run at 4:00 A.M., 12:00 P.M., and 5:00 P.M.), then you need to have each of these time values in a comma-separated list. Be sure not to type any spaces in the list. For the program running at 4:00 A.M., 12:00 P.M., and 5:00 P.M., the **Hour** values list would read **4,12,17**. Notice that **cron** uses military time format.

For the **DayOfWeek** entry, 0 represents Sunday, 1 represents Monday, and so on, all the way to 6 representing Saturday.

Any entry that has a single asterisk (*) wildcard will match any minute, hour, day, month, or day of week when used in the corresponding column.

When the dates and times in the file match the current date and time, the command is run as the user who set the **crontab**. Any output generated is e-mailed back to the user. Obviously, this can result in a mailbox full of messages, so it is important to be thrifty with your reporting. A good way to keep a handle on volume is to output only error conditions and have any unavoidable output sent to **/dev/null**.

Let's look at some examples. The following entry runs the program **/usr/bin/ping -c 5 zaphod** every four hours:

```
0 0,4,8,12,16,20 * * * /usr/bin/ping -c 5 zaphod
```

Here is an entry that runs the program **/usr/local/scripts/backup_level_0** at 10:00 P.M. on every Friday night:

```
0 22 * * 5 /usr/local/scripts/backup_level_0
```

And finally, here's a script to send out an e-mail at 4:01 A.M. on April 1 (whatever day that may be):

```
1 4 1 4 * /bin/mail dad@domain.com < /home/sshah/joke
```

NOTE: When **crond** executes commands, it does so with the **sh** shell. Thus, any environment variables that you might be used to may not work within **cron**.

SUMMARY

In this chapter, we discussed the five core services that come with every Linux system. These services do not require network support and can vary from host to host, making them very useful, since they can work regardless of whether or not the system is in multiuser mode.

A quick recap of the chapter:

▼   **init** is the father of all processes in the system with a PID of 1. It also controls runlevels and can be configured through the **/etc/iniitab** file.

■   **inetd** is the superserver that listens to server requests on behalf of a large number of smaller, less frequently used services. When it accepts a request for one of those services, **inetd** starts the actual service and quietly forwards data between the network and actual service. Its configuration file is **/etc/inetd.conf**.

■   **xinetd** is the "new" version of the classic inetd superserver that offers more configuration options and better built-in security. Its configuration file is **/etc/xinetd.conf**.

■   **syslog** is the system-wide logging daemon. Along with log entries generated by the system, **syslog** can accept log messages over the network (so long as you enable that feature). Its configuration file is **/etc/syslog.conf**.

▲   Finally, the **cron** service allows you to schedule events to take place at certain dates and times, which is great for periodic events like backups and e-mail reminders. All the configuration files on which it relies are handled via the **crontab** program.

In each section of this chapter, we discussed how to configure a different service and even suggested some uses beyond the default settings that come with the system. I highly recommend that you poke around these services and familiarize yourself with what can be accomplished with them. I've written several powerful data collection and analysis tools that required things like **cron** and **syslog** to work, as well as some wonderfully silly and useless things. *Don't be afraid to have fun with it!*

CHAPTER 10

Compiling the Linux Kernel

One of Linux's greatest strengths is that its source code is available to anyone who wishes to peer inside. The GNU GPL (general public license) under which Linux is distributed even allows you to tinker with the source code and distribute your changes! Real changes to the source code (at least, those to be taken seriously) go through the process of joining the official kernel tree. This requires extensive testing and proof that the changes will benefit Linux as a whole. At the very end of the approval process, the code gets a final yes or no from a core group of the Linux project's original developers who have the trust of Linus Torvalds. It is this extensive review process that keeps the quality of Linux's code so noteworthy.

NOTE: Linux's core development group is geographically quite diverse. Key people include Alan Cox in the U.K., Alexey Kuznetsov in Moscow, and Linus himself in Northern California's Silicon Valley.

For systems administrators who have used other operating systems, this approach to code control is a significant departure from the philosophy of waiting for the company to release a patch, service release, or some sort of "hot fix." Instead of having to wade through public relations, sales engineers, and other front-end units, you have the option of contacting the author of the subsystem directly and explaining your problem. A patch can be created and sent to you before the next official release of the kernel, and get you up and running.

Of course, the flip side of this working arrangement is that you need to be able to compile a kernel yourself rather than rely on someone else to supply precompiled code. And, of course, you won't have to do this often, because production environments, once stable, rarely need a kernel compile. But if need be, you should know what to do. Luckily, it's not difficult.

NOTE: Not so long ago, most commercial UNIX-based operating systems required that their kernels be *relinked* whenever configuration changes were made. The process of relinking the kernel essentially involves taking all of the individual components of the kernel and gluing them together. This allows sites to add and remove components should they decide to make more efficient use of their available hardware. (Note that the individual components that were linked together were pre-compiled modules, not source code.) However, since the advent of dynamically loaded modules (discussed in more detail later this chapter), most UNIX systems have removed the need for this step.

In this chapter, we'll walk through the process of acquiring a kernel source tree, configuring it, compiling it, and finally, installing the result.

CAUTION: The kernel is the first thing that loads when a Linux system is booted. If the kernel doesn't work right, it's unlikely that the rest of the system will boot. Be sure to have an emergency boot disk handy in case you need to revert to an old configuration. Also see the section on LILO in Chapter 7.

WHAT EXACTLY IS A KERNEL?

Before we jump into the process of compiling, let's back up a step and make sure you're clear on the concept of what a kernel is and the role it plays in the system. Most often, a reference to Linux is generally a reference to a Linux *distribution*. As discussed in Chapter 1, a distribution comprises everything necessary to get Linux to exist as a functional operating system in a networked environment. (For example, Red Hat Linux is a distribution.) Distributions contain code from projects that are independent of Linux; in fact, many of these projects can exist on other UNIX-like platforms as well. The GNU C Compiler, for example, which comes with all Linux distributions, also exists on many other operating systems (probably more systems than most people realize exist).

So, then, what *does* make up the pure definition of Linux? The *kernel*. The kernel of any operating system is the core of all the system's software. The only thing more fundamental than the kernel is the hardware itself.

The kernel has many jobs. The essence of its work is to abstract the underlying hardware from the software and provide a running environment for application software. Specifically, the environment must handle issues such as networking, disk access, virtual memory, and multitasking—a complete list of these tasks would take up a chapter in itself! Today's Linux kernel (2.4.0-test9) contains roughly 2.8 million lines of code (including device drivers). By comparison, the sixth edition of UNIX from Bell Labs in 1976 had roughly 9000 lines. Figure 10-1 illustrates the kernel's position in a complete system.

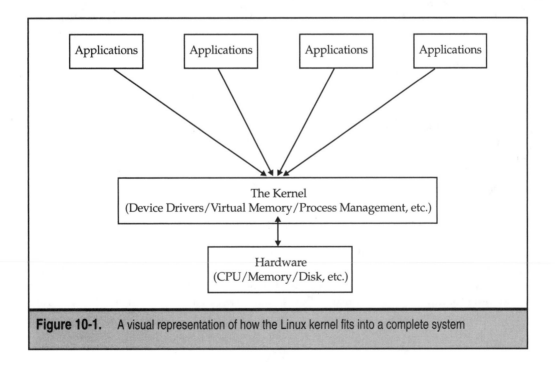

Figure 10-1.   A visual representation of how the Linux kernel fits into a complete system

Although the kernel is a small part of a complete Linux system, it is by far the most critical element. If the kernel fails or crashes, the rest of the system goes with it. Happily, Linux can boast its kernel stability. *Uptimes* (the length of time in between reboots) for Linux systems are often expressed in years. Indeed, UNIX systems in general regularly claim significantly long uptimes. (This author's personal best was 441 days on an actively used server. The reason it went down? The power supplied died.)

FINDING KERNEL SOURCE CODE

Your distribution of Linux probably has the source code to the specific kernel it installed, whatever version that may be. If you find a need to download a different (possibly newer) version, the first place to look for the source code is at the official kernel Web site: http://www.kernel.org. This site contains a listing of Web sites mirroring the kernel source as well as several free tools and general-purpose utilities.

Under the site's link for downloading the kernel, you'll find a list of mirror Web sites based on country codes. Although you can connect to any of them, you'll most likely get the best performance by sticking to your own country. Go to http://www.*xx*.kernel.org, where *xx* is the Internet country code for your country. For the United States, this address is http://www.us.kernel.org.

NOTE: Because of how the online information system distributes load across multiple sites, you may see a different Web page every time you visit. Don't be concerned—all the sites are synchronized every night. Simply follow the links to the directory that stores copies of the kernel in which you're interested.

Getting the Correct Version

The Web site listing of kernels available will contain folders for v1.0, v1.1, and so forth; and v2.2, v2.3, and so forth. Before you follow your natural inclination to get the latest version, make sure you understand how the Linux kernel versioning system works.

Because Linux's development model encourages public contributions, the latest version of the kernel must be accessible to everyone, all the time. This presents a problem, however: Software that is undergoing significant updates may be unstable and not of production quality.

To circumvent this problem, early Linux developers adopted a system of using odd-numbered kernels (1.1, 1.3, 2.1, 2.3, and so on) to indicate a design-and-development cycle. Thus, the odd-numbered kernels carry the disclaimer that they may not be stable and should not be used for situations in which reliability is a must. These kernels typically come out at a very high rate since there is so much development activity—new versions of development kernels can be released as often as twice a week! Of course, this is a good thing for developers, because it allows them to keep careful watch of how things are progressing on all fronts.

On the other hand, even-numbered kernels (1.0, 1.2, 2.0, 2.2, and so on) are considered ready-for-production systems. They have been allowed to mature under the public's usage (and scrutiny). Unlike development kernels, production kernels are released at a much slower rate and only contain bug fixes. It is rare that an even-numbered kernel contains a new feature.

As of this writing, many distributions are gearing up for the upcoming 2.4.0 kernel release. Some distributions such as Red Hat 7.0 are shipping 2.4 ready, but they're running 2.2.16. Because it is more likely that you'll be compiling a 2.4-series kernel than a 2.2-series kernel, this chapter will go through the steps of compiling 2.4.0-test9. However, the basic steps used (**make xconfig, make dep, make clean,** and **make bzImage**) are the same. The only difference will be that the 2.2-series kernel will not have as many configuration options.

CAUTION: The 2.4.0-test9 kernel is considered beta. This means the kernel development group only recommends its usage on systems that are *not* production. If you want to compile a kernel for production use, be sure to compile the latest even-numbered kernel. By the time you read this, it should hopefully be 2.4.*x* where *x* doesn't include the word "test". Because 2.4 should be ready by the time this book hits the shelves, I am covering it instead of a 2.2 kernel.

The 2.4.0-test9 kernel can be found at ftp://ftp.kernel.org/pub/linux/kernel/ v2.4/ linux-2.4.0-test9.tar.gz.

Unpacking the Kernel Source Code

Until now, you've probably seen most packages come in files with the .RPM extension, and you're most likely accustomed to using one of the tools that came with the system (such as **glint** or **gnoRPM**) to install the package. Kernel source code is a little different and requires some user participation. Let's go through the steps to unpack the kernel.

You'll start by renaming the existing tree so that you can revert back to it if the new version doesn't work out. Once the old tree is safe, you'll create a new directory for the version of Linux you're going to unpack. Only then are you ready to unpack it. Overall, it's really a straightforward process.

For the remainder of this chapter, we'll assume you are working out of the **/usr/src** directory. This is the traditional location of the kernel source tree.

Save the Current Source Tree

Before unpacking the new source tree, save and rename the current one. In the directory tree in **/usr/src**, you'll see a directory called **linux**:

```
[root@ford src]# ls -l
total 2
drwxr-xr-x   3 root     root      1024 Oct 16 09:33 linux
```

```
-rw-------    1 root      root    99502080 Oct 16 21:34 linux-2.4.9-test9.tar.gz
drwxr-xr-x    7 root      root        1024 Oct 16 09:36 redhat
[root@ford src]#
```

In the **linux** directory is the current source tree. (Note that some distributions, including Red Hat, do not install the entire source tree by default. Only the necessary files for development purposes are installed.) The safe path to upgrading is to rename the existing tree with a suffix indicating its associated version number. Find out the current version number with the **uname** command, like so:

```
[root@ford src]# uname -r
2.2.16-22
[root@ford src]#
```

In this case, we want to rename the **linux** directory **linux-2.2.16-22**:

```
[root@ford src]# mv linux linux-2.2.16-22
```

> **NOTE:** If someone has previously updated the running kernel, it's possible that the running kernel does not match the sources in **/usr/src/linux**. In this situation, you can find out the version of the kernel by looking at the file **makefile** in the **/usr/src/linux** directory. At the top of the file, you'll see lines indicating version, patch level, and sublevel. If version = 2, patch level = 3, and sublevel = 30, you have kernel version 2.3.30.

Modify the Directory Structure

Now take the opportunity to add some clarity to your directory structure. In our example, we had to use the **uname** command to find out the current version of the kernel and thus what to name the **linux** directory. This works acceptably well the first time around. However, in the event that you need to upgrade multiple times and wish to keep your older kernel source codes, you'll want to find a better way of tracking the association between directories and kernel versions.

So instead of creating a new directory called **linux**, we'll take advantage of the fact that we know we're working with the 2.4.0-test9 kernel. We'll name the directory **linux-2.4.0-test9**.

There is a slight catch to this naming convention. The kernel we've downloaded will automatically unpack into a directory called **linux**. Additionally, development tools that already exist in the system are expecting certain files to be in **/usr/src/linux**, not **/usr/src/linux-2.4.0-test9**. Thus we use a symbolic link, as follows:

```
[root@ford src]# mkdir linux-2.4.0-test9
[root@ford src]# ln -s linux-2.4.0-test9 linux
[root@ford src]# ls -l
total 3
lrwxrwxrwx    1 root      root          12 Oct 12 21:23 linux -> linux-2.4.0-test9
drwx------    2 root      root        1024 Oct 12 21:23 linux-2.4.0-test9
drwxr-xr-x    3 root      root        1024 Oct 16 09:33 linux
```

```
-rw-------    1 root      root   9502080 Oct 16 21:34 linux-2.4.9-test9.tar.gz
drwxr-xr-x    7 root      root      1024 Oct 16 09:36 redhat
[root@ford src]#
```

Unpack the Kernel

Now for the big finish: unpacking the kernel itself. This is done using the **tar** command:

```
[root@ford src]# tar -xzf linux-.2.10.tar.gz
```

You'll hear your hard disk whirl for a bit—it is, after all, a large file! On a Pentium II 350MHz with a reasonably quick IDE drive, this step takes just under two minutes.

> **TIP:** Take a moment to check out what's inside of the kernel source tree. At the very least, you'll get a chance to see what kind of documentation ships with a stock kernel. Developers can also take this chance to learn more about how Linux's innards work.

BUILDING THE KERNEL

So now you have an unpacked kernel tree just waiting to be configured. In this section, we're going to review the process of configuring a kernel. This is in contrast to operating systems such as Windows 2000, which come pre-configured and therefore contain support for many features you may not want.

The Linux design philosophy allows the individual to decide about the important parts of the kernel. (If you don't have a SCSI subsystem, what's the point in wasting memory to support it?) This individualized design has the important benefit of letting you thin down the feature list so that Linux can run on less-powerful systems with the same excellent performance. You may find that a box incapable of supporting Windows 2000 Server is more than enough for a Linux server.

Two steps are required in building a kernel: configuring and compiling. We won't get into the specifics of configuration in this chapter, which would be difficult because of the fast-paced evolution of Linux kernel distributions. However, once you understand the basic process, you should be able to apply it from version to version. For the sake of discussion, we'll cite examples from the v2.4.0-test9 kernel that we unpacked in the previous section.

The make xconfig Process

The first step in building the kernel is configuring its features. Usually your desired feature list will be based on whatever hardware you need to support. This, of course, means that you'll need a list of that hardware. The following command will list all hardware connected to the system via the PCI bus:

```
[root@ford src]# cat /poc/pci
```

NOTE: Looking at the contents of the **/proc/pci** file is not the only way to probe your hardware. I highly recommend taking a look at what else is in the **/proc** file system. Also be sure to check out Chapter 27, which highlights many of the interesting features of the **/proc** file system.

With this list of hardware, you're ready to start configuring the kernel. Begin by starting X Windows with the **startx** command. Once X Windows is up and running, open up a terminal window and enter these commands:

```
[root@ford /root]# cd /usr/src/linux
[root@ford linux]# make xconfig
```

The second command invokes the **make** utility. This development tool helps you create scripts describing all the steps necessary for compiling a program, but other uses for **make** (and many other well-designed tools for UNIX) have been found. One of these uses is to compile and execute the GUI configuration tool. Non-GUI tools exist as well and can be started with the **make config** or **make menuconfig** command.

The **make xconfig** command displays a window like that shown in Figure 10-2. In this opening window, you'll see all the top-level configuration menus. By clicking the buttons, you can open submenus listing all the specific features that you can enable. A default setting exists for most options, but it is recommended that you review all settings to make sure they're set as desired. When you've worked your way through all the menus, click the Save and Exit button.

Linux Kernel Configuration		
Code maturity level options	ATA/IDE/MFM/RLL support	Multimedia devices
Loadable module support	SCSI support	File systems
Processor type and features	IEEE 1394 (FireWire) support	Console drivers
General setup	I2O device support	Sound
Memory Technology Devices (MTD)	Network device support	USB support
Parallel port support	Amateur Radio support	Kernel hacking
Plug and Play configuration	IrDA (infrared) support	
Block devices	ISDN subsystem	Save and Exit
Multi–device support (RAID and LVM)	Old CD–ROM drivers (not SCSI, not IDE)	Quit Without Saving
Networking options	Input core support	Load Configuration from File
Telephony Support	Character devices	Store Configuration to File

Figure 10-2. Opening window for `make xconfig`

Kernel Features and Modules

Figure 10-3 illustrates the General Setup submenu in the configuration utility. The first three columns contain the option buttons Y (Yes), M (Module), and N (No). The fourth column contains the name of the option in question, and the fifth column offers a Help button that will bring up a related window explaining the feature.

Answering Yes or No to enable or disable a kernel feature is simple enough, but let's take a closer look at the very cool *module configuration* option. As a systems administrator, you will find situations where you need a kernel feature only for extremely short periods of time. (An example is support for floppy disks; you'll rarely need this feature, but it's a good idea to have it nonetheless. Enabling that support, on the other hand, means the kernel requires more room in memory, which means less room for applications.)

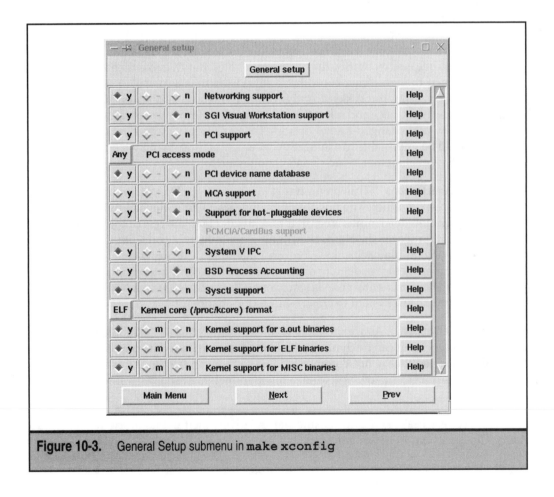

Figure 10-3. General Setup submenu in `make xconfig`

With the module system, the kernel designers have created a way for parts of the kernel, called *modules*, to be dynamically loaded and unloaded from the kernel as needed. Features not often used can thus be enabled but won't waste memory when they aren't being used. Thankfully, the kernel can automatically determine what to load and when; you enjoy the benefits of streamlined running without the burden of having additional management tasks.

NOTE: Traditionally, kernels have been written to require that all components reside in memory at all times, regardless of frequency of use. However, today's typical operating systems (including Linux) only keep in memory the absolute core of the system, which is always needed. Device drivers and certain networking features are now supported as modules.

Naturally, not everything is eligible to be compiled as a module. The kernel must know a few things before it can load and unload modules, such as how to access the hard disk and parse through the file system. If you aren't sure whether a particular feature can be compiled as a module, try it and see. (Note that not everything can be made a module. This is typically because a contributing developer opted not to make their code loadable as a module even though Linux could have supported it as a module.) As long as you have a way of accessing the system configuration (which we'll discuss later in this section), you can always go back and select Yes instead of Module for any configuration option.

Because new and changed kernel options arise as frequently as Linux distributions evolve, it would be impossible to examine every single setting. What we'll do here is take a look at the top-level menus, which don't change much.

Code Maturity Level Options   This menu has only one option: Do you want access to the latest and greatest (and therefore possibly experimental) kernel developments? Your answer to this question determines what items are available in the rest of the menus. Obviously, a production server should not be running experimental code. On the other hand, if you're planning to play with a system on your desk and are willing to take a few chances, that experimental code may offer some beneficial and interesting functions. (In general, even the experimental code is stable enough for day-to-day work. Rarely does a released feature cause a system to crash—but it does happen.)

Loadable Module Support   As we mentioned earlier in this chapter, loadable modules are pieces of the kernel that can be dynamically loaded and unloaded as needed. This is very handy for features that are not commonly used so you can use your available memory wisely. These submenus allow you to set a few parameters available in support for loadable modules.

Processor Type and Features   This is another relatively self-explanatory list of setup items. The 2.2.10 kernel has only four questions:

▼   What kind of processor are you running?

- Do you need math emulation? (Necessary for running the kernel on 386, 386SX, or 486SX systems—yes, they're still out there!)

- Do you want to take advantage of memory registers?

▲ Do you want the kernel to have SMP chipset support? (This lets you take advantage of systems with multiple CPUs.)

General Setup   This menu is critical in the grand scheme of kernel configuration. Your setup decisions here will enable and disable other menus, so choose carefully.

All the options are self-explanatory except the item for binary file-type support: Not too long ago, compiled programs were stored in a file format known as **a.out**. Unfortunately, this scheme had severe limitations when it came to shared libraries, which became more of an issue as UNIX evolved. The ELF format was created to address these limitations and then some. Linux currently uses the ELF binary format for all of its programs. Your system is unlikely to need **a.out** support, and you can safely say No to this option.

Memory Technology Devices   A feature new to the Linux kernel is support for special memory devices like flash cards. This is very handy for smaller systems that need non-volatile memory but don't want to install a disk (common in embedded systems). Unless you have a specific need for a device like that, you can safely ignore this menu.

Parallel Port Support   A lot of new devices that are coming onto the market use the PC parallel port—a domain traditionally reserved for printers—to access the system. If you have such a device, be sure to enable it in this menu. If you don't have any devices that need parallel port support, be sure to slip into this menu and disable the features.

Plug and Play Support   Sometimes this feature is more affectionately called "Plug and *Pray* Support." Linux's support for PnP devices does work; the nature of PC-based hardware, however, makes it unreliable. In general, defining what you need from the system is a safer course than relying on PnP to find it for you.

Block Devices   This menu lists the Linux support options for devices such as hard disks and CD-ROMs, including many options specific to chipsets. Unless you are certain of your particular chipset, you will want to leave these enhancement settings. Linux's default behavior should work fine.

Multi-Device Support (RAID and LVM)   If you want to configure a RAID system on your Linux server, you will need to enable the features in this menu. This includes support for software RAID (which is surprisingly fast) as well as hardware-supported RAID. The Logical Volume Manager (LVM) configuration options are also set through these menus. The LVM allows you to group together several disks and treat them as one large disk. This is different than RAID in that LVM offers no redundancy. For example, if you have two 18G disks and configure them in a RAID 0 mirror, you have a total of 18G of storage. If you tie two 18G disks together in a LVM, you get 36G of storage. However, in the RAID configuration, any one of the disks can fail and you'll still have all your data. If one of the disks fail in the LVM, you're out all 36G. Then again, that's why you have backups.

> **NOTE:**   You can read more about LVM at http://www.linuxdoc.org/HOWTO/LVM-HOWTO.html.

Networking Options   At a minimum, you should enable the UNIX Domain Sockets and TCP/IP Networking options.

One of Linux's greatest claims to fame is its support for complex networking configurations. In fact, Linux code is commonly examined by companies designing commercial networking gear such as routers and switches. (Not too long ago, a major networking manufacturer announced that its latest product is actually based on Linux!) Exploring the details of the networking options is beyond the scope of this chapter. In general, however, I do highly recommend that anyone looking for a general purpose networking solution take a look at what Linux has to offer before investing in an expensive commercial solution.

Telephony Support   This section is for folks who have hardware that supports IP telephony (VoIP). This has nothing to do with modems—you need serial support for modems. Take a gander into this menu if you do have such hardware.

ATA/IDE/MFM/RLL Support   If you have an IDE disk, you will want to peer into this section and see if extra support is available for your chipset. (The Linux default will work with all IDE disks.) If there is extra support, you should enable it so that Linux can get better performance out of your drive.

If you have an older MFM or RLL disk, this section is for you too—and you should consider upgrading soon.

SCSI Support   Set these options to add SCSI support into Linux. If you do require SCSI support, enabling the Verbose Error Reporting is well worth the additional memory required—especially when you're tracking down tricky SCSI errors.

IEEE 1394 (Firewire) Support   Linux now supports the IEEE 1394 Firewire standard, a common protocol used by digital audio/video equipment such as digital cameras. If you have such devices, be sure you have the necessary Firewire hardware for your PC and enable the correct driver in this menu.

I2O Device Support   I2O is an intelligent interface for abstracting the devices from particular operating systems. Devices that support I2O can have a single device driver that is run on special I2O hardware with simple OS-specific driver stubs in the main operating system. This results in faster hardware and less time to market, since a driver developed for I2O works on all platforms.

Despite the intentions, I2O hasn't taken off as expected and still requires special hardware to be installed in PCs in order for I2O hardware to work in them. If you have such hardware, take a look into this menu; otherwise you can safely skip it.

Network Device Support   Like the SCSI subsystem, the network subsystem needs to have a driver set up for the network card. This list of cards is a little oddly placed, but since you can see all the options whether they're available or not, it isn't hard to select your card.

If you think there might be a need for a second network interface card from a different manufacturer, or if you want to anticipate possible replacement of the card with something else, you can designate support for multiple cards. As the kernel loads, it will automatically probe for all the cards it can support and enable drivers for each card it finds.

Amateur Radio Support   Looking to take Linux into the field? Amazingly enough, you can still remain connected to a network through ham radio drivers. These settings allow you to configure a point-to-point link on top of which TCP/IP can sit. For additional details and relevant Web sites, read the help for all the options in this menu.

IrDA Support   Support for infrared devices is now a standard part of Linux, which is especially handy for laptop owners who have an IR port. If you decide to try this out, read the **/usr/src/linux/Documentation/networking/irda.txt** file that came with the Linux kernel source code.

ISDN Subsystem   Select these options if you want to take advantage of an ISDN modem. Unlike some of the preceding menus, the ISDN support entries are not separate from the device driver entries, so be careful with your settings.

Old CD-ROM Drivers   Remember when CD-ROMs weren't IDE? Linux, too, was around during those times, and many device drivers were written to deal with that media. If you are installing Linux on an older system, you may find these settings handy.

Input Core Support   The input core is the minimum amount of necessary code for Linux to talk to a keyboard. Unless you find yourself with a special reason, you can leave the default settings.

Character Devices   This menu covers a generic class of devices that communicate with the system one byte at a time (in contrast to devices such as hard disks, which communicate in blocks of bytes). You'll find support for serial ports, terminals, and watchdog timers in here.

Multimedia Devices   This menu lists the support available for high-end video devices like frame buffers and tuner cards. These drivers are not to be confused with video cards used by the X Windows system. Unless you have a special device like this, you can safely skip over this menu.

File Systems   Linux supports a great number of file systems aside from its native ext2 file system. This is especially helpful for non-PC installations, such as those using Sun SPARC or Apple Macintosh. In general, if you don't recognize a particular item, or if the file system is not native to your hardware, you can disable it. The one file system you *must* enable is support for ext2.

> *CAUTION:*   Although an option is available to compile ext2 as a module, *DON'T!* The kernel needs to know how to read modules from an ext2 file system before it can load additional modules.

Console Drivers   As Linux increases its aptitude for cross-platform environments, more options become available for multiple types of consoles. By default, Linux supports the VGA console, which is usually all PC folks will need. If you need Linux to display on other consoles, select the support in this menu.

USB Support   At long last, Linux now has support for USB devices. If your PC has USB ports and more important, if you have devices that plug into them, you will want to enable USB support and enable the driver for your device. Don't have a Linux driver for your USB device? Go harass the maker of the device and tell them to get with the times and write a driver for Linux!

Kernel Hacking   Unless you plan to do kernel development yourself, answer this question with a No.

Compiling the Kernel

This stage of the kernel building process is by far the easiest, but it also takes the most time. The compile itself works in three stages: The first stage creates the *dependency tree*, which is a fancy way of saying that the system determines which files need to be compiled and which can be ignored. The second stage is the clean up. Any previous compiles in this particular tree get tidied up, and old files are removed. Even if the tree is brand new, including this clean-up step never hurts. The last step is the compile itself. Once started, this last step doesn't need any attendance.

Because of the amount of code that needs to be compiled, be ready to wait a few minutes at the very least. A fast Pentium-based system may take upward of four to five minutes to churn through the entire source code.

Here's the command for performing the compilation stage. The compile stages in the command are separated by semicolons:

```
[root@ford linux]# make dep;make clean;make zImage;make modules
```

The start of the last stage includes the **zImage** parameter to tell the system to compress the final kernel so that it requires less space during boot time (required for PC-based Linux systems).

TIP: If you're finding that your kernel is still too big, try using `make bzImage` instead of just `make zImage`. This more aggressive compression scheme will make booting take a little longer, but the difference will be hardly noticeable on a Pentium-class system.

INSTALLING THE KERNEL

So now you have it: a fully compiled kernel just waiting to be installed. You probably have a couple of questions now: Just where *is* the compiled kernel, and where the heck do I install it?

The first question is easy to answer. Assuming you have a PC and are working out of the **/usr/src/linux** directory, the compiled kernel will be called **/usr/src/linux/arch/i386/boot/zImage**. The map file for this will be **/usr/src/linux/System.map**. You'll need both files for the install phase.

NOTE: If you did a `make bzImage` instead of `make zImage`, the compiled kernel will be **/usr/src/linux/arch/i386/bzImage**.

Now, let's install the compiled kernel. Begin by copying the **zImage** file into **/boot**, renaming **zImage** to

```
vmlinuz-x.x.xx
```

where **x.x.xx** is the version number of the kernel. For the sample kernel we're using in this chapter, the filename would be **vmlinuz-2.4.0-test9**. So the exact command for our example is as follows:

```
[root@ford linux]# cp /usr/src/linux/arch/i386/boot/zImage /boot/vmlinuz-2.4.0-test9
```

NOTE: The decision to name the kernel image **vmlinuz-2.4.0-test9** is somewhat arbitrary. It's convenient because kernel images are commonly referred to as **vmlinuz**, and the suffix of the version number is useful when you have multiple kernels available. Of course, if you want to have multiple versions of the same kernel (for instance, one with SCSI support and the other without it), then you will need to design with a more representative name.

Now that the kernel image is in place, copy over the **System.map** file. This file is useful when the kernel is misbehaving and generating "Oops" messages. These messages include a lot of detail about the current state of the system, including a lot of hexadecimal numbers. **System.map** gives Linux a chance to turn those hexadecimal numbers into readable names, making debugging easier. Though this is mostly for the benefit of developers, it can be handy when you're reporting a problem.

Using the same convention as the kernel image itself, copy the **System.map** file like so:

```
[root@ford linux]# cp /usr/src/linux/System.map /boot/System.map-2.4.0-test9
```

With the kernel in place, it is time to install the modules that we compiled earlier. To do this, simply run the following command:

```
[root@ford linux]# make modules_install
```

This will create a directory under the **/lib/modules** directory based on the version of the kernel being compiled and install the appropriate modules there.

With the proper files in place, you're ready to edit the **lilo.conf** file so that the system recognizes these kernels as options when booting. Refer to Chapter 7 for details on the **lilo.conf** file format. Let's consider a vanilla configuration in which this kernel is to be labeled **linux-2.4.0-test9**, and the **df /boot** command (see Chapter 6) tells us that the images are located on the **/dev/hda1** partition. We would insert the following lines in the **/etc/lilo.conf** file:

```
image=/boot/vmlinuz-2.4.0-test9
      label=linux-2.4.0-test9
      root=/dev/hda1
      read-only
```

To make this kernel boot by default, make sure the line

```
default=/boot/vmlinuz-2.4.0-test9
```

appears near the top of the file.

Now for the grand finale: Run **lilo**!

```
[root@ford linux]# lilo
Added linux-2.4.0-test9 *
Added linux
Added dos
[root@ford linux]#
```

The **lilo** output contains the boot options told to it by the **/etc/lilo.conf** file. The default kernel that will boot is the very first one (with the * next to it). Reboot and let it fly!

NOTE: For full details on LILO, see Chapter 7.

It Didn't Work!

The kernel *didn't* fly, you say? It froze in the middle of booting? Or it booted all the way and then nothing worked right? First and foremost, *don't panic*. This kind of problem happens to everyone, even the pros. After all, they're more likely to try untested software first. So don't panic, the situation is most definitely reparable.

First thing: Notice that when we added a new entry in the **/etc/lilo.conf** file, we *did not* remove the previous entry. We'll use that now. Reboot, and at the LILO: prompt enter the name of the previous kernel that was known to work. This is probably called **linux**. This action should bring you back to a known system state.

Now go back to the kernel configuration and verify that all the options you selected will work for your system. For example, did you accidentally enable support for the Sun UFS file system instead of Linux's ext2 file system? Did you set any options that depended on other options being set? Remember to use the Help buttons beside each kernel option in the configuration interface, making sure that you understand what each option does and what you need to do to make it work right.

When you're sure you have your settings right, step through the compilation process again and re-install the kernel. Remember to rerun `lilo` so that the changes take effect. Reboot and try again.

Don't worry: Each time you compile a kernel, you'll get better at it. When you do make a mistake, it'll be easier to go back, find it, and fix it.

PATCHING THE KERNEL

Like any other operating system, Linux gets upgrades to fix bugs, improve performance, and add new features. These upgrades come out in two forms: a complete new kernel release and a patch. The complete new kernel works well for people who don't have at least one complete kernel already downloaded. For those who do have a complete kernel downloaded, patches are a much better solution because they contain only the changed code.

Think of patches as comparable to a Windows HotFix or service pack. By itself, it's useless; but when added to an existing version of Windows, you (hopefully) get an improved product. The key difference between HotFixes and patches is that patches contain the changes in the source code that need to be made. This allows you to review the source code changes before applying them. This is much nicer than guessing whether or not a fix will break the system!

You can find out about new patches to the kernel at many Internet sites. Your distribution vendor's Web site is a good place to start; it'll list not only kernel updates, but also patches to other parts of the distribution. Another source is the official Linux Kernel Archive at http://www.kernel.org. (That's where we got the complete kernel to use as the installation section's example.)

In this section, we'll apply a patch to update our installation of the 2.4.0-test9 kernel to 2.4.0-test10.

Downloading and Unpacking Patches

Patch files are located in the same directory from which the kernel is downloaded. This applies to each major release of Linux, so the patch to update 2.4.0-test9 to 2.4.0-test10 is located in the **/pub/linux/kernel/v2.4/** directory of the Linux kernel FTP site. Likewise, the patch to take Linux from 2.3.30 to 2.3.31 is located in the **/pub/linux/kernel/v2.3** directory.

Each patch filename is prefixed with the term "patch" and suffixed with the Linux version number being installed by the patch. Note that each patch brings Linux up by only one version; thus the **patch-2.4.0-test10** file can only be applied to Linux-2.4.0-test9. If you have Linux-2.4.0-test8 and wish to bring it up to 2.4.0-test10, you'll need two patches, **patch-2.4.0-test9** and **patch-2.4.0-test10**.

Patch files are stored on the FTP server in `gzip`-compressed format. In this example, then, we'll be downloading **patch-2.4.0-test10.gz**.

Once you have the file from the FTP site, move it to the **/usr/src** directory (assuming that you unpacked the kernel from the preceding section into **/usr/src/linux**). Decompress the patch using the `gzip` command:

```
[root@ford src]# gzip -d patch-2.4.0-test10.gz
```

where `patch-2.4.0-test10.gz` is the name of your patch. This leaves a file called **patch-2.4.0-test10** in the same directory. Don't worry about having to erase **patch-2.4.0-test10.gz**; the `gzip` command automatically removes the original file for you.

Now you're ready to apply the patch.

Applying the Patch

NOTE: This section assumes you have already downloaded and unpacked the Linux kernel as described in earlier sections of this chapter. The patch in this example, **patch-2.4.0-test10**, can only be applied to Linux-2.4.0-test9. If you are patching a different version, remember to use the appropriate version numbers when issuing commands.

To apply **patch-2.4.0-test10** to Linux-2.4.0-test9 (which should be in the **/usr/src/linux** directory), issue the following command:

```
[root@ford src]# patch -p0 < patch-2.4.0-test10
```

A stream of filenames is printed out to your screen. Each of those files has been updated by the patch file. If there were any problems with the upgrade, you will see them reported here.

If the Patch Worked . . .

If the patch worked and you received no errors, you're just about done! All that needs to be done is recompiling the kernel. If you don't want to alter the configuration of the kernel, you can simply change to the **/usr/src/linux** directory and recompile the kernel as follows:

```
[root@ford linux]# make dep;make clean;make zImage;make modules
```

Once compiled, follow the directions in the "Installing the Kernel" section, earlier in this chapter.

> **NOTE:**   If the kernel you are compiling is too big, don't forget that you can use **make bzImage** instead.

If the Patch Didn't Work . . .

If you had errors during the process of patching the kernel, don't despair. This probably means one of two things:

▼ The patch version number cannot be applied to the kernel version number (for instance, you've tried to apply **patch-2.4.0-test10** to **Linux-2.4.0-test8**).

▲ The kernel source itself has changed. (This happens to developers who forget that they made changes!)

The easiest way to fix either situation is to erase the kernel located in **/usr/src/linux** and unpack the full kernel there again. This will ensure you have a pristine kernel. Then apply the patch. It's tedious, but if you've done it once, it's easier and faster the second time.

SUMMARY

In this chapter, we discussed the process of configuring and compiling the Linux kernel. This isn't a trivial matter, but doing it gives you the power to take fine control of your computer that simply isn't possible with most other operating systems. Compiling the kernel is a significant but straightforward process. The Linux development community has provided excellent tools that make the process as painless as possible.

In addition to compiling kernels, we walked through the process of upgrading kernels using the patches available from the Linux Kernel Web site, http://www.kernel.org.

When you compile a kernel for the first time, do it on a non-production machine, if possible. This gives you a chance to take your time and fiddle with the many operational parameters that are available. It also means you won't annoy your users if something goes wrong!

For programmers curious about the kernel's innards, many references are available. (Of course, the source code itself is the ultimate documentation.) Unfortunately, the last books released about the Linux kernel covered only up to the 2.0 series. Many components have changed significantly since then; nevertheless, the existing books provide general direction. A particularly good resource is *Linux Device Drivers* by Alessandro Rubini, (O'Reilly and Associates, 1998). It focuses on writing device drivers but also includes a great deal of general kernel information.

CHAPTER 11

Securing an Individual Server

You don't have to look hard to find that someone has discovered yet another new and exciting way to break into your systems. Sites such as http://www.securityfocus.com and mailing lists such as BugTraq regularly announce such new exploits for the public to consume. And to make the situation even more troublesome for system administrators is the proliferation of "script kiddies." These individuals do not themselves possess the technical knowledge to break into other sites; they use pre-built scripts instead, usually for the sole purpose of impressing friends and being a nuisance. The positive result of this behavior is the Linux community being very responsive to security issues that come up. Security patches being released in less than 24 hours of their announcement is not unheard of.

In this chapter, we discuss basic techniques for securing your server. If you follow these tips, you'll be more likely to keep out the script kiddies. But be advised: No system is perfect. New holes are discovered daily, and new tools to launch attacks come out more often than we'd like to imagine. Securing your systems is much like fighting off disease—as long as you maintain basic hygiene, you're likely to be okay, but you'll never be invulnerable.

"Hackers" versus "Crackers"

Before I get flamed to a toast from the hacking crowd, let me clarify some things here. Hackers are not evil. Most do not (usually) break into systems maliciously. Hackers show an impressive aptitude for understanding the system's internals and for finding clever solutions to perplexing problems. In fact, quick patches to a broken system are often known as "hacks" because they are clever but not necessarily clean or proper. They just work and should be appreciated for what they are.

The general term for folks who take it upon themselves to break into others' systems is *crackers*—individuals who "crack" open systems. They give hackers a bad name and have made the Internet as a whole annoyingly paranoid. Unfortunately, the media has opted to stick with the term "hackers" to classify anyone doing anything bad on the Internet. Which term should you use? Depends; if you're talking to fellow administrators, developers, or similar folk, you'll probably be better off with "cracker." If you're talking to someone who generally doesn't keep up with the lingo, stick with "hacker." (As if life weren't complicated enough...)

Nearly all network administration texts today have chapters like this one, explaining which of the neat, network-friendly features you have to turn off so that crackers can't abuse them. Because of cracker-friendly programs such as Back Orifice, IT managers must constantly remain vigilant about protecting their Windows NT/2000 systems from unauthorized access. Unfortunately, it's a sad reality we have to deal with.

TCP/IP AND NETWORK SECURITY

This chapter assumes you have experience configuring a system for use on a TCP/IP network. Because the focus here is on network security and not an introduction to networking, this section discusses only those parts of TCP/IP affecting your system's security. If you're curious about TCP/IP's internal workings, read Chapter 24.

The Importance of Port Numbers

Every host on an IP-based network has at least one IP address. In addition, every Linux-based host has many individual processes running. Each process has the potential to be a network client, a network server, or both. Obviously, if a packet's destination were identified with the IP address alone, the operating system would have no way of knowing to which process the packet's contents should be delivered.

To solve this problem, TCP/IP adds a component identifying a TCP (or UDP) *port*. Every connection from one host to another has a *source port* and a *destination port*. Each port is labeled with an integer between 0 and 65535.

In order to identify every unique connection possible between two hosts, the operating system keeps track of four pieces of information: the source IP address, the destination IP address, the source port number, and the destination port number. The combination of these four values is guaranteed to be unique for all host-to-host connections. (Actually, the operating system tracks a myriad of connection information, but only these four elements are needed to uniquely identify a connection.)

The host initiating a connection specifies the destination IP address and port number. Obviously, the source IP address is already known. But the source port number, the value that will make the connection unique, is assigned by the source operating system. It searches through its list of already open connections and assigns the next available port number. By convention, this number is always greater than 1024 (port numbers from 0 to 1023 are reserved for system uses). Technically, the source host can also select its source port number. In order to do this, however, another process cannot have already taken that port. Generally, most applications let the operating system pick the source port number for them.

Knowing this arrangement, we can see how source Host A can open multiple connections to a single service on destination Host B. Host B's IP address and port number will always be constant, but Host A's port number will be different for every connection. The combination of source and destination IPs and port numbers (a 4-tuple) is therefore unique, and both systems can have multiple independent data streams (connections) between each other.

For a server to offer services, it must run programs that listen to specific port numbers. Many of these port numbers are called *well-known services* because the port number associated with a service is an approved standard. For example, port 80 is the well-known service port for the HTTP protocol.

In "Using the netstat Command," later in this chapter, we'll look at the `netstat` command as an important tool for network security. When you have a firm understanding of what port numbers represent, you'll be able to easily identify and interpret the network security statistics provided by the `netstat` command.

For More Information on TCP/IP

In addition to Chapter 24, there are many great books that discuss TCP/IP in greater detail. The *Network Administrators Reference* by Tere' Parnell and Christopher Null (Osborne/McGraw-Hill, 1998) is a good place to start. This book discusses network administration from a high-level point of view and is a solid text all by itself (despite being very NT-centric). It discusses TCP/IP but doesn't get too far into the nuts and bolts.

The ultimate TCP/IP "bible" (referenced by network developers and administrators around the world) is W. Richard Stevens's *TCP/IP Illustrated* series (Addison-Wesley, 1994–96). These books step you through TCP/IP and related services in painstaking detail. As a systems administrator, you'll be interested mostly in *Volume 1: The Protocols*, which addresses the suite of protocols and gives a strong explanation of IP stacks. If there's a kernel-hacker inside of you who's curious about TCP/IP implementation, check out Stevens's line-by-line analysis of the BSD network code in *Volume 2: The Implementation*. (Although there's little resemblance between Linux's networking code and the code documented in *Volume 2*, the general guidance and philosophy therein is still invaluable.)

Another excellent book, *TCP/IP Network Administration* by Craig Hunt (O'Reilly & Associates, 1998), is a solid network administration reference. It has a much greater breadth of topics (but less technical depth) than Stevens's *Volume 1*.

Finally, if you're responsible for implementing a firewall (and I recommend you do), the O'Reilly & Associates text on firewall design, *Building Internet Firewalls (2000x)*, edited by D. Brent Chapman, et al., is a good one. And from Cheswick and Bellovin (who built AT&T's first firewall), *Firewalls and Internet Security* (Addison-Wesley, 2001). The first edition from 1994 is an interesting book, however it has become a bit dated. The 2001 release should prove to be more on par with O'Reilly's book.

TRACKING SERVICES

The services provided by a server are what make it a server. These services are accomplished by processes that bind to network ports and listen to the requests coming in. For example, a Web server might start a process that binds to port 80 and listens for requests to download the pages of a site. Unless a process exists to listen to a specific port, Linux will simply ignore packets sent to that port.

> **NOTE:**   Remember that when a process makes a request to another server, it opens a connection on a port, as well. The process is, in effect, listening to data coming in from that port. However, on the client the process knows to whom it's talking because it initiated the request. The client process will automatically ignore any packets sent to it that do not originate from the server to which it's connected.

This section discusses the usage of the `netstat` command, a tool for tracking network connections (among other things) in your system. It is, without a doubt, one of the most useful debugging tools in your arsenal for troubleshooting security and day-to-day network problems.

Using the netstat Command

To track what ports are open and what ports have processes listening to them, we use the `netstat` command. For example:

```
[root@ford /root]# netstat -natu
Active Internet connections (servers and established)
Proto Recv-Q Send-Q Local Address            Foreign Address          State

tcp        1      0 209.179.251.53:1297      199.184.252.5:80   CLOSE_WAIT
tcp        1      0 209.179.251.53:1296      199.184.252.5:80   CLOSE_WAIT
tcp       57      0 209.179.158.93:1167      199.97.226.1:21    CLOSE_WAIT
tcp        0      0 192.168.1.1:6000         192.168.1.1:1052   ESTABLISHED
tcp        0      0 192.168.1.1:1052         192.168.1.1:6000   ESTABLISHED
tcp        0      0 0.0.0.0:4242             0.0.0.0:*              LISTEN
tcp        0      0 0.0.0.0:1036             0.0.0.0:*              LISTEN
tcp        0      0 0.0.0.0:1035             0.0.0.0:*              LISTEN
tcp        0      0 0.0.0.0:1034             0.0.0.0:*              LISTEN
tcp        0      0 0.0.0.0:1033             0.0.0.0:*              LISTEN
tcp        0      0 0.0.0.0:1032             0.0.0.0:*              LISTEN
tcp        0      0 0.0.0.0:1031             0.0.0.0:*              LISTEN
tcp        0      0 0.0.0.0:1024             0.0.0.0:*              LISTEN
tcp        0      0 0.0.0.0:6000             0.0.0.0:*              LISTEN
tcp        0      0 0.0.0.0:80               0.0.0.0:*              LISTEN
tcp        0      0 0.0.0.0:515              0.0.0.0:*              LISTEN
tcp        0      0 192.168.1.1:53           0.0.0.0:*              LISTEN
tcp        0      0 127.0.0.1:53             0.0.0.0:*              LISTEN
tcp        0      0 0.0.0.0:98               0.0.0.0:*              LISTEN
tcp        0      0 0.0.0.0:113              0.0.0.0:*              LISTEN
tcp        0      0 0.0.0.0:23               0.0.0.0:*              LISTEN
tcp        0      0 0.0.0.0:21               0.0.0.0:*              LISTEN
tcp        0      0 0.0.0.0:111              0.0.0.0:*              LISTEN
udp        0      0 0.0.0.0:1024             0.0.0.0:*
udp        0      0 192.168.1.1:53           0.0.0.0:*
udp        0      0 127.0.0.1:53             0.0.0.0:*
udp        0      0 0.0.0.0:111              0.0.0.0:*

[root@ford /root]#
```

By default (with no parameters), **netstat** will provide all established connections for both network and domain sockets. That means we'll see not only the connections that are actually working over the network, but also the interprocess communications (which, from a security monitoring standpoint, are not useful). So in the command illustrated above, we have asked **netstat** to show us all ports (**-a**)—whether they are listening or actually connected—for TCP (**-t**) and UDP (**-u**). We have told **netstat** not to spend any time resolving hostnames from IP addresses (**-n**).

In the **netstat** output, each line represents either a TCP or UDP network port, as indicated by the first column of the output. The Recv-Q (receive queue) column lists the number of bytes received by the kernel but not read by the process. Next, the Send-Q column tells us the number of bytes sent to the other side of the connection but not acknowledged.

The fourth, fifth, and sixth columns are the most interesting in terms of system security. The Local Address column tells you your own server's IP address and port number. Remember that your server recognizes itself as 127.0.0.1 and 0.0.0.0 as well as its normal IP address. In the case of multiple interfaces, each port being listened to will show up on both interfaces and thus as two separate IP addresses. The port number is separated from the IP address by a colon. In the output from the **netstat** example shown above, one Ethernet device has the IP address 192.168.1.1, and the PPP connection has the address 209.179.251.53. (Your IP addresses will vary depending on your setup.)

The fifth column, Foreign Address, identifies the other side of the connection. In the case of a port that is being listened to for new connections, the default value will be 0.0.0.0:*. This IP address means nothing since we're still waiting for a remote host to connect to us!

The sixth column tells us the State of the connection. The man page for **netstat** lists all of the states, but the two you'll see most often are LISTEN and ESTABLISHED. The LISTEN state means there is a process on your server listening to the port and ready to accept new connections. The ESTABLISHED state means just that—a connection is established between a client and server.

Security Implications of netstat's Output

By listing all of the available connections, you can get a snapshot of what the system is doing. You should be able to explain and justify *all* ports listed. If your system is listening to a port that you cannot explain, this should raise suspicions.

If you've been using your memory cells for other purposes and haven't memorized the services and their associated port numbers, you can look up the matching info you need in the **/etc/services** file. However, some services (most notably those that use the portmapper) don't have set port numbers but are valid services. To see which process is associated with a port, use the **-p** option with **netstat**. Be on the lookout for odd or unusual processes using the network. For example, if the BASH shell is listening to a network port, you can be fairly certain that something odd is going on.

Finally, remember that you are only interested in the destination port of a connection; this tells you which service is being connected to and whether it is legitimate. Unfortunately, **netstat** doesn't explicitly tell us who originated a connection, but we can usually figure it out if we give it a little thought. Of course, becoming familiar with the applications that you do run and their use of network ports is the best way to determine who originated a connection to where. In general, you'll find that the rule of thumb is that the side whose port number is greater than 1024 is the side that originated the connection. Obviously, this general rule doesn't apply to services typically running on ports higher than 1024, such as X Windows (port 6000).

Shutting Down Services

One purpose for the **netstat** command is to determine what services are enabled on your servers. Making Linux easier to install and manage right out of the box has led to more and more default settings that are unsafe, so keeping track of services is especially important.

When you're evaluating which services should stay and which should go, answer the following questions:

1. *Do we need the service?* The answer to this question is very important. In most situations, you should be able to disable a great number of services that start up by default. A standalone Web server, for example, should not need to run NFS.

2. *If we do need the service, is the default setting secure?* This question can also help you eliminate some services—if they aren't secure and they can't be made secure, then chances are they should be removed. The Telnet service, for instance, is often a candidate for early removal because it requires that passwords be sent over the Internet without encryption.

3. *Does the service software need updates?* All software needs updates from time to time, such as that on Web and FTP servers. This is because as features get added, new security problems creep in. So be sure to remember to track the server software's development and get upgrades installed as soon as security bulletins are posted.

Shutting Down xinetd and inetd Services

To shut down a service that is started via the **xinetd** program, simply edit the service's configuration file in **/etc/xinetd** and set disable equal to Yes. If you are using a stock **inetd**, edit the **/etc/inetd.conf** file and comment out the service you no longer want. To designate the service as a comment, start the line with a number sign (#). See Chapter 9 for more information on the **xinetd** and **inetd**.

Remember to send the HUP signal to **inetd** once you've made any changes to the **/etc/inetd.conf** file and a SIGUSR2 signal to **xinetd**. If you are using Red Hat Linux, you can also type the following command:

```
[root@ford /root]# /etc/rc.d/init.d/xinetd reload
```

Shutting Down Non-inetd Services

If a service is not run by `inetd`, then a process that is probably started at boot time is running it. The easiest way to stop that from happening is to change the symlink. Go to the **/etc/rc.d/** directory and in one of the **rc*.d** directories, find the symlinks that point to the startup script. (See Chapter 7 for information on startup scripts.) Rename the symlink to start with an X instead of S. Should you decide to restart a service, it's easy to rename it again starting with an S. If you have renamed the startup script but want to stop the currently running process, use the **ps** command to find the process ID number and then the **kill** command to actually terminate the process. For example, here are the commands to kill a **portmap** process, and the resulting output:

```
[root@ford /root]# ps auxw | grep portmap
bin        255  0.0  0.1  1084  364 ?        S    Jul08   0:00 portmap
root      6634  0.0  0.1  1152  440 pts/0    S    01:55   0:00 grep portmap
[root@ford /root]# kill 255
```

NOTE: As always, be sure of what you're killing before you kill it, especially on a production server.

A Note About the syslogd Service

One non-`inetd` service that will pop up on `netstat` output but can be safely ignored is `syslogd`. This service has historically defaulted to binding to a network port and listening for network messages to log. Because of the danger of logging arbitrary messages from a network, Linux developers have added a mechanism whereby `syslogd` only logs requests sent from other hosts if it has been started with the `-r` option. By default, `syslogd` does not start with `-r`, so you can safely let it remain on your system.

MONITORING YOUR SYSTEM

The process of tying down your server's security isn't just for the sake of securing your server; it gives you the opportunity to see clearly what normal server behavior should look like. After all, once you know what normal behavior is, unusual behavior will stick out like a sore thumb (e.g., if you turned off your Telnet service when setting up the server, seeing a log entry for Telnet means something is very wrong!).

Commercial packages that perform monitoring do exist and may be worth checking out for your site as a whole, but we'll leave the discussions of their capabilities to *Network World* or *PC Week*. Here, we'll take a look at a variety of other excellent tools that help you accomplish the monitoring of your system. Some of these tools come with all Linux distributions; some don't. All are free and easily acquired.

Making the Best Use of syslog

In Chapter 9, we explored syslog, the system logger that saves messages from various programs into a set of text files for record-keeping purposes. By now, you've probably seen the type of log messages you get with syslog. These include security-related messages such as who has logged in to the system, when they logged in, and so forth.

As you can imagine, it's possible to analyze these logs to build a time-lapse image of the utilization of your system services. This data can also point out questionable activity. For example, why was the host crackerboy.nothing-better-to-do.net sending so many Web requests in such a short period of time? What was he looking for? Has he found a hole in the system?

Log Parsing

Doing periodic checks on the system's log files is an important part of maintaining security. Unfortunately, scrolling through an entire day's worth of logs is a time-consuming and unerringly boring task that reveals few meaningful events. To ease the drudgery, pick up a text on a scripting language (such as Perl) and write small scripts to parse out the logs. A well-designed script works by throwing away what it recognizes as normal behavior and showing everything else. This can reduce thousands of log entries for a day's worth of activities down to a manageable few dozen. This is an effective way to detect attempted break-ins and possible security gaps. Hopefully, it'll become entertaining to watch the script kiddies trying and failing to break down your walls.

Storing Log Entries

Unfortunately, log parsing may not be enough. If someone breaks into your system, it's likely that your log files will be promptly erased—which means all those wonderful scripts won't be able to tell you a thing. To get around this, consider dedicating a single host on your network to storing log entries. Configure your **/etc/syslog.conf** file to send all of its messages to this single host, and configure the host so that it's listening only to the syslog port (514). In most instances, this should be enough to gather, in a centralized place, the evidence of any bad things happening.

If you're *really* feeling paranoid, consider attaching a DOS-based PC to the serial port of the loghost and, using a terminal emulation package such as Telix, record all of the messages sent to the loghost. (You can also use another Linux box running **minicom** in log mode—just be sure *not* to network this second Linux box!) Have **/etc/syslog.conf** configured to send all messages to a **/dev/ttyS0** if you're using COM1 or **/dev/ttyS1** if you're using COM2. And, of course, do *not* connect the DOS system to the network. This way, in the event the loghost also gets attacked, the log files won't be destroyed. The log files will be safe residing on the DOS system, which is impossible to log in to without physical access.

For the highest degree of monitoring capability, connect a parallel-port printer to the DOS system and have the terminal emulation package echo everything it receives on the serial port to the printer. Thus, if the DOS system fails or is damaged in some way by an attack, you'll have a hard copy of the logs. (Note that a serious drawback to using the printer for logging is that you cannot easily search through the logs. If you choose to set up this arrangement, consider also keeping an electronic copy for easier searching.)

> **TIP:**   Consider using a package like `swatch` to page you when it sees a log entry that indicates trouble. You can find out more about it at http://www.stanford.edu/~atkins/swatch/.

Monitoring Bandwidth with MRTG

Monitoring the amount of bandwidth being used on your servers produces some very useful information. The most practical use for it is justifying the need for upgrades. By showing system utilization levels to your managers, you'll be providing hard numbers to back up your claims. Your data can be easily turned into a graph, too—and managers like graphs! Another useful aspect of monitoring bandwidth is to identify bottlenecks in the system, thus helping you to better balance the system load. But the most useful aspect of graphing your bandwidth is to identify when things go wrong.

Once you've installed a package such as MRTG (Multi-Router Traffic Grapher, available at http://www.mrtg.org) to monitor bandwidth, you will quickly get a criterion for what "normal" looks like on your site. A substantial drop or increase in utilization is something to investigate. Check your logs, and look for configuration files with odd or unusual entries.

COPS

The COPS tool (Computer Oracle and Password System) provides a simple and automated way of checking for unusual settings in the system. Such checks include looking for SetUID programs in home directories, unusual permission settings on home directories, configuration files that expose your system to outside access without authorization, and so on.

One of the most significant features of COPS is that it is designed to be automatically run from a `cron` entry (see Chapter 9 for more about `cron`) every night. The report, if there is anything to report, is e-mailed to you.

You can research and download the latest and greatest version of COPS at ftp://ftp.cert.org/pub/tools.

TripWire

TripWire, now a commercial package, takes a very paranoid approach to security: If something changes, TripWire tells you. This comprehensive protection removes the opportunity for someone to place a "backdoor" or "time bomb" in your system.

TripWire generates MD5 checksums of every file on your system and saves them in an encrypted format. When you want to check on differences, you can recall the saved checksums and compare all of the files on the system to their known good MD5 checksum. Differences are reported.

The idea here is for you to perform an install and then ready a system for network deployment. But before actually putting the system onto the network, you run the TripWire tool to generate and store all of the checksums. You can be confident that your list of MD5 checksums is safe in its encrypted domicile.

The process of setting up a TripWire arrangement is, of course, time consuming. However, short of cutting off network connectivity it's hard to tighten up a system any more than this.

SATAN

SATAN, the System Administrators Tool for Analyzing Networks, was released in the mid-1990s to a flurry of press suggestions that it was a hacker's toolkit. And SATAN's author, Dan Farmer, more or less declared that it *was* a hacker's toolkit—but for system administrators rather than evildoers.

SATAN works by probing your network for potential security holes. This program is especially interesting because it can be run from both inside (for you) and outside of your network (against you). It's an effective way of exposing firewall gaps when you run it from the outside, and an excellent investigation of internal weaknesses when run from an inside host.

Although SATAN is a bit older and doesn't identify many of the newer attacks that are employed today, it does do many of the "twist the door handle and see if it's open" checks that are no less important. You should assume that others will run SATAN against you, so be sure you know where your own weaknesses are and get them fixed as quickly as possible.

Like COPS, SATAN is available from ftp://ftp.cert.org/pub/tools.

HELPFUL WEB SITES AND MAILING LISTS

As with TCP/IP, substantially more security information is available than we can cover in this chapter. The best way to go about keeping yourself and your system up to snuff is to regularly visit Web sites that discuss such matters and join mailing lists that make regular announcements of developments in this area.

CERT

The first and foremost site for reliable and timely information on system security is the Computer Emergency Response Team (CERT). The CERT Web site, http://www.cert.org, maintains frequent announcements and a plethora of tools for protecting your site. Even more impressive is CERT's phone response team, which will help you deal with attacks against your site if you aren't sure about what to do. The CERT Web page tells you how to contact them.

At the very least, you'll want to join the CERT mailing list or subscribe to the comp.security.announce newsgroup; that's where moderated announcements from CERT are sent. You'll rarely ever see more than one or two announcements a month, so don't worry about getting your already full mailbox crammed with even more stuff!

BugTraq

Another good source of general system information is the BugTraq mailing list. This list gets regular traffic, but because it is moderated, you don't have to worry about useless flame wars consuming your mailbox. The discussions aren't specifically about security, but rather about serious bugs that affect all types of systems. As a systems administrator, you'll find many other useful tidbits here as well. For information on subscribing to the BugTraq list, go to http://www.securityfocus.com/forums/bugtraq/faq.html. At this site, you'll also find archives of past discussions.

Rootshell

The http://www.rootshell.com Web site has been getting more press lately because of the number of security holes that are announced there on a regular basis. This site doesn't run a mailing list, but as many as 30 to 40 security issues for all types of operating systems are posted here monthly. Many reports come complete with sample tools that help you test whether your systems are vulnerable.

Security Focus

Similar to Rootshell, the Security Focus Web site (http://www.securityfocus.com) is a full-disclosure site on security issues pertinent to all operating systems. The site is actively maintained; additions to its list of security issues occur almost daily. It also has links to security-related stories around the Internet.

ODDS AND ENDS

Before we jump into the next chapter, I want to bring up three security issues that have nothing to do with Linux but are and forever will be problematic.

The first is *security through obscurity*. This phrase describes the behavior of people who foolishly believe that by not telling anyone about what's there or how something is done, their system is secure. This is simply not true. Programs can be reverse-engineered, and probes can tell more about the insides of a system or network than we'd ever want revealed. A classic example of why security through obscurity doesn't work is PGP (Pretty Good Privacy, http://www.pgp.com). Because of its source code, and because underlying algorithms have been revealed to the world and thereby examined by countless cryptography experts, PGP is considered the most secure means of storing information. No proprietary cryptography system has ever reached this level of trust before.

The second issue is *social engineering*, the process by which a would-be intruder starts with a telephone before taking to the keyboard. It's remarkable what one can learn by making a few phone calls, showing the slightest bit of authority, and asking unsuspecting people for information. Reporters often use this technique for getting the inside scoop on news stories, because they know the average insider is far less likely to be ready to handle probing questions than is a public relations representative. Social engineering also works for questions about passwords, network infrastructure, operating systems, and so on.

The only way to help keep social engineering from getting through your site's security is by keeping your system's users educated and aware. They should be warned against revealing critical information to anyone who calls up asking for it. Policies need not be complicated to be effective—for example, "The MIS department will never ask for your password. If anyone does ask for your password, report it immediately."

Finally, there is the issue of *physical security*. That is, making sure that only trustworthy individuals have physical access to the machine. The reason this is critical is that once a person has physical access, it is possible for them to do anything with it—from the simple action of turning off a critical server (a potentially lethal move in the .com world) to the more insidious act of putting a tap onto your network connection so that all of its traffic can be monitored, passwords stolen, etc. Of course, these two are extremes. A realistic "attack" in this situation can be as simple as the attacker booting your system with a boot disk, mounting your root file system, and adding an account for herself so that she can remotely access your system with ease at a later date. And of course, there is simple theft: you could find that your system suddenly doesn't have RAM anymore or you're missing those new (and expensive) CPUs.

My point: You can have all the best electronic security you want, but the wrong person with physical access to a machine can cut through all of them with ease. Keep your machines protected.

SUMMARY

Security is one of those topics about which you can never say enough. In the course of writing this chapter, I considered touching on many topics that were clearly beyond of the scope of the book. Exploring most of these subjects would require adding many more chapters.

Don't fail to take an assertive role in exploring the issues of your system's security. It is an annoyingly time-consuming task, but it is one that cannot be ignored in this era of complex networks and operating systems. If your environment is like most today, you're probably running several different operating systems and need to contend with security for all of them.

PART III

Internet Services

CHAPTER 12

DNS

W ould the World Wide Web have become such a smashing success if you had to read "http://204.71.200.68" on the side of a bus rather than "http://www.ya-hoo.com"? Probably not. The need to map those long numerical IP addresses into people-friendly format has been an issue with TCP/IP since its creation in the 1970s. Although this translation isn't mandatory, it does make the network much more useful and easy to work with for most of us.

Initially, IP address-to-name mapping was done through the maintenance of a **hosts.txt** file that was distributed via FTP to all the machines on the Internet. As the number of hosts grew (starting back in the early 1980s), it was soon clear that a single person maintaining a single file of all of those hosts was not a realistic way of managing the association of IP addresses to host names. To solve this problem, a distributed system was devised in which each site would maintain information about its own hosts. One host at each site would be considered "authoritative," and that single host address would be kept in a master table that could be queried by all other sites. This is the essence of DNS, the *Domain Name Service*.

For example, if Host A wanted to contact Host B, the following queries would occur:

1. Host A would ask who was authoritative for all of the host names at Site B.

2. Host A would receive an answer such as "Nameserver B."

3. Host A would then ask Nameserver B, "What is Host B's IP address?"

4. Nameserver B would answer with Host B's IP address.

5. With the IP address of Host B in hand, Host A could begin direct communication with Host B.

If this seems like a lot of extra work to get something as simple as another host's IP address, realize that the only other choice would be to have a central site maintaining a master list of all hosts (numbering in the tens of millions) and having to update those host names tens of thousands of times a day—simply impossible! Even more important to consider are the needs of each site. One site may need to maintain a private DNS server because its firewall requires that IP addresses not be visible to outside networks, yet the inside network must be able to find hosts on the Internet. If you're stunned by the prospect of having to manage this for every host on the Internet, then you're getting the picture.

In this chapter, we will discuss DNS in depth, so you'll have what you need to configure and deploy your own DNS servers for whatever your needs may be.

NOTE: In this chapter, you will see the terms "DNS servers" and "name servers" used interchangeably. Technically, "name servers" is a little ambiguous because it can apply to any number of naming schemes that resolve a name to a number and vice versa. In the context of this chapter, "name server" will always mean a DNS server unless otherwise stated.

CAUTION: This chapter uses as examples many host names, domain names, and IP addresses that really do exist. Please be kind and do NOT configure your DNS server with their settings!

BEFORE DNS: THE /ETC/HOSTS FILE

Not all sites run DNS servers. Not all systems need DNS servers. In sufficiently small sites with no Internet connectivity, it's reasonable for each host to keep its own copy of a table matching all of the host names in the local network with their corresponding IP addresses. This table is stored in the **/etc/hosts** file.

TIP: Even in hosts that have access to a DNS server, you may want to keep a hosts file locally, where a particular host can look up an IP address before going out to the DNS server. Typically, this is done so that the system can keep track of hosts it needs for booting so that even if the DNS server may become unavailable, the system can still boot. Less obvious might be the simple reason that you want to give a host a name but you don't want to (or can't) add an entry to your DNS server.

The **/etc/hosts** file keeps its information in a simple tabular format. The IP address is in the first column, and all the related host names are in the second column. Only white space separates the entries. Pound symbols (#) at the beginning of a line represent comments. Here's an example:

```
#
# Host table for Steve's Internal network
#
127.0.0.1    localhost   localhost.localdomain
192.168.1.1  ford        # Steve's Linux box
192.168.1.3  toybox      # Heidi's Mac (MacOS 9/X)
192.168.1.6  tinymac     # Mac Duo 2400 (MacOS 9/PPC Linux)
192.168.1.7  assimilator # Win2k / Linux
192.168.1.8  trillian    # Firewall/Router (Linux)
192.168.1.9  arthur      # FreeBSD toy
192.168.1.20 zaphod      # Printer
```

In general, your **/etc/hosts** file should contain at the very least the necessary host-to-IP mappings to allow your system to boot up if the DNS server is not responding.

Using NIS to Distribute the Hosts File

The **/etc/hosts** file is an excellent candidate for distribution via NIS—Network Information Service, which, simply put, is a mechanism by which you can keep a centralized database of tabular information. (For more on NIS, see Chapter 19.) Any UNIX host capable of connecting to and reading tables from an NIS server can, of course, use this information. The benefit to you is simple: You can maintain a centralized list of hosts that all workstations in your network can access. When you update the central list, all hosts on the network can see it. Some sites even prefer maintaining their host lists via NIS instead of DNS, since NIS host tables are easier to manage.

If you do elect to take advantage of NIS distribution for your hosts file, it's very important that you still maintain the minimum number of entries in the locally managed **/etc/hosts** file. You always want your system to have what it needs to come up in the event it cannot contact the NIS server.

THE GUTS OF DNS

In this section, we'll explore some background material necessary to your understanding of the installation and configuration of a DNS server and client.

Domains and Hosts

Up until now, you've most likely referenced sites by their *fully qualified domain name* (FQDN), like this one: www.hyperreal.org. Each string between the periods in this FQDN is significant. Starting from the right end and moving to the left, you have first the top-level domain (.org, .com, .net, .mil, .gov, .edu, .int, and the two-letter country codes such as .us for the United States).

NOTE: Getting a new top-level domain approved is a difficult process. As of this writing, several new top-level domains have been given a go (e.g. .tv), but they are not in wide use as yet.

From these top-level domains come actual organizational boundaries. Companies, ISPs, educational communities, and nonprofit groups typically acquire unique names under one or more of the domains. Here are a few examples: redhat.com, caldera.com, planetoid.org, hyperreal.org, theorb.com, spinway.com, and clickarray.com. Assignment of these names is done by companies like register.com and networksolutions.com under the authority of the IANA (Internet Assigned Naming Authority).

Visually, you can imagine the DNS format as an upside-down tree, as shown in Figure 12-1. The root of the tree is a simple period; this is the period that's supposed to occur after every FQDN. Thus the proper FQDN for www.planetoid.org is really www.planetoid.org. (with the root period at the end). Most applications have come to assume that the user will not place the suffixing period.

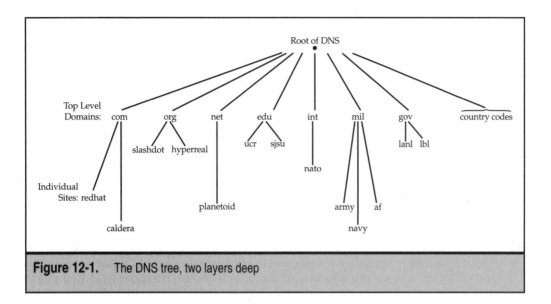

Figure 12-1. The DNS tree, two layers deep

All domains are placed in *root servers*, DNS servers scattered around the entire world. Each server contains the entire mapping of domain names up to two layers deep (planetoid.org, redhat.com, and so on) to their *primary name servers*. A primary name server for a domain is simply a DNS server that knows about all hosts and subdomains existing under its domain. For example, the root servers know that the primary name server for planetoid.org is 207.126.116.254. That's all the root server knows about planetoid.org. To find out about the hosts existing inside of planetoid.org, you have to ask the DNS server at 207.126.116.254. When asked about planetoid.org, the DNS server at 207.126.116.254 knows only about the hosts inside planetoid.org—and nothing else. If you ask it about whitehouse.gov, it will turn around and ask the primary name server for whitehouse.gov. (See the information about caching name servers in "Configuring Servers" later in this chapter.)

By keeping DNS distributed in this manner, the task of keeping track of all the hosts connected to the Internet is delegated to each site taking care of its own information. The central repository listing of all the primary name servers, called the *root server*, is the only list of existing domains. Obviously, a list of such critical nature is itself mirrored across multiple servers and multiple geographic regions. For example, an earthquake in Japan may destroy the root server for Asia, but all the other root servers around the world can take up the slack until it comes back online. The only difference noticeable to users is likely to be a slightly higher latency in resolving domain names. Pretty amazing, isn't it?

So now that you know how domains get resolved, you can begin to see the separation of hosts and domains. The host name is the very first word before the first period in an FQDN. For example, in the FQDN taz.hyperreal.org, the host name is taz, and the domain name is hyperreal.org. When a user sitting somewhere far away (in Internet terms) asks, "What's the IP address of taz.hyperreal.org?" the root servers will tell the user to ask ns.hyperreal.org. When ns.hyperreal.org is asked the same question, it can authoritatively answer "209.133.83.16."

Subdomains

"But I just saw the site www.cs.ucr.edu!" you say. "What's the host name component, and what's the domain name component?"

Welcome to the wild and mysterious world of *subdomains*. A subdomain exhibits all the properties of a domain, except that it has delegated a subsection of the domain instead of all the hosts at a site. Using the ucr.edu site as an example, the subdomain for the Department of Computer Science is cs.ucr.edu. When the primary name server for ucr.edu receives a request for a host name whose FQDN ends in cs.ucr.edu, the primary forwards the request down to the primary name server for cs.ucr.edu. Only the primary name server for cs.ucr.edu knows all the hosts existing beneath it.

Figure 12-2 shows you the relationship from the root servers down to ucr.edu, and then to cs.ucr.edu. The "www" is, of course, the host name.

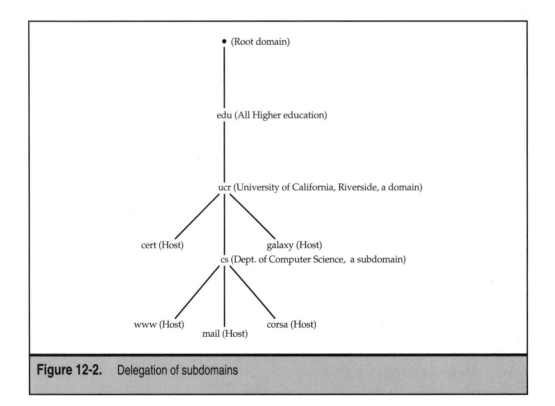

Figure 12-2.   Delegation of subdomains

To make this clearer, let's follow the path of a DNS request. A query starts with the top-level domain edu. Within edu is ucr.edu, and five authoritative DNS servers for ucr.edu are found. Let's pick (at random) the blue.ucr.edu server to be contacted and ask about www.cs.ucr.edu. blue.ucr.edu's DNS configuration is such that for anything ending with a cs.ucr.edu, the server must contact momo.cs.ucr.edu to get an authoritative answer. The request for www.cs.ucr.edu is then passed on to momo.cs.ucr.edu, which returns 138.23.169.15.

Note that when a site name appears to reflect the presence of subdomains, it doesn't mean subdomains in fact exist. Although the host name specification rules do not allow periods, the BIND name server has always allowed them (BIND is described in the upcoming section "Installing a DNS Server"). Thus from time to time, you will see periods used in host names. Whether or not a subdomain exists is handled by the configuration of the DNS server for the site. For example, www.cert.ucr.edu does not mean cert.ucr.edu is a subdomain. Rather, it means www.cert is the host name of a system in the ucr.edu domain.

in-addr.arpa Domain

DNS allows resolution to work in both directions. *Forward resolution* converts names into IP addresses, and *reverse resolution* converts IP addresses back into host names. The process of reverse resolution relies on the *in-addr.arpa* domain.

As explained in the preceding section, domain names are resolved by looking at each component from right to left, with the suffixing period indicating the root of the DNS tree. Very few top-level domains exist, but each level going down the tree fans out. Following this logic, IP addresses must have a top-level domain as well. This domain is called the in-addr.arpa.

Unlike FQDNs, IP addresses are resolved from left to right once they're under the in-addr.arpa domain. Each octet further narrows down the possible host names. Figure 12-3 gives you a visual example of reverse resolution of the IP address 138.23.169.15.

Types of Servers

DNS servers come in three flavors: primary, secondary, and caching. *Primary servers* are the ones considered authoritative for a particular domain. An *authoritative server* is the one on which the domain's configuration files reside. When updates to the domain's DNS tables occur, they are done on this server.

Secondary servers work as backups and as load distributors for the primary name servers. Primary servers know of the existence of secondaries and send them periodic updates to the tables. When a site queries a secondary name server, the secondary responds with authority. However, because it's possible for a secondary to be queried before its primary can alert it to the latest changes, some people refer to secondaries as "not quite authoritative." Realistically speaking, you can generally trust secondaries to have correct information. (Besides, unless you know which is which, you cannot tell the difference between a query response from a primary and one received from a secondary.)

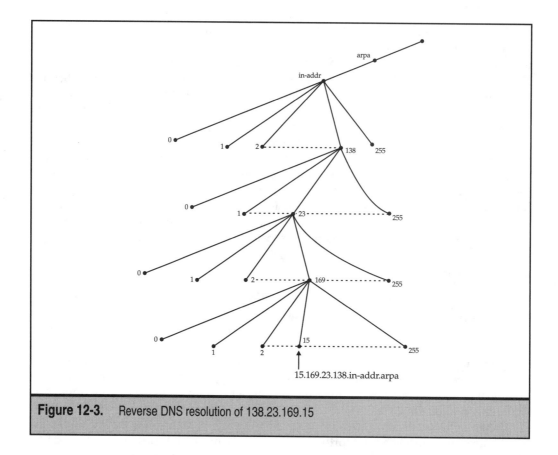

Figure 12-3.   Reverse DNS resolution of 138.23.169.15

Caching servers are just that: caching servers. They contain no configuration files for any particular domain. Rather, when a client host requests a caching server to resolve a name, that server will check its own local cache first. If it cannot find a match, it will find the primary server and ask it. This response is then cached. Practically speaking, caching servers work quite well because of the temporal nature of DNS requests. That is, if you've asked for the IP address to hyperreal.org, you are likely to do so again in the near future. (The Web has made this even more likely.) Clients can tell the difference between a caching server and a primary or secondary server, because when a caching server answers a request, it answers it "nonauthoritatively."

NOTE: A DNS server can be configured to act with a specific level of authority for a particular domain. For example, a server can be primary for domain.com but be secondary for example.net. All DNS servers act as caching servers, even if they are also primary or secondary for any other domains.

INSTALLING A DNS SERVER

Most Linux distributions come with the option to install a DNS server when the system is installed for the first time. The DNS server of choice for Linux and for almost all UNIX servers is BIND, the Berkeley Internet Name Domain server. (At one point, a rumor floated around the Internet that Windows NT's name server bore striking similarity to BIND. This rumor was never confirmed or denied.) As of this writing, the latest BIND version is 9.0.

NOTE: Because of the critical nature of the BIND software, it was taken over by the Internet Software Consortium (ISC) to ensure its continued development. You can find out more about the ISC at http://www.isc.org. As of this writing, the ISC is in charge of development of a DHCP server as well as the INN news server.

Because of the timing between writing this book and the release of new distributions, it is unlikely you have the latest version of BIND. If you're a Win2k administrator, you should be quite familiar with this since most Win2k books to date have been written for pre-releases rather than the official release. (Ah, the exciting world of frequent updates...) But if you are running the last official release of BIND (8.2.2pl5), don't worry. There were no known security problems with 8.2.2pl5, so you should be safe on that front. Plus, those configuration keywords that were correct for 8.2.2pl5 are still correct for 9.0.

NOTE: If you are running Red Hat Linux with the DNS server that shipped with it, you can skip to the "Configuring Servers" section. All you need to know is that the default location for the **named.conf** file is **/etc**, and the default location for the records files is **/var/named**. However, it is always a good idea to keep up with the latest versions of BIND, so going through the steps of downloading and compiling BIND 9 is likely to be the better choice.

The great news is that once BIND is configured, you'll rarely need to concern yourself with its operation. (Wonderful, isn't it?) Nevertheless, keep an eye out for new releases. New bugs and security issues are discovered from time to time and should be corrected. Of course, new features are released, as well, but unless you have a need for them, those releases are less critical. All new BIND releases are available at http://www.isc.org.

In this section, we'll discuss the process of downloading and compiling BIND. If your distribution uses package management software, you may want to look for the precompiled versions of the BIND software. If you do go with a precompiled version, however, be sure to download it from a trusted source.

NOTE: Although freely available with full source code to anyone who wishes to download it, BIND has the benefit of the ISC's commercial-quality management and support. Of course you'll have to pay for the commercial-level support, but the software supported by their commercial-level contracts is the same software you can download for free.

What to Download, Unpack, and Read

The first big difference you'll see between BIND 8.*x* and BIND 9.0.0 is the packaging. BIND 8 is distributed in three separate files: **bind-contrib.tar.gz**, **bind-doc.tar.gz**, and **bind-src.tar.gz** for user-contributed code, documentation, and source code, respectively. The new version of BIND ships with all three of these packages in one handy tarball: **bind-9.0.0.tar.gz**. You can download this from ftp://ftp.isc.org/isc/bind9/9.0.0.

You will want to download the tarball into a directory that has plenty of free space. For this example, I'm using **/usr/local/src**. As the root user (see the **su** command in Chapter 6), start by unpacking the archive as follows:

```
[root@ford src]# tar -xvzf bind-9.0.0.tar.gz
```

This will create a subdirectory called **bind-9.0.0** and place all of the files inside of it.

Unlike previous versions of BIND that used a build script based on what operating system you had, the new version uses the GNU autoconf scripts to automatically make those determinations and pick the appropriate configuration. To configure BIND, enter the directory created when unpacking the bind source tree and run **configure** as follows:

```
[root@ford src]# cd bind-9.0.0
[root@ford bind-9.0.0]# ./configure
```

This will allow BIND to automatically determine the configuration of your machine and place all the configuration files relative to the **/usr/local** directory. (If you want to stick to the Red Hat locations, you should run **./configure --prefix=/usr** instead. For this chapter, however, we will assume that BIND has been installed relative to **/usr/local**. If you install it the Red Hat way, be sure you adjust your path names accordingly in the remaining examples.)

Once BIND has been configured, you need to compile it by running the **make** command, like so:

```
[root@ford bind-9.0.0]# make
```

The **make** command will take a few minutes to run depending on the speed of your system. You should see a lot of commands fly across your screen—this is okay. It is simply **make** giving you a play-by-play commentary of what's going on.

Once it is done compiling, you will need to install the packages. This is done with the **make install** command:

```
[root@ford bind-9.0.0]# make install
```

And that's all! BIND is ready to be configured.

If BIND Doesn't Compile

First, don't worry. BIND is extremely unlikely to fail. I have successfully compiled BIND several times already without any problems. However, if for some reason it did not work, try removing the bind-9.0.0 directory (see the **rmdir** command in Chapter 6) and start again. Once you have gone through the steps, you'll see that starting from scratch takes only a few extra minutes. This may seem naive, but more than likely there was simply a problem in the unpacking process, or the **configure** command was not able to find things. Be sure you are doing this as the root user (see the **su** command in Chapter 6).

If it is still not working, send a copy of the last screen of output from **make** to the developers of BIND at bind9-bugs@isc.org. Remember to include as much information as you can about your configuration and the messages that you got. And of course, be nice. You'll be talking to the actual developers here—starting your message with a rant about how BIND is terrible is not a good way to get help.

What Got Installed?

A lot of things—most of which, thankfully, we can leave to the developer and hacker types who are interested in getting into the uglies of DNS. The three tools that we are interested in are:

Tool	Description
/usr/local/bin/host	Performs a simple query on a name server.
/usr/local/bin/dig	Traces the path of a name server.
/usr/local/sbin/named	This is the DNS server itself.

The remainder of the chapter will discuss each of these tools, their configurations, and their usage.

Starting DNS at Boot Time

If you are using the Red Hat–supplied DNS server, you only need to check that there exists a symlink in the **/etc/rc.d/rc3.d** directory that points to the **/etc/rc.d/init.d/named** script and that the symlink's name starts with an **S**. (See Chapter 7 for more information about startup scripts.) If this symlink is there, the Red Hat–supplied server is already in place and ready to go.

If you have installed Red Hat's server but performed the upgrade to BIND 9.0, then you will need to change the **/etc/rc.d/init.d/named** script. Using your favorite text editor, change the script so that instead of running **/usr/sbin/named**, it will run **/usr/loal/sbin/named**. (Remember to adjust the path name if you installed BIND in a different location using the **--prefix** option at configure time.) Also adjust the location of the **named.conf** file.

Note that the Red Hat script for starting and stopping BIND was originally for BIND 8.*x*. This is fine, and it will continue to start and stop the BIND 9.0 installation without a problem so long as the path names have been adjusted. However, the original script also has the feature of getting status information from BIND. The method that it used is no longer valid, and thus you cannot run **/etc/rc.d/init.d/named status** to get status information. Since the start and stop parameters do work, the script will properly start the server at boot time.

If you aren't using Red Hat, you'll find that most of the preceding comments regarding Red Hat's methods will probably work for you, too. Note, however, that you cannot simply start **named** from the **rc.local** script at the very end. This is because many other services (such as Sendmail) rely on DNS to be properly functioning in order for them to start. Be sure that BIND starts as the first network service after the IP address gets set.

Hurry Up Already! And What Are We Skipping in the Process?

If all you're looking for is a simple configuration for a simple situation, take a look at the cookbook solutions in "Putting It All Together" at the end of the chapter. One of them may be exactly what you're looking for. Of course, I still recommend reading through the chapter so that you understand how BIND interprets the configuration files so that you can more easily troubleshoot problems in the future.

If you do take the time to read the documentation that comes with BIND, you may wonder why I don't cover several of the features that are new to BIND, such as DNSSEC and IPv6 support. The reason is simple—those are very heavy topics that require a significant background in other topics to understand. Both of their discussions more or less merit a book of their own. It's unfortunate that DNS has become this complex, but the Internet isn't the friendly place it used to be, either...

BIND Documentation

BIND comes with a lot of great documentation, and I highly recommend taking the time to go through it. It's hardly light reading, but it will make you a better system administrator and a better DNS administrator. And the world needs as many good sysadmins as it can get!

All of the documentation comes as part of the original tarball that we unpacked under the **doc** directory earlier in this section. The best way to read through the files is to point your Web browser to them and click through. This is because several of the files are written in HTML and are much easier to read than their text counterparts. (By easier to read, I mean easier on the eye. The content is identical.) Assuming you unpacked the tarball in the **/usr/local/src** directory, you will want to browse to file **/usr/local/src/bind-9.0.0/doc**.

If you get a permission-denied error, this is probably because all of those files are owned by root and you're running your Web browser as a non-root user. The easiest way around this is to use the **chown** command (see Chapter 6) to make all of the files in the bind-9.0.0 directory owned by you before browsing through it.

Of the directories in the **doc** directory, the most important documentation is the **arm** subdirectory. In there you will find the BIND Administrators Reference Manual, a replacement for the BOG if you recall older versions of BIND. As the title suggests, ARM is a reference manual and not a tutorial, but as you need more complex configurations out of your DNS server, you will find it a very valuable resource.

CONFIGURING CLIENTS

In this section and the next, we'll delve into the wild and exciting process of configuring DNS clients and servers! Okay, maybe they're not that exciting—but there's no denying their significance to the infrastructure of any networked site, so you'd best be able to get a few warm and fuzzy feelings about DNS configurations.

Client-Side DNS (a.k.a. the Resolver)

So far, we've been studying servers and the DNS tree as a whole. The other part of this equation is, of course, the client—the host that's contacting the DNS server to resolve a host name into an IP address.

Under Linux, the client side of DNS is handled by the *resolver*. This is actually part of a library of C programming functions that get *linked* to a program when the program is started. Because all of this happens automatically and transparently, the user doesn't have to know anything about it. It's simply a little bit of magic that let's them start browsing the Internet.

From the system administrator's perspective, configuring the DNS client isn't magic, but it's very straightforward. There are only two files involved: **/etc/resolv.conf** and **/etc/nsswitch.conf**.

The /etc/resolv.conf file

The **/etc/resolv.conf** file contains the information necessary for the client to know what its local DNS server is. (Every site should have, at the very least, its own caching DNS server.) This file has two lines: The first indicates the default search domain, and the second line indicates the IP address of the host's name server.

The *default search domain* applies mostly to sites that have their own local servers. When the default search domain is specified, the client side will automatically append this domain name to the requested site and check that first. For example, if we specify our default domain to be yahoo.com and then try to connect to the host name my, the client software will automatically try contacting my.yahoo.com. Using the same default, if we try to contact the host www.stat.net, the software will try www.stat.net.yahoo.com (a perfectly legal host name), find that it doesn't exist, and then try www.stat.net alone (which does exist).

Of course, you may supply multiple default domains. However, doing so will slow the query process a bit, because each domain will need to be checked. For instance, if both yahoo.com and stanford.edu are specified, and we perform a query on www.stat.net, we'll get three queries: www.stat.net.yahoo.com, www.stat.net.stanford.edu, and www.stat.net.

The format of the **/etc/resolv.conf** file is as follows:

```
search domainname
nameserver IP-address
```

where ***domainname*** is the default domain name to search, and ***IP-address*** is the IP address of your DNS server. For example, here's my **/etc/resolv.conf**:

```
search planetoid.org
nameserver 127.0.0.1
```

Thus when I contact zaphod.planetoid.org, I only need to specify zaphod as the host name. Since I run a name server on my own machine, I specify the local host address.

The /etc/nsswitch.conf file

The **/etc/nsswitch.conf** file tells the system where it should look up certain kinds of configuration information (*services*). When multiple locations are identified, the **/etc/nsswitch.conf** file also specifies the order in which the information can be best found. Typical configuration files that are set up to use **/etc/nsswitch.conf** include the password file, group file, and hosts file. (To see a complete list, open the file in your favorite text editor.)

The format of the **/etc/nsswitch.conf** file is simple: The service name comes first on a line (note that **/etc/nsswitch.conf** applies to more than just host name lookups), followed by a colon. Then come the locations that contain the information. If multiple locations are identified, the entries are listed in the order in which the system needs to perform the search. Valid entries for locations are files, **nis**, **dns**, **[NOTFOUND]**, and **NISPLUS**. Comments begin with a pound symbol (#).

For example, if you open the file with your favorite editor, you'll see a line similar to this:

```
hosts:     files nisplus nis dns
```

This line tells the system that all host name lookups should first start with the **/etc/hosts** file. If the entry cannot be found there, NISPLUS is checked. If the host cannot be found via NISPLUS, regular NIS is checked, and so on. It's possible that NISPLUS isn't running at your site and you want the system to check DNS records before it checks NIS records. In this case, you'd change the line to

```
hosts:     files dns nis
```

And that's it. Save your file, and the system automatically detects the change.

The only recommendation for this line is that the hosts file (**files**) should always come first in the lookup order.

What's the preferred order for NIS and DNS? This is very much dependent on the site. Whether you want to resolve host names with DNS before trying NIS will depend on whether the DNS server is closer than the NIS server in terms of network connectivity, if one server is faster than another, firewall issues, site policy issues, and other such factors.

Using [NOTFOUND]

In the **/etc/nsswitch.conf** file, you'll see entries that end in **[NOTFOUND]**. This is a special directive that allows you to stop the process of searching for information after the system has failed all prior entries. For example, if your file contains the line **hosts: files [NOTFOUND] dns nis**, the system will try to look up host information in the /etc/hosts file only. If the requested information isn't there, NIS and DNS won't be searched.

GETTING READY FOR DNS SERVERS: THE NAMED.CONF FILE

The **named.conf** file is the main configuration file for BIND. Based on this file's specifications, BIND determines how it should behave and what additional configuration files, if any, must be read. If you've read any other books about DNS and BIND, you may be thinking that I've made a typo and what I *really* mean is **named.boot**. Not at all—the **named.boot** file is used by older versions of BIND (4.*x*, the latest of which is 4.9.3). The ISC has since stopped support for this series and now supports only the 8.*x* and 9.*x* series of BIND, which uses a completely new file format—and thus the new filename.

This section of the chapter covers what you need to know to set up a general-purpose DNS server. You'll find a complete guide to the new configuration file format in the **html** directory of BIND's documentation.

The general format of the **named.conf** file is as follows:

```
statement {
     options;      // comments
};
```

The **statement** keyword tells BIND we're about to describe a particular facet of its operation, and **options** are the specific commands applying to that statement. The curly braces are required so that BIND knows which options are related to which statements; there's a semicolon after every option and after the closing curly brace.

An example of this is as follows:

```
options {
    directory "/var/named";    // put config files in /var/named
};
```

The location of the **named.conf** file depends on what you specified the --**prefix** line to be when configuring BIND. If you left it to the default, BIND will look for it in the /usr/local/etc directory. However, if you have a Red Hat installation, you will find it by default to be in the /etc directory. I personally prefer keeping all host specific configuration files in the /etc directory, so I created a symlink (see Chapter 6) from /usr/ local/etc/ **named.conf** to **named.conf**.

The Specifics

This section documents the most common statements you will see in a **named.conf** file. The best way to tackle this is to give it a skim but then treat it as a reference guide for later sections. If some of the directives seem bizarre or don't quite make sense to you during the first pass, don't worry. Once you see them in use in later sections, the hows and whys will quickly fall into place.

NOTE: I can almost hear you saying it: "Why is this stuff so ugly to configure? Don't they have a GUI for this? Can't this be simplified!?" Well, yes and no. The hard part here is not the configuration file, but the concepts. And no GUI can simplify that for you. But once you understand the concepts, the configuration file will feel much more sane. If while you're glancing through this section you feel very lost, you may just want to skip to the next section and see these files in action. Then come back and actually see what the files are doing in better detail.

Comments

Comments may be in one of the following formats:

Format	Indicates
//	C++-style comments
/*...*/	C-style comments
#	Perl and UNIX shell script-style comments

In the case of the first and last styles (C++ and Perl/UNIX shell), once a comment begins, it continues until the end of the line. In regular C-style comments, the closing */ is required to indicate the end of comment. This makes C-style comments easier for multiline comments. In general, however, you can pick the comment format that you like best and stick with it. No one style is better than another.

statement Keywords

You can use the following **statement** keywords:

Keyword	Description
acl	Access Control List—Determines what kind of access others have to your DNS server.
include	Allows you to include another file and have that file treated like part of the normal **named.conf** file.
logging	Specifies what information gets logged and what gets ignored. For logged information, you can also specify where the information is logged.

Keyword	Description
`options`	Addresses global server configuration issues.
`controls`	Allows you to declare control channels for use by the **ndc** utility.
`server`	Sets server-specific configuration options.
`zone`	Defines a DNS zone (discussed in further detail in "Zones," later in the chapter).

ACLs

Access Control Lists (ACLs) allow you to specify a group of addresses as having access or no access to your DNS server. Each group gets a name, and you can use this name in other configuration options. The entries in an **acl** statement do not themselves change the behavior of BIND.

There are four default ACLs: **any** specifies all hosts; **none** denies all hosts; **localhost** allows the IP address of all interfaces on this BIND system; and **localnet** allows any host on a network for which this system has an interface.

To specify your own ACL, use this format:

```
acl name_of_your_acl {
     address-list
};
```

where **name_of_your_acl** is the name of the ACL you wish to define, and **address-list** is the list of addresses defined by ACL. By default, everything is denied (for this ACL only), so you just add a list of the addresses having access. This address list contains individual addresses separated by semicolons. An individual address can be formatted in one of three ways:

▼ Dotted decimal notation (192.168.1.2).

■ IP prefix notation (192.168.2/24), where the /24 represents the number of "on" bits in the netmask. For example, /24 represents the netmask 255.255.255.0. Most network gear allows this type of address specification.

▲ The name of an existing ACL. References to ACLs that are defined later in the file (*forward references*) are not allowed.

To negate an address, place an exclamation mark (!) in front of it. Address lists are evaluated from left to right, so if you specify an address as being accessible before you specify the negation, that address will be allowed access. For example, let's say you want to allow access to everyone on the 192.168.1 network access except 192.168.1.2. The statement

```
192.168.1/24; !192.168.1.2;
```

will still give access to 192.168.1.2, because it's allowed through by the first expression of 192.168.1/24. To deny 192.168.1.2 but allow the rest of 192.168.1/24, you need to specify the address list as follows:

```
!192.168.1.2; 192.168.1/24
```

Here is a sample ACL statement:

```
acl punks {
# These people thought it was funny to replace salt for the sugar
# next to the coffee machine. Little do they know to NEVER make the
# sysadmin unhappy... Mu-ha-ha-ha!
     !192.168.1.45; !192.168.1.74;
};
acl our_network {
     punks; 192.168.1/24; 192.168.2/24; // everybody but punks
};
```

Note that defining an ACL does not automatically put it to use. It simply allows you to refer to the addresses as a group instead of repeating a list of addresses over and over again.

The include Statement

If you find that your configuration file is starting to grow unwieldy, you may want to consider breaking up the file into smaller components. Each file can then be included into the main **named.conf** file. Note that you cannot use the **include** statement inside another statement.

Here's an example of an **include** statement:

```
include "/var/named/acl.conf";
```

CAUTION: To all you C and C++ programmers out there: Be sure not to begin **include** lines with the pound symbol (#), despite what your instincts tell you! That symbol is used to start comments in the **named.conf** file. (Believe me when I say this error is a *very* frustrating bug to track down!)

The logging Statement

The **logging** statement is used to specify what information you want logged, and where. When this statement is used in conjunction with the **syslog** facility, you get an extremely powerful and configurable logging system. The items logged are a number of statistics about the status of **named**. By default, they are logged to the **/var/log/messages** file.

Unfortunately, the configurability of this logging statement comes at the price of some additional complexity, but the default logging set up by **named** is good enough for most uses. If you want to reconfigure the logging process, read the BIND Administrators Reference Manual.

Configuration Options

Many options are available for your BIND configuration; these are listed in Table 12-1. Obviously, you don't need to specify all of these options in order to make your system work, but it's good to know what the choices are if you need to do some additional configuration.

Option	Description
`directory` *path-name;*	Location of the rest of the **named** configuration files.
`named-xfer` *path-name;*	Path name to the **named-xfer** program. By default, this is **/usr/sbin/named-xfer**.
`dump-file` *path-name;*	Path name of the file to which the **named** server should dump database information when the server receives a signal from the **ndc** program (**ndc dumpdb**).
`memstatistics-file` *path-name;*	Path name of the file to which memory usage statistics are written to on exit, if the **deallocate-on-exit** option (defined in this table) is set to Yes. By default, the filename is **named.memstats**.
`pid-file` *path-name;*	Path name of the file to which the **named** server writes its process ID immediately after startup. Default is **/var/run/named.pid**. This file is used by the **ndc** program.
`statistics-file` *path-name;*	Path name of the file into which the server appends statistics information when the **ndc stats** command is run.
`auth-nxdomain` *yes/no;*	If you specify Yes (the default), the server will always answer authoritatively on domain queries for which it is authoritative. Caution: Do not specify No unless you really know what you're doing.

Table 12-1. BIND Configuration Options

Option	Description
`deallocate-on-exit` *yes/no;*	When set to Yes, the server will write out a complete report of memory allocation. Results in a longer shutdown time but is useful for analysis of memory usage. Default is No.
`fake-iquery` *yes/no;*	Default is No. If Yes, the server will simulate the obsolete IQUERY query type. Like the **auth-nxdomain** option, don't turn this on unless you know what you're doing.
`fetch-glue` *yes/no;*	Yes (the default) tells the server to fetch (and cache) the necessary records to answer queries about domains on which it is not authoritative. Setting this to No, along with the **recursion** option, prevents your cache from growing and becoming corrupted by malicious attacks. However, clients have to do more work for each query.
`host-statistics` *yes/no;*	Tells BIND whether to keep track of statistics for each host that queries it. Although the information is useful, the tracking consumes substantial memory; thus the default is No.
`multiple-cnames` *yes/no;*	The specification for DNS tables does not allow for CNAME records to point to other CNAME records, so the default for this option is No. Since older versions of BIND did allow this, you can enable this backward compatibility by choosing Yes for this option. (CNAME records are host aliases, discussed in "DNS Records Types" later in the chapter.)

Table 12-1. BIND Configuration Options *(continued)*

Option	Description
`notify yes/no;`	Default is Yes. Causes a primary DNS server to send a NOTIFY message informing all the primary server's secondaries that its tables have been updated. The NOTIFY message causes the secondaries to perform zone transfers (to get the latest information from the primary) almost immediately.
`recursion yes/no;`	If Yes (the default), the server will attempt to traverse the DNS tree to get information about a requested IP address. This takes the load off the client to perform the same task. (See the `fetch-glue` option for reasons to turn recursion off.)
`forwarders { ip-list; }`	Specifies a list of IP addresses to be queried if the current server does not have the answer to a request. Forwarders are optional; the addresses generally come from an upstream provider. Example `ip-list` (with fictitious addresses): ```forwarders {\n 192.168.8.24;\n 192.168.3.12;\n};```
`forward first/only;`	Only applicable if you have set up `forwarders` (see previous listing). The default setting, First, causes the server to query forwarders for unknown information before going out on its own to resolve a request. By changing this option to Only, the server will look to forwarders only and not attempt to resolve any addresses by itself.

Table 12-1.   BIND Configuration Options *(continued)*

Option	Description
`check-names` *`type`* `action;`	Verifies the integrity of domain names based on their client contexts. Values for *`type`*: `master` = primary name servers; `slave` = secondary name servers; `response` = caching servers and clients. Values for *`action`*: `ignore` = no checking; `warn` = respond by generating a log entry; `fail` = generate a log entry and refuse to respond to the query. Defaults: `Check-names` *`master`* `fail;` `Check-names slave warn;` `Check-names` *`response`* `ignore;` The `check-names` option can be specified in the `zone` statement, in which case it overrides the configuration setup in the `options` statement for that particular zone. When used in the `zone` statement, do not specify *`type`*, because it can be derived from the `zone` information.
`allow-query {` *`address-list;`* `};`	Specifies which IP addresses are allowed to generate queries to the server. By default, all hosts are allowed. Separate addresses in *`address-list`* with semicolons (same format as for `acl`, discussed earlier in this section). You can refer to `acls` by name in this *`address-list`*, as well.
`allow-transfer {` *`address-list; }`*	Specifies which hosts can perform a zone transfer with your DNS server. In general, this list will include only hosts that are secondaries for your primaries. By default, anyone can perform a zone transfer, but I recommend you restrict this to only those with a legitimate reason to do so.

Table 12-1. BIND Configuration Options *(continued)*

Option	Description
`listen-on { address-list; }`	By default, the **named** server will listen to port 53 for DNS queries on all interfaces, but you can change this by specifying other addresses in *address-list*. Format is the same as for **acl** address list explained earlier. To select which port **named** will listen to, add **port** *portnum* right after the **listen-on** statement but before the first curly brace. Value for *portnum* is the port number you want named to listen to. For example: `Listen-on port 1031 {192.168.1.1;};` tells BIND to listen to port 1031 for DNS queries, on the interface configured to be 192.168.1.1. And `listen-on { 192.168.1.1; };` tells BIND to listen to its default port 53 for DNS queries, on the interface configured to be 192.168.1.1.
`query-source address address\ port port;`	When a server needs to contact another DNS server, it goes by default to any of the IP addresses on the system, and the source port is a random high port (port numbers 1024 to 65535). If you need a particular configuration to allow your DNS server through a firewall, you can specify a specific source *address* and *port* of origin for the message. If you need to specify one but not the other, you can use the wildcard (*) character. For example, the statement `Query-source address * port 53;` says to send the query from whatever IP address **named** wants to use but from port 53 explicitly.

Table 12-1.   BIND Configuration Options *(continued)*

Option	Description
`max-transfer-time-in` *number*;	Specifies the number of minutes a zone transfer can run before it is terminated. Default is 120 minutes.
`transfer-format\` *one-answer/many-answers*;	When the **named** process answers a request, it sends back only one answer at a time (the default), even though there may be space to pack multiple answers into one transfer. This is because old versions of BIND and other DNS servers still in use do not support multiple responses. If you know your DNS server will be working only with other BIND 8.*x* servers, you can change this option to ***many-answers*** for improved performance.
`transfers-in` *number*;	Maximum number of inbound zone transfers that can be running concurrently. Default is 10. Increasing this value may speed up the process of updates at the expense of increasing system load.
`transfers-out` *number*	Maximum number of outbound zone transfers that can be running concurrently. Default is 10. As of this writing, this option is parsed by BIND but is not yet in use.
`transfers-per-ns` *number*;	Maximum number of inbound zone transfers that can be running concurrently from a single remote name server. Default is 2. Can be increased at the expense of more load on the remote name server.

Table 12-1.   BIND Configuration Options *(continued)*

Option	Description
`coresize size;`	If **named** crashes, Linux will generate a **coredump**, an image of the memory used by the program at the instant it crashed. Data can be used for "post mortem" analysis by programmers. Be aware: This image may be quite large; if you're short on disk space for the DNS system, consider limiting the core file size. Default under Linux is unlimited. The *size* parameter can be specified in bytes (no suffix), K, MB, or GB. For example, all of the following are the same value, 1 gigabyte: `coresize 1073741824;` `coresize 1048576K;` `coresize 1024M;` and `coresize 1G;`
`datasize datasize;`	Specifies memory allocated for **named**. Default under Linux = as much memory as you have. The *datasize* value follows the same conventions as the *size* value for **coresize**. Thus `1073741824` is the same as `1048576K` is the same as `1024M` is the same as `1G`.
`files number;`	Maximum number of files **named** can open at once. Be aware: The more files BIND has open at once, the more its performance is affected by having to deal with all those file handles. (C programmers are familiar with this issue because of the **select** system call.)

Table 12-1.   BIND Configuration Options *(continued)*

Option	Description
`stacksize` *number*;	Maximum amount of memory **named** can take off the system stack (used to track temporary variables in a program). Default under Linux is no limit. For *number*, follow the same conventions as for `coresize` and `datasize`.
`cleaning-interval` *number*;	Specifies interval between server's removals of expired records from the cache. Default is every 60 minutes. If set to 0, no periodic cleaning will occur.
`interface-interval` *number*;	By default, the server scans the list of interfaces on the system every 60 minutes. If **listen-on** is enabled (defined earlier in this table), **named** begins listening for DNS requests on any new interfaces it finds. If an interface has disappeared, **named** will stop listening to requests on that interface. If this option is set to 0, the server will check for available interfaces only when **named** is started up.
`statistics-interval` *number*;	Specifies how often the **named** server generates server statistics and deposits them to the log file. Default is every 60 minutes. If set to 0, no statistics are generated.

Table 12-1. BIND Configuration Options *(continued)*

Option	Description

`topology { address-list; };`	When multiple forwarders exist, **named** shows preference to servers assumed to be closer than others. By default, the **named** server shows preference to itself and then to servers on the same subnet. You can specify another order of preference (the order of the *address-list*). You can also embed sublists representing a group of addresses. For example, in this configuration,
	
	`topology {`
	`    192.168.3.12;`
	`    { 192.168.11.25; 192.168.42/24; }`
	`    192.168.8.24;`
	`};`
	
	first choice is given to 192.168.3.12, equal preference is shown to 192.168.11.25 and all hosts on the 192.168.42.0 network, and last preference is given to 192.168.8.24.

Table 12-1.   BIND Configuration Options *(continued)*

In general, don't change the defaults for these options unless you have an explicit reason to do so.

The server Statement

The **server** statement tells BIND specific information about other name servers it might be dealing with. The format of the **server** statement is as follows:

```
server ip-address {
     bogus yes/no;
     transfer-format one-answer/many-answers;
};
```

where **ip-address** is the IP address of the server in question.

The first item in the statement, **bogus**, tells the server whether or not the other server is sending bad information. This is useful in the event you are dealing with another site that may be sending you bad information due to a misconfiguration. The second item, **transfer-format**, tells BIND whether this server can accept multiple answers in a single query response. As far as we know, the only servers that can handle multiple responses are BIND version 8.*x* servers.

A sample **server** entry might look like this:

```
server 192.168.3.12 {
     bogus no;
     transfer-format many-answers;
};
```

Zones

The **zone** statement allows you to define a DNS zone—the definition of which is often confused. Here is the fine print: *A DNS zone is not the same thing as a DNS domain*. The difference is subtle, but important.

Let's review: Domains are designated along organizational boundaries. A single organization can be separated into smaller administrative subdomains. Each subdomain gets its own zone. All of the zones collectively form the entire domain.

For example, the .bigcompany.com is a domain. Within it are the subdomains .engr.bigcompany.com, .marketing.bigcompany.com, .sales.bigcompany.com, and .admin.bigcompany.com. Each of the four subdomains has its own zone. And .bigcompany.com has some hosts within it that do not fall under any of the subdomains, thus it has a zone of its own. As a result, .bigcompany.com is actually composed of five zones in total.

In the simplest model, where a single domain has no subdomains, the definition of zone and domain are the same in terms of information regarding hosts, configurations, and so on.

The process of setting up zones in the **named.conf** file is discussed in the following section.

CONFIGURING SERVERS

Time for Big Fun: configuring a name server! Oh, you don't think it's fun? Well, wait until you find out how much people get paid for knowing this stuff.

Earlier, you learned about the differences between primary, secondary, and caching name servers. Briefly, primary name servers contain the databases with the latest DNS information for a zone. When a zone administrator wants to update these databases, the primary name server gets the update first, and the rest of the world asks it for updates. Secondaries explicitly keep track of primaries, and primaries notify the secondaries when changes occur. Primaries and secondaries are considered equally authoritative in their answers. Caching name servers have no authoritative records, only cached entries.

Updating the named.conf File for a Primary Zone

The most basic syntax for a zone entry is as follows:

```
zone domain-name  {
     type master;
     file path-name;
};
```

The **path-name** refers to the file containing the database information for the zone in question. For example, to create a zone for the domain planetoid.org, where the database file is located in **/var/named/planetoid.org.db**, we would use the following:

```
zone "planetoid.org" {
     type master;
     file "planetoid.org.db";
};
```

Note that the **directory** option for the **named.conf** file will automatically prefix the **planetoid.org.db** filename. So if we designated **directory /var/named;**, the server software will automatically look for planetoid.org's information in **/var/named/plane-toid.org.db.**

Now that's just the *forward reference*—the mechanism by which others can look up a name and get the IP address. It's proper Net behavior to also supply an IP-to-host name mapping (also necessary if you want to send e-mail to some sites!). To do this, you provide an entry in the in-addr.arpa domain.

The format of an in-addr.arpa entry is the first three octets of your IP address, reversed, followed by **in-addr.arpa**. Assuming that the network address for plane-toid.org is 192.168.1, the in-addr.arpa domain would be **1.168.192.in-addr.arpa**. Thus the **zone** statement in the **named.conf** file would be as follows:

```
zone "1.168.192.in-addr.arpa" {
     type master;
     file "planetoid.org.rev";
};
```

Now that you have your **named.conf** entries ready, it's time to actually write the **planetoid.org.db** and **planetoid.org.rev** files.

Additional Options

Primary domains may also use some of the configuration choices from the **options** statement. These options are

▼ **check-names**

■ **allow-update**

- allow-query
- allow-transfer
- notify
- ▲ also-notify

Using any of these options in a zone configuration will affect only that zone. See the "Configuration Options" subsection in the discussion of **named.conf** earlier in this chapter for more information on how these options work.

Updating the named.conf for a Secondary Zone

The zone entry format for secondary servers is very similar to that of master servers. For forward resolution, here is the format:

```
zone domain-name {
    type slave;
    masters  IP-address-list; ;
};
```

where the **domain-name** is the exact same name as the primary name server, and the **IP-address-list** is the list of IP addresses where the primary name server for that zone exists.

A recommended additional option you can list in a secondary zone configuration is

```
file path-name;
```

where **path-name** is the full path location of where the server will keep copies of the primary's zone files. By keeping a local copy, you can reduce bandwidth needs for updates and improve performance.

Additional Options

A secondary zone configuration may also use some of the configuration choices from the **options** statement. These options are

- ▼ check-names
- allow-update
- allow-query
- allow-transfer
- max-transfer-time-in
- notify
- ▲ also-notify

See the "Configuration Options" subsection in the discussion of **named.conf** earlier in this chapter for more information on how these options work.

Updating the named.conf File for a Caching Zone

A caching configuration is the easiest of all configurations. It's also required for every DNS server configuration, even if you are running a primary or secondary server. This is necessary in order for the server to recursively search the DNS tree to find other hosts on the Internet.

The two zone entries you need are for the cache, and making the local-host entry primary for itself. Here's the first entry:

```
zone "." {
      type hint;
      file "named.ca";
};
```

The line **type hint;** specifies that this is a caching zone entry, and the line **file "named.ca"**; specifies the file that will prime the cache with entries pointing to the root servers. (This **named.ca** file comes with the BIND package. You can also find the latest file at ftp://rs.internic.net.)

The second zone entry is as follows:

```
zone "0.0.127.in-addr.arpa"   {
      type master;
      file "named.local";
};
```

This is the reverse entry for resolving the local host address back to the local host name. The **named.local** file contains the following:

```
$TTL 86400
@         IN      SOA     localhost. root.localhost.   (
                                     1997022700 ; Serial
                                     28800      ; Refresh
                                     14400      ; Retry
                                     3600000    ; Expire
                                     86400 )    ; Minimum
               IN       NS      localhost.

1       IN      PTR     localhost.
```

If this doesn't make sense to you yet, don't worry. Just know that this is enough for a caching server. The following sections will help you make sense of this file.

DNS Records Types

Okay, I kind of lied. You *aren't* ready to create the **planetoid.org.db** and **plane-toid.org.rev** files—not quite yet. First you need to understand all the record types for DNS: SOA, NS, A, PTR, CNAME, MX, TXT, and RP.

SOA: Start of Authority

The SOA record starts the description of a site's DNS entries. The format of this entry is as follows:

```
domain.com. IN SOA ns.domain.com. hostmaster.domain.com. (
        1999080801          ; serial number
        10800               ; refresh rate in seconds (3 hours)
        1800                ; retry in seconds (30 minutes)
        1209600             ; expire in seconds (2 weeks)
        604800      )       ; minimum in seconds (1 week)
```

The first line contains some details we need to pay attention to:

▼ **domain.com.** is of course to be replaced with your domain name. Notice that last period at the end of **domain.com.**? It's supposed to be there—indeed, the DNS configuration files are extremely picky about it. The ending period is necessary for the sever to differentiate relative host names from fully qualified domain names (FQDNs); for example, the difference between oid and oid.planetoid.org.

■ **IN** tells the name server that this is an Internet record. There are other types of records, but it's been years since anyone has had a need for them. We can safely ignore them.

■ **SOA** tells the name server this is the Start of Authority record.

■ **ns.domain.com.** is the FQDN for the name server for this domain (that would be the server where this file will finally reside). Again, watch out and don't miss that trailing period.

▲ **hostmaster.domain.com.** is the e-mail address for the domain administrator. Notice the lack of an @ in this address. The @ symbol is replaced with a period. Thus, the e-mail address referred to in this example is hostmaster@domain.com. The trailing period is used here, too.

The remainder of the record starts after the opening parenthesis on the first line. The first line is the serial number. It's used to tell the name server when the file has been updated. Watch out—forgetting to increment this number when you make a change is a mistake frequently made in the process of managing DNS records. (Forgetting to put a period in the right place is another common error.)

TIP: To maintain serial numbers in a sensible way, use the date formatted in the following order: *YYYYMMDDxx*. The tail-end *xx* is an additional two-digit number starting with 00, so if you make multiple updates in a day, you can still tell which is which.

The second line in the list of values is the refresh rate in seconds. This value tells the secondary DNS servers how often they should query the primary server to see if the records have been updated.

The third value is the retry rate in seconds. If the secondary server tries but cannot contact the primary DNS server to check for updates, the secondary server tries again after the specified number of seconds.

The fourth value is intended for secondary servers that have cached the zone data. It tells these servers that if they cannot contact the primary server for an update, they should discard the value after the specified number of seconds. One to two weeks is a good value for this interval.

The final value, minimum, tells caching servers how long they should wait before expiring an entry if they cannot contact the primary DNS server. Five to seven days is a good guideline for this entry.

NOTE: Don't forget to place the closing parenthesis after the final value.

NS: Name Server

The NS record is used for specifying which name servers maintain records for this zone. The format of this record is as follows:

```
IN NS          ns1.domain.com.
IN NS          ns2.domain.com.
```

You can have as many backup name servers as you'd like for a domain—at least two is a good idea. Most ISPs are willing to act as secondary DNS servers if they provide connectivity for you.

A: Address Record

The A record is used for providing a mapping from host name to IP address. The format of an A address is simple:

```
host name          IN A          IP-Address
```

For example, an A record for the host oid.planetoid.org, whose IP address is 192.168.1.2, would look like this:

```
oid          IN A          192.168.1.2
```

Note that any host name is automatically suffixed with the domain name listed in the SOA record, unless this host name ends with a period. In the foregoing example for oid, if the SOA record above it is for planetoid.org, then oid is understood to be oid.planetoid.org. If we were to change this to oid.planetoid.org (without a trailing period), the name server would understand it to be oid.planetoid.org.planetoid.org. So if you want to use the FQDN, be sure to suffix it with a period.

PTR: Pointer Record

The PTR record is for performing reverse name resolution, thereby allowing someone to specify an IP address and determine the corresponding host name. The format for this record is very similar to the A record, except with the values reversed:

```
IP-Address      IN PTR     host name
```

The **IP-address** can take one of two forms: just the last octet of the IP address (leaving the name server to automatically suffix it with the information it has from the in-addr.arpa domain name); or the full IP address, which is suffixed with a period. The **host name** must have the complete FQDN. For example, the PTR record for the host oid would be as follows:

```
192.168.1.2.    IN PTR     oid.planetoid.org.
```

MX: Mail Exchanger

The MX record is in charge of telling other sites about your zone's mail server. If a host on your network generated an outgoing mail with its host name on it, someone returning a message would not send it back directly to that host. Instead, the replying mail server would look up the MX record for that site and send the message there instead.

When Internet sites were primarily composed of UNIX-based systems, with Sendmail configured as a NULL host forwarding to a mail hub, lack of an MX record was okay. But as more non-UNIX systems joined the Net, MX records became crucial. If pc.domain.com sends a message using its PC-based mail reader (which cannot accept SMTP mail), it's important that the replying party have a reliable way of knowing the identity of pc.domain.com's mail server.

The format of the MX record is as follows:

```
domainname.  IN MX weight host name
```

where **domainname.** is the domain name of the site (with a period at the end, of course); the **weight** is the importance of the mail server (if multiple mail servers exist, the one with the smallest number has precedence over those with larger numbers); and the **host name** is, of course, the name of the mail server. It is important that the **host name** have an A record, as well.

Here's an example entry:

```
domain.com.    IN MX 10 mailserver1
               IN MX 20 mailserverbackup
```

Typically, MX records occur at the top of DNS configuration files. If a domain name is not specified, the default name is pulled from the SOA record.

CNAME: Canonical Name

CNAME records allow you to create aliases for host names. This is useful when you want to provide a highly available service with an easy-to-remember name, but still give the host a real name.

Another popular use for CNAMEs is to "create" a new server with an easy-to-remember name without having to invest in a new server at all. An example: A site has a mail server named mailhost in a UNIX-like tradition. As non-UNIX people come into the Internet picture, they assume the mail server will be called mail; to accommodate this assumption, a CNAME is created rather than renaming the server, so that all requests to the host named mail will transparently resolve to mailhost.

Here's the format for the CNAME record:

```
new host name   IN CNAME   old host name
```

For example, for the mail-to-mailhost mapping mentioned just above, our entries might look like this:

```
mailhost     IN A        192.168.1.10
mail         IN CNAME    mailhost
```

CAUTION: It is a bad, bad, *bad* practice to point an MX record to a CNAME record. The official DNS specification document explicitly prohibits this. BIND will allow it, but only to keep backward compatibility with a broken feature from the past.

RP and TXT: The Documentation Entries

Sometimes it's useful to provide contact information as part of your database—not just as comments, but as actual records that others can query. This can be accomplished using the RP and TXT records.

A TXT record is a free-form text entry into which you can place whatever information you deem fit. Most often, you'll only want to put contact information in these records. Each TXT record must be tied to a particular host name. For example:

```
hhgttg.planetoid.org. IN TXT "Contact: Marvin"
                       IN TXT "SysAdmin/Android"
                       IN TXT "Voice: 800-555 -1212"
```

The RP record was created as an explicit container for a host's contact information. This record states who is the responsible person for the specific host; here's an example:

```
hhgttg.planetoid.org.   IN RP marvin.domain.com. planetoid.org.
```

As useful as these records may be, they are a rarity these days, because it is perceived that they give away too much information about the site that could lead to social engineering-based attacks. You may find such records helpful in your internal DNS servers, but you should probably leave them out of anything that one could query from the Internet.

PUTTING IT ALL TOGETHER

So now we have the entries we need in the **named.conf** file, and we know about all the DNS record types. It's time to create the actual database that will feed the server.

The database file format is not too strict, but some conventions that have jelled over time. Sticking to these conventions will make your life easier and will smooth the way for the administrator who takes over your creation.

TIP: Comment liberally. In this file, comment lines begin with a semicolon. Although there isn't a lot of mystery about what's going on in a DNS database file, a history of the changes is a useful reference about what was being accomplished and why.

Every database file must start with a $TTL entry. This entry tells BIND what the time-to-live value is for each individual record. (The TTL in the SOA record is for the SOA record only.) After the $TTL entry is the SOA record and at least one NS record. Everything else is optional. (Of course, "everything else" is what makes the file useful!) You may find the following general format helpful to follow:

```
$TTL
SOA record
NS records
MX records
A and CNAME records
```

For example, here is a complete zone configuration file for a single domain with four hosts and a time-to-live setting of 604,800 seconds (1 week):

```
$TTL 604800
@       IN      SOA     domain.com.  hostmaster.domain.com. (
                        1999022300 ; serial number
                        10800     ;Refresh every 3 hours
                        1800      ;Retry every 30 minutes
                        1209600   ;Expire in 2 weeks
                        604800 )  ;Minimum 1 week
                IN      NS      ns.domain.com.
                IN      MX 10   mail.domain.com.
imp             IN      A       192.168.1.1   ; Internet gateway
```

```
mail            IN      A       192.168.1.2   ; mail server
technics        IN      A       192.168.1.3   ; web server
www             IN      CNAME   technics
ns              IN      A       192.168.1.4   ; name server
peanutbutter    IN      A       192.168.1.5   ; firewall
```

And here is the corresponding reverse file:

```
$TTL 604800
@   IN   SOA 1.168.192.in-addr.arpa. hostmaster.domain.com. (
                    1999010501      ; Serial
                    10800           ; Refresh rate (3 hours)
                    1800            ; Retry (30 minutes)
                    1209600         ; Expire (2 weeks)
                    604800 )        ; Minimum (1 week)
            IN      NS      ns.domain.com.
1           IN      PTR     imp.domain.com.
2           IN      PTR     mail.domain.com
3           IN      PTR     technics.domain.com
4           IN      PTR     ns.domain.com
5           IN      PTR     peanutbutter.domain.com.
```

A Complete Configuration

So far, we've given you snippets of configuration files. Hopefully that has been enough to give you the big DNS picture and provide plenty of guidance for coming up with your own configuration file. Then again, a nice example never hurts.

Following is a complete configuration for a primary domain (domain.com) that also acts as a secondary to a friend, example.com. In exchange, the example.com domain acts as our secondary. We allow zone transfers to occur between our two sites, but not with any other sites. The domain.com site's ISP provides DNS service, as well, to which we forward requests when we cannot resolve information ourselves.

Here is the **named.conf** file:

```
options {
  directory "/var/named";
  forwarders {
            192.168.2.1;
            192.168.2.2;
  };
  allow-transfer  {
            10.0.0.1;   // ns1.example.com
            10.0.0.2;   // ns2.example.com
  };
};
```

```
//
// a caching only name server config
//
zone "." {
        type hint;
        file "named.ca";
};

zone "0.0.127.in-addr.arpa" {
        type master;
        file "named.local";
};


//
// our primary information
//
zone "domain.com"  {
        type master;
        file "named.domain.com.";
};
zone "1.168.192.in-addr.arpa" {
        type master;
        file "named.rev";
};


//
// our secondary information for example.com
//
zone "example.com" {
        type slave;
        file "example.com.cache";
        masters  { 10.0.0.1; 10.0.0.2; };
};
```

Here is the **/var/named/named.ca** file:

```
;   This file holds the information on root name servers needed to
;   initialize cache of Internet domain name servers
;   (e.g. reference this file in the "cache  .  <file>"
;   configuration file of BIND domain name servers).
;
;   This file is made available by InterNIC registration services
;   under anonymous FTP as
;           file                    /domain/named.root
```

```
;                   on server             FTP.RS.INTERNIC.NET
;          -OR- under Gopher at    RS.INTERNIC.NET
;            under menu               InterNIC Registration Services (NSI)
;            submenu                 InterNIC Registration Archives
;            file                      named.root
;
;        last update:    Aug 22, 1997
;        related version of root zone:    1997082200
;
;
; formerly NS.INTERNIC.NET
;
.                              3600000   IN   NS    A.ROOT-SERVERS.NET.
A.ROOT-SERVERS.NET.            3600000        A     198.41.0.4
;
; formerly NS1.ISI.EDU
;
.                              3600000        NS    B.ROOT-SERVERS.NET.
B.ROOT-SERVERS.NET.            3600000        A     128.9.0.107
;
; formerly C.PSI.NET
;
.                              3600000        NS    C.ROOT-SERVERS.NET.
C.ROOT-SERVERS.NET.            3600000        A     192.33.4.12
;
; formerly TERP.UMD.EDU
;
.                              3600000        NS    D.ROOT-SERVERS.NET.
D.ROOT-SERVERS.NET.            3600000        A     128.8.10.90
;
; formerly NS.NASA.GOV
;
.                              3600000        NS    E.ROOT-SERVERS.NET.
E.ROOT-SERVERS.NET.            3600000        A     192.203.230.10
;
; formerly NS.ISC.ORG
;
.                              3600000        NS    F.ROOT-SERVERS.NET.
F.ROOT-SERVERS.NET.            3600000        A     192.5.5.241
;
; formerly NS.NIC.DDN.MIL
;
.                              3600000        NS    G.ROOT-SERVERS.NET.
G.ROOT-SERVERS.NET.            3600000        A     192.112.36.4
```

```
;
; formerly AOS.ARL.ARMY.MIL
;
.                             3600000    NS    H.ROOT-SERVERS.NET.
H.ROOT-SERVERS.NET.           3600000    A     128.63.2.53
;
; formerly NIC.NORDU.NET
;
.                             3600000    NS    I.ROOT-SERVERS.NET.
I.ROOT-SERVERS.NET.           3600000    A     192.36.148.17
;
; temporarily housed at NSI (InterNIC)
;
.                             3600000    NS    J.ROOT-SERVERS.NET.
J.ROOT-SERVERS.NET.           3600000    A     198.41.0.10
;
; housed in LINX, operated by RIPE NCC
;
.                             3600000    NS    K.ROOT-SERVERS.NET.
K.ROOT-SERVERS.NET.           3600000    A     193.0.14.129
;
; temporarily housed at ISI (IANA)
;
.                             3600000    NS    L.ROOT-SERVERS.NET.
L.ROOT-SERVERS.NET.           3600000    A     198.32.64.12
;
; housed in Japan, operated by WIDE
;
.                             3600000    NS    M.ROOT-SERVERS.NET.
M.ROOT-SERVERS.NET.           3600000    A     202.12.27.33
; End of File
```

Here is the **/var/named/named.local** file:

```
$TTL 86400
@       IN      SOA     localhost. root.localhost.  (
                                    1997022700 ; Serial
                                    28800      ; Refresh
                                    14400      ; Retry
                                    3600000    ; Expire
                                    86400 )    ; Minimum
                IN      NS      localhost.

1       IN      PTR     localhost.
```

Here is the **/var/named/named.domain.com** file:

```
$TTL 86400
@        IN      SOA      domain.com.  hostmaster.domain.com. (
                          1999022300 ; serial number
                          10800    ;Refresh every 3 hours
                          1800     ;Retry every 30 minutes
                          1209600 ;Expire in 2 weeks
                          604800 ) ;Minimum 1 week
         IN      NS       ns.domain.com.
         IN      MX 10    mail.domain.com.
imp          IN      A        192.168.1.1    ; Internet gateway
mail         IN      A        192.168.1.2    ; mail server
technics     IN      A        192.168.1.3    ; web server
www          IN      CNAME    technics
ns           IN      A        192.168.1.4    ; name server
peanutbutter IN      A        192.168.1.5    ; firewall
```

Here is the **/var/named/named.rev** file:

```
$TTL 604800
@  IN   SOA 1.168.192.in-addr.arpa. hostmaster.domain.com. (
                       1999010501        ; Serial
                       10800             ; Refresh rate (3 hours)
                       1800              ; Retry (30 minutes)
                       1209600           ; Expire (2 weeks)
                       604800 )          ; Minimum (1 week)
           IN      NS       ns.domain.com.
1          IN      PTR      imp.domain.com.
2          IN      PTR      mail.domain.com
3          IN      PTR      technics.domain.com
4          IN      PTR      ns.domain.com
5          IN      PTR      peanutbutter.domain.com.
```

We don't have to create any files to be secondary for example.com. We only need to add the entries we already have in the **named.conf** file.

And that's it: a complete configuration for a primary domain.

THE DNS TOOLBOX

This section describes a few tools that you'll want to get acquainted with as you work with DNS. They'll help you to troubleshoot problems more quickly.

kill -HUP

If you have changed BIND's configuration files, you will need to tell it to re-read them by sending the named process a HUP signal. Begin by finding the process ID for the **named** process. This can be done by looking for it in **/usr/local/var/run/named.pid** or in **/var/run/named.pid**. If you do not see it in either place, you can run the following command to get it:

```
[root@ford /root]# ps -C named
```

This will produce output that looks something like this:

```
PID TTY          TIME CMD

14880 ?       00:00:00 named
14881 ?       00:00:00 named
14882 ?       00:00:00 named
14883 ?       00:00:00 named
14884 ?       00:00:00 named
```

Look for the lowest number in the first column and use it to send a HUP signal, like this:

```
[root@ford /root]# kill -HUP 14880
```

Of course, replace "14880" with the correct process ID from your output.

host

The **host** tool is really the master of all DNS tools. By learning all of the features host has to offer, you can eliminate the need to learn several of the smaller tools that come with BIND. Long time users of **nslookup** may be surprised to see their old friend being put away. Well, the news isn't as bad as you think—the BIND team is simply trying to leave less overlap between their tools.

In its simplest use, **host** allows you to resolve host names into IP addresses from the command line. For example:

```
[root@ford root]# host theorb.com
theorb.com has address 209.133.83.16
```

We can also use **host** to perform reverse lookups. For example:

```
[root@ford root]# host 209.133.83.16
16.83.133.209.IN-ADDR.ARPA domain name pointer taz.hyperreal.org
```

This can lead to all kinds of interesting discoveries. In this case, we see that theorb.com is the same as taz.hyperreal.org. It's likely that taz.hyperreal.org is also "virtually hosting" other domains, as well.

> **TIP:** If you are familiar with **nslookup**, don't worry—it's still there. However, since the BIND group is trying to move people away from it, consider using the **dig** tool (discussed next) instead when you need to find out about records other than A and PTR, or when you need to query servers other than your own.

dig

The domain information gopher, **dig**, is a great tool for gathering information about DNS servers. The typical format of the **dig** command is:

```
[root@ford /root]# dig @server domain query-type
```

where **@server** is the name of the DNS server you want to query, **domain** is the domain name you are interested in querying, and **query-type** is the name of the record you are trying to get (A, MX, NS, SOA, HINFO, TXT, or any).

For example, to get the **mx** record for the domain whitehouse.gov from the DNS server ns1.ucsd.edu, you would run:

```
[root@ford /root]# dig @ns1.ucsd.edu whitehouse.gov mx
```

dig is an incredibly powerful program. You should read the man page that was installed with **dig** to learn how to use some of its more advanced features.

whois

The **whois** command is used for determining ownership of a domain. Information about a domain's owner isn't a mandatory part of its records, nor is it customarily placed in the TXT or RP records. So you'll need to gather this information using the **whois** technique, which reports the actual owner of the domain, their snail-mail address, e-mail address, and technical contact phone numbers.

Due to Network Solutions, Inc. having to allow competition, the **whois** registry works a little differently than it used to. Now, when you make a query against the default **whois** database, you will be told who the registrar is and the name server for that domain. You then must make a second query to get more information about the domain itself with the appropriate **whois** server.

Let's walk through an example of getting information about the clickarray.com domain. We first query the default database and get a response like so:

```
[root@ford root]# whois clickarray.com
[whois.crsnic.net]

Whois Server Version 1.3
Domain names in the .com, .net, and .org domains can now be registered
with many different competing registrars. Go to http://www.internic.net
```

```
for detailed information.
    Domain Name: CLICKARRAY.COM
    Registrar: REGISTER.COM, INC.
    Whois Server: whois.register.com
    Referral URL: www.register.com
    Name Server: NS.STAT.NET
    Updated Date: 01-may-2000
>>> Last update of whois database: Thu, 26 Oct 2000 06:47:54 EDT <<<
The Registry database contains ONLY .COM, .NET, .ORG, .EDU domains and
Registrars.

No such file or directory while getting address for "whois.register.com"
```

From this information, we see that clickarray.com used Register.com, Inc., as their registrar. Also from this information we see that the **whois** database for Register.com is whois.register.com. So we perform a second query against whois.register.com for clickarray.com and get a response like this:

```
[root@ford /root]# whois -f whois.register.com clickarray.com
[whois.crsnic.net]
Whois Server Version 1.3
Domain names in the .com, .net, and .org domains can now be registered
with many different competing registrars. Go to http://www.internic.net
for detailed information.

    Domain Name: CLICKARRAY.COM
    Registrar: REGISTER.COM, INC.
    Whois Server: whois.register.com
    Referral URL: www.register.com
    Name Server: NS.STAT.NET
    Updated Date: 01-may-2000

>>> Last update of whois database: Thu, 26 Oct 2000 06:47:54 EDT <<<
The Registry database contains ONLY .COM, .NET, .ORG, .EDU domains and
Registrars.
[whois.register.com]
The data in Register.com's WHOIS database is provided to you by
Register.com for information purposes only, that is, to assist you in
obtaining information about or related to a domain name registration
record.  Register.com makes this information available "as is," and
does not guarantee its accuracy.  By submitting a WHOIS query, you
agree that you will use this data only for lawful purposes and that,
under no circumstances will you use this data to: (1) allow, enable,
```

or otherwise support the transmission of mass unsolicited, commercial advertising or solicitations via direct mail, electronic mail, or by telephone; or (2) enable high volume, automated, electronic processes that apply to Register.com (or its systems). The compilation, repackaging, dissemination or other use of this data is expressly prohibited without the prior written consent of Register.com. Register.com reserves the right to modify these terms at any time. By submitting this query, you agree to abide by these terms.

```
    Organization:
        Le Lu
        Le Lu
        1551 Great Tree Common
        Los Angeles, CA 92532
        US
        Phone: 213-555-2321
        Email: clickarray@yahoo.com


Registrar Name....: Register.com
Registrar Whois...: whois.register.com
Registrar Homepage: http://www.register.com


Domain Name: CLICKARRAY.COM


        Created on..............: Fri, Feb 25, 2000
        Expires on..............: Mon, Feb 25, 2002
        Record last updated on..: Fri, Jun 02, 2000


Administrative Contact:
        Fazoom, Inc.
        Le Lu
        1551 Great Tree Common
        Los Angeles, CA 92532
        US
        Phone: 213-555-2321
        Email: clickarray@yahoo.com


Technical Contact, Zone Contact:
        Register.Com
        Domain Registrar
        575 8th Avenue - 11th Floor
        New York, NY 10018
        US
        Phone: 212-798-9200
```

```
     Fax..: 212-629-930
     Email: domain-registrar@register.com
Domain servers in listed order:
NS.STAT.NET                                    207.126.116.254
Register your domain name at http://www.register.com
```

Keeping the **whois** information up-to-date for your own domain is very important. Should an extraordinary event occur, such as your site being attacked or turned into a spam relay, you'll most likely be contacted via telephone before via e-mail. In such situations, not having current, relevant information can cause you a great deal of harm.

Other References

Obviously, any protocol that's been around as long as DNS can't be summarized in a few short pages. If you need to explore DNS beyond what has been discussed in this chapter, I highly recommend the following texts:

DNS and BIND, Third Edition, by Paul Albitz and Cricket Liu (O'Reilly &Associates, 1999) does a superb job of really getting into the truly hairy details of DNS. If you're looking to subdomain, do DNS load balancing, or basically do anything out of the ordinary, pick up this book. Chapters like the one you're reading are a great way to get up and running with a reasonably solid understanding, but it's books like *DNS and BIND* that make you fly.

In Chapter 11 of this book, I recommend *TCP/IP Illustrated,* Volume 1, by Richard Stevens (Addison-Wesley, 1994-1996). It contains a chapter dedicated to DNS, with a packet-by-packet analysis and fundamental explanations of how it all works.

There are several RFCs related to DNS, most notably 1034 and 1035. Several are included with the BIND documentation in the **bind-9.0.0/doc/rfc** directory. You can also get them online from http://www.rfc-editor.org. If you're curious about the bleeding edge, visit the Internet Engineering Task Force at http://www.ietf.org to see what they are up to.

SUMMARY

In this chapter, we covered all of the information you'll need to get various types of DNS servers up and running. We discussed

▼   Name resolution over the Internet

■   Compiling the BIND name server

■   The **/etc/hosts** file (and a little about NIS)

■   The process of configuring a Linux client to use DNS

- Configuring DNS servers to act as primary, secondary, and caching servers
- The record types needed to establish a site
- Most of the configuration options in the **named.conf** file
- Tools for use in conjunction with the DNS server to do troubleshooting
- ▲ Additional sources of information

With the information available in the BIND documentation on how the server should be configured, along with the actual configuration files for a complete server presented in this chapter, you should be able to go out and perform a complete installation from start to finish.

Like any software, nothing is perfect, and problems can occur with BIND and the related files and programs discussed here. Don't forget to check out Web sites as well as the various newsgroups dedicated to DNS and BIND for additional information. Especially notable are these:

- ▼ comp.protocols.dns.bind
- ■ comp.protocols.dns.ops
- ▲ comp.protocols.dns.std

You will find plenty of people who can help you work through your problems. Remember to help someone else after you've learned it yourself!

CHAPTER 13

FTP

The File Transfer Protocol (FTP) has existed for the Internet since around 1971. Remarkably, the protocol has undergone very little change since then. Clients and servers, on the other hand, have been almost constantly improved and refined. This chapter discusses the installation and configuration of one particularly refined server, the Washington University FTP server, better known as *wu-ftpd*.

A majority of Linux distributions come with wu-ftpd as their default FTP server. Many commercial non-Linux FTP sites also use wu-ftpd instead of the server that came with their variant of UNIX for the same reasons that wu-ftpd is the server of choice under Linux: its stability, flexibility, and security.

CAUTION: Like most other services, wu-ftpd is only as secure as you make it. The authors of the program have provided all of the necessary tools to make your site secure, but a bad configuration can cause your site to become open. Remember to double-check your configuration and test it out before going live.

In this chapter, we will discuss how to download, compile, and install the latest version of wu-ftpd. We will also show how to configure it for private access as well as anonymous access. And finally, we will show how to set up virtual domains with wu-ftpd.

THE MECHANICS OF FTP

The act of transferring a file from one computer to another may seem trivial, but in reality it is not—at least, not if you're doing it right. In this section, we step through the details of the FTP client/server interaction. While this information isn't crucial to being able to get an FTP server up and running, it is important when you need to consider security issues as well as troubleshooting issues—especially troubleshooting issues that don't clearly manifest themselves as FTP-related. ("Is it the network, or is it FTP?")

Client/Server Interactions

When an FTP client wants to connect to an FTP server, it takes a random high port (a port number greater than 1024) as its source and port number 21 as its destination on the FTP server. (Port 21 is the ubiquitous FTP server port defined in the FTP standard.) Once the connection is established, the client can log in and issue commands to go through the FTP server's directories.

When the client makes a request to transfer a file, the server grabs another random high port and begins listening for connections on it. It sends this new port number to the FTP client over the existing connection. The FTP client takes this port number and initiates a new connection from one of its random high ports to the port number the server provided. The original connection is left open so that the client and server can send additional "out of band" messages to each other (for example, abort the transfer).

This design, conceived in the early 1970s, assumed something that was reasonable for a long period of time on the Internet: Internet users are a friendly bunch who know better. This was indirectly protected by the fact that the National Science Foundation (NSF) funded the Internet backbone, and therefore no commercial organizations were allowed onto it unless they were working in conjunction with a research institute. Academic- and government-funded research labs made up most of the users.

Around 1990–1991, the NSF stopped footing the bill for the Internet backbone, and the Internet went commercial. At first, it wasn't a big deal. Then the World Wide Web came along and the Net's population exploded—along with its security problems.

Many sites have now taken to using firewalls to protect their internal networks from the Big Bad Internet. Firewalls, however, consider arbitrary connections from high ports on the Internet to high ports on the internal network to be a very bad thing (rightfully so). As a result, many firewalls implement application-level proxies for FTP, which keep track of FTP requests and open up those high ports when needed to receive data from a remote site.

Of course, not all firewalls are that smart. Many sites rely on packet filtering firewalls, which don't really understand the data going through them but know that data being sent to arbitrary high ports is bad and thus bounces them out. This type of firewall promptly breaks FTP, because FTP relies on being able to open a connection back with the client on a high port. A typical symptom of this behavior occurring is when a client appears to be able to connect to the server without a problem, the connection seems to hang whenever an attempt to transfer data occurs.

Now think back to when FTP was originally created and bandwidth was at a premium. When someone wanted to get a file transferred from host A to host B while sitting at host C, the process of transferring the file from host A to C and then from C to B would end up wasting an incredible amount of bandwidth. So the designers of the FTP protocol came up with a solution: Make it possible for someone sitting on host C to transfer a file from host A to host B directly. This was done via a *passive transfer*.

Passive transfers are accomplished by having the client side rather than the server side, initiate the connection for data transfer. From the standpoint of firewalls, this allows the client to remain securely behind a firewall without the need for complex rules for allowing connections back in.

GETTING THE LATEST WU-FTPD

Like other server software, wu-ftpd undergoes updates and upgrades on a regular basis. These updates are now made available (via FTP, of course) at ftp://ftp.wu-ftpd.org. The Web site, http://www.wu-ftpd.org, is also a good place to get information on the status of the wu-ftpd daemon. As of this writing, the latest version of wu-ftpd is 2.6.1; however, many CD-ROMs have been distributed with 2.5.0. The upgrade is recommended because the wu-ftpd development group is no longer supporting prior versions. The upgrade is especially important if you've inherited a Linux system (or any UNIX system, for that matter) running any version of wu-ftpd prior to the VR14 patch, because of a widely publicized security problem that script kiddies (see Chapter 11 for a definition) have used to break into sites.

If you have installed Red Hat Linux 7.0 with the FTP server enabled, you have 2.6.1 already. If not, you can download version 2.6.1 at ftp://ftp.wu-ftpd.org/pub/wu-ftpd/wu-ftpd-2.6.1. tar.gz.

Once you have this package downloaded, you will need to un**tar** it with the following command:

```
[root@ford src]# tar -xvzf wu-ftpd-2.6.tar.gz
```

This will create a subdirectory called **wu-ftpd-2.6.1** relative to your current directory, where all of the source code files will be unpacked. For the purpose of consistency, you may want to unpack this and any other software you compile yourself into the **/usr/ local/src** directory.

Read the READMEs

You'll find that wu-ftpd comes with several documentation files in straight text format. One of these README files includes the procedure for compiling wu-ftpd on many different computing platforms (should you be interested in doing so). I highly recommend taking a few minutes to read through what is there. In this release, and as will be in future releases, the documentation that comes with the package contains a wealth of information for finding online help resources, as well as notes about the package that the developers want you to know. It also is helpful to have read the documentation that comes with the package *before* heading off to any discussion forums with questions.

Compiling and Installing wu-ftpd

From the subdirectory into which wu-ftpd unpacked, all you need to type is

```
[root@ford wu-ftpd-2.6.1]# ./build lnx
```

and you're done. The script takes care of the compilation and verification process for you. At the end of the compilation process, you should see something that looks like this:

```
Executables are in bin directory:
    text    data     bss     dec      hex filename
  134036   14080  100576  248692    3cb74 bin/ftpd
    6634     484      36    7154     1bf2 bin/ftpcount
    9020     468   10336   19824     4d70 bin/ftpshut
    6309     428   12320   19057     4a71 bin/ftprestart
    6634     484      36    7154     1bf2 bin/ftpwho
    5872     384    8256   14512     38b0 bin/ckconfig
    8384     556     352    9292     244c bin/privatepw
Done
```

If you have an existing configuration, you will want to make a backup of the configuration files so that the installation process doesn't write over them. The files you will need to save are these:

▼ /etc/ftpaccess

■ /etc/ftpgroups

■ /etc/ftphosts

▲ /etc/ftpusers

Once you have saved them, you are ready to do the install. If you aren't the root user already, use the **su** command to become the root user. Then enter the command

```
[root@ford wu-ftpd-2.6.1]# ./build install
```

This will cause all of the binaries and man pages to be installed into their appropriate locations.

With the binaries in place, we are now ready to edit the **/etc/services** file so that the system will be able to patch the port numbers for FTP to the FTP service listed in **/etc/inetd.conf** (or **/etc/xinetd.conf** if you are using Red Hat 7). Be sure **/etc/services** contains the following two lines:

```
ftp-data        20/tcp
ftp             21/tcp
```

Fixing Your inetd.conf File

If you are using a distribution of Linux that comes with a standard **inetd** program, you will want to follow these steps to edit the **/etc/inetd.conf** file so that the system will automatically launch the FTP server whenever someone tries to connect to it. To make the changes, open up **/etc/inetd.conf** with your favorite text editor. Near the top of the file, you should find a line that begins with "ftp." If you don't find any such line, then you will need to add one. You can add this line anywhere in the file, but make sure it reads as follows:

```
ftp     stream  tcp     nowait  root    /usr/sbin/tcpd  in.ftpd -l -a
```

As you might recall from Chapter 9, the **/etc/inetd.conf** file is managed by the **inetd** program, which acts as a kind of "super-server," listening for network requests on behalf of many server applications and starting the server applications once it detects a connection request for it. If its configuration file **/etc/inetd.conf** gets changed, you need to send the **inetd** process a signal to tell it to reload its configuration file. This is done in one of two ways:

▼ Run the following command:

```
kill -1 `ps -C inetd | awk 'print $2'`
```

▲ See if your distribution keeps track of the process ID for you in the **/var/run/inetd.pid** file. If it does, you can use

```
kill -1 `cat /var/run/inetd.pid`
```

Fixing Your xinetd.conf File

If you are using a distribution that comes with the **xinetd** daemon (like Red Hat 7) instead of a regular **inetd**, then you will need to follow these directions to enable the FTP service.

First, make sure there is a file called **wu-ftpd** in the **/etc/xinetd.d** directory. That file should read:

```
# description: The wu-ftpd FTP server serves FTP connections. It uses
#         normal, unencrypted usernames and passwords for authentication.
service ftp
{
        socket_type             = stream
        wait                    = no
        user                    = root
        server                  = /usr/sbin/in.ftpd
        server_args             = -l -a
        log_on_success          += DURATION USERID
        log_on_failure          += USERID
        nice                    = 10
}
```

Now we need to tell **xinetd** to re-read all of its configuration files. This is done by sending it a **SIGUSR1**. The easiest way to do this is to run:

```
[root@ford /root]# kill -SIGUSR1 `cat /var/log/xinetd.pid`
```

If you have Red Hat 7, you can also run:

```
[root@ford /root]# /etc/rc.d/init.d/xinetd reload
```

And you should now be able to **ftp** to your own system. Don't worry if you can't log in yet—we'll get to those details in the next section—but at the very least you should be able to get an FTP login prompt.

CONFIGURING WU-FTPD

The wu-ftpd package comes with several sample configuration files that are very easy to modify and deploy on your FTP server. In "Cookbook Access Solutions" later in this

One of the goals of this book is to provide a way for NT/2000 administrators to become comfortable with Linux by demonstrating system parallels. This section visualizes some of the most important concepts for both operating systems so you can see how their foundations are established.

Linux Administration Blueprints

Table of Contents

Linux vs. Windows NT/2000 Authentication...2

Linux vs. Windows NT/2000-Based Network..4

Linux vs. Windows NT/2000 Boot Process..6

Linux vs. Windows NT/2000 Shutdown Process...8

Linux vs. Windows NT/2000 Authentication

Linux Authentication

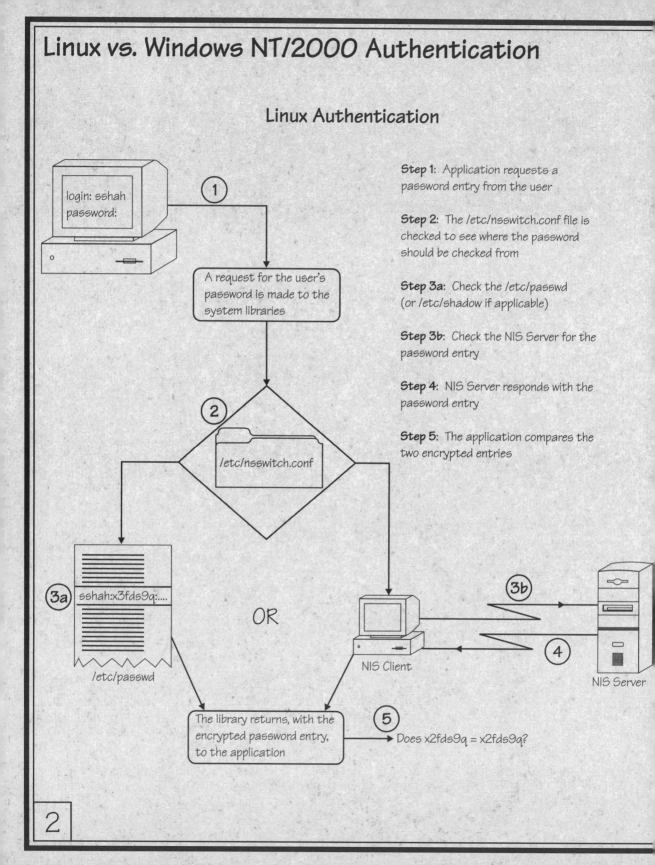

Step 1: Application requests a password entry from the user

Step 2: The /etc/nsswitch.conf file is checked to see where the password should be checked from

Step 3a: Check the /etc/passwd (or /etc/shadow if applicable)

Step 3b: Check the NIS Server for the password entry

Step 4: NIS Server responds with the password entry

Step 5: The application compares the two encrypted entries

login: sshah
password:

A request for the user's password is made to the system libraries

/etc/nsswitch.conf

sshah:x3fds9q:....

/etc/passwd

OR

NIS Client

NIS Server

The library returns, with the encrypted password entry, to the application

Does x2fds9q = x2fds9q?

Windows NT/2000 Authentication

login: sshah
password:

① A request to verify the user's password is made

Step 1: Application sends password entered by the user to the operating system

Step 2a: If it is the local domain, check the password against the local SAM

Step 2b: Otherwise, check the password against the PDC/Active Directory Server

Step 3: Return to the calling application with a message indicating whether the user was authenticated or not

2a

?

2b

Local Hard Disk

Primary Domain Controller/
Active Directory Server

OK

NT/2000 Client ③

The key difference between Linux and NT/2000 is that Linux performs all authentication issues outside of the core operating system. This gives a great deal of flexibility in how the authentication happens, and improves the stability of the system as a whole since it allows the Linux kernel to remain simple. The trade-off is consistency in the user interfaces and the need for application developers to handle their own authentication procedure.

Linux vs. Windows NT/2000-Based Network

Linux Network

Windows NT/2000-Based Network

NT/2000 File Server

NT/2000 Backups
(e.g., "Retrospect")

Primary Domain
Controller/Active
Directory Server

Windows-Based Clients

Firewall

IIS
Web Server

Print Server/
Backup Domain
Controller (NT 3/4 Only)

NT/2000 SQL
Server

WINS Server

DNS Server
(NT 3/4 Only)

Both networks are functionally equivalent: whatever NT/2000 can do, Linux can do also. However, Linux can typically do this with fewer servers and can support Windows and Macintosh clients as well. This is accomplished with the Samba package for working with Windows clients, and Netatalk for working with Macintosh clients.

Linux vs. Windows NT/2000 Boot Process

The Linux Boot Process

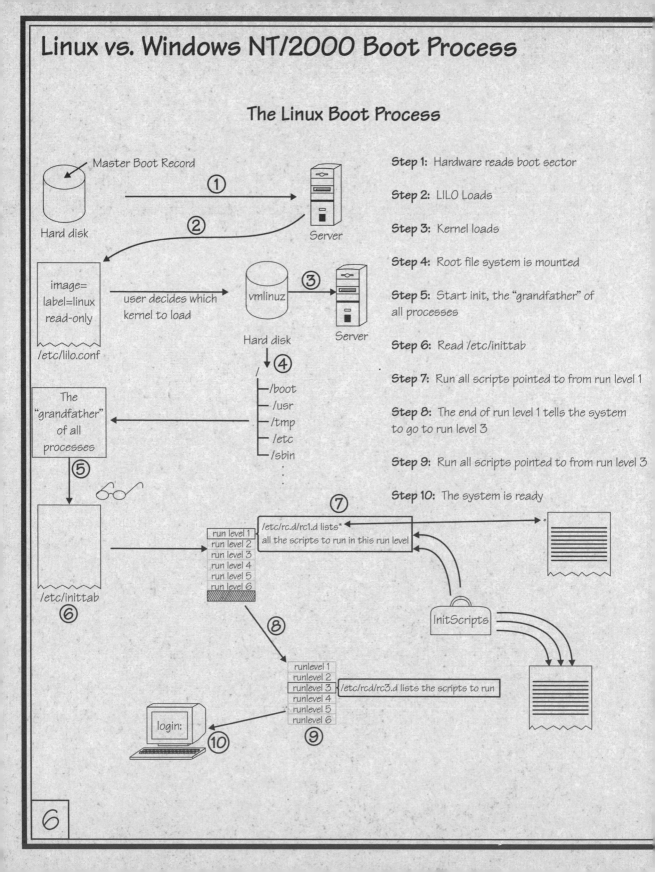

Step 1: Hardware reads boot sector

Step 2: LILO Loads

Step 3: Kernel loads

Step 4: Root file system is mounted

Step 5: Start init, the "grandfather" of all processes

Step 6: Read /etc/inittab

Step 7: Run all scripts pointed to from run level 1

Step 8: The end of run level 1 tells the system to go to run level 3

Step 9: Run all scripts pointed to from run level 3

Step 10: The system is ready

The NT/2000 Boot Process

Master Boot Record

Hard disk

NTDETECT.COM

user decides which kernel configuration to use

Server

Server

boot.ini

NTOSKRNL
HAL.DLL

Server

C:\
└── \WINNT
└── \Program Files
└── \temp

SMSS.EXE

Application

Win32

NTCORE

What services need to be loaded?

Services

Bag of Services

login:

SCREG.EXE
LSASS.EXE

Drivers

Bag of Drivers

Step 1: Hardware reads boot sector

Step 2: NTLDR loads and reads BOOT.INI (similar to LILO and /etc/lilo.conf)

Step 3: NTDETECT runs to probe the hardware

Step 4: NTLDR loads NTOSKRNL.EXE, the NT/2000 kernel and HAL.DLL, the Hardware Abstraction Layer

Step 5: NT/2000 makes the C: drive available

Step 6: SMSS.EXE, the services manager gets loaded. This reads the registry and determines which services should be loaded

Step 7: The WIN32 system is loaded

Step 8a: Winlogon, which provides login service, is started

Step 8b: SCREG, the Scan Registry Tool, and LSASS, the Local Security Authority, are started along with Winlogon. SCREG starts auto loading drivers. The system is ready

The NT/2000 and Linux boot processes do strike parallels between each other. If you understand the reasoning behind one, you can understand the reasoning behind the other. They both start by reading the MBR, and they both end by providing login: prompts for the user. Noteworthy points of similarity are the NTLDR and LILO. They look different and act different, but in the end they do the exact same thing. NTDETECT, NTOSKRNL, and HAL are three components that are all done in the Linux kernel. Although SMSS and init take very different paths, their goal is one and the same: getting the necessary services started.

Linux vs. Windows NT/2000 Shutdown Process

Linux Shutdown

RunLevels
1
2
3
4
5
6

/etc/rc.d/rc6.d

InitScripts

sync

Server

Server

The system is halted

Step 1: The shutdown or reboot command is invoked

Step 2: Init is told to change to runlevel 6

Step 3: The scripts in runlevel 6 call init scripts with the parameter "stop"

Step 4: Outstanding buffers are written for disk (sync'd)

Step 5: The file systems are unmounted

Step 6: The system is halted

NT/2000 Shutdown

WINS Server
(NT 3/4 Only)

Print
Server

File
Server

Primary
Domain
Controller/Active
Directory Server

Services

101010

SMSS.EXE

Step 1: The shutdown command is invoked

Step 2: The WINS Server (NT 3/4 Only) is notified that the machine is leaving the network

Step 3: Disconnects from all network services

Step 4: The persistent connection to the PDC/Active Directory Server is closed

Step 5: "Last Known Good" information is written to the registry

Step 6: Services are shutdown

Step 7: The system is halted

Unfortunately, the Linux and NT/2000 shutdown procedures don't show the same amount of parallels that their boot processes do. This stems from the nature of Linux's NIS, NFS, and LPR services versus NT/2000's PDC/Active Directory and SMB protocols. Linux doesn't maintain persistent connections for those services; NT/2000 does.

chapter, we'll even present some of our own simple, pre-done configurations if you just need to get off to a quick start.

This section focuses on the nitty-gritty details of what wu-ftpd has to offer. You may find it a handy reference tool rather than a tutorial, but at least one good skim through it is definitely warranted.

Controlling Access Through the /etc/ftpaccess File

The **/etc/ftpaccess** file contains five types of commands:

▼ Access control

■ Automatic banner information for clients

■ Logging configuration

■ Miscellaneous server commands

▲ Permissions

We'll examine each specific command belonging to each group.

Access Control

Being able to control who may and who may not enter your FTP server is a crucial aspect of server management. The following commands allow you to do just that.

class The **class** command defines a new class of users on your system. It does not grant or take away any particular rights, but defining a class is necessary for referencing a group of users in commands discussed later in this section.

The format of a **class** command is

```
class classname type address...
```

where the **classname** is the name of the new class you are defining. **Type** is one of three values: anonymous, real, or guest. *Anonymous users* are just that: users who may access the server without having explicit permission from you to log in. (Please note that by defining a class that allows anonymous users, you are not actually setting up anonymous FTP.) *Real users* must have an account on the system and a valid shell. (In the case of FTP, we define a valid shell to be any shell that is listed in the **/etc/shells** file.) *Guest users* are those who do not have a real account on the server but are explicitly listed in a guest group (discussed later in this section). Finally, **address** is a list of IP addresses that the defined class may originate from. The asterisk (*) is a wildcard that says all IP addresses are valid for the class being defined.

For example, the **class** statement

```
class myclass anonymous 10.10.*
```

defines the class myclass, which consists only of anonymous users whose IP addresses start with 10.10.

You can have as many **class** entries as you like.

autogroup   The **autogroup** command is used for setting which UNIX group anonymous users belong to when they log in via the FTP server. By explicitly setting the group they belong to, you can retain tight control over what files they may and may not access.

The format of the **autogroup** command is

```
autogroup groupname class...
```

where *groupname* is the name of the group that you want anonymous users to belong to (note that the *groupname* should correlate to an entry in the **/etc/group** file), and *class...* is a list of classes that you want affected by this command.

For example, if you defined three classes,

```
class a anonymous,real 10.10.*
class b anonymous,real,guest 192.168.5.*
class c anonymous,real 192.168.7.10 192.168.7.11 192.168.7.12
```

you can specify an autogroup class like so:

```
autogroup anonftp a b
```

Now anyone from class a or b who logs in as anonymous has to work within the confines of the group anonftp.

deny   The **deny** command allows you to block access to your site based on someone's originating IP address or host name. (Note that because reverse resolving host names to IP addresses is unreliable, it is recommended that you use only IP addresses.) The format of the **deny** command is as follows:

```
deny address message_file
```

where *address* is the IP address and *message_file* is the filename of the message that you want to send back to them when they try to connect. For example, the command

```
deny 192.168.66.7 /home/ftp/no_evil_crackers
```

would cause the contents of the file **/home/ftp/no_evil_crackers** to be sent to any user who tries to log in to the server from the IP address 192.168.66.7.

guestgroup   The **guestgroup** command is useful when you have real users but want them to have only restrictive FTP privileges similar to that of anonymous users. The format of the command is

```
guestgroup groupname...
```

where **groupname** is the name of one or more groups (taken from **/etc/group**) that you want restricted.

To restrict users in this manner, in addition to this entry in the **/etc/ftpaccess** file, you need to change the format of each user's **/etc/passwd** entry. The new format should have their home directory broken up by the **/./** characters. Before the split should be the effective root directory, and after the split should be the user's relative home directory. For example, the entry

```
sshah:ilhsvmt1m8wh:256:1024:Steve Shah:/ftp/./sshah:/bin/ftponly
```

would mean **/ftp** is the user's new relative root directory. This would prevent the user even seeing the actual **/home** directory, or any other directory for that matter. Because of this, you need to place **bin, etc,** and **lib** directories in **/ftp** where enough libraries and binaries exist to allow them to at least **ftp** into the system. This aspect is identical to an anonymous user configuration, which we discuss in "Setting Up the Anonymous User" later in the chapter.

Relative to **/ftp** would be a subdirectory called **sshah**, which would be their home directory for logging in via FTP. Because **/bin/ftponly** is not a real shell, they could not **telnet** into the system. However, be sure that **/bin/ftponly** is listed in the **/etc/shells** file.

limit   The **limit** command allows you to control the maximum number of users who log in to your system via FTP by class and time of day. The format of the **limit** command is

```
limit class n times message_file
```

where **class** is the name of the class affected, **n** is the maximum number, **times** is the day and times when the users are allowed to log in, and **message_file** is the file that is displayed to any users who are not allowed in.

The format of the **times** entry is a little tricky. The parameter is in the form of a comma-delimited string, where each option is for a separate day. Sunday through Saturday take the form Su, Mo, Tu, We, Th, Fr, and Sa, respectively, and all the weekdays can be referenced as Wk. Time should be kept in military format, without a colon separating the hours and minutes. A range is specified by a dash (-).

For example, to limit the class anonpeoples to a maximum of 25 on Monday through Thursday all day, and on Friday to 7 P.M., you would use the line

```
limit anonpeoples 25 MoTuWeTh,Fr0000-1900 /home/ftp/.message.too_many
```

where the contents of the file **/home/ftp/.message.too_many** is sent back to the user if the maximum is exceeded.

NOTE: Support for the `limit` command is for those servers that either have limitations in terms of available bandwidth or that need to be available for other tasks during certain times. For example, an FTP server that makes product errata sheets available should be accessible by customers during normal business hours. Only during the late-night hours, when business traffic has died down, might it be acceptable for the server to host your collection of band discographies. The `limit` command allows you to accomplish this type of configuration.

loginfails The `loginfails` command allows you to limit the number of consecutive failed logins when a user connects to your site. The format of the command is

```
loginfails n
```

where **n** is the number of login failures you are willing to tolerate. For example, if you want the system to automatically drop the connection for someone who fails to type in their password correctly three times in a row, you would use

```
loginfails 3
```

private You may find it necessary to share files with others you don't want to give an account on the system to, but at the same time you don't want to place a file into a 100% publicly accessible directory. By setting up a private group, you require the clients to use the **SITE GROUP** and **SITE GPASS** commands so that they can change into the privileged groups that require passwords. For the FTP server to support this capability, you need to set the PRIVATE flag, using the command

```
private switch
```

where **switch** is ON or OFF.

Because you need to require passwords for these special groups, you need to use the **/etc/ftpgroups** file. The format of an access group in **/etc/ftpgroups** is

```
access_group_name:encrypted_password:real_group
```

where **access_group_name** is the name that the client uses to reference the special group, **encrypted_password** is the password users need to supply (via **SITE GPASS**) to access the group, and **real_group** is the actual group referenced in the **/etc/group** file.

To generate an encrypted password entry for this file, you need to use the **crypt** function. This can be accessed through the following simple Perl script:

```
#!/usr/bin/perl
print "Enter password to encrypt: ";
chop ($password=<STDTN>);
print "The encrypted password is: ", crypt($password,$password);
```

Simply type this and save it as a file. Change the permissions on it to be executable (for example, `chmod 755 my_perl_script`) and run it. The script will prompt you for the password you want to set and then print out the resulting encrypted string.

Banner Message Control

When a user logs in to your site via FTP, you may find it handy to present some kind of message to them as they log in. In other situations, you may find it handy to be able to present a special message if they enter a particular directory or perform a certain action. This section discusses how to use the commands in wu-ftpd's **/etc/ftpaccess** file to do just that.

banner   This command allows you to present a message to a user who has connected to the FTP service but has not logged in yet. The format of the **banner** command is

```
banner filename
```

where ***filename*** is the name of the file (with full path) that you want displayed. The file should be a straight ASCII text file. For example:

```
banner /home/ftp/welcome_to_my_ftp_site
```

NOTE: Administrators who have taken care of busy FTP servers have commented that a good banner message is actually very crucial in limiting the number of one-user inquiries about your site. To quote my technical editor, "People actually do read them!"

email   The **email** command allows you to specify the e-mail address of the site maintainer. Commands such as **message** (discussed next) use this information as well. The format of this command is

```
email address
```

where ***address*** is the e-mail address of the site administrator. You should consider using a generic e-mail address here such as "ftp@ftp.*yoursite*.com" and use the **/etc/aliases** file (see Chapter 15 on Sendmail) to expand that alias to all of your real administrators. An example of the **email** command in action is

```
email ftp@ftp.yoursite.com
```

message   The **message** command is useful when you need to set up special messages for a specific class of users or for users who enter a specific directory. The format of the command is

```
message path when class...
```

where **path** is the file that is to be displayed to the user, **when** is the condition that must be true in order for you to display the message, and **class** (which is optional) is the list of classes the message applies to.

The **when** parameter is what makes this command really different from the **banner** command. **when** can take one of two forms: LOGIN or CWD=**path**. If it is LOGIN, the message is displayed after a successful login. If it is CWD=**path**, the message is displayed when a user goes into the **path** directory.

The message file itself is an ordinary text file with some special keywords. These keywords are as follows:

Option	Description
%T	Local time
%F	Free space for the partition on which path is located
%C	The current working directory
%E	The e-mail address specified with the **email** command
%R	Client host name
%L	Server host name
%U	Username provided at login time
%M	Maximum number of allowed users in the login class
%N	Number of users in the class

NOTE: Messages triggered by an anonymous login must be relative to the anonymous FTP directory.

An example of the **message** command in action is

```
message ./too.many.users LOGIN anonusers
```

where the **too.many.users** file looks like this:

```
Sorry %R, but %L's limit of %N out of %M users has been reached. We
are working on getting a larger server but in the meantime we
appreciate patience. Please try again later.
Your FTP Administrator, %E
```

readme   The **readme** command allows the server to automatically inform a user when a particular file was last updated. The command takes the form

```
readme path when class
```

where **path** is the full path name of the file that you want the FTP server to keep an eye on, **when** is when you want the user to be told (the format of **when** is the same as for the **message** command), and **class** is the class this command applies to. The **when** and **class** parameters are optional. For example:

```
readme ./README CWD=/pub/patches
```

Logging

You can use wu-ftpd to configure what information should be logged about its usage. This information is a great way of getting a handle on utilization information so that you can better lay out and organize your services.

This section discusses the commands used in customizing the log entries.

log commands   If you want to log each command entered by users connecting to your FTP service, you want to use **log commands**. Its usage is as follows:

```
log commands typelist
```

where **typelist** is the comma-separated list of the type of user whose commands you want to log, as described by the **class** command. Valid user types are anonymous, guest, and real. For example, if you want to log all the commands typed by anonymous users, you would type

```
log commands anonymous
```

log transfers   If you want to log only the files transferred between users and your server instead of all commands typed, you would use the **log transfers** command:

```
log transfers typelist directions
```

where **typelist** is the type of user whose commands you want to log as described by the **class** command (that is, anonymous, guest, and real), and **directions** is a comma-separated list of which direction the transfer must take in order for it to be logged (that is, inbound and outbound). For example, to log all guest users' inbound and outbound connections, type

```
log transfers guest inbound,outbound
```

Miscellaneous Server Commands

Of course, there are always the commands that don't really fit into any particular category. Consider the following.

alias   It is often convenient to create shortcuts to frequently accessed directories. By using the **alias** command, you can do just that. The format of the command is

```
alias alias-name actual-directory
```

where **alias-name** is the alias itself, and **actual-directory** is the full directory that you want to set up a shortcut to. For example,

```
alias redhat /pub/linux/distributions/redhat
```

would allow a user to enter the command

```
cd redhat
```

and have the system automatically take him to the **/pub/linux/distributions/redhat** directory.

cdpath   The equivalent to the shell PATH environment variable, **cdpath** allows you to establish directory paths for users who connect to your FTP service. The format of the command is

```
cdpath directory
```

where **directory** is the name of the directory you want to add to the path. For example, if you used

```
cdpath /pub/linux
cdpath /pub/recipes
```

and a user enters the command **cd microwave**, wu-ftpd would search for the following directories:

- ▼ **./microwave**
- ■ Aliases called microwave
- ■ **/pub/linux/microwave**
- ▲ **/pub/recipes/microwave**

NOTE: The key difference between an alias and a cdpath is that an alias specifies a single mapping from one directory name to another. A cdpath, on the other hand, specifies a list of directories that should be checked when a user enters the **cd** command.

compress   The wu-ftpd server offers the ability to perform file conversions on the fly. One specific conversion it can do is compress or decompress a file before it is sent to a user. This is especially useful for clients who may not have the same compression tool you used or for clients on slow links who want to compress a file before sending it over the line.

The format of the **compress** command is

```
compress switch class
```

where ***switch*** is either ON or OFF, and ***class*** is either real, anonymous, or guest.

The caveat to using this feature is that you must also have your **/etc/ftpconversions** file set up. We'll discuss this in "File Conversions on the Fly," later in the chapter.

tar   Like the **compress** command, the **tar** command allows clients to **tar** or un**tar** a file before downloading it. (See Chapter 6 for more information on using **tar**.) The format of this command is

```
tar switch class
```

where ***switch*** is either ON or OFF, and ***class*** is either anonymous, real, or guest.

> **NOTE:**   This is a great mechanism for users to recursively download subdirectories.

Permissions

Setting file permissions on an FTP server is very important. You need to make sure the correct permissions are set so that files that you don't want to share don't get shared, and files that should not be altered are not altered. The commands discussed in this section help you maintain that integrity.

chmod   The **chmod** command allows you to decide if you want to give users the right to change permissions of files on your site. (They must own the file in order to be able to change permissions on it.) The format of the command is

```
chmod switch class
```

where ***switch*** is either ON or OFF and ***class*** is anonymous, guest, or real. In general, you want to give this kind of permission only to real users. For example:

```
chmod ON real
```

delete   The **delete** command tells the server whether users have the right to delete files they own on the FTP server. The format of the command is

```
delete switch class
```

where *switch* is either ON or OFF, and *class* is either anonymous, guest, or real. For example:

```
delete ON real
```

overwrite This command allows you to decide if you want to allow users to be able to overwrite existing files with their uploads. The format of the **overwrite** command is

```
overwrite switch class
```

where *switch* is either ON or OFF, and *class* is either anonymous, guest, or real. For example:

```
overwrite ON real
```

rename The **rename** command allows you to decide if you want users to be able to rename files that they own on the FTP server. The format of the command is:

```
rename switch class
```

where *switch* is either ON or OFF and *class* is either anonymous, guest, or real. For example:

```
rename ON real
```

umask The **umask** command allows you to decide if you want users of your FTP server to be able to change their default *umask*. A user's umask determines what the default permissions are going to be for any file they create. The umask is in octal and represents the inverse of what their permissions would be. For example, a umask of 077 means that any file created can be read, written to, or executed by the owner, but not by anyone else.

    The format of the **umask** command is

```
umask switch class
```

where *switch* is either ON or OFF, and *class* is either anonymous, real, or guest. For example:

```
umask ON real
```

passwd-check Sites providing anonymous access generally request that users of the site enter their e-mail address as the password; wu-ftpd allows you to decide how strict you want to be about enforcing password-check if you run an anonymous site. The format of the **passwd-check** command is

```
passwd-check strictness enforcement
```

where ***strictness*** is either none, trivial, or rfc822, and ***enforcement*** is either warn or enforce.

If ***strictness*** is none, the user can enter anything in the password field, and it will be accepted by wu-ftpd. Trivial only requires that the e-mail address have an @ sign in it. Specifying rfc822 requires that the e-mail address be fully compliant with the Message Header Standard. (For example, sshah@domain.com is an rfc822-compliant e-mail address.)

The enforcement of this command comes in two flavors: warn, which means that wu-ftpd will warn the user if their password is not compliant and then move on, and enforce, which means that wu-ftpd will not allow the user access until they have provided a valid address.

Note that this affects only anonymous access.

path-filter The **path-filter** command allows you to apply a filter against the filenames used for files that are uploaded to the server. The format of the command is

```
path-filter typelist message allowed-regexp denied-regexp
```

where ***typelist*** is the comma-separated list of users this command affects; the user types available are anonymous, guest, and real. ***Message*** is the file that is displayed to the user if their filename does not make it past this filter. ***Allowed-regexp*** is the regular expression that a filename must match if the user wants to upload it. ***Denied-regexp*** is the regular expression that a file cannot match if the user wants to upload it. For example, the line

```
path-filter anonymous /home/ftp/.badfilename UL* gif$
```

tells us that anonymous users must set the names of the files they upload to start with the letters "UL" but cannot end in "gif." If the filename doesn't meet this criteria, the contents of **/home/ftp/.badfilename** are sent to the user.

upload You can use the **upload** command, along with **path-filter**, to control files placed onto your server. The **upload** command specifies the permissions that the client has to place files in certain directories, as well as the permissions the files will take on after they are placed there. The format of the command is

```
upload directory dirglob switch owner group perms mkdir
```

where ***directory*** is the directory that is affected by this command, ***dirglob*** is the regular expression used to determine whether a subdirectory under ***directory*** is a valid place to make an upload, and ***switch*** is either YES or NO, thereby establishing whether an upload can happen in ***directory***. The ***owner***, ***group***, and ***perms*** parameters establish just that—the file's owner, group, and permissions, respectively. Finally, you can specify the ***mkdir*** operation as either DIRS or NODIRS, determining whether the client can create subdirectories under the specified ***directory***. For example:

```
upload /home/ftp /incoming yes ftp ftp 0400 nodirs
```

NOTE: The `upload` command affects only the directory listed, not any subdirectories beneath it. This prevents remote users from being able to create arbitrary directories on your server and hiding files in there.

The Log File

As we discussed earlier, the log file is important in your day-to-day operations. With it, you can perform an analysis of your FTP site and determine things like what the most commonly accessed files are and usage patterns for the site as a whole.

The default location for the FTP log file is **/var/log/xferlog**. Each line of the log contains the entry shown in Table 13-1.

Log Title Entry	Description
`Current-time`	The time at which the entry occurred. The format of the line is *DDD MMM dd hh:mm:ss YYYY*, where *DDD* is the day of the week, *MMM* is the month, *dd* is the day of the month, *hh:mm:ss* is the time in hours, minutes, and seconds, and *YYYY* is the year.
`Transfer-time`	The number of seconds it took to perform the transfer of this particular entry.
`Remote-host`	The client's host name.
`File-size`	Size of the file being transferred.
`File-name`	Name of the file being transferred.
`Transfer-type`	Either *a* for ASCII or *b* for binary.
`Special-action-flag`	A list of actions performed on the file by the server: *C* means the file was compressed, *U* means the file was uncompressed, *T* means the file was tarred, and a hyphen (-) means that no action was taken.
`Direction`	The direction of the transfer, where *o* means outbound and *i* means inbound.
`Access-mode`	The type of user that performed the transaction: *a* for anonymous, *r* for real, and *g* for guest.
`Username`	The local user name if the User-type is set to real.

Table 13-1.   Entries Contained in Each Line of **/var/log/xferlog**

Log Title Entry	Description
Service-name	The name by which the FTP server was invoked.
Authentication-method	The type of authentication done by the server on the user. *0* means no authentication was done, and *1* means the user had to log in with a unique login/password combination.
Authenticated-user-id	If the user had to log in with a unique login/password combination, the login would be here. Anonymous transfers are listed as *anonymous*.

Table 13-1.   Entries Contained in Each Line of **/var/log/xferlog** *(continued)*

File Conversions on the Fly

Sometimes, clients will not have the necessary tools to make use of the file they are downloading because it is either compressed or archived in a format that they cannot read. (This used to especially be true with **.tar.gz** files until WinZip started unarchiving those files, as well.) Other times, the reverse is true: The client is able to handle compressed files and would prefer receiving the file in a compressed format. Of course, file compression is just one of infinite types of use that you can set up with an **/etc/ftpconversions** file.

The format of the file is:

strippre:strippost:addonpre:addonpost:external:type:options:desc

The fields are as shown in Table 13-2.

Field	Description
strippre	The strip prefix is the starting characters of a filename that are removed before the file is transferred. For example, if the strip prefix is set to wedding , and a full filename is wedding.ring, a user could simply request a file ring, and wu-ftpd would know which file to get as well as what kind of conversion to do with it.

Table 13-2.   Fields of the **/etc/ftpconversions** File

Field	Description
strippost	The strip postfix is the same as the strip prefix, except it is for the end of the file instead. For example, if the strip postfix is set to.gz and a filename on the server is ring.gz, the server would know to perform the action matching this line in the configuration file if the client requested the file ring.
addonpost	Add-on postfix is the opposite of strippost in that instead of removing the end of a filename, it appends to it. This would be used in a case where a file that isn't compressed gets .gz added to it as it is compressed and sent to the client.
addonpre	Add-on prefix is the opposite of strippre. It allows you to add a prefix to a filename before it is sent to a client.
external	This entry specifies which program (external to wu-ftpd) is run when a filter matches. In the case of downloads, the resulting file after conversion should be sent to a program's standard output (stdout). Uploads are sent to the program's standard in (stdin). You can specify the filename the client requested in the command line for the external command by using **%s** instead of the name itself. The server will automatically search and replace every occurrence of **%s** with the client's filename.
type	In the world of wu-ftpd, files exist as one of three types: regular, ASCII, and directories (T_REG, T_ASCII, and T_DIR, respectively). This field allows you to specify the type of file that wu-ftpd should act on if the filename filter matches. You can specify multiple options by separating them with a pipe symbol (	). For example, **T_REG|T_ASCII** specifies that you want the filter to be applied to any type of file.

Table 13-2.   Fields of the **/etc/ftpconversions** File *(continued)*

Field	Description
options	This field decides whether this filter is going to compress, uncompress, or **tar** files. Each option is represented by O_COMPRESS, O_UNCOMPRESS, and O_TAR, respectively. You can do multiple things to a file at once by using the pipe (	) symbol between commands. For example, **O_COMPRESS|O_TAR** means that this filter will both compress and **tar** a client request.
desc	This is a freeform field that allows you to describe what the filter does.

Table 13-2.   Fields of the **/etc/ftpconversions** File *(continued)*

A Sample Entry

The following is a sample entry that compresses files using **gzip** on demand. This would allow someone who wants to get the file **orb_discography.tar** to instead request the file **orb_discography.tar.gz** and have the server compress the file using **gzip** before sending it to her. The configuration line that does this is as follows:

```
:::.gz:/bin/gzip -9 -c %s:T_REG|T_ASCII:O_COMPRESS:GZIP
```

The first two parameters (strip prefix and strip postfix) are not necessary since we are not taking anything away from the filename. The third parameter (add-on prefix) doesn't apply since we do not want to add anything to the beginning of the filename. The fourth parameter, .gz (add-on postfix), specifies that the filename should have .gz appended to it after this filter is done executing. The fifth parameter (external command) specifies the exact invocation of the **gzip** program in order to perform the file compression. Notice that **%s** is used instead of a filename. The sixth parameter (type of file) tells wu-ftpd that it can perform compression on both straight ASCII as well as regular files. The seventh parameter, O_COMPRESS (the options field), tells the server that the file action being performed is compression. Finally, the last field is a simple human readable reminder of what this filter does: run **gzip**.

Although this appears intimidating, don't worry about it! It is unlikely you'll need to change the default configuration file that comes with wu-ftpd since it covers the most popular conversions.

Configuring Host Access

The **/etc/ftphosts** file allows you to explicitly allow or deny users based on their originating IP address. Each line in the file can take the form

```
allow username address
```

or

```
deny username address
```

where **username** is the login they use when connecting to the FTP service, and **address** is the originating IP address. You can list multiple addresses in a comma-separated list.

COOKBOOK ACCESS SOLUTIONS

With all of the options available, configuring the wu-ftpd server can appear a bit daunting when it shouldn't be. Similar to DNS configurations, the most common configurations are also some of the easiest to accommodate. In this section, we will go through these combinations to help you get going.

Anonymous Only

Under the UNIX model, every process must have an owner. In the case of an anonymous FTP user, this owner should have minimal file access rights and only be able to see the files in the designated public FTP area. To accomplish this, you need to make sure that a user called ftp is set up. (This happens automatically under Red Hat Linux.)

Setting Up the Anonymous User

> **NOTE:** If you're using Red Hat Linux, you can simply install the **anonftp-2.8-1.i386.rpm** RPM instead of going through the steps discussed in this section.

You can easily check to see whether you have an anonymous user by examining your **/etc/passwd** file. If a username ftp exists, this step is taken care of for you. If you don't, you will want to create a new user called ftp using commands similar to

```
[root@ford /root]# echo "/bin/ftponly" >> /etc/shells
```

and

```
[root@ford /root]# useradd -c "FTP User" -d /home/ftp -r -s/bin/ftponly ftp
```

The first command tells the system that **/bin/ftponly** is an acceptable user shell. This is necessary for the **useradd** command to be able to use it, even though the shell doesn't really exist. The reason why you would want to set someone's shell to a nonexistent shell but keep it listed in **/etc/shells** is so that they can log in to the system via FTP but not via Telnet.

The second command creates the ftp user account. You can change the **/home/ftp** directory to be any place where you'd prefer anonymous FTP access to occur. (A dedicated partition may be called for if you intend to make your site large.) Also recall that the **-r** option creates a system account, thus a home directory is not automatically created.

For organizational purposes, you should also create an ftp group if it doesn't exist already. This is done with the command

```
[root@ford /root]# groupadd -r ftp
```

The **-r** parameter serves the same purpose as it does in the **useradd** command.

With the accounts created, you will need to make sure the home directory for the anonymous ftp user is set up. This is the directory that users will see when connecting to the service.

Setting Up the Anonymous FTP Directory

NOTE: If you used the **anonftp-3.0-9.i386.rpm** RPM, you can skip these steps, too, since the directory structure has been set up for you.

The anonymous FTP directory should have the following subdirectories:

▼ pub

■ bin

■ etc

▲ lib

The permissions on these directories should be set with the following commands:

```
[root@ford /home/ftp]# chown root.root bin etc lib
[root@ford /home/ftp]# chown root.ftp pub
[root@ford /home/ftp]# chmod 111 bin etc
[root@ford /home/ftp]# chmod 755 lib
[root@ford /home/ftp]# chmod 2755 pub
```

When an anonymous ftp user logs in, the server performs a **chroot**, a system function that changes the definition of what the root directory is from whatever directory the anonymous FTP files are located in. In the case where the anonymous FTP files are located in **/home/ftp**, the **chroot** command could change the root directory definition to be **/home/ftp**; thus a "cd /" would really refer to **/home/ftp**. This is done so that anonymous users cannot see other files in the system, especially sensitive files such as **/etc/passwd**. The side effect of doing the **chroot** is that the programs that are running must be available in this new root directory, or they cannot be used. Thus, you must copy the files shown in the following table into the following directories. (Note: we assume that **/home/ftp** is the directory where the anonymous ftp files will be.)

Source File	Destination	Permissions
/lib/ld-2.1.1.so	/home/ftp/lib	755
/lib/libc-2.1.1.so	/home/ftp/lib	755
/lib/libnsl-2.1.1.so	/home/ftp/lib	755
/lib/libnss_files-2.1.1.so	/home/ftp/lib	755
/usr/bin/compress	/home/ftp/bin	111
/bin/cpio	/home/ftp/bin	111
/bin/gzip	/home/ftp/bin	111
/bin/ls	/home/ftp/bin	111
/bin/sh	/home/ftp/bin	111
/bin/tar	/home/ftp/bin	111

Remember to set the permissions on the above files correctly using the **chmod** command (see Chapter 6).

You will also need to create some symbolic links. The following series of commands will create them:

```
[root@ford /root]# cd /home/ftp/lib
[root@ford lib]# ln -s ld-2.1.1.so ld-linux.so.2
[root@ford lib]# ln -s libc-2.1.1.so libc.so.6
[root@ford lib]# ln -s libnsl-2.1.1.so libnsl.so.1
[root@ford lib]# ln -s libnss_files-2.1.1.so libnss_files.so.2
[root@ford lib]# cd /home/ftp/bin
[root@ford bin]# ln -s gzip zcat
```

And finally, you will need to set up simple **passwd** and **group** files. The purpose of these files is not for authentication but for appearance. Recall that every file's owner is represented as a UID and that the **/etc/passwd** file gives a mapping from UIDs to login names. The same applies for groups, GIDs, and the **/etc/group** file. Thus, you will need to create **/home/ftp/etc/group** with at least the following:

```
root::0:                                                          ftp::X:
```

where X is the GID for the ftp group as established by the **groupadd** command in the previous section.

The **/home/ftp/etc/passwd** file will need to have the following:

```
root:*:0:0:::                                                 ftp:*:XX:YY::::
```

where XX is the UID from the ftp user as created by the **useradd** command, and YY is the group number for the ftp group as established by the **groupadd** command.

Setting Up /etc/ftpaccess

The key to setting up an anonymous FTP server is the user ftp and the appropriate directories. Once set up, you need only a minimal configuration in the **/etc/ftpaccess** file. A simple file is

```
class     anonclass    anonymous   *
class     nonanon      real,guest  *
email ftp@domain.com
loginfails 3
limit nonanon 0 Wk0000-2359 /home/ftp/.norealusers
readme    README*      login
readme    README*      cwd=*
message /welcome.msg                login
message .message                    cwd=*
compress          yes             anonclass
tar               yes             anonclass
chmod             no              anonymous
delete            no              anonymous
overwrite         no              anonymous
rename            no              anonymous
log transfers anonymous inbound,outbound
passwd-check rfc822 warn
```

Not as Crazy as It Seems

You must be thinking that this is insane. Under NT, all you do is click a button and start dragging files over to a folder and TA-DA! You have an anonymous FTP server. All of this configuration stuff is just too tedious! Well, you've got a point—it is tedious. However, there is a reason why ISPs around the world still pick UNIX over NT for public FTP servers: security and configurability.

We've already seen how configurable wu-ftpd is, so let's touch on security quickly. When a user logs into a UNIX anonymous FTP server, he or she is locked into a set of subdirectories via the **chroot** instruction, which is impossible to get out of. Once the **chroot** command is issued, the system will not let a process undo it. When the wu-ftpd server accepts a login from an anonymous user, it immediately does a **chroot** before taking any requests from the anonymous user. Under Windows NT, you have to really trust the security model provided by the FTP server to not allow the client to poke their noses into other files in your system. Furthermore, since wu-ftpd's source code is under public display, you don't need to worry about back doors into your system, which is something you can never be sure about with closed-source packages. (Anyone who has dealt with networking manufacturers knows that backdoors exist in commercial systems.)

The key lines here are the class definitions where we separate non-anonymous users from anonymous users, and the limit line, which limits the non-anonymous users to 0 all days of the week for all day. (Real users who try to log in are sent the content of the file **/home/ftp/.norealusers**.) The rest of the file is pretty generic; you'll see it in many different configurations.

Setting Up an /incoming Directory

If you need to allow anonymous users to deposit files onto your system, you will need to set up a special incoming directory for them. Files placed there can be retrieved only by the root user, not by other anonymous users. This is so that individuals with dishonorable intentions don't turn your FTP server into a public access site for their stash of pornography, pirated software, or illegal content (such as stolen credit card numbers). Of course, this means there is overhead for you as a site administrator, but a human safety shield is the only way you can ensure that anonymously uploaded files are acceptable for keeping on the server for others to download.

To create this directory, go to your anonymous FTP directory (for example, **/home/ftp**) and create a subdirectory called **incoming**, like so:

```
mkdir incoming
```

Then, change the permissions so that only the user ftp can write to it, but the anonymous user cannot read from it:

```
chmod 300 incoming
chown ftp.ftp incoming
```

And last, add the following two lines to your **/etc/ftpaccess** file to control where uploads go:

```
upload /home/ftp * no
upload /home/ftp /incoming yes ftp ftp 0000 nodirs
```

The first **upload** command denies uploading to all directories on your FTP server. The second command then explicitly opens up one directory where anonymous users can upload files.

Mixed Access

It is entirely acceptable to run a server that supports mixed access; that is, it provides both anonymous users and regular users access to the server. Begin by configuring the server as you would for anonymous-only access. Once set up, change the **/etc/ftpaccess** file so that it reads

```
class   all   real,guest,anonymous   *
email ftp@domain.com
loginfails 5
readme  README*     login
```

```
readme   README*    cwd=*
message /welcome.msg           login
message .message               cwd=*
compress         yes           all
tar              yes           all
chmod            no            guest,anonymous
delete           no            guest,anonymous
overwrite        no            guest,anonymous
rename           no            guest,anonymous
log transfers anonymous,real inbound,outbound
passwd-check rfc822 warn
```

Note that this configuration does not provide upload access to anonymous users. Assuming your anonymous FTP directories are located in **/home/ftp**, you need to add the following lines to the **/etc/ftpaccess** file:

```
upload /home/ftp * no
upload /home/ftp /incoming yes ftp ftp 0000 nodirs
```

(Read the "Upload" section on setting up upload support in anonymous FTP servers for information on how to set up the incoming directory itself.)

Registered Users Only

It is also possible to configure a server with only registered users access. There are two techniques for denying access to anonymous FTP users. The first is to not have an ftp user in the **/etc/passwd** file. This method is very simple and does the job. However, if you want to keep the configuration for anonymous FTP intact, you can deny anonymous FTP access in the same way our anonymous FTP access denies real users—by using the **limit** command in the **/etc/ftpaccess** file.

The **/etc/ftpaccess** file for doing this type of configuration would be

```
class    all    real,guest   *
class anon anonymous
email ftp@domain.com
loginfails 5
limit anon 0 Wk0000-2359 /home/ftp/.noanonusers
readme   README*    login
readme   README*    cwd=*
message /welcome.msg           login
message .message               cwd=*
compress         yes           all
tar              yes           all
chmod            no            guest
delete           no            guest
```

```
overwrite       no              guest
rename          no              guest
log transfers real inbound,outbound
passwd-check rfc822 warn
```

where **/home/ftp/.noanonusers** is the text file sent to the client trying to connect as anonymous to inform them that anonymous access is not allowed.

CONFIGURING A VIRTUAL FTP SERVER

With wu-ftpd, you can set up multiple FTP servers on the same host so long as each server has its own IP address. (This is a limitation of FTP, not of the wu-ftpd implementation in particular.) The process is quite easy once you have anonymous FTP set up for your primary host. This section assumes that you have already configured an IP alias and fudged the ARP table correctly. (This is discussed later in the "Advanced Linux Networking" part of the book.) This quick jumpstart on the process assumes you have one ethernet card and want to add a single virtual IP address:

1. Make sure your new IP address exists in both the local host table (**/etc/hosts**) as well as your DNS table. (In this example, we'll call the host "earth.")

2. Run the **ifconfig** command to configure the eth0:0 device with the appropriate address, netmask, and broadcast. For example, to configure the 192.168.1.42 device on eth0:0, I would use

```
ifconfig eth0:0 192.168.1.42 netmask 255.255.255.0 broadcast 192.168.1.255
```

3. Fudge the ARP table. You will need your ethernet card's hardware address for this. Run the **ifconfig -a** command to get this information. Assuming your ethernet card's hardware address is 00:10:4B:CB:15:9F, type

```
arp -s earth 00:10:4B:CB:15:9F pub
```

With your virtual IP address established, you now need to create a directory structure similar to that of an anonymous site. This should be placed in the directory that you want to make your virtual FTP site. Then add the **virtual** command to the end of your **/etc/ftpaccess** file. The command's format is

```
virtual IP ftype directory
```

where **IP** is the IP address of your virtual FTP server, and **ftype** is the file type that **directory** refers to. The **ftype** value can be either root, banner, or logfile. If the **ftype** is root, **directory** should be the directory in which the anonymous FTP files are set up for the virtual site. If **ftype** is either banner or logfile, the **directory** entry should be the corresponding file.

For example, to set up a virtual FTP server on the IP address 192.168.1.42, I could set up my configuration to read like this:

```
virtual 192.168.1.42 root    /home/earth
virtual 192.168.1.42 banner  /home/earth/.welcome.banner
virtual 192.168.1.42 logfile /var/log/xferlog.earth
```

NOTE: All of the files that are necessary for anonymous FTP access must be set up in the virtual FTP server's root directory. In our example, this means setting up the **bin**, **etc**, **lib**, and **pub** subdirectories in the **/home/earth** directory.

SUMMARY

The Washington University FTP daemon (www.wu-ftpd.org) is a powerful FTP server offering all of the features one would need for running a commercial FTP server in a secure manner. In this chapter, we discussed the process of compiling, installing, and configuring the wu-ftpd server. Specifically, we covered:

▼ All of the configuration options for wu-ftpd

■ Details about the FTP protocol and its effects on firewalls

■ Establishing virtual FTP servers

■ Setting up anonymous FTP servers

▲ Setting up both anonymous servers in conjunction with a normal-users-only FTP server

This information is enough to keep your FTP server humming for quite a while. Of course, like any printed media about software, this text will age, and the information will slowly but surely become obsolete. Please be sure to visit the wu-ftpd Web site from time to time to learn about not only the latest developments but also the latest documentation.

CHAPTER 14

Setting Up Your Web Server Using Apache

In this chapter, we discuss the process of installing and configuring the *Apache HTTP server* (www.apache.org) on your Linux server. Apache is free software released under the GNU GPL. According to one of the most respected statistics on the Net (published by Netcraft Ltd., www.netcraft.co.uk), Apache has a market share of more than 50%. This level of respect from the Internet community comes from the following benefits and advantages provided by the Apache server software:

▼ It is stable.

■ Several major Web sites, including www.amazon.com and Microsoft's Hotmail service, are using it.

■ The entire program and related components are open-source.

■ It works on a large number of platforms (all popular variants of UNIX, some of the not-so-popular variants of UNIX, and even Windows NT).

■ It is extremely flexible.

▲ It has proved to be secure.

Before we get into the steps necessary to configure Apache, we will review some of the fundamentals of the HTTP protocol as well as some of the internals of Apache, such as its process ownership model. This information will help us understand why Apache is set up to work the way it does.

THE MECHANICS OF HTTP

HTTP (HyperText Transfer Protocol) is, of course, a significant portion of the foundation for the World Wide Web, and Apache is the server implementation of the HTTP protocol. Browsers such as Netscape Navigator and Microsoft Internet Explorer are client implementations of HTTP.

As of this writing, the HTTP protocol is at version 1.1 and is documented in RFC 2616 (for details, go to ftp://ftp.isi.edu/in-notes/rfc2616.txt).

Headers

When a Web client connects to a Web server, the client's default method of making this connection is to contact the server's TCP port 80. Once connected, the Web server says nothing; it's up to the client to issue HTTP-compliant commands for its requests to the server. Along with each command comes a *request header* including information about the client. For example, when using Netscape Navigator under Linux as a client, a Web server will receive the following information from a client:

```
GET / HTTP/1.0
Connection: Keep-Alive
User-Agent: Mozilla/4.06 [en] (X11; U; Linux 2.2.5-15 i686)
```

```
Host: localhost:8000
Accept: image/gif, image/x-xbitmap, image/jpeg, image/pjpeg,
image/png, */*
Accept-Encoding: gzip
Accept-Language: en
Accept-Charset: iso-8859-1,*,utf-8
```

The first line contains the HTTP **GET** command, which asks the server to fetch a file. The remainder of the information makes up the header, which tells the server about the client, the kind of file formats the client will accept, and so forth. Many servers use this information to determine what can and cannot be sent to the client, as well as for logging purposes.

Along with the request header, additional headers may be sent. For example, when a client uses a hyperlink to get to the server site, a header entry showing the client's originating site will also appear in the header.

When it receives a blank line, the server knows a request header is complete. Once the request header is received, it responds with the actual requested content, prefixed by a server header. The server header tells the client information about the server, the amount of data the client is about to receive, and the type of data coming in. For example, the request header shown just above, when sent to a default installation of the Apache HTTP server under Red Hat 6.0, results in the following server response header:

```
HTTP/1.1 200 OK
Date: Tue, 24 Aug 1999 12:59:46 GMT
Server: Apache/1.3.6 (UNIX) (Red Hat/Linux)
Last-Modified: Wed, 07 Apr 1999 21:17:54 GMT
ETag: "1a005-799-370bcb82"
Accept-Ranges: bytes
Content-Length: 1945
Keep-Alive: timeout=15, max=100
Connection: Keep-Alive
Content-Type: text/html
```

The response header is followed by a blank line and then the actual content of the transmission.

Nonstandard Ports

The default port for HTTP requests is port 80, but you can also configure a Web server to use a different (arbitrarily chosen) port that is not in use by another service. This allows sites to run multiple Web servers on the same host, each server on a different port. Some sites use this arrangement for multiple configurations of their Web servers, to support various types of client requests.

When a site runs a Web server on a nonstandard port, you can see that port number in the site's URL. For example, this address,

http://www.redhat.com/

with an added port number, would read

http://www.redhat.com:80/

CAUTION: Don't make the mistake of going for "security through obscurity." If your server's on a non-standard port, that doesn't guarantee that Internet troublemakers won't find your site. Because of the automated nature of tools used to attack a site, it takes fewer than 100 lines of C code to scan a server and find which ports are running Web servers. Using a nonstandard port does not keep your site "secure."

Process Ownership and Security

As discussed in other chapters, running a Web server under UNIX forces you to deal with the Linux (and UNIX in general) model. In terms of permissions, that means each process has an owner, and that owner has limited rights on the system.

Whenever a program (process) is started, it inherits the permissions of its parent process. For example, if you're logged in as root, the shell in which you're doing all your work has all the same rights as the root user. In addition, any process you start from this shell will inherit all the permissions of that root. Processes may give up rights, but they cannot gain rights.

NOTE: There is an exception to the Linux inheritance principle: Programs configured with the SetUID bit (see the **chmod** command in Chapter 6) do not inherit rights from their parent process but rather start with the rights specified by the owner of the file itself. For example, the file containing the program **su (/bin/su)** is owned by root and has the SetUID bit set. If the user sshah runs the program **su**, that program doesn't inherit the rights of sshah but instead will start with the rights of root.

How Apache Processes Ownership

To do network setups, the Apache HTTP server must start with root permissions. Specifically, it needs to bind itself to port 80 so that it can listen for requests and accept connections. Once it does this, Apache can give up its rights and run as a nonroot user, as specified in its configuration files. By default, this is the user *nobody*.

As user nobody, Apache can read only the files that user nobody has permission to read. Thus, if a file's permissions are set so that they are readable only by the file's owner, the owner must be nobody. For any file that you want available to user nobody, set that file's permission to world readable:

```
chmod a+r filename
```

where **filename** is the name of the file.

Security is especially important for sites that use CGI scripts. By limiting the permissions of the Web server, you decrease the likelihood that someone can send a malicious request to the server. And the server processes and corresponding CGI scripts can break only what they can access. As user nobody, the scripts and processes don't have access to the same key files that root can access. (Remember that root can access everything, no matter what the permissions.)

CAUTION: In the event that you decide to allow CGI scripts on your server, pay strict attention to how they are written. Be sure it isn't possible for input coming in over the network to make the CGI script do something it shouldn't. Although there are no statistics on this, most successful attacks on sites are typically possible because of improperly configured Web servers and/or poorly written CGI scripts.

INSTALLING THE APACHE HTTP SERVER

Although most distributions of Linux come with the Apache HTTP server already installed, you may need to perform an upgrade or adjust the configuration. This section walks you through the process of downloading the Apache source code, compiling it, and finally installing it. Apache configuration commands are covered in later sections.

If you want to stick with your Linux distribution's default Apache installation, you can skip this section. All you'll need to know are the locations of the Apache configuration files and the top-level pages, and how to restart the server. For Red Hat 7, these are as follows:

Configuration files	**/etc/httpd/conf**
Top-level pages	**/var/www**
Server restart	**/etc/rc.d/init.d/httpd restart**

The latest version of the Apache HTTP server is always located at http://www.apache.org/dist. As of this writing, the latest stable version is Apache 1.3.14, available in the **apache_1.3.14.tar.gz** archive file.

Let's begin by downloading the Apache source code:

1. Download the Apache archive file and place it in a working directory. Typically, **/usr/local/src** is the location used for storing and compiling programs.

2. Unarchive the program with this command:

```
[root@ford src]# tar -xzf apache_1.3.14.tar.gz
```

This will create the **apache_1.3.14** directory, which will contain the necessary files for compiling the program.

Compiling Apache

The Apache HTTP server is actually a core system with basic functionality that supports dynamically loadable modules. The modules perform tasks such as dynamic URL spelling correction, URL rewriting, cookie tracking, and so forth. The default configuration consists of the most popular modules. Because Apache is under constant development, always refer to the program's Install file to see what the current defaults are and what optional modules are available.

For this example, we'll stick with the default configuration.

1. Begin by running the **./configure** script that comes with Apache. If you aren't sure about whether an existing Web server exists on your system, you should configure Apache to install into the **/usr/local/apache** directory, like so:

   ```
   [root@ford apache_1.3.14]# ./configure --prefix=/usr/local/apache
   ```

2. Once it's configured, run **make** to compile the program:

   ```
   [root@ford apache_1.3.14]# make
   ```

3. Install Apache into the appropriate directory:

   ```
   [root@ford apache_1.3.14]# make install
   ```

And that's it! You now have Apache installed.

Apache Modules

Part of what makes Apache so powerful and flexible is that its design allows extensions through modules. Apache comes with many modules by default and automatically includes them in the default installation.

If you are interested in extending Apache's capability, visit http://httpd.apache.org/docs to see what other modules are available for inclusion as well as directions on adding them to your installation.

To give you some idea of what kinds of things people are doing with modules, visit http://modules.apache.org. There you will find modules like the LDAP Authentication Module to let your users authenticate against a LDAP server; mod_backhand to perform load balancing across multiple web servers; and mod_frontpage to provide Front Page extensions to Apache.

Installing Apache on Busy Systems

On a system with heavy traffic, you may need to upgrade a Web server "live," meaning the amount of time the Web server should be down for the upgrade is the amount of time it takes to shut off the old version and start the new one.

To accommodate such instances, create the directory **/usr/local/apache_*version***, where *version* is the Apache version number you are installing. In our example, we would create the directory **/usr/local/apache_1.3.14** and install Apache there. To do that, change the directory specified in the **--prefix** option when running **./configure**. Once you have this special directory created, make a symbolic link from **/usr/local/apache** to **/usr/local/apache_1.3.14**.

The next time you need to upgrade Apache, you can configure and install to a newer directory—perhaps **/usr/local/apache_2.0**—while the **/usr/local/apache_1.3.14** remains active. Once everything is set up in **/usr/local/apache_2.0**, you can stop the server process (discussed next), change the symbolic link so that it points to **/usr/local/apache_2.0**, and then start the new Apache. This results in upgrade downtime of only as long as it takes you to type in three commands! Even better, if the 1.4.0 version doesn't work out for you, it'll be easy to revert to the old version. Just shut down the server, point **/usr/local/apache** back to **/usr/local/ apache_1.3.14**, and start up again.

Make Sure Nobody Is There!

As mentioned earlier, Apache runs by default as user nobody. Make sure this user exists by viewing the **/etc/passwd** file and looking for the entry. (If you need to, check Chapter 5 for instructions on confirming whether a particular user exists.)

Starting Up and Shutting Down Apache

One of the nicest features of Linux is the ability to start up and shut down system services without needing to reboot. This is easy to do in the Apache server.

To start Apache, use this command:

```
[root@ford root]# /usr/local/apache/bin/apachectl start
```

To shut down Apache, enter this command:

```
[root@ford root]# /usr/local/apache/bin/apachectl stop
```

Starting Apache at Boot Time

Since so many distributions of Linux come with Apache installed, you'll need to disable the existing configuration if you want to run your newly compiled version. To do this, check the **rc.d** directories and find the symbolic links that point to existing Apache startup scripts. Existing scripts are likely to be called **httpd** or **apache**.

For example, under Red Hat Linux, the **/etc/rc.d/rc3.d/S85httpd** script points to **/etc/rc.d/init.d/httpd**, which starts up the default installation of Apache. To change this so that a recently compiled version runs instead, we would replace the link to point to **/usr/local/apache/bin/apachectl**.

Under Red Hat Linux, the commands to accomplish this update are as follows:

```
[root@ford apache_1.3.9]# cd /etc/rc.d/rc3.d
[root@ford rc3.d]# rm S85httpd
[root@ford rc3.d]# ln -s /usr/local/apache/bin/apachectl S85httpd
```

Don't forget to do the same for shutdown scripts. Here are the appropriate commands under Red Hat Linux:

```
[root@ford rc3.d]# cd /etc/rc.d/rc6.d
[root@ford rc6.d]# rm K15httpd
[root@ford rc6.d]# ln -s /usr/local/apache/bin/apachectl K15httpd
```

For details on startup and shutdown scripts, see Chapter 7.

Testing Your Installation

You can perform a quick test on your Apache installation using a default home page. To do this, start up the server (if necessary) using the command

```
[root@ford /root]# /usr/local/bin/apache/bin/apachectl start
```

Apache comes with a default home page, **index.html**, located in **/usr/local/apache/ htdocs**. To find out if your Apache installation went smoothly, start a Web browser and tell it to visit your machine. For example, for a machine with the host name franklin.domain.com, you would visit http://franklin.domain.com. There you should see a simple Web page whose title is "It Worked!" If you don't, retrace your Apache installation steps and make sure you didn't encounter any errors in the process. (Linux error messages are sometimes very terse, making them easy to miss.)

CONFIGURING APACHE

Apache supports a rich set of configuration options that, unlike Sendmail, are sensible and easy to follow. This makes it a simple task to set up the Web server in various configurations.

This section walks through a basic configuration. The default configuration is actually quite good and (believe it or not), works right out of the box, so if the default is acceptable to you, simply start creating your HTML documents! Apache allows several common customizations. After we step through creating a simple Web page, we'll see how we can make those common customizations in the Apache configuration files.

Creating a Simple Root-Level Page

If you like, you can start adding files to Apache right way in the **/usr/local/apache/htdocs** directory for top-level pages. Any files placed in that directory must be world readable.

As mentioned earlier, Apache's default Web page is **index.html**. Let's take a closer look at changing the default home page so that it reads "Welcome to ford.planetoid.org." Here are the commands:

```
[root@ford]# cd /usr/local/apache/htdocs
[root@ford]# echo "Welcome to ford.planetoid.org" >> index.html
[root@ford]# chmod 644 index.html
```

We could also use an editor such as **vi** or **pico** to edit the **index.html** file and make it more interesting.

Creating Home Pages

Users who want to create home pages have to take only the following steps:

```
[sshah@ford]$ cd
[sshah@ford]$ chmod a+x .
[sshah@ford]$ mkdir public_html
[sshah@ford]$ chmod a+x public_html
```

As a result of these commands, files placed in the **public_html** directory for a particular user and set to world readable will be on the Web with the URL

```
http://yourhostname.domain.com/~username
```

where **yourhostname.domain.com** is the user machine's fully qualified domain name, and **username** is the login of the user who created the Web page. The default filename that loads is **index.html**.

For example, user sshah would enter the following to create a home page:

```
[sshah@ford]$ cd ~/public_html
[sshah@ford]$ echo "Welcome to Steve's Homepage" >> index.html
[sshah@ford]$ chmod 644 index.html
```

If sshah's site name is ford.domain.com, his URL would be http://ford.domain.com/ ~sshah. (One hopes, of course, that he'll eventually go back and edit the **index.html** file to contain something more interesting.)

Apache Configuration Files

The configuration files for Apache are located in the **/usr/local/apache/conf** directory. There you will see the three files **srm.conf**, **access.conf**, and **httpd.conf**.

> **NOTE:**   The first two config files, **srm.conf** and **access.conf**, are stub files only and are no longer used; essentially, they're artifacts from when Apache was originally just a set of patches against the NCSA Web server many years ago. They contain only a note saying that all changes to the configuration should go into the **httpd.conf** file.

The best way to learn more about the configuration files is to read the **httpd.conf** file. The default installation file is heavily commented, explaining each entry, its role, and the parameters you can set.

Common Configuration Changes

The default configuration settings work just fine right out of the box and need no modification. Nevertheless, most site administrators will want to make the alterations described in this section.

Making Nobody Somebody

Apache's default user, nobody, allows Apache to run without root permissions. Of course, since other subsystems will use the nobody login as well, you will want to limit their access to certain files.

Create a new user whose login is clearly intended for a specific group of files; for example, www. To accompany this login, you'll want to create a group called www, as well. For the www login:

▼ Set the shell setting to **/bin/false** so that users cannot log in to the account.

▲ Set a password to * so that no one can use FTP to access the account.

(Don't worry—these settings on the user account won't keep a process from running as that user.)

Once the www account and group are created, edit the **httpd.conf** file so that the entries for **User** and **Group** are set to www. For example:

```
User www
Group www
```

Don't forget to change the permissions on all the files in the **/usr/local/apache** directory so that they are owned by www and have a group setting of www, as follows:

```
[root@ford /root]# cd /usr/local;chown -R www.www apache
```

Changing Host Names

At many sites, servers fulfill multiple purposes. An intranet Web server that isn't getting heavy usage, for example, should probably share its usage allowance with another service. In such a situation, the computer name www used in the preceding section wouldn't be a good choice, because it suggests that the machine has only one purpose.

It's better to give a server a neutral name and then establish DNS CNAME entries or multiple host name entries in the **/etc/hosts** file. In other words, you can give the system several names for accessing the server, but it needs to know only about its real name. Consider a server whose host name is dioxin.eng.domain.org that is to be a Web server, as well. You might be thinking of giving it the host name alias www.eng.domain.org. However, since dioxin will know itself only as dioxin, users who visit www.eng.domain.org will be confused by seeing in their browsers that the server's real name is dioxin.

Apache provides a way to get around this using the ServerName directive. By specifying what you want Apache to return as the host name of the Web server, a system with a name like dioxin can have an alias of www, invisible to users of the site. Here is an example of the ServerName directive:

```
ServerName www.eng.domain.org
```

Server Administrator

It's often a good idea, for a couple of reasons, to use an e-mail alias for a Web site's administrator. First, there may be more than one administrator. By using an alias, it's possible for the alias to expand out to a list of e-mail addresses. Second, if the current administrator leaves, you don't want to have to make the rounds of all those Web pages and change the name of the site administrator.

Assuming you have set up the e-mail alias so that www@domain.com represents your Web administrator(s) (see Chapter 15 for doing this using Sendmail and Linux), you need to edit the ServerAdmin line in the **httpd.conf** file so that it reads as follows:

```
ServerAdmin www@domain.com
```

NOTE: Obviously, we can't cover everything about the Apache HTTP server in a few short pages. The software's online manual comes with the distribution and will give you the information you need. It's written in HTML, so you can access it in a browser. Simply point to **file:/usr/local/apache/htdocs/manual/index.html**.

Configuring Virtual Domains

One of the most used features of Apache is its ability to support virtual domains—that is, to allow multiple domains to be hosted from the same IP address. This is accomplished by the HTTP 1.1 protocol, which specifies the desired site in the HTTP header rather than relying on the server to know what site to fetch based on its IP address.

NOTE: Don't forget that it is not merely enough to configure a virtual domain using Apache. You must also get the domain itself from a company that sells domain names like Register.com. Once you have the domain name, you can either use your registrar's DNS server or you can set up your own DNS server. Either way, you will need to establish the necessary entries so that www.yourdomain.com points to your Web server. Of course, if you are just playing around and don't want to set up a site for real, you can simply set up a local DNS server and create fictitious domains and IP addresses, or even just add the necessary entries to the **/etc/hosts** file.

To set up a new virtual domain, open the **httpd.conf** file in your favorite text editor and scroll toward the end of the file. There you will find a commented-out example of a virtual host entry that looks something like this:

```
#
# VirtualHost example:
# Almost any Apache directive may go into a VirtualHost container.
#
#<VirtualHost ip.address.of.host.some_domain.com>
#   ServerAdmin webmaster@host.some_domain.com
#   DocumentRoot /www/docs/host.some_domain.com
#   ServerName host.some_domain.com
#   ErrorLog logs/host.some_domain.com-error_log
#   CustomLog logs/host.some_domain.com-access_log common
#</VirtualHost>
```

Simply clone this entry and substitute in your own information. For example, for my domain, planetoid.org, the virtual host entry would look like this:

```
#
# Virtual Host Settings for planetoid.org
#
<VirtualHost planetoid.org>
   ServerAdmin linuxadmin@planetoid.org
   DocumentRoot /www/htdocs/planetoid.org
   ServerName planetoid.org
   ErrorLog /www/logs/planetoid.org/error_log
   CustomLog /www/logs/planetoid.org/access_log common
</VirtualHost>
```

Note that you have to do this for each host you want visible. So if I want to have both www.planetoid.org and planetoid.org resolve to the same Web page, I need to set up a second virtual host setting for www.planetoid.org, as well. (Both www.planetoid.org and planetoid.org can have the same configuration information, but they must remain separate virtual host entries.)

Once you have the information in there, simply restart Apache using the **/usr/ local/apache/bin/apachectl restart** command, and you're off!

BASIC TROUBLESHOOTING WITH APACHE

The process of changing configurations (or even the initial installation) can sometimes not work as smoothly as we'd like. Thankfully, Apache does an excellent job at reporting why it failed in its error log file.

The error log file is located in your logs directory. If you are running a stock Red Hat installation, this is in the **/var/log/httpd** directory. If you installed Apache yourself using the installation method discussed earlier in this chapter, the logs are in the **/usr/local/ apache/logs** directory. In these directories, you will find two files: **access_log** and **error_log**.

The **access_log** file is simply that—a log of which files have been accessed by people visiting your Web site. It contains information about whether the transfer completed successfully, where the request originated (IP address), how much data was transferred, and what time the transfer occurred. This is a very powerful way of determining the usage of your site.

The **error_log** file contains all of the errors that occur in Apache. Note that not all errors that occur are fatal—some are simply problems with a client connection from which Apache can automatically recover and continue operation. However, if you started Apache but still cannot visit the Web site, then take a look at this log file to see why Apache may not be responding. The easiest way to see the last 10 error messages is by using the **tail** command, like so:

```
[root@ford logs]# tail -10 error_log
```

If you need to see more log information than that, simply change the number 10 to the number of lines that you do need to see. If that number of lines exceeds the length of your screen, you can pipe the output through more so that you can see one screen at a time, like so:

```
[root@ford logs]# tail -100 error_log | more
```

This will display the last 100 lines of the error log, one screen at a time.

SUMMARY

In this chapter, we covered the process of arranging your own Web server using Apache from the ground up. This chapter by itself is enough to get you going with a top-level page and a basic configuration.

I highly recommend taking some time to page through the Apache manual. It is well written, concise, and flexible enough so that you can set up just about any configuration imaginable.

In addition to the manual documentation, several good books about Apache have been written. *Apache: The Definitive Guide*, Second Edition (O'Reilly & Associates, 1999), covers the details of Apache very well. The text focuses on Apache and Apache only, so you don't have to wade through hundreds of pages to find what you need.

CHAPTER 15

SMTP

The Simple Mail Transfer Protocol (SMTP) is the de facto standard for mail transport across the Internet. Anyone who wants to have a mail server capable of sending and receiving mail across the Internet must be able to support it. Many internal networks have also taken to using SMTP for their private mail services because of its platform independence and availability across all popular operating systems. But what may be more important for you is Sendmail's presence on the Internet—so it should comfort you to know that some of the largest sites such as Yahoo!, AOL, @Home, and Earthlink, Cisco, and Microsoft's own Hotmail service use Sendmail.

In this chapter, we'll first discuss the mechanics of SMTP as a protocol and its relationship to other mail-related protocols, such as POP and IMAP. Then we'll discuss the Internet's most popular mail server, Sendmail, which comes with virtually all distributions of Linux. As part of our discussion on Sendmail, we'll go over several popular configurations and conclude with some references to where you can get more information.

THE MECHANICS OF SMTP

The SMTP protocol defines the method by which mail is sent from one host to another. That's it. It does not define how the mail should be stored. It does not define how the mail server should send the mail readable by the recipient. Nothing.

SMTP's strength is its simplicity, and that is due to the dynamic nature of networks during the early 1980s. (The SMTP protocol was originally defined in 1982.) People were linking networks together with everything short of bubble gum and glue. SMTP was the first mail standard that was independent of the transport mechanism. This meant people using TCP/IP networks could use the same format to send a message as someone using two cans and a string.

SMTP is also independent of operating systems, which means each system can use its own style of storing mail without worrying about how the sender of a message stores his mail. You can draw parallels to how the phone system works: Each phone service provider has its own independent accounting system; however, they all have agreed upon a standard way to link their networks together so that calls can go from one network to another transparently.

Rudimentary SMTP Details

Ever had a "friend" who sent you an e-mail on behalf of some government agency informing you that you owe taxes from the previous year, plus additional penalties? Somehow a message like this ends up in a lot of people's mailboxes around April 1, better known as April Fool's Day. Well, guess what? We're going to show you how they did it. Even more fun, how you can do it yourself. (Not that I would advocate such behavior, of course.)

The purpose of this example is to show how the SMTP protocol sends a message from one host to another. After all, more important than learning how to forge an e-mail is learning how to troubleshoot mail-related problems. So in this example, you are acting as the sending host, and whichever machine you connect to is the receiving host.

The SMTP protocol requires only that a host be able to send straight ASCII text to another host. Typically, this is done by contacting the SMTP port (port 25) on a mail server. You can do this using the Telnet program. For example:

```
[root@ford /root]# telnet mailserver 25
```

where the host *mailserver* is the recipient's mail server. The "25" that follows *mailserver* tells Telnet that you want to communicate with the server's port 25 rather than the normal port 23. (Port 23 is used for remote logins, and port 25 is for the SMTP server.)

The mail server will respond with a greeting message such as this:

```
220 mail ESMTP Sendmail 8.9.3/8.9.3; 26 Aug 1999 23:17:44 -0700 (PDT)
```

You are now communicating directly with the SMTP server.

Although there are many SMTP commands, the four worth noting are

▼ **HELO**

■ **MAIL FROM:**

■ **RCPT TO:**

▲ **DATA**

The **HELO** command is used when a client introduces itself to the server. The parameter to **HELO** is the host name that is originating the connection. Of course, most mail servers take this information with a grain of salt and double-check it themselves. For example:

```
helo super-duper-strong-coffee.com
```

If you aren't coming from the super-duper-strong-coffee.com domain, many mail servers will respond by telling you that it knows your real IP address, but they will not stop the connection from continuing. (Some mail servers include a comment about why you didn't use a truthful **HELO** statement.)

The **MAIL FROM:** command requires the parameter of the sender's e-mail address. This tells the mail server the e-mail's origin. For example,

```
mail from: dilbert@domain.com
```

means the message is from dilbert@domain.com.

The **RCPT TO:** command also requires the parameter of an e-mail address. This e-mail address is of the recipient of the e-mail. For example,

```
rcpt to: pointy-hair-manager@domain.com
```

means the message is destined to pointy-hair-manager@domain.com.

Now that the server knows who the sender and recipient are, it needs to know what message to send—that is done by using the **DATA** command. Once issued, the server will expect the entire message with relevant header information followed by one empty line, a period, and then another empty line. Continuing the example, dilbert@domain.com might want to send the following message to pointy-hair-manager@domain.com:

```
DATA
354 Enter mail, end with "." on a line by itself
From: Dilbert <dilbert@domain.com>
To: Pointy Hair Manager <pointy-hair-manager@domain.com>
Subject: On time and within budget.
Date: Sat, 1 Apr 2000 04:01:00 -0700 (PDT)

Just an fyi, boss. The project is not only on time, but it is within
budget too!

.
250 NAA28719 Message accepted for delivery
```

And that's all there is to it. To close the connection, enter the **QUIT** command.

This is the basic technique used by applications that send mail—except, of course, they usually use C code rather than Telnet, but the actual content sent between the client and server remains the same.

Security Implications

Sendmail, the mail server a majority of Internet sites use, is the same package most Linux distributions use. Like any other server software, its internal structure and design are complex and require a considerable amount of care during development. In the recent years, however, the developers of Sendmail have taken a very paranoid approach to their design to help alleviate these issues. Basically, they ship the package in a very tight security mode and leave it to us to loosen it up as much as we need to loosen it up for our site. This means the responsibility falls to us of making sure we keep the software properly configured (and thus not vulnerable to attacks).

Some issues to keep in mind when deploying any mail server are:

▼ When an e-mail is sent to the server, what programs will it trigger?

■ Are those programs securely designed?

■ If they cannot be made secure, how can you limit their damage?

▲ Under what permissions do those programs run?

In Sendmail's case, we need to back up and examine its architecture.

Mail service has three distinct components. The *mail user agent* (*MUA*) is what the user sees, such as the Eudora, Outlook, and Pine programs. An MUA is responsible only for reading mail and allowing users to compose mail. The *mail transfer agent* (*MTA*) handles the process of getting the mail from one site to another; Sendmail is an MTA. Finally, the *mail delivery agent* (*MDA*) is what takes the message, once received at a site, and gets it to the appropriate user mailbox.

Many mail systems integrate these components. For example, Microsoft Exchange Server integrates the MTA and MDA functionalities into a single system. (If you consider the Web interface to Exchange Server, it is also an MUA.) Lotus Domino also works in a similar fashion. Sendmail, on the other hand, works as an MTA only, passing the task of performing local mail delivery to another external program. This allows each operating system or site configuration to use its own custom tool if necessary (that is, to be able to use a special mailbox store mechanism).

In most straightforward configurations, sites prefer using the Procmail program to perform the actual mail delivery (MDA). This is because of its advanced filtering mechanism as well as its secure design from the ground up. Many older configurations have stayed with their default **/bin/mail** program to perform mail delivery. The security issues in using that particular program vary from operating system to operating system.

Because Sendmail must run as the root user in order to bind to port 25 and accept mail there, its child processes by default run with the same level of permissions. This means the MDA must be of a secure design—and ditto for any other program that can get spawned from Sendmail through the use of mail aliases and forwarding files. (We will discuss this in "The Aliases File," later in the chapter.)

Recently, Sendmail has started shipping with a tool called **smrsh** (SendMail Restricted Shell). This special shell restricts what the child process can do, and thus can help keep any programs spawned by Sendmail from doing bad things as the root user. If you ever find yourself needing to process mail using an external program, you should consider using **smrsh** as a wrapper to prohibit bugs in your program from being exploited to do potentially dangerous things.

Sendmail itself is an open-source package, giving it the benefit of public scrutiny for bugs, security flaws, and other such design issues. It has been this way from the day it was released in the early 1980s. The base version of Sendmail is free and can be used both commercially and noncommercially. Many large sites, such as Yahoo!, use Sendmail and believe in its design methodology.

In the late 1990s, Eric Allman, the creator of Sendmail, started a company called Sendmail Inc., which sells a commercial version of the package. The commercial version of the package is different from the free version only in terms of configuration tools, installation tools, support, and documentation. The actual mail server software itself is the same.

SMTP vs. POP

SMTP is not POP. POP is not SMTP. Now that we have that straightened out, let's clarify what it all means:

▼   SMTP is a transport protocol for sending messages *only*. A user cannot connect to an SMTP server to read his or her mail.

▲   The Post Office Protocol, or POP, is just the opposite. A client *can* use POP to read mail off a POP server, but the client host *cannot* use a POP server to send e-mail. For more information on POP, see Chapter 16.

What often confuses some people is the fact that the actual machine running the SMTP server software can be the same machine running the POP server software. This is because SMTP uses port 25 to accept connections, and POP (version 3 specifically) accepts connections on port 110.

Recommended Texts

One of Sendmail's biggest features is also one of its biggest problems: configurability. (One might even argue the same for UNIX-based operating systems as a whole.) Obviously, we can't cover everything about Sendmail in this chapter; instead, we give you the information necessary to set up the most common configurations and hopefully supply enough base knowledge for you to be able to pursue more complex designs with confidence.

If you decide to take on the challenge of understanding more about Sendmail, check out the one truly authoritative book on the beast: *Sendmail, Second Edition* (O'Reilly & Associates, 1997). The book is coauthored by the main developer of Sendmail himself, Eric Allman. The downside to this text is that it's HUGE—more than 1,100 pages. This is *not* an introductory text! However, if you ever find yourself posting a question about Sendmail on an Internet discussion forum, be ready to hear at least one person telling you to get this book. (The book is also affectionately called "The Bat Book" because of the bat pictured on its cover.)

You've probably got another two or three books on system administration sitting on your bookshelf—it would be naive of me to think otherwise—that cover Sendmail, as well. One difference you may find between what I cover and what they cover is that I won't be getting into the details of all the commands in the **sendmail.cf** configuration file. This is because most configuration options should be doable through the use of the configuration macros that come with Sendmail. Not only are the macros easier for you, but they make it easier for your successors to know what you've done with the system, rather than have to worry that they are going to break some minor (undocumented) tweak you did by upgrading. If you do decide to read up more on the format of the **sendmail.cf** file, be sure to understand that a handful of pages is not going to be complete enough for you to be able to seriously play with the rule sets defined in the configuration file. As always, use good sysadmin common sense and back up any files before making changes.

Red Hat 7's Pre-Installed Version of Sendmail

As of this writing, the latest version of Sendmail is 8.11.1. For those of you who are installing Red Hat Linux 7, you should note that it comes with Sendmail 8.11.0 installed. Although there are numerous bug fixes in the newer version (see ftp://www.sendmail.org/pub/sendmail/RELEASE_NOTES), none of them was security related. Unless you are finding problems with 8.11.0, you can stick with it.

Also note that Red Hat ships with a preconfigured mail server suitable for a single-server, single-office configuration with spam filtering enabled. If that's all you want, skip to the "Fast Configure for Red Hat 7" section, later, to change a few settings to customize the default configuration for your site name.

Of course, I still encourage you to read this chapter—as any mail administrator knows, the day will come when you'll need to compile and configure a new version of Sendmail. I've been doing this for eight years now, and I've always found myself upgrading mail servers at 2 A.M. because I just read of a security announcement and corresponding patch from www.sendmail.org and don't want to wait a few days for Red Hat to ship a new RPM.

FINDING AND INSTALLING SENDMAIL

Most distributions of Linux come with Sendmail preinstalled and preconfigured for a simple server configuration. While this means you don't have to deal with installing Sendmail at the time of initial deployment, it doesn't mean you won't ever have to upgrade! This section goes through the process of downloading a clean version of the Sendmail source code, compiling it, and installing it.

Downloading Sendmail

The best place to find Sendmail is at either the main site, http://www.sendmail.org, or at one of the mirror sites listed on the Web page. As of this writing, the latest version of Sendmail is 8.11.1. We will go through the process of downloading and compiling it as an example.

The Sendmail Web site is actually quite an impressive collection of useful information regarding Sendmail. You will find the Sendmail FAQ, pointers to useful electronic documentation, and, of course, links to the commercial version of the software, at http://www.sendmail.com. I highly recommend you read through the FAQ even if you don't understand all of it or don't even have a question that needs to be answered yet. That way, when you do run across a problem, you will have a better idea of what help you can find at the Web site.

The most recent version of Sendmail can be found at ftp://ftp.sendmail.org/pub/sendmail. The file containing Sendmail 8.11.1 is ftp://ftp.sendmail.org/pub/sendmail/sendmail.8.11.1.tar.gz.

Similar to the other packages we have downloaded, you should download it to a directory where you will have enough space to unpack it and then compile it. The **/usr/local/src** directory is often good for that. For this example, we will assume that we are working in that directory.

The command for unpacking source code archive is

```
[root@ford src]# tar -xzf sendmail.8.11.1.tar.gz
```

This will create the directory **/usr/local/src/sendmail-8.11.1** to contain all the source.

Compiling Sendmail

The developers of Sendmail have done a remarkable job at making Sendmail as easy to compile as possible, especially given the number of platforms on which Sendmail works! To start the process, make sure you are in the **/usr/local/src/sendmail-8.11.1** directory. Once there, type

```
[root@ford sendmail-8.11.1]# ./Build
```

This will result in the Sendmail binary, the miscellaneous tools that work with Sendmail (**mail.local**, **mailstats**, **makemap**, **praliases**, **rmail**, **smrsh**, and **vacation**), and the corresponding man pages.

NOTE: Red Hat 7 changed one very important directory location: the man (manual) pages that once resided in **/usr/man** now reside in **/usr/share/man**. Unfortunately, this means we need to tweak one of Sendmail's configuration files before letting the **Build** script run. To fix the problem, simply edit the **./sendmail-8.11.1/devtools/OS/Linux** file so that the line that reads:

define('confMANROOT', '/usr/man/man')

will instead read:

define('confMANROOT', '/usr/share/man/man')

If you do not do this before the **./Build** procedure, the installation phase will not work.

At this point, we are about 25% done with the installation of a new version of Sendmail. The rest of the process requires us to build a configuration file, a process that is not quite as intuitive as we'd like it to be. But the benefits still outweigh the negatives, which explains the continued success of Sendmail.

Peripheral Programs

Sendmail comes with several little programs to help administer the system or to provide additional security features on top of what comes built into it. In this section, we step through the process of understanding, compiling, and installing these programs.

Table 15-1 describes each of these peripheral programs.

We will cover installing Sendmail once we have created the necessary configuration files.

Tool	Description
`mailstats`	This program presents the statistics that Sendmail tracks on its performance and throughput in a human readable form.
`mail.local`	This is a simple mail delivery agent. (Instead, consider using Procmail, which is discussed later in "The Sendmail Macros.")
`makemap`	To increase performance, Sendmail keeps many of its tables in database format. This, of course, requires that there be a tool to convert the tables (as we create them using a text editor) into the database format. `makemap` is that tool.
`praliases`	The Sendmail aliases file allows you to create alternative e-mail addresses for your users, among many other things. (See "The Aliases File" on **/etc/aliases** later in this chapter.) Although I can't figure out any really good use for this tool, especially since the aliases file is kept in a human-readable format, it is possible to use it to dump the aliases file by using `praliases`.
`smrsh`	The **smrsh** tool (and corresponding feature in Sendmail) is a great way to help secure Sendmail. It essentially restricts Sendmail so that it can run only those programs placed in a special directory. If a program isn't there, it can't be run. This keeps outsiders from trying to send Sendmail bogus information in hopes of executing a malicious operation. It is highly recommended you use this feature in Sendmail. (How to use this feature is discussed in "smrsh," later.)

Table 15-1. Sendmail Peripheral Programs

FAST CONFIGURE FOR RED HAT 7

Red Hat Linux 7 comes with Sendmail 8.11.0 preconfigured. The configuration is well suited for single mail-server environments where all of the mail is funneled through this host. The box is also configured to disallow relaying from any host, which keeps it reasonably secure. To get it running, all you need to do is give it some more identity as well as a list of hosts for which it can accept mail.

NOTE: These next sections break my rule of configuring Sendmail using the MC files in conjunction with the M4 pre-processor. This means you better document your work and keep it in a well-known "documentation" area so your successors know what's going on. As I mentioned earlier in the chapter, it is still a good idea to follow through this entire chapter and learn how to do it "the right way."

All of the following changes are in the **/etc/sendmail.cf** file unless otherwise noted. You will need to make the changes as the root user and, when you are done, restart Sendmail using the following command:

```
[root@ford /root]# /etc/rc.d/init.d/sendmail restart
```

Your Official Domain Name

In the **/etc/sendmail.cf** file, find the lines that read:

```
# my official domain name
# ... define this only if sendmail cannot automatically determine your domain
#Dj$w.Foo.COM
```

You will want to change the last line of this block to read:

```
DjMYDOMAIN.COM
```

where **MYDOMAIN.COM** is your domain name. This assumes that you have an MX record set up in your DNS records that points to this host for all e-mail related issues. Note the missing pound symbol (#) at the beginning of the line. This uncomments the line so that it becomes effective when you restart Sendmail.

As Whom Do You Masquerade?

Sendmail boasts the ability to act like another host or domain name. This is useful when you have multiple domain names or you want the mail to look like it's coming from one place when it is not. For example, if your mail server's name is mail.example.net but you want it to look like all of your mail comes from just example.net, you should use this feature to masquerade the mail server.

In the **/etc/sendmail.cf** file, find the lines that read:

```
# who I masquerade as (null for no masquerading) (see also $=M)
DM
```

You will want to change the second line to read:

```
DMmasquerade.com
```

where *masquerade.com* is the name you want to masquerade as. Note that if you masquerade as another host, you should be in administrative control of the other host, or the other host name should be an alias for your own mail server.

From Which Hosts Do You Receive Mail?

A common trick for ISPs who do domain hosting is to set up a single mail server and configure their DNS so that all of their domains' MX records point to the same mail server. (See Chapter 12 for details on DNS.) In order for Sendmail to accept mail for multiple hosts, it must be told what hostnames it should accept. This is done through the **Cw** option in the **sendmail.cf** file. The Red Hat default has the **Cw** option already configured so that it looks in the **/etc/mail/local-host-names** for a list of hosts on behalf of whom it answers mail.

NOTE: A common problem is when a host appears to be taking mail from other sites but not from itself. In this case, be sure to add **localhost** and **localhost.localdomain** to your **/etc/mail/local-host-names** file.

Differing File Locations

The Sendmail group has been pushing the migration of the two "classic" configuration files, **sendmail.cf** (Sendmail's master configuration file) and **aliases** (a simple database of mailing lists and alternate names for users), into the **/etc/mail** directory. In fact, since version 8.9, they have been installed in **/etc/mail** by default. Most other UNIX vendors have followed suit and put the configuration files into **/etc/mail**, as well.

Yet for whatever reason, Red Hat made the bad decision to keep these two configuration files out of the normal locations. Most of the newer configuration files made their way into **/etc/mail**; however, **sendmail.cf** and **aliases** have remained in the **/etc** directory. The remainder of this chapter refers to these two files as being in the **/etc/mail** directory. If you are using the stock distribution of Sendmail that comes pre-installed with Red Hat 7, you will need to remember that you are an exception and thus will have to map the filenames accordingly.

THE RIGHT WAY: CONFIGURING SENDMAIL
WITH MC FILES

Sendmail configuration files are notoriously complex, which has a lot to do with Sendmail's history as the ultimate glue between disparate mail systems during the 1980s. The *rule sets* that define Sendmail's behavior allow for headers to be rewritten and even special action to be taken on particular header entries. This level of configurability, along with the fact that it was free and distributed with source code, made Sendmail the de facto mail server for hosts on the Internet.

You might expect that as the need for connecting disparate mail systems came to a close, the configuration file would be simplified—but it wasn't. This was because of the number of people who used the flexibility of Sendmail to create powerful messaging solutions that would not be possible with any other mail server. And so we still use the basic structure of the Sendmail configuration file, almost 20 years after it was originally designed.

> **NOTE:**   This is not to say that the actual format of the configuration file has remained identical. It hasn't. Several changes have been made as far as new parameters to certain commands, and so on.

What made Sendmail's configuration file tolerable is the set of macros that were developed to make the process of generating configuration files much easier. Sendmail allows you to use the M4 macro language, which was originally developed in the 1970s and thus is available across all variants of UNIX (including Linux) to convert a short and simple configuration file, which is much easier to understand by humans, into a formal configuration file.

In this section, we will go through the process of developing the correct macro file for your site's needs.

> **TIP:**   The ultimate authority on writing MC files comes from the developers of Sendmail. A quick peek into the **cf** directory relative to the Sendmail distribution reveals a README file, which documents all the macros that come with Sendmail. While you may find this document overwhelming at first, it covers everything necessary to configure Sendmail via the M4 macros.

Enough M4 for Sendmail

The M4 language is actually a complete macro language (read the information page on M4 for the complete documentation); however, the Sendmail configuration file needs only a small subset of commands in order to build a complete configuration file. In this section, we document what those commands are and how to use them.

Any commands you use in this section should be placed in a straight text file ending with a .MC extension, such as **myconfig.mc**. In the next section, we will discuss how to convert the .MC file into a **sendmail.cf** file.

A Note from Experience: Tweaking Sendmail

If you're ever in a situation where you need to change the configuration of Sendmail, you may be tempted to edit the **/etc/sendmail.cf** file directly—especially if the change seems relatively trivial. The problem with doing such things is that small changes often get left undocumented. The fact that the mail server is "tweaked" in one way or another most likely will be communicated from one generation of sysadmin to the next, as long as there is personnel overlap. Yet there is bound to come a time when there will be no overlap; thus it is in the site's best interest to make the system as self-documenting as possible. For Sendmail, this means resisting the urge to make changes directly to the **/etc/sendmail.cf** file and instead making all of the changes to the MC file. MC files contain references to the macros that get expanded into what becomes the **/etc/sendmail.cf** file. As long as the MC file reflects the **/etc/sendmail.cf** file correctly, your successor will be able to pick up where you left off, without having to incur any unnecessary downtime trying to understand the little changes you made.

CAUTION: M4 is a stream-based language, which means it doesn't have the concept of lines. As a result, any time it sees a command it recognizes, it will expand it, regardless of context. This means that any references to commands in comments must be quoted.

divert

The **divert** command tells M4 to ignore input until it sees another **divert** command. This allows you to place free-form comments in your macro file, which is a great way to document your work: You can explain _why_ you are setting the parameters you are setting, so those future administrators who need to deal with your work will understand the reasoning behind the setup.

To mark the beginning of a comment block, use

```
divert(-1)
```

To mark the end of a comment block, use

```
divert(0)
```

For example:

```
divert(-1)
#
# mysite.mc - Sendmail configuration file
```

```
# Friday the 13th of the 13th day of the 13th month.
# See /usr/local/doc/sendmail-config.txt for additional details.
# Developed by H.D. Core (hdc@domain.com)
#
divert(0)
```

dnl

This instruction is as close as M4 gets to understanding anything about lines. The **dnl** instruction stands for Delete till New Line, and its purpose is to eliminate unnecessary white space between macro expansions. You'll see it used liberally in the .MC files that come with Sendmail. Note that using **dnl** is not required.

define

The **define** command is a basic building block that allows you to give values to a variable. The format of the command is

```
define ('variable', 'value')
```

For example, to set QUEUE_DIR to **/var/spool/mqueue**, we would use

```
define ('QUEUE_DIR', '/var/spool/mqueue')
```

undefine

This command is the opposite of the **define** command—it takes a variable that has already been defined and undoes the setting. It is useful in situations where a predefined macro that comes with Sendmail has all the settings you want (except for one or two that you don't). In these cases, you can undefine the settings you don't want rather than defining a new macro by hand.

For example, to undefine the variable PROCMAIL_PATH, we would type

```
undefine ('PROCMAIL_PATH')
```

Using Quotes

As you may have noticed by now, string definition must be in single quotes. These quotes are important to M4 in order to process strings correctly. The beginning quote mark should be the back-tick character (`). This is often found on the same key as the tilde character (~). The end of the quote should be a single quote (') that is often shared with the double quote character (").

For example:

```
OSTYPE ('linux')
```

The Sendmail Macros

M4 by itself doesn't make configuring Sendmail any easier—it's the macros that ship with the Sendmail package that you can use from within an M4 script that make it easier. In this section, we discuss those macros.

Before reading this section, take a moment to look at the .MC files that come with Sendmail so that you know what's there. Don't worry if it doesn't make sense yet—seeing what's there and then reading this section will make things work a little more smoothly than the other way around. All of the .MC files are in the **./sendmail-8.11.1/cf/cf** directory.

OSTYPE

The OSTYPE macro must be used before any of the other macros discussed in this section. It sets up the minimum number of definitions necessary for the particular operating system specified. In our case, we simply need to supply the string "linux" as its parameter, like so:

```
OSTYPE('linux')
```

By using this macro, we spare ourselves from having to configure a large number of settings by hand. The configuration options include:

▼ The location of Sendmail-related files

■ Options for the program to use to deliver mail to individual mailboxes

■ Which shell to use for executing programs outside of Sendmail

■ USENET news interfacing options

■ SMTP, UUCP, and FAX options for remailing

▲ Options for using Procmail

You can view the specific features in the **cf/README** file that comes with Sendmail. We will not elaborate on all of the options available, because their defaults for Linux don't need to be adjusted and because they can vary from version to version.

DOMAIN

If you are configuring a large number of mail servers for a single site, you may want to look into setting up a domain macro for your site. (See the **cf/domains** directory for examples.) These macros are essentially site-specific entries that you can set up and share across your network so that other administrators do not have to repeat certain configuration options.

For example, if you wanted to set up a domain configuration for your site and call it mysite.m4, you would use the DOMAIN macro as follows:

```
DOMAIN('mysite')
```

For most sites, this is unnecessary and not worth the extra work of setting up a new domain entry in the **cf/domains** directory.

MAILER

In the first section, we discussed the differences between mail transfer agents (MTAs) and mail delivery agents (MDAs). Sendmail is an MTA only, and thus it requires another program to perform the actual mail delivery. The MAILER macro allows you to specify the program to perform the delivery of messages.

There are three mailers we are interested in: local, smtp, and Procmail. The local mailer is meant for messages that need to be delivered to mailboxes. The smtp mailer is for messages that need to be relayed to other sites. For example, if you have a single mail server and many clients in your network, you may want to configure your firewall so that the only host that is allowed to communicate through the firewall on the SMTP port (25) is your mail server. This means all of the clients on your network need to relay through your mail server, thus the need for a smtp mailer.

The last mailer is the most interesting. Procmail is a general-purpose mail-filtering tool that is extremely flexible. Best of all, it is written with security issues in mind, which makes Procmail an excellent replacement for the default local mailer that comes with Linux. And the icing on the cake? Procmail probably came with your Linux distribution.

NOTE: Sendmail supports more mailers than I have presented here; however, their usage is more likely to be the exception rather than the rule. If you are running into exceptions, it is better that you read through the **cf/README** file yourself rather than depend on my interpretation (and simplification) of it.

For example, to use the smtp mailer for relays and Procmail for local delivery, you need the following lines in your .MC file:

```
MAILER('procmail')
MAILER('smtp')
```

NOTE: You *must* have a mailer macro in your .MC file.

MASQUERADE_AS

It is often necessary to give the illusion that all e-mail originates from the same location when it really may not (for example, UNIX hosts doing their own e-mail service but relaying through your server to be sent to the Internet). In such cases, you should use the MASQUERADE_AS macro to set up host-name masquerading. The format of this command is as follows:

```
MASQUERADE_AS(domainname)
```

where ***domainname*** is the name of the domain you want the messages to masquerade as.

EXPOSED_USER The EXPOSED_USER macro works in conjunction with the MASQUERADE_AS macro to set up exceptions to the masquerading for specific users. For example, you'd probably want to know if the message originated from the root user. The usage of EXPOSED_USER is

```
EXPOSED_USER(usernames)
```

where ***usernames*** is a comma-separated list of users who should not be masqueraded.

For example, to make all of your mail appear as if it is coming from example.net except for mail coming from the root user, you need the following lines in your .MC file:

```
MASQUERADE_AS('example.net')
EXPOSED_USER('root')
```

FEATURE

Sendmail comes with a number of features that need to be explicitly enabled. Each feature that you want enabled should be enabled through the FEATURE macro, like so:

```
FEATURE('feature_name')
```

where ***feature_name*** is the name of the feature that you wish to enable. In this section, we will go through the list of features that Sendmail supports.

use_cw_file If your mail server is known by multiple names, you need to let Sendmail know. This was originally communicated in a special macro placed inside the final configuration file, but that practice made it much more difficult to make changes. This feature tells Sendmail to look for the list of mail server names in the **/etc/mail/local-host-names** file. The format of the file is simply a list of host names, one host name per line.

This feature differs from masquerading because use_cw_file tells Sendmail for which hostnames to accept mail, whereas masquerading tells Sendmail as what it can send mail.

use_ct_file Sendmail has a command-line option that allows you to change an outgoing message's sender name to something other than your own. By default, Sendmail allows only the root user to do this without generating a warning in the mail header. Using this feature, you can add more people to the list of trusted users by adding them to the **/etc/mail/trusted-users** file. The format of the file is one user per line.

redirect When users leave the system, it is often necessary to provide forwarding information for them. This is done using the redirect feature in Sendmail. Messages sent to *address*.REDIRECT@*mailserver* have an SMTP code sent back to the mail sender telling them to forward e-mail to *address*. This is done using the **/etc/mail/aliases** file (discussed in

"The Aliases File" later in the chapter) to set up an alias for the user who has departed. For example, if the user jshah has left, and his new e-mail address is jshah@example.net, you can set up an entry in the **/etc/mail/aliases** file that looks like

```
jshah:      jshah@example.net.REDIRECT
```

Now when mail is received for the user jshah, the sender automatically gets a message sent back to them indicating that the user's new e-mail address is jshah@example.net.

mailertable   If you are performing virtual hosting, you may want to route your e-mail in a different way, depending on the domain to which it is being sent. The mailertable feature allows you to do this in the **/etc/mail/mailertable** file, where each line is in the format

```
receiverhost            mailer:hostname
```

where **receiverhost** is the host for which you are receiving mail, **mailer** is the mailer (as defined with the MAILER macro), and **hostname** is the machine onto which you want to pass the message. The **receiverhost** has some additional flexibility—namely, it can have wildcard host names. This is done by prefixing the **receiverhost** string with a period, which tells Sendmail to allow an arbitrary host name to be in front of the **receiverhost** string. For example, if we specified **receiverhost** to be .domain.com, it would accept messages destined to anything.domain.com. If **receiverhost** is not prefixed with a period, than the complete host name must match.

For example, to relay all messages sent to any host in the .domain.com domain to the host mail.outsourced-mail-server.com, we would create an entry that looks like

```
.domain.com                      smtp:mail.outsourced-mail-server.com
```

TIP: Although it is probably just coincidence, Sendmail was created a mere 20 miles north of the base of Silicon Valley, a mystical land where mergers and acquisitions happen daily. And as luck may have it, Sendmail's mailertable feature is very well suited to instances where a merger or acquisition has created an immediate need for a single mail server to accept mail for more than one domain name. Another popular use for this feature is for the purpose of relaying mail through a DMZ. Thus the firewall can be configured to only pass mail through if the originating IP address is the relay host.

Mailertable must be turned into Sendmail's database format before it can be used. This is done via the **makemap** program that gets compiled along with Sendmail. To use it with the mailertable file, we would say

```
[root@ford /etc]# makemap hash /etc/mail/mailertable
```

domaintable   The domaintable feature allows you to tell Sendmail to map one domain name to another domain name transparently. This is useful when your site changes its domain name. Once you enable it with the FEATURE command, you will need to set up the database containing the name information mapping. The database is typically **/etc/mail/domaintable**. The format of this file is

```
oldname.com        newname.com
```

Like the mailertable, Sendmail requires this table to be converted into a database format using the **makemap** command, like so:

```
[root@ford /etc]# makemap hash /etc/mail/domaintable
```

always_add_domain This feature tells Sendmail to always add your domain name to all delivered mail, even if it is being delivered locally. This is a good way to ensure a uniform appearance of e-mail addresses to all people, regardless of whether they are inside or outside of your domain.

virtusertable If you are hosting virtual domains, you will quickly find yourself facing name space collisions for e-mail addresses. The virtusertable feature allows you to get around this by setting up a special mapping of e-mail addresses to real user names. Thus, it becomes possible for there to be multiple info e-mail addresses (such as info@domain.com, info@example.net, and so on) hosted on the same system.

The format of the virtusertable is as follows:

```
fake-address           real-address
```

where **fake-address** is the address that you need to host, and **real-address** is where the e-mail is actually sent. So if you are hosting domain.com and example.net, you might do something like

```
info@domain.com domain-info@real-domain.com
info@example.net example-info@real-domain.com
```

so that any messages sent to info@domain.com get sent to domain-info@real-domain.com instead, and info@example.net gets sent to example-info@real-domain.com.

You can set up the additional flexibility of having the right column entry not have a username but have the @domain.com portion. This results in any messages sent to any username to @domain.com being forwarded to a single address. For example

```
@domain.com        jaffe@jaffe-networks.com
```

will cause any messages sent to any user @domain.com to have their messages forwarded to jaffe@jaffe-networks.com.

This table is like the other tables we've discussed, in that it needs to be converted into the database format using the **makemap** command, like so:

```
[root@ford /etc]# makemap hash /etc/virtusers
```

nullclient   If you have UNIX machines in your network and want them all to relay their e-mail through a central server, you will need to configure them so that they are *null clients*. Telling Sendmail that it is a null client is essentially asking it to remove its intelligence and pass the buck over to a central server. While this may appear bizarre, it's actually a good idea, because it allows you to centralize mail service. Null clients relay all of their messages to the *mail hub*, which takes care of proper delivery, even if the delivery stays local to your network. This feature also enables you to perform centralized logging of mail activity.

To specify a mail hub, use the following **define** statement in conjunction with the FEATURE macro:

```
define('MAIL_HUB', 'mailhubhost')
```

where **mailhubhost** is the name of the host acting as mail hub. For example:

```
FEATURE('nullclient')
define('MAIL_HUB', 'dune.clickarray.com')
```

where dune.clickarray.com is the mail hub.

local_procmail   This feature tells Sendmail to use Procmail as the local mailer. It can take up to three parameters: the path to Procmail (defaults to **/usr/local/bin/procmail**), parameters to Procmail (defaults to **-Y -a *hostname* -d *username***), and flags for the mailer. Realistically speaking, all you need to do is specify the location of Procmail. Don't worry about the parameters to Procmail unless you have a special need and have read the corresponding Procmail parameters. For example:

```
FEATURE('local_procmail', '/usr/bin/procmail')
```

smrsh   One of Sendmail's security problems is that we, the people who configure it, make mistakes. One of the most common mistakes is setting up programs that can be run through an alias expansion in an insecure manner that can be exploited by remote users. We are effectively hitting ourselves in the foot with a hammer.

Sendmail tries to take away the hammer with the SendMail Restricted Shell (**smrsh**). It is a very simplified shell that has limited functionality, and therefore fewer things can be exploited because of a misconfiguration.

This feature accepts a parameter specifying where **smrsh** is located. If **smrsh** is in the **/usr/sbin** directory, we would specify

```
FEATURE('smrsh', '/usr/sbin/smrsh')
```

promiscuous_relay   By default, Sendmail does not allow any site to relay mail through your site. This is done to protect you from spammers using your systems as a hopping point. If for some reason you have to allow random people to relay through your mail server, you can use this feature.

CAUTION: Allowing random people to relay through your server is a ***very bad idea***. It opens up your site to denial of service (DoS) attacks, theft of bandwidth, and the nightmare of getting floods of e-mail coming from angry recipients of unsolicited e-mail. Before opening up your system like this, understand the implications!

relay_entire_domain   Sendmail's default behavior is to relay mail only from hosts listed in the access database (discussed in "Spam Control: The "Access" Database," later in the chapter). By using this feature, you allow any host from within your domain to relay through you.

relay_based_on_MX   This feature tells Sendmail to look up the DNS MX record of a host that is asking to relay through you. If Sendmail finds that the host's MX record is the same host that Sendmail is running on, the message will be accepted for relaying.

accept_unqualified_senders   Normally, Sendmail refuses mail from e-mail addresses that are unqualified. For example, mail from sshah@domain.com is acceptable, but mail from sshah alone is not. Using this feature tells Sendmail to *not* require that sender e-mail addresses be qualified.

accept_unresolvable_domains   Sendmail defaults to verifying that the sender's domain name is resolvable via DNS. This keeps people from forging e-mail from nonexisting domains. If your site has a limited view of the Internet DNS namespace for some reason (such as if you're behind a firewall), you will want to use this feature to tell Sendmail to accept messages from unresolvable domains.

access_db   This feature enables the access database, which allows you to specify whether you want to accept, reject, drop, or reject with a special code all of your incoming e-mail, based on source domain or e-mail address. We explore the configuration file for this feature in greater detail in "Spam Control: The "Access" Database" later in this chapter, when we discuss spam control.

blacklist_recipients   There are some users who should never receive e-mail, such as nobody, bin, or lp. You can blacklist these users so that they cannot receive e-mail by using this feature in combination with the access_db feature.

The way that blacklist configuration works with the access_db is discussed later in "Spam Control: The "Access" Database."

Configurable Parameters

Sendmail offers a number of configurable parameters for its features. In this section, we review these parameters and explain what they are used for and their default values. You'll find that, for the most part, the defaults are perfectly good, and you won't need to change anything.

You can see the very long list of configurable options in the **cf/README** file; they are described in Table 15-2. However, many of those options are so incredibly rarely used that you'll probably even forget they are there when you're done with this chapter. Because of that, Table 15-2 sticks to the most common options.

Option Name	Description	Default
`confMAILER_NAME`	The name used for internally-generated mail (typically for error messages for returned mail).	MAILER-DAEMON
`confDOMAIN_NAME`	Your domain name. You should set this option only if Sendmail cannot determine your domain name by itself.	No default
`confCW_FILE`	The full path to the file containing host names that the server may be known as (see the use_cw_file feature).	/etc/sendmail.cw
`confCT_FILE`	The full path to the file containing trusted users (see the use_ct_file feature).	/etc/sendmail.ct
`confCR_FILE`	The full path to the relay-domains file. This is the list of domains for which Sendmail will relay. (You should use the access_db feature instead.)	/etc/mail/relay-domains
`confALIAS_WAIT`	When the mail aliases file is updated, it must be converted to the internal database format with the **newaliases** command. This parameter tells Sendmail how long to wait for **newaliases** to run before rebuilding the database itself.	10 minutes (10m)
`confMIN_FREE_BLOCKS`	The number of free blocks the mail storage partition must have for Sendmail to accept new messages. This option allows Sendmail to protect the system from sudden bursts of e-mail.	100 blocks, where 1 block (under Linux) is equal to 1K
`confMAX_MESSAGE_SIZE`	The maximum message size (in bytes) that Sendmail will accept.	Infinite

Table 15-2.   Sendmail's Most Common Configurable Parameters

Option Name	Description	Default
`ConfAUTO_REBUILD`	Specifies if Sendmail should automatically rebuild the aliases database if needed.	False
`ConfLOG_LEVEL`	Specifies Sendmail's level of logging. The higher the level number, the more logging performed. The level codes are as follows: 0 Minimal logging 1 Serious system failures and potential security problems 2 Lost communication (network problems) 3 Transient errors, malformed addresses, forward/include errors 4 Minor failures, out-of-date alias databases, connection rejections via check_rule sets 5 Message collection statistics 6 Creation of error messages, **VRFY** and **EXPN** commands 7 Delivery failures (host or user unknown, and so on) 8 Successful deliveries and alias database rebuilds 9 Messages being deferred 10 Database expansion (alias, forward, and user database lookups) 11 NIS errors and end-of-job processing 12 All SMTP connections 13 Bad user shells and files with improper permissions	Log level 9
`confME_TOO`	When a message is sent to an alias that has the sender as a member of the list (such as the user hdc sends a message to management, which expands to the users hdc, julia, and ceo), this option determines whether the message should be sent to the sender, too.	False (does not send message back to sender)

Table 15-2.   Sendmail's Most Common Configurable Parameters *(continued)*

Option Name	Description	Default
`confTO_INITIAL`	Timeout period Sendmail should wait when connecting to remote sites to send mail.	5 minutes (5m)
`confTO_IDENT`	Timeout period Sendmail should wait when trying to identify the username of someone trying to send mail to it via the IDENT protocol.	30 seconds (30s)
`confTO_QUEUEWARN`	Timeout period before a user is told that her message being relayed through Sendmail is being deferred because the remote site cannot be contacted.	4 hours (4h)
`ConfSMTP_LOGIN_MSG`	The greeting message sent to someone trying to connect to Sendmail. Some sites have taken to customizing this string so that remote sites don't know what kind of mail server is really being run. In essence, this is security through obscurity, where the underlying philosophy is, "Why tell them what you don't have to?" Just understand that obscuring the type of mail server does not mean a cracker will not get through if they are determined enough.	Host name of the server, the version of Sendmail, and the version of the Sendmail configuration file
`confDOUBLE_BOUNCE_ADDRESS`	If an error occurs, Sendmail delivers an e-mail notice to the site administrator. The site administrator is defined by this option. Most sites leave the default alone and use an alias to route messages to the system administrator.	Postmaster

Table 15-2. Sendmail's Most Common Configurable Parameters *(continued)*

NOTE: Some of the parameters in the configuration file represent time values. The format of these values is a number followed by a letter, where the letter is either *s* for seconds, *m* for minutes, *h* for hours, or *d* for days. For example, 10m is 10 minutes, 3d is 3 days, and so on.

For example, to set the path for the Procmail program to **/usr/bin/procmail**, we would use

```
define('PROCMAIL_MAILER_PATH', '/usr/bin/procmail')
```

A Complete Sample Configuration

Here is the complete .MC file used to build the Red Hat 7 configuration:

```
VERSIONID('linux setup for Red Hat Linux')dnl
OSTYPE('linux')
define('confDEF_USER_ID', ''8:12'')dnl
undefine('UUCP_RELAY')dnl
undefine('BITNET_RELAY')dnl
define('confAUTO_REBUILD')dnl
define('confTO_CONNECT', '1m')dnl
define('confTRY_NULL_MX_LIST',true)dnl
define('confDONT_PROBE_INTERFACES',true)dnl
define('PROCMAIL_MAILER_PATH', '/usr/bin/procmail')dnl
define('STATUS_FILE', '/var/log/sendmail.st')dnl
define('UUCP_MAILER_MAX', '2000000')dnl
define('confUSERDB_SPEC', '/etc/mail/userdb.db')dnl
dnl define('confPRIVACY_FLAGS', 'authwarnings,novrfy,noexpn')dnl
dnl define('confTO_QUEUEWARN', '4h')dnl
dnl define('confTO_QUEUERETURN', '5d')dnl
dnl define('confQUEUE_LA', '12')dnl
dnl define('confREFUSE_LA', '18')dnl
FEATURE('smrsh', '/usr/sbin/smrsh')dnl
FEATURE('mailertable', 'hash -o /etc/mail/mailertable')dnl
FEATURE('virtusertable', 'hash -o /etc/mail/virtusertable')dnl
FEATURE(redirect)dnl|
FEATURE(always_add_domain)dnl
FEATURE(use_cw_file)dnl
FEATURE(local_procmail)dnl
FEATURE('access_db')dnl
FEATURE('blacklist_recipients')dnl
dnl We strongly recommend to comment this one out if you want to
dnl protect yourself from spam. However, the laptop and users on
dnl computers that do not have 24x7 DNS do need this.
FEATURE('accept_unresolvable_domains')dnl
dnl FEATURE('relay_based_on_MX')dnl
MAILER(smtp)dnl
MAILER(procmail)dnl
```

Compiling Macros into a Configuration File

Once you have all of your macros put into a .MC file, you are ready to convert it into a complete configuration file that Sendmail can understand. The process is wonderfully straightforward:

1. Make sure your configuration file is in the **cf/cf** directory, relative to the main Sendmail directory that was created when the source code was unpacked. For the sake of discussion, let's call the file we are working with **ourconfig.mc**.

2. Run the command

   ```
   [root@ford cf]#m4 ../m4/cf.m4 ourconfig.mc > ourconfig.cf
   ```

And that's it. The file **ourconfig.cf** has been created and is ready to use.

INSTALLING SENDMAIL

We now have Sendmail compiled and its configuration files ready to go. All we need to do is actually install these creations into their place and start it up. BUT, as with any service, be sure to make backups of all of your existing binaries and configuration files *before* performing the installation. In the worst case where nothing works, you should be able to revert back to the old configuration quickly so that your users will experience minimal amounts of downtime. Ideally, you should be able to install the new version so quickly that no one even notices the mail server was down.

When you have your backup of the Sendmail binaries and configuration files, go back to the directory where you ran **./Build** the first time (**/usr/local/src/sendmail-8.11.1**) and type

```
[root@ford sendmail-8.11.1]# ./Build install
```

This will copy the Sendmail binary into **/usr/sbin** and install the man pages into the appropriate directories. With the binaries in place, you need to copy the configuration file into the **/etc** directory. Go back to the directory where you created the **ourconfig.cf** file and type

```
[root@ford cf]# cp ourconfig.cf /etc/mail/sendmail.cf
```

With the files in place, kill Sendmail and restart it. Suggested command-line parameters are **-bd** and **-q1h**. The **-bd** option tells Sendmail to go into daemon mode so that it sits quietly in the background processing e-mail, and the **-q1h** option tells it to go back and process outstanding e-mail once an hour. (The default configuration for Sendmail is to try to process the e-mail immediately, and if it cannot contact the destination host, it will queue it for future delivery.) Thus the command line to start Sendmail is:

```
[root@ford /root]# /usr/sbin/sendmail -bd -q1h
```

It is a good idea to create a startup script for Sendmail if one doesn't exist for it already. (Most likely, one was already created for you when you installed Linux.) See Chapter 7 for more information on startup and shutdown scripts.

BEYOND THE PRIMARY CONFIGURATION FILE

Reading through the features that Sendmail offers us, we saw that there are many features that enable and disable the usage of additional configuration files. Some of these files are very straightforward and are explained in a sentence or two in the previous section. But there are two files in particular that are nontrivial: the aliases file and the access database file. In this section, we examine their formats and learn how to write our own.

The Aliases File

Sendmail's mail aliases file is one of its most powerful features. It allows you to create mailing lists, give users alternative e-mail aliases, and even pipe e-mail directly to external applications. Most configurations place the aliases in either **/etc/aliases** or **/etc/mail/ aliases**. They are unlikely to be anywhere else.

The format of the aliases file is reasonably straightforward. All comment lines begin with a pound symbol (#), and the remainder of the line is free form. Lines may also be blank to help define logical blocks.

Each alias must begin with the alias's name, followed immediately by a colon. The remainder of the line is what Sendmail will expand that address to be. The content of the line can be one of six things: another alias, a list of aliases, another user, a list of users, a file, or an external application. Aliases and usernames can be intermixed. Any aliases referenced on the right side of the colon must be defined already.

Assume the domain domain.com has the users boson, yom, achan, julia, sangeet, hdc, and sshah. Let's look at a few examples and see what some of these aliases can be set up to do.

▼ We want a simple alias for Sangeet. Since she is the CEO, we set up an alias as follows:

```
ceo: sangeet
```

Now any mail sent to ceo@domain.com will transparently be sent to Sangeet.

■ We want to create an alias for three of our departments: engineering, mis, and management. We can create the aliases:

```
engineering: boson, yom
mis: achan, sshah
management: julia, hdc, ceo
```

Any mail sent to management@domain.com will automatically be forwarded to the users julia, hdc, and ceo. The ceo address will get expanded to sangeet.

■ We want to create the alias everybody so that any mail sent to it will automatically be forwarded to all of the departments. We can do that with the following alias:

```
everybody: engineering, mis, management
```

E-mail sent to everybody@domain.com will be expanded to engineering, mis, and management. Each of these aliases will expand to their respective users, with the management alias having one more expansion to convert ceo to sangeet.

Following the trend here?

CAUTION: Depending on the database backend compiled with Sendmail, you may not be able to get more than about 1000 characters-worth of addresses per alias. From the standpoint of good administrative practices, try to keep each individual alias down to a manageable size so that it's easy to follow what each one expands to.

■ If we want all of the mail sent to a particular address to be copied to a file, we simply begin the right side of an alias with a forward slash character (/), indicating that the rest of the line is a filename. So if we want messages sent to log@domain.com to be placed into a file called **/tmp/log**, we would set an alias, like so:

```
log: /tmp/log
```

▲ If we want to pipe all of the e-mail sent to a particular alias to an external program, we can do so through this file. Assume that the external program is **/etc/smrsh/external_program**.

```
abuse: "|/etc/smrsh/external_program"
```

NOTE: If you configured Sendmail to use **smrsh**, you will need to be sure to place your binaries in the correct directory so that **smrsh** knows they are there. If you are sticking with the Red Hat installation of **smrsh**, this directory is **/etc/smrsh**. If you are compiling **smrsh** yourself, the default directory is **/usr/adm**.

Once you are done creating the aliases file, you will need to use the **newaliases** command to convert the file into a database format that Sendmail can quickly read. To do so, simply type

```
[root@ford /etc]# newaliases
```

Spam Control: The "Access" Database

When configuring Sendmail, you have the option of enabling the access_db. This feature allows you to use the **/etc/mail/access** file to list special actions for particular domain names, host names, IP addresses, and users. This feature is especially interesting because it unifies all of Sendmail's spam-control mechanisms into a single configuration file.

The format of the file is simple: Lines that begin with a pound symbol (#) are comments, blank lines are allowed, and the rest of the lines contain the actual configuration information.

The default features that are enabled when using the access_db feature allow you to list either the host name, domain name, IP address, or e-mail address, and specify whether you want a specific action on e-mail originating from there. The actions are listed in Table 15-3.

Let's look at a few examples that illustrate the features listed in Table 15-3:

▼ To reject all messages from annoying-web-site.com, your entry would be

```
annoying-web-site.com                           REJECT
```

■ To discard all messages from badperson@badpeople.com, you would use

```
badperson@badpeople.com                         DISCARD
```

Action	Description
OK	Accepts the message even if there are other rules that would otherwise reject it. For example, if you enable the feature to deny messages from domain names that cannot be resolved to an IP address, you can specify a specific exception domain using the **OK** action.
RELAY	Unless explicitly turned on, the default Sendmail configuration does not relay messages for other domains. This action overrides that rule for a specific domain.
REJECT	Refuses all messages from this site/person. This will cause a brief message to be sent back to the sender informing him or her that the message was rejected.
DISCARD	Discards the message entirely. No message is sent back to the sender. For all he/she knows, the message was accepted.
SMTP-code message	*SMTP-code* must be a valid SMTP code as specified in RFC 821. *message* can be any text you want returned along with *SMTP-code*.

Table 15-3. access_db Features

- To relay all messages from the 138.23.0.0 network, you would use

```
138.23                          RELAY
```

- To reject all messages from spamathon.com with the SMTP message "550 No Spam Here.", you would use

```
spamathon.com                   550 No Spam Here.
```

▲ We can put all of these examples together into a single file:

```
#
# /etc/mail/access
# Rules for accepting/denying mail from various sites.
#
annoying-web-site.com           REJECT
badperson@badpeople.com         DISCARD
spamathon.com                   550 No Spam Here.
```

If you enabled the blacklist_recipients feature, you can list the users' e-mail addresses from whom you don't want to receive e-mail. For example:

```
myuser@domain.com               550 Been blacklisted...
```

REAL-LIFE SENDMAIL ISSUES

E-mail is usually the most often used service at any site. Given the frequency of its usage, you are bound to run across situations where you need to get some more information about the mail system. Although these situations aren't Sendmail-specific problems (disk and network problems are more often the culprit), knowing about some of the peripheral tools that come with Sendmail can be helpful in debugging the problem.

In this section, we go over some of these tools and instances where you might use them.

mailq

When Sendmail accepts a message, it immediately places it in a queue. This allows Sendmail to accept mail faster than it can process it—a feature crucial in high-volume environments.

Because a message gets queued for later processing, users can experience delays between sending a message and having it arrive at the destination. After all, there may be several queues between the sender and receiver, each with its own queue length, processing time, and bandwidth limitations.

Another cause for delay is simply that Sendmail thinks something is broken and cannot send outgoing messages. This also causes the queue to grow.

In any case, finding out how long the queue is for your server is important. With Sendmail, this is done using the **mailq** command, like so:

```
[root@ford /root]# mailq
```

This will list all of the messages in the queue, their message identifier, whom the message is from, and where the message is going.

Is Sendmail Running?

When mail seems especially slow, you may begin to question whether Sendmail is even running! The quick way to check this from any host on your network is to try to **telnet** to your mail server's port 25, as we did in the first section of this chapter. You should see a response from the server in a timely manner. If the response is slow, it may be due to a few possibilities:

▼ *The mail server is very busy.* This can be checked by logging into the server and running the **uptime** command. It will report three values representing the current load average, the load average from 5 minutes ago, and the load average from 15 minutes ago. These load averages represent the average number of processes that are waiting for CPU time. A value higher than 1.0 for each processor means that the system has more things to do than it has time to do, and that means a process has to wait longer before the CPU can get to it. Periodic bursts are normal, but a sustained load significantly greater than the number of processors means you need to look into a bigger/faster mail server solution.

■ *The mail server is so busy that Sendmail has stopped processing messages.* This is Sendmail's way of keeping the server from spiraling out of control. Instead of increasing the load by processing messages, it simply queues them for future processing. This can make mail delivery times substantially greater. The default load average at which it stops processing is 8.

■ *DNS is broken.* A typical sign of broken DNS is *extremely* sluggish performance even though the load average is near zero. Delays of minutes before server response are caused by the server making a DNS request, and then having to wait until the timeout before it gives up on resolving a host name or IP address and continuing on the best it can. In the case of message delivery, this means leaving the messages in the queue until DNS is repaired.

▲ *Out of spool space.* Sendmail gets especially grumpy when it runs out of disk space. A quick check of disk space allocation with the **df** command can reveal if this is a problem. (See Chapter 6 for more information on **df**.)

If Sendmail is not responding at all, you may need to restart it. To do so, try using the startup script:

```
[root@ford /root]# /etc/rc.d/init.d/sendmail start
```

If that does not work, you can start Sendmail by hand, like so:

```
[root@ford /root]# sendmail -bd -q15m
```

The **-bd** parameter tells Sendmail to go into daemon mode, and **-q15m** tells Sendmail to check its queues every 15 minutes.

Where Does Sendmail Keep Its Queues and Spools?

Sendmail maintains only one queue, and that queue is stored in **/var/spool/mqueue** under Linux. The mail spools themselves are stored in **/var/spool/mail**, where each user's mail spool is stored in a file with their login name.

Because the mail spool and mail queue can grow due to inputs from users and people outside of your network, it is possible that file space can get used up unexpectedly, causing Sendmail to get grumpy about not having enough working space. For this reason, it is a good idea to keep these two spools on their own partition (especially **/var/spool/mail**). By doing so, users outside your network cannot bring the entire system down if they send messages that are too large; they can only affect Sendmail's behavior.

Of course, it doesn't matter how or why the disk space is no longer available: If it isn't there, Sendmail will not behave. So be sure to check for this problem when you notice abnormal behavior.

How to Remove Entries from the Queue

In your life as a system administrator, you are bound to run across a user who insists on doing something incredibly crazy—like mailing a 100MB movie file halfway around the world to his buddy who has a very slow connection.

In those cases, you may need to purge an entry in the queue by hand. To do this, you need to first find out which message is the troublemaker. Sometimes it is obvious, as in the case of a large message in **/var/spool/mqueue**—the file size will stick out like a sore thumb. Other times, it takes a bit of intuition when looking at the mail queue with the **mailq** command. A message that has been sitting in the queue for days is unlikely to be delivered successfully and may need to be purged because it is causing Sendmail to spend time needlessly trying to send it. In either case, you should see the message ID number. (Under Sendmail, this is a mixture of letters and numbers.) You should then be able to identify the message in the mail queue by looking for the filenames that contain the message ID. A quick way to do that is

A Note from Experience: Overloaded and Overworked

I once had a user who tried to mail a 40MB PowerPoint presentation to 80 people in the office! What made this a really bad situation? My mail spool partition only had 2GB of space (80 copies times 40MB equals 3.2GB). What could make it worse? The director got four copies, which made his mail client crash when trying to download messages. How did I know something was wrong (before my users screamed)? I could *hear* the disk working hard on my poor little Sun IPX. (A Sun IPX is roughly the same in performance as a 60MHz Pentium.)

```
[root@ford /root]# ls  -1 /var/spool/mqueue | grep messageID
```

where **messageID** is the ID number of the troublemaker.

With this information, you are ready to remove the file from the queue. Simply use the **rm** command to remove the queue file. For example, if you found that message ID RAA735 was causing problems, you could remove that message like so:

```
[root@ford /root]# rm  -i /var/spool/mqueue/*RAA735
```

Don't forget to check if Sendmail is still working correctly after you do this. If Sendmail happened to be working on that particular piece of mail when you removed it, Sendmail may need to be restarted.

Flushing the Queue

If your site loses connectivity with the rest of the world (for instance, if your Internet connection is down), Sendmail will quietly accept messages from your users for future delivery. When Sendmail finds that it can once again contact other servers, it will quietly start processing the queue itself.

In most instances, you can leave Sendmail alone and let it work through its queue. Sendmail does a great job at regulating itself and making sure it processes its queue without overwhelming the system or your network connection.

However, there are instances when you need Sendmail to hurry up and get through its queue faster. One instance might be if the outage was long enough that it would take Sendmail unreasonably long to process the queue at its normal rate, especially given the flood of new e-mails coming into the system. (After all, other sites trying to contact your mail server patiently queued their messages until they could connect. Now they're all delivering!)

In these instances, you need Sendmail to churn through its queue much more quickly. To force Sendmail to process its queue faster, kill Sendmail and restart it with a much higher processing rate. For example, to start Sendmail such that it processes its queue every minute, you would enter

```
[root@ford /root]# sendmail -bd -q1m
```

Another trick is to invoke Sendmail with the **-q** option, like so:

```
[root@ford /root]# sendmail -q
```

CAUTION: If you're going to use the **-q** trick, do not kill the running Sendmail first!

Mail Logging

Keeping track of how much mail goes through your system is useful for two reasons: It provides a history of activity on the server, which is good when trying to track down bad behavior on the system (or of the users on the system!); and it provides a quantifiable metric for the demands placed on the server. The latter is especially handy when trying to convince those with the spending power that a server needs to be upgraded!

Sendmail uses the syslog mechanism for logging its activity. Most Linux distributions come preconfigured so that any messages sent to syslog that are from the mailer are placed into a separate log file called **/var/log/maillog**. (You may need to check your **/etc/syslog.conf** file to determine if this is true for your system.)

On a system that passes hundreds to thousands of messages a day, these logs will grow very quickly. Be sure you have a method of rotating your logs. (Red Hat Linux comes preconfigured to do this.) If you are doing this by hand, simply rename the current log file to something new (for example, maillog to maillog.old), and then create an empty new file called maillog. Once the files are set up, restart the syslog daemon so that it knows what to do with the new files.

SUMMARY

In this chapter, you learned how to configure the Sendmail mail server. Although it can appear intimidating at first, it doesn't take long for its methodology to make sense. More important, you learned that configuring Sendmail isn't nearly as horrible as so many people would have you believe.

The most important things you should carry with you from this chapter are:

▼ Sendmail is configured using a series of macros written in the M4 macro language.

■ Most of these macros come predefined with the Sendmail source code.

■ All of the features you need are specified, using these macros, into a file that ends with a .MC extension.

■ Once this macro file is created, you "compile" it into the final configuration file, **/etc/mail/sendmail.cf**.

■ A configuration file outside of **/etc/mail/sendmail.cf** is usually stored as a straight text file but then converted into a database format so that Sendmail can refer to it quickly.

■ There are very few binaries related to Sendmail. The server application itself is a single file called **sendmail**, located at **/usr/sbin/sendmail**. It should be started at boot time through a startup script, as described in Chapter 7.

▲ Sendmail comes with a few peripheral programs such as **smrsh**, which can really help your day-to-day sysadmin operations. The **smrsh** tool has especially notable features.

As we've seen, Sendmail is one very powerful program that can handle some remarkable configurations. Take advantage of its flexibility and let only your creativity limit what you do with it.

CHAPTER 16

Post Office Protocol (POP)

The Post Office Protocol, or POP for short, is a standardized mechanism that workstations of any operating system can use to download mail from a mail server. POP was created as a result of two developments:

▼ The proliferation on the Internet of non-UNIX PCs lacking the capability to run a fully capable SMTP server such as Sendmail

▲ The proliferation of workstations connected to the Internet via dial-up facilities that are rarely connected 100% of the time

Under POP, mail servers running an SMTP server can accept messages and store them to a mail spool; users on any type of workstation with a POP-compliant mail reader can then connect to the POP server (which can read the mail spool written to by the SMTP server) and download their mail. When a user wants to send e-mail, the workstation can contact the local SMTP server and relay outgoing messages to it. See Figure 16-1.

Figure 16-1. Sending and receiving mail with SMTP and POP

This chapter discusses the POP Version 3 (POP3) protocol in detail, along with the security implications of supporting it. We then step through the process of downloading, compiling, and installing POP3.

THE MECHANICS OF POP

Like the other services we have discussed so far, POP needs a server process to handle requests. The server process listens to these requests on port 110.

Each request to and response from the POP server is in cleartext ASCII, which means it's very easy for us to test the functionality of a POP server using Telnet. (This is especially useful when you have users who claim that the "mail server is broken," although the real problem is that they're unfamiliar with the system.) Like SMTP servers, a POP server can be controlled with a very short list of commands.

To get a look at the most common commands, let's walk through the process of connecting to a POP server, logging in, listing available messages, reading one, and then dropping the connection.

> **NOTE:** We'll use the `telnet` command to read mail only as a means of seeing the actual POP3 commands being sent to the server and the server's responses. In reality, once the server has been set up, you can read your mail with a mail reader such as Eudora or Netscape Communicator. Knowing the actual POP3 commands is helpful when you need to track down problems reported by your users. Often, it's easier to use Telnet to check quickly whether the POP server is responding than to try and use a real mail client—especially if you suspect the mail client has a bug!

Reading Mail with Telnet

We begin by **telnet**ing to the POP3 server. From a command prompt, type

```
[root@ford /root]# telnet pop3server.domain.com 110
```

The POP3 server responds as follows:

```
+OK ready.
```

The server is now waiting for you to give it a command. (Don't worry that you don't see a prompt.) First, you want to log in, and then tell the server your login name via the **USER** command:

```
USER yourlogin
```

Here **yourlogin** is, of course, your login ID. The server responds with

```
+OK Password required for yourlogin.
```

Now tell the server your password, using the **PASS** command.

CAUTION: The system will echo back your password, so don't do this if you have people looking over your shoulder!

PASS *yourpassword*

where *yourpassword* is your password. The server responds with

+OK *yourlogin* has *X* messages (*Y* octets)

where *X* and *Y* will be actual numbers. *X* represents the number of messages in your mailbox, and *Y* represents the number of bytes in your mailbox. You're now logged in and can issue commands to read your mail.

Begin by listing the messages that are waiting, using the **LIST** command. Type

LIST

and the server will list all the messages in your mailbox. The first column represents the message number, and the second column represents the site of the message. The response for my mailbox currently looks like this:

```
+OK 5 messages (13040 octets)
1 4246
2 2303
3 2334
4 1599
5 2558
.
```

Now let's try to actually read a message, using the **RETR** command. The only parameter that **RETR** needs is the message number to read. We'll start simple: To read message 1, type

RETR 1

The server responds with something like this:

```
Return-Path: <hdc@domain.com>
Received: from localhost (localhost [127.0.0.1])
        by ford.domain.com (8.9.3/8.9.3) with ESMTP id WAA08271
        for <sshah@localhost>; Wed, 23 Jun 1999 22:32:38 -0700
Received: from domain.com
        by localhost with POP3 (fetchmail-5.0.0)
        for sshah@localhost (single-drop); Wed, 23 Jun 1999 22:32:38 -0700 (PDT)
Received: (from hdc@localhost)
        by deathstar.domain.com (8.9.2/8.8.7) id IAA06752
        for sshah@domain.com; Wed, 23 Jun 1999 08:05:52 -0700 (PDT)
From: "H. D. Core" <hdc@deathstar.domain.com>
Message-Id: <199906231505.06752@deathstar.domain.com>
```

```
Subject: by the way
Date: Wed, 23 Jun 1999 08:05:52 -0700 (PDT)
Content-Type: text
Status: RO
Lines: 5

Always remember: It's a great big disco world.


.
```

Normally, mail readers do us the service of parsing out the information and presenting it in a much more readable form than what you see here. But this example gives you an idea of from whom the message is coming, the subject line, and the date.

At this point, you can issue as many **RETR** commands as you'd like to read your messages. Reading a message does not cause it to be deleted. To delete the message, you must explicitly issue a **DELE** command, with a parameter specifying the message number. Now that we've read message 1, we can delete it by typing

```
DELE 1
```

which gets this response from the server:

```
+OK Message 1 has been deleted.
```

Like the **RETR** command, you can issue the **DELE** command as many times as necessary. The messages aren't actually deleted until you quit the session using the **QUIT** command.

And that's it. Now you know enough about POP3 commands to be able to test servers and, if necessary, to read your mail without a proper mail reader!

Knowing When You Need Help

I *need* to read my mail regularly. Nothing demonstrated this more clearly than something I experienced a few years ago. The server on which my home directory resided was down, and I was prevented from logging in. This was a system on which I didn't have administrative permissions, so I had to wait for the sysadmin to fix the server. Frustrated, I downloaded the RFC specifications for POP3 (RFC 1939, ftp://ftp.isi.edu/in-notes/rfc1939.txt), from which I figured out how to read my mail via POP3 commands and Telnet. I patiently read through all of my mail using this method (several dozen messages), and even responded to a few of them by using Telnet to issue SMTP commands directly to the SMTP server. By the time the Sysadmin arrived, I had already read and replied to all of my e-mail for the morning. Sad, but true...

Conflicts Between POP and Other Protocols

IMAP is another protocol that mail readers can use to access mail stored on servers. Though it has properties similar to POP, keep in mind that IMAP is a different protocol and needs its own server daemon to service requests.

NOTE: In the event a user attempts to use both a POP mail reader and an IMAP mail reader, you as the administrator can expect to get a request to restore their mail spool. Because POP and IMAP are independent protocols, their server daemons will work independently, as well. So if both are started at the same time and reading the same mail spool, file corruption is the likely result. When introducing new users to your system, remind them never to use two mail readers at once.

Conflicts like this will happen when people use mail readers such as pine, elm, or mutt, which read the mail spool directly from the disk (typically, through an NFS-mounted spool disk; see Chapter 18 on the Network File System for additional information). Those readers make copies of the spool file, perform all the changes, and then rewrite the spool file. If another mail reader is used while the process is happening, file corruption can occur. More likely, the user will lose messages or will see old messages reappear.

QPOPPER

It's likely that your distribution of Linux already comes with some version of a POP3 server. Although you'll rarely need to update the POP3 daemon, it is something that you should know how to do. In this section, we'll walk through the process of downloading, compiling, and installing the Qpopper daemon. The UNIX version is free from Qualcomm's Eudora division. The latest version, 3.1, is available at ftp://ftp.eudora.com/eudora/servers/unix/popper/.

Installing Qpopper

The latest non-beta version of Qpopper is quite stable and dependable. I've been using this package for several years now and have yet to be able to trace a single problem to the POP daemon itself. User complaints about "the mail server" inevitably have been traced to their mail client or to some network issue. You just can't say that about a lot of software these days!

So let's begin by downloading Qpopper 3.1 from ftp://ftp.eudora.com/eudora/servers/unix/popper/qpopper3.1.tar.gz. Remember to download it to a directory large enough to unpack it and compile it. (A good choice is **/usr/local/src**.)

Next, unpack the compressed program. Assuming you've downloaded Qpopper into **/usr/local/src**, use the following command to unpack it:

```
[root@ford src]# tar -xvzf qpopper3.1.tar.gz
```

This creates a subdirectory called **qpopper3.1**, in which you'll find all the source files and documentation with the program package.

Compiling Qpopper

Before compiling Qpopper, you'll need to configure it. Qpopper comes with a configure script that does much of this for you. All it needs is for you to give it some additional directions, and the rest will take care of itself. If you want to see all of the configuration options, you can run the `configure` command with the `--help` parameter, like so:

```
[root@src qpopper3.1]# ./configure --help
```

Table 16-1 lists the options available for use with the `configure` command.

Here is an example of a configuration line to enable Authenticated POP (APOP, discussed later in "Authenticated POP"), provide support for shadow passwords, and establish the server mode (note, the code is entered on one line; it's shown on two here due to the printing requirements for this book):

```
[root@ford qpopper2.53]# configure --enable-apop=/etc/pop.auth
--with-popuid=bin --enable-specialauth --enable-servermode
```

When you run the configure script, it will display all the information it finds. Most of this is concerned with library and compiler support issues and is of no interest here.

> **TIP:** In the unlikely event that the configure process does error out and you require help, be sure to save and use the information that the script generates.

Once Qpopper is configured, simply run the **make** command to compile the entire program. It should take less than a minute, even on relatively slow systems. The **make** command

```
[root@ford qpopper3.1]# make
```

will leave you with two binary files, **popper** and **popauth**, both in the **popper** subdirectory. The first file is the actual server daemon, and the second is the tool necessary for managing APOP accounts. In addition, you'll have the man pages for **popper** and **popauth**.

Although you have the choice of installing the binaries just about anywhere, it makes the most sense to put them in the **/usr/bin** directory, since it holds many other applications, as well. Here are the commands for copying **popper** and **popauth** into **/usr/bin**:

```
[root@ford qpopper3.1]# cd popper
[root@ford popper]# cp popper /usr/bin
[root@ford popper]# cp popauth /usr/bin
```

```
[root@ford popper]# chmod 755 /usr/bin/popper
[root@ford popper]# chmod 4755 /usr/bin/popauth
[root@ford popper]# chown root.root /usr/bin/popper
[root@ford popper]# chown bin.root /usr/bin/popauth
```

Configuration Option	Description
`--enable-apop=path` `--with-popuid=user`	These two options are used in tandem. The `--enable-apop=path` option enables the APOP service, which is an extension of normal POP3. The APOP extension lets users send their passwords in an encrypted format rather than in cleartext. The **path** parameter specifies the file where the authentication file will reside, typically **/etc/pop.auth**. The **user** parameter specifies the username that will own the file. The bin user is a good choice here. (Configuring the APOP database is discussed later in "Authenticated POP.")
`--enable-bulletins= path`	*Bulletins* are a handy mechanism for making announcements to all of your users without having to hit all those mailboxes with the same message. Instead, you write a single message, and each user will see it as part of the next mail download. You'll save disk space as well as time, especially if you have many users. The **path** is the directory where new bulletins are posted. Details on bulletins are discussed in "Publishing Bulletins" later in the chapter.
`--enable-servermode`	Server mode is designed to make the Qpopper daemon run more efficiently in heavy-load environments. Consider using this option if you have a large number of active users.
`--enable-specialauth`	This option is required if you are using shadow passwords. (See "Special Authentication" later in this chapter.)

Table 16-1. Options for the `configure` command

NOTE: If you used the `--with-popuid=user` option with the `./configure` statement, make sure the user specified in that option matches the owner of the **/usr/bin/popauth** program. For this installation, I'm assuming you are using the bin user. If you want, you can change bin to your specified user in the **chown bin.root** line shown previously.

To install the manual pages, we copy the files ending in **.8** to the **/usr/man/man8** directory (or **/usr/share/man/man8** if you are using Red Hat 7), like so:

```
[root@ford popper]# cd ../man
[root@ford man]# cp *.8 /usr/man/man8
[root@ford man]# chown root.root /usr/man/man8/popper.8
[root@ford man]# chown root.root /usr/man/man8/popauth.8
[root@ford man]# chmod 644 /usr/man/man8/popper.8
[root@ford man]# chmod 644 /usr/man/man8/popauth.8
```

Setting Up Qpopper

The Qpopper service is run through the **inetd** daemon, which was discussed in Chapter 9. (Red Hat 7 users may remember this as the **xinetd** daemon.) Here is what you need to do to get Qpopper working with it:

▼ **Make sure POP is a service.** Edit the **/etc/services** file, and be sure that there exists a service called **pop3** that uses port 110/tcp. The line should look something like this:

```
pop3            110/tcp         pop-3      # POP version 3
```

If it is there, great! You're ready to go. If it is not, be sure to add it and save the **/etc/services** file.

■ **Set Up Qpopper with inetd.** If you are using the straight **inetd** daemon, you need to edit the **/etc/inetd.conf** file and be sure that a line that looks like the following exists:

```
pop3    stream tcp      nowait  root      /usr/bin/popper popper
```

Be sure that there are no other lines in the **/etc/inetd.conf** file that begin with **pop3**, or the daemon will be confused. Now send an HUP signal to the daemon, like so:

```
[root@ford /root]# kill -1 -C inetd
```

And **inetd** should be ready.

■ **Configure Qpopper with xinetd.**   If an **ipop3** file does not already exist for **xinetd** in the **/etc/xinetd.d** directory, you will need to create one. The file should look like this:

```
# description: The POP3 service allows remote users to access their mail \
#              using an POP3 client such as Netscape Communicator, mutt, \
#              or fetchmail.
service pop3
{
        socket_type             = stream
        wait                    = no
        user                    = root
        server                  = /usr/bin/popper
        log_on_success          += USERID
        log_on_failure          += USERID
}
```

Once you have the correct configuration file in place, you need to tell **xinetd** to re-read its configuration files by sending it a SIGUSR2 signal. Get the PID of **xinetd** using the **ps** command, like so:

```
[root@ford /root]# ps -C xinetd
```

Assuming your output looks like this:

```
PID TTY          TIME CMD
438 ?        00:00:00 xinetd
```

where the PID for **xinetd** is shown to be 438, you can send the SIGUSR2 signal like this:

```
[root@ford /root]# kill -SIGUSR2 438
```

Of course, you can show off your complete and utter coolness by doing it in one command with a little **awk** trickery, like so:

```
[root@ford /root]# kill -SIGUSR2 `kill -C xinetd | sed '1d' | awk '{print $1}'`
```

■ **Test Qpopper.**   Check this by using the **netstat** command to see if there is a process listening to the POP port, like so:

```
[root@ford /root]# netstat -ant | grep 110
```

One of the output lines should contain a line that looks like this:

```
tcp        0      0 0.0.0.0:110             0.0.0.0:*               LISTEN
```

You can also test this by using the Telnet trick discussed earlier in the chapter. Simply **telnet** to your own POP server on port 110, and see if you get a response.

▲ **If it doesn't work...**   Check the parameters with which you compiled Qpopper. Did you enable any features beyond what was described in this chapter? Often times, trying to add more authentication (such as authentication by using PAM) can lead to difficulty. Are you sure that your version of **inetd** was properly restarted? A typo can mean you sent an HUP or SIGUSR2 signal to the wrong process, and most other processes quietly ignore those signals. Did either **inetd** or **xinetd** have a problem with your config file and failed to start again? (Use the **ps** command to check.) If it had a problem, did you check the system logs (**/var/log/messages**) to see if any messages were written out?

ADVANCED QPOPPER CONFIGURATIONS

In the section on compiling Qpopper, the table of options available for configuring the protocol includes some advanced parameters such as server mode, special authentication, Authenticated POP, and bulletin support. In this section, we'll examine the processes of setting up these advanced functions, as well as some of the command-line options you can set for popper in **/etc/inetd.conf** or **/etc/xinetd.d/ipop3**.

Server Mode

When a user connects to the Qpopper service, Qpopper makes a backup of the mail spool being read and works with the backup. However, when a user is using a mail client that either deletes all of the mail on the server as soon as it is downloaded or simply leaves all of the mail on the server, making a backup is a waste of system resources.

In server mode, Qpopper doesn't make the backup copy; instead, it feeds the user's requests straight from the original mailbox. This is useful at sites where users tend to accumulate large mail spools. In these situations, using server mode results in faster QPopper operation and less system overhead.

To turn on server mode, set the option

```
--enable-servermode
```

when running the **./configure** script.

Special Authentication

Linux supports the use of *shadow password files*. With shadow password files, the normal **/etc/passwd** file is separated into two files: **/etc/passwd** and **/etc/shadow**. In the **/etc/passwd** file are stored the user's login, UID, GID, home directory, and shell, but not the user's encrypted password entry. That information has been moved into the **/etc/shadow** file, which is only readable by the root user (unlike **/etc/passwd**, which is world readable).

Qpopper supports the use of shadow passwords, too. To enable that support, use the

```
--enable-specialauth
```

option when running the **./configure** script.

NOTE: Certainly Qpopper's support for shadow passwords is an advantage, but it does not address the fundamental problem that the POP protocol allows for passwords to be transmitted over the network in cleartext. This, of course, poses a much greater security issue. See the following "Authenticated POP" section for additional details.

Authenticated POP

One of POP's fundamental security flaws is that it transmits passwords in cleartext over the network. This may be acceptable on a LAN, where you have tighter control of where the network can be tapped and by whom. However, the same can never be said about the Internet. Passwords in cleartext pose a real problem for remote users, who may need to access their e-mail from several remote locations and want to use their existing POP-based mail readers.

To get around this security risk, an extension to the POP protocol was created. Called *Authenticated POP*, or APOP for short, it works in much the same way as normal POP. The key exception is that, instead of authenticating users via the **user/pass** command set, the client tells the server that it's going to use APOP; the server responds by telling the client the current system time. The client then uses the server's system time as the key to encrypt the password. (Using the server's system time as the encryption key allows the client to encrypt the same password into a different value each time.) Since the server knows the key, it takes the password as it knows it and encrypts it using the same key. The resulting encrypted entries are then compared. If the password is correct, the client is allowed access. The encryption method used is an MD5 hash.

Thankfully, the process of administering the APOP service is relatively straightforward. For the user, there is only the need to use a mail reader that supports the APOP authentication method. No special work need otherwise be done.

Setting Up APOP Users

The first step in setting up users under APOP is establishing the database. This is done with the following command:

```
[root@ford /root]# /usr/bin/popauth -init
```

Once the database is created, you can add users to it with this command:

```
[root@ford /root]# /usr/bin/popauth -user user
```

where **user** is the login name of the user you are adding. To remove someone from the database, use this command:

```
[root@ford /root]# /usr/bin/popauth -delete user
```

Remember that the only people who are allowed to perform users additions and deletions are root and the APOP administrator specified by the **--with-popuid** option in

./configure. Normal users may use the **popauth** command to change their passwords only, as follows:

```
[user@ford ~]$ /usr/bin/popauth
```

Publishing Bulletins

If you need to send a message to all of your users, you can either send the same message to each user or you can use a *bulletin*. Once a bulletin is set up, the system will automatically keep track of whether or not a user has seen it. If a user has not yet seen a bulletin, it will appear as a normal mail message the next time that user checks e-mail. Once the user has downloaded the bulletin, it won't appear ever again, even if the bulletin itself remains available to other users. Slick, isn't it?

To use bulletins, simply use the

```
--enable-bulletins=path
```

line in the **./configure** script, where **path** is the directory where you intend to place bulletins. A good default location for this storage is **/var/spool/bulletins**.

Creating Bulletins

It's best to name each new bulletin with a filename that alphabetically follows the previous bulletin's filename. A good way of do this is to prefix each filename with a number, like so:

00001-welcome_to_the_system
00002-downtime_on_oct_12
00003-halloween_party_announcement

and so on. The file itself should be structured like a complete e-mail message the way Sendmail would deliver it. For example:

```
From qpop Wed Nov  9 13:31:08 1998
Date: Wed, 9 Nov 1998 13:31:07 -0800 (PST)
From: "Mail Administrator" <helpdesk@domain.com>
Subject: Welcome to the System

Welcome to Domain.Com! We're yet another wild and
exciting Internet company whose stock value will
eventually be used by roller coaster designers all
over the world. If you have any problems with your
computer, send mail to helpdesk@domain.com or call
extension 411.

Thanks, and welcome to the company.
```

> **NOTE:** In bulletins, be sure to observe the RFC 822 header formats, especially in regard to the date. A lot of mail readers tend to be picky about this element.

Bulletin Directory Maintenance

Whenever a new user signs onto the system, he or she will receive every single bulletin that is in the bulletin directory. Obviously, it doesn't make sense to send the new person an announcement to the office party from last year, so be sure to do periodic housekeeping of the bulletins directory. Orderly naming of bulletin filenames should help you with this task.

Do note, however, that Qpopper will be confused if you reuse a bulletin number. Let's say you erase the second of the three bulletins you have in the system. You erase the second bulletin, but you don't create a new bulletin to take its place in the alphabetical order. Instead, create a new bulletin number. If you're using our suggestion to make bulletin filenames with numbers, you'll want to be sure the next (fourth) bulletin starts with a 00004, even if you erased the second one (00002).

> **NOTE:** Bulletins are a great way to get a message out to all of your users, but this method requires that all of your users read mail using a POP mail reader. Depending on your site, this may not be possible. It's a good idea to verify this before using bulletins for universal announcements.

Command-Line Options for Qpopper

You can set some features of Qpopper on the command line. To do this, edit your **/etc/inetd.conf** file so that these options appear at the end of the line. And remember to give the **inetd** daemon a kick with the **kill -1** command as described earlier in this chapter.

Here are the Qpopper command-line options:

Option	Description
-b *bulldir*	Instead of the using the value **./configure --enable-bulletin** option to designate the bulletin directory, set it to the value specified in **bulldir** in this option.
-T *timeout*	Set the timeout for a connection to be *timeout* seconds instead of the default 600 seconds. Recommended values are between 30 and 120 seconds.

SUMMARY

In this chapter, we examined the steps to setting up a POP server using the Qualcomm's Qpopper server software. Compared to most other services, POP is easy to set up and manage with blessedly few exceptions. Qpopper runs well and cooperatively; I have used it at commercial sites with excellent success. In three years, I have yet to blame it for any mail server problems.

Of course, Qpopper is just like any other server software, in that you'll want to keep up with security postings and updates from Qualcomm. Version 3.1 revises a classic package that has had fewer than a small handful of security problems to date, only one of which in the last three years resulted in an exploit. Try saying that about any other Internet-related software!

Once you have the POP server running, the one important issue to address is POP authentication via cleartext passwords. Qpopper supports the use of APOP, which takes care of this security problem, so seriously consider using it. All of Eudora's mail readers support APOP. Since it's an open standard, any other developer can learn how to support it and add it to their mail client's list of supported protocols, without having to pay any licensing fees or royalties to Qualcomm.

In most other chapters, I've recommended some reading for gaining further knowledge of a particular topic. In the case of POP, there isn't a heck of a lot more to know. RFC 1939, which documents the POP protocol, can be found at ftp://ftp.isi.edu/ in-notes/rfc1939.txt.

CHAPTER 17

The Secure Shell (SSH)

O ne unfortunate side effect of bringing your computer onto a public network (such as the Internet) is that, at one point or another, some folks out there will try to break into your system. Why? Because they stupidly think it's cool to do so. This is obviously not a good thing.

In Chapter 9, we discussed techniques for securing your Linux system, all of which are designed to limit remote access to your system to the bare essentials. But what if you need to perform system administrative duties from a remote site? Telnet is woefully insecure, because it transmits the entire session (logins, passwords, and all) in cleartext. How can you reap the benefits of a truly multiuser system if you can't securely log into it?

NOTE: *Cleartext* means that the data is unencrypted. In any system, when passwords get sent over the line in cleartext, a packet sniffer could determine what a user's password is. This is especially bad if that user is root! Before the Windows NT folks reading this start insisting that their network logins are encrypted by default, let's remember this: After authentication, the PDC returns a token to the NT client for use in lieu of having to reauthenticate every time a user wants to access a network share that's used for the entire life of the login. Thus, if a packet sniffer captures the token, it can be reissued to a thief to gain access to servers. In short, a cracker doesn't even need the password to break in. In the immortal words of Homer J. Simpson, "D'OH!" Furthermore, it wasn't until Windows 2000 that the ability to log in to a host that is not in your local area network became available. Unfortunately, Win2k only offers this feature through the insecure Telnet protocol...

To tackle the issue of remote login versus password security, a package called Secure Shell (OpenSSH) was developed. (The term "Open" in the title refers to the fact that the source code is open to public inspection, and the resulting binaries can be used in both commercial and noncommercial use.) It allows users to connect to a remote server just as they would using Telnet—except that the session is 100% encrypted. Someone using a packet sniffer merely sees garbage going by. Should they capture the garbage, decrypting it could take decades.

In this chapter, we'll take a brief and general look at the cryptography concept. Then, we'll examine the versions of SSH, where to get it, and how to install and configure it.

PUBLIC KEY CRYPTOGRAPHY

Let me begin with a disclaimer: I am not a cryptography expert, and this chapter is most certainly not the definitive source for cryptography lessons. What you will find here is a general discussion along with some references to good books that approach the topic more thoroughly.

Secure Shell relies on a technology called *public key cryptography*. It works similarly to a safe deposit box at the bank: You need two keys in order to open the box. In the case of public key cryptography, you need two mathematical keys: a public one and a private one. Your public key can be published on a public Web page, printed on a T-shirt, or posted on a billboard in the busiest part of town. Anyone who asks for it can have a copy of it. On the other hand, your private key must be protected to the best of your ability. It is this piece of information that makes the data you want to encrypt truly secure. Every public key/private key combination is unique.

The actual process of encrypting data and sending it from one person to the next requires several steps. Let's watch Alice and Bob go through this process one step at a time in Figures 17-1 through 17-5.

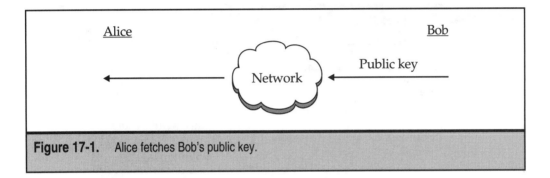

Figure 17-1.   Alice fetches Bob's public key.

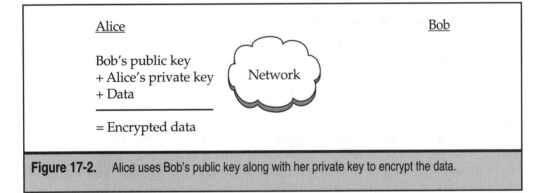

Figure 17-2.   Alice uses Bob's public key along with her private key to encrypt the data.

Figure 17-3.   Alice sends the encrypted data to Bob.

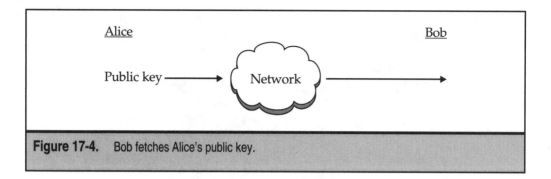

Figure 17-4. Bob fetches Alice's public key.

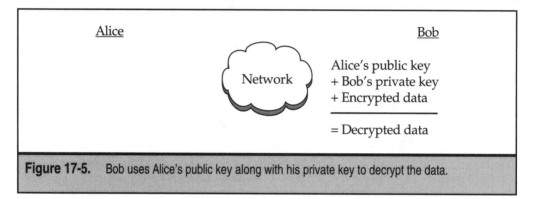

Figure 17-5. Bob uses Alice's public key along with his private key to decrypt the data.

Looking at these steps, notice that at no point was the secret key sent over the network. Also note that once the data was encrypted with Bob's public key and Alice's private key, the only pair of keys that could decrypt it were Bob's private key and Alice's public key. Thus, if someone intercepted the data in the middle of the transmission, they wouldn't be able to decrypt the data without the private keys.

To make things even more interesting, SSH regularly changes its private key so that the data stream gets encrypted differently every few minutes. Thus, even if someone happened to figure out the key for a transmission, that miracle would only be valid for a few minutes until the keys changed again.

Key Characteristics

So what exactly *is* a key? Essentially, a key is a very large number that has special mathematical properties. Whether someone can break an encryption scheme depends on their ability to find out what the key is. Thus, the larger the key is, the harder it will be to discover it.

Low-grade encryption has 56 bits. This means there are 2^{56} possible keys. To give you a sense of scale, 2^{32} is equal to 4 billion, 2^{48} is equal to 256 trillion, and 2^{56} is 65,536 trillion. While this seems like a significant number of possibilities, it has been demonstrated that a loose network of PCs dedicated to iterating through every possibility could conceivably break a low-grade encryption code in less than a month. In 1998, the Electronic Frontier Foundation (EFF) published designs for a (then) $250,000 computer capable of cracking 56-bit keys in a few seconds to demonstrate the need for higher-grade encryption. If $250,000 seems like a lot of money to you, think of the potential for credit card fraud if someone successfully used that computer for that purpose!

> **NOTE:**   The EFF published the aforementioned designs in an effort to convince the U.S. government that their laws that limited the export of crypto software were sorely outdated and hurting the U.S., since so many companies were being forced to work in other countries. This finally paid off in 2000, when the laws were loosened up enough to allow the export of higher-grade cryptography. (Unfortunately, most of the companies doing cryptography work already exported their engineering to other countries.)

For a key to be sufficiently difficult to break, experts suggest no fewer than 128 bits. Because every extra bit effectively doubles the number of possibilities, 128 bits offers a genuine challenge. And if you want to really make the encryption solid, a key size of 512 bits or higher is recommended. SSH can use up to 1024 bits to encrypt your data.

The trade-off to using higher-bit encryption is that it requires more math processing power for the computer to churn through and validate a key. This takes time and therefore makes the authentication process a touch slower—but most feel this is a worthy bargain.

> **NOTE:**   Though unproven, it is believed that even the infamous National Security Agency (NSA) can't break codes encrypted with keys higher than 1024 bits.

Cryptography References

SSH supports a variety of encryption algorithms. Public-key encryption happens to be the most interesting method of performing encryption from site to site and is arguably the most secure. If you want to learn more about cryptography, here are some good books to look into:

▼ *PGP* by Simon Garfinkel (O'Reilly and Associates, 1994)

■ *Applied Cryptography: Protocols, Algorithms and Source Code in C*, Second Edition, by Bruce Schneier (John Wiley & Sons. 1995)

▲ *Cryptography and Network Security: Principles and Practice*, Second Edition, by William Stallings (Prentice Hall, 1998)

The *PGP* book is specific to the PGP program, but it also contains a hefty amount of history and an excellent collection of general cryptography tutorials. The *Applied Cryptography* book might be a bit overwhelming to many, especially nonprogrammers, but it very successfully explains how actual cryptographic algorithms work. (This text is considered a bible among cypherheads.) Finally, *Cryptography and Network Security* is heavier on principles than on practice, but it's useful if you're interested in the theoretical aspects of cryptography rather than the code itself.

SSH VERSIONS AND DISTRIBUTIONS

Until recently (middle of 2000), the U.S. government made it illegal to develop crypto-graphic software in the U.S. and export it to other countries. With the laws having become relaxed, a lot of software has made itself much more available.

In addition to this change there has been a lot of development of the OpenSSH package. This is a completely free implementation of the Secure Shell standard in terms of both source code and its use. The first version of SSH that was made available by DataFellows restricted free use of SSH to noncommercial activities; commercial activities required that licenses be purchased. But more significant than the cost of the package is the fact that the source code to the package is completely open. This is important to cryptographic software, for it allows peers to examine the source code and make sure that there are not holes that may allow hackers to break the security. (In other words, serious cryptographers do not rely on security through obscurity.)

Because the SSH protocol has become an IETF standard, there are also other developers actively working on SSH clients for other operating systems. As of this writing, there are many MS Windows clients, Macintosh clients, and even a Palm Pilot client, in addition to the standard UNIX clients. You can find the version of OpenSSH that we will be discussing at http://www.openssh.com. You can find other implementations of SSH at http://www.openssh.org.

NOTE: As of this writing, we are up to SSH version 2. Unfortunately, most non-UNIX clients only support SSH version 1. Thus it is important that your server side understand both versions. If you plan to use OpenSSH, don't worry. It supports both.

OpenSSH and OpenBSD

The OpenSSH project is being spearheaded by the OpenBSD project. OpenBSD is a version of the BSD operating system (another UNIX variant) that strives for the best security of any operating system available. A quick trip to their Web site (http://www.openbsd.org) shows that they have gone *three years* without a remote exploit in their default installation. Unfortunately, this comes at the expense of not having the most whiz-bang-feature–rich tools available, since they require that anything added to their distribution get audited for security first. This has made OpenBSD a very popular foundation for firewalls.

The core of the OpenSSH package is considered part of the OpenBSD project, and thus is very simple and specific to the OpenBSD operating system. To make OpenSSH available to other operating systems, a separate group exists to make OpenSSH portable whenever new releases come out. Typically, this only takes a few days from the original release. (For instance, OpenSSH 2.2.0 was released on August 31, 2000. OpenSSH 2.2.0p1, the portable version, was released a mere two days later, on September 2, 2000.)

> **NOTE:** Since we are targeting Linux, we will use the versions suffixed with a "p" indicating that it has been ported.

Alternative Vendors for SSH Clients

Every day, many of you work with heterogeneous environments. It's impossible to ignore all of the Windows 95/98/NT and MacOS systems out there in the world. In order to allow these folks to work with a *real* operating system, they need some mechanism for logging in from remote sites. And because Telnet is not secure, SSH provides us with an answer.

Thankfully, DataFellows is not the only organization that makes an SSH client for non-UNIX operating systems. Here is a quick rundown of several SSH clients:

▼ **NiftySSH, for MacOS**   http://www.lysator.liu.se/~jonasw/freeware/niftyssh/
This is an extension of the NiftyTelnet program that has been available for the Macintosh for quite some time. The SSH extensions work quite nicely and are very stable, even with MacOS 9.

■ **MindTerm (Multiplatform)**   http://www.mindbright.se/mindterm
It supports up to version 1.5 of the SSH protocol. A beta version supporting 2.0 is currently available for testing. Written in 100% Java, it works on many UNIX platforms (including Linux) as well as Windows and MacOS. See the Web page for a complete list of tested operating systems.

■ **TerraTerm SSH, for Windows**   http://www.zip.com.au/~roca/ttssh.html
This package is a DLL to the TerraTerm terminal emulator. Both the DLL and main package are free. It supports up to version 1.5 of the SSH protocol.

■ **FreeSSH, for Windows**   http://www.freessh.org
A simple SSH client that works under both 16-bit as well as 32-bit Windows—handy for those folks who just can't drop Windows 3.11 quite yet!

■ **SecureCRT, for Windows**   http://www.vandyke.com/products/SecureCRT/
A commercial implementation of SSH.

▲ **PilotSSH, for Palm Pilot**   http://www.isaac.cs.berkeley.edu/pilot/
If you just gotta have connectivity from your Palm Pilot.

The Weakest Link

You've probably heard of the saying, "You're only as secure as your weakest link." This particular saying has an extremely significant meaning to OpenSSH and securing your network: OpenSSH is only as secure as the weakest connection between the user and the server. This means that if a user **telnet**s from host A to host B and then **ssh**s to host C, the entire connection can be monitored from the link between host A and host B. The fact that the link between host B and C is encrypted becomes irrelevant.

Be sure to explain this to your users when you enable logins via **ssh**, especially if you're disabling Telnet access altogether. Unfortunately, taking the time to tighten down your security in this manner will be soundly defeated if your users **telnet** to a host across the Internet so that they can **ssh** into your server. And more often than not, they won't have the slightest idea of why doing that is a bad idea.

DOWNLOADING, COMPILING, AND INSTALLING SSH

Although several distributions of Linux are now shipping with OpenSSH, you should know how to download and compile the package yourself in the event you need to upgrade. If you have a distribution that already has OpenSSH (such as Red Hat 7), then you can skip this section.

As of this writing, the latest version of OpenSSH is 2.2.0p1. You can download this from http://www.openssh.com/portable.html. Select the site that is closest to you and download **openssh-2.2.0p1.tar.gz** to a directory with enough free space. (**/usr/local/src** is a good choice, and we'll use it in this example.)

Once you have downloaded OpenSSH to **/usr/local/src**, unpack it with the **tar** command, like so:

```
[root@ford src]# tar -xvzf openssh-2.2.0p1.tar.gz
```

This will create a directory called **openssh-2.2.0p1** inside of **/usr/local/src**.

Along with OpenSSH, you will need OpenSSL 0.9.5a or later. As of this writing, the latest version is OpenSSL-0.9.6. You can download that from http://www.openssl.org. Once you have downloaded OpenSSL to **/usr/local/src**, unpack it with the **tar** command, like so:

```
[root@ford src]# tar -xvzf openssl-0.9.6.tar.gz
```

Finally, the last package you need is the Zlib library, which is used to provide compression and decompression facilities. Most distributions (such as Red Hat) have this already, but if you want the latest version, you need to download it from http://www.freesoftware.com/pub/infozip/zlib. The latest version as of this writing is 1.1.3. To unpack the package in **/usr/local/src**, usr **tar**, like so:

```
[root@ford src]# tar -xvzf zlib.tar.gz
```

Begin by going into the **zlib** directory, like so:

```
[root@ford src]# cd zlib-1.1.3
```

Then run **configure** and **make**, like so:

```
[root@ford zlib-1.1.3]# ./configure
[root@ford zlib-1.1.3]# make
```

This will result in the zlib library being built. To install it, run

```
[root@ford zlib-1.1.3]# make install
```

The resulting library will be placed in the **/usr/local/lib** directory.

Now you need to compile OpenSSL. Begin by leaving the **zlib** directory and entering the **OpenSSL** directory, like so:

```
[root@ford zlib-1.1.3]# cd ../openssl-0.9.6
```

Once you are in the **OpenSSL** directory, all you need to do is run **configure** and **make**. OpenSSL will take care of figuring out the type of system it is on and configure itself to work in an optimal fashion. The exact commands are

```
[root@ford openssl-0.9.6]# ./config
[root@ford openssl-0.9.6]# make
```

Note that this step may take a few minutes to complete. Once OpenSSL is done compiling, you can test it by running

```
[root@ford openssl-0.9.6]# make test
```

If all went well, the test should run without event. If there are any problems, OpenSSL will report them to you. If you do get an error, you should remove this copy of OpenSSL, and try the download/unpack/compile procedure again. I have successfully tested this package under several versions of Linux as well as other UNIXes and have never had a problem with the compile/test phase.

Once you have finished the test, you can install OpenSSL by running

```
[root@ford openssl-0.9.6]# make install
```

This step will install OpenSSL into the **/usr/local/ssl** directory.

We are now ready to compile and install the OpenSSH package. Move into the OpenSSH package directory, like so:

```
[root@ford openssl-0.9.6]# cd ../openssh-2.2.0p1
```

As with the other two packages, you need to begin by running the **configure** program. For this package, however, you need to specify some additional parameters. Namely, you need to tell it where the other two packages got installed. You can always run **./configure** with the **--help** option to see all of the parameters, but you'll find that the following **./configure** statement will probably work fine:

```
[root@ford openssh-2.2.0p1]#./configure --with-ssl-dir=/usr/local/ssl --with-tcp-wrappers
```

(Note that this is one continuous line and should be entered without pressing ENTER in the middle of it.)

Once OpenSSH is configured, simply run **make** and **make install** to put all of the files into the appropriate **/usr/local** directories.

```
[root@ford openssh-2.2.0p1]# make
[root@ford openssl-2.2.0p1]# make install
```

And you're set! You can now use OpenSSH.

Double Clicking on Setup Isn't Necessarily Better

While this whole process of having to download multiple packages and compile them may seem tedious as compared to "double-click on setup.exe," remember what you've got here. You have the full source code to the package. If you aren't sure about whether it is doing what they claim to do, you can always look at the source code or hire a programmer to look at it. If you are concerned about your privacy and/or security, you can always examine the code to make sure it isn't exposing anything it shouldn't. In other words, the developers have put everything out in front of you to check on if you like. You don't have to take their word on it. This translates into no surprises, which in a production environment is important. Not sure yet? Remember the outrage in mid-2000 when it was discovered that the docked version of RealPlayer under Windows was sending back usage information for the purpose of advertising to Real, Inc.? Could they have done that if their source code was available for others to browse and double check? And before you grumble about the value of your time, remember that you'll get better at this! My junior sysadmins who I've introduced to UNIX at work can now download and get most packages to compile and work in minutes after only a few months of exposure. I'm sure that before long, you'll be running through these steps just as quickly.

Server Startup and Shutdown

If you want users to be able to log in to your system via SSH, you will need to start the server process at boot time. The clean and proper way to do this is to create a startup script (as we discussed in Chapter 7) for the **/usr/local/sbin/sshd** process to start the Secure Shell server. However, for the last several years, I've been using SSH and have never once had to shut it down—so here is the "cheat" technique: You can edit the **/etc/rc.d/rc.local** file so that the last instruction in it is as follows:

```
#
# Start the SSH Server Daemon
#
/usr/local/sbin/sshd
```

If for some reason you *do* need to stop the SSH server but not the entire system, you can simply kill the **sshd** process. To find out the server's process number, use the **ps** command:

```
[root@ford /root]# ps -C sshd
  PID TTY           TIME CMD
26847 ?         00:00:00 sshd
```

In this case, the PID for **sshd** is 26847, so to kill this process, you'll type

```
[root@ford /root]# kill 26847
```

Of course, you can restart the daemon at any time by simply running

```
[root@ford /root]# /usr/local/sbin/sshd
```

USING SSH

With the **ssh** daemon started, you can simply use the **ssh** client to log in to a machine from remote in the same manner that you would with Telnet. The key difference between **ssh** and Telnet is that **ssh** will not prompt you for your login, but instead will assume that you have the same login across both machines, which is typically the case.

However, if you need to use a different login (for instance, if you are logged in as root on one host and want to **ssh** to another and log in as yourself), all you need to do is provide the **-l** option along with the desired login. For example, if I want to log in to the host ford from arthur, I would do

```
[root@arthur /root]# ssh -l sshah ford
```

and I would be prompted with a password prompt from ford for the user sshah's password. If you just want to log in to the remote host without having to change your login, you can simply run **ssh**, like so:

```
[sshah@ford ~]$ ssh arthur
```

Applications Related to SSH

The OpenSSH package actually comes with an additional program that uses the same encryption technology called Secure Copy.

Secure Copy (scp) is meant as a replacement for the **rcp** command, which allows you to do remote copies from one host to another. The most significant problem with the **rcp** command is that users tend to arrange their remote-access settings to allow far too much access into your system. To help mitigate this, instruct users to use the **scp** command instead. The format of **scp** is identical to **rcp**, so users shouldn't have problems with this transition. For example, if I'm logged in to ford as user sshah and I want to copy the **.tcshrc** file from arthur, I would type:

```
[sshah@ford ~]$ scp arthur:.tcshrc .
```

SUMMARY

The Secure Shell tool is a superior replacement to Telnet for remote logins. Adopting the OpenSSH package will put you in the company of many other sites that are disabling Telnet access altogether and allowing only OpenSSH access through their firewalls. Given the wide-open nature of the Internet, this change isn't an unreasonable thing to ask of your users.

Here are the key issues to keep in mind when you consider Secure Shell:

▼ SSH is very easy to compile and install.

■ Replacing Telnet with SSH requires no significant retraining.

■ SSH exists on many platforms, not just UNIX.

▲ Without SSH, you are exposing your system to potential network attacks in which crackers can "sniff" passwords right off your Internet connections.

In closing, let me remind you that using OpenSSH doesn't make your system secure immediately. There is no replacement for a set of good security practices. Following the lessons from Chapter 9, you should disable all unnecessary services on any system that is exposed to untrusted networks (such as the Internet); allow only those services that are absolutely necessary. And that means if you're running SSH, you should disable Telnet, **rlogin**, and **rsh**.

PART IV

Intranet Services

CHAPTER 18

Network File System (NFS)

N etwork File System (NFS) is the UNIX way of sharing files and applications across the network. The NFS concept is somewhat similar to that of Windows NT's disk sharing in that it allows you to attach to a disk and work with it as if it were a local drive—a very handy tool for sharing files or a large disk with coworkers. (Often, it's handy for both.)

Aside from their similar roles, there are some important differences between NFS and NT shares that require different approaches to their management. The tools that you use to control network drives are (of course) different, as well. In this chapter, we discuss those differences; however, the primary focus of the chapter is to show you how to deploy NFS under the Linux environment.

THE MECHANICS OF NFS

Chapter 8 covered the process of mounting and unmounting file systems. The same idea applies to NFS, except each mount request is qualified with the server from which the disk share is coming. Of course, the server must be configured to allow the requested partition to be shared with a client.

Let's look at an example. Making an NFS mount request for **/export/home** from the server nox, so that the share appears locally as the **/home** directory, is done as follows:

```
[root@ford /root]# mount nox:/export/home /home
```

Assuming that the command was run from the host named ford, all of the users on ford would be able to view the contents of **/home** as if it were just another directory. Linux would take care of making all of the network requests to the server.

Remote procedure calls (RPCs) are responsible for handling the requests between the client and server. RPC technology provides a standard mechanism for any RPC client to contact the server and find out to which service the calls should be directed. Thus, whenever a service wants to make itself available on a server, it needs to register itself with the RPC service manager, *portmapper*. Portmapper takes care of telling the client where the actual service is located on the server.

Mounting and Accessing a Partition

Several steps are involved in a client's making a request to mount a server's partition:

1. The client contacts the server's portmapper to find out which network port is assigned as the NFS mount service.

2. The client contacts the mount service and requests to mount a partition. The mount service checks to see if the client has permission to mount the requested partition. (Permission for a client to mount a partition is based on the **/etc/exports** file.) If the client does have permission, the mount service returns an affirmative.

3. The client contacts the portmapper again, this time to find out on which port the NFS server is located. (Typically, this is port 2049.)

4. Whenever the client wants to make a request to the NFS server (for example, to read a directory), an RPC is sent to the NFS server.

5. When the client is done, it updates its own mount tables but doesn't inform the server.

NOTE: Notification to the server is unnecessary, because the server doesn't keep track of all clients that have mounted its file systems. Because the server doesn't maintain state information about clients and the clients don't maintain state information about the server, clients and servers can't tell the difference between a crashed system and a really slow system. Thus, if a NFS server is rebooted, all clients will automatically continue their operations with the server as soon as the server is back online.

Security Considerations for NFS

Unfortunately, NFS is not a very secure method for sharing disks. The steps necessary to make NFS more secure are no different from those for securing any other system. The only catch is that you must be able to trust the users on the client system, especially the root user. If you're the root user on both the client and server, then there is a little less to worry about. The important thing in this case is to make sure non-root users don't become root—which is something you should be doing, anyway!

If you are in a situation where you cannot fully trust the person with whom you need to share a disk, it will be worth your time and effort to seek alternative methods of sharing resources (such as read-only sharing of the disk).

As always, stay up to date on the latest security bulletins coming from the Computer Emergency Response Team (www.cert.org), and keep up with the all the patches from your distribution vendor.

Versions of NFS

NFS is not a static protocol. Standards committees have helped NFS evolve to take advantage of new technologies as well as changes in usage patterns. Today, the standards are up to version 3.0, with 4.0 in the works. Unfortunately, Linux's NFS implementation is behind the times in this regard—it supports up to version 2.0 only. Efforts are being made to support NFS version 3.0, but this will take time.

Most other operating systems supporting NFS probably have an NFS version 2.0 mode, which allows you to use Linux servers. Some of these systems (including IRIX) require that you explicitly specify the NFS mount option (**vers=2**) for servers that only allow NFS 2.0. Refer to the appropriate vendor's documentation for details.

ENABLING NFS

As of this writing, all distributions of Linux come with the NFS server installed, usually with NFS already enabled. If you aren't sure about your system, use the **ksysv** tool. It will show NFS as started in runlevels 3 and 5.

If you aren't sure as to whether or not NFS is running, you can check by running **rpcinfo**, as follows:

```
[root@ford /root]# rpcinfo -p
```

If NFS is running on your system, you'll see something like the following:

```
program vers proto   port
 100000    2   tcp    111  rpcbind
 100000    2   udp    111  rpcbind
 100024    1   udp    965  status
 100024    1   tcp    967  status
 100011    1   udp    976  rquotad
 100011    2   udp    976  rquotad
 100005    1   udp    988  mountd
 100005    1   tcp    990  mountd
 100005    2   udp    993  mountd
 100005    2   tcp    995  mountd
 100005    3   udp    998  mountd
 100005    3   tcp   1000  mountd
 100003    2   udp   2049  nfs
 100021    1   udp   1096  nlockmgr
 100021    3   udp   1096  nlockmgr
 100021    1   tcp   2597  nlockmgr
 100021    3   tcp   2597  nlockmgr
```

If NFS isn't running on your system, the entries for **nfs** and **mountd** will be missing. To start NFS without having to reboot, enter this command:

```
[root@ford /root]# /etc/rc.d/init.d/nfs start
```

To stop NFS without having to shut down, enter this command:

```
[root@ford /root]# /etc/rc.d/init.d/nfs stop
```

If you have NFS enabled through **ksysv**, NFS will automatically start up every time you boot the system.

The Components of NFS

NFS under Linux is made up of five parts:

▼ **rpc.statd**   This daemon handles the file-locking issues between the client and
the server.

■ **rpc.quotad**   As its name suggests, **rpc.quotad** supplies the interface between
NFS and the quota manager. Users will be held to the same restrictions
regardless of whether they're working with their data through NFS.

■ **rpc.mountd**   When a request to mount a partition is made, the **rpc.mountd**
daemon takes care of verifying that the client has enough permission to make
the request. This permission is stored in the **/etc/exports** file. (The upcoming "The
/etc/exports Configuration File" section tells you more about the **/etc/exports** file.)

■ **rpc.nfsd**   The main component to the NFS system. This process actually takes
care of handling NFS requests.

▲ **rpc.lockd**   The **rpc.statd** daemon uses this daemon to handle lock recovery on
crashed systems.

Kernel Support for NFS

As of Linux 2.2, there has been kernel-based support for NFS, which runs significantly
faster than earlier implementations. Unfortunately, kernel-based NFS server support is
still considered experimental code. It is not mandatory—if you don't compile support for
it into the kernel, you will not use it. If you have the opportunity to try kernel support for
NFS, I highly recommend that you do so. If you choose not to use it, don't worry: The
`nfsd` program that handles NFS server services is completely self-contained and provides everything necessary to serve NFS.

NOTE: On the other hand, clients must have support for NFS in the kernel. This support in the kernel
has been around for a very long time and is known to be very stable. Red Hat 7 ships with kernel support for NFS enabled.

CONFIGURING NFS SERVERS

Setting up an NFS server is a two-step process. The first step is to create the **/etc/exports**
file. This file defines which parts of your server's disk get shared with the rest of your network and the rules by which they get shared. (For example, is a client allowed to only
read a partition? Are they allowed to write to a partition?) The second step is to start the
NFS server processes that read the **/etc/exports** file and follow the specifications.
    Pretty straightforward, isn't it?

The /etc/exports Configuration File

NFS servers have only one configuration file: **/etc/exports**. This file lists the partitions that are sharable, the hosts they can be shared with, and with what permissions. Here is the format of each entry in the **/etc/exports** file:

```
/dir/to/export       client1(permissions) client2(permissions) \line
                     client3(permissions) client4(permissions)
```

▼ */dir/to/export* is the directory you want to share with other users; for example, **/export/home**.

■ *client1*, *client2*, and so forth are the host names of the NFS clients.

▲ *permissions* are the corresponding permissions for each client.

Table 18-1 describes the valid permissions for each client.

TIP: A handy way of keeping UIDs in sync is by using NIS. See Chapter 19 for details.

Permission Option	Meaning
secure	The port number from which the client requests a mount must be lower than 1024. This permission is on by default.
ro	Allows read-only access to the partition.
noaccess	The client will be denied access to all directories below **/dir/to/mount**. This allows you to export the directory **/dir** to the client, and then to specify **/dir/to** as inaccessible without taking away access to something like **/dir/from**.
no_root_squash	A simple security measure causes the server to ignore, by default, requests made by the root user on an NFS mounted partition. If you want to disable this and allow the root user on the client host to access the NFS mounted directory, you need to export that directory with this permission.

Table 18-1. NFS Client Permissions for Shared Partitions

Permission Option	Meaning
squash_uids=*uid-list*	When an NFS request is made, it includes the UID of the user making the request. This allows the NFS server to enforce permissions, as well. Use this option when you want to restrict certain UIDs from accessing a particular shared partition. The variable *uid-list* is a comma-separated list of UIDs you want to deny. Ranges are acceptable, as well; for example: **squash_uids=5, 10-15,20,23**.
squash_gids=*gid-list*	This works just like **squash_uids**, except it applies to GIDs rather than UIDs.
rw	Normal read/write access.

Table 18-1.   NFS Client Permissions for Shared Partitions *(continued)*

Following is an example of a complete NFS **/etc/exports** file:

```
#
# /etc/exports for nfsserver.domain.com
#
/export/home           denon(rw) technics(rw) vestax(rw) \
                       unixadmin(rw,no_root_squash)
/export/usr/local      denon(rw,no_root_squash) \
                       technics(rw,no_root_squash) \
                       vextax(rw,no_root_squash) \
                       unixadmin(rw,no_root_squash)
/export/anonftp        ftpserver(ro,no_root_squash)
```

Telling the NFS Server Process About /etc/exports

Once you have an **/etc/exports** file written up, use the **exportfs** command to tell the NFS server processes to re-read the configuration information. The parameters for **exportfs** are as follows:

exportfs Command Option	Description
-a	Export all entries in the **/etc/exports** file.
-r	Re-export all entries in the **/etc/exports** file.

`exportfs` Command Option	Description
`-u client:/dir/to/mount`	Unexport the directory */dir/to/mount* to the host *client*.
`-o options`	Options specified here are the same as described in Table 18-1 for client permissions. These options will apply only to the file system specified on the `exportfs` command line, not to those in */etc/exports*.
`-v`	Be verbose.

Following are examples of **exportfs** command lines.

▼ To export all file systems:

```
[root@ford /root]# exportfs -a
```

▲ To export the directory **/export/stuff** to the host taos with the **read/write** and **no_root_squash** permissions:

```
[root@ford /root]# exportfs -o rw,no_root_squash taos:/export/stuff
```

NOTE: In most instances, you will simply want to use **exportfs -r**.

Common Problems

When exporting file systems, you may find that the server appears to be refusing the client access, even though the client is listed in the **/etc/exports** file. Typically, this happens because the server takes the IP address of the client connecting to it and resolves that address to the fully qualified domain name (FQDN), and the host name listed in the **/etc/exports** file isn't qualified. (For example, the server thinks the client host name is denon.domain.com, but the **/etc/exports** file lists just denon.)

Another common problem is that the server's perception of the host name/IP pairing is not correct. This can occur because of an error in the **/etc/hosts** file or in the DNS tables. You'll need to verify that the pairing is correct.

CONFIGURING NFS CLIENTS

NFS clients are remarkably easy to configure under Linux, because they don't require any new or additional software to be loaded. The only requirement is that the kernel be compiled to support NFS. All of the distributions come with this feature enabled by default. Aside from the kernel, the only other change is to the options in the **mount** command.

The mount Command

The **mount** command was originally discussed in Chapter 8. Note two changes for NFS partition mounting: the specification of the NFS server name, and the options specified after the **-o** on the **mount** command line.

Following is an example of a **mount** command line:

```
[root@ford /root]# mount -o rw,bg,intr,soft denon:/export/home /home
```

These **mount** options can also be used in the **/etc/fstab** file. This same entry in the **/etc/fstab** file would look like this:

```
denon:/export/home     /home     nfs     rw,bg,intr,soft 0 0
```

In the previous examples, **denon** is the NFS server name. The **-o** options are listed in Table 18-2.

mount -o Command Option	Description
bg	Background mount. Should the mount initially fail (for instance, if the server is down), the mount process will send itself to background processing and continue trying to execute until it is successful. This is useful for file systems mounted at boot time, because it keeps the system from hanging at the **mount** command if the server is down.
intr	Specifies an interruptible mount. If a process is pending I/O on a mounted partition, this option allows the process to be interrupted and the I/O call to be dropped. For more information, see "The Importance of the intr Option," later in this section.

Table 18-2.   NFS Partition **mount -o** Options

`mount -o` Command Option	Description
`soft`	Enables a soft mount for this partition, allowing the client to time out the connection after a number of retries (specified with the `retrans=r` option). For more information, see "Soft vs. Hard Mounts," later in this section.
`retrans=r`	The r value specifies the maximum number of connection retries for a soft-mounted system. For more information, see "Soft vs. Hard Mounts," later in this section.
`rsize=x`	Sets the read block size to x bytes; the default is 1024 bytes. Increasing this to 8192 bytes often improves performance.
`wsize=x`	Sets the write block size to x bytes; the default is 1024 bytes. Increasing this to 8192 bytes often improves performance.

Table 18-2. NFS Partition `mount -o` Options *(continued)*

NOTE: Remember that NFS servers can also be, at the same time, NFS clients.

Soft vs. Hard Mounts

By default, NFS operations are *hard*, which means they continue their attempts to contact the server indefinitely. This arrangement is not always beneficial, however. It causes a problem if an emergency shutdown of all systems is performed. If the servers happen to get shut down before the clients, the clients' shutdowns will stall while they wait for the servers to come back up. Enabling a *soft* mount allows the client to time out the connection after a number of retries (specified with the `retrans=r` option).

There is one exception to the preferred arrangement of having a soft mount with a `retrans=r` value specified: Don't use this arrangement when you have data that must be committed to disk no matter what, and you don't want to return control to the application until the data has been committed. (NFS-mounted mail directories are typically mounted this way.)

Cross-Mounting Disks

Cross-mounting is the process of having server A NFS mounting server B's disks, and server B NFS mounting server A's disks. While this may appear innocuous at first, there is a subtle danger in doing this: If both servers crash, and if both servers require mounting the other's disk in order to boot correctly, you've got a chicken and egg problem. Server A won't boot until server B is done booting, but server B won't boot because server A isn't done booting.

To get around this problem, make sure you don't get yourself into a situation where this happens. All of your servers should be able to completely boot without needing to mount anyone else's disks for anything. However, this doesn't mean you can't cross-mount at all. There are legitimate reasons for needing to cross-mount, such as needing to make home directories available across all servers.

In these situations, make sure you set your **/etc/fstab** entries to use the **bg** mount option. By doing so, you will allow each server to background the **mount** process for any failed mounts, thus giving all of the servers a chance to complete boot and then properly make their NFS mountable partitions available.

The Importance of the intr Option

When a process makes a system call, the kernel takes over the action. During the time that the kernel is handling the system call, the process has no control over itself. In the event of a kernel access error, the process must continue to wait until the kernel request returns; the process can't give up and quit. In normal cases, the kernel's control isn't a problem, because typically, kernel requests get resolved very quickly. When there's an error, however, it can be quite a nuisance. Because of this, NFS has an option to mount partitions with the interruptible flag (the **intr** option), which allows a process that is waiting on an NFS request to give up and move on.

In general, unless you have reason not to use the **intr** option, it is usually a good idea to do so.

NOTE: *Keep those UIDs in sync!* Every NFS client request to an NFS server includes the UID of the user making the request. This UID is used by the server to verify that the user has permissions to access the requested file. However, in order for NFS permission-checking to work correctly, the UIDs of the users must be synchronized between the client and server. Having the same username on both systems is not enough. (You can compare this to keeping SIDs synchronized under Windows NT.)

Performance Tuning

The default block size that gets transmitted with NFS is 1K. This is handy, since it fits nicely into one packet and, should any packets get dropped, NFS has to retransmit very few packets. The downside to this is that it doesn't take advantage of the fact that most networking stacks are fast enough to keep up with segmenting larger blocks of data for transport, and that most networks are reliable enough that it is extremely rare to lose a block of data.

Given these factors, it is often better to optimize for the case of a fast networking stack and a reliable network, since that's what you're going to have 99% of the time. The easiest way to do this with NFS is to use the **wsize** (write size) and **rsize** (read size) options. A good size to use is 8K. This is especially good if you have network cards that support jumbo frames (such as those based around the Alteon Tigon II chipset).

An example entry with **wsize** and **rsize** is as follows:

```
denon:/export/home   /home  nfs      rw,bg,intr,soft,wsize=8192,rsize=8192 0 0
```

COMMON USES FOR NFS PARTITIONS

The following ideas are, of course, just ideas. You are likely to have your own reasons for sharing disks via NFS.

▼ *To hold popular programs.* If you are accustomed to Windows NT, you've probably worked with applications that refuse to be installed on network shares. For one reason or another, these programs want every system to have their own copy of the software—a nuisance, especially if you have a lot of machines that need the software. Linux (and UNIX in general) rarely has such conditions prohibiting the installation of software on network disks. (The most common exceptions are high-performance databases.) Thus, many sites install heavily used software on a special partition that is exported to all hosts in a network. Often this partition is mounted on each client's **/usr/local** directory, since the partition contains software that is local to the site.

■ *To hold home directories.* Another common use for NFS partitions is to hold home directories. By placing home directories on NFS mountable partitions, it's possible to configure the Automounter and NIS so that users can log in to any machine in the network and have their home directory available to them. Heterogeneous sites typically use this configuration so that users can seamlessly move from one variant of UNIX to another without worrying about having to carry their data around with them.

▲ *For shared mail spools.* A disk residing on the mail server can be used to store all of the user mailboxes, and then NFS exports to all hosts on a network. Traditional UNIX mail readers then read a user's e-mail straight from the spool file. In the case of large mail servers, where multiple servers might be used for providing POP mailboxes, all the mailboxes reside on an NFS partition that is shared with all of the servers.

TROUBLESHOOTING NFS

Like any major service, NFS has mechanisms to help it cope with error conditions. In this section, I'll discuss some common error cases and how NFS handles them.

Stale File Handles

If a file or directory is in use by one process when another process removes the file or directory, the first process gets an error message from the server. Typically, this error is "Stale NFS Filehandle."

Most often, stale file handles occur when you're using a system in the X Windows environment and you have two terminal windows open. For instance, the first terminal window is in a particular directory (say, **/home/user/mydir**), and that directory gets removed from the second terminal window. The next time you press ENTER in the first terminal window, you'll see the error message.

To fix this problem, simply change your directory to one that you know exists without using relative directories (for example, **cd /tmp**).

Permission Denied

You're likely to see the "Permission denied" message if you're logged in as root and are trying to access a file that is NFS mounted. Typically, this means that the server on which the file system is mounted is not acknowledging root's permissions. (Usually, this occurs for security reasons.)

The quick way around this problem is to become the user who owns the file you're trying to control. For example, if you're root and you're trying to access a file owned by the user hdc, use the **su** command to become hdc:

```
[root@ford /root]# su - hdc
```

When you're done working with the file, you can exit out of hdc's shell and return to root.

Note that this workaround assumes that hdc exists as a user on the system and has the same UID on both the client and the server.

Hard vs. Soft Mounts

Although we covered hard and soft mounts in the section on configuring NFS clients, it's worth some additional comments here. When a server goes down, understanding the difference between hard and soft mounts over NFS is important to your troubleshooting efforts.

On an NFS file system that is *hard mounted,* the client must commit all changes to the server before allowing other operations. The client will continue trying to contact the server, until the server sends back an acknowledgment. From the user's perspective, it may look like the client system has crashed when it hasn't.

The purpose of configuring a file system as hard mounted is to make sure that data being accessed via NFS does not get lost. For crucial file systems (such as the mail spool), this is a very important attribute.

Soft mounts, on the other hand, aren't quite as persistent about getting data written to the NFS server's disk. The client will try to access the server and commit unwritten data, but after a specified timeout period (number of retries), the client will give up and return control to the user. Although this has the potential of causing data loss, it allows clients to handle failed NFS servers more gracefully.

SUMMARY

In this chapter, we discussed the process of setting up an NFS server and client. This requires very little change, so sharing your disks this way should be relatively painless. Some key points to remember:

▼ NFS is a stateless protocol. Clients can't tell the difference between a crashed server and a slow server; thus recovery is automatic when the server comes back up. (In the reverse situation, when the client crashes and the server stays up, recovery is also automatic.)

■ The key server processes in NFS are `rpc.statd`, `rpc.quotad`, `rpc.mountd`, and `rpc.nfsd`.

■ Use `rpcinfo -p` to view all the RPC services on your system.

▲ Use `exportfs -a` to export all the file systems specified in the **/etc/exports** file.

NFS is a powerful tool for sharing disks. Be sure to spend some time experimenting with it to meet your system's resource-sharing needs.

CHAPTER 19

Network Information Service (NIS)

The Network Information Service (NIS) makes possible the sharing the data of critical files across the local area network. Typically, files such as **/etc/passwd** and **/etc/group**, which ideally would remain uniform across all hosts, are shared via NIS. In this way, every network machine that has a corresponding NIS client can read the data contained in these shared files and use the network versions of these files as extensions to the local versions. However, NIS is not limited to sharing just those two files. Any tabular file where at least one column has a unique value throughout the file can be shared via NIS. You'll find many such files to exist in your system, including the Sendmail aliases file, the Automounter files, and even the **/etc/services** file.

The main benefit achieved from using NIS is that you can maintain a central copy of the data, and whenever that data is updated, it automatically propagates to all of the network users. To your users, features of NIS give the appearance of a more uniform system—no matter what host they may be working on, all of their tools and files are always there.

If you're coming from a Windows NT background, you might think of NIS as a substantially more versatile Primary Domain Controller (PDC). In fact, NIS is actually much more in line with Windows 2000 directory services than PDCs.

In this chapter, we'll explore NIS, how it works, and how it can benefit you. We will then explain how to set up the client and server portions of the NIS configuration. Finally, we'll discuss some of the tools related to NIS.

INSIDE NIS

The Network Information Service is really just a simple database that clients can query. It contains a series of independent tables. Each table originated as a straight text file, such as **/etc/passwd**, which is tabular in nature and has at least one column that is unique for every row (a database of key/pair values). NIS keeps track of these tables by name and allows querying to happen in one of two ways:

▼ Listing the entire table

▲ Pulling a specific entry based on a search for a given key

Once the databases are established on the server, clients can query the server for database entries. Typically this happens when a client is configured to look to the NIS *map* when an entry cannot be found in the client's local database. A host may have a simple file containing only those entries needed for the system to work in single-user mode (when there is no network connectivity)—for example, the **/etc/passwd** file. When a program makes a request to look up user password information, the client checks its local **passwd** file and sees that the user doesn't exist there; the client then makes a request to the NIS server to look for a corresponding entry in the passwd table. If the NIS does have an entry, it is returned to the client and then to the program that requested the information in the first place. The program itself is unaware that NIS was used. The same is true if the NIS map returns an answer that the user password entry does not exist. The program would be passed the information without its knowing how much activity had happened in between.

This of course applies to all the files that we tell NIS to share. Other popular shared files include **/etc/group** and **/etc/hosts**.

NOTE: Although it is technically correct to refer to NIS's tables as a database, they are more typically called maps. (In this context, we are mapping keys to values.) Using the **/etc/passwd** file as an example, we map a user's login name (which we know is always unique) to the rest of the password entry.

The NIS Servers

NIS can have only one authoritative server where the original data files are kept (this is somewhat similar to DNS). This authoritative server is called the *master* NIS server. If your organization is large enough, you may need to distribute the load across more than one machine. This can be done by setting up one or more *secondary* (*slave*) NIS servers. In addition to helping distribute the load, secondary servers also provide a mechanism to better handle server failures. The secondary NIS server can continue answering queries even while the master or other secondary servers are down.

NOTE: A server can be both a server and a client at the same time.

Secondary NIS servers receive updates whenever the primary NIS server is updated, so that the masters and slaves remain in sync. The process of keeping the secondary servers in sync with the primary is called a *server push*. As part of its update scripts, the NIS master also pushes a copy of the map files to the secondary server. Upon receiving these files, the secondary servers update their databases, as well. The NIS master does not consider itself completely up to date until the secondary servers are up to date, as well.

NOTE: A *server pull* mechanism also exists for NIS. However, this solution is typically reserved for more complex configurations, such as when you have hundreds of slave servers. In a smaller network, this should not be an issue.

Domains

Primary NIS servers establish *domains* that are similar to the domains of a PDC. A significant difference is that the NIS domain does not require the NIS server administrator to explicitly allow a client to join. (Bear in mind that the NIS model assumes that all clients are members of the same administrative domain and are thus managed by the same system administrators.) Furthermore, the NIS server only sends out data; it does not perform authentication. The process of authenticating users is left to each individual host; NIS merely provides a centralized list of users.

> **TIP:** Since NIS domains must be given names, it's a good practice (though not mandatory) to use names that are different from your DNS domain names. You'll have a much easier time discussing your network domains with fellow administrators when everyone knows which is which.

NIS and Yellow Pages

When NIS was originally developed in the 1980s, it was called Yellow Pages (YP for short). When Sun Microsystems, the developers of the SunOS operating system (also known as Solaris 1), started selling its systems in the U.K., a conflict occurred: The term "Yellow Pages" was a trademark of British Telecom. To avoid a lawsuit, Sun renamed the package Network Information Service, and other UNIX vendors followed suit.

Today, you'll find that all of the NIS tools are still prefixed with **yp** instead of **nis**. For whatever reason, the filenames weren't changed along with the official name of the package. So don't be confused by intermixed references to YP and NIS. It's all the same thing.

CONFIGURING THE MASTER NIS SERVER

Linux distributions typically come with NIS already compiled and installed. All that is left for you to do is enable the service (if it isn't enabled already). To do so, you use the **ksysv** tool, and make sure **ypserv** is part of the startup process in runlevels 3 and 5.

Once NIS is enabled, you'll need to configure it. There are four steps to doing this:

1. Establish the domain name.
2. Start the **ypserv** daemon to start NIS.
3. Edit the makefile.
4. Run **ypinit** to create the databases.

Establishing the Domain Name

Setting the NIS domain name is done with the **domainname** command. Let's say we're setting up a domain called orbnet.domain.com; we can tell the system the name of the NIS domain like this:

```
[root@ford /root]# domainname orbnet.domain.com
```

Of course, in order to have this established every time we reboot, we need to place the **domainname** command in an **rc** script.

▼ If you are using Red Hat, you can edit the **/etc/sysconfig/network** and add this line:

```
NIS_DOMAIN=orbnet.domain.com
```

▲ Non–Red Hat folk can edit the **/etc/rc.d/init.d/ypserv** script. Do a search for the line containing **domainname**, and if you can't find one, add one anywhere after the first line. The line should read like so:

```
domainname orbnet.domain.com
```

and you'd replace **orbnet.domain.com** with your own NIS domain name. Setting the domain name should occur before the NIS servers start.

Starting NIS

The **ypserv** daemon is responsible for handling NIS requests. If you are installing NIS onto a live server, most likely you will not want to reboot the server to complete the installation. Instead, you can simply run the **init** script yourself, like so:

```
[root@ford /root]# /etc/rc.d/init.d/ypserv start
```

If you need to stop the NIS server at any time, you can do so with the command

```
[root@ford /root]# /etc/rc.d/init.d/ypserv stop
```

Editing the Makefile

You've seen the use of the **make** command to compile programs in many other chapters. The **make** tool doesn't do the compilation, however—it simply keeps track of what files need to be compiled and then invokes the necessary program to perform the compilation. The file that actually contains the instructions for **make** is called a *makefile*.

The **make** tool is efficient because the programs it invokes are arbitrary. You can substitute your preferred compiler in place of the one that comes with a particular Linux distribution. When **make** sees that a file's date and time have been modified, **make** takes that to mean that the file's contents have been modified. If the file has been modified, that tells **make** that the file needs to be recompiled.

Putting this concept to work on NIS is very straightforward. In this case, there's a series of straight text files that need to be converted into database format. We want a tool that will reconvert any files that have been changed—you can see how **make** fits the bill!

Changing over to the **/var/yp** directory, we see a file called **Makefile** (yes, all one word). This file lists the files that get shared via NIS, as well as some additional parameters for how they get shared and how much of each one gets shared. Open up the makefile with your favorite editor, and you can see all the configurable options. Let's step through the makefile options that apply to Linux.

Designating Slave Servers: NOPUSH

If you plan to have NIS slave servers, you'll need to tell the master NIS server to push the resulting maps to the slave servers. Change the NOPUSH variable to false if you want slave servers.

> **NOTE:** If you don't need slave servers now but think you will need them later, you can change this option when you do add the servers.

```
# If we have only one server, we don't have to push the maps to the
# slave servers (NOPUSH=true). If you have slave servers, change this
# to "NOPUSH=false" and put all hostnames of your slave servers in
# the file /var/yp/ypservers.
NOPUSH=true
```

Remember to list the hostnames of your slave servers in the **/var/yp/ypservers** file. And for each hostname you list there, be sure to list a corresponding entry in the **/etc/hosts** file.

Minimum UIDs and GIDs: MINUID and MINGID

When accounts are added, the minimum UID and GID created in **/etc/passwd** and **/etc/group** files will be different depending on your Linux distribution. Be sure to set the minimum UID and GID values that you are willing to share via NIS. Obviously, you don't want to share the root entry via NIS, so the minimum should never be zero.

```
# We do not put password entries with lower UIDs (the root and system
# entries) in the NIS password database, for security. MINUID is the
# lowest uid that will be included in the password maps.
# MINGID is the lowest gid that will be included in the group maps.
MINUID=500
MINGID=500
```

Merging Shadow Passwords with Real Passwords: MERGE_PASSWD

So that NIS can be used for other systems to authenticate users, you will need to allow the encrypted password entries to be shared through NIS. If you are using shadow passwords, NIS will automatically handle this for you by taking the encrypted field from the **/etc/shadow** file and merging it into the NIS shared copy of **/etc/passwd**. Unless there is a specific reason why you do not want to enable sharing of the encrypted passwords, leave the MERGE_PASSWD setting alone.

```
# Should we merge the passwd file with the shadow file ?
# MERGE_PASSWD=true|false
MERGE_PASSWD=true
```

Merging Group Shadow Passwords with Real Groups: MERGE_GROUP

The **/etc/group** file allows passwords to be applied to group settings. Since the **/etc/group** file needs to be publicly readable, some systems have taken to supporting shadow group files—these are similar in nature to shadow password files. Unless you have a shadow group file, you need to set the MERGE_GROUP setting to false.

```
# Should we merge the group file with the gshadow file ?
# MERGE_GROUP=true|false
MERGE_GROUP=false
```

Designating Filenames

The following makefile segment shows the files that are preconfigured to be shared via NIS. Just because they are listed here, however, does not mean they are automatically shared. This listing simply establishes filenames for later use in the makefile.

Most of the entries start with

```
$(YPPWDDIR)
```

which is a variable that is set up right before this section in the makefile. The default value for this variable is **/etc**, which means any occurrence of **$(YPPWDDIR)** will be replaced with **/etc** when the makefile is run. Thus GROUP will become equal to **/etc/group**, PASSWD will become **/etc/passwd**, and so forth. The variable **$(YPSRCDIR)**, as well, is set to **/etc**.

```
# These are the files from which the NIS databases are built. You
# may edit these to taste in the event that you wish to keep your NIS
# source files separate from your NIS server's actual configuration
# files.
#
GROUP       = $(YPPWDDIR)/group
PASSWD      = $(YPPWDDIR)/passwd
SHADOW      = $(YPPWDDIR)/shadow
GSHADOW     = $(YPPWDDIR)/gshadow
ADJUNCT     = $(YPPWDDIR)/passwd.adjunct
#ALIASES    = $(YPSRCDIR)/aliases     # could be in /etc or/etc/mail
ALIASES     = /etc/aliases
ETHERS      = $(YPSRCDIR)/ethers      # ethernet addresses (for rarpd)
BOOTPARAMS  = $(YPSRCDIR)/bootparams # for booting Sun boxes
                                     # (bootparamd)
HOSTS       = $(YPSRCDIR)/hosts
NETWORKS    = $(YPSRCDIR)/networks
PROTOCOLS   = $(YPSRCDIR)/protocols
```

```
PUBLICKEYS    = $(YPSRCDIR)/publickey
RPC           = $(YPSRCDIR)/rpc
SERVICES      = $(YPSRCDIR)/services
NETGROUP      = $(YPSRCDIR)/netgroup
NETID         = $(YPSRCDIR)/netid
AMD_HOME      = $(YPSRCDIR)/amd.home
AUTO_MASTER   = $(YPSRCDIR)/auto.master
AUTO_HOME     = $(YPSRCDIR)/auto.home
```

What Gets Shared: The all Entry

In the following makefile entry, all of the maps listed after the **all:** are the maps that get shared.

```
all:  passwd group hosts rpc services netid protocols netgrp mail \
      #shadow publickey # networks ethers bootparams amd.home \
      #auto.master auto.home passwd.adjunct
```

Notice that the line continuation character, the backslash (\ ), is used to ensure that the **make** program knows to treat the entire entry as one line, even though it is really three lines. In addition, note that the second line begins with a pound sign (#), which means the rest of the line is commented out.

Based on this format, you can see that the maps configured to be shared are **passwd**, **group**, **hosts**, **rpc**, **services**, **netid**, **protocols**, **netgrp**, and **mail**. These entries correspond to the filenames listed in the preceding section of the makefile. Of course, not all sites want these entries shared, or they want some additional maps shared (such as the **automounter** files, **auto.master** and **auto.home**). To change any of the maps you want shared, alter the line so that the maps you *don't* want shared are listed after a # symbol.

For example, let's say you want only the **passwd**, **group**, **auto.master**, **auto.home**, and **netid** maps shared over NIS. You'd change the **all:** line to read as follows:

```
all: passwd group auto.master auto.home netid \
     # hosts rpc services protocols netgrp mail \
     # shadow publickey networks ethers bootparams amd.home \
     # passwd.adjunct
```

Note that the order in the **all:** line doesn't matter. The placement of the foregoing entries simply makes them easily read.

Using ypinit

Once you have the makefile ready, you need to initialize the YP (NIS) server using the **ypinit** command.

NOTE: Remember that you must already have the domain name set before you run the `ypinit` command. This is done with the `domainname` utility as shown in "Establishing the Domain Name" earlier in this chapter.

```
[root@ford /root]# /usr/lib/yp/ypinit -m
```

Here, the **-m** option tells **ypinit** to set the system up as a master NIS server. Assuming we are running this on a system named ford.domain.com, we would see the system respond as follows:

```
At this point, we have to construct a list of the hosts that
will run NIS servers. ford.domain.com is in the list of NIS
server hosts. Please continue to add the names for the other
hosts, one per line. When you are done with the list, type
a <control-D>.
        next host to add:  ford.domain.com
        next host to add:
```

Continue entering the name of all the secondary NIS servers. Press CTRL-D when you have added all necessary servers. These entries will be placed in the **/var/yp/ypservers** file for you; if needed, you can change them by editing the file later.

Once you are done, **ypinit** will run the **make** program automatically for you, to build the maps and push them to any secondary servers you have indicated.

Makefile Errors

If you made a mistake in the makefile, you may get an error when **ypinit** runs the **make** program. If you see this error:

```
gmake[1]: *** No rule to make target '/etc/shadow', needed by 'passwd.byname'.
Stop.
```

don't worry about it. This means you have specified a file to share that doesn't exist (in this error message, the file is **/etc/shadow**). You can either create the file or go back and edit the makefile so that the file is not shared. (See the previous section "What Gets Shared: The all Entry.")

Another common error message is

```
failed to send 'clear' to local ypserv: RPC: Program not registered
Updating passwd.byuid...
failed to send 'clear' to local ypserv: RPC: Program not registered
gmake[1]: *** No rule to make target '/etc/gshadow', needed by 'group.byname'.
Stop.
gmake[1]: Leaving directory '/var/yp/orbnet.planetoid.org'
```

There are actually two error messages here. You can ignore the first one, which indicates that the NIS server hasn't been started yet. The second error message is the same one described in the preceding paragraph. Once you've fixed it, type in the following command:

```
[root@ford /root]# cd /var/yp;make
```

to rebuild the maps, as described in the next section.

Updating NIS Maps

If you have updated the files configured to be shared by NIS with the rest of your network, you need to rebuild the map files. (For example, you may have added a user to the **/etc/passwd** file.) To rebuild the maps, use the following **make** command:

```
[root@ford /root]# cd /var/yp;make
```

CONFIGURING AN NIS CLIENT

Thankfully, NIS clients are much easier to configure than NIS servers! To set up an NIS client, you need to do the following:

1. Edit the **/etc/yp.conf** file.
2. Set up the startup script.
3. Edit the **/etc/nsswitch.conf** file.

Editing the /etc/yp.conf File

The **/etc/yp.conf** file contains the information necessary for the client-side daemon, **ypbind**, to start up and find the NIS server. You need to make a decision regarding how the client is going to find the server, by either using a broadcast or by specifying the hostname of the server.

The broadcast technique is appropriate when you need to move a client around to various subnets, and you don't want to have to reconfigure the client so long as an NIS server exists in the same subnet. The downside to this technique, of course, is that you must make sure that there is an NIS server in every subnet.

NOTE: When you use the broadcast method, you must have an NIS server in every subnet because broadcasts do not span multiple subnets. If you are uncertain whether a particular NIS server is in the same subnet, you can find out by pinging the broadcast address. If the NIS server is one of the hosts that responds, then you know for sure that the broadcast method will work.

The other technique for client-to-server contact is specifying the hostname of the server. This method works well when you need to subnet your network, but you don't need an NIS server in every subnet. This allows a client to move anywhere inside your network and still be able to find the NIS server—however, if you need to change a client so that it points to another NIS server (to balance the network load), you'll need to change that yourself.

▼   **Broadcast Method**   If you choose the broadcast technique, edit the **/etc/yp.conf** file so that it reads as follows:

```
domain mydomainname broadcast
```

where **_mydomainname_** is the name of your NIS domain. Remember that if you need failover support, you will need to have two NIS servers in every subnet in order for broadcast to find the second server.

▲   **Server Hostname Method**   If you want to specify the name of the NIS server directly, edit the **/etc/yp.conf** file so that it reads as follows:

```
domain mydomainname server servername
```

where **_mydomainname_** is the name of your NIS domain, and **_servername_** is the name of the NIS server to which you want this client to refer.

NOTE: Remember that you also have to have an entry for **servername** in the **/etc/hosts** file. At the time NIS is started, you may not yet have access to DNS, and you most certainly don't have access to the NIS hosts table yet! For this reason, the client must be able to do the hostname-to-IP resolution without the aid of any other services.

Setting Up the Startup Script

The NIS client runs a daemon called **ypbind** in order to communicate with the server. Typically, this is started in the **/etc/rc.d/init.d/ypbind** startup script. Check your startup scripts with the **ksysv** program and verify that **ypbind** is started at runlevel 3.

▼   To start the daemon without having to reboot, use this command:

```
[root@ford /root]# /etc/rc.d/init.d/ypbind start
```

▲   If you need to stop the daemon first, type

```
[root@ford /root]# /etc/rc.d/init.d/ypbind stop
```

Editing the /etc/nsswitch.conf File

The **/etc/nsswitch.conf** file is responsible for telling the system the order in which to search for information. The format of the file is as follows:

```
filename:    servicename
```

where **filename** is the name of the file that needs to be referenced, and **servicename** is the name of the service to use to find the file. Multiple services can be listed, separated by spaces. Here are the valid services:

files	Use the actual file on the host itself.
yp	Use NIS to perform the lookup.
nis	Use NIS to perform the lookup (**nis** is alias for **yp**).
dns	Use DNS for the lookup (applies only to hosts).
[NOTFOUND=return]	Stop searching.
nis+	Use NIS+. (Due to the experimental status of the NIS+ implementation under Linux at this writing, avoid using this option.)

Here is an example entry in the **/etc/nsswitch.conf** file:

```
passwd:     files nis
```

This setting means search requests for password entries will first be done in the **/etc/passwd** file. If the requested entry isn't found there, NIS will then be checked.

The **/etc/passwd** file should already exist and contain most of the information needed. You may need to adjust the order in which certain **servicenames** are listed in the file. (If you installed a DNS server as discussed in Chapter 12, you have already adjusted this file appropriately.)

Testing Your NIS Client Configuration

After the **/etc/yp.conf** and **/etc/nsswitch.conf** files are established, and the **ypbind** client daemon is all set up, you should be able to use the **ypcat** command to dump a map from the NIS server to your screen. To do this, type the following command:

```
[root@ford /root]# ypcat passwd
```

which dumps the **passwd** map to your screen—that is, of course, *if* you are sharing your **passwd** map via NIS. If you aren't, pick a map that you *are* sharing and use the **ypcat** command with that filename.

If you don't see the map dumped out, you need to double-check your client and server configurations and try again.

CONFIGURING A SECONDARY NIS SERVER

As your site grows, you'll undoubtedly find that there is a need to distribute the NIS service load to multiple hosts. NIS supports this through the use of secondary NIS servers. These servers require no additional maintenance once they are configured, because the master NIS server sends them updates whenever you rebuild the maps (with the **yp;make** command, as described in "Editing the Makefile" earlier in this chapter).

There are three steps to setting up a secondary NIS server:

1. Set the domain name.
2. Set up the NIS master to push to the slave.
3. Run **ypinit** to initialize the slave server.

Setting the Domain Name

Like configuring a master NIS server, you establish the NIS domain name before starting up the actual initialization process for a secondary server:

```
[root@ford /root]# domainname mydomainname
```

where **mydomainname** is the NIS domain name for your site.

Of course, the secondary server's domain name must be set up so that it automatically becomes established at boot time. If you are using Red Hat Linux, you can do this by setting the NIS_DOMAIN variable in the **/etc/sysconfig/network** file. Otherwise, you can edit your **/etc/rc.d/init.d/ypserv** file so that the first thing it does after the initial comments is set the domain name there.

NOTE: Be sure to set the domain name by hand before you continue with the **ypinit** step of the installation.

Setting Up the NIS Master to Push to Slaves

If you haven't already configured the master NIS server that will push to the slave NIS servers, you should do so now. This requires two tasks: First, edit the **/var/yp/ypservers** file so that it lists all the secondary NIS servers to which the master server will push maps. For example, if you want the master server to push maps to the hosts technics and denon, you'll edit **/var/yp/ypservers** so that it looks like this:

```
technics
denon
```

Second, you'll need to make sure the makefile has the line **NOPUSH=false**. See the section on configuring NIS master servers for details.

Running ypinit

With these set-up steps accomplished, you're ready to run the **ypinit** command to initialize the secondary server. Type the following command:

```
[root@ford /root]# /usr/lib/yp/ypinit -s master
```

where the **-s** option tells **ypinit** to configure the system as a slave server, and *master* is the name of the NIS master server.

The output of this command will complain about **ypxfrd** not running—you can ignore this. What the secondary server is trying to do is pull the maps from the master server down, using the **ypxfrd** daemon. This won't work, because you didn't configure the master NIS server to accept requests to pull maps down via **ypxferd**. Rather, you configured the master server to push maps to the secondaries whenever the master has an update. The server process at this point must be started by hand. It's the same process as for the primary server: **ypserv**. To get it started, run this command:

```
[root@ford /root]# /etc/rc.d/init.d/ypserv start
```

> **NOTE:** Be sure to have the server process start as part of the boot process. You can use the **ksysv** program to do this. The **ypserv** program should start in runlevels 3 and 5.

To test the secondary server, go back to the master server and try to do a server-side push. Do this by running the **make** program again, as follows:

```
[root@ford /root]# cd /var/yp;make all
```

This should force all of the maps to be rebuilt and pushed to the secondary servers. The output will look something like this:

```
Updating passwd.byname....
Pushed passwd.byname map.
Updating passwd.byuid...
Pushed passwd.byuid map.
Updating hosts.byname...
Pushed hosts.byname...
[etc...]
```

The **[etc...]** on the last line means the listing will go on for all the maps that you are sharing.

NIS TOOLS

To help you work with NIS, a handful of tools have been written to let you extract information from the database via the command line:

▼ ypcat

■ ypwhich

■ ypmatch

▲ yppasswd

The first tool, **ypcat**, dumps the contents of an NIS map. This is useful for scripts that need to pull information out of NIS: **ypcat** can pull the entire map down, and then **grep** can be used to find a specific entry. The **ypcat** command is also useful for simple testing of services, as demonstrated earlier in this chapter.

The **ypwhich** command returns the name of the NIS server that is answering your requests. This is also a good diagnosis tool if NIS doesn't appear to be working as expected. For example, let's say you've made a change in the master NIS tables, but your change can't be seen by a specific client. You can use **ypwhich** to see to which server the client is bound. If it's bound to a secondary server, it might be that the secondary server is not listed in the primary server's **/var/yp/ypservers** file.

An example of **ypwhich** usage is as follows:

```
[root@ford /root]# ypwhich
```

The **ypmatch** command is a close relative of **ypcat**. Rather than pulling an entire map down, however, you supply a key value to **ypmatch** and only the entry corresponding to that key is pulled down. Using the **passwd** map as an example, I can pull down the entry to sshah with this simple command:

```
[root@ford /root]# ypmatch sshah passwd
```

The **yppasswd** command is the NIS version of the standard Linux **passwd** command. The difference between the two is that the **yppasswd** command allows the user to set their password on the NIS server. The behavior is otherwise identical to **passwd**. In fact, many sites rename the standard **passwd** command to something like **passwd.local** and then create a symlink from **passwd** to **yppasswd**.

USING NIS IN CONFIGURATION FILES

One of the most popular uses of NIS is the sharing of the **/etc/passwd** file so that everyone can log in to all hosts on the network by making a single modification to the master **/etc/passwd** map. Some distributions of Linux automatically support this feature once they see NIS running. Others still require explicit settings in **/etc/passwd** so that the login program knows to check NIS as well as the base password file.

> **NOTE:** Whether a system automatically uses NIS for logins depends on which C library the system uses. The newer glibc-based distributions (such as Red Hat and Caldera) automatically use NIS, whereas libc5-based versions (such as Debian) do not. Not all distributions have settled on one library or another, and the subject is a hot topic of debate. With libc5 development stopped, however, it's inevitable that all distributions will use glibc.

Let's assume that you need to add the special tokens to your **/etc/passwd** file to allow logins from users listed in the NIS **passwd** file.

Here is the basic setting you should add to your client's **/etc/passwd** file to allow host login for all users listed in the NIS **passwd** list:

```
+:*:::::
```

> **NOTE:** glibc-based systems do not need this addition to the **/etc/passwd** file, but having it there will not confuse glibc or otherwise make it behave badly.

And here is the setting if you want to deny everyone from logging in to that host except for those listed explicitly in the **/etc/passwd** file:

```
+:::::::/bin/false
```

This overrides all the user's shell settings so that when login to the client is attempted, the login program tries to run **/bin/false** as the user's login program. Since **/bin/false** doesn't work as a shell, the user is immediately booted out of the system.

To allow a few, explicitly listed users into the system while still denying everyone else, use these commands:

```
+username
+username2
+username3
+:::::::/bin/false
```

This allows only **username**, **username2**, and **username3**, specifically, to log in to the system.

IMPLEMENTING NIS IN A REAL NETWORK

In this section, we'll discuss deployment of NIS in real networked environments. This isn't so much a cookbook as it is a collection of samples. After all, we've already described the details of configuring and setting up NIS servers and clients. No need to repeat that!

Obviously, there will be exceptions to each scenario described here. Some small networks might generate an unusually high amount of NIS traffic, for some reason. Some large networks might have such light NIS traffic that only a single master is needed. In any case, apply a liberal dose of common sense to the following, and you should be fine.

A Small Network

We define a small network to be one with fewer than 30 to 40 UNIX/Linux systems, all of which exist on the same subnet.

In this case, a single NIS master server is more than enough. Unless any of the systems in your network are generating an unreasonable amount of NIS requests, all of the other systems can be configured as clients to query the master server via either broadcast or direct connection. If you don't expect to segment your network, you'll probably want to stick with using broadcast, because it simplifies the process of adding hosts to the network.

The NIS server itself shouldn't have to be too beefy. If you do have a powerful machine handling the task, don't be afraid to have it share the load with another lightweight service or two. (DHCP is often a good candidate for load sharing.)

A Segmented Network

Segmented networks introduce complexity to the process of handling broadcast-style services (such as ARP or DHCP). For a growing network, however, segmenting is likely to be a necessity. By segmenting your traffic into two or more discrete networks, you can better keep traffic on each segment down to a controllable level. Furthermore, this arrangement helps you impose tighter security for inside systems. For instance, you can put Accounting and Human Resources onto another subnet, to make it harder for engineering to put sniffers on the network and get to confidential information.

For NIS, segmenting means two possible solutions. The first solution assumes that even though you have a larger network, it doesn't require a lot of NIS traffic. This is typically the case in heterogeneous networks where Microsoft Windows has made its way to many desktop workstations. In this case, keeping a single NIS master server is probably enough. *In any event*, this network's clients should be configured to contact the server directly instead of using broadcasts. This is because only those clients on the same subnet as the NIS server will be able to contact it via broadcasts, and it's much easier to keep all your client workstations configured consistently.

On the other hand, if you do think there is enough NIS traffic, splitting the load across multiple servers—one for each subnet—is a good idea. In this case, the master NIS server is configured to send updates to the secondaries whenever the maps are updated, and clients can be consistently configured to use broadcasts to find the correct NIS server. By using broadcasts, clients can be moved from one subnet to another without your having to reassign their NIS server.

Networks Bigger than Buildings

It isn't uncommon for networks to grow bigger than the buildings they're located in. Remote offices connected through a variety of methods mean a variety of administrative decisions—and not just concerning NIS!

For NIS, however, it is crucial that a server be located at each side of every WAN link. For example, if you have three campuses, connected to each other in a mesh by T1 links, you should have at least three NIS servers, one for each campus. This arrangement is needed because NIS relies on low-latency links in order to perform well, especially given that it is an RPC-based protocol. (Doing a simple `ls -l` command can result in hundreds of lookups, literally.) Furthermore, in the event one of the WAN links fails, it is important that each site be able to operate on its own until the link is reestablished.

Depending on the organization of your company and its administration, you may or may not want to split NIS so that multiple NIS domains exist. Once you get past this administrative decision, you can treat each campus as a single site and decide how many NIS servers need to be deployed. If you intend to keep a uniform NIS space, there should be only one NIS master server; the rest of the NIS servers at other campuses should be slaves.

SUMMARY

In this chapter, we discussed the process of installing master NIS servers, slave NIS servers, and NIS clients, as well as how to use some of the tools available on these servers. Here are the key points to remember about NIS:

▼ Although similar in nature to PDCs, NIS servers are not the same. Namely, NIS servers do not perform authentication.

■ Because anyone in your network can join an NIS domain, it is assumed that your network is already secure. Most sites find that the benefits of this arrangement outweigh the risks.

■ Once the makefile is set up and `ypinit` has been run, master NIS servers do not need additional setups. Changes to the files that you need to share via NIS (such as **/etc/passwd**) are updated and propagated by running `cd /var/yp;make`.

■ NIS slave servers are listed on the master server's file, **/var/yp/ypservers**.

■ NIS slave servers receive their information from the server via a server push.

■ Setup of an NIS slave server is little more than running the `ypinit -s` command.

■ NIS clients need their **/etc/yp.conf** and **/etc/nsswitch.conf** files to be adjusted, and then only the `ypbind` program is set running.

▲ Be sure to establish the NIS-isms in the client-side password file.

CHAPTER 20

Samba

Samba is a powerful tool for allowing UNIX-based systems (such as Linux) to interoperate with Windows-based systems. Samba does this by understanding the Microsoft networking protocol, *SMB* (Session Message Block). From a system administrator's point of view, this means being able to deploy a UNIX-based server without having to install NFS, LP, and some kind of UNIX-compatible authentication support on all the Windows clients in the network. Instead, the clients can use their native tongue to talk to the server—which means fewer hassles for you and seamless integration for your users. No wonder Samba is so popular!

This chapter covers the procedure for downloading, compiling, and installing Samba. Thankfully, Samba's default configuration requires little modification, so we'll concentrate on how to perform customary tasks with Samba and how to avoid some common pitfalls. In terms of administration, you'll get a short course on using Samba's Web Administration Tool (SWAT), and on the **smbclient** command-line utility. We'll end by documenting the process of using encrypted passwords.

No matter what task you've chosen for Samba to handle, be sure to take the time to read the program's documentation, especially since it now comes with a complete O'Reilly book! It is well written, complete, and thorough. For the short afternoon it takes to get through most of it, you'll gain a substantial amount of knowledge.

NOTE: Samba has actually been ported to a significant number of platforms—almost any variant of UNIX you can imagine, and even several non-UNIX environments. In this discussion, we are of course most interested in Samba/Linux, but keep in mind that Samba can be deployed on your other UNIX systems, as well.

THE MECHANICS OF SMB

To fully understand the Linux/Samba/Windows relationship, you need to understand the relationships of both operating systems to their files, printers, users, and networks. To better see how these relationships compare, let's examine some of the fundamental issues of working with both Linux and Windows in the same environment.

Usernames and Passwords

The UNIX login/password mechanism is radically different from the Windows PDC (Primary Domain Controller) model and the Windows 2000 Active Directory model. Thus it's important for the system administrator to maintain consistency in the logins and passwords across both systems. Users need to access both systems without having to worry about reauthentication or cached passwords that don't match a particular server.

You have several management options for handling username and password issues:

▼ **The Linux Password Authentication Module (PAM)**   Allows you to authenticate users against a PDC. This means you still have two user lists—one local and one on the PDC—but your users need only keep track of their passwords on the Windows system.

■ **Samba as a PDC** Allows you to keep all your logins and passwords on the Linux system, while all your Windows boxes authenticate with Samba. (Unfortunately, support for this still appears to be a bit unreliable.)

▲ **Rolling your own solution using Perl** Allows you to use your own custom script. For sites with a well-established system for maintaining logins and passwords, it isn't unreasonable to come up with a custom script. This would be done using WinPerl and the Perl modules that allow changes to the Security Access Manager (SAM), to update the PDC's password list. A Perl script on the Linux side can communicate with the WinPerl script to keep accounts synchronized.

In the worst-case situation, you can always maintain the two systems by hand (which some early sysadmins did indeed have to do!), but this method is error prone and not much fun to manage.

Encrypted Passwords

Starting with Windows NT 4/Service Pack 3, Windows 98, and Windows 95 OSR2, Windows uses encrypted passwords when communicating with the PDC and any server requiring authentication (including Linux and Samba). The encryption algorithm used by Windows is different from UNIX's, however, and therefore is not compatible.

Here are your choices for handling this conflict:

▼ Edit the Registry on Windows clients to disable use of encrypted passwords. The Registry entries that need to be changed are listed in the **docs** directory in the Samba package.

▲ Configure Samba to use Windows-style encrypted passwords.

The first solution has the benefit of not pushing you over to a more-complex password scheme. On the other hand, you have to apply the Registry fix on all your clients. The second option, of course, has the opposite effect: For a little more complexity on the server side, you don't have to modify any of your clients.

The process of setting up Windows-style encrypted passwords is discussed in "Encrypted Password Support" later in this chapter.

The Differences Between smbd and nmbd

The code of the Samba server is actually composed of two daemons: **smbd** and **nmbd**. The **smbd** daemon handles the actual sharing of file systems and printer services for clients. It starts by binding to port 139 and then listens for requests. Every time a client authenticates itself, **smbd** makes a copy of itself; the original goes back to listening to port 139 for new requests, and the copy handles the connection for the client. This new copy also changes its effective user ID from root to the authenticated user. (For example, if the user sshah authenticated against **smbd**, the new copy would run with the permissions of sshah, not the permissions of root.) The copy stays in memory as long as there is a connection from the client.

The **nmbd** daemon is responsible for handling NetBIOS name server requests. It begins by binding itself to port 137; unlike **smbd**, however, **nmbd** does not create a new instance of itself to handle every query. In addition to name server requests, **nmbd** also handles requests from master browsers, domain browsers, and WINS servers.

Both daemons must be started for Samba to work properly.

NOTE: With the release of Windows 2000, Microsoft moved to a pure DNS naming convention as part of its support for Active Directory in an attempt to make name services more consistent between the Network Neighborhood and the hostnames that are published in DNS. In theory, you shouldn't need **nmbd** anymore, but the reality is that you will. Especially if you intend to allow non–Windows 2000 hosts on your network to access your Samba shares. Unfortunately, it will be many years before we see the complete demise of the horror known as NetBIOS.

Compiling and Installing Samba

Samba comes installed on most Linux distributions. Nevertheless, like all the other services we've discussed in this book, you should be able to compile the software yourself in the event you want to upgrade the package to a new release. Since its inception, Samba has had users across many different UNIX platforms and so has been designed to handle various versions of UNIX (including Linux). There is rarely a problem during the compilation process.

As of this writing, the latest version of Samba is 2.0.7.

NOTE: If you are running Red Hat Linux 7, you should already have Samba 2.0.7 installed. To check, look for the **/usr/sbin/smbd** file. If it is there, you are ready to go. If it isn't, you can either install it via RPM from the CD-ROM or you can download and compile. For more information about installing via RPM, see Chapter 4, as well as the following section to find out about the differences between where a compiled version places files and where RPM places files. If you are running an older version of Red Hat or if your distribution did not come with Samba 2.0.7, you should consider uninstalling the existing package and upgrading. If you choose to remain with the version you currently have, remember that not all of the features that we discuss in this chapter will be available (although most should be).

Begin by downloading the Samba source code from http://www.samba.org into the directory where you want to compile it. For this example, we'll assume this directory is **/usr/local/src**.

1. Unpack Samba using the **tar** command:

```
[root@ford src]# tar -xvzf samba-2.0.7.tar.gz
```

2. Step 1 creates a subdirectory called **samba-2.0.7** for the source code. Change into that directory.

TIP: Using your favorite text editor, start by reading the file titled **Manifest**. This explains all the files that came with Samba and gives you the location of the Samba documentation. While this isn't immediately crucial, it will help you in the long run.

3. Within the **samba-2.0.7** directory, there will be another subdirectory called **source**. Change into that directory like so:

```
[root@ford samba-2.0.7]# cd source
```

4. Before you run **./configure**, evaluate the options that you want to configure for your Samba installation.

Samba Configuration (./configure) Options	Description
--with-smbmount	To include support for the **smbmount** command. (This feature is currently Linux-specific. Future Samba versions will include a general-purpose **mount** tool that will work across multiple operating systems.) The **smbmount** command allows you to attach shares off of NT servers (or other Samba servers) in a similar way that you can mount NFS partitions.
--with-pam	If your distribution of Linux comes with PAM (as does Red Hat), enable this feature so that Samba can take advantage of the options available through the Password Authentication Module.

5. Run the **./configure** command with the options you've chosen for your Samba installation. For example, to support both the **smbmount** and PAM features, you would enter this command:

```
[root@ford source]# ./configure --with-smbmount --with-pam
```

6. Run **make** like so:

```
[root@ford source]# make
```

7. Run **make install** like so:

```
[root@ford source]# make install
```

8. Samba is now installed in the **/usr/local/samba** directory.

9. The default location of Samba's man pages makes them inaccessible for use with **man**. If you are not using Red Hat 7, type the following commands to make them available:

```
[root@ford source]# cd /usr/local/samba/man
[root@ford man]# cp man1/* /usr/man/man1
[root@ford man]# cp man5/* /usr/man/man5
[root@ford man]# cp man7/* /usr/man/man7
[root@ford man]# cp man8/* /usr/man/man8
```

If you are using Red Hat 7, then use this set of commands to make the man pages available:

```
[root@ford source]# cd /usr/local/samba/man
[root@ford man]# cp man1/* /usr/share/man/man1
[root@ford man]# cp man5/* /usr/share/man/man5
[root@ford man]# cp man7/* /usr/share/man/man7
[root@ford man]# cp man8/* /usr/share/man/man8
```

10. Now copy the default configuration file into the **/usr/local/samba/lib** directory. Assuming you unpacked Samba into the **/usr/local/src** directory, the default configuration file will be **/usr/local/src/samba-2.0.7/examples directory**. To copy the correct file, enter these commands:

```
[root@ford man]# cd /usr/local/src/samba-2.0.7/examples
[root@ford examples]# cp smb.conf.default /usr/local/samba/lib/smb.conf
```

11. The default permissions on the Samba directories allow only the root user to access them. You will need to allow other users to access the files, except for the **private** directory. To do this, issue these commands:

```
[root@ford examples]# cd /usr/local/samba
[root@ford samba]# chmod -R 755 bin lib man var
```

NOTE: The **/usr/local/samba/bin** directory is typically not found in the search path for shells. You can either add it there or you can simply copy the binaries from **/usr/local/samba/bin** to **/usr/local/bin** (assuming, of course, that **/usr/local/bin** is in your path).

Red Hat 7 and RPM Installations

If you choose to use the version of Samba that comes pre-installed with Red Hat 7 or that gets installed via RPM, you will need to be aware of the locations of files. The following table lists where we map the filenames in the Red Hat 7 version and in the compiled version. Because this book does not focus solely on Red Hat 7, we use the directory locations that are from the compiled version. Simply map those filenames to the Red Hat–isms, and you should be fine.

Red Hat 7 Locations	Compiled Locations
/usr/bin/addtosmbpass	/usr/local/samba/bin/addtosmbpass
/usr/bin/convert_smbpasswd	/usr/local/samba/bin/convert_smbpasswd
/usr/bin/make_printerdef	/usr/local/samba/bin/make_printerdef
/usr/bin/make_smbcodepage	/usr/local/samba/bin/make_smbcodepage
/usr/sbin/nmbd	/usr/local/samba/bin/nmbd
/usr/bin/nmblookup	/usr/local/samba/bin/nmblookup
/usr/bin/smbclient	/usr/local/samba/bin/smbclient
/usr/sbin/smbd	/usr/local/samba/bin/smbd
/usr/bin/smbpasswd	/usr/local/samba/bin/smbpasswd
/usr/bin/smbspool	/usr/local/samba/bin/smbspool
/usr/bin/smbstatus	/usr/local/samba/bin/smbstatus
/usr/bin/smbtar	/usr/local/samba/bin/smbtar
/usr/sbin/swat	/usr/local/samba/bin/swat
/usr/bin/testparm	/usr/local/samba/bin/testparm
/usr/bin/testprns	/usr/local/samba/bin/testprns
/usr/share/swat/*	/usr/local/samba/swat/*
/etc/samba/codepages/*	/usr/local/samba/lib/codepages/*
/etc/samba/smbpasswd	/usr/local/samba/private/smbpasswd
/etc/samba/smb.conf	/usr/local/samba/lib/smb.conf

Samba Administration

This section describes some of the issues of administering Samba. We'll see how to start and stop Samba, how to do common administrative tasks with SWAT, and how to use **smbclient**. Finally, we'll examine the process of using encrypted passwords.

Starting and Stopping Samba

Most distributions of Linux have scripts that will start and stop Samba without your needing to pay much attention. If you're using the Samba installation that came with your Linux distribution, you shouldn't need to change the scripts. They take care of startup at boot time and stopping at shutdown. If you are using Red Hat 7, you can use the **/etc/rc.d/init.d/smb** script to start and stop the services. For example, to explicitly start the service using this script, you would run:

```
[root@ford /root]# /etc/rc.d/init.d/smb start
```

And to stop the service using this script, you would run:

```
[root@ford /root]# /etc/rc.d/init.d/smb stop
```

Make sure you have the appropriate symlinks pointing to this script in the **/etc/rc3.d** and **/etc/rc5.d** directories so that Samba starts up automatically at boot time. See Chapter 7 for details on checking for this and setting up the symlinks if you don't have them already.

NOTE: If you don't have scripts to automatically start Samba, it's a good idea to take the time to write them. See Chapter 7 for details on writing and placing the scripts.

Starting Samba takes just two steps. First, start the **smbd** process. Although you can set many parameters on the command line, it's often better to set them in the configuration file (**smb.conf**). If you're using SWAT, it will maintain that file for you. The only command-line parameter you're likely to have is the **-D** option to tell Samba to run as a daemon:

```
[root@ford samba]# /usr/local/samba/bin/smbd -D
```

Next, start the **nmbd** process. Like **smbd**, many parameters can be set through the command line, but you'll probably find it easier to maintain if you keep configuration changes in the **smb.conf** file. The only command-line parameter you're likely to have is the **-D** option to tell **nmbd** to run as a daemon.

```
[root@ford samba]# /usr/local/samba/bin/nmbd -D
```

NOTE: You should start both **smbd** and **nmbd** as the root user.

Stopping Samba is little trickier than starting it up. Use the **ps** command to list all of the Samba processes. From this list, find the instance of **smbd** that is owned by root, and kill this process. This will also kill all of the other Samba connections.

NOTE: If you make a change to the configuration of Samba, you'll need to stop and then restart Samba in order for those changes to take effect. It's the client's responsibility to reestablish the connection. This is part of the SMB protocol, and not a limitation of Samba.

Using SWAT

Prior to version 2.0 of Samba, the official way to configure it was by editing the **smb.conf** file. Though verbose in nature and easy to understand, this file was rather large and cumbersome. It also meant that setting up shares under NT was still easier than setting up shares with Samba. Many individuals developed graphical front-ends to the editing process. Many of these tools are still being maintained and enhanced—you can read more about them by visiting Samba's Web site at http://www.samba.org. As of version 2.0, however, Samba ships with SWAT, the Samba Web Administration Tool.

Using SWAT is remarkably easy. All configuration is done via a Web browser. SWAT then takes the information from the browser and builds an **smb.conf** file. For those who are used to editing configuration files, this may be a bit annoying because SWAT doesn't preserve comments in the configuration file itself. Therefore, server configuration documentation must remain external to Samba rather than embedded in the configuration file in the form of comments.

NOTE: If you prefer maintaining comments in your configuration file, or if you need to write some of your own tools to automate certain administration chores, you should not use SWAT. Herein lies the beauty of text-based configuration files. You have a choice—you don't have to use the GUI if you don't want to, and since the file format is public, anyone can write their own administration tool if they want to.

Setting Up SWAT

SWAT is the Samba Web Administration Tool with which you can manage Samba through a browser interface. It's an excellent alternative to editing the Samba configuration files by hand, but don't let it make you believe that the configuration files are complex!

What makes SWAT a little different from other browser-based administration tools is that SWAT does not rely on a Web server (like Apache). Instead, SWAT performs all the needed Web server functions without implementing a full Web server. This is mostly accomplished by running through the **inetd** daemon.

Setting up SWAT is pretty straightforward. Here are the steps:

1. Set the permissions on **/usr/local/samba/swat** to be world readable:

   ```
   [root@ford samba]# chmod -R 755 /usr/local/samba/swat
   ```

2. Edit the **/etc/services** file so that it includes the following line:

   ```
   swat    901/tcp
   ```

3. If you use a stock **inetd**, edit the **/etc/inetd.conf** file so that it includes the following line:

   ```
   swat  stream  tcp   nowait.400   root /usr/local/samba/bin/swat swat
   ```

   If you are using **xinetd** (Red Hat 7), make sure the **/etc/xinetd.d/swat** file looks like this:

   ```
   # description: SWAT is the Samba Web Admin Tool. Use swat \
   #              to configure your Samba server. To use SWAT, \
   #              connect to port 901 with your favorite web browser.
   service swat
   {
           port    = 901
   ```

```
socket_type    = stream
wait    = no
only_from = 127.0.0.1
user    = root
server  = /usr/local/samba/bin/swat
log_on_failure  += USERID
}
```

Remember that if you are using the RPM install of Samba, the **server=** line should be set to **/usr/sbin/swat**.

4. If you are using a stock **inetd**, send the HUP signal to the **inetd** process, with this command:

```
[root@ford src]# kill -1 `ps -C inetd|awk '{if (/inetd/) print $1}'`
```

If you are using **xinetd**, send a SIGUSR1 signal to the **xinetd** process with this command:

```
[root@ford src]# kill -SIGUSR1 `ps -C xinetd|awk '{if (/xinetd/) print $1}'`
```

And you're done! Simply point Netscape Navigator to your Samba server at port 901 to get a login prompt for entering SWAT. Note that if you are using **xinetd**, this configuration only allows you to connect to SWAT from the same machine on which you are running Samba. This was done for the purpose of security, since you don't want to allow random people to be able to probe at your machine remotely. But not to worry—it is most likely that you got Netscape Navigator installed with your installation. Simply run Netscape on the server itself and go to http://localhost:901/.

CAUTION: Logging in as root through SWAT causes the root password to be sent from the Web browser to the Samba server. Therefore, avoid doing administration tasks across an untrusted network. Preferably, run Navigator on the server itself, or set up an SSH tunnel between the client host and the Samba server host.

Using SWAT from Other Hosts

If you used **inetd**, then you can use SWAT from any other host as long as it has TCP/IP connectivity and a Web browser. Simply point your browser to your server's port 901. For example, if your server name is arthur, you can visit http://arthur:901/ and get to the SWAT tool. However, with this configuration, it is possible for other people to get to your SWAT install, as well. If this means that untrustworthy people can poke at your system, then this is *not good*. What you should do is use TCP Wrappers in your **inetd.conf** file (read the man pages for **tcpd**, **hosts.allow**, and **hosts.deny** for more information) so that you can specify which hosts can access that port and which cannot.

If you used **xinetd**, then you already have TCP Wrappers functionality built into the configuration file. Take a look at Chapter 9 for more information on how to limit which hosts can connect to your server.

The SWAT Menus

When you connect to SWAT and login as root, you'll see the main menu shown in Figure 20-1. From here, you can find almost all the documentation you'll need for Samba's configuration files, daemons, and related programs. None of the links point to external Web sites, so you can read them at your leisure without connecting to the Net.

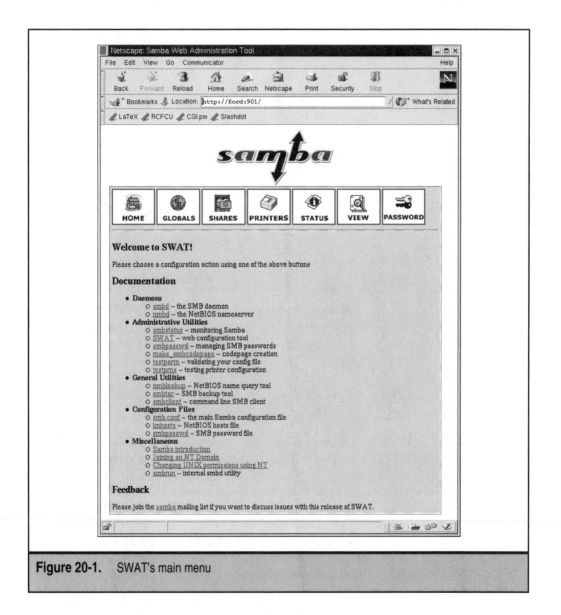

Figure 20-1.   SWAT's main menu

At the top of the window are buttons for the following menu choices:

Home	The main menu page
Globals	Configuration options that affect all operational aspects of Samba
Shares	For setting up disk shares and their respective options
Printers	For setting up printers to be accessible to NT clients
Status	The status of the **smbd** and **nmbd** processes, including a list of all clients connected to these processes and what they are doing (the same information that's listed in the **smbstatus** command-line program)
View	The resulting **smb.conf** file
Password	Password settings

Globals

The globals page lists all settings that affect all aspects of Samba's operation. These settings are divided into five groups: base, security, logging, browse, and WINS. To the left of each option is a link to the relevant documentation of the setting and its values.

Shares

Under Windows NT, setting up a *share* means creating a new folder, right-clicking it, and allowing it to be shared. Additional controls can be established by right-clicking the folder and selecting Properties.

Using SWAT, these same actions are accomplished by creating a new share. You can then select the share and click Choose Share. This brings up all the configurable parameters for the share.

Printers

Samba automatically makes all printers listed in the **/etc/printcap** file (see Chapter 21) available for use via SMB to Windows clients. Through this series of menus, you can modify Samba's treatment of these printers or even add additional printers. The one thing you cannot do here is add printers to the main system—you must do that by editing the **/etc/printcap** file. See Chapter 21 for more information on that process.

Status

The Status page shows the current status of the **smbd** and **nmbd** daemon. This information includes what clients are connected and their actions. The page automatically updates every 30 seconds by default, but you can change this rate if you like (it's an option on the page itself). Along with status information, you can turn Samba on and off or ask it to reload its configuration file. This is necessary if you make any changes to the configuration.

View

As you change your Samba configuration, SWAT keeps track of the changes and figures out what information it needs to put into the **smb.conf** file. Open the View page, and you can see the file SWAT is putting together for you.

Password

Use the Password page if you intend to support encrypted passwords. You'll want to give your users a way to modify their own passwords without having to log in to the Linux server. This page allows users to do just that.

NOTE: It's almost always a good idea to disallow access to your servers for everyone except support personnel. This reduces the chances of mistakes being made that could affect the performance or stability of your server.

Creating a Share

1. Click the Shares button on the main SWAT window. This displays a page like that in Figure 20-2.

2. In the text box next to the Create Share button, enter the name of the share you want to create and click Create Share. For instance, to create a share called MYSHARE, the screen will look like Figure 20-3.

3. Change the settings for your share. You may want to customize the share's comment (which will show up in the Windows Explorer), the directory where all the contents of the share should reside, and various security and browse options.

4. Once you've entered all the information, click the Commit Changes button near the top of the screen.

5. To make the changes appear to any systems that browse your server, restart the **smbd** daemon by going into the Status menu and clicking the Restart smbd button.

And that's it. You should now be able to see this share from Windows clients browsing the network.

Using smbclient

The **smbclient** program is a command-line tool that allows your Linux system to act as a Windows client. You can use this utility to connect to other Samba servers or even to real Windows NT/2000 servers. **smbclient** is a very flexible program and can be used to browse other servers, send and retrieve files from them, or even print to them. As you

Figure 20-2. Creating a share

can imagine, this is also a great debugging tool since you can quickly and easily check whether a new Samba installation works correctly without having to find a Windows client to test it.

In this section, we'll show you how to do basic browsing, remote file access, and remote printer access with **smbclient**. However, remember that **smbclient** is a very flexible program, limited only by your imagination.

Browsing a Server

With so many graphical interfaces around, we've come to equate browsing to mean "point and click." But when your intention is to simply find out what a server has to offer, it's not enough of a reason in itself to support an entire GUI.

Figure 20-3.   Editing MYSHARE

Using **smbclient** with the **-L** option allows you to view the offerings of an NT or Samba server without having to use a GUI. Here's the format of the command:

```
[root@ford root]# smbclient -L hostname
```

where **hostname** is the name of the server. For example, if we want to see what the host ford has to offer, we type:

```
[root@ford root]# smbclient -L ford
```

This will return information that looks something like the following:

```
Added interface ip=192.168.1.1 bcast=192.168.1.255 nmask=255.255.255.0
Password:
```

```
Domain=[MYGROUP] OS=[UNIX] Server=[Samba 2.0.5a]

        Sharename      Type        Comment
        ---------      ----        -------
        MYSHARE        Disk
        IPC$           IPC         IPC Service (Samba Server)
        lp             Printer

        Server                     Comment
        ---------                  -------
        FORD                       Samba Server

        Workgroup                  Master
        ---------                  -------
        MYGROUP
```

NOTE: Depending on server configuration, you might get prompted for a password. If the server allows guest browsing, you can simply press ENTER at the **password:** prompt and see the browse list. Otherwise, you'll need to enter your password.

Remote File Access

The **smbclient** utility allows you to access files on an NT or Samba server with a command-line hybrid DOS/FTP client interface. For its most straightforward usage, you'll simply run the following:

[sshah@ford ~]$ **/usr/local/samba/bin/smbclient //server/share**

where ***server*** is the server name and ***share*** is the share name to which you want to connect. By default, Samba automatically sets up all users' home directories as shares. (For instance, the user sshah can access his home directory on the server ford by going to **//ford/sshah**.)

Once it's connected, you'll be able to browse directories using the **cd**, **dir**, and **ls** commands. You can also use **get, put, mget**, and **mput** to transfer files back and forth. The online help explains all of the commands in detail. Simply type **help** at the prompt to see what is available.

Following are some command-line parameters you may need to use with **smbclient** to connect to a server.

Parameter for `smbclient`	Description
`-I destIP`	The destination IP address to which you want to connect.
`-U username`	The user you want to connect as, instead of the user you are logged in as.
`-W name`	Sets the workgroup name to **name**.
`-D directory`	Starts from **directory**

NOTE: `smbclient` has a `tar` mode, as well. You'll find it is easier to access this mode from the `smbtar` command, since `smbtar` provides an interface much more consistent with regular `tar`. The man page for `smbtar` will tell you more about it.

Remote Printer Access

So the head of marketing got a brand-new color laser printer, but your request for a wrist brace to help with your carpal tunnel was turned down. It's only fair that you get to use the printer, right?

If that printer is sitting on an NT server that doesn't have **lpd** configured, but it does share the printer via SMB so other Windows workstations can print to it, you're in luck. You can use **smbclient** to submit print jobs to other NT or Samba servers just as a Windows client would.

To connect to a printer on a server using **smbclient**, use the **-P** parameter and specify the service name for the printer, as shown here:

```
[root@ford root]# smbclient //ford/lp -P
```

This connects you to the service as a printer. You can then issue the **print** command along with the name of a local filename. For example, if I have a file called **blecker** in the directory from which I run **smbclient**, I can issue this command:

```
smb:> print blecker
```

to print the contents of the file **blecker**.

Possible uses for this remote printer access feature include setting up special filters in **/etc/printcap** files so that all files printed to a particular printer are automatically redirected to a Windows printer on the network. (For more information, see Chapter 21.)

Using smbmount

If your kernel is configured to support the SMB file system (as are most kernels that come with Linux distributions), you can actually mount an NT or Samba share onto your system in much the same way you would mount an NFS partition. This is very handy for accessing a large disk on a remote server without having to shuffle individual files across the network.

To use **smbmount**, simply run this command:

```
[root@ford /mnt]# smbmount //ford/sshah /mnt/sshah
```

where **//ford/sshah** is the share being mounted, and /mnt/sshah is the directory to which it is being mounted. To unmount this directory, run **umount**:

```
[root@ford /mnt]# umount /mnt/sshah
```

Encrypted Password Support

Because Windows uses a password-hashing algorithm different from Linux's, Samba needs to maintain its own password file in order to support encrypted password support. The quick way to get a list of existing users in the **/etc/passwd** file for whom to implement encrypted password support is to use the **mksmbpasswd.sh** script that comes with Samba. You can find it in the script directory of the source tree (**/usr/local/src/samba-2.0.7/source/script/mksmbpasswd.sh**) or, if you have the Red Hat 7 RPM installed, in the **/usr/bin** directory (**/usr/bin/mksmbpasswd.sh**). If you have it in the source tree directory, copy it to the Samba **/usr/local/samba/bin** directory, like so (although note that *it should be on one line*; it's two lines here, due to printing constraints for the book):

```
[root@ford /root]# cp /usr/local/src/samba-2.0.7/source/script/mksmbpasswd.sh
/usr/local/samba/bin
```

NOTE: These features require that the **/usr/local/samba/private** directory already exist. If it does not exist, create it using the **mkdir** command. Be sure that the directory has the permissions set to 0700 and is owned by root.

mksmbpasswd.sh's usage is as follows:

```
[root@ford /root]# cd /usr/local/samba/private
[root@ford private]# ../bin/addtosmbpass < /etc/passwd > smbpasswd
[root@ford private]# chmod 500 .; chmod 600 smbpasswd
```

NOTE: If you are using NIS, you will want to use `ypcat passwd` to get the password list from the NIS server and store that to a file. Then, instead of using **/etc/passwd**, use the file containing the results from `ypcat passwd`.

The foregoing command will create the **smbpasswd** list with the appropriate file permissions. Unfortunately, because UNIX passwords cannot be reversed to generate a cleartext password that can then be rehashed to work under Samba, the **smbpasswd** file's list of users does not contain valid passwords. That needs to be set by the user using the **smbpasswd** command or via SWAT's interface.

Allowing NULL Passwords

If you have a need to allow users to have no passwords (which is a bad idea), you can do so by using the **smbpasswd** program with the **-n** option, like so:

```
[root@ford /root]# smbpasswd -n username
```

where **username** is the name of the user whose password you want to set to empty.
In addition to using **smbpasswd**, you can do this via the SWAT program.

Changing Passwords with smbpasswd

Users who prefer the command line over the Web interface can use the **smbpasswd** command to change their Samba password (note that this is different from the **smbpasswd** file, which is in the **/usr/local/samba/private** directory). This program works just like the regular **passwd** program, except this program does not update the **/etc/passwd** or NIS **passwd** files. Because **smbpasswd** uses the standard protocol for communicating with the server regarding password changes, you can also use this to change your password on a remote Windows machine.

Troubleshooting Samba

There are four typical solutions to connectivity problems with Samba.

▼   **Restart Samba.**   This may be necessary because either Samba has entered an undefined state or (more likely) you've made changes to the configuration but forgot to restart Samba so that the changes take effect.

■   **Make sure the configuration options are correct.**   Errors in the **smb.conf** file are typically in directory names, usernames, network numbers, and hostnames. A common mistake is when a new client is added to a group that has special access to the server, but Samba isn't told the name of the new client being added.

- ■ **Monitor encrypted passwords**.   These may be mismatched—the server is configured to use them and the clients aren't, or (more likely) the clients are using encrypted passwords and Samba hasn't been configured to use them. If you're under the gun to get a client working, you may just want to disable client-side encryption using the **regedit** scripts that come with Samba's source code (see the **docs** subdirectory).

- ▲ **Monitor-cached passwords**.   Windows often caches passwords in files that end in **pwl**. Not only is this a security risk (the **pwl** files are poorly encrypted), but if your password has changed on the server, Windows may continue feeding the cached password instead of prompting you for a new one. Simply remove the **pwl** files to force Windows to prompt you for a password.

Summary

In this chapter, we discussed the process of compiling, installing, and configuring Samba so that your Linux server can integrate into a Windows-based network. Samba is a powerful tool with the potential to replace NT servers dedicated to disk and printer sharing.

Reading through tons of documentation probably isn't your favorite way to pass the day, but you'll find the Samba documentation to be complete, helpful, and easy reading. At least skim through the files to see what's there, so you know where you can go to get additional information when you need it. Plus, with the entire *Using Samba* book as part of the distribution, you should have everything you need for configuring even the most complex setup.

If you would rather read more about Samba in print, you can purchase the same book that is shipped with the distribution. The title of the book is *Using Samba*, by Robert Eckstein, David Collier-Brown, and Peter Kelly (O'Reilly and Associates, 1999).

CHAPTER 21

Printing

T he line printer daemon (**lpd**) is Linux's way of handling print requests. These can be requests destined for printers attached to the immediate system or printers accessible via the network. The **lpd** process can handle print requests from other clients on the network, as well (see Figure 21-1).

In this chapter, we'll document the process of setting up new printers using LPRng, the "Next Generation" print server for Linux. (Red Hat 7 ships with the latest version of this.) What makes LPRng different from other implementations is that it is much more configurable, has a better filtering mechanism, scales to large numbers of printers (the

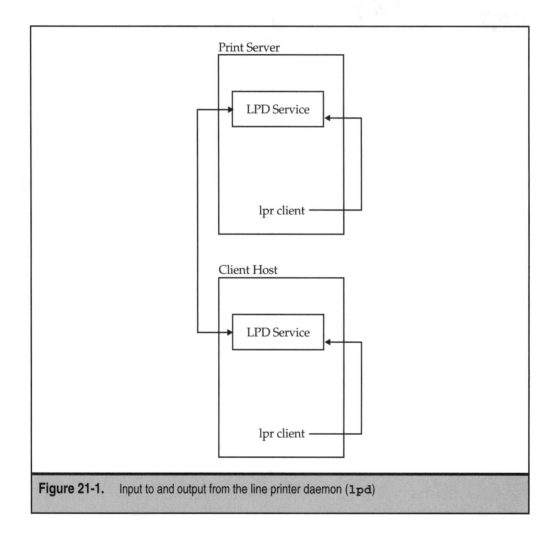

Figure 21-1.   Input to and output from the line printer daemon (**lpd**)

Dow Jones and at least one aerospace company are using it to handle over 1000 printers), and is written with security in mind.

> **NOTE:** Although `lpd` stands for line printer daemon, the program is not limited to usage with line printers only. You can use `lpd` with just about any printer that is accessible via the network or a serial or parallel port.

THE BASICS OF LPD

Linux's printing daemon follows in the footsteps of its UNIX predecessors, which gives us many benefits. Not only is our Linux system compatible with other UNIX systems' printing facilities, but we have gained exceptional flexibility.

The model used by **lpd** is actually similar to the e-mail process: The daemon quietly listens for print requests to come to it over the network. This means the daemon considers print requests coming from other hosts to be just the same as those originating from the same host as the daemon's, thus making the configuration files easier to manage.

For each print job that arrives, the file is first placed in a spool directory. Typically, this directory is **/var/spool/lpd/***printername*, where *printername* is the name of the printer to which the job is going. Once spooled, **lpd** gets the requested print job to the printer independently of the sender. This allows the sender to resume operation instead of the user having to stare at an hourglass icon.

Here are the steps of the **lpd** process for getting the print job to the printer:

1. Look up the printer configuration information in **/etc/printcap**.
2. If the printer requires that the job go through a print filter, send the file through the filter.
3. If the printer is physically attached to the server, send the filtered print request directly to the print device.
4. If the printer is remote (accessed via the network), contact the corresponding **lpd** server and send the filtered job to that server.

INSTALLING LPRNG

The latest version of LPRng is 3.6.26 and can be downloaded from http://www.astart.com/LPRng/LPRng.html. Place it in a directory where you have enough space to unpack and compile the source code. Note that if you have Red Hat 7 (which shipped with this book), the installation phase is optional. Red Hat 7 ships with 3.6.22, and the configuration options discussed in "Configuring /etc/printcap," later in this chapter, will work with both versions of LPRng.

NOTE: If you installed Red Hat 7 but did not install the print server, you can install the RPM of LPRng instead of compiling it if you don't mind being a few versions behind (though I recommend getting the most recent version). To install it, simply install the LPRng RPM from the CD-ROM. If you aren't familiar with the RPM tools available, see Chapter 4 for the necessary details.

For this discussion, we will assume that you have downloaded **LPRng-3.2.26.tgz** into the **/usr/local/src** directory. To unpack this, simply type:

```
[root@ford src]# tar -xvzf LPRng-3.6.26.tgz
```

This will create a subdirectory called **LPRng-3.6.26** and place all of the files there. Change into the **LPRng** directory, like so:

```
[root@ford src]# cd LPRng-3.6.26
```

Once you are in the directory, you will need to configure LPRng using the tools that come with the package. Most of the default options work nicely under Linux, so the only thing you will want to alter as part of the configuration step is the directories into which LPRng gets installed. To remain consistent with existing installations, you'll want to put all of the binaries relative to the **/usr** directory and the configuration files in the **/etc** directory. This is done with the following call to **configure**:

```
[root@ford LPRng-3.6.26]# ./configure --prefix=/usr --sysconfdir=/etc
```

With LPRng configured, you now want to build it using **make**, like so:

```
[root@ford LPRng-3.6.26]# make clean all
```

Once LPRng is compiled, you can install it like so:

```
[root@ford LPRng-3.6.26]# make install
```

For this chapter, we assume that you have installed LPRng using the above **configure** statement and thus have all of the binaries installed relative to the **/usr** directory. Here are the programs you've installed and their functions:

Program	Purpose
/usr/sbin/lpd	This is the print server daemon.
/usr/bin/lpr	This client tool is used for submitting print jobs.
/usr/bin/lpq	Checks the status of the print queues.
/usr/bin/lprm	Removes print jobs sitting on the queue.
/usr/sbin/lpc	Controls the print server daemon.
/usr/bin/lpstat	Shows the status of the printers.
/etc/printcap	Lists printers in the system.

Program	Purpose
/etc/lpd.conf	This file contains the LPRng configuration options used by both clients and servers.
/etc/lpd.perms	This file contains the permission information used by the **lpd** server to control user actions.
/usr/sbin/checkpc	Checks the configuration of the print system.

Starting LPRng on Boot

It is likely that your installation already has the necessary startup and shutdown scripts for the LPRng server, **lpd**. If you aren't sure, check the **/etc/rc.d/init.d** directory and look for the **lpd** file. If it isn't there, you will need to add one. A simple startup and shutdown script for **lpd** is as follows:

```
#!/bin/sh
case "$1" in
  start)
        # Start daemons.
        echo "Starting lpd: \c"; /usr/sbin!/lpd; echo;
        ;;
  stop)
        # Stop daemons.
        echo "Shutting down lpd: \c"
        server=`ps -C lpd | sed '1d' | awk '{print $1}'`
        if [ -n "$server" ]; then
            echo " lpd server pid $server";
            kill $server;
        else
            echo " no lpd server active";
        fi;
        ;;
  *)
        echo "Usage: lpd {start|stop}"
        exit 1
        ;;
esac
```

Also be sure there are appropriate symlinks from the **rc** directories. See Chapter 7 for details on startup and shutdown scripts.

Fixing Man Pages for Red Hat 7

If you did opt to install a newer release of LPRng on Red Hat 7, then you will need to adjust the installed man pages so that they are found. Since for whatever reason Red Hat felt it necessary to place man pages in **/usr/share/man**, be sure that you either move the installed LPRng man pages from **/usr/man** to **/usr/share/man** or you have your users' MANPATH environment variable include **/usr/man**. (For more information on environment variables, see Chapter 6.)

Restarting LPD on a Live System

If you have an already running system, there is no reason for you to have to shut down the system and restart it for the new printer daemon to take effect. Simply stop the existing daemon and start the new one. If you installed the startup script in **/etc/rc.d/init.d**, the process is as simple as running this:

```
[root@ford /root]# /etc/rc.d/init.d/lpd stop; /etc/rc.d/init.d/lpd start
```

Installing ifhp

LPRng supports the notion of *filters* as a way of performing pre-processing of files on their way to the printer. One of these filters is called **ifhp**.

What makes **ifhp** special is that it is a well-designed, general purpose file-type converter, able to take postscript files and convert them into the appropriate format for specific non-postscript printers. A common use of this filter is to allow desktop printers, such as HP's DeskJet, to be connected directly to a Linux system and make it appear as if it were just another postscript printer. If you have a non-postscript printer, you will need to download and install this package.

> **NOTE:** The **ifhp** package does not come with Red Hat 7 by default.

Begin by downloading the latest version of **ifhp** from ftp://ftp.astart.com/pub/LPRng/FILTERS. As of this writing, the latest version is **ifhp-3.4.2.tgz**. Assuming you have downloaded it to **/usr/local/src**, unpack it like so:

```
[root@ford src]# tar -xvzf ifhp-3.4.2.tgz
```

This will create a directory called **ifhp-3.4.2** into which the source code will be unpacked. Change into that directory and run **configure** with the same **--prefix** and **--sysconfdir** that you used for LPRng. If you are running Red Hat 7, the steps will look like this:

```
[root@ford src]# cd ifhp-3.4.2
[root@ford ifhp-3.4.2]# ./configure --prefix=/usr --sysconfdir=/etc
```

This will configure **ifhp** for your system. Once it is configured, you can compile the source code and install the binaries like so:

```
[root@ford ifhp-3.4.2]# make; make install
```

This will install the filter into **/usr/libexec/filters** and the **ifhp.conf** file into **/etc**. The details of using this package will be discussed in the following section.

CONFIGURING /ETC/PRINTCAP

The **/etc/printcap** file tells the LPRng server daemon (**lpd**) the names and characteristics of all of its printers. Every printer has an entry that looks something like this:

```
printername1|printername2|printername3:
    :command=value:
    :command:
    :command=value:
```

where **printername1** is the name of the printer, and **printername2** and **printername3** are aliases to **printername1**. Each **command** may be followed by a value.

Before we see what the final printcap file will look like, take a look at Table 21-1, which gets into the details of what each parameter in the printer configuration means. Note that this is a simplified list. You can read about the complete configuration options in the LPRng-HOWTO guide available on the Web at http://www.astart.com/LPRng/LPRng.html or in the HOWTO subdirectory of the source code.

Command	Purpose/Value
sd	Spool directory pathname. This is where the **lpd** server will place files that are being sent to the printer. Since it is possible for it to receive a new file while one is still being printed, **lpd** will queue those new files in this specified directory. Typically, this directory is **/var/spool/ lpd/**_printername_ where _printername_ is the name of the printer (e.g., sd=/var/spool/lpd/cydonia). As the files get printed, **lpd** will automatically remove them. If you expect a printer to get a lot of volume, you will want to be sure that this directory has enough space to hold all of the queued documents.
sh	Suppress banner pages. Banner pages show who printed the document and the name of the document. The idea behind this is to allow jobs arriving at high-volume printers to be easily sorted by whomever gets to the printer first. Most sites find that banner pages are not worth the wasted paper and prefer to keep this feature turned off.

Table 21-1. Commands Available in the **/etc/printcap** File for Each Printer

Command	Purpose/Value
rm	Specify the remote host. Since **lpd** can redirect print jobs to other print servers, it must be possible to specify the name of the remote print server. This command lets you do so. This is typically used in conjunction with the **rp** command.
rp	Specify the remote printer queue. When redirecting print jobs to a remote print server, you need to specify the name of the remote print queue to which you want to submit the job, as well. Typically, this is because dedicated print servers control multiple printers. This command will let you specify the name of the print queue. (Note: If you are printing to a network-enabled printer, such as an HP LaserJet with JetDirect, you do not need to specify the remote print queue.)
mx	Maximum job size in 1K blocks. 0 means no size limit.
lp	Specify the local output device (e.g. **/dev/lp0**). If your printer is connected locally, you need to specify the device name by which it can be accessed. Most printers that have a parallel port can be accessed through the **/dev/lp0** device. You will probably want to specify a filter with this parameter.
filter	Specify the filter to pass through before sending data to the local output device. You can consider a filter to be the logical equivalent to a printer driver under Windows. UNIX systems (Linux included) have a long history of working directly with postscript, and because most of the original typesetters were driven by UNIX systems, postscript became the de facto standard. (The "official" reason why UNIX was first developed at Bell Labs was so that the Patent Department could drive a typesetter. For more details, see Chapter 5 in *A Quarter Century of Unix* by Peter H. Salus (Addison-Wesley, 1994).) If your printer already understands postscript, then you can probably leave this alone. On the other hand, if your printer does not understand postscript, you will need a filter that convert postscript into your printer's format. The **ifhp** filter (available at ftp://ftp.astart.com/pub/LPRng/FILTERS) should cover just about all of the cases you can give it.

Table 21-1. Commands Available in the **/etc/printcap** File for Each Printer *(continued)*

For example, in the following **/etc/printcap** file, the printer's name is myprinter, and its alias is lp:

```
myprinter|lp:
    :sd=/var/spool/lpd/lp:
    :sh:
    :rm=intrepid:
    :rp=engprint:
```

You can have multiple printers listed in this file, like so:

```
cydonia|lp:
    :sd=/var/spool/lpd/lp:
    :sh:
    :rm=intrepid:
    :rp=engprint:
orblivion:lp2:
    :sd=/var/spool/lpd/lp2:
    :sh:
    :rm=intrepid:
    :rp=zaphod:
```

In this case, there are two printers: One is called cydonia, and the other is called orblivion.

Sample /etc/printcap Files

Here are some example configuration files that have been tested and shown to work. (Some of them are even in production use!) As you can see, the configuration files on a per-printer basis are actually quite straightforward.

▼ An HP LaserJet that supports postscript connected directly to your network:

```
cydonia|lp:
    :sd=/var/spool/lpd/lp:
    :mx#0:
    :rm=zaphod:
```

 An HP DeskJet 550C connected directly to your parallel port:

```
pommefritz|lp:
    :sd=/var/spool/lpd/lp:
    :mx#0:
    :lp=/dev/lp0:
    :ifhp=model=ghostscript,gs_device=cdj550:
    :filter=/usr/libexec/filters/ifhp:
```

▲ A postscript printer named psb connected to a print server called acen:

```
psb|lp:
        :sd=/var/spool/lpd/lp:
        :mx#0:
        :rm=acen:
        :rp=psb:
```

NOTE: For more information on what types of printers you can use with the **ifhp** filter, visit the Ghostscript Web site at http://www.cs.wisc.edu/~ghost/printer.html.

Implementing Your Changes

Once you update the **/etc/printcap** file, you need to restart **lpd** in order for your changes to take effect. To do that, find the process ID (PID) of the line printer daemon with this command:

```
[root@ford /root]# ps -C lpd
```

Then issue a **kill** statement to kill the process, like so:

```
[root@ford /root]# kill XXXX
```

where **XXXX** is the PID of **lpd**. (Of course, the PID number won't necessarily be four digits long.) Then restart **lpd**:

```
[root@ford /root]# /usr/bin/lpd
```

TIP: If you have Red Hat Linux, you can simply run the following instead of killing the process and restarting it by hand:

```
[root@ford /root]# /etc/rc.d/init.d/lpd restart
```

THE /ETC/LPD.PERMS FILE

The **/etc/lpd.perms** file allows you to control who can print to your print server. The file itself consists of a series of rules that are evaluated one at a time, in order. The first rule to match decides whether the request can or cannot be processed. The last rule should always indicate a default behavior. Any line in the **/etc/lpd.perms** file that begins with a number sign (#) is a comment.

The simplest configuration is to accept all requests. To accomplish this, the only uncommented line in the **/etc/lpd.perms** file should be

```
DEFAULT ACCEPT
```

The remainder of this section discusses more complex rules you can establish and ends with a sample set of rules you can use.

The Format of /etc/lpd.perms

The format of each rule line in the **/etc/lpd.perms** file can take one of the four following forms:

```
ACTION [not] KEY                    assigned value
ACTION [not] KEY=pattern            substring match
ACTION [not] KEY=IP/mask            IP address (with optional netmask)
```

where *ACTION* is either ACCEPT or REJECT; the **not** keyword is optional and if present, it negates the *KEY*; and the *KEY* specifies the rule we are checking against with possible parameters (*pattern* or *IP/mask*).

Confused? Don't worry, it takes everyone a few tries to understand. Let's step through a quick example to see what's going on. Say you want to refuse connections from your gateway IP address. You would write a rule that looks like this:

```
REJECT SERVICE=X IFIP=192.168.1.1
```

The action is to REJECT. There are two checks that need to match in order for the action to occur: first, the service must be a connection request (**SERVICE=X**), and second, the IP address must be 192.168.1.1 (your gateway). If these two are true, then the connection is rejected.

Taking the same example and making it more complex, let's say that you want to reject all connection requests not from your local area network (192.168.1.0/24) nor from the server itself. The rule would look like this:

```
REJECT SERVICE=X NOT IFIP=192.168.1.0/24,127.0.0.1/32
```

The action is REJECT. If the service is a connection request (**SERVICE=X**) and the IP is not in the 192.168.1.0/24 network and the IP is not 127.0.0.1, then the rule matches, and the connection is refused.

Defaults

The default behavior should always be defined. This one command breaks the standard rule format by starting with the command rather than the action. The format of **default** is as follows:

```
DEFAULT action
```

where *action* is either ACCEPT or REJECT.

Permission Keywords

With the exception out of the way, let's go through the most common keywords and their meanings. You can find the entire list and more examples in Chapter 17 of the LPRng HOWTO.

▼ **SERVICE** Tells us what services to match against. The types of services that can be matched are:

Key	Request
C	LPC Control Request
M	**lprm** Removal Request
P	Printing
Q	**Lpq** Status Request
R	**lpr** Job Transfer
X	Connection request

If you have an LPC request, you can add an LPC= clause to refine the permissions checking to allow or disallow **lpc** commands such as lpc status, printcap, active, etc. For example:

```
# Accept all lpq status requests
ACCEPT SERVICE=Q
# Reject requests to run lpc status
REJECT SERVICE=C LPC=status
# Accept everything
ACCEPT SERVICE=*
```

■ **USER** Specify which user may perform (or be rejected) for certain services. For example, to reject print requests from all users except root, you would issue this command:

```
ACCEPT SERVICE=P USER=root
REJECT SERVICE=P
```

Remember that rules are evaluated in order. Thus if root submits a print job, the first rule will match, and the print request will be accepted. If the user is not root, the second line will be evaluated, and thus all print requests from other users will be rejected.

▲ **HOST** Specify hosts for a particular action. For example, if you only want connection requests from hosts in the example.net domain, you could say:

```
ACCEPT SERVICE=P HOST=*.example.net
REJECT SERVICE=P
```

Example of /etc/lpd.perms

A common configuration is to allow your local network users to submit jobs, remove jobs, and check the status of their jobs. However, you don't want any remote users controlling the printers, and you certainly don't want any non-local network users to be submitting print jobs. This is the resulting configuration file:

```
ACCEPT SERVICE=M HOST=192.168.1.0/24
ACCEPT SERVICE=P HOST=192.168.1.0/24
ACCEPT SERVICE=Q HOST=192.168.1.0/24
ACCEPT SERVICE=R HOST=192.168.1.0/24
ACCEPT SERVICE=X HOST=192.168.1.0/24
ACCEPT SERVICE=C HOST=127.0.0.1/32 USER=root
DEFAULT REJECT
```

CLIENTS OF LPD

There are several peripheral tools that work along with **lpd** as clients. They are discussed in the following sections.

lpr

Under Linux, **lpr** is the command-line tool for performing printing operations. Most applications that offer printing services mask **lpr** behind a dialog box under X Windows.

Using **lpr** is pretty straightforward; simply type

```
[root@ford /root]# lpr filename
```

where *filename* is the name of the file you want to print. This command sends the file to the default printer (the first printer listed in the **/etc/printcap** file). If you want to send the job to another printer, use the **-P** option, like so:

```
[root@ford /root]# lpr -P printername filename
```

where *printername* is the name of the printer and *filename* is the name of the file you want to print.

Table 21-2 shows all the options available for use with **lpr**.

lpr Options	Description
-P	Send job to another printer (not the default printer).
-m	Send mail upon completion of the job.

Table 21-2. Options Available with `lpr`

`lpr` Options	Description
`-r`	Remove the file once it's been spooled for printing. (This parameter may not be used together with the `-s` option.)
`-s`	Instead of making a copy of the file for the spool, use symbolic links instead. Note: If you use this option, you cannot change the file in any way until the print job is complete; however, this is a handy option for very large files.
`-#n`	Specifies number of copies to print of each file listed; *n* is the number of copies.
`-i cols`	Indent the printed output by *cols* number of columns.

Table 21-2. Options Available with `lpr` *(continued)*

Most of the time, the only parameter you'll use with `lpr` is `-P`, which is helpful when you need to print to a printer other than your default.

lpq

The `lpq` program lists all jobs queued for the printer in the order in which they will be printed. Typically, the first job listed is actively printing. The exception is, of course, when there is a problem with the printer itself.

The only command-line parameter needed with `lpq` is the `-P` option, which is used to specify which printer's queue you want to see. The default for `lpq` is the first printer listed in the **/etc/printcap** file. Here's an example that shows what's listed in the queue for the printer zaphod:

```
[root@ford /root]# lpq -P zaphod
```

lprm

The `lprm` tool allows you to remove print jobs that have entered the print queue but have not yet started printing. Here are the command-line parameters for `lprm`.

`lprm` Parameter	Description
`-P printername`	Specifies the printer (*printername*) from which the print job should be removed. Otherwise, the default printer (the first one listed in the **/etc/printcap** file) is assumed.

lprm Parameter	Description
-	Removes all jobs that the user owns from the specified printer.
number	Removes job *number* from the queue. If you aren't sure what your job number is, use the **lpq** command to see what the print queue says.

Here's an example of an **lprm** command to remove job number 17 from the printer named zaphod:

```
[root@ford /root]# lprm -P zaphod 17
```

SUMMARY

This chapter explained how to set up the printer server software (**lpd**) under Linux, and described the corresponding client tools for use along with the software. We also discussed the required configuration files for securing your printer (**/etc/lpd.perms**) and defining what printers are available (**/etc/printcap**). However, we were only able to scratch the surface of the LPRng feature list. I highly recommend you read the LPRng HOWTO that comes with the source code distribution in the **HOWTO** directory. It's long (about 1MB), but well worth the read, as it includes more details on security options and integration with Windows environments via Samba.

Once you have printing set up on your Linux server, you'll find that it does its job very nicely and lets you focus on new and interesting challenges. Problems that arise with printing services afterward typically point to problems with the printer itself, such as paper jams and user abuse.

CHAPTER 22

DHCP

Configuring IP addresses for a handful of servers is a fairly simple task. However, manually configuring IP addresses for an entire department, building, or enterprise of heterogeneous systems can be daunting.

The Linux DHCP (Dynamic Host Configuration Protocol) client and server can assist with these tasks. The client machine is configured to obtain its IP address from the network. When the DHCP client software is started, it broadcasts a request onto the network for an IP address. If all goes well, a DHCP server on the network will respond, issuing an address and other necessary information to complete the client's network configuration.

Such dynamic addressing is also useful for configuring mobile or temporary machines. Folks who travel from office to office can plug their machines into the local network and obtain an appropriate address for their location.

In this chapter, we'll cover the process of configuring a DHCP server and client. This includes compiling and installing the necessary software and then walking through the process of writing a configuration file for it. At the end of the chapter, we'll step through a complete sample configuration.

> **TIP:** DHCP is a standard. Thus, any operating system that can communicate with other DHCP servers and clients can work with the Linux DHCP tools. One common solution that includes using the Linux DHCP server component is in office environments where there are a large number of Windows-based clients. The Windows systems can be configured to use DHCP and contact the Linux server to get their IP address. This reduces the need for yet another Windows NT server and the associated licensing costs surrounding it.

The Roots of DHCP

Long before the fad of network computers (NCs), and back when disk storage space was at a premium cost, network workstation manufacturers built machines with no local hard drives, mounting them from a shared server instead. These "diskless" machines would boot using a protocol known as BOOTP (Boot Protocol), obtaining their addresses from a server. The Dynamic Host Configuration Protocol (DHCP) was originally derived from the BOOTP protocol. In fact, much of the DHCP protocol was taken directly from BOOTP.

THE MECHANICS OF DHCP

When a client is configured to obtain its address from the network, it asks for an address in the form of a DHCP request. A DHCP server listens for client requests. Once a request is received, it checks its local database, and it issues an appropriate response. The response always includes the address and can include name servers, a network mask, and a default gateway. The client accepts the response from the server and configures its local settings accordingly.

The DHCP server maintains a list of addresses it can issue. Each address is issued with an associated *lease*, which dictates how long a client is allowed to use the address before it must contact the server to renew the address. When the lease expires, the client is not allowed to use the address.

The implementation of the Linux DHCP server includes several key features common to many DHCP server implementations. The server can be configured to issue any free address from a pool of addresses or to issue a specific address to a specific machine. In addition to serving DHCP requests, the Linux DHCP server also serves BOOTP requests.

THE DHCP SERVER

DHCPD, the DHCP server, is responsible for serving IP addresses and other relevant information upon client request. Since the DHCP protocol is broadcast-based, a server will have to be present on each subnet for which DHCP service is to be provided.

Downloading, Compiling, and Installing a DHCP Server

The ISC DHCP server is the de facto implementation for UNIX machines. This version is released with many Linux distributions. If it has not been found in a distribution, the sources for the ISC DHCP server can be obtained from the ISC site at http://www.isc.org. As of this writing, the most current version of the server is 3.0b1pl0.

Once the package is downloaded, unpack the software as shown. For this example, assume the source directory is **/usr/local/src**:

```
[root@delirium src]#  tar -xfvz dhcp-3.0b1pl0.tar.gz
```

Enter the directory and configure the package with the **configure** command:

```
[root@delirium dhcp-3.0b1pl0]#  ./configure
```

Currently, **--with-nsupdate** is the only optional parameter available to the **config-ure** command. This option is invoked if BIND 8.2 is installed and if dynamic DNS support is desired in the DHCP server.

To compile and install, issue the **make; make install** commands:

```
[root@delirium dhcp-3.0b1pl0]#  make; make install
```

Configuring the DHCP Server

The default primary configuration file of the ISC DHCP server is **/etc/dhcpd.conf**. The configuration file encapsulates two ideas:

▼   A set of declarations to describe the networks, hosts, or groups attached to the system and possibly the range of addresses issuable to each respective entity. Multiple declarations can be used to describe multiple groups of clients. Declarations can also be nested in one another when multiple concepts are needed to describe a set of clients or hosts.

▲   A set of parameters that describe the behavior of the server and configure appropriate responses. Parameters can be global, or local to a set of declarations.

NOTE: Since every site has a unique network with unique addresses, it is necessary that every site be set up with its own configuration file. If this is the first time you are dealing with DHCP, you might want to start with the sample configuration file presented toward the end of this chapter and modify it to match your network's characteristics.

Like most configuration files in UNIX, the file is ASCII text and can be modified using your favorite text editor. The general structure of the configuration file is as follows:

```
Global parameters;
Declaration1
    [parameters related to declaration1]
    [nested sub declaration]

Declaration2
    [parameters related to declaration2]
    [nested sub declaration]
```

As this outline indicates, a declaration block groups a set of clients. Different parameters can be applied to each block of the declaration.

Declarations

We may want to group different clients for several reasons, such as organizational requirements, network layout, and administrative domains. To assist with grouping these clients, we introduce the following declarations.

Group   Individually listing parameters and declarations for each host again and again can make the configuration file difficult to manage. The **group** declaration allows you to apply a set of parameters and declarations to a list of clients, shared networks, or subnets. The syntax for the **group** declaration is as follows:

```
group label
    [parameters]
    [subdeclarations]
```

where **label** is a user-defined name for identifying the group. The **parameter** block contains a list of parameters that are applied to the group. The **subdeclarations** are used in the event that a further level of granularity is needed to describe any additional clients that may be a member of the current declaration.

Ignore the parameter field for now. We will go into further detail about it in the upcoming "Parameters" section.

Host   A **host** declaration is used to apply a set of parameters and declarations to a particular host in addition to the parameters specified for the group. This is commonly used for fixed address booting, or for the BOOTP clients. The syntax for a **host** declaration is as follows:

```
host label
    [parameters]
    [subdeclarations]
```

The **label** is the user-defined name for the host group. The **parameters** and **subdeclarations** are as described in the **group** declaration.

Shared-Network   A **shared-network** declaration groups a set of addresses of members of the same physical network. This allows parameters and declarations to be grouped for administrative purposes. The syntax is

```
shared-network label
    [parameters]
    [subdeclarations]
```

The **label** is the user-defined name for the shared network. The **parameters** and **subdeclarations** are as described in the previous declaration.

Subnet   The **subnet** declaration is used to apply a set of parameters and/or declarations to a set of addresses that match the description of this declaration. The syntax is as follows:

```
subnet subnet-number netmask netmask
    [parameters]
    [subdeclarations]
```

The **subnet-number** is the network that you want to declare as being the source of IP addresses for giving to individual hosts. The **netmask** is the netmask (see Chapter 24 for more details on netmasks) for the subnet. The *parameters* and *subdeclarations* are as described in the previous declaration.

Range   For dynamic booting, the **range** declaration specifies the range of addresses that are valid to issue to clients. The syntax is as follows:

```
range [dynamic-bootp] starting-address [ending-address] ;
```

The **dynamic-bootp** keyword is used to alert the server that the following range of addresses is for the BOOTP protocol. The *starting-address* and optional *ending-address* fields are the actual addresses of the start and end blocks of IP addresses. The blocks are assumed to be consecutive and in the same subnet of addresses.

Parameters

We introduced this concept briefly earlier in the chapter. Turning on these parameters will alter the behavior of the server for the relevant group of clients. We'll discuss these parameters in the following section.

always-reply-rfc1048   This parameter's syntax is as follows:

```
always-reply-rfc1048;
```

This is used primarily for BOOTP clients. There are BOOTP clients that require the response from the server to be fully BOOTP RFC–compliant. Turning on this parameter ensures that this requirement is met.

authoritative   This parameter's syntax is as follows:

```
authoritative;
not authoritative;
```

The **authoritative** parameter is used to tag a particular network as "authoritative." By default, the server will assume that it's authoritative. When a network segment is "not authoritative," the server will send a DHCPNAK back to a client. The client will presumably retry its request at that time.

default-lease-time   This parameter's syntax is as follows:

```
default-lease-time seconds;
```

The value of *seconds* is the lease time allocated to the issued IP address if the client did not request any duration.

dynamic-bootp-lease-cutoff   This parameter's syntax is as follows:

```
dynamic-bootp-lease-cutoff date;
```

BOOTP clients are not aware of the *lease* concept. By default, the DHCP server assigns an IP address that never expires. There are certain situations where it may be useful to have the server stop issuing addresses for a set of BOOTP clients. In those cases, this parameter is used.

The *date* is specified in the form *W YYYY/MM/DD HH:MM:SS*, where *W* is the day of the week in cron format (0=Sunday, 6=Saturday), *YYYY* is the year, *MM* is the month (01=January, 12=December), *DD* is the date in two-digit format, *HH* is the two-digit hour in 24-hour format (0=Midnight, 23=11pm), MM is the the two-digit representation of minutes; and *SS* is a two-digit representation of the seconds.

dynamic-bootp-lease-length   This parameter's syntax is as follows:

```
dynamic-bootp-lease-length seconds;
```

Although the BOOTP clients don't have a mechanism for expiring the addresses they receive, it's sometimes safe to have the server assume that they aren't using the address anymore, thus freeing it for further use. This is useful if the BOOTP application is known to be short in duration. If so, the server can set the number of **seconds** accordingly and expire it after that time has past.

CAUTION: Use caution with this option, as it may introduce problems if it issues an address before another host has stopped using it.

filename   This parameter's syntax is as follows:

```
filename filename;
```

In some applications, the DHCP client may need to know the name of a file to use to boot. This is often combined with **next-server** to retrieve a remote file for installation configuration or diskless booting.

fixed-address   This parameter's syntax is as follows:

```
fixed-address  address [, address ·];
```

This parameter appears only under the **host** declaration. It specifies the set of addresses assignable to the client.

get-lease-hostname   This parameter's syntax is as follows:

```
get-lease-hostname [true | false];
```

If set to true, the server will resolve all addresses in the declaration scope and use that for the **hostname** option.

hardware   This parameter's syntax is as follows:

```
hardware [ethernet|token-ring] hardware-address;
```

In order for the server to identify a specific host, the **hardware** parameter must be used. The ***hardware-address*** (sometimes referred to as the MAC address) is the physical address of the interface, typically a set of hexadecimal octets delimited by colons. This parameter is used for fixed-address DHCP clients and is required for BOOTP clients.

max-lease-time   This parameter's syntax is as follows:

```
max-lease-time seconds;
```

A client has the option to request the duration of the lease. The request is granted as long as the lease time doesn't exceed the number of seconds specified by this option. Otherwise, it's granted a lease to the maximum of the number of seconds specified here.

next-server   This parameter's syntax is as follows:

```
next-server server-name;
```

When booting from the network, a client can be given a filename (specified by the filename parameter) and a server from which to obtain booting information. This server is specified with the **next-server** parameter.

server-identifier   This parameter's syntax is as follows:

```
server-identifier hostname;
```

Part of the DHCP response is the address for the server. On multihomed systems, the DHCP server issues the address of the first interface. Unfortunately, this interface may not be reachable by all clients of a server or declaration scope. In those rare instances, this parameter can be used to send the IP of the proper interface that the client should communicate to the server.

server-name   This parameter's syntax is as follows:

```
server-name name;
```

where ***name*** is the host name of the server that is being booted by a remote booting client. This parameter is used for remote clients or network install applications.

use-host-decl-names   This parameter's syntax is as follows:

```
use-host-decl-names [true|false];
```

This parameter is used in the same scope of other host declarations. It will add the **host-name** option to the **host** declaration, using the host name in the declaration for the option host.

use-lease-addr-for-default-route   This parameter's syntax is as follows:

```
use-lease-addr-for-default-route [true|false];
```

Some network configurations use a technique known as *ProxyARP* so that a host can keep track of other hosts that are outside its subnet. If your network is configured to support ProxyARP, you'll want to configure your client to use itself as a default route. This will force it to use *ARP* (the Address Resolution Protocol) to find all remote (off the subnet) addresses.

CAUTION: The `use-lease-addr-for-default-route` command should be used with caution. Not every client can be configured to use its own interface as a default route.

Options

Currently, the DHCP server supports more than 60 options. The general syntax of an option is as follows:

```
option option-name [modifiers]
```

Table 22-1 summarizes the most commonly used DHCP options.

Option	Description
`broadcast-address`	An address on the client's subnet specified as the broadcast address
`domain-name`	The domain name the client should use as the local domain name when performing host lookups
`domain-name-servers`	The list of DNS servers for the client to use to resolve host names
`host-name`	The string used to identify the name of the client
`nis-domain`	The NIS domain name (see Chapter 19)
`nis-servers`	A list of the available NIS servers to bind to
`routers`	A list of routers the client is to use in order of preference
`subnet-mask`	The netmask the client is to use

Table 22-1.   Common DHCP Options

A Sample dhcpd.conf File

The following is an example of a simple DHCP configuration file.

```
subnet 192.168.1.0 netmask 255.255.255.0
        # Options
        option routers 192.168.1.1;
        option subnet-mask 255.255.255.0;

        option domain-name "uidzero.com";
        option domain-name-servers delirium.uidzero.com;

        # Parameters
        default-lease-time 21600;
        max-lease-time 43200;

        # Declarations
        range dynamic-bootp 192.168.1.25 192.168.1.49;

        # Nested declarations
        host vertigo
            hardware ethernet 00:80:c6:f6:72:00;
            fixed-address 192.168.1.50;
```

In this example, a single subnet is defined. The DHCP clients are instructed to use 192.168.1.1 as their default route and 255.255.255.0 as their subnet mask. DNS information is passed to the clients; they will use uidzero.com as their domain name and delirium.uidzero.com as their DNS server. A lease time of 21600 seconds is set, but if the clients request a longer lease, they may be granted a lease that can last as long as 43200 seconds. The range of IP addresses issued starts at 192.168.1.25 and can go as high as 192.168.1.49. The machine with a MAC address of 00:80:c6:f6:72:00 will always get assigned the IP address 192.168.1.50.

General Runtime Behavior

Once started, the daemon patiently waits for a client request to arrive prior to performing any processing. When a request is processed and an address is issued, it keeps track of the address in a file called **dhcpd.leases**. In the event of a server failure, the contents of this file are used to keep track of the addresses that have been issued to specific clients.

THE DHCP CLIENT DAEMON

DHCPCD, the client daemon included with many popular Linux distributions, is the software component used to talk to a DHCP server described in the previous sections. If invoked, it will attempt to obtain an address from an available DHCP server and then configure its networking configuration accordingly.

Downloading, Compiling, and Installing a DHCP Client

In the event that the DHCPCD software is not already part of your Linux distribution, it can be obtained, compiled, and installed manually. The Linux DHCP client included with many Linux distributions can be found at http://www.phystech.com/download. As of this writing, the most current version of the software is 1.3.18-pl1.

Once downloaded, the package should be unpacked as shown:

```
[root@delirium src]# tar -xfvz dhcpcd-1.3.18-pl1.tar.gz
```

The current version of the software is not bundled with the GNU configure utility; however, its configuration is fairly simple. Edit the makefile to ensure that the proper flags are set. This can be done by running **emacs**, **vi**, or even **pico**. Run the **make** utility when done to build the client daemon. Installation is completed by using the **make install** command.

Configuring the DHCP Client

The client is typically run from the startup files, but it can also be run by hand. It's typically started prior to other network services, since other network services aren't started if the DHCP client daemon can't obtain an address. Refer to Chapter 7 for more details on creating a startup script.

On the other hand, the client can be invoked at the command line after startup. The client daemon can be started without additional options. If successful, the client will make a copy of itself in background mode and quit. Older versions print out the assigned address. Here is how to start the client from the command line:

```
[root@delirium root]# dhcpcd
```

Optionally, the client daemon can be started with additional flags that slightly modify the behavior of the software. The full syntax of the command is shown here:

```
dhcpcd [-dkrDHR] [-t timeout] [-c filename] [-h hostname]
[-i vendorClassID] [-I clientID] [-l leasetime] [interface]
```

The options are described in detail in Table 22-2.

Option	Description
-c *filename*	The client daemon will execute the specified filename after obtaining and configuring its networking. This is useful if there are services that need to be started only after the network has been configured. Typically, most network services can be started without the network being present and should behave properly when the network becomes configured.
-d	This flag turns on debug mode. In debug mode, DHCPCD will provide verbose output to syslog.
-D	If invoked with this option, DHCPCD will set the local machine's domain name to that specified by the server. The client does not do this by default.
-i *vendorClassID*	Provides additional information for the DHCP server. The vendor class is a string that can be used to help the server classify the client into a particular group. By default, DHCPCD sends system name, system release, and machine type as a string.
-I *clientID*	Instead of sending the ethernet address, you can force the client to send another identifier string. Most servers use the ethernet address as an identifier, but there are exceptions.
-h *hostname*	Includes the specified host name in the DHCP messages sent by DHCPCD. There are DHCP servers that can be configured to accept DHCP messages from a set list of clients.
-H	Forces DHCPCD to set the host name to that specified by the server. The client does not do this by default.
-k	Terminates the currently running DHCPCD client daemon.

Table 22-2.   DHCP Client Options

Option	Description
-l *leasetime*	The requested number of seconds the client wants the DHCP lease. Of course, the server can reject this value and issue a lease time less than the requested value.
-r	If invoked with this option, DHCPCD will act like a BOOTP client. This is for the rare case that there is only a BOOTP client available, or for testing.
-R	By default, DHCPCD will replace the **/etc/resolv.conf** file such that DNS resolution will be configured with the parameters returned by the server. There are situations for which you may not want this to happen. Specifying this option will prevent it.
-t *timeout*	The timeout is the number of seconds DHCPCD will try to obtain an address.
interface	Specifies an interface to have DHCPCD configure. If nothing is specified, DHCPCD will configure the first ethernet interface (eth0).

Table 22-2.   DHCP Client Options *(continued)*

SUMMARY

DHCP is a useful tool for dynamically configuring the addresses for large groups of machines or a mobile workstation. Since DHCP is an open protocol, the architecture and platform of the server and the client are irrelevant.

A computer running Linux can serve DHCP requests. The software to do this is highly configurable and has mechanisms to persist after machine failures.

Software also exists to configure the networking of a Linux machine from a DHCP server on the network. This client daemon has a number of options that make it able to speak to a variety of DHCP servers.

CHAPTER 23

Backups

A server that is not backed up is a disaster waiting to happen. Performing backups is a critical part of any server's maintenance, no matter what operating system you use. In this chapter, we discuss the backup options that come with Linux. Many commercial packages exist as well, and you can purchase them for anywhere from a few hundred to many thousands of dollars. The best package for you depends on your site and its needs.

EVALUATING YOUR BACKUP NEEDS

Developing a backup solution is no trivial task. It requires that you consider the interactions among all the parts of your network, the servers, and the resources distributed among them. Even trickier is deciding the order in which backups are performed. For example, if you want to back up multiple partitions in parallel, you could end up losing the benefits of that parallelism if there is contention on the SCSI bus! And, of course, you must arrange for backups to occur regularly and to be verified regularly.

Unfortunately, no cookbook solution exists for setting up network backup. Every organization has different needs based on its site(s), its network, and its growth pattern. To make an educated decision, you need to consider the following questions:

▼ How much data do you need to back up?

■ What kind of hardware will you use for the backup process?

■ How much network throughput do you need to support?

■ How quickly must the data be recovered?

■ How often is data expected to be recovered?

▲ What kind of tape management do you need?

How Much Data?

Determining an accurate count of the data to be backed up is the most important issue for estimating your network backup needs. What makes this question tough to answer is that you must include anticipated growth in your determination. Given that most shops have tight purse strings, when planning for backup, it's always wise to try and plan as far ahead as financially possible.

It is also important to consider how often your data changes and with what frequency. Data that changes often (such as databases) need to be backed up frequently and quickly, whereas data that rarely if ever changes (such as the **/etc** directory) doesn't need to be backed up often (if ever).

What Kind of Hardware?

Selecting the backup media can be tricky. Many of the high-density options are appealing for the obvious reason that you can cram more data onto a single tape. Of course, high-capacity tapes typically cost more. Work toward finding an optimum solution that backs up the most system data at the best price, balanced with your requirements for media capacity.

> **NOTE:** Many advertisements for tape drives boast impressive capacities, but keep in mind that these numbers are for the compressed data on the tape, not the actual data. The amount of uncompressed data on the tape is usually about half the compressed capacity. This is important to note, because compression algorithms achieve various levels of compression depending on the type of data being compressed. For example, textual data compresses very well. Certain graphics or sound formats get little to no compression at all. When you estimate the amount of data you can store on a single unit, be sure to consider the mix of data on your servers.

Another aspect of hardware to consider is your tape drive and its relationship to the backup server. Will the tape drive be in contention with other peripherals on the system? For instance, will the tape drive be on the same SCSI chain as a disk that's being backed up? This is extremely important, since it can significantly affect the time it takes to back up a site.

And finally, are you able to feed data to the tape drive fast enough so that it can stream? If the tape drive cannot stream, it will stop writing until it gets more data. This pause may be as long as several seconds on a slow mechanism, while the drive realigns itself with the tape and finds the next available position to write data. Even if the pause is brief, when it occurs thousands of times during a single backup, it can increase your backup runtimes by many hours.

How Much Network Throughput?

Unfortunately, network throughput is easily forgotten in the planning of backup operations. But what good do you get from a really fast backup server and tape drive if you feed in the data through a thin straw?

Take the necessary time to understand your network infrastructure. Look at where the data is coming from and where it's going. Use SNMP tools, such as MRTG (http://www.mrtg.org), to collect statistics about your switches and routers. If you need to back up machines that are connected via hubs, consider a backup sequence that won't back up two machines on the same collision domain at the same time.

Gathering all this information will help you estimate the bandwidth necessary to perform backups. With your analysis done, you'll be able to figure out which upgrades will net you the best return for your money.

What Speed of Recovery?

When requests to restore data from tape arrive, you're likely to be under the gun to get the data back to the user as quickly as possible. How long your users have to wait will depend on the tool used for backup. This means you need to incorporate the cost of response time into your backup evaluation. How much are you willing to spend to get the response time you need for a restore? Obviously, faster restores typically mean higher prices.

NOTE: Although this chapter mentions only tape backups, the issues covered here apply to backup on any other media, such as CD-R or even Zip disks. Each medium has its advantages and disadvantages. CD-Rs and Zip disks offer quick access to data, but they lack the high capacity of tape drives. Pick the medium that works best for your system's needs.

How Often Do I Need to Recover?

Unfortunately, this is a question that too often gets lost in the shuffle. If you have data that needs recovery only once in a blue moon and the speed at which you recover the file is not critical, then you can get away with investing in a less capable system. On the other hand, if you suspect that you'll be doing recoveries often (typically the case in office environments), then investing in a tape drive that gives you the necessary performance on reads is just as important as how quickly you can move the data to the tape in the first place. Having a manager loom over your shoulder while you wait for the tape drive to find a file is never fun…

What Kind of Tape Management?

As the size of your backups grows, so will the need to manage the data you back up. This is where commercial tools often come into play. When evaluating your choices, be sure to consider their indexing and tape management. It does you no good to have 50 tapes worth of data if you can't find the right file. And unfortunately, this problem only gets worse as you start needing more tapes for each night's backups.

MANAGING THE BACKUP DEVICE AND FILES

The tape device interacts with Linux just as most other devices do: as a file. The filename will depend on the type of tape drive, your chosen mode of operation (auto-rewind or non-rewind), and how many drives are attached to the system.

SCSI tape drives, for example, use the following naming scheme:

Device Name	Purpose
`/dev/st`X	Auto-rewinding SCSI tape device; X is the number of the tape drive. Numbering of tape drives is in the order of the drives on the SCSI chain.
`/dev/nst`X	Non-rewinding SCSI tape device; X is the number of the tape drive. Numbering of tape drives is in the order of the drives on the SCSI chain.

Let's say you have a single SCSI tape drive. You can access it using either of these filenames: **/dev/st0** or **/dev/nst0**. If you use **/dev/st0**, the drive will automatically rewind the tape after each file is written to it. If you use **/dev/nst0**, on the other hand, you can write a single file to the tape, mark the end of file, but then stay at the tape's current position. This lets you write multiple files to a single tape.

NOTE: Non-SCSI devices will obviously use a different naming scheme. Unfortunately, there is no standard for naming backup devices if they are not SCSI devices. The QIC-02 tape controller, for example, uses the **/dev/tpqic*** series of filenames. If you use a non-SCSI tape device (which is a rare thing these days), you will need to find its corresponding driver documentation to see what device name it will use.

You may find it handy to create a symbolic link from **/dev/tape** to the appropriate device name for the rewinding mode and a link from **/dev/nrtape** for the non-rewinding mode (for example, **/dev/tape** → **/dev/st0** and **/dev/nrtape**→ **/dev/nst0**). This will make it easier to remember the name of the tape device when issuing commands. See Chapter 6 for information on using the **ln** command to create symbolic links.

What makes these backup device files different from disk files is that there is no file-system structure. Files are continuously written to the tape until it's full or until an end-of-file marker is written. If a tape device is in non-rewind mode, the write head is left in the position immediately after the last end-of-file marker, ready for the next file to be written.

Think of tape devices as similar to a book with chapters. The book's binding and the paper, like the tape itself, provide a place to put the words (the files). It's the markings of the publisher (the backup application) that separate the entire book into smaller subsections (files). If you (the reader) were an auto-rewinding tape drive, you would close the tape every time you were done with a single file and then have to search through the tape to find the next position (chapter) when you're ready to read it. If, however, you were a non-rewinding tape drive, you would leave the tape open to the last page you read.

Using mknod to Create the Device Files

If you don't have the file **/dev/st0** or **/dev/nst0**, you can create one using the **mknod** command. (See Chapter 6 for an explanation of **mknod**.) The major number for SCSI tape drives is 9, and the minor number dictates which drive and whether it is auto-rewinding or not. The numbers 0 through 15 represent drive numbers 0 through 15, auto-rewinding. The numbers 128 through 143 represent drive numbers 0 through 15, non-rewinding. The tape drive is a character device.

So to create **/dev/st0**, we would type this **mknod** command:

```
[root@ford /root]# mknod /dev/st0 c 9 0
```

And to create **/dev/nst0**, we would use this command:

```
[root@ford /root]# mknod /dev/nst0 c 9 128
```

Manipulating the Tape Device with mt

The **mt** program provides simple controls for the tape drive, such as rewinding the tape, ejecting the tape, or seeking a particular file on the tape. In the context of backups, **mt** is most useful as a mechanism for rewinding and seeking.

All of the **mt** actions are specified on the command line. Table 23-1 shows the parameters for the command.

mt Command Parameter	Description
-f *tape_device*	Specifies the tape device. The first non-rewinding SCSI tape device is **/dev/nst0.**
fsf *count*	Forward-spaces a number (***count***) of files. The tape is positioned on the first block of the next file; for example, **fsf 1** would leave the head ready to read the second file of the tape.
asf *count*	Positions the tape at the beginning of the file indicated by ***count***. Positioning is done by first rewinding the tape and then forward-spacing over ***count*** file marks.
rewind	Rewinds the tape.
erase	Erases the tape.
status	Gives the status of the tape.
offline	Brings the tape offline and, if applicable, unloads the tape.
load	Loads the tape (applies to tape changers).
lock	Locks the drive door (only applies to certain tape drives).
unlock	Unlocks the drive door (only applies to certain tape drives).

Table 23-1. Parameters for the **mt** Command

NOTE: If you do not use a non-rewinding tape device, the tape drive will automatically rewind after you perform your operation with **mt**. This can be rather frustrating if you are seeking to a specific file!

▼ To rewind the tape in **/dev/nst0**, use this command:

```
[root@ford /root]# mt -f /dev/nst0 rewind
```

▲ To move the head so that it is ready to read the third file on the tape, use this command:

```
[root@ford /root]# mt -f /dev/nst0 asf 2
```

COMMAND-LINE TOOLS

Linux comes with several tools that help you perform backups. Though they lack administrative front-ends, they are simple to use—and they do the job. Many formal backup packages actually use these utilities as their underlying backup mechanism.

dump and restore

The **dump** tool works by making a copy of an entire file system. The **restore** tool can then take this copy and pull any and all files from it.

To support incremental backups, **dump** uses the concept of *dump levels*. A dump level of 0 means a full backup. Any dump level above zero is an incremental relative to the last time a **dump** with a lower dump level occurred. For example, a dump level of 1 covers all the changes to the file system since the last level 0 dump, a dump level of 2 covers all of the changes to the file system since the last level 1 dump, and so on—all the way through dump level 9.

Consider a case in which you have three dumps: the first is a level 0, the second is a level 1, and the third is also a level 1. The first dump is, of course, a full backup. The second dump (level 1) contains all the changes made since the first dump. The third dump (also a level 1) *also* has all the changes.

The **dump** utility stores all the information about its dumps in the **/etc/dumpdates** file. This file lists each backed up file system, when it was backed up, and at what dump level. Given this information, you can determine which tape to use for a restore. For example, if you perform level 0 dumps on Mondays, level 1 incrementals on Tuesday and Wednesday, and then level 2 incrementals on Thursday and Friday, a file that was last modified on Tuesday but got accidentally erased on Friday can be restored from Tuesday night's incremental backup. A file that was last modified during the preceding week will be on Monday's level 0 tape.

> **NOTE:** The **dump** tool comes with all distributions of Linux. This utility is file-system dependent, and the version for Linux only works on Linux's native file system (ext2).

Using dump

The **dump** tool is a command-line utility. It takes many parameters, but the most relevant are as shown in Table 23-2.

dump Command Parameter	Description
-n	The dump level, where *n* is a number between 0 and 9.
-b *blocksize*	Sets the dump block size to *blocksize*, which is measured in kilobytes. If you are backing up many large files, using a larger block size will increase performance.
-B *count*	Specifies a number (*count*) of records per tape to be dumped. If there is more data to dump than there is tape space, **dump** will prompt you to insert a new tape.
-f *filename*	Specifies a location (*filename*) for the resulting dumpfile. You can make the dumpfile a normal file that resides on another file system, or you can write the dumpfile to the tape device. The SCSI tape device is **/dev/st0**.
-u	Updates the **/etc/dumpdates** file after a successful dump.
-d *density*	The *density* of the tape in bits per inch.
-s *size*	The *size* of the tape in feet.

Table 23-2.   Parameters for the **dump** Command

For example, here is the command to perform a level 0 dump to **/dev/st0** of the **/dev/hda1** file system:

```
[root@ford /root]# dump -0  -f /dev/st0 /dev/hda1
```

Suppressing the Tape Size Calculation   The **dump** tool must know the size of the tape in units of bits per inch and feet per tape. It uses this information to provide multi-volume backups so that it can prompt the operator to insert the next tape when it is ready. But if you don't know the size of your tape in bits per inch and its length in feet, you may still know the dump will fit on the tape. (For example, you may know that the partition you are dumping is 2GB and the tape capacity is 5GB uncompressed.) In this situation, you can do a little trick to keep **dump** from calculating the tape size. Instead of dumping straight to the device, send the output to the standard output, and then use the **cat** program to redirect the dump to the tape. Using the example in the previous section, you would enter this command:

```
[root@ford /root]# dump -0 -f - /dev/hda1 | cat >> /dev/st0
```

Since you're sending the output to standard out, you can also use this opportunity to apply your own compression filters to the stream instead of relying on hardware compression. For example, to use **gzip** to compress your dump, you'd type

```
[root@ford /root]# dump -0 -f - /dev/hda1 | gzip --fast -c >> /dev/st0
```

CAUTION: It's considered dangerous to dump file systems that are being actively used. The only way to be 100% sure that a file system is not in use is by unmounting it first. Unfortunately, very few people can afford the luxury of unmounting a system for the time necessary to do backup. The next best thing is to go through the unappealing task of verifying backups on a regular basis. Verification is best done by testing to see if the **restore** program (discussed in "Using restore" later in this chapter) can completely read the tape and extract files from it. It's tedious, and it isn't fun. But many a system administrator has lost a job over bad backups—don't be one of them!

Using dump to Back Up an Entire System   The **dump** utility works by making an archive of one file system. If your entire system comprises multiple file systems, you need to run **dump** for every file system. Since **dump** creates its output as a single large file, you can store multiple dumps to a single tape by using a non-rewinding tape device.

Assuming we're backing up to a SCSI tape device, **/dev/nst0**, we must first decide which file systems we're backing up. This information is in the **/etc/fstab** file. Obviously, we don't want to back up files such as **/dev/cdrom**, so we skip those. Depending on our data, we may or may not want to back up certain partitions (such as **swap** and **/tmp**).

Let's assume this leaves us with **/dev/hda1**, **/dev/hda3**, **/dev/hda5**, and **/dev/hda6**. To back up these to **/dev/nst0**, compressing them along the way, we would issue the following series of commands:

```
[root@ford /root]# mt -f /dev/nst0 rewind
[root@ford /root]# dump -0uf - /dev/hda1 | gzip --fast -c >> /dev/nst0
[root@ford /root]# dump -0uf - /dev/hda3 | gzip --fast -c >> /dev/nst0
[root@ford /root]# dump -0uf - /dev/hda5 | gzip --fast -c >> /dev/nst0
[root@ford /root]# dump -0uf - /dev/hda6 | gzip --fast -c >> /dev/nst0
[root@ford /root]# mt -f /dev/nst0 rewind
[root@ford /root]# mt -f /dev/nst0 eject
```

The first **mt** command is to make sure the tape is completely rewound and ready to accept data. Then come all the **dump** commands run on the partitions, with their outputs piped through **gzip** before going to the tape. To make the backups go a little faster, the **--fast** option is used with **gzip**. This results in compression that isn't as good as normal **gzip** compression, but it's much faster and takes less CPU time. The **-c** option on **gzip** tells it to send its output to the standard out. We then rewind the tape and eject it.

Using restore

The **restore** program reads the dumpfiles created by **dump** and extracts individual files and directories from them. Although restore is a command-line tool, it does offer a more intuitive interactive mode that lets you go through your directory structure from the tape.

Table 23-3 shows the command-line options for the **restore** utility.

restore Utility Option	Description
-i	Enables interactive mode for **restore**. The utility will read the directory contents of the tape and then give you a shell-like interface in which you can move directories around and tag files you want to recover. When you've tagged all the files you want, **restore** will go through the dump and restore those files. This mode is handy for recovering individual files, especially if you aren't sure which directory they're in.

Table 23-3. Command-Line Options for the **restore** Utility

`restore` Utility Option	Description
`-r`	Rebuilds a file system. In the event you lose everything in a file system (a disk failure, for instance), you can simply re-create an empty file system and restore all the files and directories of the dump.
`-b blocksize`	Sets the dump's block size to **blocksize** kilobytes. If you don't supply this information, **restore** will figure this out for you.
`-f filename`	Reads the dump from the file **filename**.
`-T directory`	Specify the temporary workspace **(directory)** for the restore. The default is **/tmp**.
`-v`	The verbose option; it shows you each step **restore** is taking.
`-y`	In the event of an error, automatically retries instead of asking the user if he or she wants to retry.

Table 23-3.   Command-Line Options for the `restore` Utility *(continued)*

A Typical Restore   A typical invocation of **restore** is as follows:

```
[root@ford /root]# restore -ivf /dev/st0
```

This will pull the dump file from the device **/dev/st0** (the first SCSI tape device), print out each step **restore** takes, and then provide an interactive session for you to decide which files from the dump get restored.

A Complete Restore   Should a complete file system be lost, you can re-create the file system using the **mke2fs** command and then **restore** to populate the file system. For example, let's say our external SCSI drive (**/dev/sda**), which has a single partition on it (**/dev/sda1**), fails. After replacing it with a new drive, we would re-create the file system, like so:

```
[root@ford /root]# mke2fs /dev/sda1
```

Next, we have to mount the partition in the appropriate location. We'll assume this is the /**home** partition, so we type the following:

```
[root@ford /root]# mount /dev/sda1 /home
```

Finally, with the dump tape in the SCSI tape drive (**/dev/st0**), we perform the restoration using the following command:

```
[root@ford /root]# cd /home; restore -rf /dev/st0
```

> **TIP:** If you used **gzip** to compress your dump, you'll need to decompress it before **restore** can do anything with it. Simply tell **gzip** to uncompress the tape device and send its output to the standard out. Standard out should then be piped to **restore**, with the **-f** parameter set to read from standard in. Here's the command:
>
> ```
> [root@ford /root]# gzip -d -c /dev/st0 | restore -ivf -
> ```

tar

In Chapter 6, we discussed the use of **tar** for creating archives of files. What we didn't discuss is the fact that **tar** was originally meant to create archives of files onto tape (**tar** = tape **ar**chive). Because of Linux's flexible approach of treating devices the same as files, we've been using **tar** as a means to archive and unarchive a group of files into a single disk file. Those same **tar** commands could be rewritten to send the files to tape instead.

The **tar** command can archive a subset of files much more easily than **dump** can. The **dump** utility works only with complete file systems, but **tar** can work on mere directories. Does this mean **tar** is better than **dump** for backups? Well, sometimes…

Overall, **dump** turns out to be much more efficient than **tar** at backing up entire file systems. Furthermore, **dump** stores more information about the file, requiring a little more tape space but making recovery that much easier. On the other hand, **tar** is truly cross-platform—a **tar** file created under Linux can be read by the **tar** command under any other UNIX. And **gzip**ped **tar** files can even be read by the WinZip program!

Whether you are better off with **tar** or **dump** depends on your environment and needs.

> **NOTE:** For more information on using **tar**, see Chapter 6.

SUMMARY

Backups are one of the most important aspects of system maintenance. Your systems may be superbly designed and maintained, but without solid backups, the whole package could be gone in a flash. Think of backups as your site's insurance policy.

This chapter covered the fundamentals of tape drives under Linux, along with some of the command-line tools for controlling tape drives and for backing up data to tape drives. With this information, you should be able to perform a complete backup of your system. Thankfully, **dump**, **restore**, and **tar** are not your only options for backup under Linux. Many commercial and noncommercial backup packages exist, as well. High-end packages such as Legato and Veritas have provided Linux backup support for quite some time now and offer some impressive solutions. Simpler programs such as bru and Lonetar are good for the handful of servers that are manageable by a single person.

However you decide to go about the task of backing up your data, just make sure that you do it.

PART V

Advanced Linux Networking

CHAPTER 24

TCP/IP for System Administrators

One of the things that many system administrators miss when learning the ropes is that networks have such a significant role in how we administer our systems that we *have* to learn more about them in order to be effective.

This chapter is an introduction to the guts of Transmission Control Protocol/Internet Protocol, better known as TCP/IP. It is grounded in theory, though I will use real-life examples from **tcpdump**. Ideally, this will give you some ideas of where you can use your knowledge of TCP/IP to troubleshoot system problems.

Please note that the intent of this chapter is not to be a complete replacement for the many books on TCP/IP, but rather an introduction from the standpoint of someone who needs to worry about systems administration. If you want a more complete discussion on TCP/IP, I highly recommend *TCP/IP Illustrated Vol. 1* by Richard Stevens (Addison-Wesley, 1994).

Ethereal: The GUI Packet Analyzer

The **tcpdump** program is a command-line utility that reads raw packets off the network and dissects them into a more human-readable format. It comes with every Linux distribution. You will find many of the examples in this chapter to be quite useful in getting a handle on how to use **tcpdump**, but for more details on its usage, see the man page on **tcpdump**.

Additionally, I highly recommend getting a copy of Ethereal from http://ethereal.zing.org. Unfortunately, Ethereal doesn't seem to be shipping with most Linux distributions, which is a shame; it is a wonderful version of **tcpdump** that provides a graphical interface and better protocol dissectors. From the Ethereal Web site, you can find pre-compiled binaries for various operating systems (including Windows!).

Because Ethereal and **tcpdump** both use the underlying system **libpcap** to capture packets from the network, both programs use the same filter keywords. So as you get a handle of **tcpdump** (or walk through my examples), you can use the same filters in Ethereal to get the same effect. Note that the filters do not include command-line arguments that start with a dash.

THE LAYERS

TCP/IP is built in a layered manner, thus the references to TCP/IP *stacks*. In this section, we take a look at what the TCP/IP layers are, their relationship to one another, and finally, why they really don't match the ISO's seven-layer OSI model. We'll also translate the marketing-speak of the OSI layers into meanings that are relevant to your network.

Packets

At the very bottom of the layering system is the smallest unit of data that networks like dealing with: *packets*. Packets contain both the data that we want to transmit between our systems as well as some control information that helps networking gear determine where the packet should go.

NOTE: The terms "packet" and "frame" are often interchanged when discussing networks. In these situations, people referring to a frame often mean packet. The difference is subtle. A frame is the space in which packets go on a network. At the hardware level, frames on a network are separated by preambles and postambles that tell the hardware where one frame begins and ends. A packet is the data that is contained within the frame.

A typical TCP/IP packet flowing in an ethernet network looks like Figure 24-1.

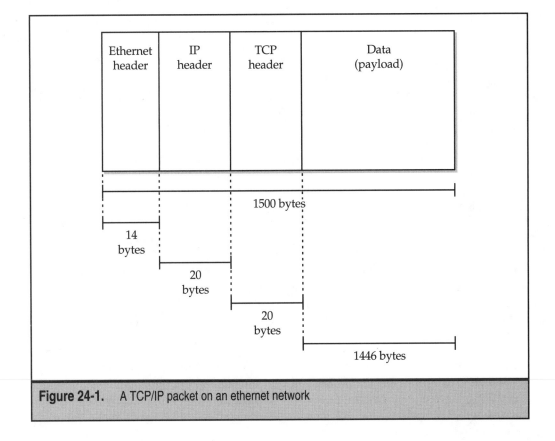

Figure 24-1.   A TCP/IP packet on an ethernet network

As we can see in this diagram, packets are layered by protocol, with the lowest layers coming first. Each protocol uses a *header* to describe the information needed to move data from one host to the next. Packet headers tend to be small—the headers for TCP, IP, and ethernet in their simplest (most common) form only take 54 bytes of space from the packet, thus leaving the rest of the 1446 bytes of frame to the data.

NOTE: In the last few years, the ethernet specification has been updated to allow frames larger than 1500 bytes. These frames are appropriately called *jumbo frames* and can hold up to 9000 bytes. This, conveniently, is enough space for a complete set of TCP/IP headers, ethernet headers, NFS control information, and one page of memory (4K to 8K, depending on your system's architecture; Intel uses 4K pages). Because servers can now push one complete page of memory out of the system without having to break it up into tiny packets, throughput on some applications (such as remote disk service) can go through the roof! The downside to this is that not everyone uses jumbo frames, so you need to make sure your network cards are compatible with your switches, etc. Furthermore, jumbo frames are typically only used in gigabit ethernet environments. Linux supports the use of jumbo frames with the AceNIC driver (**acenic.o**). See http://jes.home.cern.ch/jes/gige/acenic.html for more information about that driver.

Figure 24-2 illustrates how a packet is passed up the protocol stack. Let's look into this process a little more closely.

When a host's network card receives a packet, it first checks to see if it is supposed to accept the packet. This is done by looking at the destination addresses located in the packet's headers. (More about that in "Headers," later in the chapter.) If the network card thinks that it should accept the packet, it keeps a copy of it in its own memory and generates an interrupt to the operating system.

Upon receiving this interrupt, the operating system calls on the device driver of the network interface card (NIC) to process the new packet. The device driver copies the packet from the NIC's memory to the system's memory. Once it has a complete copy, it can examine the packet and determine what type of protocol is being used. Based on the protocol type, the device driver makes a note to the appropriate handler for that protocol that it has a new packet to process. The device driver then puts the packet in a place where the protocol's software ("the stack") can find it and returns to the interrupt processing.

Note that the stack does not begin processing the packet immediately. This is because the operating system may be doing something important that it needs to finish before letting the stack process the packet. Since it is possible for the device driver to receive many packets from the NIC quickly, a *queue* exists between the driver and the stack software. The queue simply keeps track of the order in which packets arrive and notes where they are in memory. When the stack is ready to process those packets, it grabs them from the queue in the appropriate order.

As each layer processes the packet, appropriate headers are removed. In the case of a TCP/IP packet over ethernet, the driver will strip the ethernet headers, IP will strip the IP header, and TCP will strip the TCP header. This will leave just the data that needs to be delivered to the appropriate application.

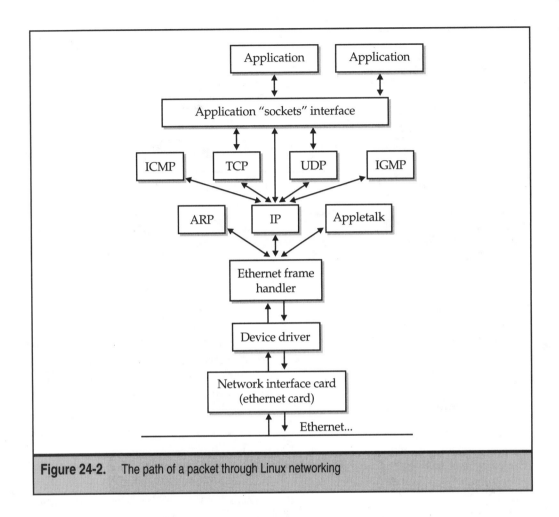

Figure 24-2.   The path of a packet through Linux networking

TCP/IP Layers and the OSI Model

The ISO (International Standards Organization) OSI (Open Systems Interconnection) Reference Model is a well-known model for describing the various abstraction layers in networking. The OSI model has seven layers (see Figure 24-3) that unfortunately don't map to TCP/IP very well. However, marketingese has managed to do it, and a general understanding of what each layer represents has emerged.

Layer 1   Layer 1, the physical layer, describes the actual medium on which the data flows. In a network infrastructure, a pile of CAT 5 ethernet cable is considered the physical layer.

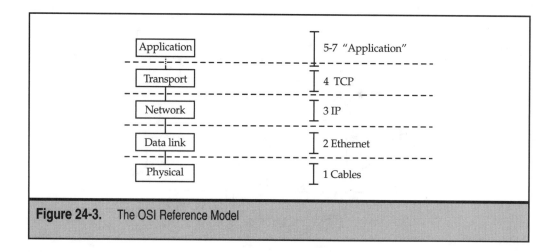

Figure 24-3.   The OSI Reference Model

Layer 2   Layer 2, the data link layer, is used to describe the ethernet protocol. The difference between the OSI model and ethernet is that ethernet only concerns itself with sending frames and providing a valid *checksum* for them. The purpose of the checksum is to allow the receiver to validate whether the data arrived as it was sent. This is done by adding all the values in the packet and comparing them against the checksum that was provided by the sender. If the receiver gets a corrupted frame (that is, the checksums do not match), it is up to the higher-level protocols to ask the sender to retransmit the data. OSI's data link layer formally specifies this level to have that feature built into it.

Layer 3   Layer 3 is the network layer. In TCP/IP lingo, we refer to this as the IP (Internet Protocol) layer. Like layer 2, IP doesn't live up to the formal definition of a network layer. IP merely worries about getting packets from one host to another across multiple subnetworks. The formal definition calls for accounting and congestion control, neither of which IP is capable of. (Note that the accounting can be done by the stack, but it is not a requirement to comply with the IP standard.)

Layer 4   TCP and UDP (User Datagram Protocol) are mapped to layer 4, the transport layer. TCP actually maps to this OSI layer quite well. It provides a reliable transport from one *session*—a single connection from a client program to a server program—to another. (For example, **telnet**ing to a server creates a session. You can have multiple windows running Telnet from the same client to the same server, each instance of Telnet having its own session.) UDP, however, doesn't map quite as nicely. While it understands the concept of sessions, it does not provide reliability (UDP won't detect lost or duplicate packets, for instance).

Layers 5–7   Technically, OSI's layers 5–7 each have a specific purpose, but in TCP/IP lingo, they're all clumped together into the application layer. HTTP cookies, for instance, are considered a layer 7 feature.

So given this horrible mismatching of the OSI model to the TCP/IP stack, why does the marketplace continue to compare the two? Good question. The answer, unfortunately, probably started with an MBA student's thesis and got progressively worse. It's become a de facto standard when describing the various functions of TCP/IP—sadly, it's best to get used to them.

THE PROTOCOLS

So far we have briefly mentioned the purpose of each TCP/IP stack protocol in relation to the OSI model and discussed how they differed. In this section, we discuss the intended purpose of each protocol—ethernet, IP, TCP, UDP, and ICMP—as thought by its designers.

Ethernet

Ethernet's responsibility is simple: get the packet from one host on a LAN (local area network) to another host on a LAN. Ethernet has no concept of a global network because of limitations on the timing of packets, as well as the number of hosts that can exist on a single network segment. You'll be pressed to find more than 200 or so hosts on any given segment due to bandwidth issues and simple management issues. It's easier to manage smaller groups of machines.

IP

The Internet Protocol (IP) is more wise to the world around it. It understands how to communicate with both hosts inside the immediate LAN as well as with hosts that are connected to you via routers (for example, hosts on other subnets, the Internet, etc.). This means that an IP packet can make its way to any other host connected to the same IP network so long as there exists a route to that host.

IP by itself, however, only guarantees that it will *try* to get a packet to its destination. This means that packets can be delivered out of order, sent after a long delay, or even dropped along the way. Furthermore, IP only understands how to get a packet to another host. Once a packet arrives at the host, there is no information in the IP header to tell it which application to deliver the data to.

The reason why IP does not provide any more features than as a simple transport protocol is that it was meant to be a foundation for other protocols to rest on. Of these protocols that use IP, not all of them need reliable connections or guaranteed packet order. Thus, it is the responsibility of higher-level protocols to provide those features if needed.

TCP

The Transmission Control Protocol (TCP) uses IP to send packets of data from one host to another. TCP itself adds the necessary features to provide a reliable connection that guarantees the order of packets, the validity of the data within the packet, and the automatic retransmission of packets that are dropped in transit. Another important concept TCP introduces is *port numbers*, which allow data to be transmitted between specific applications rather than just from host to host.

The most important feature of TCP is the idea of *connections*. This is akin to telephone conversations between two offices. The main phone number to the building is like the IP address, and the extension is the port number. For example, let's say you want to order a music CD. The ordering department of that store has a well-known phone number and extension that you call directly. When you pick up the phone and dial the number, your phone system automatically picks an available extension out of which to send the call. When your call comes in, the company doesn't want to have only one operator taking orders on that extension, so the phone system is configured to automatically route the call to the next available operator. (Note that you still dialed a well-known extension number.) Once the operator picks up the phone, you have established a connection.

The combination of your phone number, the extension that you called from (that was chosen by your phone system), the destination phone number, and the destination extension are the four values that guarantee the unique connection between you and the operator. So when the person sitting in the cubicle next to you decides to order a CD at the same time you are talking with an operator, he can make a call to the same company and same extension, but because your phone system will pick a free extension for him to dial out of—different than the one you're using—his connection will be unique. This allows the phone system to be able to sort out who is talking to whom, even though you and your cube-buddy are in the same office building calling the same company to order CDs.

Now take this scenario and substitute IP address for phone number, port for extension, musiccompany.com for the music company, and Apache Web server for operator. What do you get? A perfect example of how TCP connections work.

Given this tremendously useful protocol, you can see why it is very common on the Internet. However, the set of features that it offers comes at the price of performance. The overhead required to manage connection information, the retransmission of packets, and the automatic reordering of packets, if necessary, takes time. As a result, TCP isn't quite the speed demon we'd wish it were. It also means that it isn't the most appropriate protocol for all types of data that need to be transmitted over the network.

UDP

Like TCP, the User Datagram Protocol (UDP) uses IP to send packets of data from one host to another. Yet unlike TCP, UDP does not guarantee the order or delivery of packets, nor does it support the concept of connections. What it does add to IP is the concept of *ports*, so that applications can communicate with one another, making UDP much faster than TCP and useful for situations where lost packets are acceptable. UDP also provides a checksum, so that the data that does arrive at its destination can be verified for data integrity.

A very popular use of UDP is streaming media. This is because UDP requires less overhead than TCP, and when you're trying to stream audio and video, you need as much time for decompression and display of images as you can get. Furthermore, a dropped packet in an audio stream means a quick blip in sound. We, as users of this technology, would much rather hear a small blip in sound than hear perfect sound that keeps getting delayed due to a few packets needing to be retransmitted!

ICMP

The Internet Control Message Protocol (ICMP) was especially designed for one host to communicate to another host on the state of the network. Since the data is used only by the operating system and not by users, ICMP does not support the concept of port numbers, reliable delivery, or guaranteed order of packets. (In reality, ICMP packets make up for less than 0.3% of the Internet's traffic.)

Every ICMP packet contains a *type* that tells the recipient what the nature of the message is. The most popular type is "Echo-Request," which is used by the infamous PING program. When a host receives the ICMP "Echo-Request" message, it responds with an ICMP "Echo-Reply" message. This allows the sender to confirm that the other host is up, and since we can see how long it takes the message to be sent and replied to, we get an idea of the latency of the network between the two hosts.

HEADERS

Earlier in the chapter, we learned that a TCP/IP packet over ethernet was a series of *headers* for each protocol followed by the actual data being sent. "Packet headers," as they are typically referred to, are simply those pieces of information that tell the protocol how to handle the packet.

The following sections detail the headers found in a TCP/IP packet over ethernet, what each protocol sees in them, and what, as system administrators, we can do with this knowledge.

Ethernet

Ethernet has a very interesting history. As a result, there are two types of ethernet headers: 802.3 and Ethernet II. Thankfully, they both look similar, and there is a simple test to tell them apart. Let's begin by looking at the contents of the ethernet header (see Figure 24-4).

The ethernet header contains three entries: the destination address, the source address, and the packet's protocol type.

Ethernet addresses—also called MAC (Medium Access Control) addresses; no relation to the Apple Macintosh—are 48-bit (6 bytes) numbers that uniquely identify every ethernet card in the world. This is important since, when putting together a LAN using ethernet, this is the only unique value you can be sure of.

NOTE: A packet that is sent as a *broadcast* (meaning all network cards should accept this packet) has the destination address set to ff:ff:ff:ff:ff:ff.

Figure 24-4. The ethernet header

The packet's protocol type is a 2-byte value that tells us what protocol this packet should be delivered to on the receiver's side. For IP packets, this value is hex 0800 (decimal 2048).

The packet we have just described here is an Ethernet II packet. (Typically, it is just called *ethernet*.) 802.3 packets changed the format a little. The destination and source MAC addresses remained in place, but instead of telling us what protocol the packet should be delivered to, it told us the length. The way you can tell the difference between the two types is that there is no protocol type with a value of less than 1500. Thus, any ethernet header where the protocol type is less than 1500 is really a 802.3 packet. Realistically, you probably won't see many (if any) 802.3 packets anymore.

Viewing Ethernet Headers

To see the ethernet headers on your network, run the following command:

```
[root@orb ~]# tcpdump -e
```

This tells **tcpdump** to dump the ethernet headers along with the TCP and IP headers.

Now generate some traffic by visiting a Web site or **telnet**ing to another host. Doing so will generate output like this:

```
15:46:08.026966 0:d0:b7:6b:20:17 0:10:4b:cb:15:9f ip 191: orb.telnet > 10.2.2.2.4769:
P 5259:5396(137) ack 1 win 17520 (DF) [tos 0x10]

15:46:08.044151 0:10:4b:cb:15:9f 0:d0:b7:6b:20:17 ip 60: 10.2.2.2.4769 > orb.telnet:
. ack 5396 win 32120 (DF)
```

The start of each line is a timestamp of when the packet was seen. The next two entries in the lines are the source and destination MAC addresses, respectively, for the packet. In the first line, the source MAC address is 0:d0:b7:6b:20:17, and the destination MAC address is 0:10:4b:cb:15:9f.

After the MAC address is the packet's type. In this case, **tcpdump** saw 0800 and automatically converted it to ip for us so that it would be easier to read. If you don't want **tcpdump** to convert numbers to names for you (especially handy when your DNS resolution isn't working), you can run

```
[root@orb ~]# tcpdump -e -n
```

where the **-n** option tells **tcpdump** to not do name resolution. The same two lines above without name resolution would look like:

```
15:46:08.026966 0:d0:b7:6b:20:17 0:10:4b:cb:15:9f 0800 191: 10.2.2.1.23 > 10.2.2.2.4769:
P 5259:5396(137) ack 1 win 17520 (DF) [tos 0x10]
```

```
15:46:08.044151 0:10:4b:cb:15:9f 0:d0:b7:6b:20:17 0800 60: 10.2.2.2.4769 > 10.2.2.1.23:
. ack 5396 win 32120 (DF)
```

Notice that in each line, the ip became 0800, the hostname orb became 10.2.2.1, and the port number telnet became 23. We will discuss the meaning of the rest of the lines in the "TCP" section later in this chapter.

IP

The Internet Protocol has a slightly more complex header than ethernet, as we can see in Figure 24-5. Let's step through what each of the header values signifies.

The first value in the IP header is the version number. The version of IP that is in most common use today is version 4 (IPv4); however, you will be seeing more of version 6 over the next few years. Version 6 offers many improvements (and changes) to version 4 that are best left to books dedicated on the subject. (Version 5, by the way, was an experimental version designed for multimedia that never made it outside of the lab.)

The next value is the length of the IP header itself. We need to know how long the header is because there may be optional parameters appended to the end of the base header. The header length tells us how many, if any, options are there. To get the byte count of the total IP header length, multiply this number by 4. (For instance, typical IP headers will have the header length value set to 5, indicating that there are 20 bytes in the complete header.)

The Type Of Service (TOS) header tells IP stacks what kind of treatment should be given to the packet. As of this writing, the only defined values are minimized delay, maximized throughput, maximized reliability, and minimized cost. See RFCs 1340 (ftp://ftp.isi.edu/in-notes/rfc1340.txt) and 1349 (ftp://ftp.isi.edu/in-notes/rfc1349.txt) for more details.

The total length value tells us how long the complete packet is, including the IP and TCP headers, but not including the ethernet headers. This value is represented in bytes. An IP packet cannot be longer than 65,536 bytes.

The identification number is supposed to be a unique number used by a host to identify a particular packet. This is used by IP to reassemble packets that have been fragmented.

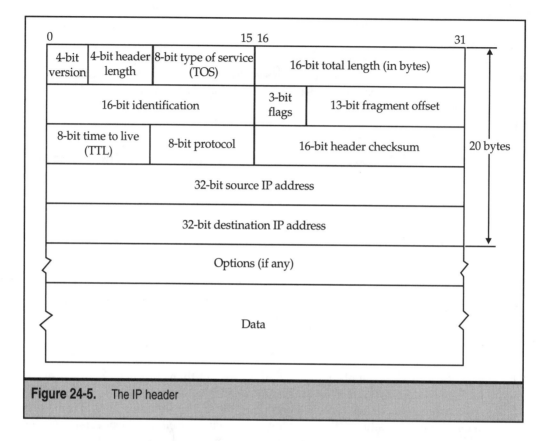

Figure 24-5. The IP header

The flags in the IP packet tell us whether the packet is fragmented or not. Fragmentation occurs when an IP packet is larger than the smallest *MTU* (maximum transmission unit) between two hosts. MTU defines the largest packet that can be sent over a particular network. For example, ethernet's MTU is 1500 bytes. Thus, if we have a 4000-byte IP packet that needs to be sent over ethernet, the packet will be fragmented into three smaller packets. The first two packets will be 1500 bytes, and the last packet will be 1000 bytes.

The fragment offset value tells us which part of the complete packet we are receiving. Continuing with the 4000-byte IP packet example, the first fragment offset we'll receive will be 0. The second will be 1500, and the third will be 3000. The receiving IP stack will take these three packets and reassemble them into one large packet before passing it up the stack.

The time-to-live field (TTL) is a number between 0 and 255 that signifies how much time a packet is allowed to have on the network before being dropped. The idea behind this is that in the event of a routing error, when the packet is going around in a circle, the TTL would cause the packet to eventually time out and be dropped, thus keeping the network from becoming completely congested with circling packets. As each router processes the packet, the TTL value is decreased by one. When the TTL reaches zero, the router at which this happens sends a message via the ICMP protocol (refer to "ICMP" earlier in the chapter), informing the sender of this.

The protocol field in the IP header tells us which higher-level protocol this packet should be delivered to. Typically this has a value for TCP, UDP, or ICMP. In the **tcpdump** output we've seen, it is this value that determines whether the output reads udp or tcp after displaying the source and destination IP/port combination.

The last small value in this IP header is the checksum. This field holds the sum of every byte in the IP header, including any options. When a host builds an IP packet to send, it computes the IP checksum and places it into this field. The receiver can then do the same math and compare values. If the values mismatch, the receiver knows that the packet was corrupted during transmission. (For example, a lightning strike creating electrical disturbance might create packet corruption.)

Finally, the numbers that matter the most in an IP header: the source and destination IP addresses. These values are stored as 32-bit integers instead of the more human readable, dotted decimal notation (for example, instead of 192.168.1.1, the value would be hexadecimal c0a80101).

tcpdump and IP

Because of IP's simple nature, **tcpdump** doesn't have a lot to say about it in its output. The most interesting things that **tcpdump** displays about IP headers are the source IP, destination IP, TTL, Identification, and whether the packet is a fragment or not. To illustrate this, let's walk through an example using **traceroute** and **tcpdump**.

The **traceroute** program works by initially setting the TTL value of a UDP packet to 1 and then sending it off to the destination host. This causes the first router along the path to drop the packet and send back an ICMP message. **traceroute** sees the ICMP message and now knows the first router in the path between the source host and the destination host. Another packet is built, this time with a TTL value of 2, and sent off. Of course, this packet causes the second router along the path to announce itself by means of an ICMP message.

traceroute repeats this process until the destination host itself generates an ICMP message about the packet having a TTL of 0. Having received an ICMP message from every router in between two hosts, it can display this list to you. For example, if we want to see every router between www.planetoid.org and www.hyperreal.org, we would see the following **traceroute** output:

```
[sshah@planetoid.org:~]% traceroute -n www.hyperreal.org
traceroute to hyperreal.org (209.133.83.16), 30 hops max, 40 byte packets
 1   209.133.3.3   1.105 ms   0.984 ms   0.689 ms
 2   209.133.83.16   0.785 ms   0.866 ms   0.772 ms
```

The **tcpdump** command used to generate this output was:

```
[root@planetoid.org]# tcpdump -vv -t -i eth0 -n udp or icmp
```

Here are what the command-line options tell **tcpdump** to do: **-vv** tells **tcpdump** to be as verbose as possible, **-t** says to not print out the time stamp, **-i eth0** says to capture the packets from the network card configured as **eth0** only, and **-n** says to not do DNS resolution on any of the IP addresses seen. Finally, the parameter that tells **tcpdump** what type of packets to capture is the string **udp or icmp**. As the string implies, it tells **tcpdump** to print out only UDP/IP or ICMP/IP packets.

The resulting **tcpdump** output of this connection shows us this:

```
207.126.116.254.41373 > 209.133.83.16.33435: udp 12 [ttl 1] (id 41374)
209.133.3.3 > 207.126.116.254: icmp: time exceeded in-transit [tos 0xc0] (ttl 255, id 54485)
207.126.116.254.41373 > 209.133.83.16.33436: udp 12 [ttl 1] (id 41375)
209.133.3.3 > 207.126.116.254: icmp: time exceeded in-transit [tos 0xc0] (ttl 255, id 54486)
207.126.116.254.41373 > 209.133.83.16.33437: udp 12 [ttl 1] (id 41376)
209.133.3.3 > 207.126.116.254: icmp: time exceeded in-transit [tos 0xc0] (ttl 255, id 54487)
```

The format of the first line is quite simple:

Example	Description
207.126.116.254	Source IP address
41373	Source port number (ports are covered in the "TCP" and "UDP" sections under "The Protocols," earlier in the chapter)
>	Separator between source and destination addresses
209.133.83.16	Destination IP address

Example	Description
33435	Destination port (ports are covered in the "TCP" and "UDP" sections under "The Protocols," earlier in the chapter)
udp 12	A UDP packet that is 12 bytes long
[ttl 1]	The TTL (time-to-live) is set to 1 (refer to the previous section on IP)
Id 41374	A packet ID that is 41374 (refer to the previous section on IP)

Subsequent lines are, of course, similar to the first line.

In these packets, we see planetoid.org (207.126.116.254) generate three UDP packets destined to host www.hyperreal.org (209.133.83.16). Notice that those three UDP packets are sent on three different port numbers (33435, 33436, and 33437). Each of these packets has a TTL set to 1. As a result, each of these UDP packets caused an intermediate router (209.133.3.3) to generate an ICMP message back to the source saying that it had received a packet where time exceeded in-transit. In other words, the TTL had reached 0. The reason why three packets were sent was to generate three separate times that are printed in **traceroute**'s output.

Now let's look at the second hop, which in our case turns out to be the destination:

```
207.126.116.254.41373 > 209.133.83.16.33438: udp 12 (ttl 2, id 41377)
209.133.83.16 > 207.126.116.254: icmp: 209.133.83.16 udp port 33438 unreachable (ttl 254,
id 53507)
207.126.116.254.41373 > 209.133.83.16.33439: udp 12 (ttl 2, id 41378)
209.133.83.16 > 207.126.116.254: icmp: 209.133.83.16 udp port 33439 unreachable (ttl 254,
id 53508)
207.126.116.254.41373 > 209.133.83.16.33440: udp 12 (ttl 2, id 41379)
209.133.83.16 > 207.126.116.254: icmp: 209.133.83.16 udp port 33440 unreachable (ttl 254,
id 53509)
```

Here we see that UDP packets are still sent to the same destination IP, except this time with a TTL of 2. A different set of port numbers (33438, 33439, and 33440) was used to help **traceroute** differentiate these packets from the previous set of packets. Since the TTL is set to 2, the packet makes it past the first router from which we received an ICMP message (209.133.3.3) and makes it to our destination (209.133.83.16). However, the destination finds that there is no application that is ready to accept any data on those ports. As a result, the host sends back an ICMP message stating udp port 33438 unreachable. As with the first set of packets, this is done three times to get a feel for how fast the response is on average.

TCP

The TCP header is similar to the IP header in that it packs quite a bit of information into a little bit of space. Let's start by looking at Figure 24-6.

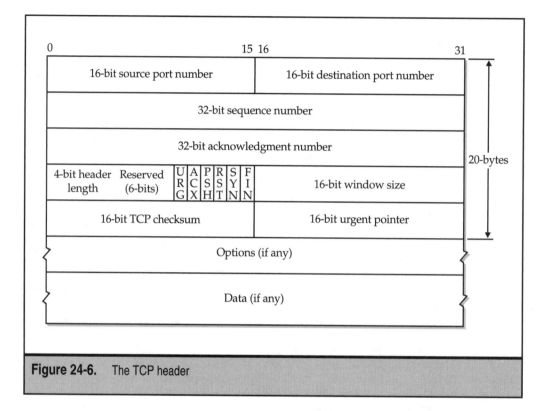

Figure 24-6.   The TCP header

The first two pieces of information in a TCP header are the source and destination port numbers. Because these are only 16-bit values, their range is 0 to 65535. Typically, the source port is a value greater than 1024, since ports 1 to 1023 are reserved for system use on most operating systems (including Linux, Solaris, and the many variants of MS Windows). On the other hand, the destination port is typically low; most of the popular services reside there, although this is not a requirement.

In **tcpdump**'s output, we see port numbers immediately after the IP address. For example, in the output from **tcpdump -n -t**:

```
192.168.1.1.2046 > 192.168.1.12.79: . 1:1(0) ack 1 win 32120 (DF)
```

the source port number is 2046, and the destination port number is 79.

The next two numbers in the TCP header are the sequence and acknowledgment numbers. These values are used by TCP to ensure the order of packets is correct and to let the sender know which packets have been properly received. In day-to-day administrative tasks, you shouldn't have to deal with them.

In **tcpdump**'s output, we see sequence numbers in packets containing data. The format is *starting* number:*ending* number. Look at the following **tcpdump** output from **tcpdump -n –t**:

```
192.168.1.1.2046 > 192.168.1.12.79: P 1:6(5) ack 1 win 32120 (DF)
```

We see that the sequence numbers are 1:6, meaning that the data started at sequence number 1 and ended at sequence number 6. In the parenthesized number immediately following the sequence numbers, we can see the length of the data being sent (5 bytes in this example).

In this sample output, we also see the acknowledgment number. Whenever the packet is acknowledging data it has received (refer to the discussion of the ACK flag later in this section), **tcpdump** prints ack followed by the acknowledgment number. In this case, that number is 1, meaning that 192.168.1.1 is acknowledging the first byte sent to it by 192.168.1.12 in the current connection.

NOTE: In order to make the output more readable, **tcpdump** uses *relative values*. Thus a sequence number of 1 really means that the data contained within the packet is the first byte being sent. If you want to see the actual sequence number, use the **-s** option.

Similar to IP's header length, TCP's header length tells us how long the header is, including any TCP options. Whatever value is in the header length field is multiplied by 4 to get the byte value.

This next part is a bit tricky. TCP uses a series of flags to indicate whether the packet is supposed to initiate a connection, contain data, or terminate a connection. The flags (in the order they appear) are: Urgent (URG), Acknowledge (ACK), Push (PSH), Reset (RST), Synchronize (SYN), and Finish (FIN). Their meanings are as follows:

Flag	Meaning
URG	Message that there is urgent data in the packet that should receive priority processing
ACK	Acknowledgment of successfully received data
PSH	Request to immediately process any received data
RST	Immediately terminates the connection
SYN	Request to start a new connection
FIN	Request to finish a connection

These flags are typically used in combination with one another. For example, it is common to see PSH and ACK together. This combination is essentially the sender telling the receiver two things:

▼ There is data in this packet that needs to be processed, and

▲ I am acknowledging that I have received data from you successfully.

You can see which flags are in a packet in **tcpdump**'s output immediately after the destination IP address and port number. For example:

```
192.168.1.1.2046 > 192.168.1.12.79: P 1:6(5) ack 1 win 32120 (DF)
```

In this line, we see the flag is P for PSH. **tcpdump** uses the first character of the flag's name to indicate the flag's presence (such as S for SYN, F for FIN, etc.). The only exception to this is ACK, which is actually spelled out as ack later in the line. (If the packet has only the ACK bit set, a period is used as a placeholder where the flags are usually printed.) ACK is an exception because it makes it easier to find what the acknowledgment number is for that packet. (See the discussion on acknowledgment numbers earlier in this section; we will discuss flags in greater detail when we discuss connection establishment and tear down.)

The next entry in the header is the window size. TCP uses a technique called *sliding window*, which allows each side of a connection to tell the other how much buffer space it has available for dealing with connections. When a new packet arrives on a connection, the available window size decreases by the size of the packet until the operating system has a chance to move the data from TCP's input buffer to the receiving application's buffer space. Window sizes are computed on a connection-by-connection basis. Let's look at some output from **tcpdump -n -t** as an example:

```
192.168.1.1.2046 > 192.168.1.12.79:  . 6:8(2) ack 1 win 32120 (DF)
192.168.1.12.79 > 192.168.1.1.2046:  . 1:494(493) ack 8 win 17520 (DF)
192.168.1.1.2046 > 192.168.1.12.79:  . 8:8(0) ack 495 win 31626 (DF)
192.168.1.1.2046 > 192.168.1.12.79:  . 8:8(0) ack 495 win 32120 (DF)
```

In the first line, we can see that 192.168.1.1 is telling 192.168.1.12 that it currently has 32120 bytes available in its buffer for this particular connection. In the second packet, 192.168.1.12 sends 493 bytes to 192.168.1.1. (At the same time, 192.168.1.12 tells 192.168.1.1 that its available window is 17520 bytes.) 192.168.1.1 responds to 192.168.1.12 with an acknowledgment saying it has properly accepted everything up to the 495th byte in the stream, which in this case includes all of the data that has been sent by 192.168.1.12. It's also acknowledging that its available window is now 31626, which is exactly the original window size (32120) minus the amount of data that has been received (493 bytes). A few moments later, in the fourth line, 192.168.1.1 sends a note to 192.168.1.12 stating that it has successfully transferred the data to the application's buffer and that its window is back to 32120.

A little confusing? Don't worry too much about it. As a system administrator, you shouldn't have to deal with this level of detail, but it is helpful to know what the numbers mean.

> **NOTE:** You may have noticed an off-by-one error in my math above. 32120 − 493 is 31627, not 31626. This has to do with the nuances of sequence numbers, calculations of available space, etc. For the full ugliness of how the math works, read RFC 793 (ftp://ftp.isi.edu/in-notes/rfc793.txt).

The next element in the TCP header is the checksum. This is similar to the IP checksum in that its purpose is to provide the receiver a way of verifying that the data received isn't corrupted. Unlike the IP checksum, the TCP checksum actually takes into account both the TCP header as well as the data being sent. (Technically, it also includes the TCP pseudo-header, but being system administrators, that's another mess we can skip over.)

Finally, the last piece of the TCP header is the *urgent pointer*. This value is observed when the URG flag is set and tells the receiving TCP stack that some very important data starts at the offset pointed to by the urgent pointer, relative to the sequence number. The TCP stack is supposed to relay this information to the application so that it knows it should treat that data with special importance.

In reality, you'll be pressed to see a packet that uses the URG bit. Ever. Most applications have no way of knowing whether data sent to it is urgent or not, and most applications don't really care. As a result, a small chord of paranoia should strike you if you do see urgent flags in your network. Make sure it isn't part of a probe from the outside trying to exploit bugs in your TCP stack and cause your servers to crash. (Don't worry about Linux—it knows how to handle the urgent bit correctly.)

UDP

In comparison to TCP headers, UDP headers are much simpler. Let's start by looking at Figure 24-7.

The first fields in the UDP header are the source and destination ports. These are conceptually the same thing as the TCP port numbers. In **tcpdump** output, they appear in a very similar manner. Let's look at a DNS query to resolve "www.djdan.com" into an IP address as an example with the command **tcpdump -n -t port 53**:

```
192.168.1.1.1096 > 192.168.1.8.53: 25851+ A? www.djdan.com. (31)
```

Figure 24-7. The UDP packet header

In this output, we can see that the source port of this UDP packet is 1096, and the destination port is 53. The rest of the line is the DNS request broken up into a human readable form.

The next field in the UDP header is the length of the packet. **tcpdump** does not display this information.

Finally, the last field is the UDP checksum. This is used by UDP to validate that the data has arrived to its destination without corruption. If the checksum is corrupted, **tcpdump** will tell you.

Unfortunately, there is no definitive way of telling a TCP packet apart from a UDP packet in **tcpdump**'s output. Aside from relying on intuition (for example, DNS is typically port 53 in UDP), you must explicitly filter out one of them; you can do that by specifying not udp or not tcp as a parameter to **tcpdump**. If you want a better breakdown of the packet as well as detail on all of the header values, you should use Ethereal instead.

So then why use **tcpdump** at all? For quick ad-hoc dumps of what's flying over your network, it does the job. Furthermore, since the output is straight text, you can dump the output to a file and do post-processing with Perl scripts.

A great example of **tcpdump**'s usefulness comes from my master's thesis (http://www.planetoid.org/thesis). To prove a point, I let **tcpdump** run on a large network for 27 hours, collecting data. The resulting 850MB text file allowed me to do all kinds of analysis on the type of traffic that no other packet sniffing tool was (or is) capable of doing.

A COMPLETE TCP CONNECTION

As we discussed earlier, TCP supports the concept of a *connection*. Each connection must go through a sequence to get established; once both sides are done sending data, they must go through another sequence to close the connection.

In this section, we review the complete process of a simple HTTP request and view the process as seen by **tcpdump**. Note that all of the **tcpdump** logs in this section were generated with the **tcpdump -n -t port 80** command. Unfortunately, because of the complex nature of TCP, we cannot cover every possible scenario that a TCP connection can take. However, the coverage given here should be enough to help you determine when things are going wrong at the network level rather than at the server level.

A Note from Experience: Troubleshooting with tcpdump

Being very network-centric, I tend to break out **tcpdump** early in troubleshooting sessions. While it may seem extreme, I've found that in many instances, it allowed me to narrow down the possible problems much more quickly.

One example of this was a problem one of my peers brought to me. It seemed a new mail server was delivering some mail very quickly, and others would never get delivered. A quick **tcpdump** on the mail server revealed that DNS requests for hosts inside our network would resolve correctly and quickly, whereas DNS requests for hosts outside of our network were timing out. Not only did we immediately figure out that DNS was the culprit, but we found out what specific types of DNS problem we had.

This was, of course, much easier to solve than if we had to step through the mail configuration file first!

Opening a Connection

TCP goes through a *three-way handshake* for every connection that it opens up. The reason for this is to allow both sides to send each other their state information and give each other a chance to acknowledge the receipt of that data.

The first packet is sent by the host that wants to open the connection with a server. For this discussion, we will call this host the *client*. The client sends a TCP packet over IP and sets the TCP flag to SYN. The sequence number is the initial sequence number that the client will use for all of the data it will send to the other host (which we'll call the *server*).

The second packet is sent from the server to the client. This packet contains two TCP flags set: SYN and ACK. The purpose of the ACK is to tell the client that it has received the first (SYN) packet. This is double checked by placing the client's sequence number in the acknowledgment field. The purpose of the SYN is to tell the client with which sequence number the server will be sending its responses.

Finally, the third packet goes from the client to the server. It has only the ACK bit set in the TCP flags for the purpose of acknowledging to the server that it received its SYN. This ACK packet has the client's sequence number in the sequence number field and the server's sequence number in the acknowledgment field.

Sound a little confusing? Don't worry—it is. Let's try to clarify it with a real example from **tcpdump**. The first packet is sent from 192.168.1.1 to 207.126.116.254, and it looks like this (note that both lines are actually one very long line):

```
192.168.1.1.1367 > 207.126.116.254.80: S 2524389053:2524389053(0)
win 32120 <mss 1460,sackOK,timestamp 26292983 0,nop,wscale 0> (DF)
```

We can see the client's port number is 1367 and the server's port number is 80. The S means that the SYN bit is set and that the sequence number is 2524389053. The 0 in the parentheses after the sequence number means that there is no data in this packet. After the window is specified as being 32120 bytes large, we see that **tcpdump** has kindly shown us which TCP options were a part of the packet. However, as system administrators, we don't need to concern ourselves with them.

Notice that there is no acknowledgment bit set and no acknowledgment field to print. This is because the client has no sequence number to acknowledge yet! Time for the second packet from the server to the client:

```
207.126.116.254.80 > 192.168.1.1.1367: S 1998624975:1998624975(0)
ack 2524389054 win 32736 <mss 1460>
```

Like the first packet, the second packet has the SYN bit set, meaning that it is telling the client what it will start its sequence number with (in this case, 1998624975). It's okay that the client and server use different sequence numbers. What's important, though, is that the server acknowledges receiving the client's first packet by turning the ACK bit on and setting the acknowledgment field to 2524389054 (the sequence number that the client used to send the first packet).

Now that the server has acknowledged receiving the client's SYN, the client needs to acknowledge receiving the server's SYN. This is done with a third packet that has only the ACK bit set in its TCP flags. This packet looks like this:

```
192.168.1.1.1367 > 207.126.116.254.80: . 1:1(0) ack 1 win 32120 (DF)
```

We can clearly see that there is only one TCP bit set: ACK. The value of the acknowledgment field is shown as a 1. But wait! Shouldn't it be acknowledging 1998624975? Well, don't worry—it is. **tcpdump** has been kind enough to automatically switch into a mode that prints out the relative sequence and acknowledgment numbers instead of the absolute numbers. This makes the output much easier to read. So in this packet, the acknowledgment value of 1 means that it is acknowledging the server's sequence number plus one.

We now have a fully established connection.

So why all the hassle to start a connection? Why can't the client just send a single packet over to the server stating "I want to start talking, okay?" and have the server send back an "okay"? The reason is that without all three packets going back and forth, neither side is sure that the other side received the first SYN packet—and that packet is crucial to TCP's ability to provide a reliable and in-order transport.

Transferring Data

With a fully established connection in place, both sides are able to send data. Since we are using an HTTP request as an example, we will first see the client generate a simple request for a Web page. The **tcpdump** output looks like this:

```
192.168.1.1.1367 > 207.126.116.254.80: P 1:8(7) ack 1 win 32120 (DF)
```

Here we see the client sending 7 bytes to the server with the PSH bit set. The intent of the PSH bit is to tell the receiver to immediately process the data, but because of the nature of the Linux network interface to applications (sockets), setting the PSH bit is unnecessary. Linux (and all socket-based operating systems) automatically processes the data and makes it available for the application to read as soon as it can.

Along with the PSH bit is the ACK bit. This is because TCP always sets the ACK bit on outgoing packets. The acknowledgment value is set to 1 which, based on the connection setup we observed in the previous section, means that there has been no new data that needs acknowledging.

Given that this is an HTTP transfer, it is safe to assume that since it is the first packet going from the client to the server, it is probably the request itself.

Now the server sends a response to the client with this packet:

```
207.126.116.254.80 > 192.168.1.1.1367: P 1:767(766) ack 8 win 32736 (DF)
```

Here the server is sending 766 bytes to the client and acknowledging the first 8 bytes that the client sent to the server. This is probably the HTTP response. Since we know that the page we requested is very small, this is probably all of the data that is going to be sent in this request.

The client acknowledges this data with the following packet:

```
192.168.1.1.1367 > 207.126.116.254.80: . 8:8(0) ack 767 win 31354 (DF)
```

This is a *pure acknowledgment,* meaning that the client did not send any data, but it did acknowledge up to the 767th byte that the server sent.

The process of the server sending some data and then getting an acknowledgment from the client can continue as long as there is data that needs to be sent.

Closing the Connection

TCP connections have the option of ending ungracefully. That is to say, one side can tell the other "stop *now!*" Ungraceful shutdowns are accomplished with the RST (reset) flag, which the receiver does not acknowledge upon receipt. This is to keep both hosts from getting into a "RST war" where one side resets and the other side responds with a reset, thus causing a never ending ping-pong effect.

Let's start with examining a clean shutdown of the HTTP connection we've been observing so far. In the first step in shutting down a connection, the side that is ready to close the connection sends a packet with the FIN bit set indicating that it is finished. Once a host has sent a FIN packet for a particular connection, it is not allowed to send anything other than acknowledgments. This also means that even though it may be finished, the other side may still send it data. It is not until both sides send a FIN that both sides are finished. And like the SYN packet, the FIN packet must receive an acknowledgment.

In the next two packets, we see the server tell the client that it is finished sending data, and the client acknowledges this:

```
207.126.116.254.80 > 192.168.1.1.1367: F 767:767(0) ack 8 win 32736
192.168.1.1.1367 > 207.126.116.254.80: . 8:8(0) ack 768 win 31353 (DF)
```

We then see the reverse happen. The client sends a FIN to the server, and the server acknowledges it:

```
192.168.1.1.1367 > 207.126.116.254.80: F 8:8(0) ack 768 win 32120 (DF)
207.126.116.254.80 > 192.168.1.1.1367: . 768:768(0) ack 9 win 32735 (DF)
```

And that's all there is to a graceful connection shutdown.

As I indicated earlier, an ungraceful shutdown is simply one side sending another the RST packet, which looks like this:

```
192.168.1.1.1368 > 207.126.116.254.80: R 93949335:93949349(14) win 0
```

In this example, 192.168.1.1 is ending a connection with 207.126.116.254 by sending a reset. After receiving this packet, running **netstat** on 207.126.116.254 (which happens to be another Linux server) affirmed the connection was completely closed.

HOW ARP WORKS

The Address Resolution Protocol (ARP) is a mechanism that allows IP to map ethernet addresses to IP addresses. This is important because when you send a packet on an ethernet network, it is necessary to put in the ethernet address of the destination host.

The reason we separate ARP from ethernet, IP, TCP, and UDP is that ARP packets do not go up the normal packet path. Instead, because ARP has its own ethernet header type (0806), the ethernet driver sends the packet to the ARP handler subsystem, which has nothing to do with TCP/IP.

The basic steps of ARP are as follows:

1. The client looks in its ARP cache to see if it has a mapping between its IP address and its ethernet address. (You can see your ARP cache by running **arp -a** on your system.)

2. If an ethernet address for the requested IP address is not found, a broadcast packet is sent out requesting a response from the person with the IP we want.

3. If the host with that IP address is on the LAN, it will respond to the ARP request, thereby informing the sender of what its ethernet address/IP address combination is.

4. The client saves this information in its cache and is now ready to build a packet for transmission.

We can see an example of this from **tcpdump** with the command **tcpdump -e -t -n arp**:

```
0:a0:cc:56:fc:e4 0:0:0:0:0:0 arp 60: arp who-has 192.168.1.1 tell 192.168.1.8
0:10:4b:cb:15:9f 0:a0:cc:56:fc:e4 arp 42: arp reply 192.168.1.1 (0:10:4b:cb:15:9f)
is-at 0:10:4b:cb:15:9f
```

The first packet is a broadcast packet asking all of the hosts on the LAN for 192.168.1.1's ethernet address. The second packet is a response from 192.168.1.1 giving its IP/MAC address mapping.

This, of course, begs the question: "If we can find the MAC address of the destination host using a broadcast, why can't we just send all packets to the broadcast?" The answer has two parts. The first is that the broadcast packet requires that hosts on the LAN receiving the packet take a moment and process it. This means that if two hosts are having a very intense conversation (such as a large file transfer), all of the other hosts on the same LAN would incur a lot of overhead checking on packets that don't belong to them. The second reason is that networking hardware (such as switches) relies on ethernet addresses in order to quickly forward packets to the right place and to minimize network congestion. Any time a switch sees a broadcast packet, it must forward that packet to *all* of its ports. This makes a switch no better than a hub.

"Now, if I need the MAC address of the destination host in order to send a packet to it, does that mean I have to send an ARP request to hosts that are sitting across the Internet?" The answer is a reassuring *no*.

When IP figures out where a packet should head off to, it first checks the routing table. If it can't find the appropriate route entry, IP looks for a *default route*. This is the path that, when all else fails, should be taken. Typically, the default route points to a router or firewall that understands how to forward packets to the rest of the world.

This means that when a host needs to send something to another server across the Internet, it only needs to know how to get the packet to the router, and therefore, it only needs to know the MAC address of the router.

To see this happen on your network, do a **tcpdump** on your host and then visit a Web site that is elsewhere on the Internet, such as www.clickarray.com. You will see an ARP request from your machine to your default route, a reply from your default route, and then the first packet from your host with the destination IP of the remote Web server.

The ARP Header: ARP Works with Other Protocols, Too!

The ARP protocol is not specific to ethernet and IP. To see why, let's take a quick peek at the ARP header (see Figure 24-8).

The first field that we see in the ARP header is the hard type. The hard type field specifies the type of hardware address. (Ethernet has the value of 1.)

The next field is the prot type. This specifies the protocol address being mapped. In the case of IP, this is set to 0800 (hexadecimal).

The hard size and prot size fields that immediately follow tell ARP how large the addresses it is mapping are. Ethernet has a size of 6, and IP has a size of 4.

The op field tells ARP what needs to be done. ARP requests are 1, and ARP replies are 2.

NOTE: There is a variant of ARP called RARP that stands for Reverse ARP. RARP has different values for the op field.

Figure 24-8. The ARP packet header

Finally, there are the fields that we are trying to map. A request has the sender's ethernet and IP addresses as well as the destination IP address filled in. The reply fills in the destination ethernet address and responds to the sender.

BRINGING IP NETWORKS TOGETHER

Now that we have some of the fundamentals of TCP/IP under our belt, let's take a look at how they work to let us glue networks together. In this section, we cover the differences between hosts and networks, netmasks, static routing, and some basics in dynamic routing.

The purpose of this section is not to show you how to configure a Linux router (that is covered in Chapter 26), but to introduce the concepts. Although you may find it less exciting than actually playing, you'll realize that understanding the basics makes playing a little more interesting. More important, should you be looking to apply for a Linux system administrator's job, these could be things that pop up as part of the interview questions. Well, if you ever get interviewed by me, you can *expect* it!

Hosts and Networks

The Internet is a large group of interconnected networks. All of these networks have agreed to connect with some other network, thus allowing everyone to connect to one another. Each of these component networks is assigned a network address.

Traditionally, in a 32-bit IP address, the network component typically takes up either 8, 16, or 24 bits to encode a class A, B, or C network, respectively. Since the remainder of the bits in the IP address are used to enumerate the host within the network, the fewer bits that are used to describe the network, the more bits are available to enumerate the hosts. For example, class A networks have 24 bits left for the host component, which means there can be upwards of 16,777,214 hosts within that network. (Classes B and C have 65,534 and 254 nodes, respectively.)

NOTE: There are also class D and class E ranges. Class D is used for multicast, and class E is reserved for experimental usage.

To better organize the various classes of networks, it was decided early in IP's life that the first few bits would decide to which class the address belonged. For the sake of readability, the first *octet* of the IP address specifies the class.

NOTE: An octet is 8 bits, which in the typical dotted decimal notation of IP means the number before a dot. For example, in the IP address 192.168.1.42, the first octet is 192, the second octet is 168, and so on.

The ranges are as follows:

Class	Octet Range
A	0–126 (except 10)
B	128–192.167 (except 172)
C	192.169–223

You probably noted some gaps in the ranges. This is because there are some special addresses that are reserved for special uses. The first special address is one you are likely to be familiar with: 127.0.0.1. This is also known as the *loopback address*. It is set up on every host using IP so that it can refer to itself. It seems a bit odd to do it this way, but just because a system is capable of speaking IP doesn't mean it has an IP address allocated to it! On the other hand, the 127.0.0.1 address is virtually guaranteed. (If it isn't there, more likely than not, something has gone wrong.)

Three other ranges are notable: Every IP in the 10.0.0.0 network, the 172.16 through 172.31 networks, and the 192.168 network is considered a *private IP*. These ranges are not allowed to be allocated to anyone on the Internet, and therefore, you may use them on your internal networks.

NOTE: We define internal networks as networks that are behind a firewall—not really connected to the Internet—or that have a router performing network address translation at the edge of the network connecting to the Internet. (Most firewalls perform this address translation as well.)

Subnetting

Imagine a network with a few thousand hosts on it, which is not unreasonable in a medium-sized company. Trying to tie them all together into a single large network would probably lead you to pull out all your hair, beat your head into a wall, or possibly both. And that's just the figurative stuff.

The reasons for not keeping a network as a single large entity range from very technical issues to very political ones. On the technical front, there are limitations to every technology on how large a network can get before it becomes too large. Ethernet, for instance, cannot have more than 1024 hosts on a single collision domain. Realistically, having more than a dozen on an even mildly busy network will cause serious performance issues. Even migrating hosts to switches doesn't solve the entire problem since switches, too, have limitations on how many hosts they can deal with.

Of course, you're likely to run into management issues before you hit limitations of switches; managing a single large network is very difficult. Furthermore, as an organization grows, individual departments will begin compartmentalizing. Human Resources is usually the first candidate to need a secure network of their own so that nosy engineers don't peek into things they shouldn't. In order to support a need like that, you need to create subnetworks, a task more commonly referred to as *subnetting*.

Assuming our corporate network is 10.0.0.0, we could subnet it by setting up smaller class C networks within it, such as 10.1.1.0, 10.1.2.0, 10.1.3.0, and so on. These smaller networks would have 24-bit network components and 8-bit host components. Since the first 8 bits would be used to identify our corporate network, we could use the remaining 16 bits of the network component to specify the subnet, giving us 65,534 possible subnetworks. Of course, you don't have to use all of them!

NOTE: As we've seen earlier in this chapter, the host component of an IP address is typically set to all zeros. This convention makes it easy for other humans to recognize which addresses correspond to entire networks and which addresses correspond specifically to hosts.

Netmasks

The purpose of a *netmask* is to tell the IP stack which part of the IP address is the network and which part is the host. This allows the stack to determine whether a destination IP address is on the LAN or if it needs to be sent to a router for forwarding elsewhere.

The best way to start looking at netmasks is to look at IP addresses and netmasks in their binary representations. Let's look at the 192.168.1.42 address with the netmask 255.255.255.0:

Dotted Decimal	Binary
192.168.1.42	11000000 10101000 00000001 00101010
255.255.255.0	11111111 11111111 11111111 00000000

Converting Numbers

The easiest way to convert a number from decimal (base 10 math) to binary (base 2) is to find a calculator that can do it for you. GNOME and KDE both have calculator programs that are able to do this. However, if you don't happen to have a calculator handy, you can do it by hand.

Binary into Decimal

To convert a binary number into decimal, begin by assigning each placeholder a value. Starting left to right in an 8-bit number, these values would be 128, 64, 32, 16, 8, 4, 2, and 1. Next, read through the actual number you are converting. For each digit that is 1, add in the placeholder's value. For example, to convert the binary value 10101000, we would do this:

Placeholder	128	64	32	16	8	4	2	1	
Binary	1	0	1	0	1	0	0	0	10101000
Decimal	+128	+0	+32	+0	+8	+0	+0	+0	= **168**

Decimal into Binary

Converting decimal into binary is equally straightforward. Start by trying to subtract 128 from the decimal number. If you can, the placeholder for 128 is set to 1. Then try to subtract 64. If that can be done, set the placeholder for 64 to 1. If you find that you can't subtract out a particular placeholder number, set that place holder to 0.

For example, if you want to convert the number 74 into binary, do the following: 74 – 128 is less than 0, set the 128 placeholder to 0. Since 74 – 64 = 10, set the 64 placeholder to 1. Neither 32 nor 16 can be subtracted from 10, so their placeholders are 0. And 10 – 8 = 2, so 8's placeholder is set to 1. The placeholder for 4 is set to 0. Since 2 – 2 = 0, the placeholder for 2 is set to 1. And, of course, this means that 1's place holder is 0. The results in the binary number are as follows:

Placeholder	128	64	32	16	8	4	2	1	
Binary	0	1	0	0	1	0	1	0	10101000
Decimal	+0	+64	+0	+0	+8	+0	+2	+0	= **74**

See, I told you using a calculator is easier!

In this example, we want to find out what part of the IP address 192.168.1.42 is network and what part is host. Now, according to the definition of netmask, those bits that are zero are part of the host. Given this definition, we see that the first three octets make up the network address and the last octet makes up the host.

In discussing network addresses with other people, it's often handy to be able to state the network address without having to give the original IP address and netmask. Thankfully, this network address is computable given the IP address and netmask using a bitwise AND operation.

The way the bitwise AND operation works can be best explained by observing the behavior of two bits being ANDed together. If both bits are 1, then the result of the AND is also 1. If either bit (or both bits) is zero, the result is zero. We can see this more clearly in this table:

Bit 1 to Be ANDed	Bit 2 to Be ANDed	Result of AND Operation
0	0	0
0	1	0
1	0	0
1	1	1

So computing the bitwise AND operation on 192.168.1.42 and 255.255.255.0 yields the bit pattern 11000000 10101000 00000001 00000000. Notice that the first three octets remained identical and the last octet became all zeros. In dotted decimal notation, this reads 192.168.1.0.

NOTE: Remember that we need to give up one IP to the network address and one IP to the broadcast address. In this example, the network address is 192.168.1.0, and the broadcast address is 192.168.1.255.

Let's walk through another example. This time, we want to find the address range available to us for the network address 192.168.1.176 with a netmask of 255.255.255.240. (This type of netmask is commonly given by ISPs to business DSL and T1 customers.)

A quick breakdown of the last octet in the netmask shows us that the bit pattern for 240 is 11110000. This means that the first three octets of the network address plus 4 bits into the fourth octet are held constant. (255.255.255.240 in binary is 11111111 11111111 11111111 11110000.) Since the last four bits are variable, we know we have 16 possible addresses ($2^4 = 16$). Thus, our range goes from 192.168.1.176 to 192.168.1.192 ($192 - 176 = 16$).

Because it is so tedious to type out complete netmasks, many people have started using an abbreviated format where the network address is followed by a slash and the number of bits in the netmask. So the network address 192.168.1.0 with a netmask of 255.255.255.0 would be abbreviated to 192.168.1.0/24.

NOTE: The process of using netmasks that do not fall on the class A, B, or C boundaries is also known as Classless Inter-Domain Routing (CIDR). You can read more about CIDR in RFC 1817 (http://www.rfc-editor.org/rfc/rfc1817.txt).

Static Routing

When two hosts on the same LAN want to communicate, it is quite easy for them to find each other: Simply send out an ARP message, get the other host's MAC address, and you're off. But when the second host is not local, things become trickier.

In order to get two or more LANs to communicate with one another, a router needs to be put into place. The purpose of the router is to know about the topology of both networks. When I want to communicate with the other network, my machine will set the destination IP as the host on the other network, but the destination MAC address will be for the router. This allows the router to receive the packet and examine the destination IP, and since it knows that IP is on the other network, it will forward the packet. The reverse is also true for packets that are coming from the other network to my network (see Figure 24-9).

The router must in turn know what networks it is plugged into. This information is called its *route table*. When the router is manually informed about what paths it can take, the table is called *static*, thus the term *static routing*. Once routes are plugged into the routing table by a human, they cannot be changed until a human operator comes back to change them.

Unfortunately, routers are rather expensive devices. They are typically dedicated pieces of hardware that are highly optimized for the purpose of forwarding packets from one interface to the another. You can, of course, make a Linux-based router (we discuss this in Chapter 26) using a stock PC that has two or more network cards. Such configurations are fast and cheap enough for smaller networks. In fact, many companies are already starting to do this, since older PC's that are too slow to run the latest Web browsers and word processing applications are still plenty fast to perform routing. (A low-end Pentium-class machine is fast enough to keep a 100Mb ethernet connection full! Many dedicated routers use even simpler, slower hardware.)

The downside to Linux-based routers has more to do with PC hardware than Linux. By their nature, PCs are built to be less robust than dedicated network hardware. Furthermore, having an operating system that allows users to log in to do things other than routing

Figure 24-9. Two networks connected by a router

means you run the risk of junior administrators adding load to a router that they shouldn't be touching. (This problem is independent of your operating system. Watch your PC router's performance drop through the floor when someone thinks that an OpenGL-based screen saver would be a cute addition!)

Routing Tables

As mentioned earlier, routing tables are lists of network addresses, netmasks, and destination interfaces. A simplified version of a table might look like this:

Network Address	Netmask	Destination Interface
192.168.1.0	255.255.255.0	Interface 1
192.168.2.0	255.255.255.0	Interface 2
192.168.3.0	255.255.255.0	Interface 3
Default	0.0.0.0	Interface 4

When a packet arrives at a router that has a routing table like this, it will go through the list of routes and apply each netmask to the destination IP address. If the resulting network address is equal to the network address in the table, the router knows to forward the packet on that interface.

So let's say that the router receives a packet with the destination IP address set to 192.168.2.233. The first table entry has the netmask 255.255.255.0. When this netmask is applied to 192.168.2.233, the result is not 192.168.1.0, so the router moves on to the second entry. Like the first table entry, this route has the netmask of 255.255.255.0. The router will apply this to 192.168.2.233 and find that the result network address is equal to 192.168.2.0. So now the appropriate route is found. The packet is forwarded out of interface 2.

If a packet arrives that doesn't match the first three routes, it will match the default case. In our sample routing table, this will cause the packet to be forwarded to interface 4. More than likely, this is a gateway to the Internet.

Limitations of Static Routing

The example of static routing we've used is pretty typical of smaller networks. There are only a handful of networks that need to communicate with one another, and they aren't going to change often.

However, there are limitations to this technique. The biggest limitation is human—you are responsible for updating all of your routers with new information whenever you make any changes. Although this is usually very easy to do in a small network, it means that there is room for error. Furthermore, as your network grows and more routes get added, it is more likely that the routing table will become trickier to manage this way.

The second—but almost as significant—limitation is that the time it takes the router to process a packet is linear to the number of routes there are. With only 3–4 routes, this isn't a big deal. But as you start getting into dozens of routes, the overhead can become noticeable.

Given these two limitations, it is best to use static routes only in small networks.

Dynamic Routing with RIP

As networks grow, the need to subnet them grows, too. Eventually, you'll find that you have a lot of subnets that can't all be tracked easily, especially if they are being managed by different administrators. One subnet, for instance, may need to break their network in half for security reasons. In a situation this complex, going around and telling everyone to update their routing tables would be a real nightmare and would lead to all sorts of network headaches.

The solution to this problem is to use *dynamic routing*. The idea behind dynamic routing is that each router only knows about one network when it starts up. It then announces to other routers connected to it what it knows, and the other routers reply back with what they know. Think of it as "word of mouth" advertising for your network. You tell the people around you about your network, they then tell their friends, and their friends tell their friends, and so on. Eventually, everyone connected to the network knows about your new network.

On campus-wide networks (such as a large company with many departments) you'll typically see this method of announcing route information. As of this writing, the two most commonly used protocols are RIP and OSPF.

RIP is short for Routing Information Protocol and is currently up to version 2. It is a very simple protocol that is easy to configure. Simply tell the router information about one network (making sure each subnet in the company has a connection to a router that knows about RIP), and then have the routers connected to one another. RIP broadcasts happen at regular time intervals (usually less than a minute), and in only a few minutes, the entire campus network knows about you.

Let's see how a smaller campus network with four subnets would work with RIP. Figure 24-10 shows how the network is connected.

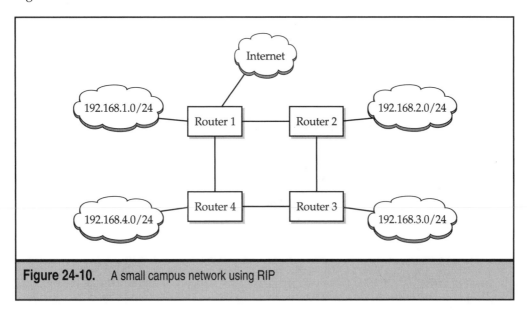

Figure 24-10. A small campus network using RIP

NOTE: For simplicity sake, I'm serializing the events. In reality, many of these events would happen in parallel.

As illustrated in this figure, router 1 would be told about 192.168.1.0/24 and about the default route to the Internet. Router 2 would be told about 192.168.2.0/24, router 3 would know about 192.168.3.0/24, and so on. At startup, each router's table looks like this:

Router	Table
Router 1	192.168.1.0/24 Internet Gateway
Router 2	192.168.2.0/24
Router 3	192.168.3.0/24
Router 4	192.168.4.0/24

Router 1 then makes a broadcast stating what routes it knows about. Since routers 2 and 4 are connected to it, they update their routes. This makes the routing table look like this (new routes in *italics*):

Router	Table
Router 1	192.168.1.0/24 Internet Gateway
Router 2	192.168.2.0/24 *192.168.1.0/24 via router 1* *Internet Gateway via router 1*
Router 3	192.168.3.0/24
Router 4	192.168.4.0/24 *192.168.1.0/24 via router 1* *Internet Gateway via router 1*

Router 2 then makes its broadcast. Routers 1 and 3 see these packets and update their tables as follows (new routes in *italics*):

Router	Table
Router 1	192.168.1.0/24 Internet Gateway *192.168.2.0/24 via router 2*

Router	Table
Router 2	192.168.2.0/24 192.168.1.0/24 via router 1 Internet Gateway via router 1
Router 3	192.168.3.0/24 *192.168.2.0/24 via router 2* *192.168.1.0/24 via router 2* *Internet Gateway via router 2*
Router 4	192.168.4.0/24 192.168.1.0/24 via router 1 Internet Gateway via router 1

Router 3 then makes its broadcast, which routers 2 and 4 hear. This is where things get interesting, since this introduces enough information for there to be multiple routes to the same destination. The routing tables now look like this (new routes in *italics*):

Router	Table
Router 1	192.168.1.0/24 Internet Gateway 192.168.2.0/24 via router 2
Router 2	192.168.2.0/24 192.168.1.0/24 via router 1 Internet Gateway via router 1 *192.168.3.0/24 via router 3*
Router 3	192.168.3.0/24 192.168.2.0/24 via router 2 192.168.1.0/24 via router 2 Internet Gateway via router 2
Router 4	192.168.4.0/24 192.168.1.0/24 via router 1 *or 3* Internet Gateway via router 1 *or 3* *192.168.3.0/24 via router 3* *192.168.2.0/24 via router 3*

Next, router 4 makes its broadcast. Routers 1 and 3 hear this and update their tables to the following (new routes in *italics*):

Router	Table
Router 1	192.168.1.0/24 Internet Gateway 192.168.2.0/24 via router 2 *or 4* *192.168.3.0/24 via router 4* *192.168.4.0/24 via router 4*
Router 2	192.168.2.0/24 192.168.1.0/24 via router 1 Internet Gateway via router 1 192.168.3.0/24 via router 3
Router 3	192.168.3.0/24 192.168.2.0/24 via router 2 192.168.1.0/24 via router 2 *or 4* Internet Gateway via router 2 *or 4* *192.168.4.0/24 via router 4*
Router 4	192.168.4.0/24 192.168.1.0/24 via router 1 Internet Gateway via router 1 192.168.3.0/24 via router 3 192.168.2.0/24 via router 3

Once all the routers go through another round of broadcasts, the complete table would look like this:

Router	Table
Router 1	192.168.1.0/24 Internet Gateway 192.168.2.0/24 via router 2 or 4 192.168.3.0/24 via router 4 or 2 192.168.4.0/24 via router 4 or 2
Router 2	192.168.2.0/24 192.168.1.0/24 via router 1 or 3 Internet Gateway via router 1 or 3 192.168.3.0/24 via router 3 or 1

Router	Table
Router 3	192.168.3.0/24
	192.168.2.0/24 via router 2 or 4
	192.168.1.0/24 via router 2 or 4
	Internet Gateway via router 2 or 4
	192.168.4.0/24 via router 4 or 2
Router 4	192.168.4.0/24
	192.168.1.0/24 via router 1 or 3
	Internet Gateway via router 1 or 3
	192.168.3.0/24 via router 3 or 1
	192.168.2.0/24 via router 3 or 1

Why is this mesh important? Let's say router 2 fails. If router 3 was relying on router 2 for sending packets to the Internet, it can immediately update its tables reflecting that router 2 is no longer there and then forward Internet-bound packets through router 4.

RIP's Algorithm (and Why You Should Use OSPF Instead)

Unfortunately, when it comes to figuring out the most optimal path from one subnet to another, RIP is not the smartest protocol. Its method of determining which route to take is based on the fewest number of routers (hops) between it and the destination. Although that sounds optimal, what this algorithm doesn't take into account is how much traffic is on the link or how fast the link is.

Looking back at Figure 24-10, we can see where this situation might play itself out. Let's assume that the link between routers 3 and 4 becomes very congested. Now if router 3 wants to send a packet out to the Internet, RIP will still evaluate the two possible paths (3 to 4 to 1 and 3 to 2 to 1) as being equidistant. As a result, the packet may end up going via router 4 when clearly the path through router 2 (whose links are not congested) would be much faster.

OSPF (Open Shortest Path First) is very similar to RIP in how it broadcasts information to other routers. What makes it different is that instead of keeping track of how many hops it takes to get from one router to another, it keeps track of how quickly each router is talking to one another. Thus, in our example where the link between routers 3 and 4 becomes congested, OSPF will realize that and be sure to route a packet destined to router 1 via router 2.

Another feature of OSPF is its ability to realize when a destination address has two possible paths that would take an equal amount of time. When it sees this, OSPF will share the traffic across both links—a process called *load balancing*—thereby making optimal use of available resources.

Unfortunately, because OSPF is much newer than RIP, you may find that some of your older hardware does not support OSPF.

SUMMARY

This chapter covered the fundamentals of TCP/IP and other protocols, ARP, subnetting and netmasks, and routing. It's a lot to digest, but hopefully this simplified version should make it easier to understand.

Specifically, we discussed:

▼ How TCP/IP relates to the ISO OSI 7-layer model

■ The composition of a packet

■ The specifications of packet headers and how to get them using the **tcpdump** tool

■ The complete process of a TCP connection setup, data transfer, and connection teardown

■ How to calculate netmasks

■ How static routing works

▲ And how dynamic routing works with RIP

Because the information here is (substantially) simplified from the real-deal, you may want to take a look at some other books for more information regarding this topic. This is especially important if you have complex networks that your machines need to live in or if you need to understand the operation of your firewall.

One book I recommend to everyone is *TCP/IP Illustrated Vol. 1* by Richard Stevens (Addison-Wesley, 1994). This book covers TCP/IP in depth and several popular protocols that send their data over IP. Stevens does a fantastic job of explaining this complex subject in a very clear and methodical manner. I have yet to meet a single person who read this and didn't understand what he said. A system administrator who has read this book can easily make him/herself much more valuable in the job market.

If you need to start out with something a little less meaty, try *TCP/IP For Dummies, Fourth Edition* by Leiden, et al (Hungry Minds, 2000). Although it is a "dummies" book, you'll be pleased to see that the coverage does get deep, just at a much slower rate. And thankfully, the authors didn't slip on correctness to make it simpler. (Marketing and sales folk who need to sell networking hardware should be required to read this book!)

My last recommendation is specific to those who need to configure Cisco equipment (which according to Cisco's sales figures is a lot of you!): *Cisco TCP/IP Routing Professional Reference* by Chris Lewis (McGraw-Hill, 2000). Chris does a solid job at explaining both the protocols as well as configuration issues for Cisco equipment.

CHAPTER 25

Network Configuration

Knowing how to configure your network services by hand can be terribly important for multiple reasons. First and foremost is that when things are breaking and you can't start your favorite GUI, being able to handle network configuration from the command line is crucial. Another reason is remote administration: You may not be able to run a graphical configuration tool from a remote site. Issues such as firewalls and network latency will probably restrict your remote administration to command line only. Finally, it's always nice to be able to perform network configuration through scripts, and command-line tools are best suited for scriptability.

In this chapter, we will tackle the two tools necessary for performing command-line administration of your network interface: **ifconfig** and **route**.

MODULES AND NETWORK INTERFACES

Network devices under Linux break the tradition of accessing all devices through the file metaphor. Not until the network driver initializes the card and registers itself with the kernel does there exist a mechanism for anyone to access the card. Typically, Ethernet devices register themselves as being eth$X$, where X is the device number. The first device is eth0, the second is eth1, and so on.

Depending on how your kernel was compiled, the device drivers for your network interface cards may have been compiled as a module. For most distributions, this is the default mechanism for shipping since it makes it much easier to probe for hardware.

If the driver is configured as a module, and you have autoloading modules set up, you will need to tell the kernel the mapping between device names and the module to load in the **/etc/conf.modules** file. For example, if my eth0 device is a 3Com 3C905 Ethernet card, I would add the following line to my **/etc/conf.modules** file:

```
alias eth0 3c59x
```

where 3c59x is the name of the device driver.

> **TIP:** If you purchased Red Hat 6.0 and a brand new 3Com 3C905C network card, you may be unpleasantly surprised to find that the driver does not work. This is because the new network card came out right after Red Hat 6.0, and the new driver that needed to go with it didn't make it onto the distribution CD. You can download this driver (and many others) from http://cesdis.gsfc.nasa.gov/linux/.

You will need to set this up for every network card you have. For example, if you have a network card based on the DEC Tulip chip set and an SMC-1211 (based on the RealTek 8139 chip set, a popular chip set amongst cheap 100BaseT cards) in the same machine, you would need to make sure your **/etc/conf.modules** file includes the lines

```
alias eth0 tulip
alias eth1 rtl8139
```

where tulip refers to the NIC with the DEC Tulip chip on it, and rtl8139 refers to the SMC 1211 card.

NOTE: These alias commands will not be the only entries in the **/etc/conf.modules** file.

IFCONFIG

The **ifconfig** program is responsible for setting up your network interface cards (NICs). All of its operations can be performed through command-line options, and in its native format, it has no menus or graphical interface.

Many tools have been written to wrap around **ifconfig**'s command-line interface to provide menu-driven or graphical interfaces, many of which are shipped with distributions of Linux. For example, Caldera users can configure their network interface through COAS, and Red Hat users can use the **netcfg** program.

In this section, we focus on the command-line version of **iconfig** only.

Simple Usage

In its simplest usage, all you need to do is provide the name of the interface being configured and the IP address. The **ifconfig** program will deduce the rest of the information based on the IP address. Thus, you could enter

```
[root@ford /root]# ifconfig eth0 192.168.1.42
```

to set the eth0 device to the IP address 192.168.1.42. Because 192.168.1.42 is a class C address, the calculated netmask will be 255.255.255.0, and the broadcast address will be 192.168.1.255.

If the IP address you are setting is a class A or class B address that is subnetted differently, you will need to explicitly set the broadcast and netmask address on the command line, like so:

```
[root@ford /root]# ifconfig dev ip netmask nmask broadcast bcast
```

where **dev** is the network device you are configuring, **ip** is the IP address you are setting it to, **nmask** is the netmask, and **bcast** is the broadcast address. For example,

```
[root@ford /root]# ifconfig eth0 1.1.1.1 netmask 255.255.255.0 broadcast 1.1.1.255
```

will set the eth0 device to the IP address 1.1.1.1 with a netmask of 255.255.255.0 and a broadcast address of 1.1.1.255.

TIP: You can list all of the active devices by running `ifconfig` with no parameters. You can list all devices, regardless of whether they are active, by running `ifconfig -a`.

Setting Up NICs at Boot Time

Unfortunately, each distribution has taken to automating their setup process for network cards a little differently. We cover Red Hat Linux in the next section due to its popularity and because you get a copy of Red Hat with this book. But for other distributions, you need to handle this procedure in one of two ways:

▼   Use the administrator tool that comes with that distribution to add network card support. This is probably the easiest and most reliable method. Caldera Linux, for example, uses the COAS tool.

▲   Find the startup script that is responsible for configuring network cards. (Using the **grep** tool to find which script runs `ifconfig` works well.) At the end of the script, add the necessary `ifconfig` statements. Another common place to add `ifconfig` statements is in the **rc.local** script—not as pretty, but it works equally well.

Setting Up NICs Under Red Hat Linux

Red Hat Linux has a system setup that makes it easy to configure network cards at boot time. It is done through the creation of files in the **/etc/sysconfig/network-scripts** directory that are read at boot time. All of the graphical tools under Linux create these files for you, but for the power-user inside of you just dying to edit the files by hand, the follwing is what you need to know.

For each network interface, there is an **ifcfg** file in **/etc/sysconfig/network-scripts**. This filename is suffixed by the name of the device, thus **ifcfg-eth0** is for the eth0 device, **ifcfg-eth1** is for the eth1 device, and so on.

The format of each of these files is as follows:

```
DEVICE="eth0"
IPADDR="192.168.1.1"
NETMASK="255.255.255.0"
NETWORK=192.168.1.0
BROADCAST=192.168.1.255
ONBOOT="yes"
BOOTPROTO="none"
IPXNETNUM_802_2=""
IPXPRIMARY_802_2="no"
IPXACTIVE_802_2="no"
IPXNETNUM_802_3=""
IPXPRIMARY_802_3="no"
IPXACTIVE_802_3="no"
IPXNETNUM_ETHERII=""
```

```
IPXPRIMARY_ETHERII="no"
IPXACTIVE_ETHERII="no"
IPXNETNUM_SNAP=""
IPXPRIMARY_SNAP="no"
IPXACTIVE_SNAP="no"
```

All of the entries that start with an IPX are for the IPX protocol suite. In this section, we are interested only in the IP-related information, which is at the top of the file. Specifically, we are interested in the following fields:

```
DEVICE="eth0"
IPADDR="192.168.1.1"
NETMASK="255.255.255.0"
NETWORK=192.168.1.0
BROADCAST=192.168.1.255
ONBOOT="yes"
```

These fields determine the IP configuration information for the eth0 device. Note how each of these values corresponds to the parameters in **ifconfig**. To change the configuration information for this device, simply change the information in the **ifcfg** file and run

```
[root@ford /root]# cd /etc/sysconfig/network-scripts
[root@ford network-scripts]# ./ifdown ifcfg-eth0
[root@ford network-scritps]# ./ifu!p ifcfg-eth0
```

If you need to configure a second network interface card, copy the **ifcfg-eth0** file to **ifcfg-eth1** and change the information in **ifcfg-eth1** to reflect the second network card's information. Once there, Red Hat will automatically configure it during the next boot. If you need to activate the card immediately, run

```
[root@ford /root]# cd /etc/sysconfig/network-scripts
[root@ford network-scripts]# ./ifup ifcfg-eth1
```

Additional Parameters

The format of the **ifconfig** command is as follows:

```
[root@ford /root]# ifconfig device address options
```

where **device** is the name of the Ethernet device (for instance, eth0), **address** is the IP address you wish to apply to the device, and **options** are one of the following:

Option	Description
up	Enables the device. This option is implicit.
down	Disables the device.

Option	Description
arp	Enables this device to answer **arp** requests (default).
-arp	Disables this device from answering arp requests.
mtu *value*	Sets the maximum transmission unit (MTU) of the device to ***value***. Under ethernet, this defaults to 1500. (See the following "Tip" regarding certain gigabit ethernet cards.)
netmask *address*	Sets the netmask to this interface to ***address***. If a value is not supplied, **ifconfig** calculates the netmask based on the class of the IP address. A class A address gets a netmask of 255.0.0.0, class B gets 255.255.0.0, and class C gets 255.255.255.0.
broadcast *address*	Sets the broadcast address to this interface to ***address***. If a value is not supplied, **ifconfig** calculates the broadcast address based on the class of the IP address in a similar manner to netmask.
pointtopoint *address*	Sets up a point-to-point connection (PPP) where the remote address is ***address***.

TIP: Many gigabit ethernet cards now support jumbo ethernet frames. A jumbo frame is 9000 bytes in length, which (conveniently) holds one complete NFS packet. This allows file servers to perform better, since they have to spend less time fragmenting packets to fit into 1500-byte ethernet frames. Of course, your network infrastructure as a whole must support this in order to benefit. If you have a network card and appropriate network hardware to set up jumbo frames, it is very much worth reading into how to toggle those features on. Some popular NICs based on the Tigon II chipset (such as the Alteon AceNIC, 3Com 3C985, NetGear GA620, Farallon PN9000SX, and SGI AceNIC) can set the frame size to 9000 bytes by changing the MTU setting when configured with **ifconfig** (for example, **ifconfig eth0 192.168.1.1 mtu=9000**).

USING ROUTERS

If your host is connected to a network with multiple subnets, you need a *router*. This box, which sits between networks, redirects packets toward their actual destination. (Typically, most hosts don't know the correct path to a destination; they only know the destination itself.)

In the case where a host doesn't even have the first clue about where to send a packet, it uses its *default route*. This path points to a router, which ideally does have an idea of where the packet should go, or at least knows of another router that can make smarter decisions.

A typical Linux host knows of three routes: the first is the loopback route, which simply points toward the loopback device. The second is the route to the local area network so that packets destined to hosts within the same LAN are sent directly to them. Finally, the third route is the default route. This route is used for packets that need to leave the local area network to communicate with other networks.

If you set up your network configuration at install time, this setting is most likely already taken care of for you, so you don't need to change it. However, this doesn't mean you can't . . .

NOTE: There are actually instances where you will need to change your routes by hand. Typically, this is necessary when multiple network cards are installed into the same host where each NIC is connected to a different network. You should know how to add a route so that packets can be sent to the appropriate network based on the destination address.

Simple Usage

The typical **route** command is structured as follows:

```
[root@ford /root]# route cmd type addy netmask mask gw gway dev dn
```

The parameters are as follows:

Parameter	Description
cmd	Either **add** or **del** depending on whether you are adding or deleting a routing. If you are deleting a route, the only other parameter you need is **addy**.
type	Either **-net** or **-host** depending on whether **addy** represents a network address or a router address.
addy	The destination network to which you want to offer a route.
netmask *mask*	Sets the netmask of the **addy** address to *mask*.
gw *gway*	Sets the router address for **addy** to *gway*. Typically used for the default route.
dev *dn*	Sends all packets destined to **addy** through the network device *dn* as set by **ifconfig**.

▼ Here's how to set the default route on a sample host, which has a single ethernet device and a router of 192.168.1.1:

```
[root@ford /root]# route add -net default gw 192.168.1.1 dev eth0
```

■ This command line sets up a system so that all packets destined to 192.168.1.42 are sent through the first PPP device:

```
[root@ford /root]# route add -host 192.168.1.42 netmask 255.255.255.255 dev ppp0
```

▲ Here's how to delete the route destined to 192.168.1.42:

```
[root@ford /root]# route del 192.168.1.42
```

NOTE: If you are using a gateway, you need to make sure a route exists to the gateway before you reference it for another route. For example, if your default route uses the gateway at 192.168.1.1, you need to be sure you have a route to get to the 192.168.1.0 network first.

Displaying Routes

There are two ways you can display your route table: the **route** command and **netstat**.

Route

Using **route** is the easiest way to display your route table—simply run **route** without any parameters. Here is a complete run, along with the output:

```
[root@ford /root]# route
Kernel IP routing table
Destination     Gateway       Genmask         Flags Metric Ref Use Iface
10.10.2.0       *             255.255.255.0   UH    0      0   0   eth1
192.168.1.0     *             255.255.255.0   U     0      0   0   eth0
127.0.0.0       *             255.0.0.0       U     0      0   0   lo
default         firewall      0.0.0.0         UG    0      0   0   eth1
```

You see two networks. The first is the 192.168.1.0 network, which is accessible via the first ethernet device, eth0. The second is the 10.10.2.0 network, which is connected via the second ethernet device, eth1. The default route is 10.10.2.4; however, because the IP address resolves to the host name firewall in DNS, **route** prints its host name instead of the IP address.

We have already discussed the destination, gateway, netmask (referred to as **genmask** in this table), and **Iface** (interface, set by the dev option on **route**). The other entries in the table have the following meanings:

Entry	Description
Flags	A summary of connection status, where each letter has a significance:
	U The connection is up.
	H The destination is a host.
	G The destination is a gateway.

Entry	Description
`Metric`	The cost of a route, usually measured in hops. This is meant for systems that have multiple paths to get to the same destination, but one path is preferred over the other. A path with a lower metric is typically preferred. The Linux kernel doesn't use this information, but certain advanced routing protocols do.
`Ref`	The number of references to this route. This is not used in the Linux kernel. It is here because the route tool itself is cross-platform. Thus it prints this value, since other operating systems do use it.
`Use`	The number of successful route cache lookups. To see this value, use the `-F` option when invoking **route**.

Note that **route** displayed the host names to any IP addresses it could look up and resolve. While this is nice to read, it presents a problem when there are network difficulties, and DNS or NIS servers become unavailable. The **route** command will hang on, trying to resolve host names and waiting to see if the servers come back and resolve them. This wait will go on for several minutes until the request times out.

To get around this, use the **-n** option with **route** so that the same information is shown, but **route** will make no attempt to perform host name resolution on the IP addresses.

netstat

Normally, the **netstat** program is used to display the status of all of the network connections on a host. However, with the **-r** option, it can also display the kernel routing table. You should note that most other UNIX-based operating systems require that you use this method of viewing routes.

Here is an example invocation of **netstat -r** and its corresponding output:

```
[root@trillian /root]# netstat -r
Kernel IP routing table
Destination     Gateway       Genmask         Flags MSS Window  irtt Iface
192.168.1.0     0.0.0.0       255.255.255.0 U     0   0       0 eth0
127.0.0.0       0.0.0.0       255.0.0.0     U     0   0       0 lo
default         192.168.1.1 0.0.0.0         UG    0   0       0 eth0
```

In this example, you see a simple configuration. The host has a single network interface card, is connected to the 192.168.1.0 network, and has a default gateway set to 192.168.1.1.

Like the **route** command, **netstat** can also take the **-n** parameter so that it does not perform host name resolution.

SUMMARY

In this chapter, we covered the four major components necessary to understanding how basic network services are set up on your Linux system:

▼   Kernel modules and their application to network device drivers

■   Using `ifconfig`

▲   Using `route`

Although we covered kernel modules earlier in this book, we revisited the topic this time with the specific intent of understanding kernel modules and their relationship to network device drivers. Remember the **/etc/conf.modules** file when setting up new network interfaces!

We ended the chapter with two sections on the command-line tools used for configuring network interface cards and setting up routes. Although graphical versions of these tools exist in various forms for different distributions, becoming familiar with them on the command line (especially the **route** command) is an important part of becoming a proficient Linux system administrator. It's also especially handy for remote administration!

CHAPTER 26

Advanced Linux Networking

L inux not only makes a great server platform but is a great network router, too. It supports all of the key features needed in commercial-grade routers without the expense of being a commercial-grade router. Even networking companies are starting to use Linux in their products; for example, Yago Systems, a company purchased by Cabletron, used Linux in one of its early routing platforms.

Part of what makes Linux so popular as a networking platform is the stability of its code base and the large user base installation, which regularly finds new and creative ways to deploy Linux (thus testing all aspects of its functionality). This means you can deploy a Linux-based routing system like you would any other network appliance.

Unfortunately, the problem with these advanced features is that they require you to have a fairly strong understanding of TCP/IP. (This is true of all networking equipment, regardless of vendor or operating system.) The tools themselves are very straightforward, but the concepts can be difficult to grasp at times. At the very least, you should understand IP addresses, netmasks, and port numbers. A knowledge of how routing tables work is a bonus. An understanding of the TCP packet structure means you'll finish this chapter craving more. (So read Chapter 24 if you want to learn more about TCP/IP.)

In this chapter, we discuss three specific components of the Linux networking code: IP aliasing, packet filtering, and IP Masquerading. The first concept is common among many operating systems: it's the ability of a single network interface to take on multiple IP addresses. Packet filtering is a little more complex, and most other operating systems require it to be purchased as a separate package or are unable to perform the task altogether. In short, packet filtering allows you to decide whether to accept and process a packet based on various attributes, such as the source and destination addresses. Finally, IP Masquerading is a variation on network address translation (NAT) that allows you to represent an entire network using only one IP address.

All of these features are supported in the kernel; however, they need user space tools to manipulate their configurations. The user space tools are explained in this chapter, but I do assume that you already have these features enabled in the kernel. If you are using the same kernel that came with our distribution of Linux, it is unlikely that you'll need to change anything. On the other hand, if you have recompiled your kernel, be sure you have included support for all of the previously mentioned features. They are all selectable in the Networking menu of the kernel configuration tool.

I can already hear some of you saying, "Really, I don't care about the details. Just help me protect my home network, and leave me alone!" Don't worry, this chapter is still for you. Skip to the "Cookbook Solutions" section for some quick solutions that will secure a simple, single subnet network connected to the Internet via a single IP address.

NOTE: All the tools and features cited assume that you are using kernel version 2.2 or later. If you have an older Linux system, it is highly recommended that you upgrade to take advantage of the features and performance improvements in the latest developments.

IP ALIASING

Linux can respond to multiple IP addresses using only one network card. Typical uses of this feature are for Web servers that must be able to support the HTTP/1.0 protocol, thus requiring that every domain have its own IP address. (Support for HTTP/1.0 is necessary for SSL service since most certificates issued by Certificate of Authorities are tied to a specific IP address.) Since a reasonably powerful PC running Linux is perfectly capable of hosting multiple domains on a single server, it makes sense to set up the system so that it is capable of responding to multiple IP addresses.

NOTE: By default, the kernel that came with your distribution should allow you to perform IP aliasing; however, if you need to compile your own kernel for whatever reason, be sure to enable IP aliasing in the Networking options.

To set up an IP alias, you need to use the `ifconfig` command with a special device name: Instead of using the actual device name of the network card (for instance, eth0), aliasing requires that you give the device name a suffix with a colon and a number (such as eth0:0). Every aliased device should have a unique number. For example, the first aliased device should be eth0:0, the second eth0:1, then eth0:2, and so on. The default kernel setting for the maximum number of IP aliases per device is 127.

NOTE: You must have configured the device before you create aliases for it. In other words, eth0 must be configured before eth0:0 can be configured.

The rest of the `ifconfig` line works just as it does for normal devices.

▼   To configure eth0:0 as 10.1.1.2 with a netmask of 255.255.255.0 and a broadcast address of 10.1.1.255, you would type

```
[root@ford /root]# ifconfig eth0:0 10.1.1.2 netmask 255.255.255.0
broadcast 10.1.1.255
```

▲   To configure eth1:3 as 10.1.2.3 with a netmask of 255.255.255.0 and a broadcast address of 10.1.2.255, you would type

```
[root@ford /root]# ifconfig eth1:3 10.1.2.3 netmask 255.255.255.0
broadcast 10.1.2.255
```

PACKET FILTERING

In a perfect world, you wouldn't have to worry about who is sending you data, because in a perfect world, no one would be malicious. Unfortunately, this is an imperfect world, and you need to worry about individuals on the Internet bent on sending your servers packets of data that could compromise site security. For example, unless you have purposely configured your machine to NFS export its disks to the world, there should be no reason why someone across the Internet should want to contact your NFS mount daemon. Ditto for other services such as IMAP, POP, Telnet, and so on.

Also in a perfect world, all pieces of software would be bulletproof and would, by themselves, reject connections or packets that would cause problems. But you know you don't live in a perfect world, so you need to use a mechanism for refusing questionable packets before your server software even sees them.

To make matters even more interesting, Linux can be configured and used as a router. In this configuration, you may need to provide protection for not only your server but for all of the machines on one particular side of the network. Common scenarios include Linux systems acting as firewalls.

So how do you do this? Enter packet filtering.

> **CAUTION:**   *Do not even begin to think that reading this chapter will make you a firewall expert!* People have managed to write multi-volume books on network security, firewalls, and packet filtering. This being a general-purpose system administration book, we are not interested in all of the fine details of running a secure firewall. What we *are* interested in is understanding the basic packet-filtering tools that are available to us under Linux. With this knowledge, you should be able to pick up a firewalls book and figure out how to make Linux a truly secure firewall. If your interest is in setting up a simple firewall for a home network or small office network, this chapter will be enough to get you through the process and have a reasonably secure site. As with any security issue, a little paranoia can go a long way. Keep up with security patches and updates and make sure to apply them in a timely manner.

More In-Depth Firewall Resources

If you are interested in setting up a more elaborate firewall configuration, check out *Building Internet Firewalls, Second Edition*, by Chapman and Zwicky (O'Reilly & Associates, 1999). Another good read is *Firewalls and Internet Security* by Cheswick and Bellovin (Addison-Wesley, 2000). This book discusses a lot of philosophical issues on security. One of the chapters in the first edition (1994), "An Evening with Berferd," documents their attempts to capture a hacker in the act. Finally, you can check out a non-technical book that is simply entertaining to read: *The Cuckoo's Egg: Tracking a Spy Through the Maze of Computer Espionage* by Clifford Stoll (Pocket Books, 1995). This story tracks a hacker prior to the Web and the massive commercialization of the Internet. There isn't much technical information, but what is there is real.

How Packet Filtering Works

A packet filter is simply a component in the operating system that examines each packet and checks it against some set of criteria. Based on those criteria, if the packet is allowed through, the operating system delivers it to the application. On the other hand, a packet that is not allowed through can either trigger a failure response to the sender or simply be thrown away as if it never happened. The action that is taken depends on the settings of the packet filter (see Figure 26-1).

Before we get into the process of understanding how to set up packet filter rules, we need to step back and look at what information a packet tells us so that we know which criteria we can use to decide whether to accept a packet.

Each packet that goes through an IP network has an IP header. This header carries information about the source of the packet as well as the destination. If the packet is also a TCP or UDP packet, it has the corresponding header for those protocols, as well (see Figure 26-2).

The purpose of all of the information within these packets is to help network equipment figure out how to direct packets from the source host to the destination host. Once the packet makes it to the destination host, it allows the host to decide whether it wants to accept it. The IP header specifies which host should receive it, and the TCP header specifies which application on the destination host should get the data (see Figure 26-3).

Looking at the IP and TCP headers, we see the fields we can use to decide whether we want to accept a packet. The most interesting of these fields are

▼   Source/destination IP address

▲   Source/destination port number

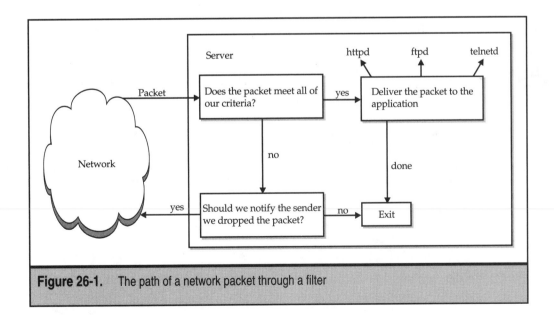

Figure 26-1.   The path of a network packet through a filter

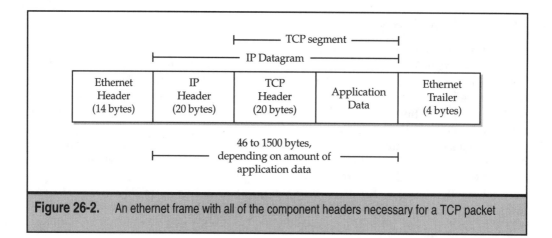

Figure 26-2.   An ethernet frame with all of the component headers necessary for a TCP packet

The source and destination numbers are obvious—where the packet is coming from and where it is going. Being able to filter on the destination may sound silly; after all, if you have received the packet, aren't you the destination? But you must not forget about the possibility of Linux being used as a router. In that case, the source and destination IP addresses may not include your IP address.

Checking against a source and destination port number allows you to pick which services you want to allow. For example, if you're running a large Web site where content is kept on a centralized NFS server, you need to allow your internal hosts to communicate with each other using the NFS protocol; however, people from outside the network should have no reason to contact your NFS-related services. Thus, you can block packets destined to port 111 (portmapper) and 2049 (where NFS typically responds).

These are not the only items you may want to check, of course, but they are certainly the most common.

> **NOTE:**   These options apply to both TCP and UDP. Some sites also filter on ICMP packets. We will discuss that in further detail in "Filtering Out the Ping of Death" later in this chapter.

In this section, we discuss the process of setting up a packet filter using the **ipchains** tool. When used in conjunction with IP Masquerading, you have a complete packet-filtering firewall solution. Note that the default kernel that gets shipped with most distributions has packet-filtering support already in the kernel. If you have to compile your own kernel for whatever reason, be sure to enable the network firewall when performing the configuration.

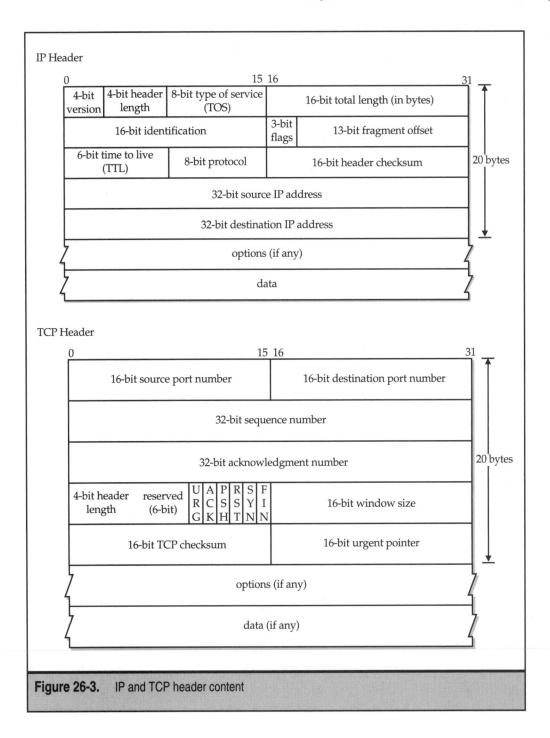

Figure 26-3. IP and TCP header content

CAUTION: You should always run the latest kernel versions available on a firewall. Hackers prey on sites that fail to keep up with the latest software releases and exploit holes in older releases.

IP Chains, Tables, and Packet Filtering

The history of Linux firewalling is a bit tricky to follow, because the developers have had to redo their implementation twice now. The first time Linux saw these features was in the 2.0 series of kernels. Back then, the tool that controlled the firewalling features was called **ipfwadm**. Because of limitations, the firewalling code was rewritten in the 2.2 series, and the **ipchains** tool was born. However, as anyone who has had the misfortune to see the resulting code can attest to, this solution was not pretty. But more important, it was hard to extend. The result is the 2.4 series that, because of the new methods of manipulating the rules that make it much more flexible, needs a new tool called **iptables**.

Because the 2.4 series is so new, we will cover both **ipchains** as well as **iptables**. Let's start with **ipchains**.

In Linux 2.2, the set of rules that decide whether a packet is allowed to enter the system, or is forwarded on, are stored in a series of *chains*. Each chain defines a set of rules that determine whether a packet may enter or leave a system. All of these chains are linked together to form a complete rule base. When a packet goes through the system, each rule for each applicable chain is applied to the packet in order. When a packet matches a rule, the system looks at what the corresponding action is and does it.

Unfortunately, these chains are only stored in memory, which means that you'll lose all of your settings upon reboot. Thus, if you want to keep your settings, you will need to write a simple script to re-create them at boot time. Don't worry, though: Scripts of this nature are very straightforward to write, and we'll step through a few of them along the way.

ipchains

The actual tool that performs the chain manipulation is (appropriately) called **ipchains**. Depending on your distribution, you may or may not have gotten it as part of your installation. Not to worry either way—you can download the latest version from http://netfilter.filewatcher.org/ipchains/. From this Web site, you will want to get two files: the latest **ipchains** (which is 1.3.10 as of this writing) and the latest helper scripts (which is 1.1.2 as of this writing). The **ipchains** program is now only distributed in source code format, so if your distribution did not come with **ipchains**, you will need to download it and install it. (Note that Red Hat Linux comes with **ipchains** preinstalled in the **/sbin** directory.) Because the helper scripts are written in shell script, they do not need compilation.

Once we have **ipchains** ready, we'll learn about what command-line options exist and then give some examples of how to use it. In the next section, we'll go through some cookbook situations so you can see **ipchains** in use.

▼ *TIP:*   Much of this chapter is derived from my fiddling around with **ipchains** to make my own firewall, the **ipchains** man page, and the **ipchains** HOWTO guide. The guide is available at the **ipchains** Web page. Another good place to get help with **ipchains** is **http://snafu.freedom.org/linux2.2**.

Compiling and Installing ipchains

For this section, we will assume that you have downloaded **ipchains-1.3.10.tar.gz** into the **/usr/local/src** directory. Note that Red Hat 6.0+ users have version 1.3.9 already installed. The commands in this chapter will work for 1.3.9, so you don't need to upgrade unless you find a specific problem.

Begin by unpacking the archive using the **tar** command, like so:

```
[root@ford src]# tar -xvzf ipchains-1.3.10.tar.gz
```

This will create a directory called **/usr/local/src/ipchains-1.3.10**. Go into that directory using the **cd** command and run **make all**:

```
[root@ford src]# cd ipchains-1.3.10
[root@ford ipchains-1.3.10]# make all
```

The compile will take only a few seconds. Once it is done, run **make install**:

```
[root@ford ipchains-1.3.10]# make install
```

This will install the **ipchains** binary into **/sbin** and the **ipchains** man page into **/usr/man/man8**.

Installing the Helper Scripts   For this section, let's assume that you have downloaded **ipchains-scripts-1.1.2.tar.gz** into the **/usr/local/src** directory. They can also be found at the http://netfilter.filewatcher.org/ipchains site. Note that Red Hat 6.0+ users have this installed already.

Begin by unpacking the archive using the **tar** command, like so:

```
[root@ford src]# tar -xvzf ipchains-scripts-1.1.2.tar.gz
```

This will create a directory called **/usr/local/src/ipchains-scripts-1.1.2**. Inside it will be three scripts: **ipchains-restore**, **ipchains-save**, and **ipfwadm-wrapper**, each with its corresponding man page. All we need to do is simply copy them into their appropriate locations, like this:

```
[root@ford src]# cd ipchains-scripts-1.1.2
[root@ford ipchains-scripts-1.1.2]# cp ipchains-restore /usr/bin
[root@ford ipchains-scripts-1.1.2]# cp ipchains-save /usr/bin
[root@ford ipchains-scripts-1.1.2]# cp ipfwadm-wrapper /usr/bin
[root@ford ipchains-scripts-1.1.2]# cp ipchains-restore.8 /usr/man/man8
[root@ford ipchains-scripts-1.1.2]# cp ipchains-save.8 /usr/man/man8
[root@ford ipchains-scripts-1.1.2]# cp ipfwadm-wrapper.8 /usr/man/man8
```

Using ipchains

The **ipchains** program is a command-line tool that allows manipulation of packet-filtering (also referred to as *firewalling*) *chains*. There are four types of chains: input chains, forwarding chains, output chains, and user-defined chains. Input chains are sets of rules that are applied to packets that enter the system from the network. Forwarding chains apply to packets that are passing through the Linux system when Linux is configured as a router. And, of course, output chains apply to packets that are headed out of the system. User-defined chains can apply to input, forwarding, or output packets. Figure 26-4 shows this relationship.

Actions To set up these chains, we need to pass certain parameters to the **ipchains** program. The format of the parameters depends on the action you want to take—the action is always the first parameter. Valid actions are shown in Table 26-1.

Before we go through the actions that need specific parameters, let's define the parameter types in Table 26-2.

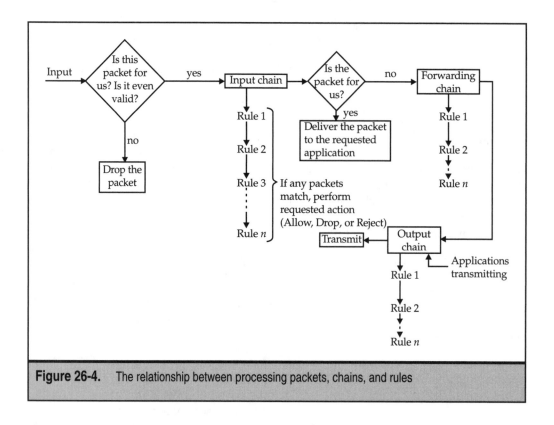

Figure 26-4.   The relationship between processing packets, chains, and rules

Parameter	Action
-A	Appends one or more rules to the end of the selected chain. If the rule applies to more than one set of IP address and port number combination, the rule will be added for each combination.
-D	Deletes one or more rules from the selected chain. You can either specify a rule number or specify the parameters for which a rule should be deleted. (For instance you can delete all rules that apply to IP address 192.168.3.19.)
-R	Replaces a rule in the selected chain. If the source and/or destination names match more than one entry, the replacement will fail, and the program will return an error.
-I	Inserts one or more rules in the selected chain at a given rule number.
-L	Lists a chain. If no specific chain is requested, all of the chains are listed.
-F	Flushes the selected chain. This is the same as deleting all of the entries in a particular chain.
-Z	Zeros out all the counters that **ipchains** keeps for accounting purposes.
-N	Creates a new chain.
-X	Deletes a chain. A chain must be empty before you can do this—that is, you need to flush the chain first.
-P	Sets the default policy for a given chain.

Table 26-1.   Parameters for the **ipchains** Program and Their Actions

Type of Parameter	Meaning
Chain	The name of the chain that the invocation of **ipchains** is going to work on. The three default chains are input, forward, and output.
Rulespec	The rule specification. The format of a rule specification is explained later in this section.

Table 26-2.   Parameter Types

Type of Parameter	Meaning
`Rulenum`	The number of the rule you want to work on. (This assumes the rule number already exists.)
`Target`	The action the kernel should take when it finds a packet that matches a rule listed in the chain. Valid targets are ACCEPT, REJECT, and DENY. ACCEPT means that the packet is allowed to pass through whatever chain is currently being processed. DENY means the packet is dropped, and the system simply pretends it never got it. REJECT is the friendly version of DENY: It refuses to accept the packet, but it sends an ICMP message to the sender indicating so.
`Options`	Additional modifiers that can be applied to each rule. These are, of course, not required. Options are discussed later in this section.

Table 26-2. Parameter Types *(continued)*

Now that you understand these definitions, let's examine the parameters that each action needs:

▼ To add a rule, use

```
[root@ford /root]# ipchains -A chain rulespec options
```

■ To delete a rule, use

```
[root@ford /root]# ipchains -D chain rulespec options
[root@ford /root]# ipchains -D chain rulenum options
```

■ To replace a rule, use

```
[root@ford /root]# ipchains -R chain rulenum rulespec options
```

■ To insert a rule, use

```
[root@ford /root]# ipchains -I chain rulenum rulespec options
```

■ To list rules, use

```
[root@ford /root]# ipchains -L chain options
```

■ To flush a selected chain, use

```
[root@ford /root]# ipchains -F chain options
```

- To zero out a set of counters for a chain, use

  `[root@ford /root]# ipchains -Z chain options`

- To create a new chain, use

  `[root@ford /root]# ipchains -N chain options`

- To delete a chain, use

  `[root@ford /root]# ipchains -X chain options`

▲ To set the policy for a given chain, use

  `[root@ford /root]# ipchains -P chain target options`

Rule Specifications The rule specification (or *rulespec*, as we have abbreviated it) is made up of a series of individual command-line parameters. These parameters are as follows:

▼ **-p protocol** Specifies the type of IP packet to which this rule should apply. Valid protocols are those that are listed in the **/etc/protocols** file or a numeric value for any protocol that isn't listed there. Typical values are **tcp**, **udp**, **icmp**, or **all**, where **all** refers to all of the valid protocols. If you prefix the **protocol** with an exclamation point (!), you invert the test. For example, saying **-p !icmp** effectively means "for all protocols that are not icmp."

■ **-s source/mask port** Specifies what the source IP address (or network address) must be for this rule to match. Typical uses are to deny networks that are known to be hostile or untrustworthy. In this option, **source** is the IP address, and **mask** is the netmask that can be represented either by using dotted decimal notation (such as 255.255.255.0) or by specifying the number of bits in the netmask (for example, 25 is equal to a netmask of 255.255.255.128). Note that the **mask** is optional if you want to specify a specific host. The **port** value allows you to specify the source port number on which you want to act. You can use a range of values by using the format **port1:port2**, where **port1** is the lower bound and **port2** is the upper bound. Port numbers are optional. For example, to specify any ports in the range of 1024 to 65535 from any host in the 192.168.42.0 network, you would say **-s 192.168.42.0/24 1024:65535**. Prefixing either the IP/netmask combination or the port number with an exclamation point (!) negates the expression. For example, to specify any host except 192.168.42.7, you would say **-s !192.168.42.7**. This is useful when you want to explicitly allow a certain set of hosts or networks and deny everyone else.

■ **--source-port port** Specifies a port (or port range of **port** is in the format of **port1:port2**, where **port1** is the lowest port number and **port2** is the highest port number) without having to specify an IP address. If you want to set up a rule for all hosts whose source port is 0 to 1023, for example, you would use `--source-port 0:1023`.

■ `-d destination/mask port`   The same as the `-s` option, except this is for the destination instead of the source IP address.

■ `--destination-port port`   The same as the `--source-port` option, except this option applies to the destination port rather than the source port.

■ `--icmp-type typename`   Applies a rule to a ICMP packet whose type is *typename*. You can run `ipchains -h icmp` to see a list of types. The most common type is the echo-reply, which is used for the ping program. Prefixing *typename* with an exclamation point (!) inverts the rule. For example, to set up a rule for all ICMP packets except port-unreachable messages, you would say `--icmp-type ! port-unreachable`.

■ `-j target`   Specifies that the action to perform if a rule matches should be *target*, where *target* is either a use-defined chain or one of the predefined targets (ACCEPT, DENY, REJECT).

■ `-i interface`   Specifies the interface to which this rule should apply, where *interface* is the name of the device (such as eth0). If this option is not specified for a rule, it is the name of the device (such as eth0). If this option is not specified for a rule, it is assumed that the rule will apply to all interfaces. If *interface* is prefixed with an exclamation point (!), it inverts the rule. For example, to apply a rule to all interfaces except ppp1, you would say `-I ! ppp1`.

▲ `-f`   Applies this rule to any packet fragment. Because the header information in an IP fragment is not included with each fragment, it is impossible to apply any existing rules to it. You can avoid this mess altogether by configuring the kernel to defragment all packets before delivering them. If you do want to allow fragments from certain interfaces, use this in conjunction with the `-I` option. By prefixing the `-f` with an exclamation point (!), you can invert the meaning. For example, to say that we want to reject all fragments except those coming from eth0, we would use `! -f -i eth0 -j ALLOW`.

Options   Additional options, shown in Table 26-3, may be specified for a rule.

Examples of Using ipchains   As we've seen so far, `ipchains` can be a bit hair-raising to figure out. Usually, though, it takes only a few examples of it in action to better understand the relationship between all of the actions and their corresponding options. So let's step through some examples.

Option	Description
-b	Applies the rule bidirectionally. This is effectively the same as setting up an additional rule where the source and destination information are reversed.
-v	Verbose output.
-n	Gives numeric output. Normally, listing all of the rules or changing the rules with the verbose option will result in all of the IP addresses getting their names resolved so that the output will be more readable. If you are debugging a problem and host name resolution is not available, you should use this option so the system doesn't stall while waiting for DNS requests to time out.
-l	Turns on kernel logging for all packets that match the rules.
-x	Shows exact numbers when printing rule information with the **-L** action. Typically, output is rounded to the nearest 1,000 or 1,000,000.
-y	Matches only packets with the SYN bit set but not the ACK or FIN bits set. The SYN bit in a TCP header is used to initiate connections. Typically, this option is used to block incoming connections but allow outgoing connections. You can prefix this option with a exclamation mark (!) to invert it, thereby matching all packets where the SYN bit isn't set and the ACK or FIN bit is set.

Table 26-3   Additional Options That May Be Specified for a Rule

▼ You want to set up a rule so that connections coming from the 192.168.1.8 are dropped, but you are allowed to open up a connection to them:

```
[root@ford /root]# ipchains -A input -p tcp -s 192.168.1.8 -j DENY -y
```

■ You want to block all connections to our port 8080 from anyone and log all attempts:

```
[root@ford /root]# ipchains -A input -p tcp --destination-port 8080 -j DENY -l
```

▲ You want to block all packets coming from ntp.ucsd.edu except those coming from port 123. This is done with two filters: The first allows packets from ntp.ucsd.edu port 123; the second denies everything else coming from ntp.ucsd.edu. This works because rules are checked in order—if a packet comes from ntp.ucsd.edu from port 123, it will match the first rule and immediately accept the packet. The second rule will not be checked. On the other hand, if the packet is from ntp.ucsd.edu port 124, the first rule will not apply causing **ipchains** to check the packet against the second rule. Because it will match the second rule, **ipchains** will drop the packet.

```
[root@ford /root]# ipchains -A input -p tcp -s ntp.ucsd.edu 123 -j ACCEPT
[root@ford /root]# ipchains -A input -p tcp -s ntp.ucsd.edu -j DENY
```

iptables

From a user's point of view, the **ipchains** tool in the Linux 2.2 series did its job pretty well. No real complaints, per se. But inside the kernel was a whole other story. The code was difficult at best to follow and very difficult to extend. And this is where the beauty of open source comes into play: Instead of just complaining about why things are the way they are, other developers were able to look into the code and give their feedback. This in conjunction with some great ideas from the code TCP/IP developers resulted in the 2.4 series of kernels getting what amounts to a new TCP/IP stack with much better support for firewalls. (It's also a lot faster!) Because of the drastic internal changes, some changes had to be seen by the users, and this comes in the form of a new command-line tool called **iptables**.

But before we all sigh and groan about having two different systems, we should take note that a lot of effort went into making the two similar to users. So moving from **ipchains** should not be too drastic after all.

▼ **NOTE:** "But I don't want to change—period!" Okay, you got it. The developers realized that not everyone was in a hurry to adopt the new system, although they may want to begin using the new kernel. To accommodate this, the firewall code was written as a kernel module, and the old **ipchains** code was fixed up to work as a module, as well. Thus, by simply loading the correct module, you can pick and choose which firewall code you want to use. (There is even support for the **ipfwadm** code!) To get the **ipchains** code, simply use **insmod ipchains.o** instead of **ip_tables.o**. (See Chapter 10 for more information on modules.) If you want to bring back **ipfwadm** support, use **insmod ipfwadm.o**. Note that all of these are mutually exclusive. This means you can have any one loaded, but not more. For instance, if you have **ip_tables.o** loaded, you cannot load **ipchains.o** or **ipfwadm.o**.

In this section, we will cover the differences in how **ipchains** and **iptables** work, getting **iptables**, the command-line usage of **iptables**, and then finally some examples of using **iptables**.

The Differences Between ipchains and iptables

Most of the differences between **ipchains** and **iptables** are internal. This makes the transition much more painless. However, the most significant change is in how the rules get applied depending on whether a packet is destined to the host or only being passed forward (routed). Figure 26-5 illustrates this for us.

The first thing to note is that the capitalization has changed. This is important—the three core chains, INPUT, FORWARD, and OUTPUT, are capitalized so that it is clear that they must always be there. User-added chains remain in lowercase.

The second thing to note is that not all packets go through all chains. In **ipchains**, packets that would get forwarded would be subject to all of the same input and output rules that packets local to the host would get. However, this isn't always desirable in the case where you have a Linux system acting as router. For instance, you may want to allow more free access to a particular host inside your network while keeping the router itself simply inaccessible to everyone else. Note, however, that this does not keep you from using the INPUT and OUTPUT chains from within FORWARD, if you like. Simply set up a rule so that all packets jump to the INPUT chain, and then at the end of your FORWARD chain, set up a second rule so that all packets jump to the OUTPUT chain. (How to do this is discussed in "Using iptables," later in the chapter.)

The remaining changes are mostly cosmetic in the form of differing command-line options. Specifics will be covered later in this section.

Downloading and Installing iptables

Before we even begin discussing this step, you must be running a 2.4 series kernel for this to work. Red Hat Linux 7.0 ships with the 2.2.16 kernel, because the 2.4.0 kernel was not ready at the time they needed to ship. (The current best guess for 2.4.0 to ship is for

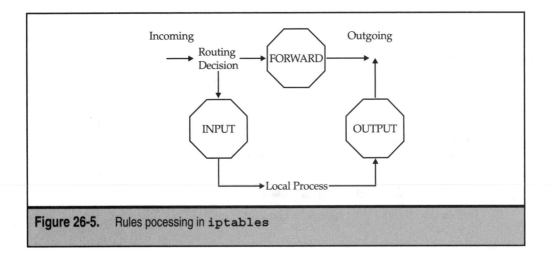

Figure 26-5. Rules pocessing in `iptables`

early 2001.) Thankfully, Red Hat 7.0 is already equipped to handle the 2.4.0 series, so if you want to try out the kernel while it's in beta, go for it! Read Chapter 10 to see how to download and compile the kernel yourself. Also note that if you are running Red Hat 7.0, you already have **iptables** compiled for you in the **/sbin** directory.

Assuming you have a 2.4.0test9 or better, here are the steps you need to take to compile **iptables**:

1. Download **iptables-1.1.2.tar.bz2** (the most recent version as of this writing) from http://netfilter.filewatcher.org to a directory where you have enough space to compile the package. For this example, let's assume you have downloaded this to **/usr/local/src**. Note that this archive was compressed with the **bzip2** program and not **gzip**. This requires a slightly different method of unpacking.

   ```
   [root@ford src]# tar --user-compress-program bzip2 -xvf iptables-1.1.2.tar.bz2
   ```

   This will create a directory called **iptables-1.1.2** in which the source code will be.

2. Run **make**. Doing do requires that you know where the kernel source tree is. For this example, let's assume that it is in **/usr/src/linux**.

   ```
   [root@ford src]# cd iptables-1.1.2
   [root@ford iptables-1.1.2]# make KERNEL_DIR=/usr/src/linux
   ```

   This will leave you with the **iptables** binary in the current directory.

3. Install the binaries.

   ```
   [root@ford iptables-1.1.2]# make install
   ```

   This will install the binaries into the **/usr/local/bin** directory, the man pages into **/usr/local/man/man8**, and the relevant libraries that it needs into **/usr/local/lib/iptables**.

Using iptables

The **iptables** tool is actually almost letter-for-letter identical in options to the **ipchains** tool. Thus, in this section, we only cover the differences between the two rather than repeat large parts of the original **ipchains** section.

▼ The first significant change you'll see in **iptables** is that instead of using lowercase names for the input and output chains, you will see uppercase chain names: INPUT and OUTPUT.

■ The **-i** flag refers to the interface used for the INPUT and FORWARD chains.

■ The **-o** flag refers to the interface used for the OUTPUT chain.

■ The source and destination ports should be specified using the `--source-port` and `--destination-port` respectively, instead of immediately after the source IP address (`-s`) and destination IP address (`-d`).

■ IP address and port specifications must come after the `-p` option. (The `-p` option specifies the protocol; e.g., `-p tcp`.)

■ The `-y` flag is now `--syn`.

▲ The DENY target is now called DROP. (e.g., `-j DROP`)

In general, you will find that most of your scripts will work with little to no modification under **iptables**.

Cookbook Solutions

This section is dedicated to folks looking for examples or just plain wanting to skip the "how-to" component and get a simple firewall going.

Rusty's Really Quick Guide to Packet Filtering

Paul "Rusty" Russell, one of the lead developers of the packet-filtering tools for Linux, offers this simple solution for someone who has a single PPP connection to the Internet and doesn't want anyone coming back into their network. Simply add the following lines to the end of your rc.local script so that they automatically take effect at boot up time.

The first script is for the Linux 2.4 series of kernels using **iptables**. The second script is for the Linux 2.2 series of kernels using **ipchains**.

```
### Rusty's Script for Linux 2.4 kernels using ipchains
### Insert connection tracking modules
insmod ip_tables
insmod ip_conntrack
insmod ip_conntrack_ftp


### Create chain that blocks new connections, except if coming
## from the inside network
iptables -N block
iptables -A block -m state --state ESTABLISHED,RELATED -j ACCEPT
iptables -A block -m state --state NEW -i ! ppp0 -j ACCEPT
iptables -A block -j DROP


## Jump to that chain from INPUT and FORWARD chains
iptables -A INPUT -j block
iptables -A FORWARD -j block
```

If you are still using Linux 2.2 or want to continue using **ipchains** instead of **iptables**, then you'll want the following version of the script instead.

```
### Steve's Script for Linux 2.2 kernels using ipchains
ipchains -F input
ipchains -A input -j ACCEPT -f -i ppp0
ipchains -A input -j ACCEPT -p TCP ! -y -i ppp0
ipchains -A input -j ACCEPT -p UDP -d 0/0 53 -i ppp0
ipchains -A input -j ACCEPT -p TCP -d 0/0 53 -i ppp0
ipchains -A input -j REJECT -l -i ppp0
```

If you are using this on a cable modem or DSL line where your outside connection is a second ethernet interface card, be sure to change **ppp0** to reflect the proper ethernet device (probably eth1).

Also note that these settings are quite strict and will break a lot of protocols that rely on opening a connection back into your network. Active FTP and Napster are two popular ones that will not work. FTP is easy to fix—simply use passive FTP. Napster on the other hand . . . Well, just buy the record or read the prior sections on how to set up holes in your firewall and forward connections to inside hosts.

Filtering Out the Ping of Death

The Ping of Death has been around for quite a while now. Although most operating systems have had patches released that fix this problem, you may still have some older systems that are not protected on your network. If your Linux system is acting as a router for them, you will want to offer protection by using packet filtering.

But before we can build a filter for the Ping of Death, we must first understand what it is. To understand that, we have to understand what a ping is.

As we saw in Chapter 24, IP packets encapsulate many other protocols, such as TCP and UDP. Another common IP packet type is ICMP, which stands for Internet Control Message Protocol, which allows transmissions of out-of-band messages from one host to another telling of a possible problem it is having with a transmission. The most common usage, though, is informational—the *ICMP echo-reply*. An ICMP echo-reply is a special type of packet that, when received, is immediately returned. No special daemons or user-level processes must service these packets; all of the work is done in the kernel. The purpose of this message is twofold: to make sure the system is up and running and to time the response so that the sender can determine the network latency. The tool that can generate and send ICMP messages is called *ping*.

Normally, ICMP packets are very small. They must contain only enough information to get the packet to the destination (the IP header) and then a few bytes to describe the message. As a result, many systems assumed that the packet would never surpass a certain size.

The Ping of Death is a very large ICMP packet. Because this size exceeds the buffer allocation in many systems, the kernel fails to process correctly and the usual result is a system crash.

To protect your system (or systems for which you are performing routing) from the Ping of Death, you can simply filter for ICMP fragments, because there is no reasonable condition under which an ICMP packet is so large that it needs to be fragmented. The exact invocation for **ipchains** to do this is

```
[root@ford /root]# ipchains -A input -p icmp -j DENY -f
```

The way to do this with **iptables** is

```
[root@ford /root]# iptables -A input -p icmp -j DROP -f
```

Keeping It Less Strict

One very popular use of Linux is *IP Masquerading*. This is when a Linux system represents an entire network of machines using one IP address. All of the machines in the network point to the Linux system as their default gateway and route through it. In fact, as I write this, my wife is surfing the Net from her Macintosh through my Linux system, which is connected to the Internet via DSL. Her Mac is configured just like any other machine on a local area network. (Configuring IP Masquerading is discussed in "IP Masquerading" later in this chapter.)

Because I have several other machines on my network at home, I like keeping services like NFS and Samba available so that we can effectively share resources. But keeping these services available makes my system vulnerable to outside attack when it is connected to the Internet.

To protect ourselves, we have set up packet filtering for all of the services that we want to keep available to our local area network but inaccessible to everyone on the Internet. Specifically, we want to block access to the following:

▼ Portmapper (port 111)

■ NTP server (port 123)

■ Telnet (port 23)

■ Finger (port 79)

■ Auth (port 113)

▲ X Windows (ports 6000-6010)

To make things interesting, we don't want to block access to these services to people on our internal network, and we do want to allow ntp.ucsd.edu to contact our port 123, since we use it to synchronize our clocks. Furthermore, our IP address changes every time we dial up to the Internet. When we aren't connected, the ppp0 interface also goes away, so we need a script to automatically re-enable the rules when we start our connection and another script to flush these rules when we are done using our Internet connection.

The first script using **ipchains** looks like this:

```
#!/bin/sh
#
# Setup firewalling for eth1 on tcp ports 111, 123, 23, 21,
# 79, 113, and 6000-6010
```

```
# Also deny any incoming ICMP echo-reply packets.
# Use -l option so that all packets that match these criteria
# get logged.
#

# Where is ipchains
IPC=/sbin/ipchains

# Start by making sure there are not residual rules
$IPC -F input

# Deny all outside portmapper requests (111)
$IPC -A input -p tcp --destination-port 111 -j DENY -l -i eth1

# Allow ntp.ucsd.edu to connect to our port 123 so long as its
# originating port is 123. Deny everyone else trying to contact
# our port 123.
$IPC -A input -p tcp -s ntp.ucsd.edu 123 --destination-port 123 -j ALLOW -l -i eth1
$IPC -A input -p tcp --destination-port 123 -j DENY -l -i eth1

# Deny telnet from everyone
$IPC -A input -p tcp --destination-port 23 -j DENY -l -i eth1

# Deny FTP from everyone
$IPC -A input -p tcp --destination-port 21 -j DENY -l -i eth1

# Deny finger from everyone
$IPC -A input -p tcp --destination-port 79 -j DENY -l -i eth1

# Deny ident from everyone
$IPC -A input -p tcp --destination-port 113 -j DENY -l -i eth1

# Deny X-Windows from everyone
$IPC -A input -p tcp --destination-port 6000:6010 -j DENY -l -i eth1
```

TIP: You may have noticed that we used the **-l** option in all of our calls to **ipchains**. As discussed earlier, this option logs all packets that match the rule to the system logger (syslogd). Doing this serves two purposes: the first is debugging. Trying to figure out which rules are getting triggered by certain types of connections is much easier if you see a log entry for the rule that handled it. The second purpose is informational—it is always good to see when someone comes knocking at our filter/firewall! (Sadly, you will see this a lot. Even on dial-up connections.)

You can save this file as /**usr/local/bin/start_firewall**. Make sure to use **chmod** to set this file as executable, like so:

```
[root@ford /root]# chmod 0755 /usr/local/bin/start_firewall
```

When we are done with our Internet connection, we flush our firewall rules using the following script:

```
#!/bin/sh
# Remove all of the input files from the firewall.
/sbin/ipchains -F input
```

You can save this file as **/usr/local/bin/stop_firewall**. Make sure to use **chmod** to set this file as executable, like so:

```
[root@ford /root]# chmod 0755 /usr/local/bin/stop_firewall
```

To get the same effect using **iptables**, you would use the following script instead:

```
#!/bin/sh
#
# Set up firewalling for ppp0 on tcp ports 111, 123, 23, 21,
# 79, 113, and 6000-6010
# Also deny any incoming ICMP echo-reply packets.
# Use -l option so that all packets that match these criteria
# get logged.
#

IPT=/sbin/iptables
$IPT -F INPUT
$IPT -A INPUT -p tcp --destination-port 111 -j DROP -l -i eth1
$IPT -A INPUT -p tcp --destination-port 123 -j DROP -l -i eth1
$IPT -A INPUT -p tcp --destination-port 23  -j DROP -l -i eth1
$IPT -A INPUT -p tcp --destination-port 21  -j DROP -l -i eth1
$IPT -A INPUT -p tcp --destination-port 79  -j DROP -l -i eth1
$IPT -A INPUT -p tcp --destination-port 113 -j DROP -l -i eth1
$IPT -A INPUT -p tcp --destination-port 6000:6010 -j DROP -l -i eth1
```

The corresponding script to stop this kind of firewall looks a lot like the one for **ipchains**:

```
#!/bin/sh
/sbin/iptables -F INPUT
```

Choice of Rules   The first set of firewall scripts that we looked at used a technique known as *explicit allow*. This means that we set up the firewall so that unless a port is explicitly allowed through, it is denied by default. This method is considered to be the best way to secure a network, since it allows you to more easily track what is allowed into your network rather than you having to figure out what you need to deny. The downside to this is that you must be ready to work with users who want access to some feature that requires that a hole be poked through the firewall. As with any security-related change, take the time to look at the situation, and try to find a better solution, but if push comes to shove, document the change very carefully, and watch it for any suspicious activity. Some may consider this behavior overly paranoid, but it's always nicer to be overly paranoid than it is to get rid of a hacker.

The second set of firewall scripts that we discussed used another technique called *explicit deny*. Of course, this is the exact opposite of explicit allow: All packets are allowed unless explicitly denied. What's handy about this way of securing networks is that it makes dealing with a wide variety of traffic easier, since you don't need to keep dealing with exceptions to your firewall rules. The tricky part is knowing in advance what you need to lock up. In networks where your users require you to be open (e.g., ISPs), firewalls are a handy way of allowing your users to get full access to the world while allowing you to set up rules to protect specific machines on your internal network.

A blend of these two methods is to explicitly deny specific types of traffic but add to those rules deny filters for invalid networks (e.g., private networks). Invalid networks include 127.0.0.0/8, 192.168.0.0/16, 172.16.0.0/16 to 172.31.0.0/16, and 10.0.0.0/8 because they are private IPs that should not be used for source IP addresses for packets coming in over your Internet connection.

To add these rules to the start_firewall script in the "Keeping It Less Strict" section, you would add these **iptables** rules:

```
iptables -A INPUT -p all -s 127.0.0.0/8    -j DROP
iptables -A INPUT -p all -s 192.168.0.0/16 -j DROP
iptables -A INPUT -p all -s 10.0.0.0/8     -j DROP
iptables -A INPUT -p all -s 172.16.0.0/16  -j DROP
iptables -A INPUT -p all -s 172.17.0.0/16  -j DROP
iptables -A INPUT -p all -s 172.18.0.0/16  -j DROP
iptables -A INPUT -p all -s 172.19.0.0/16  -j DROP
iptables -A INPUT -p all -s 172.20.0.0/16  -j DROP
iptables -A INPUT -p all -s 172.21.0.0/16  -j DROP
iptables -A INPUT -p all -s 172.22.0.0/16  -j DROP
iptables -A INPUT -p all -s 172.23.0.0/16  -j DROP
iptables -A INPUT -p all -s 172.24.0.0/16  -j DROP
iptables -A INPUT -p all -s 172.25.0.0/16  -j DROP
iptables -A INPUT -p all -s 172.26.0.0/16  -j DROP
iptables -A INPUT -p all -s 172.27.0.0/16  -j DROP
iptables -A INPUT -p all -s 172.28.0.0/16  -j DROP
iptables -A INPUT -p all -s 172.29.0.0/16  -j DROP
iptables -A INPUT -p all -s 172.30.0.0/16  -j DROP
iptables -A INPUT -p all -s 172.31.0.0/16  -j DROP
```

If you are using **ipchains** instead, you can use the following series of commands:

```
ipchains -A input -p all -s 127.0.0.0/8     -j REJECT
ipchains -A input -p all -s 192.168.0.0/16 -j REJECT
ipchains -A input -p all -s 10.0.0.0/8      -j REJECT
ipchains -A input -p all -s 172.16.0.0/16  -j REJECT
ipchains -A input -p all -s 172.17.0.0/16  -j REJECT
ipchains -A input -p all -s 172.18.0.0/16  -j REJECT
ipchains -A input -p all -s 172.19.0.0/16  -j REJECT
ipchains -A input -p all -s 172.20.0.0/16  -j REJECT
ipchains -A input -p all -s 172.21.0.0/16  -j REJECT
ipchains -A input -p all -s 172.22.0.0/16  -j REJECT
ipchains -A input -p all -s 172.23.0.0/16  -j REJECT
ipchains -A input -p all -s 172.24.0.0/16  -j REJECT
ipchains -A input -p all -s 172.25.0.0/16  -j REJECT
ipchains -A input -p all -s 172.26.0.0/16  -j REJECT
ipchains -A input -p all -s 172.27.0.0/16  -j REJECT
ipchains -A input -p all -s 172.28.0.0/16  -j REJECT
ipchains -A input -p all -s 172.29.0.0/16  -j REJECT
ipchains -A input -p all -s 172.30.0.0/16  -j REJECT
ipchains -A input -p all -s 172.31.0.0/16  -j REJECT
```

IP MASQUERADING

A common scenario for home and small office users is that of having a single dial-up account and multiple computers that want to use it—often at the same time. To make matters even trickier, the dial-up gives you only a single IP address.

IP Masquerading solves this problem by allowing your Linux system to do two tricks: act as a router and perform network address translation (NAT).

NOTE: With the 2.4 series of kernels, the developers of the **iptables** tool have implemented the "correct" version of NAT. They differentiate this from IP Masquerading by name only. If you are reading other documentation, you will want to keep an eye out for this.

Here is how it works: Your local area network uses a bank of private IP addresses. For small networks, the 192.168 range works nicely. For this example, we'll use the 192.168.1.0 network with a 24-bit netmask. The network map will look like Figure 26-6.

Figure 26-6. Our example network

The Linux system on 192.168.1.1 ("Ford") is going to be our IP Masquerader. It has a modem in it and is configured to perform PPP dial-up to an Internet service provider. When it is dialed up, it has two interfaces in it: eth0 to connect to the local area network and ppp0 to connect to the Internet. At this point, there is no forwarding of packets between one and the other.

What we want to do is make Ford route packets on behalf of the hosts on the local area network in such a way that when the packets are sent towards the Internet, they look like they originated from Ford. When a packet comes back in response, Ford should realize that it is really meant for one of the machines on the inside network and forward it to the appropriate host. Figure 26-7 illustrates this from a broad perspective, showing the relationship between all of the hosts on the network. Figure 26-8 focuses on Ford and its IP Masquerading engine.

Figure 26-7.   Relationship between hosts on the network

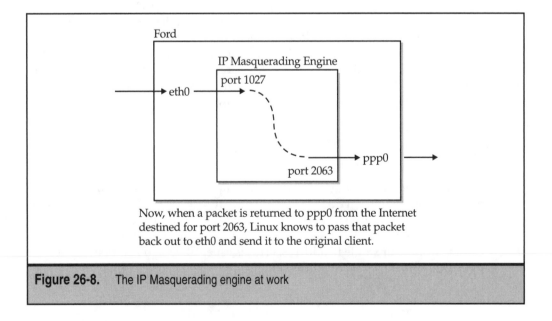

Now, when a packet is returned to ppp0 from the Internet
destined for port 2063, Linux knows to pass that packet
back out to eth0 and send it to the original client.

Figure 26-8.   The IP Masquerading engine at work

NOTE: Don't assume that the only way IP Masquerading works is with a dial-up modem. The ppp0 interface could be any type of network interface. In a firewall configuration, for example, the outside interface could simply be a second ethernet card that is plugged into the corporate network.

The Three-Line IP Masquerading Solution

If your home network is similar to the one just described (internal network on 192.168.1.0 and a Linux machine with a modem set to do dial-up PPP on the ppp0 interface), you need to add only three lines to your **/etc/rc.d/rc.local** boot script to enable IP Masquerading using **ipchains**:

```
ipchains -P forward DENY
ipchains -A forward -i ppp0 -j MASQ
echo 1 > /proc/sys/net/ipv4/ip_forward
```

NOTE: If your outside network connection is on a different interface, change ppp0 to reflect that. Also note that this script assumes that your ppp0 interface is already enabled. If it is not, enable the interface, then run this script.

The first invocation of **ipchains** sets the default forwarding behavior to DENY so that when IP forwarding is turned on, the only packets that make it through are those we explicitly allow. The second invocation of **ipchains** actually adds the Masquerading rule. This introduces a new target that was not discussed in the packet filtering section. (You have to know what IP Masquerading is before you can understand why it should be a target!) This is very simple: Add a rule to the forwarding chain that applies to the ppp0 interface only. All packets that are passed through this chain are masqueraded. The last line simply enables IP forwarding in the kernel. The reason the second rule works is a little tricky, so don't feel bad if you find it confusing and choose to ignore it!

The same script using **iptables** is done as follows:

```
modprobe iptable_nat
iptables -t nat -A POSTROUTING -o ppp0 -j MASQUERADE
echo 1 > /proc/sys/net/ipv4/ip_forward
```

In this series of commands, the first command simply probes the kernel and asks it to load the iptable_nat module if it doesn't already have it. The second line is what does the magic; it tells the networking system to enable Masquerading on the ppp0 interface. Thus, if you have a dial-up PPP connection, your entire internal network will appear as if it were coming from your single IP address. (This is especially handy since many service providers charge extra for extra IP addresses.)

So now that you know what to type, let's examine what's happening under the hood. When a PPP session is started, the default route is changed so that it points toward the ppp0 device and the first hop on the other side of the PPP connection (your ISP). So when a packet enters your system from the local area network, and IP forwarding is enabled, Linux tries to figure out where to send it. Looking at the route table, it sees that the default route is to send the packet to the ppp0 device so that it gets sent on to the Internet. The process of forwarding the packet from the local area network interface to the PPP interface requires that the packet be passed through the forwarding chain.

As Linux steps through the forwarding chain, it finds that the first rule matches the criteria: The packet is destined towards the ppp0 device. Thus, Linux goes to the target specification, which in this case is MASQ (short for masquerade). The Masquerading engine takes care of rewriting the packet, as described earlier in this section, and lets the packet be forwarded on to the Internet as a whole.

When a packet comes into the ppp0 interface from the Internet, Linux checks the with the Masquerading engine to see if the packet is really destined for someone else. If it is, the packet is demasqueraded and then sent on to the original sender on the local area network.

Masquerading Proxies

Unfortunately, not all protocols masquerade nicely. FTP is a perfect example of this: When an FTP client contacts an FTP server, it begins by contacting the server's port 21. The client passes all the login and password information through this port. However, when the client requests the server to send a file, the server initiates a new connection back to the client. Uh oh! If the client is masqueraded, then the IP Masquerader will be the machine that really gets the new connection request. The IP Masquerader will most likely reject the new connection because it doesn't have a program listening to that port, and the transfer will promptly break. (Read Chapter 13 on FTP servers for more information on this and other modes FTP can use.)

FTP is one of many protocols that do strange things like this. In order to allow these protocols to be masqueraded, a special proxy must be put in place. Linux comes with several of the most common proxies: FTP, Real Audio, IRC, Quake, VDO Live, and others (see the following list).

Module Name	Description
`ip_masq_ftp`	FTP service
`ip_masq_irc`	IRC masquerading
`ip_masq_quake`	Allows the game Quake to be played through a masqueraded network
`ip_masq_raudio`	Forwards Real Audio packets correctly
`ip_masq_vdolive`	Forwards VDO Live packets correctly

To use the modules, simply make sure to **insmod** them at boot time. For example, if you want to support Real Audio and FTP Masquerading, add the following to your boot scripts:

```
insmod ip_masq_ftp
insmod ip_masq_raudio
```

NOTE: Most distributions come with these kernel modules precompiled. If you choose to compile your own kernel, be sure to select these features while configuring the kernel, or you'll have nothing to **insmod**!

SUMMARY

In this chapter, we discussed the tools needed to perform advanced network administration under Linux. Specifically, we covered the techniques for using IP aliasing, packet filters, and IP Masquerading. Given what we have discussed, it is possible for you to set up a simple Linux router with multiple IP addresses and perform basic firewalling and NAT functions for a network.

If you are interested in learning more about Linux networking, there are plenty of Web sites you can learn from. At the top of the list is http://snafu.freedom.org/linux2.2, which contains a wonderful summary of tools, documentation, and links to more information about Linux networking. The http://netfilter.samba.org site is an excellent place for more information about the netfilter (**iptables**) system.

If you're impressed with Linux networking (and you should be!), but you don't have time to administer a Linux-based router/firewall yourself, take a look at the Firebox at http://www.watchguard.com.

CHAPTER 27

The /proc File System

Every operating system offers a mechanism for system administrators to probe the insides of the operating system and to set operational parameters when needed. In Linux, this mechanism is the **/proc** file system. Windows NT allows this to some degree through the Registry, and Solaris allows this through the **ndd** tool. (Solaris has a **/proc** file system, as well.)

In this chapter, we discuss the **/proc** file system and how it works under Linux 2.4. We'll step through some overviews and study some interesting entries in **/proc**, and then we'll end with some notes on common administrative tasks using **/proc**.

WHAT'S INSIDE THE /PROC DIRECTORY?

Since the Linux kernel is such a key component in server operations, it's important that there be a method for exchanging information with the kernel. Traditionally, this is done through *system calls*—special functions written for programmers to use in requesting the kernel to perform functions on their behalf. In the context of system administration, however, system calls mean a developer needs to write a tool for us to use (unless, of course, you like writing your own tools). When all you need is a simple tweak or to extract some statistics from the kernel, having to write a custom tool is a lot more effort than should be necessary.

To improve communication between users and the kernel, the **/proc** file system was created. The entire file system is especially interesting because it doesn't really exist on disk anywhere; it's purely an abstract of kernel information. All of the files in the directory correspond to either a function in the kernel or to a set of variables in the kernel.

> **NOTE:**   That **/proc** is abstract doesn't mean it isn't a file system. It does mean that a special file system had to be developed to treat **/proc** differently than normal disk-based file systems.

For example, to see a report on the type of processor in our servers, we can read the **/proc/cpuinfo** file with the following command:

```
[root@ford /root]# cat /proc/cpuinfo
```

The kernel will dynamically create the report showing processor information and hand it back to **cat** so that we can see it. This is a simple yet powerful way for us to examine the kernel. The **/proc** directory supports an easy-to-read hierarchy using subdirectories, so finding information is easy. For example, the **/proc/scsi** directory offers reports about the SCSI subsystem.

Even more of an advantage is that the flow of information goes both ways: The kernel can generate reports for us, and we can easily pass information back into the kernel. For instance, performing an **ls -l** in the **/proc/sys/net/ipv4** directory will show us a lot of files that are not read-only, but read-write.

"Hey! Most the **/proc** files have 0 bytes, and one is HUGE! What gives?" Don't worry if you've noticed all those 0-byte files—most of the files in **/proc** are 0 bytes because **/proc** doesn't really exist on disk. When you use `cat` to read a **/proc** file, the content of the file is dynamically generated by a special program inside the kernel. As a result, the report is never saved back to disk and thus does not take up space. Think of it in the same light as CGI scripts for Web sites, where a Web page generated by a CGI script isn't written back to the server's disk but regenerated every time a user visits the page.

CAUTION: That one huge file you see in **/proc** is **/proc/kcore**, which is really a pointer to the contents of RAM. So if you have 128MB of RAM, the **/proc/kcore** file is also 128MB. Reading **/proc/kcore** is like reading the raw contents of memory (and, of course, requires root permissions). This also means that if you try to erase **/proc/kcore**, you'll be erasing your memory! In other words, **don't!**

Tweaking Files Inside of /proc

The files in **/proc/sys/net/ipv4** represent parameters in the TCP/IP stack that can be "tuned" dynamically. Use the `cat` command to look at a particular file, and you'll see that most of the files contain nothing but a single number. But by changing these numbers, you can affect the behavior of the Linux TCP/IP stack!

For example, the file **/proc/sys/net/ipv4/ip_forward** contains a 0 (Off) by default. This tells Linux not to perform IP forwarding when there are multiple network interfaces. But if you want to set up something like IP Masquerading (see Chapter 26), you need to allow forwarding to occur. In this situation, you can edit the **/proc/sys/net/ipv4/ip_forward** file and change the number to 1 (On).

A quick way to make this change is by using the **echo** command like so:

```
[root@ford /root]# echo "1" > /proc/sys/net/ipv4/ip_forward
```

CAUTION: Be very careful when tweaking parameters in the Linux kernel. There is no safety net to keep you from making the wrong settings for critical parameters, which means it's entirely possible that you can crash your system. If you aren't sure about a particular item, it's safer to leave it be until you've found out for sure what it's for.

SOME USEFUL /PROC ENTRIES

Table 27-1 lists some **/proc** entries that you may find useful in managing your Linux system. Note that this is a far cry from an exhaustive list. For more detail, peruse the directories yourself and see what you find. Or you can also read the **proc.txt** file in the Documentation directory of the Linux kernel source code.

Unless otherwise stated, you can simply use the `cat` program to view the contents of a particular file in the **/proc** directory.

Filename	Contents
/proc/cpuinfo	Information about all of the CPUs in your system.
/proc/interrupts	IRQ usage in your system.
/proc/mdstat	Status of your RAID configuration.
/proc/meminfo	Status of memory usage.
/proc/modules	Same information produced as output from `lsmod`.
/proc/pci	Old-style report of all known PCI devices in a system.
/proc/rtc	Status of your Real-Time-Clock.
/proc/sound	Information about currently active sound cards and system resources supporting them.
/proc/swaps	Status of swap (virtual memory) partitions and/or files.
/proc/version	Current version number of the kernel, the machine on which it was compiled, and the date and time of compilation.
/proc/ide/*	Information about all of your IDE disks.
/proc/scsi/*	Information about all of your SCSI disks.
/proc/net/arp	ARP table (same as output from `arp -a`).
/proc/net/dev	Information about each network device (packet counts, error counts, and so on).
/proc/net/snmp	SNMP statistics about each protocol.
/proc/net/sockstat	Statistics on network socket utilization.
/proc/sys/dev/cdrom/info	Information about installed CD-ROMs.
/proc/sys/fs/*	Settings for file system utilization by the kernel. Many of these are writable values; be careful about changing them unless you are sure of the repercussions of doing so.

Table 27-1. Useful Entries in the **/proc** File

Filename	Contents
/proc/sys/net/core/ netdev_max_backlog	When the kernel receives packets from the network faster than it can process them, it places them on a special queue. By default, a maximum of 300 packets is allowed on the queue. Under extraordinary circumstances, you may need to edit this file and change the value for the allowed maximum.
/proc/sys/net/ipv4/ icmp_echo_ignore_all	Default = 0, meaning that the kernel will respond to ICMP echo-reply messages. Set this to 1 to tell the kernel to stop replying to those messages.
/proc/sys/net/ipv4/ icmp_echo_ignore_broadcasts	Default = 0, meaning that the kernel will allow ICMP responses to be sent to broadcast or multicast addresses. This creates a risk of your machine's being used in a denial of service attack. Change this value to 1 to prevent this risk.
/proc/sys/net/ipv4/ ip_forward	Default = 0, meaning the kernel will not forward packets between network interfaces. To allow forwarding (for routing or IP Masquerading), change this to 1.
/proc/sys/net/ipv4/ ip_local_port_range	Range of ports Linux will use when originating a connection. Default = 1024–4096. For high-usage systems, change this to 31000-61000 with this command: echo "31000 61000" > ip_local_port_range
/proc/sys/net/ipv4/ syn_cookies	Default = 0 (Off). Change to 1 (On) to enable protection for your system against SYN Flood attacks. The kernel must have TCP_SYN_COOKIES enabled during compile—(the usual status in most distributions).

Table 27-1.   Useful Entries in the **/proc** File (*continued*)

NOTE: Changes to default settings in **/proc** do not survive reboots. If you need to change a value permanently, edit your boot scripts so that the change is made at boot time. For example, to enable SYN Flood protection every time the system is booted, add the following line to the end of your **/etc/rc.d/rc.local** file:

```
echo "1" > /proc/sys/net/ipv4/tcp_syncookies
```

Enumerated /proc Entries

A listing of the **/proc** directory will reveal a large number of directories whose names are just numbers. These numbers are the PIDs for each running process in the system. Within each of the process directories are several files describing the state of the process. This information can be useful in finding out how the system perceives a process and what sort of resources the process is consuming. (From a programmer's point of view, the process files are also an easy way for a program to get information about itself.)

COMMON REPORTS AND SETTINGS DONE WITH /PROC

In this section, we step through a few things you can do with **/proc** to complement day-to-day administrative tasks. Reports and tunable options available through **/proc** are especially useful in network-related tasks.

SYN Flood Protection

When TCP initiates a connection, the very first thing it does is send a special packet to the destination, with the flag set to indicate the start of a connection. This flag is known as the SYN flag. The destination host responds by sending an acknowledgment packet back to the source, called (appropriately) a SYNACK. Then the destination waits for the source to return an acknowledgment showing that both sides have agreed on the parameters of their transaction. Once these three packets are sent (a *three-way handshake*), the source and destination hosts can transmit data back and forth.

Because it's possible for multiple hosts to simultaneously contact a single host, it's important that the destination host keep track of all the SYN packets it gets. SYN entries are stored in a table until the three-way handshake is complete. Once this is done, the connection leaves the SYN tracking table and moves to another table tracking established connections.

A SYN Flood occurs when a source host sends a large number of SYN packets to a destination with no intention of responding to the SYNACK. This results in overflow of the destination host's tables, thereby making the operating system unstable. Obviously, this is not a good thing.

Linux can prevent SYN Floods by using a *syncookie*, a special mechanism in the kernel that tracks the rate at which SYN packets arrive. If the syncookie detects the rate going above a certain threshold, it begins to aggressively get rid of entries in the SYN table that don't move to the "established" state within a reasonable interval. A second layer of protection is in the table itself: If the table receives a SYN request that would cause the table to overflow, the request is ignored. This means it may happen that a client will be temporarily unable to connect to the server—but it also keeps the server from crashing altogether and kicking *everyone* off!

To turn on syncookie support, enter this command:

```
[root@ford /root]# echo "1" > /proc/sys/net/ipv4/tcp_syncookies
```

Because **/proc** entries do not survive system reboots, you should add the following line to the end of your **/etc/rc.d/rc.local** boot script:

```
echo "1" > /proc/sys/net/ipv4/tcp_syncookies
```

Issues on High-Volume Servers

Like any operating system, Linux has finite resources. If the system begins to run short of resources while servicing requests (such as Web access requests), it will begin refusing new service requests.

The following entries in **/proc** allow you to handle a larger load:

▼ **/proc/sys/fs/file-max**

■ **/proc/sys/net/ipv4/ip_local_port_range**

▲ **/proc/sys/net/ipv4/tcp_max_syn_backlog**

The first entry in this list, **/proc/sys/fs/file-max**, specifies the maximum number of open files that Linux can support at any one time. The default value is 4096, but this may be quickly exhausted on a very busy system with a lot of network connections. Raising it to a larger number, such as 8192 or 16384, will help.

If you are increasing the number of possible open files, you will need to increase the available ports your system can use. The lower and upper boundaries are set in the **/proc/sys/net/ipv4/ip_local_port_range** file; defaults are 1024 (lower) and 4096 (upper), respectively. On a loaded system, you'll want to change these defaults to 31000 and 61000 by adding the following line to the end of your **/etc/rc.d/rc.local** boot file:

```
echo "31000 61000" >/proc/sys/net/ipv4/ip_local_port_range
```

Finally, if you're getting a large number of connections, you're getting them quickly, as well. A burst of new connections can easily take some time to handle, and those connections on the queue must wait. As the queue grows, so does the possibility that your queue will run out of space. The default length of the queue is 256 connections. You can increase it if you see connections getting refused on a regular basis.

NOTE: Before changing the length of the connection queue, be sure to look at your server process first. Make sure the reason your system is refusing connections isn't because the CPU load is too high. If that's the case, increasing the number of available connections isn't going to help. You can monitor CPU utilization with the **vmstat** command; read the man page on it for more information.

Debugging Hardware Conflicts

Debugging hardware conflicts is always a chore. You can ease the burden by using some of the entries in **/proc**. These three entries are specifically designed to tell you what's going on with your hardware:

▼ **/proc/pci**, which details all the PCI devices in your system, is very handy when you don't know the make and model of a device—and you don't want to have to open the machine!

■ **/proc/ioports** tells you the relationships of devices to I/O ports, and whether there are any conflicts. With PCI devices becoming dominant, this isn't as big an issue. Nevertheless, as long as you can buy a new motherboard with ISA slots, you'll always want to have this option.

▲ **/proc/interrupts** shows you the association of interrupt numbers to hardware devices. Again, like **/proc/ioports**, PCI is making this less of an issue.

SUMMARY

In this chapter, you learned about the **/proc** file system and how you can use it to get a peek inside the Linux kernel as well as to influence the kernel's operation. The tools used to accomplish these tasks are relatively trivial (**echo** and **cat**), but the concept of a pseudo-file system that doesn't exist on disk can be a little difficult to grasp.

Looking at **/proc** from a system administrator's point of view, you learned to find your way around the **/proc** file system, and how to get reports from various subsystems (especially the networking subsystem). You learned how to set kernel parameters to accommodate possible future enhancements.

If you are interested in delving further into the **/proc** file system, take a look at the Kernel Guide at the Linux Documentation Project (http://www.linuxdoc.org/LDP/tlk/tlk.html). Even without a background in operating systems, you may find this an interesting and enlightening read. To get the most out of it, you should have some familiarity with data structures in C.

PART VI

Appendixes

APPENDIX A

Programming Languages That Accompany Red Hat Linux

This appendix describes some of the programming languages that accompany Red Hat Linux.

The C/C++ Programming Suite

Red Hat Linux comes with the egcs compiler tools that provide a complete C and C++ programming suite. They include the compilers (gcc/g++), preprocessors (cpp), and debugger (gdb/xxgdb). The compilers come with a complete set of header files and libraries, including an implementation of the STL library. Migrating code from other C compilers to gcc is reasonably straightforward. Migrating other code from C++ compilers to g++ is not quite as clean, mostly due to continuing disagreements over the C++ standards. The official C++ standard was established at the end of 1998, so hopefully we will see an easier transition path soon.

Linux's fully integrated development environment that works with the C and C++ compilers is the K Develop Environment (www.kdevelop.org), which has a striking resemblance to Microsoft's Visual Studio. The entire environment is available under the GNU Public License and supports KDE/Qt, GNOME, and plain C/C++ projects.

NOTE: Objective C is also supported using the egcs compiler suite; however, it is mainly used on systems running the NeXTSTEP operating system.

GNU Fortran 77

Part of the egcs programming suite is the g77 compiler that implements Fortran 77. If you need this tool, you should be sure that the egcs C/C++ development tools are installed, too, since they share a common backend optimizer and code generator.

An Historical Aside

GNU Fortran 77 started in the mid-1980s as part of the Free Software Foundation's (FSF) GNU Project. FSF championed the project through the 1990s; however, as time went on, the rate at which bugs were fixed and new features were added to the compiler slowed down. This frustrated a group of developers who were fixing bugs and writing new features, only to find their work sitting on the sidelines, waiting for the maintainers to integrate them into the main distribution. Fed up, this group of programmers took the base source code, applied all of their changes, and released the updates under the name "egcs." Realizing that the egcs package was better for the free software movement, FSF decided to bless it as the official GNU C/C++ compiler in April 1999. Without the great work from both teams, we would not have the world-class compiler we have today.

tcl

tcl is a multiplatform scripting language that is relatively easy to learn. With built-in primitives for building graphical user interfaces, it is becoming increasingly popular for tool builders, since it makes it easy to create easy-to-use frontends that work across UNIX, Windows, and Macintosh. For example, to write the infamous "Hello, World" program in tcl, you would only need the following lines of code:

```
button .b -text "Hello, World!" -command exit
pack .b
```

tcl is also object-oriented and easily extensible. See http://www.tcltk.com and http://www.tclconsortium.org for more information.

Expect

An extension of tcl, Expect is a scripting language geared toward automating other applications, such as Telnet and **ftp**. It essentially allows you to have the script send certain inputs to the application upon seeing certain outputs. If you're used to some of the scripting tools that come with terminal emulation packages like ProComm or Telix, you should feel right at home with Expect. And because it has the full power of tcl behind it, you can perform some very interesting feats, given a little creativity. You must have tcl installed to use Expect.

iTcl

An extension to tcl, iTcl offers an impressive array of object-oriented functionality to the base tcl language, such as local name spaces and true inheritance. Developers writing programs longer than a few thousand lines in tcl will most likely find iTcl to be a very useful addition. You must have tcl installed to use iTcl.

TclX

TclX is a series of extensions to the tcl language that make it easier to access files, perform network operations, debug code, and perform higher-level math functions. You must have tcl installed to use TclX.

Tk

The Tk Widget Set is a series of widgets that make it even easier to write GUIs that work in the UNIX, Windows, and Macintosh environments. The designer's goal is to provide an environment where writing GUIs takes only a little longer than writing text-based applications. You must have tcl installed to use Tk.

TiX

TiX (the Tk Interface Extension) is an extension to the tk package that provides many more widgets including an MS Windows–style file-select box. Using this library is a great way of being able to focus on your program and not have to deal with the details of building the interface. To use TiX, you need to have both tcl and tk installed.

Jikes

Jikes is a Java source-code-to-bytecode compiler originally written by IBM Research Labs. (It is still maintained by IBM using an open source model—see http://www.ibm.com/research/jikes for more information on the project.) Features include strict adherence to the language specification, extremely fast compile speed, and a sophisticated dependence analysis that allows incremental compilation and automatic makefile generation.

Kaffe

Kaffe is a Java Virtual Machine that allows you to execute Java bytecode. What makes Kaffe especially interesting is that it sports a Just-in-Time (JIT) compiler that converts Java bytecode to a machine's native code before executing it. This conversion results in a slight hit in performance to start the program, but the overall execution of the program proceeds at nearly the same speed as a compiled C program. Kaffe offers all of this and the benefit of machine independence. If you're looking for a way to get into Java or have a need to execute Java programs, look into Kaffe and Jikes.

Perl

Perl is a multiplatform scripting language that is especially powerful for string manipulation and quick prototyping. Programmers with a background in C, awk, and Bourne Shell will feel right at home with Perl, as it combines the best of all of these languages into a unified package.

Given Perl's influences, it makes for a great systems administration language. People moving from a hodgepodge of Shell and awk will notice a significant improvement in speed with Perl, because it doesn't require the creation of any additional processes at runtime, unlike Shell script.

In addition to systems administration, Perl has become the language of choice for Web developers. With many modules available to make Perl even easier to use as a CGI scripting language, as well as Apache's built-in support for it via the mod_perl module, you're more likely to see Perl than any of the other languages listed here (except possibly C). If you are interested in learning more about Perl, visit http://www.perl.com.

awk

awk is a scripting language similar to Perl, but it's not nearly as feature rich. Most folks who use awk generally use it in conjunction with Shell script since it provides a quick and easy way to perform complex filtering that typically requires multiple lines in Perl. However, for more complex solutions, Perl is typically a better choice.

Python

Python is a scripting language that has boasted object-oriented design from day one and, as many of its users say, is much easier to learn than most other programming languages. Like Perl and tcl, it offers cross-platform compatibility and an easy interface to GUI toolkits.

First-time programmers may find Python more intuitive than C, C++, and even Perl. Most of Red Hat's tools are written in Python for the same reason.

Scheme

According to the documentation that comes with Scheme, it is "a statically scoped and properly tail-recursive dialect of the Lisp programming language, designed with clear and simple semantics and a minimal number of ways to form expressions." The version that ships with Red Hat is called UMB-Scheme, which is a public-domain implementation and can be invoked with the **umb-scheme** command when installed.

APPENDIX B

Getting the Usual Done

The focus of this book is taking care of systems administration duties under Linux. While that's all fun and nice, it doesn't address the recent trend of companies trying to make Linux more friendly to the desktop and their goal of removing the need for anyone to have to reboot their systems to start Microsoft Windows.

Taking your fearless author as an example, his humble home managed to stay Windows-free for the greater part of four years. I personally used Linux the entire time to perform basic, day-to-day chores such as word processing, Internet browsing, and so on. Not until my lovely wife was commanded by the almighty California State University system to take a course in Visual Basic did Windows 98 creep onto the network. (The new machine has been affectionately named "assimilator.")

The point of this rambling introduction is to show that *it is possible* to live in a Windows world using Linux as your desktop operating system. And the purpose of this appendix is to introduce some of the tools that allow you to do so. While it is a far cry from an exhaustive list, it is nonetheless a good start.

StarOffice

StarOffice is a complete MS Office–like suite of tools that includes a word processor, spreadsheet, presentation maker, calendar, e-mail, HTML authoring tool, and browser. Folks who are familiar with MS Office should find it a very easy transition, especially with its support for importing and exporting MS Office documents.

In addition to being free for use, the source code of the package (which is owned by Sun Microsystems) is also available under the GNU Public License. You can download either the "ready to install" version or the source code version from Sun's Web site at http://www.sun.com. If the download is too hefty for you, you can also buy a CD from Sun for slightly less than $20. This price is to cover the cost of packaging (the CD, etc.) and shipping. StarOffice is also available for Solaris and Windows.

Stability-wise, StarOffice is a relatively solid package. The first draft of this book was written in it, using a template developed in Word 7.0. Very neat stuff.

ApplixWare

The ApplixWare suite is another competitor to the MS Office series, as well as to StarOffice. It isn't quite as heavy as StarOffice in terms of memory or disk consumption, and as a result, it tends to respond much faster. This speed comes at the expense of features, but if you need an Office-like package that isn't overly complex, you may find this is a great tool to work with.

You can find out more about ApplixWare at http://www.applix.com.

Corel WordPerfect

For those who remember when WordPerfect was king (I still have WordPerfect 5.1), there is WordPerfect for Linux. It looks quite impressive. You can find out more about it (and the Corel Linux distribution) at http://www.corel.com.

Web Browsers

Netscape has offered its browser for Linux for a very long time. (Remember mcom.com?) As far as Web browsers go, Netscape's is a complete package that supports e-mail, netnews, and browsing. And because the Windows version of Netscape is derived from the same source code, you will find the two versions identical feature-for-feature and menu-for-menu.

Red Hat Linux and Caldera Linux both ship with Netscape preinstalled. If you want to get the latest information on Netscape, check out http://www.netscape.com. There you will also find information on the latest plug-ins, including Macromedia's Flash module, that are available for Linux.

The Opera browser is a recent addition to the Web browser market. The most significant difference between Opera and the other offerings is that it is not free. Once the 30-day trial period is over, you must pay for the browser in order to continue using it. However, those who have paid for it claim that it is worth the price. Opera was designed with efficient memory utilization in mind and thus, unlike all of the other browsers available, offers a very small memory footprint. Because Opera is small, it also tends to be faster than the others as well.

The Konquerer browser is the KDE group's contribution. Based on the Mozilla engine, its goal is to provide tight integration between the Web and the desktop similar to how Internet Explorer does for Windows. This browser is free and is available from www.kde.org.

Painting/Image Manipulation Tools

Five great tools exist for painting and image manipulation. On the painting front is kpaint, which bears a striking resemblance to the Windows Paint tool. You can also use xpaint, which is slightly more flexible, but which uses a different (and still intuitive) interface.

On the image viewing/manipulation front are Electric Eyes (ee) and xv. The first is a simple viewer and has started to ship with Red Hat Linux as a replacement to xv because of licensing restrictions on xv. The xv tool is still available on the Internet and is quite a bit more powerful and flexible than Electric Eyes; however, commercial usage requires that you buy a license.

The GNU Image Manipulation Program (GIMP) is a full-featured package aimed at being the Photoshop for Linux. It offers many filters and tools for manipulating photo-realistic images.

Finance Tools

Spreadsheets are, of course, every finance person's dream tool, and both StarOffice and ApplixWare come with a spreadsheet that is capable of reading and writing Excel files. Beyond these two packages, there are several noteworthy tools: BB Stock Tool from Falkor Technologies is a comprehensive stock tracking and analysis tool that is available for Linux, Windows, Solaris, and Irix. You can see more about it at http://www.falkor.com.

For home finances, there is GnuCash. It isn't yet quite where Quicken is, but it does offer basic functionality, and for those of us who don't need the advanced features of Quicken, it is a welcome simplification. The GnuCash Web site is at http://www.gnucash.org.

Desktop Tools

Korganizer is a personal information manager that allows you to easily store calendar and scheduling information, contacts, and other miscellaneous things you would stash into your Palm Pilot or use Outlook for. What makes Korganizer especially nice is that it uses the vCalendar file format, which is a standard supported by all of the big name PIM tools, such as Lotus Notes, Netscape, Outlook, and Palm Pilot. This makes exchanging your information very straightforward. You can get more information about Korganizer at http://people.redhat.com/pbrown/korganizer/.

Another useful program is XnotesPlus, which essentially provides "yellow sticky" notes on your screen. One of its most useful features (besides its wonderful interface) is its ability to synchronize notes against a Palm Pilot. You can find out more about this tool at http://www.graphics-muse.org.

E-Mail Clients

The most popular graphical e-mail–based client under UNIX is Netscape Communicator's package. Besides the fact that it is already there with Netscape and is free, the feature set is quite nice. It comes with a spell checker, good folder management, and a generally pleasant interface. Communicator comes preinstalled with many distributions of Linux, but you can always see the latest version at http://www.netscape.com.

Folks used to Eudora or similar mail clients will probably be more at home with Arrow. It offers a fully graphical interface while maintaining compatibility with the mail folder files from text-based mail clients, such as Pine, Mutt, or Elm. The address book is well done and the feature set is wonderfully rich. You can get more information about this package at http://www.cco.caltech.edu/~glenn/arrow/.

Another great mail reader is Mahogany Mail. It offers a comprehensive graphical interface and provides the capabilities of commercial-grade software. Even nicer, this mail reader is cross-platform between Windows and Linux, with a MacOS version in the works. So for heterogeneous sites trying to find a standard, this could be your answer. You can find out more about Mahogany Mail at http://www.phy.hw.ac.uk/~karsten/M/index.html.

Audio Tools

What desktop is complete without a nifty tool to play music with? For those interested in MP3s, XMMS makes a spiffy tool that is comparable to WinAmp. You can find out more about XMMS at http://www.xmms.org.

If your favorite Web site/radio station uses Real Audio, you can download the Linux version of Real Player at http://www.real.com.

A nice CD player (for real CDs) is kscd, which comes with the KDE environment.

Real-Time Chat

Two notable entries in the real-time chat arena have Linux clients: Yahoo offers a Linux client for their chat technology, which you can download at http://www.yahoo.com. If you are already familiar with Yahoo, you won't find any differences between the various Yahoo clients, since they are all the same program written in a platform-independent language.

For the ICQ folks, take a look at GnomeICQ at http://gnomeicu.gdev.net/. It is a complete ICQ client that is compatible with existing ICQ specifications.

Suggested Web Sites

The amount of new software that comes out for Linux grows daily. Especially with the recent development of KDE and GNOME, many programmers have taken an interest in graphical-based development of user tools.

If you're looking for new software, here's a handful of active sites that you can visit to find out about the latest goings on:

▼ **http://www.linuxapps.com**   A complete guide to new Linux applications that are in various stages of development. The site is very neatly organized, which makes finding the tool you need quite easy.

■ **http://www.freshmeat.net**   Freshmeat is a great mixture of applications and small tools. As a system administrator, you'll find plenty of reasons to visit this site to see what new and exciting developments have come about to make your life a little easier.

■ **http://www.kde.org/apphomepages.html**   Here's the KDE applications list. You'll find the latest applications developed to take advantage of the KDE environment.

■ **http://www.linuxjournal.com**   Although this is really a magazine's Web site, the editors and writers do a great job of profiling a lot of software, both commercial and noncommercial. The articles themselves are pretty nice, too.

■ **http://www.linuxsoftware.org**   Here's another well-organized site containing pointers to applications and tools for all sorts of interests and needs.

■ **http://www.linuxberg.com**   Linuxberg offers a slightly different way of organizing a collection of software. Specifically, they break down their software into user interface categories at the highest level, which is great when the application you are looking for must work within certain criteria. (For example, the application must be command-line driven, and so on.)

▲ **http://www.rpmfind.net**   This site is a very comprehensive collection of packages that are available for quick install in the RPM format. It's not as pretty as some of the other sites, but it's well worth a look.

INDEX

SYMBOLS & OPTIONS

` (backticks), BASH (Bourne Again Shell) and commands as parameters, 117-118

-a option, mount command, *172*

-A parameter, ipchains tool, *569*

-arp option, ifconfig program, 554

-b *blocksize* parameter
 dump tool, *502*
 restore tool, *505*

-b *bulldir* command-line option, Qpopper daemon, 396

-B *count* parameter, dump tool, *502*

-b option, ipchains tool, *573*

-b *superblock* parameter, e2fsck tool, *177*

-c comment command-line option, user management tools, *91*

-C *config-file* command-line option, LILO (Linux Loader) boot manager, *156*

-c *filename* option, DHCP (Dynamic Host Configuration Protocol) clients, *492*

-c parameter, e2fsck tool, *177*

-D command-line parameter, smbclient program, *461*

-d command-line parameter, syslogd daemon, *213*

-d *density* parameter, dump tool, *502*

-d *homedir* command-line option, user management tools, *91*

-d option, DHCP (Dynamic Host Configuration Protocol) clients, *492*

-D option, DHCP (Dynamic Host Configuration Protocol) clients, *492*

-D parameter, ipchains tool, *569*

-e *expire-date* command-line option, user management tools, *91*

-f command-line option, user management tools, *94*

-f *config* command-line parameter, syslogd daemon, *213*

-f *filename* parameter
 dump tool, *502*
 restore tool, *505*

-f inactive-time command-line option, user management tools, *91*

-f parameter, e2fsck tool, *177*

-F parameter, ipchains tool, *569*

-g *gid* command-line option, user management tools, *94*

-G group[, . . .] command-line option, user management tools, *91*

-g *initial-group* command-line option, user management tools, *91*

-h command-line option, RPM (Red Hat Package Manager), *72*

-h command-line parameter, syslogd daemon, *213*

-h *hostname* option, DHCP (Dynamic Host Configuration Protocol) clients, *492*

-H option, DHCP (Dynamic Host Configuration Protocol) clients, *492*

-I *clientID* option, DHCP (Dynamic Host Configuration Protocol) clients, *492*

-i command-line option
 restore tool, *504*
 RPM (Red Hat Package Manager), 71, 72

-I command-line parameter, smbclient program, *461*

-I parameter, ipchains tool, *569*

-i *vendorClassID* option, DHCP (Dynamic Host Configuration Protocol) clients, *492*

-k option, DHCP (Dynamic Host Configuration Protocol) clients, *492*

-l *hostlist* command-line parameter, syslogd daemon, *213*

-l *leasetime* option, DHCP (Dynamic Host Configuration Protocol) clients, *493*

-l option, ipchains tool, *573*

-L option, smbclient program, 459-460

-L parameter, ipchains tool, *569*

-m [-k skel-dir] command-line option, user management tools, *92*

-M command-line option, user management tools, *92*

-m *interval* command-line parameter, syslogd daemon, *213*

-m option, ypinit command, 435

-n command-line option, user management tools, *92*

-n option, ipchains tool, *573*

-n parameter, dump tool, *502*

-N parameter, ipchains tool, *569*

-nodeps command-line option, RPM (Red Hat Package Manager), *72*

-o option, mount command, *173, 188, 421-422*

-p option, netstat command, 248-249

-P parameter, ipchains tool, *569*

-r command-line option

    restore tool, *505*

    user management tools, *94*

-r command-line parameter, syslogd daemon, *213*

-r option

    DHCP (Dynamic Host Configuration Protocol) clients, *493*

    netstat command, *557*

-R option, DHCP (Dynamic Host Configuration Protocol) clients, *493*

-R parameter, ipchains tool, *569*

-r *root-directory* command-line option, LILO (Linux Loader) boot manager, *156*

-s command-line parameter, syslogd daemon, *213*

-s option, ypinit command, 440

-s shell command-line option, user management tools, *92*

-s *size* parameter, dump tool, *502*

-t command-line option, LILO (Linux Loader) boot manager, *156*

-T *directory* command-line option, restore tool, *505*

-t option, mount command, *173*

-T *timeout* command-line option, Qpopper daemon, 396

-t *timeout* option, DHCP (Dynamic Host Configuration Protocol) clients, *493*

-U command-line option

    RPM (Red Hat Package Manager), 71

    smbclient program, *461*

-u parameter, dump tool, *502*

-u uid command-line option, user management tools, *92*

-v command-line option

    LILO (Linux Loader) boot manager, *156*

    restore tool, *505*

    RPM (Red Hat Package Manager), *72*

-v option, ipchains tool, *573*

-W command-line parameter, smbclient program, *461*

-x option, ipchains tool, *573*

-X parameter, ipchains tool, *569*

-y command-line option, restore tool, *505*

-y option, ipchains tool, *573*

-y parameter, e2fsck tool, *177*

▼ A

-a option, mount command, *172*

-A parameter, ipchains tool, *569*

A (Address) records, DNS record types, 289-290

accept_unqualified_senders feature, FEATURE macro, 369

accept_unresolvable_domains feature, FEATURE macro, 369

access control

    /etc/ftpaccess file, 311-315

    wu-ftpd (Washington University FTP Server), 326-332

Access Control Lists. *See* ACLs

access.conf file, Apache HTTP server, 344

access_db database, 369, 376-378

    See also Sendmail

    actions, 377

access_log file, Apache HTTP server, 347

Account module, PAM (Pluggable Authentication Modules), *105*

accounts, installing Red Hat Linux, 35

acl keyword, named.conf file, 272

ACLs (Access Control Lists), 273-274

    default, 273

    named.conf file, 273-274

    negating addresses, 273-274

action field options, /etc/inittab file, *201-202*

actions, ipchains tool, 568-571

AD (Active Directory), Windows versus Linux, 12

addonpost field, /etc/ftpconversions/ file, *324*

addonpre field, /etc/ftpconversions/ file, *324*

Address Resolution Protocol. *See* ARP

addresses

    IP. *See* IP addresses

    MAC (Medium Access Control), 519

addy parameter, route command, 555

advanced Linux networking, 559-588

    IP aliasing, 561

    IP Masquerading, 583-588

    network configuration, 549-558

    overview, 560

    packet filtering, 562-583

    /proc file system, 589-596

    summary, 588

    TCP/IP for system administrators, 511-548

alias command, /etc/ftpaccess file, 318

aliases database, 359, 375-376

    See also Sendmail

    format of, 375

    smrsh tool and, 376

aliasing, IP, 561

all: entry, NIS (Network Information Service) and shares, 434

Allman, Eric, creator of Sendmail, 353

allow-query {address list; }; option, BIND servers, *278*

allow-transfer {address list; }; option, BIND servers, *278*

always-reply-rfc1048 parameter, DHCPD (Dynamic Host Configuration Protocol server), 486 always_add_domain feature, FEATURE macro, 367

Amateur Radio Support menu, kernel features and modules, 233

AMD (Auto-Mounter Daemon), as alternative to Automounter, 192

AND operations, netmasks and bitwise, 540

anonymous FTP directories, 327-328
    See also FTP (File Transfer Protocol); wu-ftpd (Washington University FTP Server)
    chmod command, 328
    chroot command, 327-328, 329
    groupadd command, 328
    setting up /etc/ftpaccess file, 329-330

anonymous users, wu-ftpd (Washington University FTP Server), 326-327

Apache HTTP server, 335-348
    See also Internet services
    access.conf, 344
    access_log file, 347
    changing host names, 345
    common configuration changes, 344-345
    compiling, 340-341
    configuring, 342-347
    error_log file, 347
    home (root-level) pages, 342-343
    host names, 345
    HTTP (HyperText Transfer Protocol) and, 336-338
    httpd.conf, 344, 345, 346
    index.html, 343
    installing, 339-342
    installing on busy systems, 340-341
    make command, 340
    modules, 340
    nobody user, 341, 344
    overview, 336
    process ownership and security, 338-339
    root-level (home) pages, 342-343
    ServerAdmin line of httpd.conf file, 345
    srm.conf, 344
    starting at boot time, 341-342
    starting up/shutting down, 341-342
    summary, 347-348
    testing installations, 342
    troubleshooting, 347
    /usr/local/apache/conf directory, 344
    /usr/local/apache/htdocs directory, 342-343
    /usr/local/apache_*version* directory, 340-341
    virtual domains, 345-347

APOP users, Authenticated POP, 394-395

applications
    compiling, 74-78
    installing, 69-74
    starting from KDE (K Desktop Environment), 53-54

ApplixWare, Linux tools, 606

ARP (Address Resolution Protocol), 534-536
    See also IP addresses; TCP/IP
    default routes, 535
    headers, 535-536
    overview, 534-535
    tcpdump program and, 534-535

arp option, ifconfig program, 554

-arp option, ifconfig program, 554

ATA/IDE/MFM/RLL Support menu, kernel features and modules, 232

audio tools, 608

Auth module, PAM (Pluggable Authentication Modules), *105*

auth-nxdomain *yes/no;* option, BIND servers, *275*

Authenticated POP, 394-395
    See also POP (Post Office Protocol); Qpopper daemon
    APOP users, 394-395

authentication configuration, installing Red Hat Linux, 35-38

authentication modules, Pluggable. *See* PAM

authoritative parameter, DHCPD (Dynamic Host Configuration Protocol server), 486

authoritative servers, DNS (Domain Name Service) and, 263

autofs script, starting Automounter, 190-191

autogroup command, /etc/ftpaccess file, 312

Automounter, 188-192
    See also network file systems
    alternatives to, 192
    AMD (Auto-Mounter Daemon) and, 192
    autofs script, 190-191
    /etc/auto.home file, 189-190
    /etc/auto.master file, 189-190, 191-192
    /home directories and, 189
    overview, 188-190
    starting, 190-191

awk, programming languages accompanying Red Hat Linux, 602

▼ B

-b *blocksize* parameter
    dump tool, *502*
    restore tool, *505*

-b *bulldir* command-line option, Qpopper daemon, 396

-B *count* parameter, dump tool, *502*

-b option, ipchains tool, *573*

-b *superblock* parameter, e2fsck tool, *177*

Background menu option, KDE (K Desktop Environment), 55

Background panel, GNOME (GNU Network Object Model Environment), 63

backgrounding tasks, BASH (Bourne Again Shell), 113

backticks (`), BASH (Bourne Again Shell) and commands as parameters, 117-118

backups, 495-507
    See also Intranet services
    command-line tools, 501-506
    data types and, 496
    dump tool, 501-504
    hardware and, 496-497
    managing backup device and files, 498-501
    mknod command and creating device files, 499
    mt command, 500-501
    overview, 496-498
    recovery frequency, 498

restore command, 504-506

speed of recovery and, 497-498

summary, 506-507

tape management and, 498

tape naming scheme, 498-499

throughput and, 497

banner command, /etc/ftpaccess file, 315

banner message control, /etc/ftpaccess file, 315-317

BASH (Bourne Again Shell), 112-118

backgrounding tasks, 113

backticks (`) and commands as parameters, 117-118

command-line shortcuts, 116-118

environment variables, 114-115

environment variables as parameters, 117

export command, 115

filename expansion, 117

job control, 113-114

multiple commands, 117

overview, 112-113

pipes, 115-116

printenv command, 114

redirection, 116

unset command, 115

wildcard characters, 117

binary numbers, converting to decimal, 539

BIND (Berkeley Internet Domain Name) servers, 265-297

See also DNS (Domain Name Service)

allow-query {address list; }; option, *278*

allow-transfer {address list; }; option, *278*

auth-nxdomain *yes/no;* option, *275*

check-names *type* action; option, *278*

chown command, 268

cleaning-interval *number;* option, *282*

configuration options, 275-283

configure command, 266

configuring, 284-292

coresize *size;* option, *281*

datasize *datasize;* option, *281*

deallocate-on-exit *yes/no;* option, *276*

directory *path-name;* option, *275*

DNS record types, 288-292

documentation, 268

dump-file *path-name;* option, *275*

fake-iquery *yes/no;* option, *276*

fetch-glue *yes/no;* option, *276*

files *number;* option, *281*

forwarders *first/only;* option, *277*

forwarders {*ip-list;*} option, *277*

host-statistics *yes/no;* option, *276*

installing, 265-268

interface-interval *number;* option, *282*

listen-on {address list; } option, *279*

make command, 266

make install command, 266

max-transfer-times-in *number;* option, *280*

memstatistics-file *path-name;* option, *275*

multiple-cnames *yes/no;* option, *276*

named-xfer *path-name;* option, *275*

named.conf file, 271-287, 292-297

notify *yes/no;* option, *277*

overview, 265

pid-file *path-name;* option, *275*

query-source *address* address\ port port; option, *279*

recursion *yes/no;* option, *277*

Red Hat Linux and, 265

resolver (client-side DNS), 269-271

stacksize *number;* option, *282*

starting DNS at boot time, 267-268

statistics-file *path-name;* option, *275*

statistics-interval *number;* option, *282*

tarballs, 266

tools, 267

topology *address-list;* option, *283*

transfer-format\ *one-answer/many-answers;* option, *280*

transfers-in *number;* option, *280*

transfers-out *number;* option, *280*

transfers-per-ns *number;* option, *280*

unsuccessful compilations, 266-267

what to download, unpack, and read, 266

bitwise AND operations, netmasks and, 540

blacklist_recipients feature, FEATURE macro, 369

block devices, files and directory types, 122

Block Devices menu, kernel features and modules, 231

blocking. *See* packet filtering

blocks, superblocks and file systems, 169-170

boot disks, creating for Red Hat Linux, 21, 42, *44*

boot managers, LILO (Linux Loader), 31-33, 150-156

boot process

partitions and, 171-172

quota management and, 193

Red Hat Linux and, 20

boot records, master. *See* MBRs

boot time

starting Apache HTTP server, 341-342

starting DNS (Domain Name Service) at, 267-268

bootable CD-ROMs, Red Hat Linux, 21

booting and shutting down, 149-165

See also single-host administration

fsck tool, 163, 164-165

LILO (Linux Loader) boot manager, 150-156

mount command, 165

overview, 150

Single-user ("Recovery") mode, 164-165

steps to booting, 156-163

summary, 165

unmount command, 165

BOOTP protocol, DHCP (Dynamic Host Configuration Protocol), 482

broadcast *address* option, ifconfig program, 554

broadcast methods, NIS (Network Information Service), 437

broadcast-address option, DHCP (Dynamic Host Configuration Protocol), *489*

browsers, Web, 607

browsing servers via smbclient program, 458-460

BugTraq mailing list, securing individual servers, 252

./Build command

compiling Sendmail, 356

installing Sendmail, 374

wu-ftpd (Washington University FTP Server), 308-309

building the kernel, 227-235

See also compiling the kernel

bzImage parameter, 235
cat command, 227-228
compilation stages, 234-235
dependency tree and, 234
kernel features and modules, 229-234
make *xconfig* command, 227-228
overview, 227
/proc file system and, 228
zImage parameter, 234
bulletins, 395-396
See also POP (Post Office Protocol); Qpopper daemon
creating, 395
directory maintenance, 396
/var/spool/bulletins directory, 395
bzImage parameter, compiling the kernel, 235

▼ C

-c comment command-line option, user management tools, *91*
-C *config-file* command-line option, LILO (Linux Loader) boot manager, *156*
-c *filename* option, DHCP (Dynamic Host Configuration Protocol) clients, *492*
-c parameter, e2fsck tool, *177*
C/C++ programming suite, programming languages accompanying Red Hat Linux, 600
caching servers, DNS (Domain Name Service) and, 264
caching zones, named.conf file, 287
calls
remote procedure. *See* RPCs
system. *See* system calls
cat command, 133
See also file management and manipulation
building the kernel, 227-228
concatenating files, 133
dump tool and, 503
cdpath command, /etc/ftpaccess file, 318
CERT (Computer Emergency Response Team), securing individual servers, 251-252
chain parameter type, ipchains tool, *569*
chain types, ipchains tool, 568
chains, ipchains tool, 564, 566-574
character devices, files and directory types, 122-123
Character Devices menu, kernel features and modules, 233
chat, real-time, 609
check-names *type* action; option, BIND servers, *278*
checksums, IP headers, 523
chgrp command, changing groups, 123
chmod command
anonymous FTP directories, 328
/etc/ftpaccess file and permissions, 319
ipchains tool and packet filtering, 580-581
permissions and, 124, *125*
chown command, 123
BIND (Berkeley Internet Domain Name) server documentation, 268
changing ownership, 123
chroot command, anonymous FTP directories, 327-328, 329

CIDR (Classless Inter-Domain Routing), netmasks, 541
class command, /etc/ftpaccess file, 311-312
cleaning-interval *number*; option, BIND servers, *282*
cleartext, SSH (Secure Shell) and, 400
client configuration
NFS (Network File System), 420-424
NIS (Network Information Service), 436-438
client daemon, DHCP (Dynamic Host Configuration Protocol), 491-493
client-side DNS. *See* resolver
client/server interaction
connections and, 531
FTP (File Transfer Protocol) and, 306-307
cmd parameter, route command, 555
CNAME (Canonical Name) records, DNS record types, 291
code, source. *See* source code
Code Maturity Level Options menu, kernel features and modules, 230
color scheme, KDE (K Desktop Environment), 55-58
command-line backup tools, 501-506
See also backups
dump tool, 501-504
restore tool, 504-506
command-line interface, 111-148
See also GUIs (graphical user interfaces); single-host administration
BASH (Bourne Again Shell), 112-118
chgrp command, 123
chmod command and permissions, 124, *125*
chown command, 123
documentation tools, 118-120
editors, 145-147
file management and manipulation, 126-136
file permission combinations, *125*
file permissions, 124
files and directory types, 121-123
ls command (listing files), 121
miscellaneous tools, 140-145
networking tools, 142-145
overview, 112
process manipulation, 136-140
su command, 142
summary, 147-148
uname utility, 141
w command, 142
who command, 141-142
command-line options
LILO (Linux Loader) boot manager, *156*
Qpopper daemon, 396
restore tool, *504-505*
smbclient program, *461*
syslogd daemon, 212, *213-214*
user management tools, 89-94
command-line shortcuts, BASH (Bourne Again Shell), 116-118
commenting-out unneeded services, /etc/inetd.conf file, 206
comments, named.conf file, 272
compilation stages, building the kernel, 234-235
compiling
Apache HTTP server, 340-341
DHCP (Dynamic Host Configuration Protocol) clients, 491

DHCPD (Dynamic Host Configuration Protocol server), 483-484
ipchains tool, 567-568
Qpopper daemon, 389-391
Samba, 448-450
Sendmail, 356-357
SSH (Secure Shell), 406-409
wu-ftpd (Washington University FTP Server), 308-309
compiling the kernel, 221-239
See also kernel; single-host administration
building the kernel, 227-235
compilation stages, 234-235
distributions, 223
finding kernel source code, 224-227
installing the kernel, 235-237
overview, 222-224
patching the kernel, 237-239
review process for kernel changes, 222
summary, 239
compiling software, 74-78
See also installing software
cleanup, 78
configuring packages, 76
distribution files, 75-76
documentation and, 75-76
gzip command, 74, 75
make install command, 77
make tool, 76-77
more command, 76
overview, 74
pico command, 76
rm command and cleanup, 78
SSH tarball, 74-75
tar command, 74, 75
tarballs, 74-75
unpacking packages, 74-75
compress command, /etc/ftpaccess file, 318-319
compression
gzip command, 74, 75, 129-130
tar command and, 74, 75, 103, 132-133
concatenating files, cat command, 133
configurable parameters, Sendmail, 369, *370-372*
configuration files
LinuxConf package, 95-99
NIS (Network Information Service) and, 441-442
PAM (Pluggable Authentication Modules), 105-109
Windows versus Linux, 10-11
./configure command
BIND servers, 266
LPRng file, 468
packages, 76
Qpopper daemon, 389, *390*
Samba, 449
SSH (Secure Shell), 407
configuring
LILO (Linux Loader) boot manager, 150-155
networks. *See* network configuration
Sendmail. *See* MC files
conflicts
debugging hardware via /proc file system, 596

POP (Post Office Protocol) and other protocols, 388
connections, 518, 530-534
See also TCP (Transmission Control Protocol); TCP/IP
client/server interaction, 531
closing, 533-534
opening, 531-532
RST (reset) flag, 533
tcpdump and, 530-532
three-way handshakes, 531, 594
transferring data, 532-533
Console Drivers menu, kernel features and modules, 234
Control Center, KDE (K Desktop Environment), 51-58
control flags, PAM (Pluggable Authentication Modules), *106*
controls keyword, named.conf file, 273
converting numbers, 539
COPS (Computer Oracle and Password System), monitoring systems, 250
copying files, cp command, 126
core system services, 199-220
See also single-host administration
cron program, 217-219
/etc/inittab file, 200-202
inetd daemon, 203-207
init process, 200
overview, 200
summary, 219-220
syslogd daemon, 212-217
telinit command, 203
xinetd daemon, 203-204, 207-211
Corel WordPerfect, Linux tools, 606
coresize *size;* option, BIND servers, *281*
cp command
See also dd command
copying files, 126
cps variable, /etc/xinetd.conf file, 211
"crackers" versus "hackers," securing individual servers, 242
cron program, 217-219
See also core system services
COPS (Computer Oracle and Password System) and, 250
crontab file, 218-219
overview, 217-218
cross-mounting disks, NFS (Network File System), 423
cryptography
public key, 400-403
Samba encrypted passwords, 447, 462-463
Cw option, /etc/sendmail.cf file, 359

▼ D

-D command-line parameter, smbclient program, *461*
-d command-line parameter, syslogd daemon, *213*
-d *density* parameter, dump tool, *502*
-d homedir command-line option, user management tools, *91*
-d option, DHCP (Dynamic Host Configuration Protocol) clients, *492*

-D option, DHCP (Dynamic Host Configuration Protocol) clients, *492*

-D parameter, ipchains tool, *569*

d command, fdisk utility, 181

DATA command, SMTP (Simple Mail Transfer Protocol), 351-352

Data Encryption Standard (DES), passwords and, 83

databases
    quota, 194
    user, 86-89

datasize *datasize;* option, BIND servers, *281*

dd command, 128-129
    See also cp command; file management and manipulation
    installing Red Hat Linux and floppy disk boot images, 21
    parameters, *129*

deallocate-on-exit *yes/no;* option, BIND servers, *276*

Debug argument, PAM (Pluggable Authentication Modules), *107*

debugging
    hardware conflicts and /proc file system, 596
    PAM (Pluggable Authentication Modules), 109

decimal numbers, converting to binary, 539

default routes
    ARP (Address Resolution Protocol), 535
    routers, 554

default-lease-time parameter, DHCPD (Dynamic Host Configuration Protocol server), 486

defaults block, /etc/xinetd.conf file, 208

define command, MC files (configuring Sendmail), 362

DELE command, telnet service, 387

delete command, /etc/ftpaccess file and permissions, 319-320

deleting groups, LinuxConf package, 99

deleting users, LinuxConf package, 98, *99*

deny command, /etc/ftpaccess file, 312

dependency tree, building the kernel and, 234

DES (Data Encryption Standard), passwords and, 83

desc field, /etc/ftpconversions/ file, *325*

desktop color scheme, KDE (K Desktop Environment), 55-58

desktop tools, 608

destination ports, TCP/IP and, 243

/dev/hdX, device names for disks, 179-180

/dev/hda3 partition, /etc/fstab file, 175-176

device files, creating via mknod command, 499

device information, Disk Druid partitioning tool, 28

device names for disks, 179-180

/dev/pts entry, /etc/fstab file, 176

df command
    See also file management and manipulation
    disk free space, 135

DHCP (Dynamic Host Configuration Protocol), 481-493
    See also Intranet services
    BOOTP protocol, 482
    broadcast-address option, *489*
    client daemon, 491-493
    dhcpd.leases file, 490
    domain-name option, *489*
    domain-name-servers option, *489*
    general runtime behavior, 490

    host-name option, *489*
    mechanics of, 483
    nis-domain option, *489*
    nis-servers option, *489*
    options, 489
    overview, 482-483
    routers option, *489*
    servers, 483-490
    subnet-mask option, *489*
    summary, 493

DHCP (Dynamic Host Configuration Protocol) clients, 491-493
    -c *filename* option, *492*
    -d option, *492*
    -D option, *492*
    -h *hostname* option, *492*
    -H option, *492*
    -I *clientID* option, *492*
    -i *vendorClassID* option, *492*
    -k option, *492*
    -l *leasetime* option, *493*
    -r option, *493*
    -R option, *493*
    -t *timeout* option, *493*
    configuring, 491
    downloading, compiling, and installing, 491
    interface option, *493*
    make command, 491
    make install command, 491
    options, *492-493*

DHCPD (Dynamic Host Configuration Protocol server), 483-490
    always-reply-rfc1048 parameter, 486
    authoritative parameter, 486
    configuring, 484-489
    declarations, 484-486
    default-lease-time parameter, 486
    downloading, compiling, and installing, 483-484
    dynamic-bootp-lease-cutoff parameter, 486-487
    dynamic-bootp-lease-length parameter, 487
    /etc/dhcpd.conf file, 484, 490
    filename parameter, 487
    fixed-address parameter, 487
    get-lease-hostname parameter, 487
    group declaration, 485
    hardware parameter, 488
    host declaration, 485
    make install command, 484
    max-lease-time parameter, 488
    next-server parameter, 488
    overview, 483
    parameters, 486-489
    range declaration, 486
    sample dhcpd.conf file, 490
    server-identifier parameter, 488
    server-name parameter, 488
    shared-network declaration, 485
    subnet declaration, 485-486
    use-host-decl-name parameter, 488
    use-lease-addr-for-default-route parameter, 489

dig command, DNS tools, 299

directories
    files and directory types, 121
    mkdir command, 131

rmdir command, 131
    showing present working via pwd
        command, 131
    unpacking kernel source code and naming,
        226-227
directory location of files
    whereis command, 135
    which command, 134-135
directory *path-name;* option, BIND servers, 275
Disable variable, /etc/xinetd.conf file, 208
disabling services
    find command, 162
    steps to booting, 161-162
DISCARD action, access_db database, *377*
Disk Druid partitioning tool, 27-30
    See also installing Red Hat Linux; partitions
    adding partitions, 29-30
    device information, 28
    editing/deleting partitions, 30
    menu choices, 29
    mount point information, 27
disk utilization, du command, 134
disks
    adding, 178-179
    device names for, 179-180
    fdisk utility for creating partitions, 180-186
    free space and df command, 135
    mounting/unmounting local, 171-176
    partitioning, 26-31, 179-187
    quotas. *See* quota management
    sync command, 135-136
displaying routes
    netstat command, 557
    route command, 556-557
distributions
    compiling software and, 75-76
    GNOME (GNU Network Object Model
        Environment), 59
    Linux, 4, 223
    SSH (Secure Shell), 404-406
divert command, MC files (configuring Sendmail),
    361-362
dmesg command, loading drivers, 179
dnl instruction, MC files (configuring Sendmail), 362
DNS (Domain Name Service), 257-303
    See also Internet services; IP addresses
    authoritative servers and, 263
    BIND servers, 265-297
    caching servers and, 264
    client-side. *See* resolver
    /etc/hosts file and, 259, 260
    forward resolution, 263
    FQDNs (fully qualified domain names),
        260-262
    hosts and domains, 260-262
    IP addresses and, 258
    named.conf file, 271-287, 292-297
    overview, 258, 260-264
    primary name servers and, 261
    primary servers and, 263
    record types, 288-292
    reference resources, 302
    reverse resolution, 263, *264*

root servers and, 261, 262
    secondary servers and, 263
    Sendmail, and, 379
    server types, 263-264
    starting at boot time, 267-268
    subdomains, 262-263
    summary, 302-303
    tools, 297-303
DNS record types, 288-292
    A (Address) records, 289-290
    CNAME (Canonical Name) records, 291
    MX (Mail Exchanger) records, 290-291
    NS (Name Server) records, 289
    PTR (Pointer Record) records, 290
    RP (Responsible Person) records, 291
    SOA (State of Authority) records, 288-289
    TXT records, 291
DNS tools, 297-303
    dig command, 299
    host command, 298
    kill -HUP command, 298
    nslookup command, 298, 299
    whois command, 299-302
documentation
    BIND servers, 268
    compiling software and, 75-76
documentation tools, 118-120
    See also command-line interface
    info command, 118, 120
    man command, 118, 119-120
DOMAIN macro, Sendmail macros, 363-364
Domain Name Service. *See* DNS
domain names, fully qualified. *See* FQDNs
domain names for secondary servers, NIS (Network
    Information Service), 439
domain-name option, DHCP (Dynamic Host
    Configuration Protocol), *489*
domain-name-servers option, DHCP (Dynamic Host
    Configuration Protocol), *489*
domainname command, NIS (Network Information
    Service) and, 430-431, 439
domains
    NIS (Network Information Service), 429-430
    virtual (Apache HTTP server), 345-347
    Windows versus Linux, 11
domaintable feature, FEATURE macro, 366-367
down option, ifconfig program, 553
du command
    See also file management and manipulation
    disk utilization, 134
dump tool, 501-504
    See also command-line backup tools
    -b *blocksize* parameter, *502*
    -B *count* parameter, *502*
    -d *density* parameter, *502*
    -f *filename* parameter, *502*
    -n parameter, *502*
    -s *size* parameter, *502*
    -u parameter, *502*
    backing up entire systems via, 503-504
    cat command and, 503
    /etc/dumpdates file, 501
    mt command and, 504

parameters, *502*
suppressing tape size calculation, 503
tar command and, 506
dump-file *path-name;* option, BIND servers, 275
Dynamic Host Configuration Protocol. *See* DHCP
dynamic routing. *See* RIP (Routing Information
  Protocol)
dynamic-bootp-lease-cutoff parameter, DHCPD
  (Dynamic Host Configuration Protocol server),
  486-487
dynamic-bootp-lease-length parameter, DHCPD
  (Dynamic Host Configuration Protocol server), 487

▼ **E**

-e expire-date command-line option, user
  management tools, *91*
e2fsck tool, 177-178
    See also fsck tool
    parameters, *177*
e-mail
    clients, 608
    SMTP (Simple Mail Transfer Protocol), 349-382
    user management, 85-86
echo-replies, ICMP (Internet Control Message
  Protocol), 578
editors, 145-147
    See also command-line interface; tools
    emacs, 146
    joe, 146
    overview, 145
    pico, 146-147
    vi, 145-146
edquota command, quota management, 195-197
emacs editor, 146
encrypted passwords
    See also public key cryptography
    Samba, 447, 462-463
environment variables, BASH (Bourne Again Shell),
  114-115, 117
error_log file, Apache HTTP server, 347
errors. *See* troubleshooting
/etc/auto.home file, Automounter, 189-190
/etc/auto.master file, Automounter, 189-190, 191-192
/etc/conf.modules file, modules and network
  interfaces, 557-558
/etc/dhcpd.conf file, DHCPD (Dynamic Host
  Configuration Protocol server), 484, 490
/etc/dumpdates file, dump tool, 501
/etc/exports file
    common problems, 420
    exportfs command and, 419-420
    NFS (Network File System) servers, 417-420
/etc/fstab file, 174-176
    See also file system management; mount
      command
    /dev/hda3 partition, 175-176
    /dev/pts entry, 176
    elements, *175*
    mount command and, 176
    none entry and /proc file system, 176
    sample file, 175
/etc/ftpaccess file, 311-322, 329-332

See also FTP (File Transfer Protocol); wu-ftpd
  (Washington University FTP Server)
access control, 311-315
alias command, 318
autogroup command, 312
banner command, 315
banner message control, 315-317
cdpath command, 318
chmod command, 319
class command, 311-312
compress command, 318-319
delete command, 319-320
deny command, 312
guestgroup command, 312-313
incoming subdirectory, 330
limit command, 313-314
log *commands* command, 317
log *transfers* command, 317
loginfails command, 314
message command, 315-316
mixed access, 329-330
overwrite command, 320
passwd-check command, 320-321
path-filter command, 321
permissions, 319-322
private command, 314-315
readme command, 316-317
registered users, 331-332
rename command, 320
setting up, 329-330
tar command, 319
umask command, 320
upload command, 321-322
/etc/ftpconversions/ file, 323-325
    See also wu-ftpd (Washington University FTP
      Server)
    addonpost field, *324*
    addonpre field, *324*
    desc field, *325*
    external field, *324*
    gzip command and, 325
    options field, *325*
    sample entry, 325
    strippost field, *324*
    strippre field, *323*
    type field, *324*
/etc/ftphosts file, wu-ftpd (Washington University
  FTP Server), 326
/etc/group file, user databases, 88-89
/etc/hosts file
    DNS (Domain Name Service) and, 259, 260
    NIS (Network Information Service) and, 260
/etc/inetd.conf file, 203, 204-207
    See also core system services; inetd daemon
    commenting-out unneeded services, 206
    elements and service descriptions, *204-205*
    ftp service, 206
    kill command, 207
    protocol element, *205*
    ps command, 206
    security, 206-207
    service_name element, *204*
    sock_type element, *205*
    srvr_prog element, *205*

srvr_prog_args element, *205*
telnet service, 206
user element, *205*
wait/nowait element, *205*
wu-ftpd (Washington University FTP Server),
    309-310
/etc/inittab file, 200-202
    See also core system services; init process
    action field options, *201-202*
    item descriptions, *201*
/etc/lilo.conf file, installing the kernel, 236
/etc/lpd.perms file, 474-477
    See also printing
    defaults, 475
    format of, 475
    HOST permission keyword, 476
    sample file, 477
    SERVICE permission keyword, 476
    USER permission keyword, 476
/etc/mail directory, Sendmail, 359
/etc/nsswitch.conf file
    NIS (Network Information Service), 438
    resolver (client-side DNS), 270
/etc/pam.d/login file, PAM (Pluggable Authentication
Modules) configuration file, 107-109
/etc/pam.d/other file, PAM (Pluggable
Authentication Modules), 109
/etc/passwd file
    See also passwords
    installing Red Hat Linux and authentication
        configuration, 35-36
    NIS (Network Information Service) and,
        428-429, 441-442
    Samba and encrypted passwords, 462-463
    UIDs (user IDs) and, 87, 101
    user databases, 86-88
/etc/printcap file, 471-474
    See also printing
    filter parameter, *472*
    kill command and, 474
    lp parameter, *472*
    mx parameter, *472*
    overview, 471
    rm parameter, *472*
    rp parameter, *472*
    sample files, 473-474
    sd parameter, *471*
    sh parameter, *471*
/etc/resolv.conf file, resolver (client-side DNS),
    269-270
/etc/sendmail.cf file
    Cw option, 359
    Sendmail and domain names, 358
    "tweaking," 361
/etc/shadow file, user databases, 88
/etc/shells file, user management, 85
/etc/syslog.conf file, 212-217
    See also core system services; syslogd daemon
    facility value, 212, *214*
    format of, 215-217
    location entries example, 215, *216*
    log message classifications, 212-214

overview, 212
priority levels, 212, 214, *215*
sample file, 217
string equivalents for facility value, 212, *214*
string equivalents for priority levels, *215*
wildcards and, 214
/etc/xinetd.conf file, 207-211
    See also core system services; xinetd daemon
    cps variable, 211
    defaults block, 208
    Disable variable, 208
    entry example, 211
    example file, 207-208
    Group variable, 209
    Id variable, 208
    includedir directive, 207
    instances block, 208
    Instances variable, 209
    Interface variable, 210
    log_on_failure block, 208
    log_on_success variable, 210
    log_type variable, 210
    no_access variable, 209
    only_from variable, 209
    Port variable, 210
    Protocol variable, 209
    Server variable, 209
    server_args variable, 209
    socket_type variable, 208
    Type variable, 208
    User variable, 209
    variables, 208-211
    Wait variable, 209
    wu-ftpd (Washington University FTP
        Server), 310
/etc/yp.conf file, NIS (Network Information Service),
    436-437
Ethereal program, TCP/IP and, 512
Ethernet frames
    jumbo, 554
    packet filtering and, *564*
Ethernet headers, 519-521
    See also headers; TCP/IP
    MAC (Medium Access Control) addresses
        and, 519
    tcpdump program and, 520-521
    viewing, 520-521
Ethernet protocol, TCP/IP and, 517
-exec parameter, find command, 127
Expect, programming languages accompanying Red
    Hat Linux, 601
explicit allow, packet filtering rules, 581-582
explicit deny, packet filtering rules, 582
export command, BASH (Bourne Again Shell) and
    environment variables, 115
exportfs command
    See also NFS (Network File System)
    /etc/exports file and, 419-420
EXPOSED_USER macro, Sendmail macros, 365
ext2 file system, 170, 171
    See also file systems

ext3 file system, 170
    See also file systems
external field, /etc/ftpconversions/ file, *324*

▼ F

-f command-line option, user management tools, *94*
-f *config* command-line parameter, syslogd
    daemon, *213*
-f *filename* parameter
        dump tool, *502*
        restore tool, *505*
-f inactive-time command-line option, user
    management tools, *91*
-f parameter, e2fsck tool, *177*
-F parameter, ipchains tool, *569*
facility value, /etc/syslog.conf file, 212, *214*
fake-iquery *yes/no;* option, BIND servers, *276*
fdisk utility, 180-186
        See also partitions
        d command, 181
        disk partitions listing, *182*
        n command, 183, 184-185
        options, 180-181
        overview, 180
        p command, 181-183, 184, 185
        partitions listing, *182*
        t command, 183-184
        w command, 186
FEATURE macro, 365-369
        See also Sendmail; Sendmail macros
        accept_unqualified_senders feature, 369
        accept_unresolvable_domains feature, 369
        access_db feature, 369
        always_add_domain feature, 367
        blacklist_recipients feature, 369
        domaintable feature, 366-367
        local_procmail feature, 368
        mailertable feature, 366
        nullclient feature, 368
        overview, 365
        promiscuous_relay "feature," 368-369
        redirect feature, 365-366
        relay_based_on_MX feature, 369
        relay_entire_domain feature, 369
        smrsh feature, 368
        use_ct_file feature, 365
        use_cw_file feature, 365
        virtusertable feature, 367
fetch-glue *yes/no;* option, BIND servers, *276*
FHS (File Hierarchy Standard), 147
file compression
        gzip command, 74, 75, 129-130
        tar command and, 74, 75, 103, 132-133
file management and manipulation, 126-136
        See also command-line interface
        cat command, 133
        cp command, 126
        dd command, 128-129
        df command, 135
        du command, 134
        find command, 127, *128*
        gzip command, 129-130

ln command, 127
        mkdir command, 131
        mknod command, 130
        more command, 134
        mv command, 126
        pwd command, 131
        rmdir command, 131
        sync command, 135-136
        tar command, 132-133
        whereis command, 135
        which command, 134-135
file permissions. *See* permissions
file system management, 171-178
        /etc/fstab file, 174-176
        fsck tool, 176-178
        mount command, 172-174
        mounting/unmounting local disks, 171-176
        overview, 171
        partitions, 26-31, 179-187
        partitions and boot process, 171-172
        root directory and, 171, *172*
        unmount command, 174
file systems, 167-198
        See also single-host administration
        adding disks, 178-179
        components of, 168-171
        dmesg command, 179
        ext2, 170, 171
        ext3, 170-171
        fsck tool and, 170
        i-nodes and, 168, *169*
        managing, 171-178
        mke2fs command, 186-187
        mkswap command, 186-187
        network, 187-192
        overview, 168
        partitions and, 186-187
        /proc. *See* /proc file system
        quota management, 192-198
        ReiserFS, 170
        superblocks and, 169-170
File Systems menu, kernel features and modules, 234
filename expansion, BASH (Bourne Again Shell), 117
filename parameter, DHCPD (Dynamic Host
    Configuration Protocol server), 487
filenames, NIS (Network Information Service), 433-434
files and directory types, 121-123
        See also command-line interface
        block devices, 122
        character devices, 122-123
        directories, 121
        hard links, 122
        named pipes, 123, 130
        normal files, 121
        symbolic links, 122
files *number;* option, BIND servers, *281*
filter parameter, /etc/printcap file, 472
filtering packets. *See* packet filtering
filters, installing ifhp from LPRng file, 470-471
finance tools, 607-608
find command, 127
        command options, *128*
        disabling services, 162
        -exec parameter, 127

finding kernel source code, 224-227
    See also compiling the kernel
    overview, 224
    unpacking kernel source code, 225-227
    versions, 224-225
    Web site, 224
fips tool, installing Linux in a server configuration, 18-19
firewalls
    See also packet filtering
    FTP (File Transfer Protocol) and, 307
    ipchains tool, 564, 566-574
Firewire, IEEE 1394 (Firewire) Support menu, 232
fixed-address parameter, DHCPD (Dynamic Host
    Configuration Protocol server), 487
flags entry, route command, 556
flushing queues, Sendmail, 381
force command-line option, RPM (Red Hat Package
    Manager), *72*
Fortran 77, programming languages accompanying
    Red Hat Linux, 600
forward resolution, DNS (Domain Name Service), 263
forwarders *first/only;* option, BIND servers, 277
forwarders {*ip-list;*} option, BIND servers, 277
FQDNs (fully qualified domain names), 260-262
    See also DNS (Domain Name Service)
fragmentation, IP headers and, 522
frames
    jumbo Ethernet, 554
    packet filtering and Ethernet, *564*
free nature of Linux, 5, 6-7
free space, df command, 135
fsck tool, 176-178
    See also file system management
    booting and shutting down, 163, 164-165
    e2fsck tool and, 177-178
    file systems and, 170
    lost+found directory and, 178
    troubleshooting, 178
FTP (File Transfer Protocol), 305-333
    See also Internet services
    anonymous directories, 327-328
    anonymous users, 326-327
    client/server interactions, 306-307
    /etc/ftpaccess file, 311-322
    firewalls and, 307
    overview, 306-307
    passive transfer, 307
    wu-ftpd (Washington University FTP Server),
        307-333
ftp command, networking tools, 145
ftp service, /etc/inetd.conf file, 206
fully qualified domain names. *See* FQDNs

▼ G

-g *gid* command-line option, user management
    tools, *94*
-G group[, . . .] command-line option, user
    management tools, *91*
-g initial-group command-line option, user
    management tools, *91*
General Setup menu, kernel features and modules, 231

GET command, HTTP request headers, 337
get-lease-hostname parameter, DHCPD (Dynamic
    Host Configuration Protocol server), 487
GIDs (group IDs)
    See also UIDs (user IDs)
    MINGID and NIS (Network Information
        Service), 432
    SetGID bits and user management, 100
    user management, 82
global options, lilo.conf and LILO (Linux Loader) boot
    manager, 152-153
Globals button, SWAT (Samba Web Administration
    Tool), 456
GNOME (GNU Network Object Model Environment),
    59-66
    See also KDE; Red Hat Linux; X Windows
    Background panel, 63
    Configuration Tool, 62-66
    distributions, 59
    GUIs (graphical user interfaces), 61
    overview, 59-61
    Screen Saver menu, 64
    summary, 67
    Themes menu, 65
    Window Manager panel, 66
    X Windows and, 48
gnome-help-browser interface, man command, 120
gnorpm command, RPM (Red Hat Package Manager)
    and, 73-74
GNU Fortran 77, programming languages
    accompanying Red Hat Linux, 600
GNU project, 5
GPL (GNU Public License), 5-6
graphical user interface. *See* GUI
grep command
    pipes and BASH (Bourne Again Shell), 115-116
    RPM (Red Hat Package Manager) and, 73
group command-line option, user management tools, *94*
group declaration, DHCPD (Dynamic Host
    Configuration Protocol server), 485
Group variable, /etc/xinetd.conf file, 209
groupadd command
    anonymous FTP directories, 328
    user management tools, 93
groupdel command, user management tools, 93-94
groupmod command, user management tools, 94
groups
    changing via chgrp command, 123
    deleting, 99
    /etc/group file and user databases, 88-89
    managing via LinuxConf package, 98-99
    package, 38-39
grpquota option, quota management, 194
guestgroup command, /etc/ftpaccess file, 312-313
GUIs (graphical user interfaces)
    See also command-line interface
    GNOME (GNU Network Object Model
        Environment), 61
    separation of kernel and, 8-9
gw *gway* parameter, route command, 555
gzip command, 129-130
    See also file management and manipulation; tar
        command

compiling software, 74, 75
/etc/ftpconversions/ file and, 325
restore tool and, 506

▼ H

-h command-line option, RPM (Red Hat Package Manager), 72
-h command-line parameter, syslogd daemon, *213*
-h *hostname* option, DHCP (Dynamic Host Configuration Protocol) clients, *492*
-H option, DHCP (Dynamic Host Configuration Protocol) clients, *492*
"hackers" versus "crackers," securing individual servers, 242
handshakes, three-way, 531, 594
hard disks. *See* disks
hard links, files and directory types, 122
hard versus soft mounts
    See also mount command
    NFS (Network File System), 422, 425-426
hardware conflicts, debugging via /proc file system, 596
hardware parameter, DHCPD (Dynamic Host Configuration Protocol server), 488
headers, 519-530
    See also TCP/IP
    ARP (Address Resolution Protocol), 535-536
    Ethernet, 519-521
    HTTP (HyperText Transfer Protocol), 336-337
    IP (Internet Protocol), 521-525
    overview, 519
    packet, 514
    TCP (Transmission Control Protocol), 525-529
    UDP (User Datagram Protocol), 529-530
HELO command, SMTP (Simple Mail Transfer Protocol), 351
help
    installing Linux in a server configuration, 19-20
    installing Red Hat Linux, 43
    POP (Post Office Protocol), 387
hexadecimal numbers, converting, 539
high-volume servers, /proc file system and, 595-596
/home directories
    See also root directory
    Apache HTTP server and, 342-343
    Automounter and, 189
    partitions and, 27, *182*
    user management and, 83
host command, DNS tools, 298
host declaration, DHCPD (Dynamic Host Configuration Protocol server), 485
host names
    Apache HTTP server, 345
    NIS (Network Information Service), 437
HOST permission keyword, /etc/lpd.perms file, 476
host-name option, DHCP (Dynamic Host Configuration Protocol), *489*
host-statistics *yes/no;* option, BIND servers, *276*
hosts
    DNS (Domain Name Service), 260-262
    networks and, 536-537
    Sendmail, 359

HTTP (HyperText Transfer Protocol), 336-338
    See also Apache HTTP server
    headers, 336-337
    obscurity and security, 338
    overview, 336
    port numbers and, 337-338
    request headers, 336-337
httpd.conf file, Apache HTTP server, 344, 345, 346

▼ I

-I *clientID* option, DHCP (Dynamic Host Configuration Protocol) clients, *492*
-i command-line option
    restore tool, *504*
    RPM (Red Hat Package Manager), 71, 72
-I command-line parameter, smbclient program, *461*
-I parameter, ipchains tool, *569*
-i *vendorClassID* option, DHCP (Dynamic Host Configuration Protocol) clients, *492*
i-nodes, file systems and, 168, *169*
I2O Device Support menu, kernel features and modules, 232-233
ICMP (Internet Control Message Protocol)
    echo-replies, 578
    Ping of Death, 578-579
    TCP/IP and, 519
ICQ tools, 609
Id variable, /etc/xinetd.conf file, 208
IDs
    See also user management
    group. *See* GIDs
    user. *See* UIDs
IEEE 1394 (Firewire) Support menu, kernel features and modules, 232
ifconfig program, 551-554
    See also network configuration
    Arp option, 554
    -arp option, 554
    broadcast *address* option, 554
    down option, 553
    IP addresses and, 551
    IP aliasing, 561
    mtu *value* option, 554
    netmask *address* option, 554
    NICs (Network Interface Cards) setup, 552-553
    options, 553-554
    overview, 551
    pointtopoint *address* option, 554
    simple usage of, 551
    up option, 553
ifhp filter, installing from LPRng file, 470-471
image/painting tools, 607
in-addr.arpa domain, reverse DNS resolution, 263, *264*
include keyword, named.conf file, 272
include statements, named.conf file, 274
includedir directive, /etc/xinetd.conf file, 207
incoming subdirectory, /etc/ftpaccess file, 330
index.html, Apache HTTP server, 343
inetd daemon, 203-207
    See also core system services; xinetd daemon
    /etc/inetd.conf file, 203, 204-207

overview, 203-204
Qpopper daemon and, 391
shutting down services, 247
SWAT (Samba Web Administration Tool) and,
453-454
info command, 118, 120
See also documentation tools
init process
core system services, 200
steps to booting, 157
telinit command, 203
Input Core Support menu, kernel features and
modules, 233
insmod command, IP Masquerading proxies and, 588
installing
Apache HTTP server, 339-342
DHCP (Dynamic Host Configuration Protocol)
clients, 491
DHCPD (Dynamic Host Configuration
Protocol server), 483-484
DNS servers, 265-268
ifhp filter, 470-471
ipchains tool, 567-568
iptables tool, 575-576
LPRng file, 467-469
PAM (Pluggable Authentication Modules),
102-103
Qpopper daemon, 388-389
Samba, 448-450
Sendmail, 374-375
SSH (Secure Shell), 406-409
installing the kernel, 235-237
See also compiling the kernel
/etc/lilo.conf file, 236-237
make modules_install command, 236
naming kernels, 235
troubleshooting, 236-237
/usr/src/linux/arch/i386/boot/zImage
file, 235
installing Linux in a server configuration, 15-44
fips tool, 18-19
help, 19-20
methods, 19
overview, 16-20
Red Hat Linux, 20-44
uptime command, 18
installing packages
make install command, 77
Red Hat Linux groups, 38-39
RPM (Red Hat Package Manager), 71-72
installing Red Hat Linux, 20-44
See also installing Linux in a server
configuration
accounts, 35
authentication configuration, 35-38
boot disk creation, 21, 42, *44*
boot process, 20
bootable CD-ROMs, 21
dd command, 21
Disk Druid partitioning tool, 27-30
/etc/passwd file, 35-36
help, 43
Kerberos authentication, 37
keyboard types, 23

language choice, 22-23
LDAP servers for storing passwords, 37
LILO boot manager, 31-33
mouse types, 24
networking, 33-34
overview, 20-21
package groups, 38-39
partitions, 26-31
passwords, 35-37
resolving prerequisite packages, 39, *40*
root account, 35
root passwords, 35, *36*
selecting package groups, 38-39
start of, 21-22
status indicator, *29*, 42
summary, 44
time zone configuration screen, 34
upgrading versus installing, 25-26
X Windows configuration, 39-41
installing software, 69-78
compiling software, 74-78
overview, 70
RPM (Red Hat Package Manager), 70-74
summary, 78
instances block, /etc/xinetd.conf file, 208
Instances variable, /etc/xinetd.conf file, 209
interface option, DHCP (Dynamic Host Configuration
Protocol) clients, *493*
Interface variable, /etc/xinetd.conf file, 210
interface-interval *number;* option, BIND servers, *282*
interfaces
command-line. *See* command-line interface
graphical user. *See* GUIs
network, 557-558
network cards. *See* NICs
Internet Control Message Protocol (ICMP), TCP/IP
and, 519
Internet services, 255-410
See also Intranet services
Apache HTTP server, 335-348
DNS (Domain Name Service), 257-303
FTP (File Transfer Protocol), 305-333
POP (Post Office Protocol), 383-397
SMTP (Simple Mail Transfer Protocol), 349-382
intr option, NFS (Network File System), 423
Intranet services, 411-507
See also Internet services
backups, 495-507
DHCP (Dynamic Host Configuration
Protocol), 481-493
NFS (Network File System), 413-426
NIS (Network Information Service), 427-444
printing, 465-479
Samba, 445-464
IP (Internet Protocol)
addresses, 536-537
headers, 521-525
ifconfig command and aliasing, 561
Masquerading, 583-588
TCP/IP and, 517
IP addresses, 536-537
See also networking; TCP/IP
aliasing, 561
ARP (Address Resolution Protocol), 534-536

DHCP (Dynamic Host Configuration
  Protocol), 481-493
DNS (Domain Name Service) and, 258
ifconfig program and, 551
loopback addresses, 537
private, 537
IP headers, 521-525
  checksums, 523
  content of, *565*
  fragmentation and, 522
  overview, 521-523
  tcpdump program and, 523-525
  TOS (Type Of Service) header, 521
  traceroute program and, 523-525
  TTL (time-to-live) field, 523
  versions, 521
IP Masquerading, 583-588
  See also advanced Linux networking;
    MASQUERADE_AS macro
  engine, *585*
  example network, *584*
  insmod command and, 588
  ipchains tool and, 586
  iptables tool and, 586
  NAT (network address translation) and, 583
  overview, 583-584
  packet filtering and, 579
  proxies, 587-588
  relationship between hosts on network, *585*
  Sendmail, 358-359
  "three-line" solution, 586-587
ipchains tool, 564, 566-574
  See also advanced Linux networking; firewalls;
    iptables tool; packet filtering
  -A parameter, *569*
  -b option, *573*
  -D parameter, *569*
  -F parameter, *569*
  -I parameter, *569*
  -l option, *573*
  -L parameter, *569*
  -n option, *573*
  -N parameter, *569*
  -P parameter, *569*
  -R parameter, *569*
  -v option, *573*
  -x option, *573*
  -X parameter, *569*
  -y option, *573*
  -Z parameter, *569*
  actions, 568-571
  chain parameter type, *569*
  chain types, 568
  chmod command and, 580-581
  compiling and installing, 567-568
  examples, 572-574
  IP Masquerading and, 586
  iptables tool comparison, 575, 576-577
  make install command, 567
  options, *573*
  options parameter type, *570*
  overview, 566
  parameter types, *569-570*
  parameters, *569*

port specifications, 574
rulenum parameter type, *570*
rules, 583
rulespec parameter type, *569*, 571-572
scripts, 579-581
tar command and, 567
target parameter type, *570*
iptables tool, 574-577
  See also ipchains tool; packet filtering
  downloading and installing, 575-576
  installing, 575-576
  IP Masquerading and, 586
  ipchains tool comparison, 575, 576-577
  overview, 574
  rules, 582
IrDA Support menu, kernel features and modules, 233
ISDN Subsystem menu, kernel features and
  modules, 233
iTcl, programming languages accompanying Red Hat
  Linux, 601

▼ J

Jikes, programming languages accompanying Red Hat
  Linux, 602
job control, BASH (Bourne Again Shell), 113-114
joe editor, 146
jumbo frames, NICs (Network Interface Cards)
  and, 554

▼ K

-k option, DHCP (Dynamic Host Configuration
  Protocol) clients, *492*
Kaffe, programming languages accompanying Red
  Hat Linux, 602
kcore file, /proc file system, 591
KDE (K Desktop Environment), 49-58
  See also GNOME; X Windows
  Background menu option, 55
  color scheme, 55-58
  Command box, *54*
  Control Center, 51-58
  keyboard shortcuts, 53
  kpanel, 51
  ksysv program and, 48
  licensing issues, 49
  multiple desktops, 51-52, *53*
  overview, 49
  removing GNOME banner, 50
  Screensaver option, 57-58
  starting applications from, 53-54
  starting X Windows and, 49-50
  startx command, 49
  summary, 67
  X Windows and, 48
Kerberos authentication, installing Red Hat Linux, 37
kernel, 4, 223-224
  See also compiling the kernel
  booting via LILO (Linux Loader) boot
    manager, 154-155
  building, 227-235

compiling, 221-239
features and modules, 229-234
finding source code, 224-227
installing, 235-237
LILO (Linux Loader) boot manager
    options, 156
naming, 235
NFS (Network File System) support, 417
patching, 237-239
review process for changes, 222
separation of GUI and, 8-9
unpacking source code, 225-227
kernel execution, steps to booting, 156-157
kernel features and modules, 229-234
    See also building the kernel
    Amateur Radio Support menu, 233
    ATA/IDE/MFM/RLL Support menu, 232
    Block Devices menu, 231
    Character Devices menu, 233
    Code Maturity Level Options menu, 230
    Console Drivers menu, 234
    File Systems menu, 234
    General Setup menu, 231
    I2O Device Support menu, 232-233
    IEEE 1394 (Firewire) Support menu, 232
    Input Core Support menu, 233
    IrDA Support menu, 233
    ISDN Subsystem menu, 233
    Kernel Hacking menu, 234
    Loadable Module Support menu, 230
    Memory Technology Devices menu, 231
    module configuration option, 229-230
    Multi-Device Support (RAID and LVM) menu,
        231-232
    Multimedia Devices menu, 233
    Network Device Support menu, 233
    Networking Options menu, 232
    Old CD-ROM Drivers menu, 233
    overview, 229-230
    Parallel Port Support menu, 231
    Plug and Play Support menu, 231
    Processor Types and Features menu, 230-231
    SCSI Support menu, 232
    Telephony Support menu, 232
    USB Support menu, 234
Kernel Hacking menu, kernel features and
    modules, 234
kernel loading, steps to booting, 156
key characteristics, public key cryptography, 402-403
keyboard shortcuts, KDE (K Desktop Environment)
    Control Center, 53
keyboard types, installing Red Hat Linux, 23
kill command, 139-140
    See also process manipulation
    /etc/inetd.conf file, 207
    /etc/printcap file and, 474
    examples, 140
    overview, 139
    security issues, 140
    signals, 140
kill -HUP command, DNS tools, 298
Konquerer browser, Linux tools, 607

kpanel, KDE (K Desktop Environment), 51
ksysv command
    enabling/disabling services, 161, *162*
    KDE (K Desktop Environment) and, 48
    NFS (Network File System) and, 416

▼ L

-l *hostlist* command-line parameter, syslogd daemon, *213*
-l *leasetime* option, DHCP (Dynamic Host
    Configuration Protocol) clients, *493*
-l option, ipchains tool, *573*
-L option, smbclient program, 459-460
-L parameter, ipchains tool, *569*
language choice
    See also programming languages
        accompanying Red Hat Linux
        installing Red Hat Linux, 22-23
layers
    OSI (International Standards Organization)
        model, 515-517
    TCP/IP, 512-517
LDAP servers, storing passwords with, 37
libraries, PAM (Pluggable Authentication Modules),
    101-109
licensing issues, KDE (K Desktop Environment), 49
LILO (Linux Loader) boot manager, 31-33, 150-156
    See also booting and shutting down; installing
        Red Hat Linux
    adding new kernels to boot, 154-155
    command-line options, *156*
    configuring, 150-155
    /etc/lilo.conf file, 152-153, 236-237
    global options in /etc/lilo.conf file, 152-153
    kernel options, 156
    MBRs (master boot records) and, 32, 151
    operating systems and, 33
    overview, 150
    per-block options in /etc/lilo.conf file, 153
    prompt command, 151
    running, 155
    Single-user ("Recovery") mode, 164-165
    stopping after "LI", 163-164
    summary, 165
    timeout command, 151
    Use Linear Mode option, 32
limit command, /etc/ftpaccess file, 313-314
linking, ln command, 127
links, symbolic and hard, 122
Linux, 4-13
    advanced networking, 559-588
    advantages of free software, 6-7
    Apache HTTP server, 335-348
    Automounter, 188-192
    backups, 495-507
    booting and shutting down, 149-165
    command-line interface, 111-148
    compiling the kernel, 221-239
    compiling software, 74-78
    core system services, 199-220

DHCP (Dynamic Host Configuration Protocol), 481-493
distributions, 4, 223
DNS (Domain Name Service), 257-303
editors, 145-147
file systems, 167-198
free nature of, 5, 6-7
FTP (File Transfer Protocol), 305-333
GNU project, 5
GPL (GNU Public License), 5-6
installing as server, 15-44
installing software, 69-78
Internet services, 255-410
Intranet services, 411-507
kernel, 4, 223-224
mounting shares, 9-10
network configuration, 549-558
NFS (Network File System), 9-10, 413-426
NIS (Network Information Service), 11, 427-444
overview, 4
partitions, 26-31, 179-187
POP (Post Office Protocol), 383-397
printing, 465-479
/proc file system, 589-596
programming languages accompanying Red Hat Linux, 599-603
Red Hat. *See* Red Hat Linux
reference resources, 12
Samba, 445-464
securing individual servers, 241-253
single-host administration, 79-253
SMTP (Simple Mail Transfer Protocol), 349-382
SSH (Secure Shell), 399-410
standards, 147
summary, 13
TCP/IP for system administrators, 511-548
tools, 605-609
user management, 81-110
versions and finding kernel source code, 224-225
window managers, 46-66
Windows comparison, 7-12
X Windows, 39-41, 46-48
linux directory, unpacking kernel source code, 225-226
Linux Loader. *See* LILO boot manager
LinuxConf package, 95-99
See also user management tools
adding groups, 98-99, *100*
adding users, 96-97
deleting groups, 99
deleting users, 98, *99*
modifying groups, 99
modifying users, 97, *98*
opening window, *95*
overview, 95
Privileges tab, 96, *97*
LIST command, telnet service, 386
listen-on {address list; } option, BIND servers, *279*
listing files, ls command, 121
listing processes, ps command, 136-138
ln command, linking, 127
load balancing, OSPF (Open Shortest Path First) protocol, 547

Loadable Module Support menu, kernel features and modules, 230
Loader, Linux. *See* LILO boot manager
loading drivers, dmesg command, 179
local disks, mounting/unmounting, 171-176
local_procmail feature, FEATURE macro, 368
location entries example, /etc/syslog.conf file, 215, *216*
log *commands* command, /etc/ftpaccess file, 317
log message classifications, /etc/syslog.conf file, 212-214
log parsing, syslogd daemon, 249
log *transfers* command, /etc/ftpaccess file, 317
logging, Sendmail, 381-382
logging keyword, named.conf file, 272
logging statements, named.conf file, 274
Login command-line option, user management tools, *92*
loginfails command, /etc/ftpaccess file, 314
log_on_failure block, /etc/xinetd.conf file, 208
log_on_success variable, /etc/xinetd.conf file, 210
log_type variable, /etc/xinetd.conf file, 210
loopback addresses, IP addresses, 537
lost+found directory, fsck tool and, 178
lp parameter, /etc/printcap file, 472
lpd clients, 477-479
    See also printing
    lpq command, 478
    lpr command, 477-478
    lprm command, 478-479
lpd printer daemon, 466-467
    See also printing
    /var/spool/lpd/*printername*, 467
LPRng file, 467-471
    See also printing
    configure command, 468
    installing, 467-469
    installing ifhp filter, 470-471
    make command, 468
    make install command, 468
    man pages for Red Hat Linux version 7, 469-470
    programs installed via, 468-469
    starting on boot, 469
ls command, listing files, 121
LSB (Linux Standard Base Specification), 147
LVM, Multi-Device Support (RAID and LVM) menu, 231-232

▼ M

-m [-k skel-dir] command-line option, user management tools, *92*
-M command-line option, user management tools, *92*
-m *interval* command-line parameter, syslogd daemon, *213*
-m option, ypinit command, 435
M4 language, MC files (configuring Sendmail) and, 360
MAC (Medium Access Control) addresses, Ethernet headers and, 519
macros, Sendmail, 363-369, 374
mail
    clients, 608

SMTP (Simple Mail Transfer Protocol), 349-382
    user management, 85-86
mail command, networking tools, 144
MAIL command, SMTP (Simple Mail Transfer
    Protocol), 351
mail delivery agents. *See* MDAs
mail transfer agents. *See* MTAs
mail user agents. *See* MUAs
MAILER macro, Sendmail macros, 364
mailertable feature, FEATURE macro, 366
mail.local tool, Sendmail, *357*
mailq command, Sendmail and, 378-379
mailstats tool, Sendmail, *357*
make command
    Apache HTTP server, 340
    BIND servers, 266
    bzImage parameter, 235
    compiling software and, 76-77
    DHCP (Dynamic Host Configuration Protocol)
        clients, 491
    LPRng file, 468
    NIS (Network Information Service), 431, 435-436
    PAM (Pluggable Authentication Modules), 103
    Qpopper daemon, 389
    Samba, 449
    SSH (Secure Shell), 406-407
    zImage parameter, 234, 235
make install command
    BIND servers, 266
    compiling software and, 77
    DHCP (Dynamic Host Configuration Protocol)
        clients, 491
    DHCPD (Dynamic Host Configuration
        Protocol server), 484
    ipchains tool, 567
    LPRng file, 468
    packages and, 77
    PAM (Pluggable Authentication Modules), 103
    Samba, 449
    SSH (Secure Shell), 407, 408
make modules_install command, installing the
    kernel, 236
make *xconfig* command, building the kernel, 227-228
makefile errors, NIS ypinit command and, 435-436
Makefile file, NIS (Network Information Service),
    431-432
makemap tool, Sendmail, *357*
man command, 118, 119-120
    See also documentation tools
    gnome-help-browser interface, 120
man pages for Red Hat Linux version 7, LPRng file,
    469-470
managing file systems. *See* file system management
mapping
    makemap tool, *357*
    NIS (Network Information Service), 436
    use_mapped_pass argument, *107*
MASQUERADE_AS macro
    See also IP Masquerading
    Sendmail macros, 364-365
max-lease-time parameter, DHCPD (Dynamic Host
    Configuration Protocol server), 488
max-transfer-times-in *number;* option, BIND
    servers, *280*

MBRs (master boot records), LILO (Linux Loader)
    boot manager and, 32, 151
MC files (configuring Sendmail), 360-374
    define command, 362
    divert command, 361-362
    dnl instruction, 362
    M4 language and, 360
    overview, 360
    quote marks and, 362
    rule sets, 360
    Sendmail macros, 363-369
    undefine command, 362
MDAs (mail delivery agents), Sendmail, 353
Memory Technology Devices menu, kernel features
    and modules, 231
memstatistics-file *path-name;* option, BIND servers, *275*
MERGE_GROUP setting, NIS (Network Information
    Service), 433
MERGE_PASSWORD setting, NIS (Network
    Information Service), 432
message command, /etc/ftpaccess file, 315-316
metric entry, route command, 557
MINGID, NIS (Network Information Service), 432
MINUID, NIS (Network Information Service), 432
mkdir command, 131
    See also file management and manipulation
mke2fs command, creating ext2 file systems, 186-187
mknod command, 130
    See also file management and manipulation
    creating device files, 499
    named pipes, 123, 130
mksmbpasswd.sh script, Samba encrypted
    passwords, 462
mkswap command, creating swap file systems,
    186-187
module configuration option, kernel features and
    modules, 229-230
modules
    See also kernel features and modules
    Apache HTTP server, 340
    network interfaces and /etc/conf.modules file,
        557-558
    overview, 229-230
    Pluggable Authentication. *See* PAM
monitoring systems, 248-251
    See also securing individual servers
    CERT (Computer Emergency Response Team),
        251-252
    COPS (Computer Oracle and Password
        System), 250
    MRTG (Multi-Router Traffic Grapher), 250
    overview, 248
    SATAN (System Administrators Tool for
        Analyzing Networks), 251
    syslogd daemon, 249-250
    TripWire, 250-251
more command, 134
    See also file management and manipulation
    documentation and compiling software, 76
    installing PAM (Pluggable Authentication
        Modules), 103
    RPM (Red Hat Package Manager) and, 73

mount command, 172-174, 421-422
See also file system management; NFS
(Network File System); unmount command
-a option, 172
-o option, 173, 188, 421-422
-t option, 173
booting and shutting down, 165
/etc/fstab file, 174-176
NFS partitions, 187-188
options, 172, 173
retrans=r value, 422
soft versus hard mounts, 422, 425-426
mount point information, Disk Druid partitioning
tool, 27
mount process, Windows versus Linux, 26
mounting
Automounter, 188-192
cross-mounting disks, 423
shares, 9-10
mouse types, installing Red Hat Linux, 24
moving files, mv command, 126
MRTG (Multi-Router Traffic Grapher), monitoring
systems, 250
mt command
backups and tape devices, 500-501
dump tool and, 504
MTAs (mail transfer agents), Sendmail, 353
mtu value option, ifconfig program, 554
MUAs (mail user agents), Sendmail, 353
Multi-Device Support (RAID and LVM) menu, kernel
features and modules, 231-232
Multi-Router Traffic Grapher (MRTG), monitoring
systems, 250
Multimedia Devices menu, kernel features and
modules, 233
multiple desktops, KDE (K Desktop Environment),
51-52, 53
multiple-cnames yes/no; option, BIND servers, 276
multiusers, Windows versus Linux, 8
mutt command, networking tools, 145
mv command, moving files, 126
MX (Mail Exchanger) records, DNS record types,
290-291
mx parameter, /etc/printcap file, 472

▼ **N**

-n command-line option, user management tools, 92
-n option, ipchains tool, 573
-n parameter, dump tool, 502
-N parameter, ipchains tool, 569
n command, fdisk utility, 183, 184-185
name servers
primary, 261, 263
secondary, 263
named pipes
See also pipes
files and directory types, 123
mknod command, 123, 130
named-xfer path-name; option, BIND servers, 275
named.conf file, 271-287, 292-297
See also BIND servers; DNS (Domain Name
Service)

acl keyword, 272
ACLs (Access Control Lists), 273-274
BIND configuration options, 275-283
caching zones, 287
comments, 272
controls keyword, 273
database creation, 292-297
include keyword, 272
include statements, 274
logging keyword, 272
logging statements, 274
named.ca file and, 294-296
named.local file and, 296-297
options keyword, 273
overview, 271
primary zones, 285-286
sample listing, 292-294
secondary zones, 286-287
server keyword, 273
server statements, 283-284
statement keywords, 272-273
zone configuration file, 292-293
zone keyword, 273
zone statements, 284
zones, 285-287
names
fully qualified domain. See FQDNs
host. See host names
naming directories, unpacking kernel source code
and, 226-227
naming kernels, installing the kernel and, 235
NAT (network address translation), IP Masquerading
and, 583
netmask address option, ifconfig program, 554
netmask mask parameter, route command, 555
netmasks, 538-541
See also networking; TCP/IP
bitwise AND operations, 540
CIDR (Classless Inter-Domain Routing), 541
shorthand, 540
Netscape browser, Linux tools, 607
netstat command, 244, 245-7, 557
See also port numbers; route command;
securing individual servers; tracking
services
-p option, 248-249
-r option, 557
columns overview, 246
overview, 245-246
security implications of output, 246-247
syslogd service and, 248
testing Qpopper daemon, 392
network address translation (NAT), IP Masquerading
and, 583
network configuration, 549-558
See also advanced Linux networking
/etc/conf.modules file, 557-558
ifconfig program, 551-554
overview, 550
routers, 554-557
summary, 558
Network Device Support menu, kernel features and
modules, 233
Network File System. See NFS

network file systems, 187-192
    Automounter and, 188-192
    mounting NFS partitions, 187-188
    overview, 187
Network Information Service. *See* NIS
Network Interface Cards. *See* NICs
network interfaces and modules, /etc/conf.modules
  file, 557-558
network users, Windows versus Linux, 8
networking, 536-547
    See also IP addresses; TCP/IP
    advanced. *See* advanced Linux networking
    dynamic routing with RIP (Routing
      Information Protocol), 543-547
    hosts and, 536-537
    installing Red Hat Linux, 33-34
    IP addresses and, 536-537
    netmasks, 538-541
    NIS (Network Information Service), 442-444
    overview, 536
    RIP (Routing Information Protocol), 543-547
    static routing, 541-542
    subnetting, 537-538
    Windows versus Linux, 9-10
Networking Options menu, kernel features and
  modules, 232
networking tools, 142-145
    See also command-line interface
    ftp command, 145
    mail command, 144
    mutt command, 145
    pine command, 144-145
    rsh command, 143
    telnet command, 142-143
    xhost command, 143-144
next-server parameter, DHCPD (Dynamic Host
  Configuration Protocol server), 488
NFS (Network File System), 9-10, 413-426
    See also Intranet services
    client configuration, 420-424
    client permissions for shared partitions, *418-419*
    common uses for partitions, 424
    components of, 417
    cross-mounting disks, 423
    enabling, 416-417
    /etc/exports file, 417-420
    exportfs command, 419-420
    hard versus soft mounts, 422, 425-426
    intr option, 423
    kernel support for, 417
    ksysv command, 416
    mount command and, 187-188, 421-422
    noaccess permission option, *418*
    no_root_squash permission option, *418*
    overview, 414-415
    partitions, 414-415, 424
    performance tuning, 423-424
    "Permission denied," 425
    ro permission option, *418*
    rpcinfo command, 416
    rpc.lockd daemon, 417
    rpc.mountd daemon, 417
    rpc.nfsd daemon, 417
    rpc.quotad daemon, 417

    RPCs (remote procedure calls) and, 414
    rpc.statd daemon, 417
    rsize option, 424
    secure permission option, *418*
    security considerations, 415
    server configuration, 417-420
    soft versus hard mounts, 422, 425-426
    squash_gids=*gid-list* permission option, *420*
    squash_uids=*uid-list* permission option, *420*
    "Stale NFS Filehandle," 425
    summary, 426
    troubleshooting, 425-426
    versions, 415
    wsize option, 424
NICs (Network Interface Cards)
    ifconfig program, 552-553
    jumbo frames and, 554
NIS (Network Information Service), 11, 427-444
    See also Intranet services
    all: entry, 434
    broadcast methods, 437
    client configuration, 436-438
    configuration files and, 441-442
    designating filenames, 433-434
    designating slave servers, 432
    domain names for secondary servers, 439
    domainname command and, 430-431, 439
    domains, 429-430
    /etc/hosts file and, 260
    /etc/nsswitch.conf file, 438
    /etc/passwd file and, 428-429, 441-442
    /etc/yp.conf file, 436-437
    filenames, 433-434
    host names, 437
    large networks and, 444
    make command, 431, 435-436
    Makefile file, 431-432
    map updates, 436
    master server configuration, 430-436
    MERGE_GROUP setting, 433
    MERGE_PASSWORD setting, 432
    MINGID, 432
    MINUID, 432
    NOPUSH=false option, 439
    NOPUSH variable, 432
    NT domains comparison, 11
    overview, 428-430
    pushing to slaves, 439
    real networked environments and, 442-444
    secondary server configuration, 439-440
    segmented networks and, 443
    server configuration, 430-436, 439-440
    server push, 429
    slave servers, 432
    small networks and, 443
    starting via ypserv daemon, 431
    startup scripts, 437
    summary, 444
    testing client configurations, 438
    tools, 441
    /var/yp/ypservers file, 439
    Windows NT domains comparison, 11
    YP (Yellow Pages) and, 430
    ypbind daemon, 436, 437

ypcat command, 438, 441
ypinit command, 434-436, 440
ypmatch command, 441
yppasswd command, 441
ypwhich command, 441
ypxfrd daemon, 440
nis-domain option, DHCP (Dynamic Host Configuration Protocol), *489*
nis-servers option, DHCP (Dynamic Host Configuration Protocol), *489*
nmbd daemon, Samba, 447-448, 452
noaccess permission option, NFS (Network File System), *418*
nobody user, 341
    See also Apache HTTP server
    making "somebody," 344
-nodeps command-line option, RPM (Red Hat Package Manager), *72*
nodes, i-nodes and file systems, 168, *169*
none entry, /proc file system and, 176
NOPUSH=false option, NIS (Network Information Service), 439
NOPUSH variable, NIS (Network Information Service), 432
normal files, files and directory types, 121
no_root_squash permission option, NFS (Network File System), *418*
[NOTFOUND], resolver (client-side DNS) and, 270-271
notify *yes/no;* option, BIND servers, *277*
no_warn argument, PAM (Pluggable Authentication Modules), *107*
NS (Name Server) records, DNS record types, 289
nslookup command, DNS tools, 298, 299
NT domains versus NIS domains, 11
nullclient feature, FEATURE macro, 368
numbers, converting between decimal and binary, 539

O

-o option, mount command, *173*, *188*, 421-422
obscurity and security
    HTTP (HyperText Transfer Protocol), 338
    securing individual servers, 252
OK action, access_db database, *377*
Old CD-ROM Drivers menu, kernel features and modules, 233
only_from variable, /etc/xinetd.conf file, 209
Open Shortest Path First. *See* OSPF protocol
OpenSSH and OpenBSD, SSH (Secure Shell), 404
Opera browser, Linux tools, 607
operating systems, LILO boot manager and, 33
Optional control flag, PAM (Pluggable Authentication Modules), *106*
options field, /etc/ftpconversions/ file, *325*
options keyword, named.conf file, 273
options parameter type, ipchains tool, *570*
OSI (International Standards Organization) model
    See also TCP/IP
    layers, 515-517
OSPF (Open Shortest Path First) protocol

load balancing, 547
    RIP (Routing Information Protocol) comparison, 547
OSTYPE macro, Sendmail macros, 363
overwrite command, /etc/ftpaccess file and permissions, 320
ownership
    Apache HTTP server and process, 338-339
    chown command and, 123

P

-p option, netstat command, 248-249
-P parameter, ipchains tool, *569*
p command, fdisk utility, 181-183, 184, 185
package groups, installing Red Hat Linux, 38-39
packages
    configure command, 76
    installing. *See* installing packages
    querying, 72-73
    resolving prerequisite, 39, *40*
    RPM (Red Hat Package Manager), 70-74
    uninstalling, 73
    unpacking, 74-75
packet filtering, 562-583
    See also advanced Linux networking; firewalls
    blocking examples, 579-583
    "cookbook" solutions, 577-583
    Ethernet frames and, *564*
    explicit allow, 581-582
    explicit deny, 582
    ICMP echo-replies and, 578
    IP Masquerading and, 579
    ipchains tool, 564, 566-574
    iptables tool, 574-577
    mechanics of, 563-566
    overview, 562-566
    path through filter, *563*
    Ping of Death and, 578-579
    reference resources, 562
    rules, 581-583
    Russell, Paul "Rusty" and, 577-578
packets, 513-514
    See also TCP/IP
    headers, 514
    path of through protocol stacks, 514, *515*
    queues and, 514
painting/image tools, 607
PAM (Pluggable Authentication Modules), 101-109
    See also user management
    Account module, *105*
    arguments, 106, *107*
    Auth module, *105*
    configuration files, 105-109
    control flags, *106*
    Debug argument, *107*
    debugging, 109
    downloading and installing, 102-103
    /etc/pam.d/login file, 107-109
    /etc/pam.d/other file, 109
    example configuration file, 107-109

files and locations, 104
module types and their functions, *105*
no_warn argument, *107*
Optional control flag, *106*
overview, 101-102
Password module, *105*
Required control flag, *106*
Requisite control flag, *106*
Session module, *105*
Sufficient control flag, *106*
troubleshooting, 109
try_first_pass argument, *107*
use_first_pass argument, *107*
use_mapped_pass argument, *107*
Parallel Port Support menu, kernel features and
modules, 231
parsing logs, syslogd daemon, 249
partitions, 26-31, 179-187
See also installing Red Hat Linux
boot process and file system management,
171-172
common uses for NFS, 424
creating, 180-186
creating via fdisk utility, 180-186
destructive nature of creating, 180
/dev/hdX device names for disks, 179-180
Disk Druid partitioning tool, 27-30
editing/deleting, 30
fdisk utility, 180-186
file systems and, 186-187
formatting, 31
/home directory and, 27, *182*
listing of, *182*
mount process, 26
NFS (Network File System), 414-415, 424
overview, 179
quota management and, 193-198
swap, 27, *182*
/tmp directory and, 27, *182*
/usr directory and, 26, 27, *182*
/var directory and, 27, *182*
PASS command, telnet service, 385-386
passive transfer, FTP (File Transfer Protocol), 307
passwd-check command, /etc/ftpaccess file and
permissions, 320-321
Password button, SWAT (Samba Web Administration
Tool), 457
Password module, PAM (Pluggable Authentication
Modules), *105*
passwords, 83-84
See also /etc/passwd file; user management
DES (Data Encryption Standard), 83
encrypted Samba, 447, 462-463
/etc/passwd file, 35-36, 86-88
installing Red Hat Linux, 35-37
LDAP servers and storing, 37
NULL, 463
root, 35, *36*
Samba encrypted, 446-447
shadow, 84
patching the kernel, 237-239
See also compiling the kernel
applying patches, 238-239
downloading and unpacking patches, 237-238

overview, 237
/pub/linux/kernel/v2.4/ directory, 238
troubleshooting, 239
path-filter command, /etc/ftpaccess file and
permissions, 321
percent command-line option, RPM (Red Hat Package
Manager), *72*
performance tuning, NFS (Network File System),
423-424
Perl, programming languages accompanying Red Hat
Linux, 602
"Permission denied," troubleshooting NFS (Network
File System), 425
permissions, 124, *125*
/etc/ftpaccess file, 319-322
/etc/lpd.perms file, 476
shared NFS partitions, *418-419*
physical security, securing individual servers, 253
pico editor, 146-147
documentation and compiling software, 76
pid-file *path-name;* option, BIND servers, 275
pine command, networking tools, 144-145
Ping of Death
See also ICMP (Internet Control Message
Protocol)
packet filtering and, 578-579
pipes
BASH (Bourne Again Shell), 115-116
named. *See* named pipes
Plug and Play Support menu, kernel features and
modules, 231
Pluggable Authentication Modules. *See* PAM
pointtopoint *address* option, ifconfig program, 554
POP (Post Office Protocol), 383-397
See also SMTP (Simple Mail Transfer Protocol)
authenticated, 394-395
conflicts with other protocols, 388
help, 387
mechanics of, 385-388
overview, 384-388
Qpopper daemon, 388-397
SMTP (Simple Mail Transfer Protocol)
comparison, 354
summary, 397
telnet service and, 385-387
port numbers
HTTP (HyperText Transfer Protocol) and,
337-338
netstat command and, 244, 245-7
TCP (Transmission Control Protocol) and, 518
TCP/IP and security, 243-244
well-known services and, 243
port specifications, ipchains tool, 574
Port variable, /etc/xinetd.conf file, 210
ports, UDP (User Datagram Protocol) and, 518
praliases tool, Sendmail, *357*
primary name servers, DNS (Domain Name Service)
and, 261, 263
primary zones, named.conf file, 285-286
print command, smbclient program and remote
printer access, 461
printenv command, BASH (Bourne Again Shell) and
environment variables, 114
printers, remote access via smbclient program, 461

Printers button, SWAT (Samba Web Administration Tool), 456
printing, 465-479
    See also Intranet services
    /etc/lpd.perms file, 474-477
    /etc/printcap file, 471-474
    lpd clients, 477-479
    lpd printer daemon, 466-467
    LPRng file, 467-471
    overview, 466-467
    summary, 479
priority levels, /etc/syslog.conf file, 212, 214, *215*
private command, /etc/ftpaccess file, 314-315
private IP addresses, 537
Privileges tab, LinuxConf package, 96, *97*
problems. *See* troubleshooting
/proc file system, 589-596
    See also advanced Linux networking
    building the kernel and, 228
    common reports and settings done via, 594-596
    contents of, 590-591
    debugging hardware conflicts, 596
    enumerated entries, 594
    high-volume servers and, 595-596
    kcore file, 591
    none entry and, 176
    overview, 590
    /proc/sys/fs/file-max directory, 595
    /proc/sys/net/ipv4 directory, 590, 591, *593*
    /proc/sys/net/ipv4/ip_local_port_range directory, 595
    /proc/sys/net/ipv4/tcp_max_syn_backlog directory, 595
    summary, 596
    SYN flood protection, 594-595
    system calls and, 590
    "tweaking" files within, 591
    "useful" entries, 591, *592-593*
procedure calls, remote. *See* RPCs
process manipulation, 136-140
    See also command-line interface
    kill command, 139-140
    overview, 136
    ps command, 136-138
    top command, 138-139
process ownership and security, Apache HTTP server, 338-339
Processor Types and Features menu, kernel features and modules, 230-231
programming languages accompanying Red Hat Linux, 599-603
    awk, 602
    C/C++ programming suite, 600
    Expect, 601
    GNU Fortran 77, 600
    iTcl, 601
    Jikes, 602
    Kaffe, 602
    Perl, 602
    Python, 603
    Scheme, 603
    tcl, 601
    TclX, 601

TiX (Tk Interface Extension), 601-602
Tk Widget Set, 601
promiscuous_relay "feature," FEATURE macro, 368-369
prompt command, LILO (Linux Loader) boot manager, 151
protocol element, /etc/inetd.conf file, *205*
Protocol variable, /etc/xinetd.conf file, 209
protocols, TCP/IP, 517-519
proxies, IP Masquerading, 587-588
ps command
    command-line parameters, *137*
    /etc/inetd.conf file, 206
    listing processes, 136-138
    shutting down services, 248
    STAT entry, 138
PTR (Pointer Record) records, DNS record types, 290
public key cryptography, 400-403
    See also encrypted passwords; SSH (Secure Shell)
    key characteristics, 402-403
    overview, 400-402
    reference resources, 403
/pub/linux/kernel/v2.4/ directory, patching the kernel, 238
pushing to slaves, 439
    See also NIS (Network Information Service)
    NOPUSH=false option, 439
    NOPUSH variable, 432
pwd command
    See also file management and manipulation
    showing present working directory, 131
Python, programming languages accompanying Red Hat Linux, 603

▼ Q

Qpopper daemon, 388-397
    See also Internet services; POP (Post Office Protocol)
    -b *bulldir* command-line option, 396
    -T *timeout* command-line option, 396
    advanced configurations, 393-396
    Authenticated POP, 394-395
    bulletins, 395-396
    command-line options, 396
    compiling, 389-391
    configure command, 389, *390*
    inetd daemon and, 391
    installing, 388-389
    make command, 389
    netstat command, 392
    overview, 388
    server mode, 393
    setting up, 391-393
    shadow password files, 393-395
    summary, 397
    troubleshooting, 392-393
    /usr/bin directory, 389-391
    xinetd daemon and, 392
query-source *address* address\ port port; option, BIND servers, *279*
querying packages, RPM (Red Hat Package Manager), 72-73

queues, packets and, 514
queues (Sendmail), 380-381
    See also Sendmail
    file locations, 380
    flushing, 381
    removing entries from, 380-381
quota management, 192-198
    See also file systems
    cd command, 194
    configuring individual partitions, 193-198
    edquota command, 195-197
    grpquota option, 194
    overview, 192-193
    preparing disks for quotas, 193-198
    quota command, 197-198
    quota database, 194
    quotacheck command, 197
    quota.user and quota.group files, 194
    repquota command, 197
    setting up boot process, 193
    usrquota option, 194
quote marks, MC files (configuring Sendmail) and, 362

▼ R

-r command-line option
    restore tool, *505*
    syslogd daemon, *213*
    user management tools, *94*
-r option
    DHCP (Dynamic Host Configuration Protocol)
      clients, *493*
    netstat command, 557
-R option, DHCP (Dynamic Host Configuration
    Protocol) clients, *493*
-R parameter, ipchains tool, *569*
-r *root-directory* command-line option, LILO (Linux
    Loader) boot manager, *156*
RAID, Multi-Device Support (RAID and LVM) menu,
    231-232
range declaration, DHCPD (Dynamic Host
    Configuration Protocol server), 486
rc scripts, 157-161
    See also steps to booting
    runlevel directories, 158
    writing, 159-161
RCPT command, SMTP (Simple Mail Transfer
    Protocol), 351
readme command, /etc/ftpaccess file, 316-317
real-time chat, 609
record types, DNS (Domain Name Service), 288-292
records, master boot. *See* MBRs
recovery, backups and speed of, 497-498
recursion *yes/no;* option, BIND servers, 277
Red Hat Linux
    BIND servers and, 265
    fast Sendmail configure, 358-359
    GNOME (GNU Network Object Model
      Environment), 59-66
    installing, 20-44
    LPRng file and man pages for version 7,
      469-470
    NICs (Network Interface Cards) setup, 552-553

    programming languages accompanying,
      599-603
    Samba and, 450-451
Red Hat Package Manager. *See* RPM
redirect feature, FEATURE macro, 365-366
redirection, BASH (Bourne Again Shell), 116
ref entry, route command, 557
reference resources
    DNS (Domain Name Service), 302
    Linux, 12
    packet filtering, 562
    public key cryptography, 403
    Sendmail, 354
    TCP/IP, 244
registered users, /etc/ftpaccess file, 331-332
Registry versus text files, Windows versus
    Linux, 10-11
ReiserFS file system, 170
    See also file systems
REJECT action, access_db database, *377*
RELAY action, access_db database, *377*
relay_based_on_MX feature, FEATURE macro, 369
relay_entire_domain feature, FEATURE macro, 369
remote file access, smbclient program, 460-461
remote printer access, smbclient program, 461
remote procedure calls. *See* RPCs
rename command, /etc/ftpaccess file and
    permissions, 320
reports, /proc file system and, 594-596
repquota command, quota management, 197
request headers, HTTP (HyperText Transfer Protocol),
    336-337
Required control flag, PAM (Pluggable Authentication
    Modules), *106*
Requisite control flag, PAM (Pluggable Authentication
    Modules), *106*
resolution, forward and reverse, 263, *264*
resolver (client-side DNS), 269-271
    See also BIND servers; DNS (Domain Name
      Service)
    /etc/nsswitch.conf file, 270
    /etc/resolv.conf file, 269-270
    [NOTFOUND] and, 270-271
    overview, 269
restore tool, 504-506
    See also backups; command-line backup tools;
      dump tool
    -b *blocksize* command-line option, *505*
    -f *filename* command-line option, *505*
    -i command-line option, *504*
    -r command-line option, *505*
    -T *directory* command-line option, *505*
    -v command-line option, *505*
    -y command-line option, *505*
    complete restore, 505
    gzip command and, 506
    typical restore, 505
RETR command, telnet service, 386-387
retrans=r value, mount command, 422
reverse resolution, DNS (Domain Name Service),
    263, *264*
review process for kernel changes, 222
    See also compiling the kernel

RIP (Routing Information Protocol), 543-547
    See also networking; TCP/IP
    algorithm, 547
    OSPF (Open Shortest Path First) protocol
        comparison, 547
    overview, 543-547
    sample routes, 544-547
    small campus network, *543*
rm command, cleanup after compiling software, 78
rm parameter, /etc/printcap file, *472*
rmdir command, 131
    See also file management and manipulation
ro permission option, NFS (Network File System), *418*
root account, installing Red Hat Linux, 35
root directory
    See also /home directories
    file system management and, 171, *172*
root passwords, installing Red Hat Linux, 35, *36*
root servers, DNS (Domain Name Service) and,
    261, 262
root users, 82
rootshell Web site, securing individual servers, 252
route command, 555-557
    See also netstat command; routers
    addy parameter, 555
    cmd parameter, 555
    dev *dn* parameter, 555
    displaying routes, 556-557
    flags entry, 556
    gw *gway* parameter, 555
    metric entry, 557
    netmask *mask* parameter, 555
    overview, 555-556
    parameters, 555
    ref entry, 557
    type parameter, 555
    use entry, 557
route tables, static routing, 541, 542
routers, 554-557
    See also network configuration
    default routes, 554
    overview, 554-555
    route command, 555-557
routers option, DHCP (Dynamic Host Configuration
    Protocol), *489*
routes
    default. *See* default routes
    displaying. *See* displaying routes
routing
    dynamic. *See* RIP (Routing Information Protocol)
    static, 541-542
Routing Information Protocol. *See* RIP
rp parameter, /etc/printcap file, *472*
RP (Responsible Person) records, DNS record
    types, 291
rpcinfo command, NFS (Network File System), 416
rpc.lockd daemon, NFS (Network File System), 417
rpc.mountd daemon, NFS (Network File System), 417
rpc.nfsd daemon, NFS (Network File System), 417
rpc.quotad daemon, NFS (Network File System), 417
RPCs (remote procedure calls), NFS (Network File
    System) and, 414
rpc.statd daemon, NFS (Network File System), 417

RPM (Red Hat Package Manager), 70-74
    See also installing software
    command-line options, 72
    force command-line option, *72*
    gnorpm command and, 73-74
    grep command and, 73
    -h command-line option, *72*
    -i option, 71
    installing packages, 71-72
    more command and, 73
    -nodeps command-line option, *72*
    overview, 70-71
    percent command-line option, *72*
    querying packages, 72-73
    rpm command and, 73
    Samba and, 450-451
    test command-line option, *72*
    -U option, 71
    uninstalling packages, 73
    -v command-line option, *72*
rsh command, networking tools, 143
rsize option, NFS (Network File System), 424
RST (reset) flag, connections, 533
rule sets, MC files (configuring Sendmail), 360
rulenum parameter type, ipchains tool, *570*
rules
    ipchains tool, 583
    iptables tool, 582
    packet filtering, 581-583
rulespec parameter type, ipchains tool, *569*, 571-572
runlevel directories, rc scripts and steps to
    booting, 158
Russell, Paul "Rusty," packet filtering and, 577-578

▼ **S**

-s command-line parameter, syslogd daemon, *213*
-s option, ypinit command, 440
-s shell command-line option, user management
    tools, *92*
-s *size* parameter, dump tool, *502*
Samba, 445-464
    See also Intranet services; Windows comparison
    administration, 451-452
    compiling and installing, 448-450
    ./configure command, 449
    encrypted passwords, 447, 462-463
    /etc/passwd file, 462-463
    make command, 449
    make install command, 449
    mksmbpasswd.sh script, 462
    nmbd daemon, 447-448, 452
    overview, 446
    Red Hat Linux and, 450-451
    RPM (Red Hat Package Manager) and, 450-451
    SMB (Session Message Block), 446-450
    smbclient program, 457-461
    smbd daemon, 447-448, 452
    smbmount command, 462
    smbpasswd command, 463
    smbpasswd files, 463
    source subdirectory, 449

starting/stopping, 451-452
summary, 464
SWAT (Samba Web Administration Tool),
452-457
tar command, 448-449
troubleshooting, 463-464
umount command, 462
usernames and passwords, 446-447
/usr/sbin/smbd file, 448
SATAN (System Administrators Tool for Analyzing
Networks), monitoring systems, 251
saving current source tree, unpacking kernel source
code and, 225-226
scheduling, cron program and, 217-219
Scheme, programming languages accompanying Red
Hat Linux, 603
scp (Secure Copy), SSH (Secure Shell) comparison,
409-410
Screen Saver menu, GNOME (GNU Network Object
Model Environment), 64
Screensaver option, KDE (K Desktop Environment),
57-58
scripts
    ipchains tool, 579-581
    rc, 157-161
    startup. *See* startup scripts
SCSI Support menu, kernel features and modules, 232
sd parameter, /etc/printcap file, *471*
secondary servers, DNS (Domain Name Service)
and, 263
secondary zones, named.conf file, 286-287
Secure Copy (scp), SSH (Secure Shell) comparison,
409-410
secure permission option, NFS (Network File
System), *418*
Secure Shell. *See* SSH
securing individual servers, 241-253
    See also security; single-host administration
    BugTraq mailing list, 252
    CERT (Computer Emergency Response Team)
        Web site, 251-252
    "hackers" versus "crackers," 242
    monitoring systems, 248-251
    obscurity and security, 252
    overview, 242-244
    physical security and, 253
    rootshell Web site, 252
    Security Focus Web site, 252
    social engineering and, 253
    summary, 253
    TCP/IP, 243-244
    tracking services, 244-248
security
    Apache HTTP server process ownership and,
        338-339
    /etc/inetd.conf file, 206-207
    implications of netstat command's output,
        246-247
    kill command and, 140
    NFS (Network File System), 415
    obscurity and, 252, 338
    Sendmail, 352-353
Security Focus Web site, securing individual
servers, 252

segmented networks, NIS (Network Information
Service) and, 443
Sendmail, 352-382
    See also SMTP (Simple Mail Transfer Protocol)
    access_db database, 369, 376-378
    aliases database, 359, 375-376
    Allman, Eric, 353
    ./Build command, 356, 374
    compiling, 356-357
    compiling macros into configuration files, 374
    configurable parameters, 369, *370-372*
    configuring. *See* MC files
    Cw option, 359
    determining if running, 379-380
    DNS (Domain Name Service) and, 379
    downloading, 355-356
    /etc/mail directory, 359
    /etc/sendmail.cf file, 358, 361
    fast configure for Red Hat Linux 7, 358-359
    finding and installing, 355-357
    flushing queues, 381
    hosts, 359
    installing, 374-375
    IP Masquerading, 358-359
    logging, 381-382
    macros, 363-369, 374
    mail logging, 381-382
    mail.local tool, *357*
    mailq command and, 378-379
    mailstats tool, *357*
    makemap tool, *357*
    MC files, 360-374
    MDAs (mail delivery agents), 353
    MTAs (mail transfer agents), 353
    MUAs (mail user agents), 353
    peripheral programs, 357
    praliases tool, *357*
    queues, 380-381
    "real-life" issues, 378-382
    reference resources, 354
    sample configuration, 373
    security, 352-353
    sendmail.cf configuration file, 354
    smrsh tool, 353, *357*
    spool space outage, 379
    spools, 380
    startup scripts, 379-380
    summary, 382
    telnet service and, 379
    text recommendations, 354
    "tweaking," 361
    uptime command and, 379
    /var/spool/mail directory, 380
    /var/spool/maillog directory, 382
    /var/spool/mqueue directory, 380-381
Sendmail macros, 363-369
    See also MC files (configuring Sendmail)
    compiling into configuration files, 374
    DOMAIN macro, 363-364
    EXPOSED_USER macro, 365
    FEATURE macro, 365-369
    MAILER macro, 364
    MASQUERADE_AS macro, 364-365
    OSTYPE macro, 363

server keyword, named.conf file, 273
server mode, Qpopper daemon, 393
server push, 429
    See also NIS (Network Information Service)
    NOPUSH=false option, 439
    NOPUSH variable, 432
server statements, named.conf file, 283-284
Server variable, /etc/xinetd.conf file, 209
server-identifier parameter, DHCPD (Dynamic Host
    Configuration Protocol server), 488
server-name parameter, DHCPD (Dynamic Host
    Configuration Protocol server), 488
ServerAdmin line, httpd.conf file and Apache HTTP
    server, 345
server_args variable, /etc/xinetd.conf file, 209
servers
    Apache HTTP, 335-348
    authoritative, 263
    BIND (Berkeley Internet Domain Name),
        265-297
    browsing via smbclient program, 458-460
    caching, 264
    DHCP (Dynamic Host Configuration
        Protocol), 483-490
    DNS (Domain Name Service), 263-268
    NFS (Network File System), 417-420
    NIS (Network Information Service), 429,
        430-436, 439-440
    primary name, 261, 263
    /proc file system and high-volume, 595-596
    root, 261, 262
    secondary, 263
    securing individual, 241-253
    SSH (Secure Shell) and startup/shutdown,
        408-409
    storing passwords with LDAP, 37
    wu-ftpd (Washington University FTP Server),
        307-333
SERVICE permission keyword, /etc/lpd.perms
    file, 476
service_name element, /etc/inetd.conf file, *204*
services
    commenting-out unneeded, 206
    core system. *See* core system services
    disabling, 161-162
    enabling, 161, 163
    Internet. *See* Internet services
    shutting down, 247-248
    tracking, 244-248
Session Message Block. *See* SMB
Session module, PAM (Pluggable Authentication
    Modules), *105*
SetGID bits, user management, 100
SetUID bits, user management, 100-101
sh parameter, /etc/printcap file, *471*
shadow passwords, 84
    See also passwords; user management
    /etc/shadow file, 88
    Qpopper daemon and, 393-395
shared-network declaration, DHCPD (Dynamic Host
    Configuration Protocol server), 485
shares
    mounting, 9-10

NIS (Network Information Service) and all:
    entry, 434
Shares button, SWAT (Samba Web Administration
    Tool), 456, 457, *458*, *459*
shells
    BASH (Bourne Again Shell), 112-118
    remote via rsh command, 143
    Secure Shell. *See* SSH
    user management, 84-85
shutting down services, 247-248
    See also booting and shutting down; securing
        individual servers; tracking services
    inetd daemon, 247
    non-inetd services, 248
    overview, 247
    ps command, 248
    xinetd daemon, 247
shutting down/starting up, Apache HTTP server,
    341-342
signals, kill command and, 140
single users, Windows versus Linux, 8
single-host administration, 79-253
    booting and shutting down, 149-165
    command-line interface, 111-148
    compiling the kernel, 221-239
    core system services, 199-297
    file systems, 167-198
    securing individual servers, 241-253
    user management, 81-110
Single-user ("Recovery") mode, 164-165
    See also booting and shutting down
slave servers, NIS (Network Information Service), 432
sliding window technique, TCP headers, 528
SMB (Session Message Block), 446-450
    See also Samba
smbclient program, 457-461
    See also Samba; SWAT (Samba Web
        Administration Tool)
    -D command-line parameter, *461*
    -I command-line parameter, *461*
    -L option, 459-460
    -U command-line parameter, *461*
    -W command-line parameter, *461*
    browsing servers via, 458-460
    command-line parameters, *461*
    overview, 457-458
    print command, 461
    remote file access, 460-461
    remote printer access, 461
smb.conf files, SWAT (Samba Web Administration
    Tool) and, 453
smbd daemon, Samba, 447-448, 452
smbmount command, Samba, 462
smbpasswd command
    Samba and changing passwords, 463
    Samba and NULL passwords, 463
smbpasswd files, Samba encrypted passwords, 463
smrsh tool
    aliases database and, 376
    FEATURE macro, 368
    Sendmail, 353, *357*
SMTP (Simple Mail Transfer Protocol), 349-382
    See also Internet services; POP (Post Office
        Protocol)

DATA command, 351-352
HELO command, 351
MAIL command, 351
overview, 350-352
POP (Post Office Protocol) comparison, 354
RCPT command, 351
security, 352-353
Sendmail, 352-382
telnet service and, 351
SMTP-code *message* action, access_db database, *377*
SOA (State of Authority) records, 288-289
   See also DNS record types
social engineering, securing individual servers
  and, 253
socket_type variable, /etc/xinetd.conf file, 208
sock_type element, /etc/inetd.conf file, *205*
soft versus hard mounts
   See also mount command
   NFS (Network File System), 422, 425-426
software. *See* applications
source code
   advantages of, 408
   compiling software, 74-78
   finding kernel, 224-227
   unpacking kernel, 225-227
source ports, TCP/IP and, 243
source subdirectory, Samba, 449
source trees, saving current, 225-226
speed of recovery, backups and, 497-498
spool space outage, Sendmail and, 379
spools, Sendmail, 380
squash_gids=*gid-list* permission option, NFS
  (Network File System), *420*
squash_uids=*uid-list* permission option, NFS
  (Network File System), *420*
srm.conf, Apache HTTP server, 344
srvr_prog element, /etc/inetd.conf file, *205*
srvr_prog_args element, /etc/inetd.conf file, *205*
SSH (Secure Shell), 399-410
   advantages of source code, 408
   alternative vendors for clients, 405
   applications related to, 409-410
   cleartext and, 400
   configure command, 407
   downloading, compiling, and installing,
     406-409
   make command, 406-407
   make install command, 407, 408
   OpenSSH and OpenBSD, 404
   overview, 400
   public key cryptography, 400-403
   Secure Copy (scp) comparison, 409-410
   server startup/shutdown, 408-409
   ssh daemon, 409-410
   summary, 410
   tar command and, 406
   telnet service and, 405-406
   versions and distributions, 404-406
   weakest links and, 405-406
SSH tarball, compiling software, 74-75
stacks, TCP/IP, 512
stacksize *number*; option, BIND servers, *282*
"Stale NFS Filehandle," troubleshooting NFS
  (Network File System), 425

standards
   FHS (File Hierarchy Standard), 147
   LSB (Linux Standard Base Specification), 147
StarOffice, Linux tools, 606
starting
   Apache HTTP server, 341-342
   applications from KDE (K Desktop
     Environment), 53-54
   DNS at boot time (BIND servers), 267-268
   NIS (Network Information Service) via ypserv
     daemon, 431
   Samba, 451-452
startup scripts
   NIS (Network Information Service), 437
   Sendmail, 375, 379-380
   user management, 85
startx command, KDE (K Desktop Environment) and
  X Windows, 49
STAT entry, ps command, 138
statement keywords, named.conf file, 272-273
static routing, 541-542
   See also networking; TCP/IP
   limitations of, 542
   route tables, 541, 542
statistics-file *path-name*; option, BIND servers, *275*
statistics-interval *number*; option, BIND servers, *282*
Status button, SWAT (Samba Web Administration
  Tool), 456
status indicator, installing Red Hat Linux, *29, 42*
steps to booting, 156-163
   See also booting and shutting down
   disabling services, 161-162
   enabling services, 161, 163
   init process, 157
   kernel execution, 156-157
   kernel loading, 156
   ksysv command, 161, *162*
   overview, 156
   rc scripts, 157-161
   runlevel directories, 158
strippost field, /etc/ftpconversions/ file, *324*
strippre field, /etc/ftpconversions/ file, *323*
su command, switching users, 142
subdomains, DNS (Domain Name Service), 262-263
subnet declaration, DHCPD (Dynamic Host
  Configuration Protocol server), 485-486
subnet-mask option, DHCP (Dynamic Host
  Configuration Protocol), *489*
subnetting, 537-538
   See also networking; TCP/IP
Sufficient control flag, PAM (Pluggable
  Authentication Modules), *106*
superblocks, file systems and, 169-170
superusers, defined, 82
swap file systems, creating via mkswap command,
  186-187
swap partition, *27, 182*
SWAT (Samba Web Administration Tool), 452-457
   See also Samba
   Globals button, 456
   inetd daemon and, 453-454
   menus, 455-457
   overview, 452-453
   Password button, 457

Printers button, 456
setting up, 453-454
Shares button, 456, 457, *458*, *459*
smbclient program, 457-461
smb.conf files and, 453
Status button, 456
using from other hosts, 454
View button, 457
xinetd daemon and, 454
switching users, su command, 142
symbolic links, files and directory types, 122
SYN flood protection, /proc file system, 594-595
sync command, 135-136
See also file management and manipulation
syslogd daemon, 212-217, 249-250
See also core system services; monitoring
systems
command-line parameters, 212, *213-214*
/etc/syslog.conf file, 212-217
log parsing, 249
netstat command and, 248
overview, 212
storing log entries, 249-250
/var/log directory and, 212
system calls, /proc file system and, 590
system services. *See* core system services
systems, monitoring. *See* monitoring systems

▼ **T**

-t command-line option, LILO (Linux Loader) boot
manager, *156*
-T *directory* command-line option, restore tool, *505*
-t option, mount command, *173*
-T *timeout* command-line option, Qpopper
daemon, 396
-t *timeout* option, DHCP (Dynamic Host Configuration
Protocol) clients, *493*
t command, fdisk utility, 183-184
tape devices, mt command and backups, 500-501
tape management, backups and, 498
tape naming scheme, backups and, 498-499
tar command, 132-133
See also file management and manipulation;
gzip command
compiling software, 74, 75
dump tool, 506
/etc/ftpaccess file, 319
installing PAM (Pluggable Authentication
Modules), 103
ipchains tool, 567
options, 132
Samba, 448-449
SSH (Secure Shell), 406
unpacking kernel source code, 227
tarballs
BIND servers, 266
compiling software and SSH (Secure Shell),
74-75
target parameter type, ipchains tool, *570*
tcl, programming languages accompanying Red Hat
Linux, 601

TclX, programming languages accompanying Red Hat
Linux, 601
TCP (Transmission Control Protocol)
connections, 518, 530-534
headers, 525-529
port numbers and, 518
TCP/IP, 517-518
TCP (Transmission Control Protocol) headers, 525-529
content of, *565*
sliding window technique, 528
tcpdump program and, 526-528
urgent pointer, 529
TCP/IP, 243-244, 511-548
See also advanced Linux networking
ARP (Address Resolution Protocol), 534-536
connections, 518, 530-534
destination ports, 243
Ethereal program, 512
Ethernet protocol, 517
headers, 519-530
ICMP (Internet Control Message Protocol)
and, 519
IP (Internet Protocol), 517
layers, 512-517
netstat command and, 244
networking and, 536-547
OSI (International Standards Organization)
model, 515-517
overview, 512
packets, 513-514, *515*
port numbers and, 243-244
protocols, 517-519
reference resources, 244
securing individual servers, 243-244
source ports, 243
stacks, 512
summary, 548
TCP (Transmission Control Protocol), 517-518
tcpdump program, 512
UDP (User Datagram Protocol), 518-519
Web sites, 251-252
well-known services and port numbers, 243
tcpdump program
ARP (Address Resolution Protocol) and,
534-535
Ethernet headers and, 520-521
IP headers and, 523-525
TCP connections, 530-532
TCP headers and, 526-528
TCP/IP and, 512
troubleshooting via, 530-531
UDP headers and, 529-530
Telephony Support menu, kernel features and
modules, 232
telinit command, 203
See also core system services; init process
telnet service, 385-387
DELE command, 387
/etc/inetd.conf file, 206
LIST command, 386
networking tools, 142-143
PASS command, 385-386
POP (Post Office Protocol) and, 385-387
reading mail via, 385-387

RETR command, 386-387
    Sendmail and, 379
    SMTP (Simple Mail Transfer Protocol) and, 351
    SSH (Secure Shell) and, 405-406
test command-line option, RPM (Red Hat Package Manager), 72
testing
    Apache HTTP server installations, 342
    NIS client configurations, 438
text files versus Registry, Linux versus Windows, 10-11
Themes menu, GNOME (GNU Network Object Model Environment), 65
three-way handshakes
    connections, 531
    SYN flood protection, 594
time zone configuration screen, installing Red Hat Linux, 34
timeout command, LILO (Linux Loader) boot manager, 151
TiX (Tk Interface Extension), programming languages accompanying Red Hat Linux, 601-602
Tk Widget Set, programming languages accompanying Red Hat Linux, 601
/tmp directory, partitions and, 27, *182*
tools, 605-609
    ApplixWare, 606
    audio, 608
    BIND servers, 267
    command-line backup, 501-506
    Corel WordPerfect, 606
    desktop, 608
    DNS (Domain Name Service), 297-303
    documentation, 118-120
    e-mail clients, 608
    editors, 145-147
    finance, 607-608
    ICQ, 609
    Konquerer browser, 607
    Netscape browser, 607
    networking, 142-145
    NIS (Network Information Service), 441
    Opera browser, 607
    overview, 606
    painting/image, 607
    real-time chat, 609
    StarOffice, 606
    user management, 89-99
    Web browsers, 607
    Web sites, 609
    WordPerfect, 606
top command
    See also process manipulation
    interactive process lists, 138-139
topology *address-list;* option, BIND servers, *283*
TOS (Type Of Service) header, IP headers, 521
traceroute program, IP headers and tcpdump program, 523-525
tracking services, 244-248
    See also securing individual servers
    netstat command, 244, 245-7
    overview, 244-245
    shutting down services, 247-248

transfer-format\ *one-answer/many-answers;* option, BIND servers, *280*
transfers-in *number;* option, BIND servers, *280*
transfers-out *number;* option, BIND servers, *280*
transfers-per-ns *number;* option, BIND servers, *280*
trees, saving current source, 225-226
TripWire, monitoring systems, 250-251
troubleshooting
    Apache HTTP server, 347
    fsck tool, 178
    installing the kernel, 236-237
    networks via tcpdump program, 530-531
    NFS (Network File System), 425-426
    PAM (Pluggable Authentication Modules), 109
    patching the kernel, 239
    Qpopper daemon, 392-393
    Samba, 463-464
try_first_pass argument, PAM (Pluggable Authentication Modules), *107*
TTL (time-to-live) field, IP headers, 523
tuning performance, NFS (Network File System), 423-424
TXT records, DNS record types, 291
type field, /etc/ftpconversions/ file, *324*
type parameter, route command, 555
Type variable, /etc/xinetd.conf file, 208

▼ U

-U command-line parameter, smbclient program, *461*
-U option, RPM (Red Hat Package Manager), 71
-u parameter, dump tool, *502*
-u uid command-line option, user management tools, *92*
UDP (User Datagram Protocol)
    headers, 529-530
    ports and, 518
    TCP/IP and, 518-519
UIDs (user IDs)
    See also GIDs (group IDs)
    /etc/passwd file and, 87
    mapping to /etc/passwd file, 101
    MINUID and NIS (Network Information Service), 432
    SetUID bits and user management, 100-101
    user management, 82
umask command, /etc/ftpaccess file and permissions, 320
umount command, Samba, 462
uname command
    showing system name, 141
    unpacking kernel source code, 226
undefine command, MC files (configuring Sendmail), 362
uninstalling packages, RPM (Red Hat Package Manager), 73
unmount command, 174
    See also file system management; mount command
    booting and shutting down, 165
unpacking kernel source code, 225-227
    See also compiling the kernel; finding kernel source code

linux directory, 225-226
modifying directory structure, 226-227
naming directories, 226-227
overview, 225
saving current source tree, 225-226
tar command, 227
uname command, 226
unpacking packages, compiling software and, 74-75
unpacking patches, patching the kernel and, 237-238
unset command, BASH (Bourne Again Shell) and
environment variables, 115
up option, ifconfig program, 553
upgrading versus installing Red Hat Linux, 25-26
upload command, /etc/ftpaccess file and
permissions, 321-322
uptime command
installing Linux in a server configuration, 18
Sendmail and, 379
urgent pointer, TCP headers, 529
USB Support menu, kernel features and modules, 234
use entry, route command, 557
use-host-decl-name parameter, DHCPD (Dynamic
Host Configuration Protocol server), 488
use-lease-addr-for-default-route parameter, DHCPD
(Dynamic Host Configuration Protocol server), 489
use_ct_file feature, FEATURE macro, 365
use_cw_file feature, FEATURE macro, 365
use_first_pass argument, PAM (Pluggable
Authentication Modules), *107*
use_mapped_pass argument, PAM (Pluggable
Authentication Modules), *107*
user databases, 86-89
See also user management
/etc/group file, 88-89
/etc/passwd file, 86-88
/etc/shadow file, 88
overview, 86
user element, /etc/inetd.conf file, *205*
user interfaces, graphical. *See* GUIs
user management, 81-110
See also single-host administration
databases, 86-89
e-mail, 85-86
/etc/shells file, 85
GIDs (group IDs), 82
/home directories, 83
LinuxConf package, 95-99
mail, 85-86
overview, 82-86
PAM (Pluggable Authentication Modules),
101-109
passwords, 83-84
root users, 82
SetGID bits, 100
SetUID bits, 100-101
shells, 84-85
startup scripts, 85
summary, 110
superusers, 82
tools, 89-99
UIDs (user IDs), 82
user types, 82

/var/spool/mail directory, 85-86
user management tools, 89-99
-c comment command-line option, *91*
-d homedir command-line option, *91*
-e expire-date command-line option, *91*
-f command-line option, *94*
-f inactive-time command-line option, *91*
-g *gid* command-line option, *94*
-G group[, . . .] command-line option, *91*
-g initial-group command-line option, *91*
-m [-k skel-dir] command-line option, *92*
-M command-line option, *92*
-n command-line option, *92*
-r command-line option, *94*
-s shell command-line option, *92*
-u uid command-line option, *92*
command-line options, 89-94
group command-line option, *94*
groupadd command, 93
groupdel command, 93-94
groupmod command, 94
LinuxConf package, 95-99
Login command-line option, *92*
overview, 89
useradd command, 90
userdel command, 90
usermod command, 92-93
USER permission keyword, /etc/lpd.perms file, 476
User variable, /etc/xinetd.conf file, 209
useradd command
user management tools, 90
wu-ftpd (Washington University FTP Server)
and anonymous users, 326-327
userdel command, user management tools, 90
usermod command, user management tools, 92-93
users
deleting, 98, *99*
managing via LinuxConf package, 95-99
switching via su command, 142
Windows versus Linux, 8
/usr directory
creating, 184
creating partitions and, 26, 27
mounting/unmounting local disks, 171-172
partitions and, *182*
/usr/bin directory, Qpopper daemon, 389-391
/usr/local/apache/conf directory, Apache HTTP
server, 344
/usr/local/apache/htdocs directory, Apache HTTP
server, 342-343
/usr/local/apache_*version* directory, Apache HTTP
server, 340-341
usrquota option, quota management, 194
/usr/sbin/smbd file, Samba, 448
/usr/src/linux/arch/i386/boot/zImage file,
installing the kernel, 235

▼ V

-v command-line option
LILO (Linux Loader) boot manager, *156*

restore tool, *505*
RPM (Red Hat Package Manager), *72*
-v option, ipchains tool, *573*
/var directory, partitions and, *27*, *182*
variables
    environment, *114-115*, *117*
    /etc/xinetd.conf file, *208-211*
/var/log directory, syslogd daemon and, *212*
/var/log/xferlog log file, wu-ftpd (Washington
    University FTP Server), *322-323*
/var/spool/bulletins directory, POP bulletins, *395*
/var/spool/lpd/*printername*, lpd printer daemon, *467*
/var/spool/mail directory
    mail and user management, *85-86*
    Sendmail, *380*
/var/spool/maillog directory, Sendmail, *382*
/var/spool/mqueue directory, Sendmail, *380-381*
/var/yp/ypservers file, NIS (Network Information
    Service), *439*
versions
    finding kernel source code, *224-225*
    IP headers and, *521*
    NFS (Network File System), *415*
    SSH (Secure Shell), *404-406*
vi editor, *145-146*
View button, SWAT (Samba Web Administration
    Tool), *457*
virtual command, wu-ftpd (Washington University
    FTP Server), *332-333*
virtual domains, Apache HTTP server, *345-347*
virtusertable feature, FEATURE macro, *367*

▼ W

-W command-line parameter, smbclient program, *461*
w command
    fdisk utility, *186*
    variation on who command, *142*
Wait variable, /etc/xinetd.conf file, *209*
wait/nowait element, /etc/inetd.conf file, *205*
Washington University FTP Server. *See* wu-ftpd
Web browsers, *607*
Web sites, *609*
    CERT (Computer Emergency Response Team),
        251-252
    finding kernel source code, *224*
    help for installation problems, *20*
    help for installing Red Hat Linux, *43*
    rootshell, *252*
    securing individual servers, *251-252*
    Security Focus, *252*
    Sendmail, *355-356*
    TCP/IP, *251-252*
    tools, *609*
well-known services, port numbers and, *243*
whereis command, *135*
    See also file management and manipulation
    directory location of files, *135*
which command, *134-135*
    See also file management and manipulation
    directory location of files, *134-135*

who command
    determining logged parties, *141-142*
    w command and, *142*
whois command, DNS tools, *299-302*
wildcard characters
    BASH (Bourne Again Shell) and, *117*
    /etc/syslog.conf file and, *214*
Window Manager panel, GNOME (GNU Network
    Object Model Environment), *66*
window managers, *46-66*
    GNOME (GNU Network Object Model
        Environment), *59-66*
    KDE (K Desktop Environment), *49-58*
    X Windows, *39-41*, *46-48*
Windows comparison, *7-12*
    See also Linux; Samba
    Active Directory, *12*
    configuration files, *10-11*
    domains, *11*
    mount process, *26*
    mounting shares, *9-10*
    multiusers, *8*
    network users, *8*
    networking, *9-10*
    NT domains versus NIS domains, *11*
    overview, *7-8*
    Registry versus text files, *10-11*
    Samba and Linux interoperation, *445-464*
    separation of GUI and kernel, *8-9*
    single users, *8*
    users, *8*
WordPerfect, Linux tools, *606*
wsize option, NFS (Network File System), *424*
wu-ftpd (Washington University FTP Server), *307-333*
    See also FTP (File Transfer Protocol); Internet
        services
    anonymous FTP directories, *327-328*
    anonymous users, *326-327*
    ./build command, *308-309*
    compiling and installing, *308-309*
    configuring, *310-322*
    "cookbook" access solutions, *326-332*
    /etc/ftpaccess file, *311-322*, *329-332*
    /etc/ftpconversions/ file, *323-325*
    /etc/ftphosts file, *326*
    /etc/inetd.conf file, *309-310*
    /etc/xinetd.conf file, *310*
    overview, *307-308*
    README files, *308*
    summary, *333*
    useradd command, *326-327*
    /var/log/xferlog log file, *322-323*
    virtual command, *332-333*

▼ X

-x option, ipchains tool, *573*
-X parameter, ipchains tool, *569*
X Windows, *46-48*
    See also GNOME; KDE
    difficulty of programming for, *47-48*

GNOME (GNU Network Object Model Environment) and, 48
history of, 46-48
KDE (K Desktop Environment) and, 48
starting KDE (K Desktop Environment) and, 49-50
summary, 67
window managers, 46-47
X Windows configuration, 39-41
See also installing Red Hat Linux
Xconfigurator tool, *41*
xhost command, networking tools, 143-144
xinetd daemon
See also core system services; inetd daemon
/etc/xinetd.conf file, 207-211
overview, 203-204
Qpopper daemon and, 392
shutting down services, 247
SWAT (Samba Web Administration Tool) and, 454

▼ Y

-y command-line option, restore tool, *505*
-y option, ipchains tool, *573*
-y parameter, e2fsck tool, *177*
YP (Yellow Pages), NIS (Network Information Service) and, 430
ypbind daemon, NIS (Network Information Service), 436, 437

ypcat command, testing NIS client configurations, 438, 441
ypinit command, 434-436, 440
See also NIS (Network Information Service)
-m option, 435
-s option, 440
makefile errors, 435-436
overview, 434-435
ypxfrd daemon and, 440
ypmatch command, NIS (Network Information Service), 441
yppasswd command, NIS (Network Information Service), 441
ypserv daemon, starting NIS (Network Information Service) via, 431
ypwhich command, NIS (Network Information Service), 441
ypxfrd daemon, ypinit command and, 440

▼ Z

-Z parameter, ipchains tool, *569*
zImage parameter, compiling the kernel, 234, 235
zone configuration file, named.conf file, 292-293
zone keyword, named.conf file, 273
zone statements, named.conf file, 284
zones, named.conf file, 285-287

redhat®

www.redhat.com

ABOUT THE CD

The CD-ROM included with this book contains the Publisher's Edition of the Red Hat Linux 7 distribution for the Intel i386 (or better) platform. It comes with everything you need to install Red Hat Linux and to start working with the operating system. To begin the installation process, simply insert the CD and reboot your computer.

> **NOTE:** You may need to configure your system to boot from the CD-ROM before trying to boot from the hard disk. If you aren't sure how to do this, check the manual that came with your system.

If your system cannot boot from a CD-ROM directly (this is true of older PCs), you will need to create a boot disk. See the section "Creating a Boot Disk" in Chapter 2 for details.

Red Hat Linux 7 tries to start its graphical installation program after you have booted from the CD-ROM. However, if your system does not contain a compatible video card, the installation process will stop and you will be prompted to reboot. Go ahead and reboot—when you see the opening installation screen, simply type the word **text** and then press ENTER. This will perform a text-based install that should work on just about any computer out there.

For the full details on the installation process, see the section "Installing Red Hat Linux" in Chapter 2.

All the software on this CD-ROM is copyrighted by the respective owners. Most of the software is also distributed under the GNU General Public License, version 2. See the COPYING file in the root directory of the CD-ROM for the full text of the license agreement. (Chapter 1 includes a summary of the license agreement.)

Unlike most other software, the Linux community (Red Hat included) encourages you to make and distribute copies of the CD. Using the installation CD to install however many systems for any purpose is also encouraged. If one day you find that you don't need this CD, you can give it to someone who can use it—like your local public library. After all, you can download the latest version from the Internet for free.

For additional details about Red Hat Linux, visit the company's Web site at http://www.redhat.com.

This book includes a copy of the Publisher's Edition of Red Hat Linux from Red Hat Software, Inc., which you may use in accordance with the GNU General Public License. The Official Red Hat Linux, which you may purchase from Red Hat Software, includes the complete Official Red Hat Linux distribution, Red Hat Software's documentation, and 90 days of free e-mail technical support regarding installation of Official Red Hat Linux. You also may purchase technical support from Red Hat Software on issues other than installation. You may purchase Official Red Hat Linux and technical support from Red Hat Software through the company's Web site (www.redhat.com) or its toll-free number: 1 (888) REDHAT1.

Due to space considerations on the Red Hat 7.0 CD-ROM, some rarely used files such as TeX, some foreign-language Xfree86 fonts, a DOS emulator, and some Alpha and Sparc source code files are not included. Check README.publishers-edition file on the CD-ROM for all listings. Should you happen to want any of these files, they can be downloaded from ftp.redhat.com.